College Accounting Fundamentals

Chapters 1–28

College Accounting Fundamentals

Chapters 1–28

James Don Edwards, Ph.D., C.P.A.
School of Accounting
University of Georgia

Lynn Thorne, M.B.A., C.P.A.
Department of Economics and Business
North Carolina State University

Third Edition   1986

Homewood, Illinois   60430

The first edition of this book was published under the title
College Accounting: Principles and Procedures

© RICHARD D. IRWIN, INC., 1977, 1981, and 1986

ISBN 0-256-03188-6

Library of Congress Catalog Card No. 85–61010

Printed in the United States of America

1 2 3 4 5 6 7 8 9 0 K 3 2 1 0 9 8 7 6

Dedicated to
Clara, Jim, Lisa, and Frank

Preface

College Accounting Fundamentals, Third Edition—Chapters 1–28 has been designed for students of accounting, business administration, and secretarial science. The goals of the book are twofold: (1) to provide a general practical background for secretarial and other business students who do not intend to become accountants but who need a general insight into accounting and (2) to provide career-oriented preparation for students intending to become accountants. Persons in a wide variety of fields are facing an increasing amount of financial information, and an understanding of the accounting process is crucial for success in business and in many other careers. A primary aim of the authors has been to present accounting information as an essential element of the business decision-making process.

College Accounting Fundamentals, Third Edition—Chapters 1–28 is student oriented. *Understandability* was one of the authors' primary targets. Many students have difficulty in comprehending accounting texts. The authors believe that this difficulty has been overcome in this text. The text is written to be clear and easy to read, and no prior knowledge of accounting is assumed. Every chapter has been classroom tested, and this edition incorporates answers to the questions most frequently asked by students. Numerous illustrations and examples that were developed through classroom experience have been included to aid the student in understanding complex material.

Forms and documents have been illustrated to demonstrate how accounting fills the need for various types of information. Chapters have also been reviewed by leading classroom teachers, and they have been edited carefully for understandability.

This book is designed to present the total accounting process—from recording business transactions in the books of original entry to the preparation of periodic financial reports. Basic concepts of the accounting cycle are discussed in the initial chapters. Later chapters deal with specific accounting problems found in service and merchandising enterprises. Also, there is substantial discussion of accounting procedures relating to the various forms of business organization—sole proprietorships, partnerships, and corporations. Finally, there is an introduction to cost accounting and to the accounting for a manufacturing firm.

Features of the third edition

Because of the importance of laying a firm foundation for future learning in the first few chapters, Chapter 1 of the previous edition has been divided into two chapters in the third edition. Chapter 1 now presents an *introduction.* The student can study and absorb the nature and purpose of accounting before being introduced to double-entry accounting in Chapter 2.

The *worksheet* is not introduced until Chapter 9 when adjusting and closing entries are explained.

Cash and checking account procedures are introduced in Chapter 5. This chapter emphasizes the cash account and the need for control in the handling of cash. In order to simplify this chapter, discussion of *cash receipts and cash disbursements* journals has been moved to Chapter 10.

The two *payroll* chapters have been streamlined by omitting many of the rules and regulations that were included in the previous edition.

Four chapters deal with the *accounting for a merchandising firm.* The accounting for purchase transactions is presented first, followed by the accounting from the seller's point of view. The necessity of using the accrual form of accounting for these transactions is stressed, and the accounts that arise as a result of the application of accrual accounting are introduced. The last of these four chapters presents end-of-period procedures for merchandising firms.

Four new chapters have been added to the third edition. These chapters deal with *financial statement analysis—*how to use the accumulated data in various decision-making processes. The *effect of inflation* on the historical financial statements and the provision of supplemental statements is also discussed. There is also an introduction to *cost accounting* and the *accounting for a manufacturing business.*

Two appendices have been added. Appendix A deals with computers in accounting, and Appendix B discusses the statement of changes in financial position.

Learning objectives. Learning objectives are stated at the beginning of each chapter. These both preview and review the chapter content.

Lists. Lists are used to introduce new material or to review material that has already been discussed in the chapter.

Key terms. Key terms are given at the end of each chapter. These glossaries serve as a review of the new and important terms in that particular chapter.

Supplementary materials—learning aids for students

Manual study guides. Two manual study guides are available, one for Chapters 1–14 and a second for Chapters 15–28. Included in each chapter of the study guides are chapter goals; reference outline; chapter review; matching, true-false, multiple choice, and fill-in-the-blank questions; demonstration problem; exercises; and answers.

Computerized study guides. An innovation in the third edition is the introduction of microcomputer study guides. Two different study guides are available, one for Chapters 1–14 and a second for Chapters 15–28. Versions are available for Apple and for IBM PC microcomputers.

Working papers. Two sets of working papers are available for working assigned problems, one set for Chapters 1–14 and a second set for Chapters 15–28. The working papers in many instances are partially filled in to reduce the "pencil pushing" required to solve the problems. *The format and spacing used in the working papers are identical to the Instructor's Solutions Manual and to the solutions* *transparencies.* This feature makes it easier to compare the students' solutions to the authors' solutions.

Manual practice sets. Two different manual practice sets are available for use with this text. Practice Set I is designed for use after Chapter 9, and Practice Set II is designed for use after Chapter 14.

Computerized practice set. A computerized practice set illustrating a professional medical practice is available for use with this text. It is designed for use after Chapter 10. Versions are available for use with Apple and with IBM PC microcomputers.

Check figures. The list of check figures gives key amounts for the A and B series problems in the text. The student can determine whether they are on the right track when working a problem by comparing their solutions to the key amount given for a particular problem.

Supplementary materials—teaching aids for instructors

Instructor's manual. The instructor's guide contains a summary of major concepts; chapter goals; lecture notes; and the estimated time, level of difficulty, and content of exercises and problems.

Instructor's solutions manuals. The instructor's solutions manuals contains sample course syllabi. For each chapter, the manual contains an outline and answers to the questions, exercises, and Series A and B problems. The spacing and format are identical to the work papers used by the students.

Transparencies. Very clear transparencies of solutions to problems are available to adopters. The transparencies are in two sets, one set for Chapters 1–14 and a second set for Chapters 15–28. These transparencies can be especially useful when covering problems involving worksheets and for use in large classroom situations.

Solutions manual to manual practice sets. A solutions manual is available for each of the manual practice sets.

Teacher's manual for the computerized practice set. A teacher's manual is available for the computerized practice set. In addition to providing solutions, the manual provides the instructor with information to assist the student in running the practice set on the microcomputer.

Instructor's manual for the microcomputer study guides. An instructor's manual is available for each of the microcomputer study guides. In addition to providing solutions, the manual provides the instructor with information to assist the student in running the study guides on the microcomputer.

The authors have also provided the following testing options:

Examination booklet

Computest

Teletest

Acknowledgments

We are grateful for the assistance provided by the following individuals: Charles Strain, Ocean County College; Dee Sorenson, Sierra College; Loretta Rojo, Central Piedmont Community College; Stephen Schaefer, Contra Costa College; Donald Foster, Henry Ford Community College; Albert Arsenault, Hillsborough Community College; Stuart Fukushege, Leeward County Community College; Rita Edmond; and Dennis Allen.

James Don Edwards
Lynn Bergold-Thorne

Contents

and services. Note received for an extension of payment time on a previous obligation. Note discounted before maturity. Reporting a contingent liability. Collection of a note at maturity. Renewal of a note at maturity. Dishonored notes. Notes receivable register. Notes Receivable account. Endorsement of notes. Accounting for notes payable. Notes issued for a cash loan: *Note issued in exchange for goods and services. Note issued for extension of payment time on a previous obligation. Payment of a note at maturity. Renewal of a note at maturity.* Notes payable register. Notes Payable account. Accrual of interest receivable. Accrual of interest payable.

ing. Closing entries—posting. Post-closing trial balance. Reversing entries.

College Accounting Fundamentals

Chapters 1–28

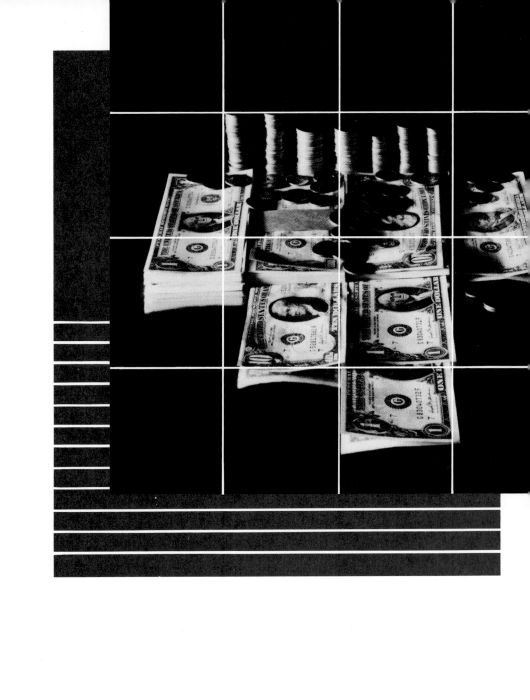

CHAPTER 1

The nature and purpose of accounting

LEARNING OBJECTIVES

In this chapter you will learn some basic information about the accounting process. After studying this chapter, you should be able to:

1. Tell who uses accounting information and why such information is important.
2. Define the three basic elements of accounting. *Assets = liabilities + OE*
3. Define the accounting equation and describe its use in accounting for business transactions.
4. Explain how revenues and expenses relate to owner's equity.
5. Explain how various business transactions affect assets, liabilities, owner's equity, revenues, and expenses.
6. Identify an income statement and its contents.
7. Identify a balance sheet and its contents.

Without realizing it, you have probably participated in some accounting transactions today. If you bought a meal on the way to class or purchased a newspaper, you were involved in an accounting transaction. Broadly speaking, the purpose of accounting is to provide useful and timely information about the financial activities of an individual, a business, or another organization. This accounting information, stated in terms of dollars, is used by a variety of people in making a wide range of personal and/or business decisions. For example:

1. Owners and prospective owners use accounting information in deciding whether to increase, decrease, retain, or acquire an ownership interest in a business.
2. Managers (who may also be owners) use accounting information in deciding how a business is operating, what its problems are, and whether additional financing is needed.
3. Creditors use accounting information in deciding whether to increase, decrease, or limit the amount of credit granted, or if credit should be extended at all.
4. Governments use accounting information in determining if tax laws and other regulatory requirements have been met.
5. Workers and unions use accounting information in deciding salary issues and whether to accept or continue employment with a given business.

Other users of accounting information include consumers, stock exchanges, lawyers, trade associations, financial reporters, and financial analysts. Because their purposes vary, different users want different information. Most, however, will want information concerning the profits or losses of the most recent period and about the financial condition of the business at the present time. The accumulation and presentation of such information are known as **financial accounting,** which is the primary subject of this book. Two other important areas of accounting are **management accounting**—the accumulation and presentation of information for internal management purposes—and **governmental accounting**—the accumulation and presentation of information about the financial affairs of governmental agencies.

While there are three basic areas of accounting, there are more than three areas of specialization for professional accountants. For example, an accountant may be employed by a private business enterprise, a public accounting firm, or a government agency as a specialist in taxation, cost accounting, budgeting, systems design and installation, or auditing.

Auditing is the testing and checking of an organization's accounting records to see whether proper policies and practices have been followed. This is the primary activity of the **certified public accountant (CPA).** In all states, an accountant may be licensed to practice as a CPA upon fulfilling certain educational requirements, passing a rigorous uniform examination, and acquiring specified amounts of actual accounting experience. Most states now require CPAs to take a certain number of hours of continuing education each year in order to renew their CPA licenses.

A public accounting firm will provide the services of a CPA for a fee. Public accounting firms typically offer tax planning, filing of tax returns, and a wide range of services designed to assist clients in managing their financial affairs.

The accounting skills that you acquire in this course will enable you to keep records of your own business and personal financial affairs. You might also keep records for lawyers, doctors, plumbers, beauticians, mechanics, and other small business owners.

THE ACCOUNTING PROCESS

Accounting is a measurement and communication process designed to provide useful and timely financial information. This process includes identifying, recording, classifying, summarizing, and interpreting business transactions. The first step is the *identification* of those events that are financial in nature and that should be recorded. *Recording* may be done by hand, or with the help of typewriters, bookkeeping machines, word processors, and machines for encoding information on magnetic tape, paper tape, or cards. Computers are also used for recording transactions. *Classifying* is the grouping of similar items together in order to make the recording of many different events and transactions more efficient. *Summarizing* is the stating of groups of data in concise form. *Interpretation* provides explanations and develops relationships that give meaning to the information.

ACCOUNTING VERSUS BOOKKEEPING

Accounting includes designing forms, records, and accounting systems; data analysis; decision making; report and financial statement preparation; and the interpretation of reports and statements. An accountant is involved with or responsible for all of these functions.

Bookkeeping is the recording phase of the accounting process, and the person who actually records information in the books is a bookkeeper. Often, especially in small businesses, the accountant also serves as the bookkeeper.

THE BASIC ELEMENTS OF ACCOUNTING

Financial information is commonly classified into the categories of assets, liabilities, owner's equity, revenues, expenses, and net income (or net loss). We will concentrate first on assets, liabilities, and owner's equity.

Assets

An **asset** is anything of value that is owned by a business. It is used in producing income for the business. Common examples of assets include cash, accounts receivable (a promise of a future cash receipt), merchandise, machinery, building, land, and furniture. The kinds and quantity of assets vary with the enterprise. A manufacturer may have a large building with many machines and other assets. A doctor may require only a small office with relatively few pieces of equipment or furniture.

Liabilities

A **liability** is a legal obligation to pay a debt. It is what a business owes to other businesses or individuals. Any asset may be used to pay a debt, but cash is most commonly used. Accounts payable and notes payable are the most common liabilities. An **account payable** is an unwritten promise to pay for something at a later date. It arises when an item, such as merchandise, equipment, supplies, or services, is purchased on credit. A **note payable** is a written promise to pay a specified amount of money at a fixed future date. When an account payable is repaid, the creditor issues a written receipt, which cancels the obligation.

Owner's equity

Owner's equity is an owner's interest in, or claim to, the assets of a business. It is the difference between the amount of assets and the amount of liabilities. Thus, assets are something owned, liabilities are something owed, and the difference is the owner's equity. *Proprietorship, capital,* and *net worth* are other terms for owner's equity.

It is important to separate a company's business activities from its owner's personal activities. A business is a distinct economic unit that exists separately from its owner. This is known as the **entity concept.** For accounting purposes, only the assets, liabilities, and economic activities of a single economic unit are considered. Thus, if one person owns several businesses, each business is treated as a separate entity, and care must be taken to separate each one's accounting. It is also important that the owner's personal economic activities not be included in the businesses's records.

THE ACCOUNTING EQUATION

All accounting information is recorded within the framework of the **accounting equation.** This equation is:

$$\textbf{Assets} = \textbf{Liabilities} + \textbf{Owner's Equity}$$
$$\textbf{A} = \textbf{L} + \textbf{OE}$$

Remember, assets are items of value that are owned by a business. Liabilities are claims by creditors to a business's assets; they are debts. A business's owners have a claim to its assets after creditors have been paid. Owner's equity is the asset value left over after all debts have been paid.

For example, if Messere Company has $30,000 of assets and $10,000 of liabilities, its owners have a right to the remaining $20,000 of assets. Thus:

$$\frac{A}{\$30,000} = \frac{L}{\$10,000} + \frac{OE}{\$20,000}$$

If the business owed $15,000 rather than $10,000, the equation would read:

$$\frac{A}{\$30,000} = \frac{L}{\$15,000} + \frac{OE}{\$15,000}$$

Note that the accounting equation must always *balance*. That is, the dollar amount on one side of the equal sign must always equal the dollar amount on the other side of the equal sign. If assets increase, liabilities and/or owner's equity must increase by the same amount.

Similarly, if assets decrease, liabilities and/or owner's equity must also decrease.

If the owner contributes $10,000 more to the business, the dollar amounts in the equation will change to:

$$\frac{A}{\$40,000} = \frac{L}{\$15,000} + \frac{OE}{\$25,000}$$

Assets have increased by $10,000. Since the owner has put the cash into the business and debts have remained the same, the owner's equity increases by $10,000. The accounting equation shows $40,000 of assets and a total of $40,000 of liabilities and owner's equity. Note again that the equation balances.

An alternative form often used to express the accounting equation is:

Assets − Liabilities = Owner's Equity
A − L = OE

If the last example is restated using the new format, it becomes:

$$\frac{A}{\$40,000} - \frac{L}{\$15,000} = \frac{OE}{\$25,000}$$

This illustrates the "leftover effect" of owner's equity. If the company pays its creditors the $15,000 it owes them, there is $25,000 of assets left over for the owners:

Assets	$40,000
− Liabilities	15,000
= Owner's Equity . . .	$25,000

If, a year later, $5,000 is owed and assets are still the same, owner's equity will be:

Assets	$40,000
− Liabilities	5,000
= Owner's Equity . .	$35,000

The relationship between assets, liabilities, and owner's equity could also be stated as:

$$\frac{OE}{\$35,000} = \frac{A}{\$40,000} - \frac{L}{\$5,000}$$

The equation continues to balance at all times. Both sides of the equal sign *must* always equal the same dollar amount.

One last way to show the basic equation of A = L + OE is:

$$\frac{L}{\$5,000} = \frac{A}{\$40,000} - \frac{OE}{\$35,000}$$

Each equation says the same thing: both creditors and owners have claims on and rights to a firm's assets. The creditors must be paid first; then the owners have a right to the remaining assets.

We will return to the basic accounting equation

$$A = L + OE$$

for the rest of this chapter's discussion.

TRANSACTIONS

An accounting **transaction** takes place when a business exchanges one thing of value for another. Transactions include cash receipts from the sale of products and services, payment of wages, and cash received from creditors. Transactions cause changes in assets, liabilities, and owner's equity. Since the accounting equation must always balance, each transaction involves giving up something in order to receive something else. It is the accountant's job to keep track of all transactions. Some common business transactions are shown in Illustration 1–1, on page 10.

EXAMPLES OF THE ACCOUNTING EQUATION

We will illustrate the accounting equation by assigning dollar values to transactions in Illustration 1–1. Each transaction affects the financial position of the Speedy TV Repair Shop.

Transaction *a* took place when owner Phil Wind invested $5,000 in cash to start the business. The assets that an owner contributes to a business are referred to as **capital.** Thus, the expression **Phil Wind, Capital** will be used to indicate Wind's interest in the assets. Assets and owner's equity both increase by $5,000.

	Assets	= Liabilities +	Owner's Equity
Transactions	Cash		Phil Wind, Capital
a.	$5,000		$5,000
	$5,000 =		$5,000

	Transaction	The Business Receives	The Business Gives Up
ILLUSTRATION 1–1	*a.* Phil Wind, owner, invests cash to start the business	Cash	Ownership rights
Business Transactions for Speedy TV Repair Shop	*b.* Wind purchases TV parts for cash	Parts	Cash
	c. Wind purchases equipment on account	Equipment	A promise to pay (Accounts Payable)
	d. Wind pays for part of the equipment purchased on account	A reduction in its promise to pay (Accounts Payable)	Cash
	e. Customers pay cash for repair services	Cash	Services
	f. Wind repairs TVs on account	A customer's promise to pay (Accounts Receivable)	Services
	g. Wind pays rent	The right to occupy a building	Cash

Notice that the equation balances, with $5,000 of cash (asset) equaling $5,000 of capital (owner's equity).

Transaction *b* is the exchange of one asset (cash) for another (TV parts). Phil Wind spent $500 to buy TV parts. The composition of the assets changes, but their total amount did not change; liabilities and owner's equity were unaffected.

	Assets	= Liabilities +	Owner's Equity
Transactions	Cash + Parts =		Phil Wind, Capital
a.	$5,000		$5,000
b.	− 500 $500		
	$4,500 $500		$5,000
	$5,000	=	$5,000

There is still $5,000 of assets, but there are two assets now, cash of $4,500 and parts of $500. Their total is still $5,000, the total of the owner's equity.

In Transaction *c,* Phil bought equipment on account. This increased both assets and liabilities by $1,000. Owner's equity did not change.

	Assets			=	Liabilities	+	Owner's Equity
	Cash	+ Parts +	Equipment	=	Accounts Payable	+	Phil Wind, Capital
Transactions							
a.	$5,000						$5,000
b.	− 500	$500					
c.			**$1,000**		**$1,000**		
	$4,500 +	$500 +	$1,000	=	$1,000	+	$5,000
		$6,000		=		$6,000	

Assets are composed of cash of $4,500, parts of $500, and equipment of $1,000, for a total of $6,000. Liabilities of $1,000 and owner's equity of $5,000 also equal $6,000. Thus, the accounting equation remains in balance, as it must at all times.

In Transaction *d,* Wind paid $300 of the amount he owed from transaction *c.* He still owes $700.

	Assets			=	Liabilities	+	Owner's Equity
	Cash	+ Parts +	Equipment	=	Accounts Payable	+	Phil Wind, Capital
Transactions							
a.	$5,000						$5,000
b.	− 500	$500					
c.			$1,000		$1,000		
d.	**− 300**				**− 300**		
Ending balance	$4,200 +	$500 +	$1,000	=	$ 700	+	$5,000
		$5,700		=		$5,700	

There has been a reduction of $300 in an asset (cash) and a reduction of $300 in a liability (accounts payable). Owner's equity remains unchanged, and the accounting equation still balances.

OTHER WAYS OF STATING THE BASIC ACCOUNTING EQUATION

As mentioned earlier, one way of restating the accounting equation is:

$$\text{Assets} - \text{Liabilities} = \text{Owner's Equity}$$

So the results of Transactions *a, b, c,* and *d* could also be shown as:

	Assets	—	Liabilities	=	Owner's Equity
Transactions	Cash + Parts + Equipment	—	Accounts Payable	=	Phil Wind, Capital
a.	$5,000				$5,000
b.	− 500 $500				
c.	$1,000		$1,000		
d.	− 300		− 300		
Ending balance	$4,200 + $500 + $1,000	—	$ 700	=	$5,000
	$5,700	—	$ 700	=	$5,000

They could also be restated as:

$$OE \ = \ A \ - \ L$$
$$\$5,000 = \$5,700 - \$700$$

or

$$L \ = \ A \ - \ OE$$
$$\$700 = \$5,700 - \$5,000$$

If two elements of the accounting equation are known, the third element can always be determined.

REVENUES AND EXPENSES *Temporary* O E

So far, the only change in owner's equity has come from Phil Wind's capital contribution. Of course, owner's equity could be reduced if Wind withdrew assets from the business. But such capital transactions are only one way of changing the owner's portion of the accounting equation. The other way is through the operation of the business.

When a business sells its product or service, the resulting cash receipts or other assets received are called **revenue**. Revenues are inflows of assets from sources other than the owner that affect owner's equity. Most revenues take the form of cash receipts. Since liabilities are not changed, there must be a corresponding increase in owner's equity so that the accounting equation will remain in balance.

Cash spent or a liability incurred in order to produce revenue is called an **expense**. Expenses are outflows of assets from business transactions that affect owner's equity. Thus, when an asset decreases as a result of paying expenses, owner's equity is reduced.

To illustrate revenue and expense transactions, let's return to the Speedy TV Repair Shop and examine Transactions *e* through *g* of Illustration 1–1. After Transaction *d,* the balances in assets, liabilities, and owner's equity were:

Assets = Liabilities + Owner's Equity

Cash	+ Parts	+ Equipment	= Accounts Payable	+ Phil Wind, Capital
$4,200	+ $500	+ $1,000 =	$700 +	$5,000

We could record revenues and expenses directly to Phil Wind, Capital, but as the number of transactions increased, it would become increasingly difficult to determine which changes came from business operations and which resulted from contributions and withdrawals by the owner. This distinction is of great importance, so the owner's equity portion of the accounting equation is expanded to include revenues and expenses. Thus:

Owner's Equity = Phil Wind, Capital + Revenues − Expenses

The last three transactions of Speedy TV Repair Shop are summarized below:

Transaction	The Business Receives	The Business Gives Up
e. Customers pay $1,000 cash for repair services	Cash	Services
f. Wind repairs TVs for $800 on account	Customer's promise to pay (Accounts Receivable)	Services
g. Wind pays $700 rent	Right to occupy building	Cash

In Transaction *e,* Speedy TV Repair Shop received $1,000 in cash from customers for services performed. The cash increases assets, which must be reflected by a corresponding increase in owner's equity. Thus, cash is increased on the left side of the accounting equation, while revenues are increased on the right side. The ultimate purpose of providing repair services is to increase owner's equity. The performance of such services produces revenue. Rather than placing the increase directly in owner's equity, it is classified as revenue.

	Assets			= Liabilities +		Owner's Equity		
Transactions	Cash	+ Parts +	Equipment =	Accounts Payable	+	Phil Wind, Capital	+ Revenues −	Expenses
Beginning balance	$4,200	$500	$1,000	$700		$5,000	$ 0	$ 0
e.	1,000						1,000	
	$5,200 +	$500 +	$1,000	= $700	+	$5,000	+ $1,000	− $ 0
		$6,700				$6,700		

After Transaction *e,* assets total $6,700, and liabilities and owner's equity total $6,700. The accounting equation is still in balance.

In a similar manner, the $800 of services rendered on account in Transaction *f* is recorded as an increase in assets (accounts receivable) and as an increase in revenue. The fact that cash has not yet been received does not prevent us from recording revenue when it is earned. A new asset is added, accounts receivable. An account receivable is a customer's promise to pay at a later date. It has value to the business, so it is an asset.

	Assets				= Liabilities +		Owner's Equity		
Transactions	Cash +	Accounts Receivable +	Parts +	Equipment =	Accounts Payable	+	Phil Wind, Capital	+ Revenues −	Expenses
Beginning balance	$4,200	$ 0	$500	$1,000	$700		$5,000	$ 0	$0
e.	1,000							1,000	
f.		800						800	
	$5,200 +	$800	+ $500 +	$1,000	= $700	+	$5,000	+ $1,800 −	$0
		$7,500					$7,500		

The total of the assets after this transaction is $7,500, which is also the total of the liabilities and owner's equity.

Transaction *g* is the payment of $700 in rent. This is an expense and thus decreases owner's equity. Assets now total $6,800, as does the combination of liabilities and owner's equity. Remember that owner's equity is composed of the capital and revenues, less expenses.

Transactions	Assets				= Liabilities +		Owner's Equity		
	Cash +	Accounts Receivable +	Parts +	Equipment =	Accounts Payable +	Phil Wind, Capital +	Revenues −	Expenses
Beginning balance	$4,200	$ 0	$500	$1,000	$700	$5,000	$ 0	$ 0
e.	1,000						1,000	
f.		800					800	
g.	− 700							700
	$4,500 +	$800	+ $500 +	$1,000 =	$700 +	$5,000 +	$1,800 −	$700
	$6,800					$6,800		

Revenues and expenses are treated as separate parts of the owner's equity to make it easier to accumulate data. Revenue items represent increases in owner's equity, while expense items represent decreases in owner's equity. The revenues and expenses are matched to determine the net increase or decrease in owner's equity. For the Speedy TV Repair Shop, owner's equity is composed of $5,000 of capital + $1,800 of revenue − $700 of expenses, or $6,100.

Owner's Equity

Phil Wind, Capital	+ Revenues	− Expenses
$5,000	$ 0	$ 0
	1,000	
	800	
		700
$5,000 +	$1,800 −	$700
	$6,100	

FINANCIAL STATEMENTS

One function of accounting records is to serve as the basis for financial statements. The ending balance in each column of the final accounting equation represents the total amount in each category—assets, liabilities, and owner's equity. Note that the total assets ($6,800) equal the total of all liabilities and owner's equity items ($6,800). Using this information, the two most basic financial statements, the income statement and the balance sheet, can be prepared.

The income statement

An **income statement** is a summary of a firm's revenues and expenses and their effect on income during a specified period of time. As mentioned earlier, revenues are increases in owner's equity resulting from operations, and expenses are decreases in owner's equity resulting from operations. Expenses are subtracted from revenues to determine the firm's net income for the period. **Net income** is the excess of revenues over expenses. If expenses exceed revenue, a **net loss** has occurred. An income statement is sometimes called a *profit and loss statement,* an *operating statement,* or an *earnings statement.* The Speedy TV Repair Shop's income statement for the month of October is shown in Illustration 1–2. It is based on Transactions *e* through *g* from Illustration 1–1 and the discussion on pages 12 through 15.

ILLUSTRATION 1–2

SPEEDY TV REPAIR SHOP
Income Statement
For the Month Ended October 31, 1987

Revenue:
   TV repair fees $1,800
Expenses:
   Rent 700
Net income $1,100

Every income statement opens with a heading that includes the company's name, the label Income Statement, and the period of time the statement covers, usually a specific month or year. For example, Speedy TV Repair Shop's income statement covers the month of October 1987.

The revenue amounts are listed first and labeled by source. Expenses are similarly listed. The difference between the revenues and the expenses represents the net income or net loss. Speedy TV Repair Shop had income of $1,100 for the month of October.

The balance sheet

A **balance sheet** presents a financial picture of a business at a particular date. It is like a photograph that represents one moment in time. This is in contrast to an income statement, which covers an extended period of time. The balance sheet lists the resources available to a firm (assets) and the sources that provided them (liabilities and owner's equity). The totals of the assets and their sources are equal, or balance; hence, the name *balance sheet*. The figures also reflect the accounting equation (A = L + OE). Thus, the accounting equation is sometimes called the *balance sheet equation*.

The Speedy TV Repair Shop's balance sheet for October 31, 1987, is shown in Illustration 1–3. As with the income statement, the name of the company and the type of statement, balance sheet, are listed as part of the heading. Since the Balance Sheet applies to one day only, the exact date of the totals is listed. In the case of Speedy TV Repair Shop, it is October 31, 1987.

ILLUSTRATION 1–3

SPEEDY TV REPAIR SHOP
Balance Sheet
October 31, 1987 *on that particular day*

Assets

Cash	$4,500
Accounts receivable	800
Parts	500
Equipment	1,000
Total assets	$6,800

Liabilities

Accounts payable	$ 700

Owner's Equity

Phil Wind, capital, October 1, 1987	$5,000	
Add net income for October	1,100	
Phil Wind, capital, October 31, 1987		6,100
Total liabilities and owner's equity		$6,800

All assets are listed with their respective dollar amounts. A total of the assets is taken. Then the liabilities and the owner's equity are listed. Note that owner's equity is composed of the amount contributed by the owner, $5,000, and the amount of the net income found on the income statement, $1,100. Total owner's equity is the sum of the two, $6,100.

SUMMARY

The primary purpose of accounting is to provide useful and timely information about the financial activities of an individual or a business. This accounting information is used by a variety of people in making business decisions.

There are three major areas of accounting: (1) **financial accounting,** (2) **management accounting,** and (3) **governmental accounting.** Within these three classifications are many areas of specialization. These areas include private enterprise, public accounting, taxation, cost accounting, budgeting, systems design, and auditing.

Auditing is the testing and checking of an organization's accounting records to ensure that proper policies and procedures have been followed. Audits are usually performed by **certified public accountants,** highly trained accountants who have earned the CPA designation by fulfilling rigorous requirements regarding education, examination, and experience.

The **accounting** process includes identifying, recording, classifying, summarizing, and interpreting business **transactions.** The recording phase of this process is called **bookkeeping.** Accounting also includes the designing of forms, records, and accounting systems; data analysis; and financial statement preparation. It is important to separate a company's business activities from its owner's personal activities. Under the **entity concept,** a business is a distinct economic unit that exists separately from its owner.

Financial information is usually classified into the categories of assets, liabilities, and owner's equity. Owner's equity may be further broken down into owner's capital, revenue, and expenses. **Assets** are items of value that are owned by a business and used in producing income. Some examples of assets are cash, **accounts receivable,** merchandise, machinery, buildings, land, and furniture. **Liabilities** are legal obligations to pay debts. Some examples of liabiltiies are **accounts payable** and **notes payable. Owner's equity** is an owner's claim to the assets of the business; it is the difference between total assets and total liabilities.

All accounting information is recorded within the framework of the **accounting equation,** which is:

$$\textbf{Assets} = \textbf{Liabilities} + \textbf{Owner's Equity}$$
$$\textbf{A} = \textbf{L} + \textbf{OE}$$

The accounting equation must always remain in balance. That is, the left side of the equation must always equal the right side.

Owner's equity can be changed by contributions or withdrawals of capital by the owner. The other way to change owner's equity is through the operations of the business. Operations create revenues and expenses.

Revenues are inflows of assets resulting from the sale of goods or services. Revenues increase owner's equity. Cash spent or a liability incurred in order to produce revenue is called an **expense.** Expenses are outflows of assets from the business. Thus, when an asset is decreased by paying expenses, owner's equity is reduced.

After the transactions for a period are summarized, financial statements are prepared. The two most common financial statements are the income statement and the balance sheet. The **income statement** is a summary of a firm's expenses and revenues and their effect on income during a specified period of time. The income statement shows whether the company had a **net income** or a **net loss.** The **balance sheet** is a financial picture of a business on a given date. The balance sheet is an illustration of the accounting equation, Assets = Liabilities + Owner's Equity.

KEY TERMS

Accounting—The process of collecting, measuring, and reporting useful and timely financial information of a business unit or organization. It includes identifying, recording, classifying, summarizing, and interpreting business transactions.

Accounting Equation—Assets = Liabilities + Owner's Equity.

Accounts Payable—An unwritten promise to pay for something at a later date.

Accounts Receivable—An asset account used to record amounts due from customers. It is a customer's promise to pay at a later date.

Asset—Anything that is owned by and has value to a business (or other organization or entity). Assets are used in producing income.

Auditing—The testing and checking of an organization's accounting records to ensure that proper policies and procedures were followed.

Balance Sheet—A financial statement that presents the assets, liabilities, and owner's equity of a business unit as of a specific date.

Bookkeeping—The recording phase of the accounting process.

Capital—Investment in a business by its owner(s).

Certified Public Accountant (CPA)—An accountant who has passed a rigorous examination, has met other requirements, and has been granted a special license. He or she is often called upon to attest to the fairness of financial information that organizations prepare.

Entity Concept—The principle that a business is a distinct economic unit that exists separately from its owner.

Expense—A cost incurred in the production of revenues; outflow of assets from business transactions that affects owner's equity.

Financial Accounting—The area of accounting that reports financial information to interested parties outside the organization.

Governmental Accounting—The area of accounting that reports the financial affairs of government agencies.

Income Statement—A summary of a firm's revenues and expenses and their effect on income during a specified period of time, such as a month or a year. It is also called a *profit and loss statement, an operating statement,* or an *earnings statement.*

Liability—A debt or obligation owed by a business to a creditor.

Management Accounting—The area of accounting that reports information to an organization's management for internal decision-making purposes.

Net Income—The amount by which the revenues of a business exceed its expenses over a specified period of time.

Net Loss—The amount by which the expenses of a business exceed its revenues over a specified period of time.

Note Payable—A written promise to pay a specified amount of money at a future date.

Owner's Equity—An owner's interest in the assets in the business.

Revenue—The cash receipts or claims to assets that result from selling a product or service to customers.

2accounts

—**Transaction**—An exchange that affects the assets, liabilities, or owner's equity of an organization.

QUESTIONS AND EXERCISES

1. What is the purpose of accounting?
2. Name some common users and uses of financial information.
3. Distinguish between bookkeeping and accounting.
4. List the three major areas of accounting.
5. Define the following terms and give some examples of each:
   a. Asset.
   b. Liability.
   c. Owner's equity.
6. What is the entity concept? Why is it important?
7. What are transactions? What are some typical examples of transactions?
8. What are revenues and expenses?
9. Define the following:
   a. Income statement.
   b. Balance sheet.
10. What items (assets, liabilities, owner's equity) in the accounting equation will increase and/or decrease in each of the following transactions?
    a. Purchased supplies on account.
    b. Cash received for services performed.
    c. Owner invested cash in the business.
    d. Paid electric bill.
    e. Purchased a car for the business.
11. What items (assets, liabilities, owner's equity) in the accounting equation will increase and/or decrease in each of the following transactions?
    a. Purchased equipment for the business.
    b. Paid the water bill.
    c. Owner invested an automobile in the business.
    d. Cash received for services performed.
    e. Purchased auto parts on a credit basis.
12. Indicate whether each of the following will increase or decrease owner's equity.
    a. Paid the electric bill.

b. Received cash for services rendered.

c. Paid the telephone bill.

PROBLEMS

1–1. J. L. Tollie is an insurance salesman. As of September 30, Tollie owned the following business-related property:

Cash	$1,350	Office supplies	$ 350
Office equipment	9,200	Automobile	12,000

22,900

As of the same date, Tollie owed business creditors as follows:

Myers Office Supply Co.	$ 120
Boyce Equipment Co.	1,250

1,390

21,530

a. On the basis of the above information, fill in the following blanks in the accounting equation:

Assets $_____ = Liabilities $_____ + Owner's Equity $_____

b. Assuming that during the month of October there is an increase in business assets of $350 and an increase in business liabilities of $510, compute the resulting accounting equation:

Assets $_____ = Liabilities $_____ + Owner's Equity $_____

c. Assuming that during November there is a decrease in business assets of $250 and a decrease in business liabilities of $260, give the resulting accounting equation:

Assets $_____ = Liabilities $_____ + Owner's Equity $_____

1–2. Alice Gibson is a beautician. As of June 30, Alice owned the following business-related property.

Cash	$ 850	Building	$30,000
Equipment	6,800	Beauty supplies	300

As of the same date, Alice owed business creditors $900.

a. On the basis of the above information, fill in the following blanks in the accounting equation:

Assets $_____ = Liabilities $_____ + Owner's Equity $_____

b. Assuming that during the month of July there is an increase in business assets of $400 and an increase in business liabilities of $250, compute the resulting accounting equation:

Assets $_____ = Liabilities $_____ + Owner's Equity $_____

c. Assuming that during August there is a decrease in business assets of $250 and a decrease in business liabilities of $350, give the resulting accounting equation:

Assets $_____ = Liabilities $_____ + Owner's Equity $_____

1–3. During July, R. H. Pawson completed the following transactions. Record the dollar amount under the appropriate heading below to show the effect of each transaction on the accounting equation. A dollar amount should be preceded by a plus sign if it is an increase and by a minus sign if it is a decrease.

a. Purchased an automobile for business purposes, $8,000.

b. Sold a used desk from the office for $350.

c. Purchased a typewriter on account, $450.

d. Paid $150 for July advertising expense.

	Assets			= Liabilities +	Owner's Equity		
	Cash	+ Office Equipment	+ Auto-mobile	= Accounts Payable	+ R. H. Pawson Capital	+ Revenue	− Expense
Bal.	$10,000	$14,000	$0	$3,000	$21,000	$0	$0
a.	_____	_____	_____	_____	_____	_____	_____
Bal.							
b.	_____	_____	_____	_____	_____	_____	_____
Bal.							
c.	_____	_____	_____	_____	_____	_____	_____
Bal.							
d.	_____	_____	_____	_____	_____	_____	_____
Bal.	_____	_____	_____	_____	_____	_____	_____

1–4. W. C. Smith is a barber, and on February 1, 1987, Smith's business, Smith's Barbershop, had the following balance sheet.

SMITH'S BARBERSHOP
Balance Sheet
February 1, 1987

Assets

Cash	$ 1,500
Equipment	2,350
Building	25,000
Total assets	$28,850

Liabilities

Accounts payable	$ 250

Owner's Equity

W. C. Smith, capital	28,600
Total liabilities and owner's equity	$28,850

The following transactions were made during the month. Indicate their effect on the accounting equation:

a. Purchased equipment on account, $1,150.

b. Withdrew $300 for personal expenses.

c. Paid $250 on accounts payable.

d. Receipts for the month totaled $3,500 (all in cash).

e. Cash expenses for the month totaled $1,200.

	Assets			=	Liabilities +		Owner's Equity		
	Cash	+ Equipment	+ Building	=	Accounts Payable	+	W. C. Smith, Capital	+ Revenue	− Expense
Bal.	$1,500	$2,350	$25,000		$250		$28,600	$0	$0
a.	___	___	___		___		___	___	___
Bal.									
b.	___	___	___		___		___	___	___
Bal.									
c.	___	___	___		___		___	___	___
Bal.									
d.	___	___	___		___		___	___	___
Bal.									
e.	___	___	___		___		___	___	___
Bal.	___	___	___		___		___	___	___

1–5. J. E. Drake owns and operates Reelow Cleaners. At the beginning of the month, the books show the following totals:

Cash	$ 3,000
Accounts receivable	1,600
Dry cleaning equipment	17,500
Office equipment	4,000
Delivery truck	12,000
Accounts payable	1,000
J. E. Drake, capital	33,100
Revenue	6,000
Expense	2,000

Set up an accounting equation form using the given totals, and then record the effects of the following transactions on the equation (using plus, minus, and equal signs). Compute new totals after each transaction. (See Problem 1–3.)

a. Rendered services for cash, $600.

b. Paid salaries, $1,500.

c. Performed services worth $2,800.

d. Purchased adding machine for office on account, $400.
e. Received $2,600 from customers in payment of their accounts.
f. Paid creditors, $450.
g. Paid rent, $1,000.
h. Purchased a new steam press on account, $4,500.

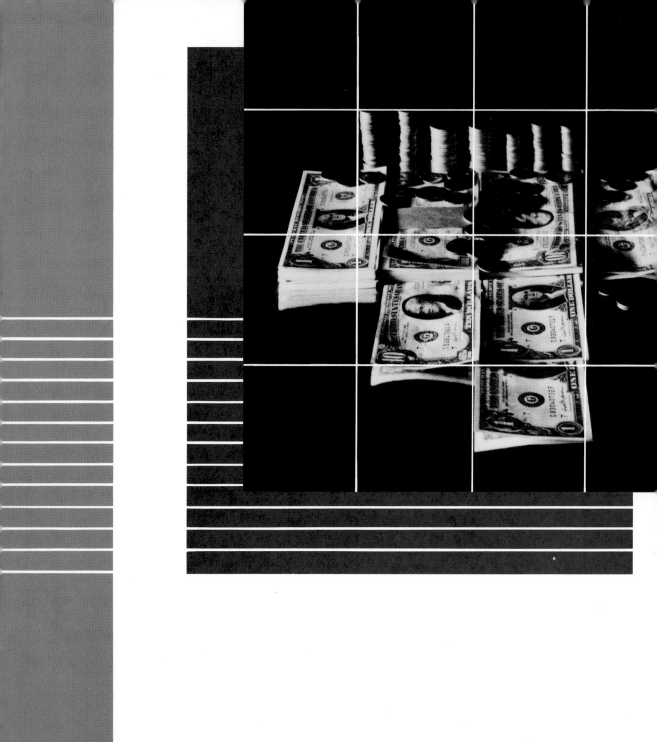

CHAPTER 2

Double-entry accounting

LEARNING OBJECTIVES

In this chapter you will learn the basic rules and procedures of double-entry accounting. After studying this chapter, you should be able to:

1. Explain the basic principles of double-entry accounting.
2. Record transactions in accounts.
3. Total the accounts and determine their balances.
4. Prepare a trial balance.

THE INTRODUCTION

In Chapter 1 the accounting equation was introduced:

$$\text{Assets} = \text{Liabilities} + \text{Owner's Equity}$$

Assets are property and other items that are owned by and add value to a business. Liabilities are the debts or obligations of a business. The amount left over after obligations are paid is owner's equity, or the owner's interest in the firm's assets.

A series of transactions was illustrated in Chapter 1. Phil Wind started a TV repair business by investing cash (an asset). He purchased some parts and repaired some TVs. In the process, Phil's business generated revenues and incurred expenses.

Totals were taken of the assets, liabilities, owner's equity, revenues, and expenses that arose from Speedy TV Repair's business transactions. An income statement was prepared which summarized the effect of revenue and expense transactions for the month of October and showed that income exceeded expenses by $1,100. This amount was Speedy TV Repair's net income for the month.

A balance sheet was also prepared. It listed all the assets, liabilities, and owner's equity amounts as of October 31, 1987. Remember that the total of the assets, $6,800, was the same as the total of the liabilities and owner's equity. Assets must always equal the sum of the liabilities and owner's equity to satisfy the accounting equation.

DOUBLE-ENTRY ACCOUNTING

Double-entry accounting evolved from the accounting equation Assets = Liabilities + Owner's Equity. As shown in Chapter 1, each transaction has a double effect on the accounting equation. At least two items are affected by each transaction. When Phil Wind invested $5,000 cash in his TV repair business, both an asset (cash) and owner's equity (capital) were increased by $5,000. Each side of the equation was affected, and the equation balanced after that transaction and after every other transaction in Chapter 1. This double effect is the basis of double-entry accounting. The double-entry system also provides a check on the arithmetic accuracy of recorded business transactions. Without this automatic check, locating an error would be very time consuming and costly.

ACCOUNTS

A business's financial records must contain more detailed information than just the totals of assets, liabilities, and owner's equity. Each of these three basic classifications is composed of many subclassifications. For example, the Speedy TV Repair Shop's total assets were composed of cash, accounts receivable, parts, and equipment. Each of these assets requires a separate set of records kept in a separate account. An **account** is the record used to classify and store information about increases and decreases in an item.

The number of accounts depends on the amount of detail desired in the financial records. For example, the asset classification *Cash* could be composed of cash on hand, a checking account balance, a savings account balance, and a petty cash fund for paying small expenses. In a TV repair shop, the Parts account might cover tubes, transistors, resistors, wires, and so on. Or, if desired, separate accounts could be kept for each specific part. Because it is more expensive to keep elaborate records, the additional cost must be weighed against the benefits of the additional information available that more detailed records provide.

An account is often represented in a form called a **T account.** The T account received its name from its shape:

Account Title

Debits	Credits

The left side of a T account is the **debit** side, and the right side is the **credit** side. Thus, to debit an account is to record a dollar amount on the left side of the account, and to credit an account is to record a dollar amount on the right side. Debit is often abbreviated **Dr.;** credit is abbreviated **Cr.**

When T accounts are used, increases and decreases are recorded by debiting and crediting the accounts in question. The general classification T accounts below are set up in the form of the accounting equation, $A = L + OE$. They show the rules for increasing and decreasing each kind of account.

Assets		=	**Liabilities**		+	**Owner's Equity**	
Debit	Credit		Debit	Credit		Debit	Credit
Increase	Decrease		Decrease	Increase		Decrease	Increase
+	−		−	+		−	+

To show an increase in an asset, one must debit the account; that is, enter the dollar amount on the left side of the T account. Since both sides of the accounting equation must balance, an increase in an asset account must be accompanied by an increase in a liability or owner's equity account or a decrease in another asset account. To show an increase in a liability or owner's equity, the dollar amount must be credited, or entered on the right side of the T account. When transactions are properly recorded in T accounts, the accounting equation will always balance, and the dollar values of the debits and credits will always be equal.

An asset account will usually have a debit balance, while liability and owner's equity accounts will usually have credit balances. An account has a **debit balance** when the sum of the transactions recorded on the left side (debits) of the T account is greater than the sum of the transactions recorded on the right side (credits). Conversely, an account has a **credit balance** when the sum of the transactions on the right side (credits) are greater than those on the left (debits). Asset accounts tend to have debit balances because increases to assets are recorded as debits and increases usually outvalue decreases. The opposite is usually true for liabilities and owner's equity, because increases in those accounts are recorded as credits. To determine an account's balance, the total value on one side of the account is subtracted from the total value on the other side.

USING T ACCOUNTS

Assets

Increases in assets are debits and are recorded on the left side of the account.

Assets

Dr.	Cr.
Increase	Decrease
+	−

An asset may be increased in any of the following ways:

1. Cash or other property may be invested by the owner.
2. Liabilities may increase.
3. Another asset may be decreased.

Decreases in assets are credits and are recorded on the right side of the account. An asset may be decreased in any of the following ways:

1. Cash or other property may be withdrawn from the business by the owner.
2. Liabilities of the business may decrease.
3. Another asset may be increased.

Liabilities

Increases in liabilities are credits and are recorded on the right side of the account.

Liabilities

Dr.	Cr.
Decrease	Increase
−	+

Liabilities may be increased in any of the following ways:

1. Assets may increase.
2. Other liabilities may be decreased.

Decreases in liabilities are debits and are recorded on the left side of the account. Liabilities may be decreased in either of the following ways:

1. Assets may decrease.
2. Other liabilities may increase.

Owner's equity

Since liabilities and owner's equity are on the same side of the accounting equation, owner's equity is increased just like a liability— by recording the amount on the right side of the account. Owner's equity is increased when the owner invests cash or other assets in the business.

Owner's Equity

Dr.	Cr.
Decrease	Increase
−	+

Owner's equity is decreased by recording an entry on the left side of the account. A decrease occurs when the owner withdraws cash or other assets from the business.

In summary, the left side of an account is the debit side, and the right side is the credit side. The accounting equation must balance, so debits must always equal credits. Asset accounts usually show debit balances, while liability and owner's equity accounts usually have credit balances.

RECORDING TRANSACTIONS IN T ACCOUNTS

The process of increasing and decreasing accounts with debits and credits will be illustrated by reworking the Speedy TV Repair Shop transactions using T accounts.

The first four transactions of the Speedy TV Repair Shop, as presented in Chapter 1, are summarized below:

	Transaction	The Business Receives	The Business Gives Up
a.	Phil Wind, owner, invests $5,000 cash to start the business	Cash	Ownership rights
b.	Wind purchases TV parts for $500 cash	Parts	Cash
c.	Wind purchases $1,000 of equipment on account	Equipment	A promise to pay (Accounts Payable)
d.	Wind pays $300 for part of the equipment purchased on account	A reduction in its promise to pay	Cash

The asset accounts

Transaction *a* was the original investment of $5,000 cash by the owner, Phil Wind. The $5,000 increase in cash is recorded as a debit to the Cash account, which is an asset. Since the owner put the cash into the business, the $5,000 increase is also credited to his capital account.

Assets		=	Liabilities	+	Owner's Equity	
Cash					**Phil Wind, Capital**	
Dr.	Cr.				Dr.	Cr.
(a) 5,000						(a) 5,000
Balance 5,000						Balance 5,000

By debiting the asset Cash and crediting the Phil Wind, Capital account for the same amount, the accounting equation is kept in balance. At this point, there is only one asset (cash), no liabilities, and the owner's capital account.

In Transaction *b,* Wind bought some TV parts for $500 cash. This transaction involves an increase in an asset (debit) offset by a decrease in another asset (credit). As a result of this transaction, a new asset, Parts, was acquired. This acquisition, however, was offset by a decrease in the asset Cash. In recording the transaction, the Parts account is debited for $500 and Cash is credited for $500, thus keeping the accounting equation in balance. Total assets still equal $5,000 (Cash $4,500 + Parts $500), and Owner's Equity equals $5,000.

Assets				=	Liabilities	+	Owner's Equity		
Cash							**Phil Wind, Capital**		
Dr.		Cr.					Dr.	Cr.	
(a)	5,000	(b)	500					(a)	5,000
Balance	4,500							Balance	5,000
Parts									
Dr.		Cr.							
(b)	500								
Balance	500								

The liability account

Phil Wind bought $1,000 of equipment on credit in Transaction *c.* This transaction causes an increase in an asset (debit) that is offset by an increase in a liability (credit). As a result of this transaction, a new asset, Equipment, was acquired, and, at the same time, a liability, Accounts Payable, was incurred. Again, separate accounts are maintained. In recording the transaction, Equipment is debited for $1,000, and Accounts Payable is credited for $1,000.

Assets =

	Cash				Parts				Equipment	
Dr.		Cr.		Dr.		Cr.		Dr.		Cr.
(a)	5,000	(b)	500	(b)	500			(c)	1,000	
Balance	4,500			Balance	500			Balance	1,000	

	Liabilities		+		**Owner's Equity**	
	Accounts Payable				**Phil Wind, Capital**	
Dr.		Cr.		Dr.		Cr.
		(c)	1,000			(a)	5,000
		Balance	1,000			Balance	5,000

As a result, the accounting equation is kept in balance with assets totaling $6,000 (Cash $4,500 + Parts $500 + Equipment $1,000) and liabilities (Accounts Payable $1,000) plus owner's equity (Phil Wind, Capital $5,000) adding up to the same $6,000 total.

Transaction *d* is the repayment of $300 of the debt incurred in Transaction *c*. The asset cash is reduced (credited) by $300, leaving a debit balance of $4,200. At the same time, the Accounts Payable account is reduced (debited) by $300, leaving a credit balance of $700.

Assets =

	Cash				Parts				Equipment	
Dr.		Cr.		Dr.		Cr.		Dr.		Cr.
(a)	5,000	(b)	500	(b)	500			(c)	1,000	
		(d)	300							
Balance	4,200			Balance	500			Balance	1,000	

	Liabilities		+		**Owner's Equity**	
	Accounts Payable				**Phil Wind, Capital**	
Dr.		Cr.		Dr.		Cr.
		(c)	1,000			(a)	5,000
(d)	300						
		Balance	700			Balance	5,000

The accounting equation still balances because total assets equal total liabilities plus owner's equity. This can be proven by comparing the total balances in the asset T accounts with the total balances in the T accounts for liabilities and owner's equity. For example, if we take the debit amount of $5,000 in the Cash account and subtract the credit total of $800, we get a debit balance of $4,200. The Parts account has a debit balance of $500, while the Equipment account has a debit balance of $1,000. Thus total assets are $5,700.

The liability account, Accounts Payable, has a credit amount of $1,000 and a debit amount of $300; thus the credit balance is $700. The Account Payable of $700 plus the $5,000 in the Phil Wind, Capital account added together equal $5,700, the same total as the total assets.

Before proceeding with Transactions *e* through *g,* we must expand the accounting equation to include revenue and expense accounts.

The revenue and expense accounts

Recall that to increase an asset account, you record the amount on the left side of the T account (debit the account). To increase a liability or an owner's equity account, you record the amount on the right side of the T account (credit the account).

We said earlier that owner's equity increases when the owner invests cash or other property in the business. This is only one of two ways in which owner's equity can be increased. An increase in owner's equity also occurs when revenue is earned from the sale of goods and services or from other sources. Thus, there are two ways for owner's equity to be increased:

1. The owner may invest additional cash or other property (assets) in the business.
2. Revenue may be earned from the sale of goods and services or from other sources.

Earning revenue also causes an increase in assets. Page 30 listed three ways in which assets could be increased. The fourth way to increase an asset is through revenue earned from the sale of goods and services or other sources.

Similarly, there are two ways in which owner's equity may be decreased. The first, the owner's withdrawal of cash or other property (assets) from the business, was mentioned on page 31. But owner's equity also decreases when expenses are incurred in the course of operating the business. By increasing expenses (which decreases own-

er's equity), assets may also be decreased. An alternative effect of
increasing expenses is to increase a liability.

Because an increase in revenue reflects an increase in owner's equity,
a revenue T account is treated the same as an owner's equity T
account. An increase in a revenue account is shown by a credit,
while a decrease is shown by a debit.

Revenues

Dr.	Cr.
Decrease	Increase
−	+

Expenses decrease owner's equity. So an increase to an expense
account is shown by a debit, and a decrease is shown by a credit.

Expenses

Dr.	Cr.
Increase	Decrease
+	−

When revenues and expenses are added to the accounting equation,
the expanded equation is:

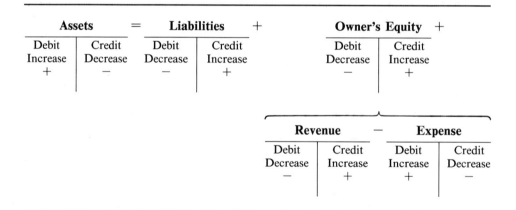

The expanded equation still balances, and the dollar amounts of the
debits and credits will always be equal. The asset and expense accounts
will normally have debit balances. The liability, owner's equity, and
revenue accounts will normally have credit balances.

After Transaction *d,* the Speedy TV Repair Shop's accounts had
the following balances:

| Assets | | | | | | = |

Cash		+	Parts		+	Equipment	
Dr.	Cr.		Dr.	Cr.		Dr.	Cr.
4,200				500			1,000	

Liabilities		+	Owner's Equity	
Accounts Payable			Phil Wind, Capital	
Dr.	Cr.		Dr.	Cr.
	700			5,000

The last three transactions of Speedy TV Repair Shop are summarized below:

Transaction	The Business Receives	The Business Gives Up
e. Customers pay $1,000 cash for repair services	Cash	Services
f. Wind repairs TVs for $800 on account	Customer's promise to pay (Accounts Receivable)	Services
g. Wind pays $700 rent	Right to occupy building	Cash

The revenue account. Transaction *e* occurred when customers paid the shop $1,000 in cash for TV repair services. This transaction involves an increase in an asset offset by an increase in owner's equity resulting from revenue. Cash was increased as a result of customers' payments for services, and, at the same time, owner's equity increased as a result of revenue generated. In recording the transaction, Cash is debited for $1,000, and Revenue is credited for $1,000, thus keeping the accounting equation in balance.

				Assets					
	Cash		+		**Parts**		+		**Equipment**

Dr.		Cr.		Dr.		Cr.		Dr.		Cr.
	4,200				500				1,000	
(e)	**1,000**									
Balance	5,200			Balance	500			Balance	1,000	

	Liabilities		+			**Owner's Equity**			
	Accounts Payable				**Phil Wind, Capital**		+		**Revenue**

Dr.		Cr.		Dr.		Cr.		Dr.		Cr.	
			700				5,000				
									(e)		**1,000**
		Balance	700			Balance	5,000			Balance	1,000

Total assets are now $6,700 (Cash $5,200, Parts $500, and Equipment $1,000). Liabilities are $700 (Accounts Payable), and owner's equity is composed of $5,000 of capital and $1,000 of revenue, or $6,000.

In Transaction *f,* repair services were performed on account. Because payment won't be received until a later date, a fourth kind of asset, accounts receivable, must be recorded. Providing services to customers on account created an increase in an asset offset by an increase in owner's equity. Accounts receivable was increased due to the promise to pay, and, at the same time, owner's equity was increased due to the revenue generated. In recording the transaction, Accounts Receivable is debited for $800, and Revenue is credited for $800. As a result, the accounting equation remains in balance (see page 39).

Total assets are now $7,500 (Cash $5,200, Accounts Receivable $800, Parts $500, and Equipment $1,000). Revenue now totals $1,800, and when it is added to the $5,000 in the Capital account, total owner's equity equals $6,800. The $6,800 of owner's equity added to the $700 of Accounts Payable equal $7,500, the total of liabilities and owner's equity.

The expense account. Transaction g is the payment of $700 of rent, which is an expense. Here, a decrease in an asset is offset by a decrease in owner's equity. As a result of this transaction, cash

Assets = Liabilities + Owner's Equity

Assets

Cash				Accounts Receivable				Parts				Equipment	
Dr.	Cr.			Dr.	Cr.			Dr.	Cr.			Dr.	Cr.
4,200								500				1,000	
(e) 1,000				(f) 800									
Balance 5,200				Balance 800				Balance 500				Balance 1,000	

Liabilities + Owner's Equity

Accounts Payable

Dr.	Cr.
	700
Balance	700

Phil Wind, Capital

Dr.	Cr.
	5,000
Balance	5,000

Revenue

Dr.	Cr.
	(e) 1,000
	(f) 800
Balance	1,800

39

Assets =

Cash			Accounts Receivable			Parts			Equipment	
Dr.		Cr.	Dr.		Cr.	Dr.		Cr.	Dr.	Cr.
4,200			(f) 800			500			1,000	
(e) 1,000	(g)	700								
Balance 4,500			Balance 800			Balance 500			Balance 1,000	

Liabilities

Accounts Payable	
Dr.	Cr.
	700
	Balance 700

Owner's Equity

Phil Wind, Capital		Revenue		Rent Expense	
Dr.	Cr.	Dr.	Cr.	Dr.	Cr.
	5,000		(e) 1,000	(g) 700	
			(f) 800		
	Balance 5,000		Balance 1,800	Balance 700	

was decreased by the rent payment, and owner's equity was decreased by the expense that was incurred. In recording the transaction, Rent Expense is debited for $700, and Cash is credited for $700 (see page 40). The accounting equation remains in balance. Cash is now $4,500. This amount added to Accounts Receivable of $800, Parts of $500, and Equipment of $1,000 equals $6,800. Owner's equity is now the $5,000 in the Capital account plus the $1,800 in the Revenue account. However, Rent Expense reduces owner's equity, so the $700 subtracted from the $6,800 leaves $6,100 of owner's equity to be added to the $700 of Accounts Payable. Liabilities and owner's equity also equal $6,800.

The account balances

After all transactions have been entered in the appropriate T accounts, each account must be totaled to determine its **balance.** When there is only one transaction recorded in a T account, the balance is that figure. The balance is a debit or credit depending on whether the amount is on the left (debit) side or the right (credit) side of the T account.

When there have been many transactions in an account, the balance is not so readily apparent. In that case, the balance is found by adding first the debit column and then the credit column and subtracting the smaller amount from the larger amount. If the total is on the left side of the T account, it is a debit balance. If it is on the right side, it is a credit balance.

For example, let's look at Speedy TV Repair's Cash account. The debit side adds up to $6,000 and the credits total $1,500. A double line is placed under each amount to indicate that it is the total for its side of the account. Since the debit side is larger, the $1,500 of credits is subtracted from the $6,000 of debits, and the net debit balance of $4,500 is written on the debit side.

		Cash		
(a)	5,000	*(b)*		500
(e)	1,000	*(d)*		300
		(g)		700
	6,000			1,500
Balance	4,500			

The next page shows how the Speedy TV Repair Shop's T accounts would look after balances are determined in all of the accounts. Note

Assets =

Cash

Dr.		Cr.	
(a)	5,000	(b)	500
(e)	1,000	(d)	300
		(g)	700
	6,000		1,500
Balance	4,500		

+

Accounts Receivable

Dr.		Cr.	
	800	(f)	

+

Parts

Dr.		Cr.	
(b)	500		

+

Equipment

Dr.		Cr.	
(c)	1,000		

Liabilities

+

Accounts Payable

Dr.		Cr.	
(d)	300	(c)	1,000
		Balance	700

+

Owner's Equity

Phil Wind, Capital

Dr.		Cr.	
		(a)	5,000

+

Revenue

Dr.		Cr.	
		(e)	1,000
		(f)	800
		Balance	1,800

−

Rent Expense

Dr.		Cr.	
(g)	700		

that Accounts Payable has amounts on both the debit and the credit side. There is no need to write the totals in since only one amount is on each side, but the balance should be determined as a $700 credit. The Revenue account has amounts on only the credit side, but the $1,800 credit balance is recorded (see page 42).

As you can see, the asset accounts all have debit balances. The liability and owner's equity (capital) account have credit balances. Because the Revenue account increases owner's equity, it has a credit balance. However, because the Expense account decreases owner's equity, it has a debit balance.

The revenue and expense accounts would be used to prepare the income statement. The balances in the asset, liability, and owner's equity accounts would be combined with the net income figure to prepare the balance sheet. In summary, the debit and credit rules are:

	Assets	Liabilities	Owner's Equity	Revenues	Expenses
Increase	Debit	Credit	Credit	Credit	Debit
Decrease	Credit	Debit	Debit	Debit	Credit

THE TRIAL BALANCE

As a result of the accounting equation and the rules of debits and credits in double-entry accounting, total debit balances in all accounts always equal total credit balances in all accounts. A way of verifying that the account totals are equal is to prepare a trial balance. A **trial balance** is a listing of all the asset, liability, capital, revenue, and expense account balances at one point in time. All debits are summed, as are all credits, to ensure that total debits equal total credits. A trial balance may be prepared at any time you want to know the balances in the accounts. The trial balance for the Speedy TV Repair Shop would appear as shown in Illustration 2–1. Note the order in which the accounts are listed: assets, liabilities, owner's equity, revenues, and expenses. Thus, balance sheet items are listed first, followed by items for the income statement. Also note that the accounts balance; that is, total debits ($7,500) equal total credits ($7,500).

A trial balance is also often used as a worksheet to help in the

**ILLUSTRATION
2–1**

	SPEEDY T.V. REPAIR SHOP		
	Trial Balance		
	October 31, 1987		

ACCT. NO.	ACCOUNT NAME	DEBIT	CREDIT
	Cash	4 5 0 0 00	
	Accounts receivable	8 0 0 00	
	Parts	5 0 0 00	
	Equipment	1 0 0 0 00	
	Accounts payable		7 0 0 00
	Phil Wind, capital		5 0 0 0 00
	Revenue		1 8 0 0 00
	Rent expense	7 0 0 00	
		7 5 0 0 00	7 5 0 0 00

preparation of financial statements. Refer to the income statement on page 16 and to the balance sheet on page 17. Note that the figures from the trial balance are repeated in these financial statements.

SUMMARY

The accounting equation is the basis for **double-entry accounting.** Every transaction affects at least two accounts, and the debit must equal the credit. Thus, each transaction has a double effect on the equation. This double effect is the basis for double-entry accounting. The double-entry system provides a check on arithmetic accuracy, since debit amounts and credit amounts must be equal.

An **account** is a record of each item within the three major accounting classifications: assets, liabilities, and owner's equity. Each account has a debit side and a credit side. The account can be represented in the form of a **T account** with **debits** on the left side and the **credits** on the right side. The T account received its name from its shape:

Account Title

Debits	Credits

Assets are increased by debits and decreased by credits. Liabilities and owner's equity are decreased by debits and increased by credits.

Owner's equity is affected by investments and withdrawals by the owner and by the results of business operations. As a result of operations, revenues are earned and expenses are incurred. Owner's equity is increased by revenues and decreased by expenses. The owner's equity section of the accounting equation can be expanded to include revenues and expenses.

Each transaction is entered in the proper T accounts as either a debit or credit. The effect the transaction has on the account determines its placement on either the debit or the credit side. An increase in cash requires the amount to be placed on the debit side of the account. A decrease in cash requires placement of the dollar amount on the credit side.

After all the transactions have been recorded in the T accounts for a period of time, the debit and credit sides of each account are totaled. Each account's **balance** is determined by subtracting the smaller amount from the larger amount, and the difference (balance) is placed in the proper debit or credit side. An account has a **debit balance** if its total debits are greater than its total credits. This is the usual balance for asset and expense accounts. An account has a **credit balance** if its total credits are greater than its total debits. Liability, owner's capital, and revenue accounts usually have a credit balance. Once each account's balance is determined, a trial balance can be prepared. A **trial balance** is a listing of all the account balances at a specific point in time. All debits are summed, as are all credits, to ensure that total debits equal total credits. Financial statements can be prepared from the trial balance.

KEY TERMS

Account—A form or record kept for each item within the three major account classifications: assets, liabilities, and owner's equity. Accounts are used to classify and store information about increases and decreases in an item.

Balance—The subtraction of one side of a T account from the other in order to determine the final total for the account.

Credit (Cr.)—The right-hand side of an account; placing an amount on the right-hand side of an account.

Credit Balance—The balance that occurs when an account's total credits are greater than its total debits. The usual balance of a liability, owner's capital, and revenue accounts.

Debit (Dr.)—The left-hand side of an account; placing an amount on the left-hand side of an account.

Debit Balance—The balance that occurs when an account's total debits are greater than its total credits. The usual balance of asset and expense accounts.

Double-Entry Accounting—An accounting system in which every transaction affects at least two accounts. There is a debit and a credit in each transaction. This system provides a check on the arithmetic accuracy of each transaction. It shows that each transaction has a double effect on the accounting equation.

T account—The physical form an account might take:

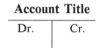

Account Title

| Dr. | Cr. |

Trial Balance—A listing of all the asset, liability, capital, revenue, and expense account balances at one point in time. All debits are summed, as are all credits, to ensure that their totals are equal.

QUESTIONS AND EXERCISES

1. What is the accounting equation?
2. What does a double-entry accounting system provide?
3. What is an account?
4. What are debits and credits? Which accounts normally have debit balances, and which accounts normally have credit balances?
5. List four ways assets may be:
   a. Increased.
   b. Decreased.
6. List three ways liabilities may be increased.
7. List two ways liabilities may be decreased.
8. List two ways owner's equity may be:
   a. Increased.
   b. Decreased.
9. How do you total an account?

10. What is a trial balance?

11. Check the correct answer in the following:

	Debit	Credit
a. To increase an asset	_____	_____
b. To increase a liability	_____	_____
c. To decrease owner's equity	_____	_____
d. To increase revenue	_____	_____
e. To increase expense	_____	_____

12. Check the correct answer in the following:

	Debit	Credit
a. To decrease a liability	_____	_____
b. To increase expense	_____	_____
c. To increase owner's equity	_____	_____
d. To decrease an asset	_____	_____
e. To increase revenue	_____	_____

PROBLEMS

2–1. J. T. Carol, M.D., has just retired from the U.S. Navy and established a local practice. Carol's business transactions during the first month were:

a. Invested $9,000 in the business.

b. Paid office rent for one month, $1,500.

c. Purchased professional equipment from Super Medical Supplies, $27,500, on account.

d. Received $12,350 for services rendered to patients during the month.

e. Paid $900 salary to office secretary.

f. Paid telephone bill, $150.

Required:

1. Set up eight T accounts with the following titles: Cash; Professional Equipment; Accounts Payable; J. T. Carol, Capital; Professional Fees; Rent Expense; Telephone Expense; and Salaries Expense.

2. Record Transactions *a* through *f* directly in these accounts.

3. Total the accounts and enter balances as necessary.

4. Prepare a trial balance of the accounts as of April 30, 1987.

2–2. F. T. Lewis has opened a business as a consulting forester. Lewis's business transactions for the month of March 1987 were:
   a. Invested $8,000 in the business.
   b. Gave car worth $7,000 to the business.
   c. Paid office rent for one month, $450.
   d. Purchased office furniture on account, $1,500.
   e. Purchased professional equipment, $500 on account.
   f. Paid $400 salary to part-time office secretary.
   g. Received $2,000 for consulting services for the month.
   h. Paid telephone bill, $120.

Required:

   1. Set up 10 T accounts with the following titles: Cash; Office Furniture; Professional Equipment; Automobile; Accounts Payable; F. T. Lewis, Capital; Consulting Fees; Rent Expense; Telephone Expense; and Salary Expense.
   2. Record Transactions **a** through **h** directly to these accounts.
   3. Total the accounts and enter balances as necessary.
   4. Prepare a trial balance of the accounts, as of March 31, 1987.

2–3. Dr. D. A. Kyle opened a dentist's office on February 1, 1987. During the month of February, Dr. Kyle completed the following transactions:
   a. Invested $25,000 in the business.
   b. Paid office rent for February, $1,000.
   c. Purchased professional equipment, $15,000.
   d. Purchased office furniture, $2,000.
   e. Paid the receptionist for the month, $700.
   f. Paid the utilities bill, $100.
   g. Paid the telephone bill, $60.
   h. Received $8,400 for services rendered to patients during the month.

Required:

   1. Set up 9 T accounts with the following titles: Cash; Office Furniture; Professional Equipment; D. A. Kyle, Capital; Professional Fees; Rent Expense; Telephone Expense; Utilities Expense; and Salaries Expense.
   2. Record Transactions **a** through **h** directly in these accounts.
   3. Total the accounts and enter balances as necessary.
   4. Prepare a trial balance of the accounts, as of February 28, 1987.

2–4. R. W. Friedl started a real estate business on June 1, 1987, and during the month Friedl made the following transactions:

a. Invested $8,000 into the business.
b. Paid $1,200 rent for the office building for the month of June.
c. Sold a house and received a commission of $1,000.
d. Purchased office furniture for the business giving a note for $11,500. (Friedl agreed to pay $1,150 at the end of each month.)
e. Purchased office equipment and agreed to pay for the office equipment within 30 days. Total bill, $1,450.
f. Sold a building and received a commission of $3,000.
g. Paid telephone bill, $300.
h. Paid for advertising in the local newspaper, $125.
i. Sold a house, receiving a commission, $700.
j. Paid electric bill, $300.
k. Paid the water bill, $25.
l. Put car worth $8,000 into the business.
m. Paid for gasoline and oil for the car, $135.
n. Paid secretary for the month, $700.
o. Sold a house and received a commission of $1,500.
p. Paid the monthly installment of $1,150 on the office furniture.
q. Paid for the office equipment in Transaction e, $1,450.

Required:

Part A

1. Set up 14 T accounts with the following titles: Cash; Office Furniture; Office Equipment; Automobile; Notes Payable; Accounts Payable; R. W. Friedl, Capital; Commission Earned; Rent Expense; Advertising Expense; Wages Expense; Utilities Expense; Gasoline and Oil Expense; and Telephone Expense.
2. Record Transactions **a** through **q.**
3. Total the accounts and enter balances as necessary.
4. Prepare a trial balance of the accounts, as of June 30, 1987.

Part B

From the trial balance, what is the amount of:

1. Assets.
2. Liabilities.
3. Owner's Equity + Revenue − Expenses.

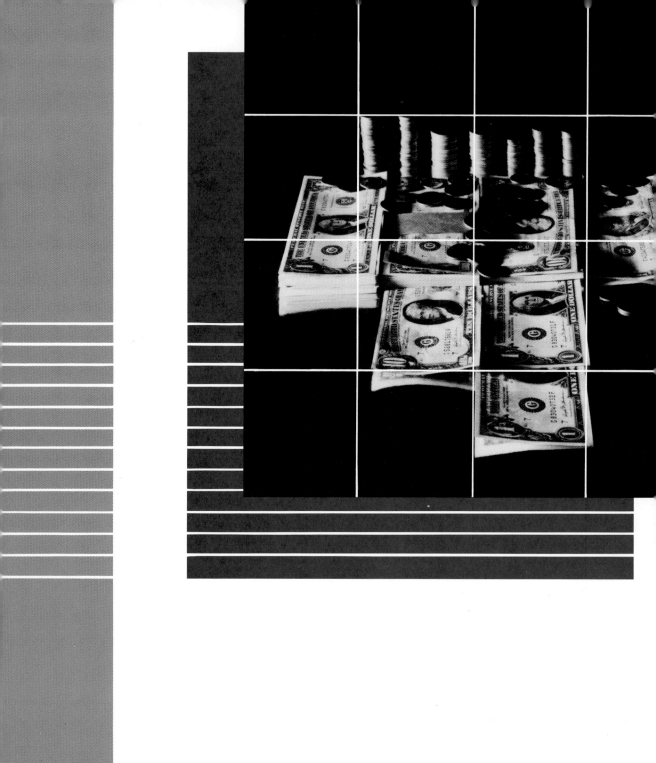

CHAPTER 3

Recording accounting information

LEARNING OBJECTIVES

In this chapter you will be introduced to several procedures and practices used in recording accounting information. After studying this chapter, you should be able to:

1. Record (journalize) transactions in the general journal.
2. Prove the general journal.
3. Post from the general journal to the general ledger.
4. Calculate and keep a running balance in each ledger account.
5. Prepare a trial balance.
6. Identify and correct errors in a trial balance.

Chapters 1 and 2 introduced the basic accounting elements—assets, liabilities, owner's equity, revenues, and expenses—and the basic accounting equation. Different kinds of transactions were analyzed for their effects on the accounting equation. Every transaction has a dual effect, and the recording of these two effects is a distinguishing feature of the double-entry system of accounting. In Chapters 1 and 2, little attention was paid to recording procedures because the focus was on the basic elements of accounting and their relationships in double-entry accounting. Now it is time to examine some of the most common recording procedures.

RECORDING TRANSACTIONS

Information about a business transaction flows from (1) business papers, source documents, or other recording devices to (2) the journal entries to (3) the accounts to (4) the trial balance to (5) the financial statements.

(1) Source Document		(2) Journal Entry		(3) Ledger Accounts		(4) Trial Balance		(5) Financial Statements
	$\rightarrow$		$\rightarrow$		$\rightarrow$		$\rightarrow$	

Business papers, or source documents

In almost every business, a written record is prepared for every transaction that takes place. These **business papers,** or source documents, may be handwritten or prepared mechanically. Among the most common business papers are payroll timecards, purchase and sales invoices, cash register tapes, deposit slips, check stubs or carbon copies of checks, duplicate sales tickets, and similar items.

The journal

Although a transaction may originally be noted on a business paper or in a business machine, its first recording in terms of double-entry accounting occurs in the journal. For this reason, the journal is called a *book of original entry.* The **journal** is the place where all transactions are initially recorded. It is a chronological record of the day-to-day transactions. An accountant analyzes each transaction to determine its debit and credit effects upon the accounts and then prepares the journal entry. Every journal entry states:

1. The date of the transaction.
2. The titles of the accounts to be debited and credited.
3. The dollar amounts of the debits and credits.
4. A brief explanation of the transaction.

The process of transferring the information contained in a business document to the journal is known as **journalizing.**

The actual form of a journal may vary among firms of different size and with different business activities. The simplest form of journal—often called a **general journal**—contains only two money columns, one for debit amounts and one for credit amounts.

A sample of a general journal is shown below. At the top of each page is a heading that identifies the book as a general journal (1). Each page is numbered (2) in consecutive order. There is a Date column (3) for the year, month, and day. The Account and Explanation column (4) is used to record the account titles of each transaction and an explanation of the transaction. There are two money columns—a Debit column (5) and a Credit column (6)—and a Posting Reference (P.R.) column (7) for cross-referencing. Note that the lines of the journal are numbered for easy reference (8). We will explain each of these items as we prepare a journal entry.

Preparing journal entries

When a **journal entry** is made, information about the transaction is taken from some form of business paper. For example, let's assume that G. Hunter invests $8,000 to start a plumbing business and that the business paper is a bank deposit receipt for $8,000. Now we want to record this transaction in the general journal. The top of the page has a heading identifying it as a general journal. The number

1 is written as the page number since this is the first transaction of a new business. The lines of the journal are numbered for easy reference. The first item entered in the Date column is the year, in our case, 1987. The year is not repeated on the page unless an entry for a transaction in a new year is recorded. The next items entered in the Date column are the month and the day of the transaction. Our transaction takes place on May 1. The month is not repeated on the page unless a transaction in a new month is recorded. Instead, only the day of each transaction is entered in the Date column.

	GENERAL JOURNAL			PAGE 1
DATE	ACCOUNT AND EXPLANATION	P.R.	DEBIT	CREDIT
1 1987				
2 May 1	Cash		8 0 0 0 00	
3	G. Hunter, Capital			8 0 0 0 00
4	Investment by owner.			
5				
6 1	Equipment		4 0 0 00	
7	Cash			4 0 0 00
8	Purchase of typewriter.			
9				

The Account and Explanation column is used to record the titles of the accounts (at least two) affected by each transaction. It is also used to provide a brief explanation of the transaction. Each account title is recorded on a separate line. The title of the account debited is entered first and is started at the left margin of the Account and Explanation column. The title of the account credited is placed on the next line, starting approximately one-half inch to the right of the margin. The explanation of the transaction is written on the next line and is usually indented slightly, but not as much as the title of the account credited.

The first money column is labeled the Debit column. It is used to record the dollar amount of each account that is to be debited. Similarly, the second money column is called the Credit column. It is used to record the dollar amount of each account that is to be credited. The dollar amount of the debit should be written on the same line as the title of the account to be debited. Likewise, the dollar amount of the credit should be written on the same line as the title of the account to be credited.

In our first entry, Cash is the account to be debited, so Cash is written against the left margin of the Account and Explanation column. The amount of $8,000 is then entered in the Debit column.

G. Hunter, Capital is the credit account that is entered on the second line, indented one-half inch from the margin. And $8,000 is entered in the credit column. Finally, an explanation, slightly indented, is entered on the third line of the journal. The fourth line is left blank because a line is always skipped between transactions.

Immediately after starting the business, Hunter purchased a typewriter for $400. In doing so, he increased the asset account Equipment, which must be debited, and decreased the Cash account, which must be credited. Since this transaction takes place on the same day as the first one, only the day, the first, is entered in the Date column. The account to be debited, Equipment, is written first, next to the left margin, and $400 is entered in the Debit column. Then the account to be credited, Cash, is entered on the next line, indented one-half inch from margin and $400 is entered in the credit column. Again a brief explanation is entered.

The P.R. (Posting Reference) column is not used during the journalizing process. It is used for cross-referencing, as explained later in this chapter.

To summarize, the complete journalizing procedure consists of several distinct steps. Each transaction must be analyzed to:

1. Determine the kinds of accounts affected—asset, liability, owner's equity, revenue, or expense.
2. Identify the specific accounts affected.
3. Determine and record the dollar amount of the increase or decrease in terms of debits and credits.
4. Write the required explanation.

The entry is then written in the journal *(journalized)*. The entry is made either at the time the transaction takes place or very shortly thereafter. In either case, the transactions are entered in the journal in chronological order—that is, according to the dates on which they occurred.

In journalizing, the debit portion of an entry is traditionally recorded first. Indenting the title of the account that is credited helps the accountant identify where the credit part of the entry begins.

The chart of accounts

Because even a small business may have many different accounts, a system must be established that permits accounts to be easily identified and quickly located. In such a system, each account is labeled with both a number and a name. A list of all the accounts and their numbers is known as a **chart of accounts.**

The names chosen for the accounts and the total number of accounts employed depend on the amount of detail required, the size of the firm, and the nature of its activities. Generally, a separate account is kept for each form of asset, liability, owner's equity, revenue, and expense. In a chart of accounts, the individual accounts are usually grouped into these five major classifications and assigned numbers. The numbering system allows every account to be easily identified as either an asset, a liability, an owner's equity, a revenue, or an expense. For example, all accounts may be assigned a three-digit number with all asset accounts beginning with 1, all liabilities with 2, all owner's equities with 3, all revenues with 4, and all expenses with 5. The other two digits in the number identify a specific account within the general classification.

Presented in Illustration 3–1 is the chart of accounts established by J. D. Staple when she opened her law office. Note that the accounts within a given classification are not numbered in exact numerical order. The gaps in numbering permit the easy insertion of additional accounts when they are needed. Also note that a chart of accounts makes it easy for an accountant to locate the appropriate accounts when a journal entry must be made.

ILLUSTRATION 3–1

J. D. STAPLE LAW FIRM
Chart of Accounts

Account No.	Name of Account
100–199	*Assets:*
110	Cash
112	Accounts Receivable
147	Office Furniture
200–299	*Liabilities:*
212	Accounts Payable
300–399	*Owner's Equity:*
320	J. D. Staple, Capital
330	J. D. Staple, Drawing
400–499	*Revenue:*
420	Fees Earned
500–599	*Expenses:*
505	Office Rent Expense
514	Advertising Expense
521	Office Supplies Expense
523	Dial-A-Phone Expense
570	Wages Expense
590	Miscellaneous Expense

HOW TO JOURNALIZE

To illustrate the journalizing procedure, we will record the transactions of the J. D. Staple Law Firm from July 1, 1987, through July 31, 1987. The firm's general journal with all of its recorded entries is reproduced in Illustration 3–2, at the end of the step-by-step analysis.

J. D. Staple opened her law office on July 1, 1987, by investing $5,000 in the business. Thus, the firm acquired an asset, Cash, in the amount of $5,000, in exchange for an equal amount of ownership rights. This increase in the Cash account is recorded by a debit of $5,000. The owner's equity account, J. D. Staple, Capital, is also increased by $5,000. An increase in an owner's equity account is recorded by a credit. The required entry in the general journal is:

	GENERAL JOURNAL				PAGE 1
DATE	ACCOUNT AND EXPLANATION	P.R.	DEBIT	CREDIT	
1 1987					
2 July 1	Cash		5 0 0 0 00		
3	J.D. Staple, Capital			5 0 0 0 00	
4	Investment by owner.				

The journalizing process consisted of the following steps:

1. The year, 1987, was written at the top of the Date column because this is the first transaction recorded in 1987.
2. The month and the day were entered in the Date column.
3. On the same line as the month and day, the title of the account to be debited, Cash, was written at the far left of the Account and Explanation column. The amount of asset increase—$5,000—was entered in the Debit column on the same line.
4. Indented about one-half inch on the next line is the title of the account to be credited, J. D. Staple, Capital. The amount of the increase in the owner's equity—$5,000—was entered on the same line in the Credit column. (Note: Only the title of the account is entered in the Account and Explanation column on the line where a debit or credit is entered.)
5. Indented slightly on the next line is a brief explanation of the transaction.

July 1, 1987

Office rent of $350 for the month of July was paid in cash.

		GENERAL JOURNAL				
DATE		ACCOUNT AND EXPLANATION	P.R.	DEBIT	CREDIT	
5						
6 July	1	Office Rent Expense		3 5 0 00		
7		Cash			3 5 0 00	
8		Paid rent for July 1987.				

The effect of this transaction is to decrease the asset Cash and to decrease owner's equity. The decrease in owner's equity is made by increasing Office Rent Expense. Remember that expense accounts have the effect of decreasing owner's equity, while revenue accounts have the effect of increasing owner's equity.

July 1, 1987

Office furniture is ordered from the Brand Furniture Store. Because the furniture must be ordered from the factory, the store cannot specify a delivery date. No journal entry is necessary until delivery of the furniture and receipt of the bill.

July 1, 1987

Dial-A-Phone, Inc., installed a telephone in the office. Both the $35 installation fee and the $25 July service charge are paid on this date.

9						
10	1	Dial-A-Phone Expense		6 0 00		
11		Cash			6 0 00	
12		Payment of installation and service charge.				

The transaction results in a decrease in the asset Cash and an increase in an expense. The journal entry consists of a debit to Dial-A-Phone Expense for $60 and a credit to Cash for $60.

July 2, 1987

Office supplies costing $72 were purchased on account from Big Fudd's Supply.

13						
14	2	Office Supplies Expense		7 2 00		
15		Accounts Payable			7 2 00	
16		Purchased office supplies from Big Fudd's				
17		Supply Store.				

This transaction results in an account payable, which is a promise to pay a creditor (Big Fudd's Supply) at some future date. It is the incurrence of an expense.

July 3, 1987

Cash of $125 was received for legal services rendered to J. P. Crowell.

18									
19		3	Cash			1 2 5 00			
20			Fees Earned					1 2 5 00	
21			Revenue received for services.						

The transaction resulted in an increase in the asset Cash and an increase in the revenue account Fees Earned. The journal entry consists of a debit to Cash and a credit to Fees Earned for $125.

July 7, 1987

Brand Furniture Store delivered the office furniture that was ordered on July 1, 1987. J. D. Staple promised to pay them in 90 days.

22									
23		7	Office Furniture			1 1 4 0 00			
24			Accounts Payable					1 1 4 0 00	
25			Purchased office furniture from Brand Furniture						
26			Store; amount payable in 90 days.						

This transaction increases the asset account Office Furniture by $1,140 and increases the liability account Accounts Payable by $1,140.

July 8, 1987

Membership dues of $500 were paid to the Bar Association.

27									
28		8	Miscellaneous Expense			5 0 0 00			
29			Cash					5 0 0 00	

Assets are decreased. Expenses are increased and have the ultimate effect of decreasing owner's equity. The journal entry shows a debit to Miscellaneous Expense and a credit to Cash for $500.

July 15, 1987

Cash of $1,050 was received for professional legal services rendered for various clients. The entry is shown as a lump-sum amount. However, individual client records will be maintained to support the entry.

31						
32	15	Cash		1 0 5 0 00		
33		Fees Earned			1 0 5 0 00	
34		Revenue received for services.				

This transaction results in an increase in the asset Cash and an increase in the revenue account Fees Earned. Remember this ultimately increases the owner's equity account.

July 18, 1987

Cash of $73 was paid to a local newspaper for advertising.

35						
36	18	Advertising Expense		7 3 00		
37		Cash			7 3 00	
38		Advertising payment.				

This transaction results in a decrease in owner's equity (expense increase) and a reduction in the asset Cash. Thus, journalizing requires a debit to Advertising Expense and a credit to Cash for $73.

July 18, 1987

A part-time secretary is hired at a salary of $5 per hour. No journal entry is necessary at this time because no monetary transaction has taken place. Only after the secretary has begun work will the business be obligated to pay for his services.

July 29, 1987

Clients are billed for professional legal services for the period of July 16 through July 29. Cash of $1,640 will be received at a later date.

39						
40	29	Accounts Receivable		1 6 4 0 00		
41		Fees Earned			1 6 4 0 00	
42		Revenue billed for services.				

This transaction increases assets and increases the revenue account.

July 31, 1987

The secretary is paid wages of $90 for work during July.

43						
44	31	Wages Expense		9 0 00		
45		Cash			9 0 00	
46		Secretary's salary.				

This transaction results in a decrease in the asset account Cash and an increase in the expense account Wages Expense.

July 31, 1987

Staple withdraws $800 from the firm.

47						
48	31	J.D. Staple, Drawing		8 0 0 00		
49		Cash			8 0 0 00	
50		Withdrawal by owner.				

The owner's equity is decreased and so is the asset Cash. Withdrawal of any assets by an owner is recorded in the **owner's drawing account.** This procedure separates the owner's investment of assets from his or her withdrawals during an accounting period and simplifies the preparation of the balance sheet. Remember, investment of asset value by the owner is recorded in the capital account.

All of these transactions are shown in Illustration 3–2 as they would appear when entered in the general journal of the J. D. Staple Law Firm. Note that a line is skipped between each journal entry. Disregard the numbers in the P.R. column. They will be explained later.

Proving the journal

As each page in the journal is filled with entries, the accuracy of the journalizing process should be checked. This is done by first adding all the debits in the Debit column and then adding all the credits in the Credit column. The adding of the two columns is known as **footing** the columns. If the total of the Debit column equals the total of the Credit column, the journal has been proved; that is, the debits are equal to the credits in the entries on that page. The

ILLUSTRATION 3–2

**J. D. Staple
Law Firm
General
Journal**

	DATE		ACCOUNT AND EXPLANATION	P.R.	DEBIT	CREDIT
1	1987					
2	July	1	Cash	110	5 0 0 0 00	
3			J.D. Staple, Capital	320		5 0 0 0 00
4			Investment by owner.			
5						
6		1	Office Rent Expense	505	3 5 0 00	
7			Cash	110		3 5 0 00
8			Paid rent for July 1987.			
9						
10		1	Dial-A-Phone Expense	523	6 0 00	
11			Cash	110		6 0 00
12			Payment of phone installation.			
13						
14		2	Office Supplies Expense	521	7 2 00	
15			Accounts Payable	212		7 2 00
16			Purchased office supplies from Big Fudd's			
17			Supply Store.			
18						
19		3	Cash	110	1 2 5 00	
20			Fees Earned	420		1 2 5 00
21			Revenue received for services.			
22						
23		7	Office Furniture	147	1 1 4 0 00	
24			Accounts Payable	212		1 1 4 0 00
25			Purchased office furniture from Brand			
26			Furniture Store; amount payable in			
27			90 days.			
28						
29		8	Miscellaneous Expense	590	5 0 0 00	
30			Cash	110		5 0 0 00
31			Paid membership dues.			
32						
33		15	Cash	110	1 0 5 0 00	
34			Fees Earned	420		1 0 5 0 00
35			Revenue received for services.			
36						
37		18	Advertising Expense	514	7 3 00	
38			Cash	110		7 3 00
39			Advertising payment.			
40						
41		29	Accounts Receivable	112	1 6 4 0 00	
42			Fees Earned	420		1 6 4 0 00
43			Revenue billed for services.			
44						
45		31	Wages Expense	570	9 0 00	
46			Cash	110		9 0 00
47			Secretary's salary.			
48						
49		31	J.D. Staple, Drawing	330	8 0 0 00	
50			Cash	110		8 0 0 00
51			Withdrawal by owner.			
52					1 0 9 0 0 00	1 0 9 0 0 00
53						
54						
55						

totals are expected to be equal because the debits must equal the credits in each individual entry.

The totals, or footings, are entered on the last line of each filled page of the journal. Footings are also entered on the last horizontal line below the last entry on a partially filled page. These figures are written in smaller figures than the dollar amounts recorded for each entry. A double line is placed under the total in each column. In Illustration 3–2, note that the total is $10,900 in both the Debit and Credit columns.

POSTING

We have seen how the accountant prepares a chronological record of the business transactions by making entries in a journal. But in a sense, the information contained in a journal is still not in usable form for financial statement preparation. To be of any value, the data must be summarized. It would make little sense to offer as a financial statement a listing of several thousand individual cash receipts. However, when properly categorized and summarized, the details of the various transactions can yield useful information. This summarization/categorization process is carried out through the use of ledger accounts.

The general ledger

Ledger accounts are printed forms on sheets of paper or computer cards. If on sheets of paper, the accounts may be kept in a loose-leaf notebook or bound in a book. If the accounts are in card form, they are kept in a tray. A business's entire collection of account records is referred to as its **general ledger,** or simply as its **ledger.** The accounts are usually grouped in the ledger according to their classification as assets, liabilities, owner's equity, revenues, or expenses. The groupings are arranged to aid in the preparation of the financial statements, and the individual accounts are kept in the numerical order stated in the chart of accounts.

The T account ledger format, as shown in Illustration 3–3, has a place for the:

1. Account name.
2. Account number.

3. Date of debit entry.
4. Amount of debit entry.
5. Posting reference to the journal page where the debit amount was originally recorded.
6. Date of credit entry.
7. Amount of credit entry.
8. Posting reference to the journal page where the credit amount was originally recorded.

The Explanation column is used to write the word *balance* or other explanations when needed.

ILLUSTRATION 3–3

General Ledger: T Account Format

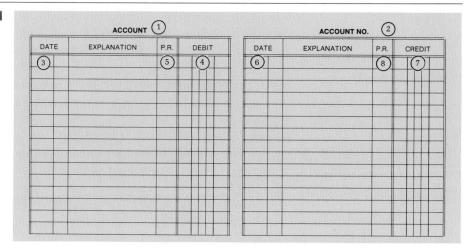

This T account format has been used to illustrate the concept that debits are recorded on the left side of the account and credits are recorded on the right. In Chapter 2, each side was added, a balance was determined, and the amount was written on the debit side if the total was a debit balance (debit amount being larger than the credit amount) or on the credit side if the total was a credit balance.

In actual practice, the T account format is seldom used in ledgers. Instead, a **balance-column account form** with one date column, separate debit and credit columns, and separate debit and credit balance columns is used. (See Illustration 3–4.) As each transaction is put into the appropriate ledger account, the dollar amount is added to or subtracted from the previous balance depending on whether the transaction is a debit or a credit and whether the previous balance is a debit or a credit. Thus, a **running balance** is kept that shows the total value in the ledger account as of the most recent transaction. The kind of account usually determines if the balance is shown in the debit or the credit column. Remember, asset and expense accounts normally have debit balances, while liability, owner's equity, and revenue accounts normally have credit balances.

As shown in Illustration 3–4, the balance-column account form has places for the:

1. Account name.
2. Account number.
3. Date of entry (debit or credit).
4. Amount of debit entry.
5. Amount of credit entry.
6. Running balance after each entry.
7. Posting reference for each entry.

ILLUSTRATION 3–4

General Ledger: Balance-Column Account Form

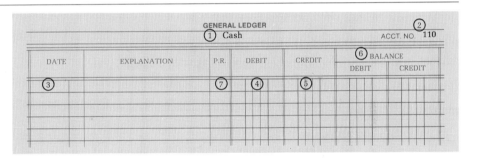

Opening accounts in the general ledger

To open an account in the general ledger, the account's title is written at the top of the account form, and the number of the account is entered to the right of the title. This information is taken from the chart of accounts. Cash is the account shown in Illustration 3–4.

Posting and cross-referencing

In a sense, a journal entry is a set of written instructions that tells what dollar amounts should be entered in which accounts and whether the accounts should be debited or credited. The process of transferring the journal entries to the accounts is known as **posting.** Through posting, information about a transaction recorded in the journal is transferred to the ledger accounts. Journal entries may be posted (1) immediately after the entry is recorded in the journal, (2) at the end of a specific period of time, such as a day, a week, or a month, or (3) after each journal page is filled.

In posting, the information transferred from the journal to the ledger consists of (1) the date of the transaction, (2) the dollar amount of the debit or credit, and (3) the number of the journal page that contains the item posted. The journal page number is recorded in the **P.R. (Posting Reference)** column in the ledger account. It provides a **cross-reference** between the journal and the ledger. After a dollar amount has been posted to a ledger account, the number of the account is entered in the P.R. column in the journal on the same line as the amount just posted. This shows that the journal entry has been posted and serves as a check on the completeness of the posting process. A transaction can be quickly traced from the journal to the ledger or vice versa by using the cross-reference numbers in the P.R. columns. Errors that may occur in the posting process can then be readily corrected.

In Illustration 3–5, the first transaction from the general journal of the J. D. Staple Law Firm, is properly posted and cross-referenced. The first line of the first entry on page 1 of the general journal indicates that a transaction occurred on July 1 that caused cash to increase by $5,000. This means that a posting must be made for $5,000 as a debit in the Cash account in the ledger. The posting was properly made by entering the date and the dollar amount in the Cash account (1). The P.R. column in the Cash account contains the number 1 to show that it was posted from page 1 of the general journal. Next, the number of the Cash account, 110, was entered in the P.R. column in the journal on the same line as the $5,000 debit (2). This shows the cross-reference of the debit part of the entry.

In like manner, the second line of the journal entry was properly posted to the J. D. Staple, Capital account (3), and the proper journal page number was inserted in the P.R. column (4). Also, the number of the capital account to which the dollar amount was posted was entered in the P.R. column in the journal on the same line as the $5,000 credit (4). This cross-references the credit part of the journal entry.

The dollar amounts in both the Cash and capital accounts are brought over to the proper Balance columns. The balance in the

**ILLUSTRATION
3–5**

**The Posting
Process**

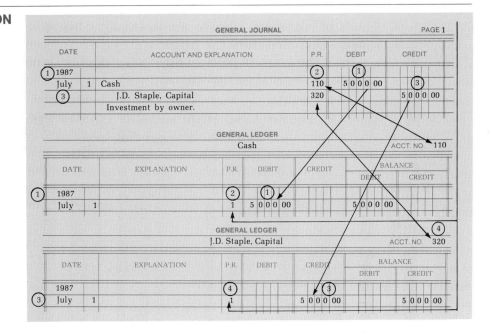

Cash account is entered in the Debit column. Assets normally carry a debit balance. The balance in the capital account is entered in the Credit column. The capital account normally has a credit balance.

The account numbers 110 and 320 in the P.R. column of the journal indicate that the entry has been completely posted. The absence of such numbers in the P.R. column immediately signals that a journal entry has not been posted to the general ledger.

The complete ledger of the J. D. Staple Law Firm is shown in Illustration 3–6 with all items properly posted from its journal (as shown in Illustration 3–2). The year 1987 has been entered at the top of the Date column in every account. Note, also, that in the Cash account and in the Fees Earned account the name of the month, July, was entered only once in the Date column even though a number of transactions occurred during the month. The Explanation column is seldom used in a general ledger. It is not necessary to repeat the explanation contained in the journal. The cross-referencing system allows any posting to be easily traced back to the general journal. Informational comments, such as those shown in the Accounts Payable ledger account, can be made to suit various purposes. In the case of Accounts Payable, for example, a list of creditors could be easily prepared from the ledger.

To summarize, in posting, three items of information are transferred from the journal to the ledger:

1. The date of the transaction.
2. The debit and credit amounts and whether each increases or decreases the corresponding account.

ILLUSTRATION 3–6

GENERAL LEDGER

Cash   ACCT. NO. 110

DATE		EXPLANATION	P.R.	DEBIT	CREDIT	BALANCE DEBIT	BALANCE CREDIT
1987							
July	1		1	5 0 0 0 00		5 0 0 0 00	
	1		1		3 5 0 00	4 6 5 0 00	
	1		1		6 0 00	4 5 9 0 00	
	3		1	1 2 5 00		4 7 1 5 00	
	8		1		5 0 0 00	4 2 1 5 00	
	15		1	1 0 5 0 00		5 2 6 5 00	
	18		1		7 3 00	5 1 9 2 00	
	31		1		9 0 00	5 1 0 2 00	
	31		1		8 0 0 00	4 3 0 2 00	

Accounts Receivable   ACCT. NO. 112

DATE		EXPLANATION	P.R.	DEBIT	CREDIT	BALANCE DEBIT	BALANCE CREDIT
1987							
July	29		1	1 6 4 0 00		1 6 4 0 00	

Office Furniture   ACCT. NO. 147

DATE		EXPLANATION	P.R.	DEBIT	CREDIT	BALANCE DEBIT	BALANCE CREDIT
1987							
July	7		1	1 1 4 0 00		1 1 4 0 00	

Accounts Payable   ACCT. NO. 212

DATE		EXPLANATION	P.R.	DEBIT	CREDIT	BALANCE DEBIT	BALANCE CREDIT
1987							
July	2	Big Fudd's Supply Store	1		7 2 00		7 2 00
	6	Brand Furniture Store	1		1 1 4 0 00		1 2 1 2 00

**ILLUSTRATION
3–6 (continued)**

J.D. Staple, Capital — ACCT. NO. 320

DATE		EXPLANATION	P.R.	DEBIT	CREDIT	BALANCE DEBIT	BALANCE CREDIT
1987							
July	1		1		5 000 00		5 000 00

J.D. Staple, Drawing — ACCT. NO. 330

DATE		EXPLANATION	P.R.	DEBIT	CREDIT	BALANCE DEBIT	BALANCE CREDIT
1987							
July	31		1	800 00		800 00	

Fees Earned — ACCT. NO. 420

DATE		EXPLANATION	P.R.	DEBIT	CREDIT	BALANCE DEBIT	BALANCE CREDIT
1987							
July	3		1		125 00		125 00
	15		1		1 050 00		1 175 00
	29		1		1 640 00		2 815 00

Office Rent Expense — ACCT. NO. 505

DATE		EXPLANATION	P.R.	DEBIT	CREDIT	BALANCE DEBIT	BALANCE CREDIT
1987							
July	1		1	350 00		350 00	

Advertising Expense — ACCT. NO. 514

DATE		EXPLANATION	P.R.	DEBIT	CREDIT	BALANCE DEBIT	BALANCE CREDIT
1987							
July	18		1	73 00		73 00	

Office Supplies Expense — ACCT. NO. 521

DATE		EXPLANATION	P.R.	DEBIT	CREDIT	BALANCE DEBIT	BALANCE CREDIT
1987							
July	2		1	72 00		72 00	

ILLUSTRATION 3–6 (concluded)

				Dial-a-Phone Expense			ACCT. NO. 523

DATE		EXPLANATION	P.R.	DEBIT	CREDIT	BALANCE	
						DEBIT	CREDIT
1987							
July	1		1	6 0 00		6 0 00	

				Wages Expense			ACCT. NO. 570

DATE		EXPLANATION	P.R.	DEBIT	CREDIT	BALANCE	
						DEBIT	CREDIT
1987							
July	31		1	9 0 00		9 0 00	

				Miscellaneous Expense			ACCT. NO. 590

DATE		EXPLANATION	P.R.	DEBIT	CREDIT	BALANCE	
						DEBIT	CREDIT
1987							
July	8		1	5 0 0 00		5 0 0 00	

3. The page number in the journal where the transaction is originally recorded.

When this information is transferred, the appropriate ledger account numbers are entered in the journal's P.R. column. Thus, after posting is completed, both the journal and the ledger contain the same information. When the proper cross-referencing has been done, the entries can be easily traced from the journal to the ledger or from the ledger to the journal.

THE TRIAL BALANCE

After a period's transactions have been journalized and posted, it is customary to prepare a trial balance. The **trial balance** is a listing of all the accounts in the general ledger and the sum of the debit and credit amounts of their balances. A simple explanation and an example of a trial balance were given in Chapter 2.

The purposes of the trial balance

A trial balance serves three purposes:

1. It indicates if the ledger is in balance by showing whether the total in the accounts with debit balances equals the total in the accounts with credit balances.
2. It aids in locating errors.
3. It assists in the preparation of financial statements.

Before preparing financial statements, the accountant tests the arithmetic accuracy of the financial records. Since every journal entry must contain an equal amount of debits and credits, the accounts must have equal debit and credit balances. In other words, the books must *balance*. This means that the debits and credits of a trial balance must balance. If they do not balance, at least one error has been made. The error can be traced to the period following the date of the last correct trial balance. A trial balance may be prepared daily, weekly, monthly, or at the end of a longer period of time. At a minimum, a trial balance is usually prepared monthly, and one is always prepared at the end of the accounting period before the preparation of financial statements.

Preparing the trial balance

To draw up a proper trial balance, the following procedures should be carefully observed:

1. The heading of the trial balance should state the name of the business, the words Trial Balance, and the date. Usually a trial balance is prepared a few days after the last day of the period in which its transactions occurred.
2. The number and title of each account should be listed after the heading in the order in which the accounts are found in the ledger.
3. The account balances should be listed in parallel columns— debit balances on the left and credit balances on the right.
4. Each column should be totaled, and the totals should be entered at the bottom of the column. A single line should be drawn above each total and a double line below each total.

The trial balance of the J. D. Staple Law Firm, prepared in accordance with these procedures, is shown in Illustration 3–7. The trial balance serves a useful purpose in the preparation of financial statements, as will be shown in Chapter 4.

ILLUSTRATION 3–7

	J. D. STAPLE LAW FIRM		
	Trial Balance		
	July 31, 1987		

ACCT. NO.	ACCOUNT NAME	DEBIT	CREDIT
110	Cash	4 3 0 2 00	
112	Accounts Receivable	1 6 4 0 00	
147	Office Furniture	1 1 4 0 00	
212	Accounts Payable		1 2 1 2 00
320	J. D. Staple, Capital		5 0 0 0 00
330	J. D. Staple, Drawing	8 0 0 00	
420	Fees Earned		2 8 1 5 00
505	Office Rent Expense	3 5 0 00	
514	Advertising Expense	7 3 00	
521	Office Supplies Expense	7 2 00	
523	Dial-A-Phone Expense	6 0 00	
570	Wages Expense	9 0 00	
590	Miscellaneous Expense	5 0 0 00	
		9 0 2 7 00	9 0 2 7 00

ERRORS

A trial balance in which debits equal credits is not necessarily error-free. A trial balance may contain errors but still look correct if:

1. No entry was made for a given transaction.
2. An entry was posted twice.
3. An amount was journalized or posted to the wrong account.
4. An incorrect amount was recorded for a given transaction.

Since a common reason for an out-of-balance trial balance is an arithmetic error, care should be taken in computing the running balance of each account. Also, if the accounts are hand-posted, the writing should be clear and legible so that it will not be misread.

Transpositions and slides

Two common recording errors are transpositions and slides. A **transposition error** occurs when digits are incorrectly arranged. For example, there would be a transposition error if the proper dollar amount of $864 were written as $684 or $468. A **slide error** occurs when the decimal point is put in the wrong place. If the proper amount is $684.00, but it is written as $68.40 or $6.84, there would be a slide error.

If either a transposition or a slide occurs and there are no other errors, the trial balance totals will be off by an amount that is evenly divisible by 9. For example, if the $350 for Office Rent Expense in Illustration 3–7 were written as $530, the Debit column of the trial balance would total $9,207 rather than $9,027. The Credit column would still total $9,027, so debits would exceed credits by $180. Since $180 is evenly divisible by 9, the chances are that a slide or transposition error has occurred. In this case, it was a transposition error.

A slide error in the trial balance in Illustration 3–7 would occur if Accounts Receivable were recorded as $164 rather than $1,640. The debit column would then total $7,551 instead of $9,027. By subtracting the debit of $7,551 from the credit balance of $9,027, we would discover an error in the amount of $1,476. Since this figure is divisible by 9 ($1,476 ÷ 9 = $164), we know that either a slide or a transposition has occurred, and we can check our figures accordingly.

Other clues may lead us to other kinds of errors. For example, if the amount of an error is evenly divisible by 2, a debit may have been posted as a credit, or vice versa. If a column is off by 10, 100, or 1,000, an error in addition was probably made. These are just a few ways errors may occur and may be traced.

SUMMARY

This chapter introduced the basic procedures used to record accounting information. Any information about a business transaction flows from the business papers to the journal entries, the accounts, the trial balance, and, finally, the financial statements.

Business papers, or source documents, are written records of business transactions. These papers may be handwritten or mechanically prepared. Some examples are payroll timecards, purchase and sales invoices, and deposit slips.

The **journal** is the place where all transactions are initially recorded. The simplest form of journal—often called a **general journal**—contains only two money columns, one for debit amounts and one for credit amounts. Every **journal entry** states:

1. The date of the transaction.
2. The titles of the accounts to be debited and credited.
3. The dollar amounts of the debits and credits.
4. A brief explanation of the transaction.

The process of transferring the information contained in a business paper to the journal is called **journalizing.** As each journal page is filled, the accuracy of its entries should be checked by **footing.** If the total of the Debit column entries equals the total of the Credit column entries, the journal has been proved.

A list of all the accounts and their numbers is known as a **chart of accounts.** In the chart of accounts, the individual accounts are usually grouped into the five major classifications—assets, liabilities, owner's equity, revenues, and expenses.

The general ledger, or **ledger,** is the entire collection of account records for a business. The accounts are usually grouped according to their classification as assets, liabilities, owner's equity, revenues, or expenses. A separate **balance column account form** is kept for each account. This form contains separate debit and credit columns and separate debit and credit balance columns. As each transaction is put into the appropriate ledger account, the dollar amount is added to or subtracted from the previous balance to arrive at a running balance. The **running balance** shows the total value in the ledger account as of the most recent transaction.

The process of transferring the journal entries to the accounts in the ledger is known as **posting.** Through the posting process, three items of information are transferred from the journal to the ledger:

1. The date of the transaction.
2. The debit and credit amounts and whether they increase or decrease the account.
3. The page number in the journal where the transaction was originally recorded.

The page number of the journal is listed in the **P.R. (posting reference)** column of the ledger, and the ledger account number is listed in the P.R. column of the journal. This is a way of **cross-referencing** the transactions.

After the period's transactions have been journalized and posted, a **trial balance** is prepared. The trial balance is a listing of all accounts in the general ledger and the sums of the debit or credit amounts of their balances. There are three reasons for preparing a trial balance.

1. To see if the total debits in all the ledger accounts is equal to the total credits.
2. To aid in locating errors.
3. To assist in the preparation of financial statements.

In locating errors, if the difference between the debit and credit columns is evenly divisible by 9, there is probably a transposition or slide error. Remember, a **slide error** occurs when a decimal point is put in the wrong place. A **transposition error** occurs when digits are incorrectly arranged.

KEY TERMS

Balance-Column Account Form—A ledger account that has separate Debit and Credit columns and separate debit and credit Balance columns. A running debit or credit balance is maintained in the last columns.

Business Papers—The written records, either handwritten or mechanically prepared, for every transaction that takes place in a business. They consist of payroll timecards, purchases and sales invoices, cash register tapes, deposit slips, check stubs or carbon copies of checks, duplicate sales tickets, and similar items.

Chart of Accounts—A complete listing of all the accounts in the ledger and their identifying numbers.

Cross-referencing—The act of entering in the P.R. column of the journal the ledger account number where the entry was posted and entering in the ledger account P.R. column the page number of the journal where the entry is found.

Footing—The process of adding the Debit and Credit columns of the general journal to determine if the Debit column total equals the Credit column total.

General Journal—The simplest form of journal. It contains two money columns, one for the debit amount and one for the credit amount.

Journal—A book of original entry that contains a chronological record of business transactions showing the changes to be recorded in terms of debits and credits as a result of each transaction.

Journal Entry—An entry recorded in a journal that analyzes the effect of a business transaction in terms of debits and credits.

Journalizing—The act of entering a transaction in a journal.

Ledger—The entire collection of the account records of a business; often referred to as the general ledger.

Owner's Drawing Account—An owner's equity account used to record an owner's withdrawal of assets from a business.

Posting—The act of transferring journal entry amounts to ledger accounts.

P.R. (Posting Reference) Column—A column in both the journal and the ledger where the page number of the journal is recorded in the ledger and the ledger account number is recorded in the journal. It serves as a cross-reference between the journal and the ledger.

Running Balance—The continually changing balance in each ledger account that shows the total value in the account as of the most recent transaction.

Slide Error—An error that occurs when a decimal point is put in the wrong place in a number.

Transposition Error—An error that occurs when digits in a number are put in incorrect order.

Trial Balance—A listing of all the accounts in the general ledger and the sums of the debit or credit amounts of their balances.

QUESTIONS AND EXERCISES

1. Describe the flow of information concerning transactions of a business.
2. Why is a journal called a book of original entry?
3. Describe the journalizing procedure.
4. Define the following terms:
   a. Chart of accounts.
   b. Posting.
   c. Cross-referencing.
5. When may journal entries be posted?
6. Describe the posting procedure.
7. What are three reasons for preparing a trial balance?
8. Elaine Combs has just prepared a trial balance for her business. The total of the Debit column equals the total of the Credit column. Does this mean that no errors have been made? Explain.

9. Define and give an example of the following:
   a. Transposition error.
   b. Slide error.
10. What journal entries should be made to record the following transactions?
    a. Office supplies costing $55 were purchased on account from Selby's Supply Company.
    b. Cash of $22 was received for services rendered to customers.
    c. The secretary was paid wages of $105.
11. What is a drawing account? What journal entry should be made when M. C. Owner withdraws $600 from the firm?
12. What are four procedures that should be carefully observed when preparing a trial balance?
13. What journal entries should be made to record the following transactions?
    a. T. Wall invested $8,000 in the business.
    b. Cash of $45 was received for services rendered to customers.
    c. Purchased $75 of supplies on account from M. Spencer.
14. From the following, select the proper accounts and prepare an income statement for the month ended May 31, 1987, for M. J. Proctor Co.

Cash.	$2,000
Revenue from services.	4,000
Rent expense.	400
Accounts payable	1,000
Salary expense	800
Supplies expense.	300
Supplies.	200

15. From the following, select the proper accounts and prepare a balance sheet for Bill Davis's Maintenance Service on June 30, 1987.

Revenue.	$3,000
Accounts payable	400
Cash.	1,500
Wage expense.	1,000 –
Accounts receivable.	600
Bill Davis, capital	1,700
Rent expense.	300 –

PROBLEMS

3–1. L. B. Hunter, a local CPA, completed the following transactions during August 1987. The following account titles are to be used.

Cash   Computer Rental Expense
Accounts Receivable   Donations Expense
Office Supplies   Dues Expense
Office Equipment   Gas and Oil Expense
Office Furniture   License Expense
Notes Payable   Rent Expense
Accounts Payable   Repairs Expense
L. B. Hunter, Capital   Telephone Expense
L. B. Hunter, Drawing   Utilities Expense
Fees Earned   Wages Expense

Required:

Journalize each transaction.

August 1   Paid July's telephone bill, $80.
         1   Paid the rent for August, $400.
         4   Paid July's electric bill, $127.
         4   Received $75 for services from G. D. Jones. *fees*
         5   Paid dues to the AICPA, $85. *dues e/p*
         5   Received $95 for services from Tom Bowers. *fees*
         6   Paid business license fee, $100.
         6   Received $75 for services from Bob Holmes.
         7   Received $50 for services from Sue Smith.
         7   Paid the secretary's weekly salary, $200.
         8   Withdrew $250 from the business.
         8   Received $65 for services from Willie Brown. *drawing Dr*
       11   Gave $40 to the United Way.
       11   Purchased a new duplicating machine for the business, giving a note for $2,520.
       12   Purchased office supplies on account, $60.
       12   Paid secretary's weekly salary, $200.
       15   Billed Sam Williams for services, $520. *acct r dr fees Cr.*
       15   Borrowed $450 from the bank giving a 60-day note. *cash dr notes Cr*
       15   Paid gasoline bill for car used in the business, $70.
       15   Sold an old typewriter for $125.
       15   Billed R. H. Farnsworth Company for services, $475.
       18   Paid $50 for maintenance on the new duplicating machine.
       18   Paid $25 for repair services on the typewriter.
       18   Withdrew $210 for living expenses.
       19   Paid for office supplies purchased on August 12. *acc pay dr cash Cr.*
       19   Received $50 for services from S. T. Maledon.
       19   Paid monthly rent on computer terminal, $150.

August 19 Received Sam Williams's payment for services billed on the 15th. *Cash dr acc rec cr.*

19 Invested $1,600 in the business. *dr cash cr capital*

20 Billed Clayton Company for services, $750.

20 Paid the note on the duplicating machine bought August 11.

20 Received $70 for services from E. V. Sells.

20 Purchased a dictaphone on account, $165.

21 Paid the secretary's weekly salary, $200.

21 Received a check from R. H. Farnsworth Company for services previously billed on the 15th.

21 Purchased a new office desk and chair for $850.

21 Hired a student to post ledgers at $4.50 per hour. He worked 10 hours and was paid $45.

22 Received check from Clayton Company in payment of their bill on the 20th.

22 Paid for the dictaphone purchased on the 20th.

22 Paid personal fuel bill on company check, $75.

25 Paid water bill, $12.

25 Withdrew $220 for personal expenses. *cr cash drawing dr.*

26 Paid secretary's weekly salary, $200.

3–2. J. M. Spencer Company had the following trial balance as of April 1, 1987. None of the journal entries for the month of April have been posted or included in the trial balance.

J. M. SPENCER COMPANY
Trial Balance
April 1, 1987

Account No.	Account Title	Debit	Credit
111	Cash	$1,200	
130	Office equipment	1,830	
211	Accounts payable		$ 450
310	J. M. Spencer, capital . . .		2,720
350	J. M. Spencer, drawing . . .	480	
410	Fees earned		1,780
511	License expense	50	
532	Wages expense	300	
540	Utilities expense	135	
565	Office supplies expense . . .	55	
588	Rent expense	775	
590	Telephone expense	125	
		$4,950	$4,950

Required:

1. Open general ledger balance column accounts for the accounts listed in the trial balance. Post the April 1, 1987, balances to the accounts.

GENERAL JOURNAL   Page 11

Date		Account and Explanation	P.R.	Debit	Credit
1987 April	1	Office Supplies Expense . . .	565	80	
		Accounts Payable . . .	211		80
		Purchased office supplies on account.			
	2	Wages Expense	532	150	
		Cash	111		150
		Paid payroll.			
	3	Rent Expense	588	275	
		Cash	111		275
		Paid rent for June.			
	4	Cash	111	280	
		Fees Earned	410		280
		Received fees for professional services.			
	7	J. M. Spencer, Drawing . . .	350	180	
		Cash	111		180
		Withdrew money for personal expense.			

GENERAL JOURNAL   Page 12

Date		Account and Explanation	P.R.	Debit	Credit
1987 April	7	Telephone Expense.	590	90	
		Cash	111		90
		Paid telephone bill.			
	8	Cash	111	195	
		Fees Earned	410		195
		Received fees for professional services.			
	9	Accounts Payable	211	80	
		Cash	111		80
		Paid for office supplies.			
	10	Utilities Expense	540	15	
		Cash	111		15
		Paid for water.			

GENERAL JOURNAL   Page 13

Date		Account and Explanation	P.R.	Debit	Credit
1987					
April	14	Office Equipment	13 0	60	
		Accounts Payable . . .	2 1 1		60
		Purchased a file cabinet on account.			
	16	Cash	1 1 1	500	
		J. M. Spencer, Capital . .	3 1 0		500
		Invested cash in business.			
	18	Accounts Payable	2 1 1	60	
		Cash	1 1 1		60
		Paid for the file cabinet.			
	21	Cash	1 1 1	450	
		Fees Earned	4 1 0		450
		Received fees for professional services.			
	21	License Expense.	5 1 1	35	
		Cash	1 1 1		35
		Paid for business license.			

GENERAL JOURNAL   Page 14

Date		Account and Explanation	P.R.	Debit	Credit
1987					
April	22	Wages Expense	5 3 2	300	
		Cash	1 1 1		300
		Paid payroll.			
	24	Utilities Expense	5 4 0	95	
		Cash	1 1 1		95
		Paid electric bill.			
	25	Cash	1 1 1	105	
		Fees Earned	4 1 0		105
		Received fees for professional services.			

2. Post the journal entries to the ledger.

3. Prepare a trial balance as of April 30, 1987.

3–3. W. R. Dixon, a local business executive, owns a small business. During the month of July several transactions were made that are listed below. The trial balance for July 1, 1987, is also listed below.

W. R. DIXON
Trial Balance
July 1, 1987

Account No.	Account Title	Debit	Credit
101	Cash	$ 2,350	
110	Accounts receivable.	1,750	
140	Office equipment.	2,750	
152	Automobile	–0–	
201	Accounts payable		$ 850
301	W. R. Dixon, capital		6,210
310	W. R. Dixon, drawing.	1,100	
405	Fees earned		4,300
508	Rent expense	2,100	
515	Utilities expense	125	
517	Telephone expense	285	
541	Wages expense	900	
		$11,360	$11,360

Required:

1. Journalize the transactions.
2. Post from the journal to the ledger.
3. Prepare a trial balance as of July 31, 1987.

July 1 Paid the monthly rent, $350.
    2 Received from Robert Rawlings a check for $750 for services previously billed.
    3 Paid electric bill of $125.
    5 Billed Dorothy Hazeltine $850 for services rendered.
    5 Paid telephone bill, $65.
    8 Paid the secretary's salary, $250.
    9 W. R. Dixon put personal car worth $5,000 into the business.
    15 Billed Walter Haller $1,500 for services rendered.
    18 Received a check for $850 from Dorothy Hazeltine.
    19 Paid water bill, $15.
    25 Withdrew $200 for personal expense.
    28 Purchased a typewriter on credit for $450.

3–4. C. P. Jones, a local attorney, completed the following transactions during July.

July 1 Paid June's electric bill, $128.
    1 Paid June's telephone bill, $80.
    2 Paid the rent for July, $300.
    3 Received $200 for services from Jay Haynes.
    3 Paid $60 for office supplies.

July 3   Received $90 for services from Connie Clark.

       7   Billed Joe Lynch for services, $150.

       7   Purchased a new typewriter on account, $800.

       7   Received $115 for services from Katherine Rogers.

       7   Withdrew $250 for living expenses.

       7   Received $250 for services from Smithbro Company.

       8   Paid gasoline bill for car used in the business, $85.

       8   Sold the old typewriter for $100. It was listed on the books at $100.

    10   Billed Tom Adams for services, $70.

    11   Received $150 from Joe Lynch for services previously billed.

    11   Paid for typewriter purchased on the 7th.

    11   Paid insurance premiums on policies taken out in the name of the business, $90.

    14   Paid the secretary's salary, $275.

    14   Paid home electric bill on a company check, $85.

    15   Invested $600 in the business.

    16   Received a check from Tom Adams for services previously billed, $70.

    18   Paid the water bill, $20.

    18   Received $70 from Barbara Clay for services rendered.

    20   Purchased office supplies on account, $50.

    20   Hired a person to clean the office once a week and paid $40 for the service.

    21   Billed Glenn Taylor for services, $300.

    22   Paid home telephone bill on a company check, $75.

    23   Paid business license fee, $65.

    24   Withdrew $150 for living expenses.

    25   Received $85 from Wesley Company for services.

    25   Paid for office supplies purchased on the 20th.

    28   Received check from Glenn Taylor for services previously billed on the 21st.

    28   Paid the cleaning person, $25.

    28   Paid the secretary's salary, $275.

    29   Received $110 for services from Gail Cox.

    29   Received $80 for services from Gary West.

    30   Gave $50 to the United Way.

    31   Withdrew $300 for living expenses.

Required:

Journalize each transaction.

3–5. R. A. Edwards, a management consultant, had the following trial balance on November 1, 1987.

R. A. EDWARDS
Trial Balance
November 1, 1987

Account No.	Account Title	Debit	Credit
101	Cash.	$ 2,300	
121	Accounts receivable.	2,500	
151	Office equipment.	1,900	
221	Accounts payable		$ 700
301	R. A. Edwards, capital		4,500
321	R. A. Edwards, drawing	3,800	
421	Consulting fees earned.		15,500
501	Rent expense	2,500	
511	Telephone expense	650	
521	Salaries expense	6,000	
531	Utilities expense	800	
541	Office supplies expense.	250	
		$20,700	$20,700

During November, Edwards completed the following transactions:

Nov. 3 Paid November rent, $250.
     3 Paid October phone bill, $85.
     3 Billed Allen Reeves for services rendered, $475.
     4 Paid $80 for office supplies.
     6 Received $300 for services from Olsen Company.
     7 Purchased a calculator on account, $400.
    10 Withdrew $300 for living expenses.
    11 Paid electric bill, $125.
    12 Paid water bill, $20.
    14 Paid secretary's salary, $300.
    17 Invested $800 in the business.
    20 Received check from Allen Reeves for services previously billed.
    21 Received $600 for services from Carmen Company.
    26 Received $50 for services from Jean Wilson.
    28 Paid for calculator purchased on the 7th.
    28 Paid home electric bill with a company check, $75.
    28 Paid secretary's salary, $300.
    28 Withdrew $300 for living expenses.

Required:

1. Open general ledger balance column accounts for the accounts listed in the trial balance. Post the November 1, 1987, balances into accounts.

2. Journalize the above transactions.
3. Post the journal entries to the accounts.
4. Prepare a trial balance for November 30, 1987.

3–6. On July 31, 1987, Ruth Hines prepared the following trial balance for her service business:

RUTH HINES
Trial Balance
July 31, 1987

Account No.	Account Title	Debit	Credit
101	Cash		$ 5,000
110	Accounts receivable	$12,000	
115	Office equipment		20,000
201	Accounts payable	10,000	
301	Ruth Hines, capital	6,000	
310	Ruth Hines, drawing		4,100
410	Fees earned	31,000	
510	Wages expense		4,400
520	Rent expense		1,400
530	Telephone expense	100	
		$59,100	$34,900

Required:

It is apparent that the trial balance does not balance. Given the following information, prepare a corrected trial balance.

1. All of the accounts have normal balances.
2. The debits to the Cash account total $14,000, and the credits to the Cash account total $8,900.
3. A $200 cash receipt from a customer was not posted to the Accounts Receivable account.
4. The balance in the Fees Earned account is $13,000 instead of $31,000.
5. The debits to the Office Equipment account total $30,900, and the credits to the Office Equipment account total $18,800.
6. The balance in Ruth Hines's capital account is $16,000.

3–7. As of July 1, 1987, the R. C. Riggins Company had the following trial balance.

During the month of July, R. C. Riggins completed the following transactions:

1987

July 1 Paid the rent for July, $225.
    1 Paid the electricity bill for June, $125.
    2 Received $65 from Jane Allison for services rendered.

R. C. RIGGINS COMPANY
Trial Balance
July 1, 1987

Account No.	Account Title	Debit	Credit
101	Cash	$ 2,450	
110	Accounts receivable	700	
115	Office supplies	105	
150	Office furniture	2,050	
201	Accounts payable		$ 750
301	R. C. Riggins, capital		2,255
310	R. C. Riggins, drawing	2,000	
410	Revenue from services		8,750
510	Gas and oil expense	320	
520	Telephone expense	280	
530	Utilities expense	250	
540	Salaries expense	2,000	
550	Rent expense	1,600	
		$11,755	$11,755

July 2 Billed Joe Stevens for services, $135.
    3 Paid the secretary's salary, $325.
    3 Purchased office supplies on account, $125.
    3 Received $150 from Julie Harmon for services rendered.
    7 Paid home electric bill by company check, $85.
    7 Received $70 for services from Jack Hall.
    7 Received $60 from Alice Kahn for services rendered.
    7 Paid the water bill, $15.
    8 Received a check from Joe Stevens for services previously billed on the 2d.
    8 Received $25 from Al Grey for services.
   10 Paid the secretary's salary, $325.
   11 Purchased new office furniture on account. $335.
   14 Received for services from Susan Carr, $50.
   15 Paid for gasoline and oil for car used in business, $70.
   15 Received $105 from Jack Hall for services rendered.
   16 Paid $85 for part-time office worker.
   17 Paid the secretary's salary, $325.
   18 Billed Jan North for services, $145.
   18 Received $70 from Hall French for services.
   21 Paid telephone bill for July, $60.
   21 Paid for office furniture purchased on the 14th.

23 Withdrew $500 for personal expenses.

23 Paid for office supplies purchased on the 3d.

24 Paid the secretary's salary, $325.

25 Received $40 for services from David Newell.

25 Received check from Jan North for services billed on the 18th.

28 Billed Bob Haley for services, $120.

31 Received $115 from Simon Trent for services.

Required:

1. Open general ledger balance column accounts for the accounts listed in the trial balance. Post the July 1, 1987, balance into accounts.
2. Journalize the above transactions.
3. Post journal entries to the accounts.
4. Prepare the trial balance for July 31, 1987.

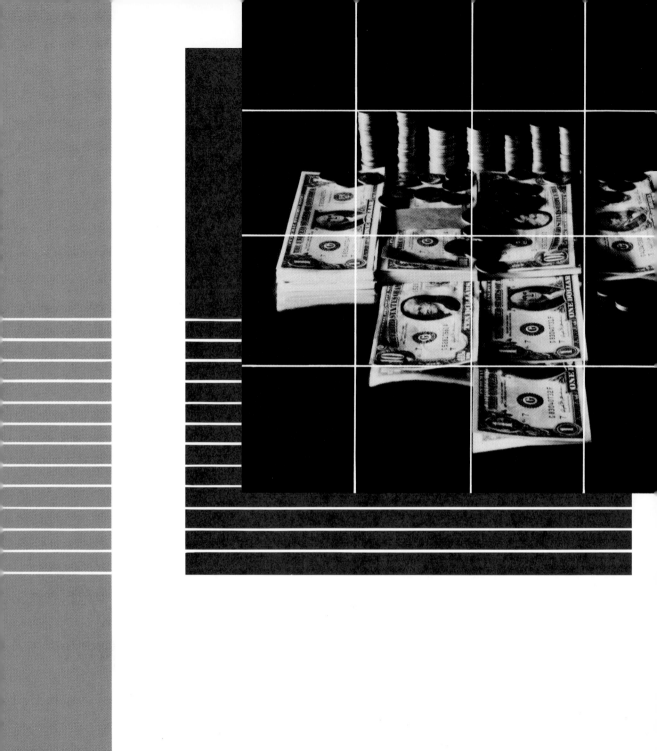

CHAPTER 4

Preparing financial statements and closing the books

LEARNING OBJECTIVES

In this chapter you will complete the procedures used in preparing financial statements from the accounting records. In particular you will:

1. Record (journalize) transactions in the general journal.
2. Post from the general journal to the general ledger.
3. Prepare closing entries.
4. Prepare a trial balance.
5. Prepare an income statement.
6. Prepare a balance sheet.
7. Prepare a statement of owner's equity.

A primary objective of every accounting system is the preparation of financial statements—income statements, balance sheets, and statements of owner's equity. Such statements may be prepared daily, weekly, monthly, quarterly (every three months), semiannually (every six months), or annually. Financial statements that cover a full year are called **annual reports,** while those that cover less than a full year are called **interim reports.**

Most businesses must prepare annual reports based on a 12-month period. If the 12-month period runs from January 1 through December 31, the reports are based on a **calendar year.** If the reports cover any other 12-month period of time, for example, from April 1 through March 31, they are based on a **fiscal year.**

In order to explain income statements, balance sheets, and statements of owner's equity, we will continue the example of the J. D. Staple Law Firm from Chapter 3. For your reference, Staple's trial balance, with accounts listed in numerical order, is presented in Illustration 4–1. Recall that the trial balance is an important aid in preparing financial statements and that the total in its debit column must always equal the total in its credit column.

FINANCIAL STATEMENTS

The general journal, general ledger, and trial balance all provide important financial information about a firm. But they are insufficient because their meaning is often obscured by too much detail. To report financial information in more easily usable form, a company prepares an income statement and a balance sheet. We first presented income statements and balance sheets in Chapter 1, but we will now look at them in more detail in order to trace the progress of the J. D. Staple Law Firm for the month of July.

The income statement

One measure of a firm's progress is the change in owner's equity that occurred as a result of operations during a specified time period. The effects that doing business has on owner's equity are recorded in the revenue and expense accounts. The summary of the revenue and expense account balances and their effect on the firm are presented in the **income statement.** If revenues have been greater than expenses, the income statement will show a **net income,** or profit. But if expenses

ILLUSTRATION 4-1

	J. D. STAPLE LAW FIRM		
	Trial Balance		
	July 31, 1987		

ACCT. NO.	ACCOUNT NAME	DEBIT	CREDIT
110	Cash	4 3 0 2 00	
112	Accounts Receivable	1 6 4 0 00	
147	Office Furniture	1 1 4 0 00	
212	Accounts Payable		1 2 1 2 00
320	J. D. Staple, Capital		5 0 0 0 00
330	J. D. Staple, Drawing	8 0 0 00	
420	Fees Earned		2 8 1 5 00
505	Office Rent Expense	3 5 0 00	
514	Advertising Expense	7 3 00	
521	Office Supplies Expense	7 2 00	
523	Dial-A-Phone Expense	6 0 00	
570	Wages Expense	9 0 00	
590	Miscellaneous Expense	5 0 0 00	
		9 0 2 7 00	9 0 2 7 00

have been greater than revenues, the income statement will show a **net loss.**

Some people believe the income statement is the most important financial statement. It shows how well a business has done in its primary activity—selling a product or rendering a service to earn a profit. A firm's ability to generate net income may also be the best measure of its ability to meet future obligations, such as mortgage payments, and, if it is a corporation, dividend payments.

Net income must be considered in reference to some time period. The statement that a person earned $2,000 means little without a time reference. If the $2,000 was earned in one year, the person earned well below the national average. But if the $2,000 was earned in one month, the person earned much more than the national average. All income statements must state the period of time that they cover.

Every income statement should have a heading that includes (1) the firm's name, (2) the statement title, and (3) the time period covered. A proper statement shows the total of the individual expenses incurred deducted from the total of the revenues earned. If the expense total exceeds the revenue total, the business suffers a net loss and a decrease in owner's equity. If the revenue total is greater than the expense total, the business has a net income and an increase in owner's equity.

The income statement for the J. D. Staple Law Firm for the period July 1 to July 31, 1987, has been reproduced in Illustration 4–2.

The trial balance on page 91 served as its source; all revenue and expense account balances were taken directly from it. Since the revenue total ($2,815) exceeded the expense total ($1,145), the firm had a net income, or increase in owner's equity, of $1,670 during this time period. Note that a double line is placed under the dollar total.

ILLUSTRATION 4–2

J. D. STAPLE LAW FIRM
Income Statement
For the Month Ended July 31, 1987

Revenues:		
Fees earned		$2,815
Expenses:		
Office rent expense	$350	
Advertising expense	73	
Office supplies expense	72	
Dial-A-Phone expense	60	
Wages expense	90	
Miscellaneous expense	500	1,145
Net income		$1,670

The balance sheet

The **balance sheet** is a statement of the basic accounting equation, Assets = Liabilities + Owner's Equity. It summarizes a firm's asset, liability, and owner's equity accounts on a given date. A firm's progress may be evaluated by comparing its balance sheets from period to period.

A balance sheet reflects a firm's financial position at a single point in time. At any other point in time, the accounts in the statement may have different balances. A trained investment analyst can often obtain a great deal of information about a firm by noting the changes in the account balances from one statement to another.

Every balance sheet should have a heading that includes (1) the firm's name, (2) statement title, and (3) the date of the statement. When presented in **account form,** a balance sheet lists all asset accounts and their balances on the left side and all liability and owner's equity accounts and their balances on the right side. Totals are computed and recorded for each side to test the equality of the accounting equation. Illustration 4–3 shows the J. D. Staple Law Firm's balance sheet as of July 31, 1987, in account form. Note that this format presents the balance sheet in the form of a T account; that is, assets are listed on the left side of the statement and liabilities and owner's equity are listed on the right side. The trial balance on page 91 was the source of all the information presented in the balance sheet.

ILLUSTRATION 4–3

J. D. STAPLE LAW FIRM
Balance Sheet
July 31, 1987

Account form

Assets		Liabilities and Owner's Equity		
Cash	$4,302	Accounts payable		$1,212
Accounts receivable	1,640	J. D. Staple, capital, June 30, 1987	$5,000	
Office furniture	1,140	Net income	$1,670	
Total assets	$7,082	Less withdrawals	800	870
		J. D. Staple, capital, July 31, 1987		$5,870
		Total liabilities and owner's equity		$7,082

A balance sheet may also be given in **report form,** a vertical format in which assets, liabilities, and owner's equity are each listed and totaled one beneath the other, as shown in Illustration 4–4. The total of the assets must equal the total of the liabilities and owner's equity in either the account form or the report form.

The owner's equity section of the balance sheet explains how any change in total owner's equity, either through operations or through the owner's investments or withdrawals, has occurred. A net income will increase total equity, while a net loss will decrease total equity. Similarly, an owner's additional investment increases total equity, while an owner's withdrawal of assets decreases total equity.

Statement of owner's equity

The **statement of owner's equity** explains in detail how changes in income and owner's investments affected owner's equity during

**ILLUSTRATION
4–4**

J. D. STAPLE LAW FIRM
Balance Sheet
July 31, 1987

statement or report form

Assets

Cash	$4,302
Accounts receivable	1,640
Office furniture	1,140
Total assets	$7,082

Liabilities and Owner's Equity

Accounts payable			$1,212
J. D. Staple, capital, July 1, 1987		$5,000	
Net income	$1,670		
Less withdrawals.	800	870	
J. D. Staple, capital, July 31, 1987.			5,870
Total liabilities and owner's equity.			$7,082

a specified period of time. The statement starts with the owner's equity (or capital) at the beginning of the period. To this amount are added any additional investments of capital that the owner made. If there was a net income for the period, that amount is also added. Or, if there was a net loss, that amount is subtracted. Finally, any withdrawals of capital made by the owner are subtracted. The resulting figure is the amount of owner's equity, or capital, at the end of the period. This procedure involves five steps:

1. Begin with the amount of capital at the beginning of the period.
2. Add additional capital investments by the owner.
3. Add the net income for the period or subtract the net loss.
4. Subtract capital withdrawals by the owner.
5. Finish with the amount of capital, or owner's equity, at the end of the period.

The statement of owner's equity for the J. D. Staple Law Firm is shown in Illustration 4–5. The first figure, $5,000, was taken from the firm's trial balance account, J. D. Staple, Capital. The net income of $1,670 was taken from the firm's income statement. It represents the link between the balance sheet and the income statement. The $800 withdrawal came from the trial balance account, J. D. Staple, Drawing. The total equity, $5,870, may be checked by solving the accounting equation for owner's equity. Total assets minus total liabil-

**ILLUSTRATION
4–5**

J. D. STAPLE LAW FIRM
Statement of Owner's Equity
For the Month Ended July 31, 1987

J. D. Staple, capital, July 1, 1987		$5,000
Net income	$1,670	
Less withdrawals	800	870
J. D. Staple, capital, July 31, 1987		$5,870

ities equals total owner's equity ($7,082 − $1,212 = $5,870). When a statement of owner's equity is prepared, only the total of $5,870 is shown in the balance sheet as J. D. Staple, Capital.

CLOSING THE BOOKS

Revenue and expense accounts are **temporary owner's equity accounts.** They are used to record the increases and decreases in owner's equity that occur over a period of time due to operations. The owner's drawing account is also a temporary owner's equity account. At the end of each accounting period, the balances in the revenue and expense accounts and the owner's drawing account are transferred to the permanent owner's capital account. This transfer process is called **closing the books.** It is accomplished by making journal entries known as **closing entries** or clearing entries.

Closing the books serves two purposes. First, it reduces the balances in all the revenue and expense accounts to zero. Because the income statement covers a specified period of time, it is essential that it contain only revenues and expenses of that period. The revenue and expense accounts must be closed at the end of one accounting period so that they will have a zero balance at the start of the next accounting period.

Second, closing the books helps bring the owner's capital account up to date at the end of each period. In updating the capital account, the owner's drawing account must also be considered. It is neither a revenue nor an expense account, but since it records the owner's withdrawal of assets for the same period of time covered by the income statement, it is also considered a temporary account. Like revenue and expense accounts, it needs to be closed out so that it will have a zero balance at the beginning of the next period. Therefore, to bring the owner's capital account completely up to date, the drawing account must be closed to it. The ending capital balance of one period becomes the beginning balance of the next period because only an instant in time elapses between the two periods.

Compound journal entries

So far, we have discussed only journal entries that have one debit account and one credit account with the dollar amounts of the debit and credit being equal. But some transactions result in debits and/ or credits to more than one account. Any time more than two accounts need to be recorded simultaneously in the journal, a **compound entry** is used. For example, if furniture costing $4,500 is purchased with a down payment of $500 in cash and a note payable is given for the balance of $4,000, a **compound entry** would be required. This transaction would be recorded as follows:

							GENERAL JOURNAL						
DATE		ACCOUNT AND EXPLANATION	P.R.	DEBIT				CREDIT					
1987													
July	7	Furniture		4	5	0	0	00					
		Cash							5	0	0	00	
		Note Payable							4	0	0	0	00
		Purchased furniture with down payment											
		and note.											

In this compound entry, three accounts are involved: one account—Furniture—must be debited, and two accounts—Cash and Note Payable—must be credited. Note, however, that the debit ($4,500) is still equal to the sum of the credits ($500 + $4,000). In *all* journal entries, the dollar amount of debits must equal the dollar amount of credits. Compound journal entries are commonly used in closing the books.

The income summary account

The revenue and expense accounts are usually not closed directly to the owner's capital account. Instead, they are closed to another temporary account called the **Income Summary** account. When all the revenue and expense accounts are closed, the balance in the Income Summary account is equal to the net income or loss for the period. This provides an additional check for errors. If no errors are found, the Income Summary account is closed to the owner's capital account.

Closing revenue accounts

A revenue account is closed by transferring its credit balance to the Income Summary account. Each revenue account is reduced to zero by debiting it for its balance and crediting the Income Summary account for the same amount.

In the case of the J. D. Staple Law Firm, the journal entry to close the Fees Earned account would be:

GENERAL JOURNAL

DATE		ACCOUNT AND EXPLANATION	P.R.	DEBIT	CREDIT
1987					
July	31	Fees Earned		2 8 1 5 00	
		Income Summary			2 8 1 5 00
		To close the revenue account.			

Fees Earned		Income Summary
2,815	2,815	2,815

When this entry is posted, the revenue account has a zero balance, and the Income Summary has a $2,815 credit balance. (T accounts are used here for illustration purposes only. In reality, all closing entires would be made in the journal before posting to the general ledger.)

In this case, the J. D. Staple Law Firm had only one revenue account. If there had been several revenue accounts, they would have been handled in the same manner in a compound entry.

Closing expense accounts

An expense account is closed by transferring its debit balance to the Income Summary account. Each expense account is reduced to zero by crediting it for its debit balance and debiting the Income Summary for the same amount. Since the J. D. Staple Law Firm has six expense accounts, the following compound journal entry would be required:

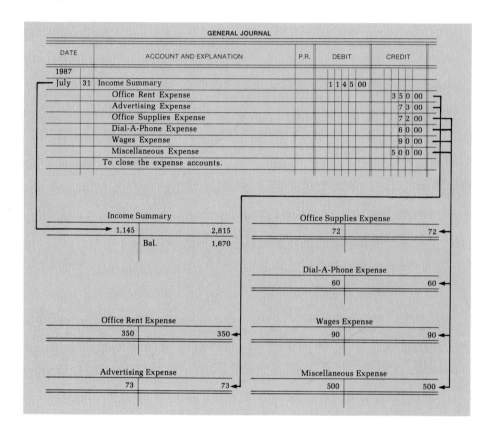

Each account could have been closed with a separate journal entry. But since each entry would have included a debit to the Income Summary account, the compound entry saves time and space. After posting this entry, the expense accounts all have zero balances, and the Income Summary account has a $1,670 credit balance. You will recall that this was the net income figure for the period.

Closing the income summary account

The Income Summary account is closed by transferring its balance to the owner's capital account. If the Income Summary account has a credit balance, it will be debited and the J. D. Staple, Capital account will be credited for the amount of the balance. If a loss has occurred, the Income Summary must be credited and J. D. Staple, Capital debited. Since there is a net income of $1,670 for the J. D.

Staple Law Firm, the closing entry is as shown. The amount of the net income is closed to the capital account. When this entry is posted, the Income Summary account has a zero balance, and the capital account has a balance of $6,670, which represents the amount of the beginning investment plus the net income.

	GENERAL JOURNAL			
DATE	ACCOUNT AND EXPLANATION	P.R.	DEBIT	CREDIT
1987				
July 31	Income Summary		1670 00	
	J.D. Staple, Capital			1670 00
	To close the income summary account.			

Income Summary		J.D. Staple, Capital	
1,145	2,815		5,000
1,670			1,670
2,815	2,815	Bal.	6,670

Closing the drawing account

If the owner has made withdrawals during the period, the drawing account should be closed to the capital account. This is done by crediting the drawing account and debiting the capital account for the amount of the withdrawals.

The J. D. Staple, Drawing account is closed out below:

	GENERAL JOURNAL			
DATE	ACCOUNT AND EXPLANATION	P.R.	DEBIT	CREDIT
1987				
July 31	J.D. Staple, Capital		800 00	
	J.D. Staple, Drawing			800 00
	To close out the J.D. Staple drawing account.			

J.D. Staple, Capital		J.D. Staple, Drawing	
800	5,000	800	800
	1,670		
Bal.	5,870		

This $800 will be posted as a debit to J. D. Staple, Capital and a credit to J. D. Staple, Drawing. This will leave the drawing account with a zero balance at the end of the period.

The closing procedure is summarized in Illustration 4–6. This illustration should help you better understand the transfer process in closing entries. In the closing process, recall that:

1. Revenue accounts have credit balances. A revenue account is closed by making a journal entry to debit the specific revenue account and credit the Income Summary account for the same amount. If there is more than one revenue account, a compound entry must be made in which each account is debited and the total of the accounts is credited to the Income Summary account.

2. Expense accounts have debit balances. An expense account is closed by crediting it and debiting the Income Summary account for the same amount. Compound entries are commonly used for this purpose.

3. The Income Summary account is closed to the capital account. If there is a credit balance, the Income Summary account is debited, and the capital account is credited. If the balance is a debit, then the Income Summary account must be credited and the capital account debited.

ILLUSTRATION 4–6

Summary of Closing Procedures

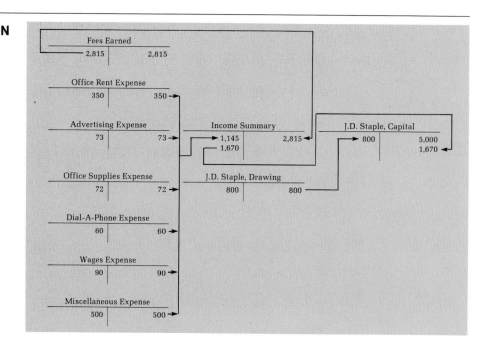

4. The drawing account is closed to the capital account by crediting it and debiting capital.

Posting the closing entries

After the journal entries are recorded, they must be posted to the ledger accounts, as shown in Illustration 4–7. The first journal entry was to close Fees Earned to Income Summary. In the ledger, the debit to Fees Earned is posted by recording the day, 31, and the amount of $2,815 in the debit column. The number 2 is placed in the P.R. column because this transaction is recorded on page 2 of the general journal. Note that debiting this account for $2,815 leaves a balance of zero. Enter the zero and put a double line under the balance column to show that the account is closed. In the general journal, the account number 420 is put in the P.R. column, as shown in Illustration 4–8. This indicates that the posting process of the debit part of the entry is complete.

The credit for $2,815 is posted to the new ledger account called Income Summary. (See Illustration 4–7.) Because the Income Summary has no balance before the posting of this first closing entry, the full date must be written in. The amount, $2,815, is written in the credit column, and the balance is entered in the credit balance column. The number 2 is put in the P.R. column because the entry

ILLUSTRATION 4–7

Posting Closing Entries—The Fees Earned Account

Fees Earned — ACCT. NO.

DATE		EXPLANATION	P.R.	DEBIT	CREDIT	BALANCE DEBIT	BALANCE CREDIT
1987							
July	3		1		1 2 5 00		1 2 5 00
	15		1		1 0 5 0 00		1 1 7 5 00
	29		1		1 6 4 0 00		2 8 1 5 00
	31		2	2 8 1 5 00			-0-

Income Summary — ACCT. NO. 340

DATE		EXPLANATION	P.R.	DEBIT	CREDIT	BALANCE DEBIT	BALANCE CREDIT
1987							
July	31		2		2 8 1 5 00		2 8 1 5 00

ILLUSTRATION 4–8

Posting Closing Entries— The General Journal

		GENERAL JOURNAL																
DATE		ACCOUNT AND EXPLANATION	P.R.	DEBIT					CREDIT					
1987														
July	31	Fees Earned	420	2	8	1	5	00						
		Income Summary	340						2	8	1	5	00	
		To close the revenue account.												
	31	Income Summary	340	1	1	4	5	00						
		Office Rent Expense	505							3	5	0	00	
		Advertising Expense	514								7	3	00	
		Office Supplies Expense	521								7	2	00	
		Dial-A-Phone Expense	523								6	0	00	
		Wages Expense	570								9	0	00	
		Miscellaneous Expense	590							5	0	0	00	
		To close the expense accounts.												
	31	Income Summary	340	1	6	7	0	00						
		J.D. Staple, Capital	320						1	6	7	0	00	
		To close the income summary account.												
	31	J.D. Staple, Capital	320		8	0	0	00						
		J.D. Staple, Drawing	330							8	0	0	00	
		To close out J.D. Staple's drawing account.												

is on page 2 of the journal. The account number 340 is placed in the P.R. column of the journal to indicate that the posting is complete for the credit portion of the entry. (See Illustration 4–8.)

Illustration 4–8 shows all the closing entries for the J. D. Staple Law Firm after they have been posted to the ledger accounts. Each account number has been placed in the P.R. column to indicate that the corresponding amount has been posted to the appropriate ledger account.

As we have discussed, only revenue, expense, and owner's equity accounts are involved in the closing process. Illustration 4–9 shows these ledger accounts for the J. D. Staple Law Firm after the closing entries have been posted. Each revenue and expense account has an entry dated July 31 and the number 2 in the P.R. column. This shows that the closing entry posted to this account was found on page 2 of the general journal. Note that the drawing, Income Summary, and expense accounts each have a zero balance. They are all closed out. Only the capital account has a balance in this portion of the ledger after the closing process is complete.

ILLUSTRATION 4–9

Posting Closing Entries— The General Ledger

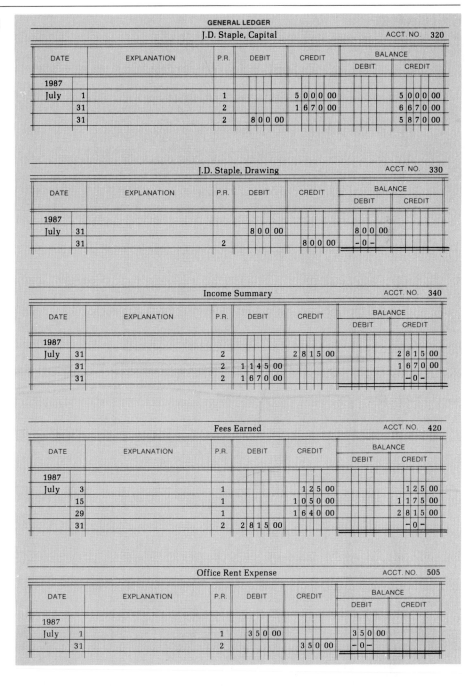

GENERAL LEDGER

J.D. Staple, Capital — ACCT. NO. 320

DATE		EXPLANATION	P.R.	DEBIT	CREDIT	BALANCE DEBIT	BALANCE CREDIT
1987							
July	1		1		5 000 00		5 000 00
	31		2		1 670 00		6 670 00
	31		2	800 00			5 870 00

J.D. Staple, Drawing — ACCT. NO. 330

DATE		EXPLANATION	P.R.	DEBIT	CREDIT	BALANCE DEBIT	BALANCE CREDIT
1987							
July	31			800 00		800 00	
	31		2		800 00	– 0 –	

Income Summary — ACCT. NO. 340

DATE		EXPLANATION	P.R.	DEBIT	CREDIT	BALANCE DEBIT	BALANCE CREDIT
1987							
July	31		2		2 815 00		2 815 00
	31		2	1 145 00			1 670 00
	31		2	1 670 00			– 0 –

Fees Earned — ACCT. NO. 420

DATE		EXPLANATION	P.R.	DEBIT	CREDIT	BALANCE DEBIT	BALANCE CREDIT
1987							
July	3		1		125 00		125 00
	15		1		1 050 00		1 175 00
	29		1		1 640 00		2 815 00
	31		2	2 815 00			– 0 –

Office Rent Expense — ACCT. NO. 505

DATE		EXPLANATION	P.R.	DEBIT	CREDIT	BALANCE DEBIT	BALANCE CREDIT
1987							
July	1		1	350 00		350 00	
	31		2		350 00	– 0 –	

**ILLUSTRATION
4–9
(concluded)**

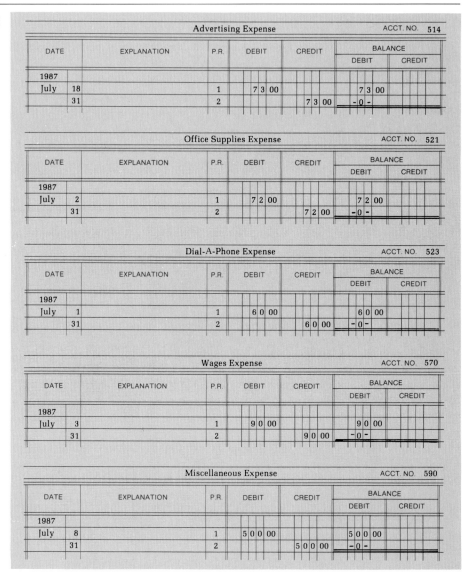

DATE		EXPLANATION	P.R.	DEBIT	CREDIT	BALANCE DEBIT	BALANCE CREDIT
		Advertising Expense				ACCT. NO.	514
1987							
July	18		1	7 3 00		7 3 00	
	31		2		7 3 00	- 0 -	

DATE		EXPLANATION	P.R.	DEBIT	CREDIT	BALANCE DEBIT	BALANCE CREDIT
		Office Supplies Expense				ACCT. NO.	521
1987							
July	2		1	7 2 00		7 2 00	
	31		2		7 2 00	- 0 -	

DATE		EXPLANATION	P.R.	DEBIT	CREDIT	BALANCE DEBIT	BALANCE CREDIT
		Dial-A-Phone Expense				ACCT. NO.	523
1987							
July	1		1	6 0 00		6 0 00	
	31		2		6 0 00	- 0 -	

DATE		EXPLANATION	P.R.	DEBIT	CREDIT	BALANCE DEBIT	BALANCE CREDIT
		Wages Expense				ACCT. NO.	570
1987							
July	3		1	9 0 00		9 0 00	
	31		2		9 0 00	- 0 -	

DATE		EXPLANATION	P.R.	DEBIT	CREDIT	BALANCE DEBIT	BALANCE CREDIT
		Miscellaneous Expense				ACCT. NO.	590
1987							
July	8		1	5 0 0 00		5 0 0 00	
	31		2		5 0 0 00	- 0 -	

THE POST-CLOSING TRIAL BALANCE

A **post-closing trial balance** is prepared after all closing entries have
been journalized and posted. Errors can easily be made in the closing
process, so a post-closing trial balance is one good way to check

for correctness. A post-closing trial balance also ensures that the books will be in balance at the start of the new accounting period. If subsequent trial balances are not in balance, it must be due to errors in the new accounting period.

The post-closing trial balance should include only the ledger accounts that appear on the balance sheet—assets, liabilities, and the owner's capital account. Income statement accounts, which are all revenue and expense accounts, and the owner's drawing account have been closed and hence have zero balances. The post-closing trial balance for the J. D. Staple Law Firm is presented in Illustration 4–10.

ILLUSTRATION 4–10

J. D. STAPLE LAW FIRM
Post-Closing Trial Balance
July 31, 1987

ACCT. NO.	ACCOUNT NAME	DEBIT	CREDIT
110	Cash	4 3 0 2 00	
112	Accounts Receivable	1 6 4 0 00	
147	Office Furniture	1 1 4 0 00	
212	Accounts Payable		1 2 1 2 00
320	J. D. Staple, Capital		5 8 7 0 00
		7 0 8 2 00	7 0 8 2 00

SUMMARY

To be optimally helpful, accounting information must be presented in the simplest, most easy-to-use form possible. Although the general journal, ledger, and trial balance contain much useful data for accountants, they are too detailed and complicated for most other users of accounting information. To overcome this problem, accountants prepare financial statements—income statements, balance sheets, and statements of owner's equity—to report a firm's financial progress. Financial statements that cover a full year are called **annual reports.** They may be based on either a **calendar year** or a **fiscal year.** Financial statements that cover less than a full year are called **interim reports.**

They may cover a day, a week, a month, three months, six months, or any other period of time that interests a company.

An **income statement** summarizes a firm's revenues and expenses and their effect on income during a specified period of time. Total expenses are subtracted from total revenues to arrive at a **net income** or a **net loss.** The information for the income statement can be transferred from the trial balance.

The **balance sheet** reflects the basic accounting equation. It summarizes a firm's assets, liabilities, and owner's equity accounts at a specific point in time. The balance sheet may be presented in one of two formats: the account form or the report form. The **account form** presents assets on the left and liabilities and owner's equity on the right. The **report form** is a vertical format—assets, liabilities, and owner's equity are listed and totaled one beneath the other. No matter which format is used, total assets should equal total liabilities and owner's equity. The information for the balance sheet can also be transferred from the trial balance.

A **statement of owner's equity** explains in detail how changes in income and owner's investments affected owner's equity during a specified period of time. Any net income and additional capital investments are added to the owner's capital balance at the beginning of the period, and any owner's withdrawals are subtracted to determine the ending balance in the capital account. If this statement is prepared, only the final balance in the capital account is shown on the balance sheet.

At the end of an accounting period the books are closed. During the **closing process,** all of the **temporary accounts**—revenue, expense, and drawing accounts—are closed into the owner's capital account using **closing entries.** First the revenue and expense accounts are closed to the **Income Summary.** Then the Income Summary and drawing accounts are closed to the owner's capital account. **Compound entries,** which involve three or more accounts, are usually necessary to record these transfers. After the closing process is completed, only asset accounts, liability accounts, and the owner's capital account have balances to carry forward to the next accounting period.

After all closing entries have been journalized and posted, the **post-closing trial balance** is prepared. It lists only the accounts that remain after closing—assets, liabilities, and the owner's equity capital account. All other accounts have a zero balance.

Many errors made in the closing process are revealed by an out-of-balance post-closing trial balance.

In summary, the accounting process consists of the following steps:

1. Analyze source documents to determine what accounts are involved in the transactions.
2. Journalize the transactions.
3. Post to the ledger accounts.
4. Determine the balances in each account.
5. Prepare a trial balance. *make sure debits = credits*
6. Prepare the income statement by copying the information from the trial balance.
7. Prepare the statement of owner's equity.
8. Prepare the balance sheet by copying the information from the trial balance.
9. Close the revenue and expense accounts to the Income Summary account.
10. Close the Income Summary account to the capital account.
11. Close the drawing account to the capital account.
12. Post the closing entries to the general ledger and place a double line under the zero in the balance columns.
13. Prepare a post-closing trial balance.

the accounting cycle

KEY TERMS

Account Form Balance Sheet—A balance sheet presented in the form of a T account. Assets are listed on the left side of the statement, and liabilities and owner's equity are listed on the right side.

Annual Report—A financial statement that covers a full year of transactions.

Balance Sheet—A financial statement that presents the assets, liabilities, and owner's equity of a business unit as of a specified date.

Calendar Year—A 12-month financial reporting period that begins on January 1 and ends on December 31.

Closing Entries—Journal entries that transfer the balances in the temporary accounts into the owner's capital account.

Closing the Books—The process of transferring the balances in all temporary accounts into the owner's capital account. First, revenue and expense accounts are closed into the Income Summary account. Then, the Income Summary and owner's drawing accounts are closed into owner's capital.

Compound Entry—A journal entry that involves three or more accounts. Debits must still equal credits. An example is:

```
Equipment . . . . . . . . . . . . . . . . .   5,000
      Cash  . . . . . . . . . . . . . . .            500
      Note payable. . . . . . . . . . . .           4,500
```

Fiscal Year—A 12-month financial reporting period that begins with any date other than January 1.

Income Statement—A summary of a firm's revenues and expenses and their effect on income during a specified period of time, such as a month or a year. It is also called a **profit and loss statement** or an **earnings statement.**

Interim Report—A financial statement that covers a period of time shorter than one year, such as one month, three months, or six months.

Net Income—The amount by which the revenues of a business exceed its expenses over a specified period of time.

Net Loss—The amount by which the expenses of a business exceed its revenues over a specified period of time.

Post-closing Trial Balance—A trial balance taken after all temporary accounts have been closed. It lists only assets, liabilities, and the owner's capital account.

Report Form Balance Sheet—A balance sheet presented in a vertical format in which assets, liabilities, and owner's equity are each listed and totaled one beneath the other.

Statement of Owner's Equity—A financial statement that explains in detail how changes in income and owners' investments affected owner's equity during a specified period of time. Any net income and additional capital investments are added to the owner's capital balance at the beginning of the period, and any net loss or owner's withdrawals are subtracted to determine the ending balance in the owner's capital account.

Temporary Owner's Equity Accounts—The revenue, expense, and owner's drawing accounts, which are closed into the owner's capital account when financial statements are prepared.

QUESTIONS AND EXERCISES

1. Which of the following accounts would appear on the income statement, and which of the following accounts would appear on the balance sheet?

a. Wages Expense. *I*   f. Cash. *B*
b. Accounts Payable. *B*   g. John Ames, Capital. *B*
c. Office Equipment. *A* *B*   h. John Ames, Drawing. *B*
d. Advertising Expense. *I*   i. Fees Earned.   *I*
customer e. Accounts Receivable. *B*   j. Office Supplies Expense. *I*

2. Define the following:
   a. Fiscal year. *12 month period*
   b. Quarterly. *3 month period*
   c. Semiannually. *6 month "*
3. Income statement expense total is $4,456, and revenue total is $8,600. What does the difference represent? *4/144*
4. The Corner Rental Agency earned revenue of $2,500 during April. It also incurred the following expenses during April: advertising, $200; office supplies, $300; wages, $600; telephone, $50; and utilities, $30. Compute the Corner Rental Agency's net income or loss for the month of April.
5. What effect does each of the following items have on owner's equity?
   a. Net income. *R*
   b. Net loss. *L*
   c. Additional investment by the owner. *R*
   d. Withdrawal of assets by the owner. *L*
   e. The purchase of office equipment on account. *none*
   f. The purchase of office furniture for cash. *none*
6. What is a statement of owner's equity? What information does it contain?
7. What is a compound entry? Give an illustration of one.
8. What two fundamental goals are accomplished by closing the books?
9. Given the account balances shown below, make the entries to (a) close the revenue account, (b) close the expense accounts, (c) close the Income Summary account, and (d) close the drawing account.

Cash	$ 6,000
Fees earned	14,000
Telephone expense	120
Wages expense	4,840
Rent expense.	2,400
Insurance expense	200
Accounts payable	1,000
R. M. Nifer, drawing	6,000

All of the accounts have normal balances.

10. At what point in the accounting cycle is a post-closing trial balance prepared?
11. What accounts appear on the post-closing trial balance?
12. From the following accounting balances select the ones needed in preparing closing entries and make the necessary closing entries:

Cash	$ 4,000
Fees earned	12,000
Accounts payable	3,000
Rent expense	5,000
Salary expense	5,000
Accounts receivable	4,000
D. A. Smith, drawing	3,000
D. A. Smith, capital	10,000
Income summary	–0–

13. Prepare the following compound entries:
    a. Purchased an automobile. Paid $1,000 cash and gave a note for $9,000.
    b. Purchased $300 of supplies and $400 of machine parts for $700 cash.

PROBLEMS

4–1. The R. L. Burns Company had the following account balances at the end of the year 1987:

Account Title	Debit	Credit
Accounts payable		$ 1,750
Accounts receivable	$ 2,050	
Cash	1,750	
Notes payable		1,700
Office equipment	4,150	
Office furniture	2,300	
Rent expense	1,800	
Revenue from services		14,250
R. L. Burns, capital		5,550
R. L. Burns, drawing	1,100	
Salaries expense	10,000	
Taxes payable		400
Utilities expense	500	
	$23,650	$23,650

Required:

Prepare a balance sheet.

4–2. The M. R. Francis Company had the following account balances at December 31, 1987.

Gas and oil expense	$ 225
Miscellaneous expense	50
Rent expense	1,200
Salaries expense	5,000
Service fees	9,500
Supplies expense	750
Telephone expense	375
Utilities expense	350

Required:

1. Prepare an income statement for the year ended December 31.
2. Prepare closing entries.

4–3. The R. J. Williams Company had the following account balances on December 31, 1987.

Account Title	Debit	Credit
Accounts payable		$ 700
Accounts receivable	$2,250	
Cash	1,850	
Rent expense	250	
Revenue from services		2,600
R. J. Williams, capital		2,400
R. J. Williams, drawing	380	
Salary expense	750	
Telephone expense	85	
Utilities expense	135	
	$5,700	$5,700

Required:

1. Prepare in good form an/a
  a. Income statement.
  b. Statement of owners' equity.
  c. Balance sheet.
2. Prepare the closing entries.

4–4. The J. C. Barnes Company had the following account balances at December 31, 1987.

Account Title	Debit	Credit
Accounts payable		$ 1,675
Accounts receivable	$ 1,500	
Cash	1,050	
Gas and oil expense	300	
J. C. Barnes, capital		6,100
J. C. Barnes, drawing	1,900	
Supplies on hand	1,850	
Miscellaneous expense	75	
Mortgage payable		2,500
Notes payable		4,000
Notes receivable	3,500	
Office equipment	4,000	
Office furniture	1,500	
Repair parts expense	2,000	
Revenue from services		4,000
Taxes payable		550
Telephone expense	125	
Utilities expense	250	
Wages expense	775	
	$18,825	$18,825

Required:

1. Prepare in good form an/a
   a. Income statement.
   b. Statement of owner's equity.
   c. Balance sheet.
2. Prepare the closing entries.

4–5. J. F. Bell, owner of Bell Company, has just given you the following list of accounts and wants you to prepare a balance sheet for December 31, 1987. Each account has a normal balance.

Accounts payable	$ 500
Accounts receivable	1,400
Cash	1,250
J. F. Bell, capital	1,700
J. F. Bell, drawing	800
Revenue from services	13,250
Rent expense	1,800
Wages expense	9,600
Miscellaneous expenses	600

4–6. J. C. Athens, owner of Athens Company, has just given you the following list of accounts and wants you to prepare an income statement for the year ended December 31, 1987. Each account has a normal balance.

Gas and oil expense.	. . . . .	$ 300
Rent expense .	. . . . . .	450
Repair parts expense	. . . .	1,500
Revenue from services .	. . .	2,500
Salaries expense .	. . . . .	500
Telephone expense .	. . . .	150

4–7. The E. D. Hopkins Company had the following trial balance as of December 1, 1987:

THE E. D. HOPKINS COMPANY
Trial Balance
December 1, 1987

Account No.	Account Title	Debit	Credit
101	Cash	$ 1,200	
110	Accounts receivable	1,700	
130	Office equipment	3,750	
201	Accounts payable.		$ 350
202	Notes payable		100
301	E. D. Hopkins, capital		4,395
310	E. D. Hopkins, drawing . . .	4,400	
340	Income summary.		–0–
410	Revenue from services		13,750
510	Rent expense	1,825	
515	Salaries expense	5,500	
520	Utilities expense	220	
		$18,595	$18,595

Required:

1. Open general ledger balance column accounts for the accounts listed in the trial balance. Post the December 1, 1987, balances to the accounts. Income summary has no balance.
2. Journalize the following transactions.
3. Post the journal entries to the ledger.
4. Prepare a trial balance as of December 31, 1987.
5. Prepare in good form an/a
   a. Income statement.
   b. Statement of owner's equity.
   c. Balance sheet.
6. Prepare the necessary closing entries. *accts from income statement*
7. Post the closing entries. ⟶ *from General journal*
8. Prepare a post-closing trial balance.

Transactions:

Dec.   2   Paid for December's rent, $275.

        5   Billed B. L. Knapp $575 for services rendered.

        8   Purchased file cabinet on account, $85.

        9   Paid electricity bill for November, $220.

     12   Received $450 from L. R. Richards for services.

     12   Purchased new piece of office equipment costing $3,000. Paid $500 in cash and gave a note payable for $2,500.

     16   Withdrew $400 for personal expenses.

     18   Paid for file cabinet.

     22   Received check from B. L. Knapp for services previously billed.

     29   Received from P. R. Preston for services, $60.

     30   Paid employee's salary, $500.

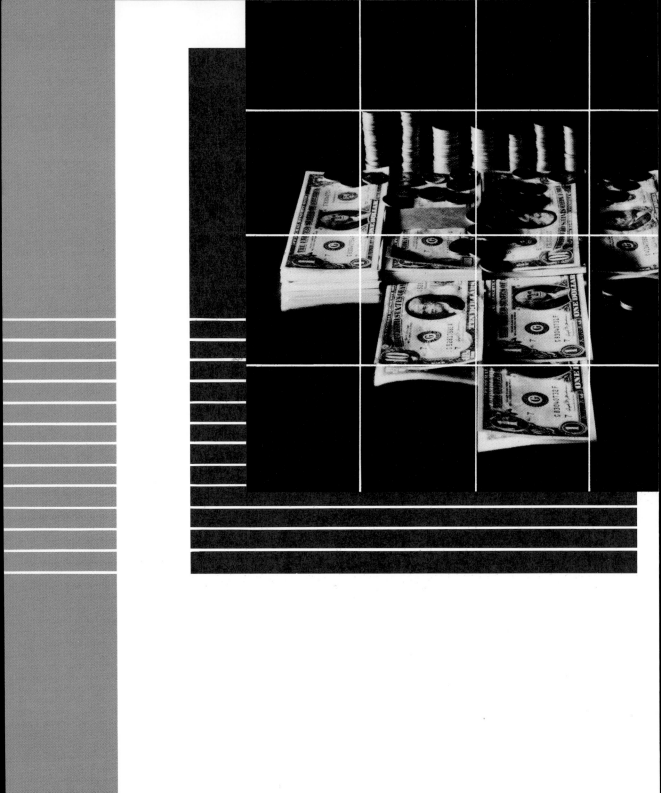

CHAPTER 5

Handling cash—checking accounts and petty cash

LEARNING OBJECTIVES

In this chapter, you will learn some basic information about how businesses handle cash, including how to use and maintain a checking account and a petty cash fund. After studying this chapter, you should be able to:

1. Define the term *cash* as it is used in business.

2. Operate a checking account.

3. Read a bank statement, prepare a bank reconciliation, and journalize the results.

4. Maintain records for a petty cash fund, including vouchers and a petty cash book.

5. Prepare journal entries to establish and reimburse a petty cash fund.

All businesses must have cash in order to make purchases and pay bills. To most individuals, cash consists of coins and currency. But in a business, cash usually has a much broader meaning. The **Cash** account includes currency and coins on hand as well as the amount of cash the company has deposited in a bank. Thus, in this broader sense, cash includes any item a bank will accept on deposit, including personal checks, traveler's checks, cashier's checks, money orders, bank drafts, and credit card receipts from sales.

Some people try to handle some items that are not really cash as if they were cash. Stamps, IOUs, and postdated checks are examples. (A check received on July 6 and dated July 8 is a postdated check. It cannot be deposited or cashed before July 8.) Stamps and IOUs will not be accepted by a bank as a deposit to your account. Thus, these items should not be debited to the Cash account but rather to Office Supplies and Accounts Receivable.

On a balance sheet it is customary to list assets in the order of their *liquidity.* **Liquidity** refers to the ease with which an asset may be converted to cash without losing value. The easier an asset can be converted to cash without losing value, the more liquid it is. Thus, cash is always listed first because it is the most liquid and the most readily spendable form of asset if there are no legal restrictions on its use. Most businesses have a large number of cash transactions. Cash is commonly received from cash sales, payments for services rendered, collections on accounts receivable, and the cash sale of other assets. Such receipts are debited to the Cash account, thus increasing that asset. Some common uses of cash that are credited to the Cash account and thus decrease it are the payment of wages, the payment of accounts payable, the cash purchase of assets, and the payment of various expenses.

Because currency cannot be identified if it is stolen and because cash transactions are quite numerous, businesses establish special procedures to handle and account for cash. Usually, the handling of cash and the recording of entries to account for cash are performed by different people. This helps to prevent stealing because the people who handle cash do not have access to the company books and thus cannot falsify entries. Such safety measures also provide a double check on all cash transactions.

THE NATURE AND PURPOSE OF CHECKING ACCOUNTS

In order to control cash disbursements, most business transactions are conducted by check. A **check** is a written document, signed by an authorized person, directing a company's bank to pay a specified amount of money to a particular party. Checks are widely used because of their great convenience and safety. In contrast, currency is very difficult to control because it is hard to determine its true owner. To avoid difficulties, a company should keep a minimum amount of currency on hand to pay small expenditures and make change for cash transactions and deposit the rest of its cash in a checking account at the bank. The use of checks greatly reduces the risk of a firm's cash being misused. With proper control procedures which include the use of checks, a firm can be relatively certain that its cash disbursements are being properly handled.

ELEMENTS OF A CHECKING ACCOUNT

A checking account (sometimes referred to as a *bank* or *commercial account*) is opened by filling out forms furnished by the bank and making a deposit. As mentioned earlier, the items that banks commonly accept for deposit are money, checks, bank drafts, and money orders. Bank drafts and money orders are forms similar to checks that represent cash to the company. A bank will accept them at face value on deposit. Each bank determines the restrictions that apply to the checking accounts it offers. For example, a bank might require the signatures of two different company officials on each check over a specified amount. The customer selects checks and deposit tickets from various alternatives provided by the bank.

The signature card

When a firm opens a checking account, each person who is authorized to sign checks against the account must sign a **signature card.** The bank is authorized to honor any check that has been signed by any individual whose signature appears on the signature card. It will not honor a check that is signed by anyone else. The bank will check the signature card if there is any doubt about the authenticity of a signature on a check. The signature card thus protects both the bank and the depositor.

The deposit tickets

A **deposit ticket** must be filled out whenever a customer wishes to deposit cash in his or her checking account. It shows (1) the

ILLUSTRATION 5–1   Sample Deposit Ticket

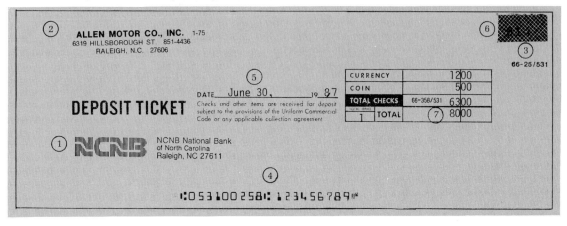

name of the bank, (2) the company's name, (3) the transit and routing numbers assigned to the bank by the American Bankers Association, (4) the account number, (5) and the date. The first four items are usually preprinted on the deposit ticket. It might also have a pre-printed deposit ticket number (6). The customer inserts the date when filling out the ticket.

Illustration 5–1 shows a deposit ticket for the Allen Motor Co., Inc. Note the company's name and the transit number 66–25/531. The numbers above the line designate the bank where this company has its account—the NCNB (North Carolina National Bank). The numbers below the line indicate the Federal Reserve District in which NCNB is located and other routing information. This deposit was made on June 30, 1987, and includes $12 in currency, $5 in coins, and one check in the amount of $63. The transit and routing numbers of the check are listed for identification purposes (7). The currency, coins, and check are added together for a total of $80.

Endorsements

A check must contain an **endorsement** before a bank will accept it for deposit. When a person endorses a check, he or she transfers its ownership to a bank or another party and guarantees its payment. To endorse a check, the depositor places his or her signature on the reverse side of the check at the end opposite the check writer's signature. A check is usually endorsed whenever it is transferred from one person to another.

The simplest form of endorsement is a *blank endorsement* in which the current owner of the check merely signs his or her name. This makes the check payable to the person who presents it for payment. A check that has a blank endorsement can be cashed by anyone regardless of the name specified on the check. For this reason, it is best to wait until arriving at the bank before endorsing a check. If a check with a blank endorsement is lost, anyone who finds it can cash it and receive the designated amount of money.

If a check is to be transferred to another party and will be sent by mail, a blank endorsement is not very safe. Instead a *full endorsement* should be used. The phrase "Pay to the order of" should precede the name of the person to whom the check is being transferred. The owner should then sign his or her name as before.

Another form of endorsement is the *restrictive endorsement.* Such an endorsement terminates further negotiation of the check and specifies the use of the check's proceeds. Restrictive endorsements are usually used on checks being deposited in a firm's account. Examples of all these endorsements are shown below:

Blank	Full	Restrictive
J. Q. Jones	Pay to the order of Merchants National Bank J. Q. Jones	Pay to the order of Merchants National Bank For deposit only J. Q. Jones

Endorsements such as these are commonly placed on a check by means of a rubber stamp. The phrase "For deposit only" limits the use of the check to that purpose.

Dishonored checks

The receipt of a check is not actual payment. If the writer of the check does not have sufficient funds in his or her account to cover the check, the bank will refuse to pay it, and the check will be **dishonored.** An account that contains insufficient funds to pay a check is said to be *overdrawn.* Its owner has written checks in an amount that is greater than the amount on deposit in the account. The issuance of such a check, which would result in the account's having a negative balance, is called an **overdraft.**

If a dishonored check is included in a bank deposit, it will be charged against the depositor's account. Thus, the total amount of any deposit depends on the deposited checks clearing the bank on which they were drawn since a depositor guarantees all checks he or she deposits. A depositor must adjust his or her records for dishonored or NSF (not sufficient funds) checks charged against his or her account. For example, if a customer used a dishonored check to pay off a purchase made on credit, the store would have to reverse the original entry and debit Accounts Receivable and credit Cash. They would then contact the customer and try to collect the account once more.

Mail and night deposits

Some firms are not able to take their daily cash receipts to the bank before the bank closes. Since it is usually not wise to leave the receipts on the firm's premises until morning, many banks provide night depository service. The deposit slip and cash receipts are assembled and dropped through a night deposit slot at the bank. The duplicate deposit slip is returned to the depositor the following day. Often a special depository is available to commercial customers for overnight safekeeping. Valuables, including cash, can be picked up the next morning or deposited as desired.

Bank by mail services are similar. If the entire deposit is made up of checks, the depositor may choose to mail the deposit. The duplicate deposit slip would then be returned by mail. It is unwise to use this approach if the deposit includes coins and currency because they can be easily stolen.

Checks and checkbooks

As stated earlier, a check is a written document, signed by an authorized person, directing the company's bank to pay a specified amount of money to a particular party (known as the *payee*). Checks are widely used in business because of their great convenience and safety. Checks can be written for exact amounts. Since the payee is specified, checks are safe to mail. They are returned to the company after clearing the bank, and, hence, serve as a receipt. Cleared checks are traceable documents in evaluating past transactions.

Checks and checkbooks may take a variety of forms. They come in various sizes and a multitude of colors. One format that is popular with small businesses has three checks to a page with a stub attached to each check. This format is shown in Illustration 5–2. The circled

ILLUSTRATION 5–2

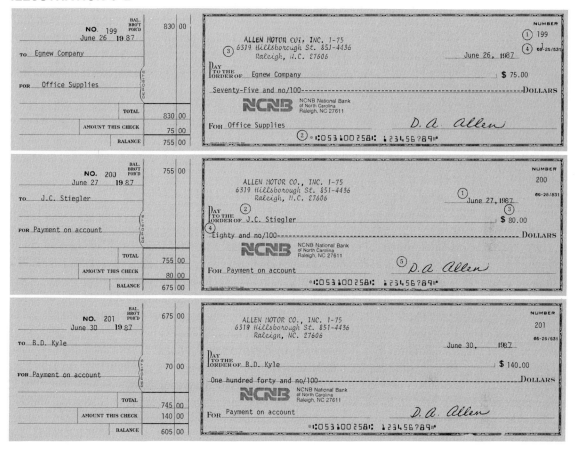

numbers on check 199 correspond to the numbers in the following explanation. The basic characteristics of these checks are standard regardless of the format. For control purposes, the checks are prenumbered in consecutive order (1). For example, the checks in Illustration 5–2 are numbers 199, 200, and 201. Because they are prenumbered, no two checks written on a given account will have the same number. All numbers should be accounted for, with none missing. The account and code numbers preprinted on the lower part of the check are printed in magnetic ink (2). This allows all checks to be processed through magnetic ink character recognition (MICR) equipment. This makes the check-sorting process quicker. The MICR characters include the identifying code of the Federal Reserve District of the bank, the identity code of the bank, and the checking account number of the firm. The company name is also preprinted on the check (3). The fractionlike number below the check number is the bank transit number and routing information (4). This was explained in the section on deposit tickets.

The firm must fill in the following information on the check:

1. Date.
2. Payee (the company or individual entitled to the check's proceeds).
3. Amount in figures.
4. Amount in words.
5. Authorized signature.

These items are identified on check number 200 in Illustration 5–2. Note that check 200 is dated June 27, 1987 (1) . The payee is J. C. Stiegler (2) . The amount of $80 is first written in figures (3) and then in words (4) . The person authorized to sign, D. A. Allen, has signed the check (5) . Recall that D. A. Allen's name must be on the signature card submitted by the company.

Checks 199–201 are in a checkbook that has a record-keeping system attached to each check. The necessary information is filled in on the check stub before the check is written. Then, when the check is detached along the perforated line, the check stub remains in the checkbook for record-keeping purposes. Note that the balance in the account after check number 198 was written—$830—is entered at the top of the stub for check no. 199. The amount of check 199 is subtracted from the $830 and the new balance of $755 is entered. As each check is written, it is subtracted from the previous balance to provide a running total that shows how much money the firm has on hand. When a deposit is made, it is entered on the stub and added to the previous balance, and a new total is derived. A deposit of $70 is illustrated on the stub for check 201.

Every checkbook should provide a sequentially numbered record of *all* checks written. Sequentially numbered checks are easier to account for. If a check is spoiled or destroyed, it should be explained in the records and marked "void." Whether valid or void, all checks should be accounted for.

The writing of a check does not automatically enter the information in the firm's journal. Thus, a journal entry must be made to record every check written. When a check is written, a credit is made to cash and a debit is recorded for either an asset acquired, an expense incurred, or the payment of an account payable.

As cash is received each day, entries are made in the journal. At the end of the day, a deposit is made to the bank. The amount of this deposit is entered in the checkbook, and a running balance of cash is kept in the checkbook. Entries are then posted to the Cash account and other related accounts.

A few simple procedures will greatly reduce the possibility of a check's being altered by a dishonest person. When the amount of a check is written in numbers, care should be taken to write the numbers so close together that no extra numbers can be inserted. When the check amount is written out in words, the words should start at the far left of the line. If any blank space remains on the line after the amount is written, a straight line should be drawn up to the word *Dollars*. Many companies use a machine called a **checkwriter** to print the amount in numbers and in words on the check. This machine is designed to prevent check alterations. When a company wishes to draw currency out of its own account the check is often made out to "Cash." Making a check payable to cash allows any holder of a check to cash it, and is a convenient way of replenishing cash funds, but it is not recommended. When a company issues a check to an outside party, that person's name should always be recorded.

A bank may directly charge or credit a customer's account. If a customer's deposit contained an endorsed check that was subsequently returned as dishonored, the bank would charge the account for the amount of the check and issue a **debit memo.** This memo would be mailed to the company along with the dishonored check as notification of the reduction in the account balance. A charge is called a debit memo because it reduces the bank's liability to the customer. An example of a debit memo is shown in Illustration 5–3.

A **credit memo** may also be prepared if a bank increases a firm's account for any reason except the receipt of a deposit. Its format is very similar to the debit memo.

Certified checks

Sometimes an ordinary check is not an acceptable form of payment. Perhaps the person receiving the check is concerned that the check will be dishonored. In such a case, the recipient may require a certified

---

ILLUSTRATION 5–3 Debit Memo

NCNB North Carolina National Bank	Checking Account Debit
NCNB 2525C Rev. 12-81	
We charge your account for the following reason:	Date
Dishonored check, NSF	May 29, 1987
	City
	Raleigh, NC
	Prepared By
	Eve May
	Approved By
	P. Dawson
	FRB-ABA Number Account Number
	053100258 123456789
	TC Amount
Allen Motor Co., Inc 1-75	20 00
6319 Hillsborough St.	
Raleigh, NC 27606	

---

check. **A certified check** is similar to a regular check except that the bank on which the check is drawn guarantees its payment by stamping "certified" and the bank's name on the check. When the bank certifies a check, it examines the writer's account to see that sufficient funds are available to cover it. Then the bank immediately deducts the amount of the check from the writer's account.

THE BANK STATEMENT

A bank must keep a record of all transactions that affect each account. Periodically the bank sends a **bank statement** to each customer to report on the status and transactions of each account over a certain period of time. The periodic reports may be monthly, weekly, or even daily, depending on the agreement between the customer and the bank. Monthly statements are the most common.

Statements may vary in format, but basically each reports:

1. The balance at the beginning of the period.
2. Deposits and other additions to the account.
3. Checks paid and other deductions from the account.
4. The balance at the end of the period.

ILLUSTRATION 5-4

NCNB

NCNB National Bank

Statement Of Account

Page

Account Number _123456789_

Period Ending _06/30/87_

Allen Motor Co., INC. I-75
6319 Hillsborough St. 851-4436
Raleigh, N.C. 27606

Note "+" Indicates Break In Numerical Sequence

① ③ ② ④

Statement Period	Beginning Balance	Withdrawals Number	Deposits Number	No. of Items Enclosed	Service Charge	Ending Balance
From 5/31/87 Thru 6/30/87	902.00	$ 686.00	$ 580.00	8.00		788.00

Date	Check No.	Amount
6- 3	195	$ 70
6-11	197	5
6-18	193	38
6-20	194	207
6-23	189	95
6-27	187	45
6-30	188	42
6-30	199	75
6-30	198	65

		$642
NSF check returned		44

Deposits		$686
6-2		$ 70
6-6		100
6-13		200
6-17		65
6-24		85
6-27		60

		$580

Daily Checking Account Balances

Also included in the bank statement will be the canceled checks that were paid by the bank during the period. Illustration 5–4 shows a bank statement for the Allen Motor Co. The circled numbers on the bank statement correspond to the numbered items in the list above.

The bank reconciliation

The bank prepares a customer's statement as of a specific time. The statement shows all the transactions that affected the account since the last bank statement, according to the bank's records. The balance in the Cash account on the company's books probably is not the same as the balance reported on the bank statement.

There are several reasons for this discrepancy. Some items that have been recorded as cash disbursements on the company books have not had time to clear the bank. A common example is outstanding checks. These are checks that have been written by the company but have not yet reached the company's bank for payment.

Other sources of discrepancy may not be known to the company until the bank statement arrives. The bank service charge is a good example of this.

Sometimes, errors are made by the bank or by the company. The bank may charge one company's account with a check written by another company. This can sometimes happen when two firms have very similar names. The company may make an error in recording a check. It is easy to transpose two figures (18 as 81) when recording a check.

As a result of these items, the bank statement balance and the checkbook balance may not be equal at a given point in time. Thus, a **bank reconciliation** is prepared whenever a bank statement is received. It explains the difference between the bank's figures and the company's figures. This reconciliation provides a check on the accuracy of the records kept by both parties. When errors do arise, they can be quickly recognized and corrected.

To prepare a bank reconciliation:

1. Compare the deposits shown by the bank during the month to those shown on the company's books. If some have not been recorded by the bank yet, add them to the *bank balance.* These are *deposits in transit*—that is, deposits made too late to appear on this statement.

2. Take all checks returned with the bank statement and compare them to the corresponding check stubs. Place a check mark ($\checkmark$) on the check stub to indicate each check that has *cleared* (been paid by the bank). Deduct those that have not cleared from the *bank balance*. List the check number and the dollar amount.

3. Check to see if there is a service charge on the bank statement. This must be subtracted from the *checkbook balance*.

4. Look at last period's bank reconciliation. Determine that all deposits in transit at that time have been properly credited to the bank. Also place a check mark beside last month's outstanding checks that have been paid this month. Any checks from the previous reconciliation that are still outstanding must be included in the new reconciliation and deducted from the bank balance.

5. Add to or subtract from the book balance any items that have been properly recorded by the bank but not by the company. Similarly, any items properly recorded on the company's books but not on the bank statement should be added to or subtracted from the bank balance.

Assume that the following information is taken from the checkbook of the Allen Motor Co. (see Illustration 5–2):

Balance June 30, 1987 . . . . $605
Deposit on June 30 70

The bank statement shown in Illustration 5–4 shows a balance of $788. It does not reflect the deposit made by the company on June 30. This deposit of $70 must be added to the balance of the bank statement. In comparing the checks returned with the bank statement and the checks written during the month, the following checks are found outstanding:

Check no. 196 $ 60
          200   80
          201   140

These amounts must be deducted from the balance of the bank statement.

In comparing checks, it is discovered that check number 197 was incorrectly recorded as $50 in the checkbook and journal. The proper amount of the payment on account was $5. The difference of $45 must be added to the checkbook balance. Check no. 188 was written for $42, but was incorrectly recorded in the company's records as

$22. This check was written for office supplies. The $20 difference must be subtracted from the checkbook balance.

The bank statement reflects a deduction from Allen's checking account of $8 for a service charge. This must be subtracted from the checkbook balance. Also enclosed in the bank statement is a check from a customer marked NSF. That person's checking account had insufficient funds to pay this check. The bank has subtracted this $44 from Allen's account, so it must also be subtracted from the checkbook balance.

The Allen Company's bank reconciliation is presented as an example in Illustration 5–5. Note that reconciliations are always made at a specific date. The information needed to complete the reconciliation is accumulated from the company records and the bank statement.

ILLUSTRATION 5–5

THE ALLEN COMPANY
Bank Reconciliation
June 30, 1987

Balance per books, June 30, 1987		$605
Add:		
Error in check recording—197		45
		$650
Subtract:		
Service charge	$ 8	
Error on check recording—188	20	
NSF check	44	72
Adjusted book balance, June 30, 1987.		$578
Balance per bank statement, June 30, 1987		$788
Add:		
Deposit in transit		70
		$858
Subtract:		
Outstanding checks:		
No. 196	$ 60	
No. 200	80	
No. 201	140	280
Adjusted bank statement balance, June 30, 1987 . . .		$578

The example in Illustration 5–5 is relatively simple. Many bank reconciliations have many checks outstanding and many other items in the statement. Regardless of its complexity, when a reconciliation is completed, the adjusted checkbook and bank balances should be equal. If they are not, an error has been made, and an additional search must be made to locate the cause of the difference.

Journalizing the reconciliation

The items that appeared in the checkbook's side of the reconciliation must be journalized to correct the company's accounts. The Cash account along with other affected accounts must be brought to their correct balances. The journal entry for the additions and the deductions to the Cash account would be:

		GENERAL JOURNAL			
DATE		ACCOUNT AND EXPLANATION	P.R.	DEBIT	CREDIT
July	1	Cash		45 00	
		Accounts Payable			45 00
		To correct cash.			
	1	Accounts Receivable		44 00	
		Bank Service Charge		8 00	
		Accounts Payable		20 00	
		Cash			72 00
		To correct cash.			

After these two entries are posted, all accounts are up to date.

The items on the bank's side of the reconciliation affect the bank's books. Thus, the firm makes no journal entry for these items. However, if the bank has made an error, the company should notify the bank so that the error can be corrected on the bank's books.

SPECIAL CHECKING ACCOUNTS

Many firms have more than one checking account. Keeping several accounts may aid in an appropriate division of responsibility and ensure proper control. Commonly, accounts are separated by the function that they serve. A payroll cash account is often used in addition to a regular cash account. This account is typically used to pay the payroll when it comes due. A separate ledger account is usually established for each bank account.

For example, the payroll account will usually have a small balance, say $100, to ensure against minor errors that might cause the account to be overdrawn. When the total of the payroll checks is determined, a check for the total is written on the general checking account and deposited in the payroll account. When the payroll checks are prepared, they are written on the payroll account. If any serious errors have been made in preparing the payroll checks, it will be easier to trace the errors than if the checks were written directly on the general account, which may have a large number of checks drawn on it for a variety of purposes.

The number of special checking accounts a firm has depends on the needs of management. A firm may choose to have several payroll accounts—one for each plant, for example. The added control over cash should be weighed against the increased cost of multiple accounts.

SAVINGS ACCOUNTS

Banks also offer **savings accounts.** Also known as time deposits, such accounts usually pay a stated rate of interest while checking accounts do not. Deposits in a savings account are usually recorded in a *passbook,* which must be presented in order to make a withdrawal. There are a large variety of plans that may loosely be defined as savings accounts. Interest rates differ from plan to plan, from town to town, and from time period to time period.

A firm may have a separate checking and savings account, or it may have a **NOW account** (negotiable order of withdrawal account). In effect, a NOW account is a combination checking and savings account. If a minimum dollar amount is maintained in such an account, the bank pays interest on it. **Interest** is a payment for the use of money. A bank pays a certain percentage rate for the use of the money in a depositor's account. For example, if a bank requires a minimum balance of $500 in a NOW account at all times and pays interest of 5½ percent, the account will earn at least $27.50 by the end of the year ($500 × .055 = $27.50). The bank pays interest on all the money on deposit in a NOW account, not just the required minimum balance. So if a customer keeps an average of $700 on deposit throughout the year and never lets her balance drop below $500, she will earn more than the minimum interest payment ($700 × .055 = $38.50). Most small firms do not have NOW accounts. Instead, they maintain separate checking and savings accounts.

Money may be withdrawn from a checking account at any time. But advance notice may have to be given to a bank before withdrawing money from a savings account. Thus, the money in a savings account may not be readily accessible. Checking accounts, savings accounts, and NOW accounts may be offered by savings and loan associations as well as from banks.

PETTY CASH

We have seen that for control purposes, most cash disbursements are made by check. But, for some small expenditures, the convenience of having coins and currency immediately available outweighs the safety of using checks. The amounts expended are not usually large. Hence, a small supply of cash, called a **petty cash fund,** can be maintained. Whenever the fund becomes low, or at the end of an accounting period, the cash supply is replenished. The petty cash fund, like all assets, should be carefully controlled to ensure its proper use. Usually one person, called the *petty cash custodian,* is given the responsibility of operating the petty cash fund. This person makes the disbursements and keeps a record of the fund's activities.

Each time a disbursement is made from the petty cash fund, a **petty cash voucher** is filled out. The exact form of the voucher may vary from firm to firm. However, several characteristics are quite common. Vouchers are often prenumbered for control purposes and they require the date of the disbursement, the name of the recipient, and the purpose. Sometimes an authorizing signature may also be needed. Illustration 5–6 shows a typical petty cash voucher.

ILLUSTRATION 5–6

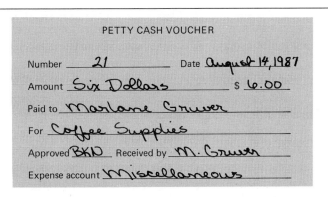

PETTY CASH VOUCHER

Number ___21___ Date August 14, 1987

Amount _Six Dollars_ $ 6.00

Paid to _Marlane Gruver_

For _Coffee Supplies_

Approved BKD   Received by _M. Gruver_

Expense account _Miscellaneous_

At any point in time, the coins and currency plus the total of the completed petty cash vouchers on hand should equal the amount originally placed in the fund. This voucher system, known as the *imprest fund* method of handling petty cash, is the most common system used by firms.

Keeping a petty cash fund

To begin a petty cash fund, a check is cashed to furnish the original supply of currency. For example, suppose that a fund is created for $100. The necessary journal entry is shown below. Note that one cash account is decreased while another one is created.

DATE		ACCOUNT AND EXPLANATION	P.R.	DEBIT	CREDIT
1987					
Aug.	1	Petty Cash		100 00	
		Cash			100 00
		To establish fund.			

GENERAL JOURNAL — PAGE 10

The petty cash custodian maintains a record of petty cash expenditures in a **petty cash book.** This book is *not* a journal. It is merely a listing of how all petty cash is spent. A petty cash voucher, similar to the one in Illustration 5–6, supports each amount that is recorded in the petty cash book. A sample petty cash book is shown in Illustration 5–7. Column headings vary from company to company, depending on the frequency of certain transactions.

ILLUSTRATION 5–7

PETTY CASH BOOK

DATE	VOUCHER NO.	RECEIPTS	PAYMENTS	POSTAGE	OFFICE SUPPLIES	GENERAL	
						AMOUNT	DESCRIPTION

Assume that during the first part of August, the following items were paid from the Allen Motor Company's petty cash fund:

August 4 Coffee supplies . . . . $ 6
       5 Postage stamps   20
       8 Office supplies   30
      12 Contribution to United Way   25

The petty cash custodian listed each item in the petty cash book after an appropriate voucher was signed. The filled-in petty cash book is shown in Illustration 5–8.

**ILLUSTRATION
5–8**

						GENERAL	
DATE	VOUCHER NO.	RECEIPTS	PAYMENTS	POSTAGE	OFFICE SUPPLIES	AMOUNT	DESCRIPTION
1987 Aug. 1	—	100					
4	1		6.00			6.00	Misc.
5	2		20.00	20.00			
8	3		30.00		30.00		
12	4		25.00			25.00	Contributions

PETTY CASH BOOK

Note that the original amount of $100 was written in the receipts column along with the date. As each disbursement was made, its date was listed and the amount of its payment was entered in the Payments column. The amount of the payment was then repeated in the appropriate explanatory column or in the General column. If the amount was entered in the General column, a description of the transaction was given.

When a petty cash fund runs short of currency, the petty cash book and the vouchers are totaled for each type of expense. The total amount of the vouchers should equal the amount in the payments column. This should be the amount of cash needed to bring the petty cash fund to its *original balance*. At Allen Motor Co., cash totaling $19 and petty cash vouchers of $81 made up the fund at the time of replenishment.

Illustration 5–9 shows the petty cash book totaled. The sum of the explanatory columns—postage ($20), office supplies ($30), and general ($31)—equals the sum of the payments column ($81). The custodian then subtracts the $81 from the $100 indicated in the receipts column and counts the cash on hand to determine if $19 still

ILLUSTRATION 5-9

			PETTY CASH BOOK				
DATE	VOUCHER NO.	RECEIPTS	PAYMENTS	POSTAGE	OFFICE SUPPLIES	GENERAL AMOUNT	DESCRIPTION
1987 Aug.1	–	100					
4	1		6.00			6.00	Misc.
5	2		20.00	20.00			
8	3		30.00		30.00		
12	4		25.00			25.00	Contributions
			81.00	20.00	30.00	31.00	

remains. A check in the amount of $81 must then be written to replenish the fund to its original balance of $100.

Illustration 5–10 shows the journal entry that would be made to replenish the petty cash fund. The information about the accounts to be debited is taken from the petty cash book. Remember, the petty cash book is not a journal. The journal entry is made when the fund is replenished.

ILLUSTRATION 5-10

		GENERAL JOURNAL				
DATE		ACCOUNT AND EXPLANATION	P.R.	DEBIT		CREDIT
Aug.	12	Postage Expense		20 00		
		Office Supplies		30 00		
		Miscellaneous Expense		6 00		
		Contributions Expense		25 00		
		Cash				81 00
		To reimburse petty cash fund.				

Note that no additional debit has been made to the petty cash fund. The fund is debited only when it is *created* or *increased* in size. The petty cash fund is credited only when it is *decreased* in size. Changes in the fund size would be made if it became apparent that the fund was either too small or too large to meet the firm's needs.

A statement of petty cash disbursements can be made by listing the totals of each type of disbursement and summing them for the grand total.

Cash short and over

When cash is handled, mistakes are likely to occur. For example, too much or too little change may have been given to a customer. As a result, actual cash collections may differ from the amount of cash that should be on hand. This difference is recorded in a separate ledger account called **Cash Short and Over.** In the long-run, shortages and overages tend to balance each other out. When financial statements are prepared at the end of an accounting period, the Cash Short and Over account is closed out to the Income Summary account. If there is a debit balance in the Cash Short and Over account, it is treated as an expense. A credit balance is handled as a revenue account.

For example, assume that the accounting record showed cash receipts for services rendered for a given day of $100 but only $98 in coins, currency, and checks was actually on hand. The entry in the journal would look like this:

		GENERAL JOURNAL			
DATE		ACCOUNT AND EXPLANATION	P.R.	DEBIT	CREDIT
Aug.	15	Cash		98 00	
		Cash Short and Over		2 00	
		Service Revenue			100 00
		To record revenue.			

SUMMARY

All businesses must have cash to operate. In business, the term **cash** means more than just coins and currency. It includes anything a bank will accept at face value on deposit, such as **certified checks,** money orders, and bank drafts. Because it is customary on a balance sheet to list assets in the order of their **liquidity,** cash is always listed first.

Since careful control of cash is important, companies develop special procedures to safeguard their cash. For example, a person who handles cash will rarely be allowed to record cash transactions in the company books. Keeping the two functions separate helps to prevent theft.

Most businesses maintain a checking account because **checks** are a convenient and safe way to handle money. A **signature card** is presented to the bank with the signatures of the people who are authorized to write checks for the company. The bank will not cash a check unless an authorized signature is on the check.

To deposit cash in its account, a company must make out a **deposit ticket** and endorse each check. There are three kinds of **endorsements:** blank endorsements, full endorsements, and restrictive endorsements. The endorsement transfers ownership of the check and guarantees its payment.

If a company writes a check for an amount that is greater than the balance in its checking account, its bank may refuse to pay it, and the check will be **dishonored.** The issuance of such a check, which would result in the account's having a negative balance, is called an **overdraft.** If a company includes a dishonored check in a deposit, its bank will charge it for the amount of the check and issue a **debit memo.** On the other hand, if the bank increases the company's account for any reason other than the receipt of a deposit, it will issue a **credit memo.**

There are many forms of checks, but the most common form among small businesses is one that has an attached stub. As checks are written, information about the date, payee, and amount are recorded on both the check and the stub. This allows the company to maintain a running balance of cash on deposit right in the checkbook. Bank deposits are also entered on the check stubs. Some companies use a **checkwriter** to prevent the alteration of check amounts. Once a deposit or check is written in the checkbook, a journal entry must be made to record it in the company books.

The bank keeps a record of all transactions on each account. Generally, once a month, the bank mails a **bank statement** to each account holder indicating the monthly activity in the account and the amount of cash on deposit. Often the account total on the bank statement does not agree with the company's records, but there are logical reasons for the discrepancy. The company may have made a deposit that arrived too late for the bank to record. Or it may have written checks that did not clear the bank as of the statement date. The bank may also add a service charge for handling the account. Finally, errors made on either bank or company records can create a difference in the balances. Thus, a company must prepare a **bank reconciliation** to explain the difference between its figures and those of the bank. A reconciliation also provides a check on the accuracy of both sets of books. Based on the reconciliation, the company can bring its checkbook and its accounts up to date.

A company may have separate checking accounts for payroll and other special uses. It may also maintain **savings accounts,** and, in rare cases, **NOW accounts.** Both savings accounts and NOW accounts earn **interest.**

Rather than write checks for small amounts, a company will maintain a **petty cash fund.** A set dollar amount is put under the control of a petty cash custodian, who keeps a record of all disbursements in a **petty cash book.** A **petty cash voucher** must support each disbursement. When the fund gets low, an entry is made in the journal to record the information from the petty cash book and reimburse the fund for the amount of cash spent. This brings the total cash in the petty cash fund back to its original amount.

Businesses may make mistakes in handling cash with customers and they may have more or less cash at the end of each day that they should have taken in or given out. In this case, since entries must have equal debits and credits, an entry is made to an account called **Cash Short and Over** for the amount to balance out the entry. If at the end of the period it has a debit balance it is shown as an expense. If it has a credit balance it is a revenue item.

KEY TERMS

Bank Reconciliation—A process that identifies and explains the differences between the checking account balance shown on a company's books and the checking account balance shown on its bank's books.

Bank Statement—A periodic statement sent by a bank to a customer that shows the current balance of a checking account and provides a detailed list of transactions for a specified period of time. Monthly statements are most common.

Cash—Coins, currency, and anything else a bank will accept for immediate deposit. This includes personal checks, traveler's checks, cashier's checks, money orders, bank drafts, and credit card receipts from sales or services rendered.

Cash Short and Over—A separate account used to record the difference between actual cash collections and the amount that should be on hand.

Certified Check—A check whose payment has been guaranteed by the bank on which it is drawn.

Check—A written document, signed by an authorized person, directing an account holder's bank to pay a specified amount of money to a particular party.

Checkwriter—A machine used to print a check's amount in numbers and words to prevent alteration.

Credit Memo—A form issued by a bank notifying a firm of an increase in its account for any reason other than the receipt of a deposit.

Debit Memo—A form issued by a bank notifying a firm of a decrease in its account for any reason other than the writing of a check.

Deposit Ticket—A document that must accompany any deposit made into a checking account, which shows the owner and number of the account, the date, and the items that make up the deposit.

Dishonored Check—A check that a bank has refused to pay because its writer lacks sufficient funds (NSF) in his or her checking account to cover the check's amount.

Endorsement—The placement of one's signature on the back of a check that is to be cashed or deposited. The endorsement transfers ownership of the check to a bank or other party and guarantees its payment.

Interest—A payment for the use of money; a percentage rate paid by a bank for the use of funds in a depositor's account.

Liquidity—The ease with which an asset can be converted into cash without loss of value.

NOW Account (Negotiable Order of Withdrawal Account)—A combination savings and checking account that pays a stated rate of interest as long as a specified minimum balance is maintained.

Overdraft—The issuance of a check in an amount that is greater than the amount of deposit in the issuer's checking account.

Petty Cash Book—A list of amounts spent from the petty cash fund. It is not a journal.

Petty Cash Fund—A small sum of money established as a separate fund from which minor cash disbursements for authorized purposes are made. When the *imprest fund* method is used, the cash in the fund plus the vouchers covering the disbursements must equal the amount originally placed in the fund.

Petty Cash Voucher—A form for recording data about disbursements from a petty cash fund. Commonly included are the amount of the disbursement, the recipient, the purpose, and, sometimes, an authorizing signature.

Savings Account—A time deposit account that pays a stated rate of interest and may require advance notification in order to make a withdrawal.

Signature Card—A card kept on file by a bank, which records the signature of each person authorized to sign checks drawn against a firm's checking account.

QUESTIONS AND EXERCISES

1. What are the components of cash from the viewpoint of a business?
2. Why is cash listed first in the balance sheet?
3. Why are special procedures established to handle the Cash account? What are some of these special procedures?
4. What is the purpose of a checking account?
5. What is a signature card?
6. Distinguish among a blank endorsement, a full endorsement, and a restrictive endorsement.
7. Give some precautions that should be taken in order to reduce the possibility of a check being altered by dishonest persons.
8. When might a customer receive a debit memo from a bank?
9. Define the following types of checks:
   a. Dishonored.
   b. Certified.
10. What are the basic parts of a bank statement?
11. Usually there is a difference between the balance in the Cash account on the company's books and the balance on the bank statement. Why might this difference exist?
12. How does a savings account differ from a checking account?
13. When is it necessary to debit an account called Cash Short and Over? When should the account be credited?
14. What is a petty cash fund? What is the imprest fund method?

15. When is the Petty Cash account debited, and when is it credited?
16. The Martin Company established a petty cash fund of $100. At the end of May, the total of the completed petty cash vouchers was $85. Coins and currency amounted to $15. The expenses were as follows:

Telephone expense $25
Office supplies expense 20
Postage expense 15
Freight expense 25

What entry should be made in the general journal to replenish the petty cash fund on May 31?
17. The Acton Company's Cash account has a balance of $1,100. The balance per the bank statement is $1,070. The difference is because of a $10 service charge and a $20 NSF check. What journal entry is necessary to correct the company's cash account?
18. The Barnett Company's Cash account has a balance of $1,645. The balance per the bank statement is $1,085. The difference is the result of the following items:

$ 10   Service charge
   50   Outstanding check
  235   NSF check
  365   Deposit in transit

What journal entry is required to correct the respective accounts on the company's books?
19. The Sherry Company established a petty cash fund of $150. At the end of July, the total of the completed petty cash vouchers was $125. Coins and currency amounted to $23. The expenses were as follows:

Postage expense $40
Office supplies expense 55
Printing expense 30

What entries should be made to

a. Establish the fund.
b. Reimburse the fund.
20. The Wall Company's Cash account has a balance of $2,470. The balance per the bank statement is $2,315. The difference is the result of the following:

$ 15   Service charge
  310   Outstanding checks
   30   NSF check
  420   Deposit in transit

a. What is the correct amount of cash?
b. What journal entry is necessary to bring the account balances up to date?

PROBLEMS

5–1. Hunter Christie, a plumber, completed the following transactions with the Walton Street Bank during the month of April 1987.

Apr.	1	Balance in bank per checkbook	$2,500.00
	4	Check no. 627	56.25
	4	Check no. 628	113.00
	4	Check no. 629	582.70
	7	Check no. 630	705.00
	7	Deposit	1,680.00
	7	Check no. 631	269.50
	7	Check no. 632	444.00
	8	Check no. 633	115.65
	8	Check no. 634	393.90
	11	Check no. 635	245.00
	14	Deposit	1,373.00
	15	Check no. 636	129.56
	15	Check no. 637	692.72
	15	Check no. 638	507.39
	18	Deposit	1,876.00
	21	Check no. 639	468.79
	22	Check no. 640	291.81
	22	Check no. 641	312.37
	22	Check no. 642	802.15
	25	Check no. 643	120.43
	25	Deposit	1,298.00
	25	Check no. 644	316.98
	28	Check no. 645	723.04
	28	Check no. 646	187.70
	28	Check no. 647	200.00
	30	Check no. 648	310.06
	30	Deposit	1,989.00

The April bank statement showed a balance of $2,517.05 on April 30. Check nos. 639, 642, 647, and 648 were outstanding. A service charge of $2.95 was made by the bank during April.

The deposit on April 30 was still in transit on that date.

Required:

Prepare a bank reconciliation on April 30.

5–2. Prepare a bank reconciliation from the following information:

Balance per bank statement of Morris & Caughman Co., Inc.,

March 31, 1987.	$3,881.00
Balance per checkbook	3,762.00

Checks outstanding:

No. 750	$ 43.87
No. 752	68.13
No. 757	140.45
No. 759	650.80
No. 760	73.25
No. 762	49.50

Returned check NSF	68.00
Deposit of March 31, 1987, not recorded on bank statement .	843.00
Check no. 753 for $212 returned with statement had been recorded in the books as $221.	
Bank service charge	5.00

5–3. D. L. Eve, an interior decorator, has just received the October bank statement. It shows a balance of $1,672. Eve's books show a balance of $1,776. Given the information below, prepare a bank reconciliation as of October 31, 1987.
   a. The bank had not received the October 31 deposit of $600.
   b. A bank service charge of $25 was not recorded on the books.
   c. The following checks were outstanding on October 31, 1987.

Check no. 176	$156
179	78
183	94
184	202

   d. A customer's check for $9 had been stamped "NSF" and had been returned with the bank statement.

5–4. Dr. P. M. Lawson, a veterinarian, completed the following transactions with the Barber Street Bank during the month of July:

July	1	Balance in bank per Cash account . . .	$8,290.00
	1	Deposit	500.00
	4	Check no. 448	25.76
	4	Check no. 449	102.50
	7	Check no. 450	400.00
	8	Check no. 451	75.24

July 8	Deposit	600.00
11	Check no. 452	55.75
11	Check no. 453	84.25
14	Check no. 454	26.00
15	Check no. 455	94.68
15	Check no. 456	82.32
18	Deposit	300.00
21	Check no. 457	500.00
25	Check no. 458	101.67
25	Deposit	600.00
28	Check no. 459	93.33
28	Check no. 460	45.00
29	Check no. 461	78.00
31	Check no. 462	12.00
31	Deposit	406.00

The bank statement for July showed a balance of $8,726.33. Check nos. 459, 460, 461, and 462 were outstanding. The deposit on July 31 was still in transit at that date. The bank service charge for July was $15.50.

Required:

1. Prepare a bank reconciliation for the month ended July 31, 1987.
2. Prepare the general journal entries that are necessary to adjust Dr. Lawson's account balance to the reconciled figures.

5–5. Prepare a bank reconciliation from the following information:

Balance per bank statement of George Hunter Company,
January 31, 1987 . . . . $6,777.77
Balance per checkbook, January 31, 1987 . . . . 7,333.10
Check outstanding: No. 179 . . . . 31.00
Deposit of $400 on January 31, 1987, has not been
recorded by the bank.
Returned check NSF 55.23
Bank service charge 14.10

The bookkeeper for George Hunter Company had recorded several checks incorrectly:

Check No.	Amount Recorded on Books	Correct Amount
159	$112	$211
173	58	85
180	76	67

5–6. The Denton Company's Cash in Bank account has a balance of $6,745 on February 28, 1987. The balance shown on the bank statement is $4,600. Using the following information, (1) prepare a bank reconciliation for the Denton Company on February 28, 1987, and (2) prepare the general journal entries that are required to correct the company's Cash in Bank account.

Checks outstanding:
No. 762	$100
No. 770	25
No. 772	50
No. 779	35

Deposit of February 28, 1987, not recorded on the bank statement	$1,000
Returned check NSF	300
Bank service charge	15

Check no. 766, returned with the bank statement, had been written for $851 but had been recorded in the books at $581. It was written in payment of an account.

The bank had charged the Denton Company with two checks written by the Benton Company. The checks were for $360 and $410.

5–7. On January 31, 1987, the Francis Company had a Cash account balance of $1,794. The bank statement for January showed a balance of $697. The deposit of $1,850 made on January 31 was still in transit. The following information was also available:

Returned check NSF	$ 53
Bank service charge	8

Check no. 346 had been written for $362 but had been recorded in the books at $632. It had been written in payment of an account.

The bank incorrectly credited our account for the Frances Co. deposit of $250.

The following checks were outstanding:

No. 350	$ 57
No. 354	112
No. 355	125

Required:

1. Prepare a bank reconciliation for the Francis Company on January 31, 1987.

2. Prepare the general journal entries necessary to correct the Cash account.

5–8. Give the general journal entry for the replenishment of a $150 petty cash fund. The cashier reports the following authorized disbursements and the cash on hand at the time of replenishment was $23.75.

Postage	$56.75
Office supplies	23.40
Taxicabs	12.75
Telephone	3.50
Repairs	26.85

5–9. The A. B. Cohen Company wants to have a petty cash fund and you have been asked to set it up and handle the transactions for it. The transactions are as follows:

1987
June 2 Set up petty cash fund with $75.
     30 Replenish petty cash with the following expenses:

Postage	$25
Office supplies	28
Miscellaneous	15

July 15 Replenish petty cash with the following expenses:

Postage	$ 3
Travel expense	55
Office supplies	2
Miscellaneous	5

July 31 Replenish petty cash with the following expenses:

Travel expense	$45
Postage	15
Office supplies	5

Required:

Journalize the transactions in the general journal.

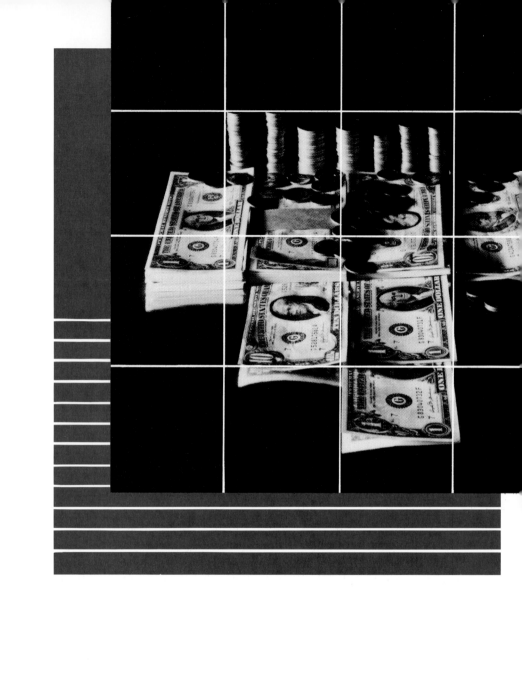

CHAPTER 6

Payroll accounting—the employee

LEARNING OBJECTIVES

In this chapter, you will learn how employees' payroll records are kept and how various laws affect employees' earnings and take-home pay. After studying this chapter, you should be able to:

1. Compute gross pay for both regular and overtime hours.
2. Calculate payroll deductions and net pay.
3. Record payroll transactions in the payroll register.
4. Prepare individual earnings records.
5. Record gross pay and payroll deductions in the accounts.

Many businesses find that wages, salaries, and related payments add up to one of their biggest expenses. In accounting, such payments to employees in exchange for their services are known as payroll transactions. Because payroll transactions are such a large expense, it is very important that they be recorded properly. This requires knowledge of the laws related to payroll computation, reporting requirements, and payroll deductions.

EARNINGS AND PAYROLL DEDUCTIONS

Payroll accounting is the computing and recording of disbursements for wages and salaries and their related payroll taxes. Payroll transactions occur only when payments are made to employees for their services. An **employee** is any individual who is hired to provide his or her services under the direct supervision and control of an employer. An employee receives wages or a salary as compensation. In contrast, an **independent contractor,** such as a lawyer or a public accountant, also offers services to a firm, but once the nature of the service is defined, an independent contractor is free to choose how the service will be accomplished. Independent contractors receive fees for their services. Thus, a significant difference between employees and independent contractors is the degree of control a company exercises over how they do their work. This distinction is important because different laws apply to each category of worker. The laws and regulations discussed in this chapter apply only to *employees*— not to independent contractors.

The starting point of payroll accounting is **gross pay,** the total amount of an employee's wages or salary before payroll deductions. Gross pay usually serves as the basis for payroll deductions. A **payroll deduction** is an amount subtracted from an employee's gross pay before a paycheck is issued that is used by the employer to cover a specified cost. Typical payroll deductions include federal income taxes, state income taxes, the employee's share of social security taxes, and miscellaneous deductions such as insurance premiums and charitable contributions. **Net pay** is the amount of pay an employee actually receives. It is gross pay minus all applicable payroll deductions.

The four phases of payroll accounting

Payroll accounting has four principal phases. The first is the computation of each employee's gross pay for the payroll period. A payroll period may vary from firm to firm and from one category of employees to another within a given firm. Payrolls are most commonly computed on a weekly, biweekly, semimonthly, or monthly basis. For example, in a manufacturing business, the production-line employees are usually paid on a weekly basis; the supervisors and middle management are usually paid either biweekly or semimonthly; and the executives are usually paid once a month.

Secondly, after gross pay has been calculated, the deductions must be determined. The deductions will be based on government regulations and employee instructions.

The results of the first two steps must be recorded in the company's permanent payroll records. This third step is essential to meet government requirements. Finally, the total payroll activity must be summarized to ease recording in the company's general records.

Computing wages and salaries

Compensation for skilled and unskilled workers is typically classified as **wages.** Wages are usually expressed as an individual hourly rate. When an employee's hourly rate is multiplied by the total hours worked during the payroll period, the resulting figure is the employee's gross pay. In contrast, compensation for administrative and managerial personnel is usually termed a **salary.** Salaries are customarily expressed as monthly or annual amounts.

The basic salary or hourly wage is sometimes supplemented by sales commissions or bonuses, production piece rate payments, cost-of-living adjustments, and profit sharing plans. These payments vary from firm to firm because each company has a unique computational formula.

Each employee's basic compensation is based on the total time worked during a particular payroll period. If the number of people is small, this time figure might be a mental record kept by the manager or a brief entry in his or her memorandum book. However, such informal records are not recommended. Good payroll records should be maintained to avoid disputes with employees, to simplify bookkeeping, and to satisfy regulations established by the government, insurance companies, labor unions, and the company itself.

Many businesses use time clocks to keep track of the hours their employees work. A **timecard** inserted into the time clock provides a printed record of when each employee arrived for work and when he or she departed for the day. A specimen timecard is shown in Illustration 6–1. Time clocks are infrequently used with *salaried* per-

ILLUSTRATION
6-1

**Specimen
Timecard**

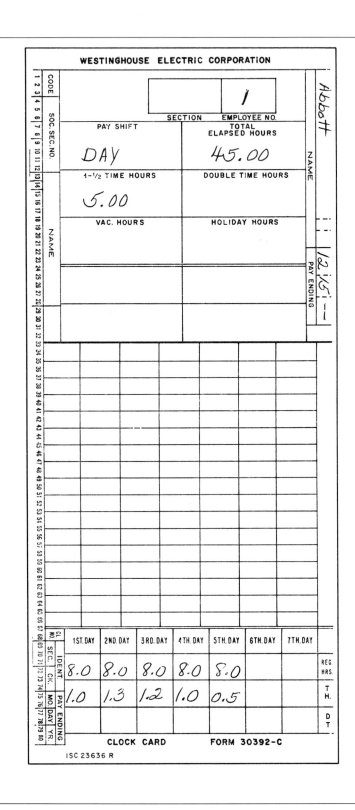

Illustration 6-1 — Specimen Timecard. Westinghouse Electric Corporation Clock Card, Form 30392-C. Employee No. 1, Name: Abbott, Pay Shift: DAY, Total Elapsed Hours: 45.00, 1-½ Time Hours: 5.00, Pay Ending 12/15.

	1ST. DAY	2ND. DAY	3RD. DAY	4TH. DAY	5TH. DAY	6TH. DAY	7TH. DAY	
REG HRS.	8.0	8.0	8.0	8.0	8.0			
T H.	1.0	1.3	1.2	1.0	0.5			
D T								

sonnel. Instead, such employees or their immediate supervisor will submit a written summary of hours worked.

Wages and salaries for employees who have not worked overtime are easy to compute using the recorded hours. The gross pay of an hourly employee is simply the base rate per hour times the total hours the employee has worked during the period. For salaried employees, it is simply their prescribed salary for the payroll period.

Usually, hourly employees are entitled to extra compensation for working overtime. The **Federal Fair Labor Standards Act,** passed in 1938, is commonly known as the Wages and Hours Law. It establishes a minimum wage that must be paid by employers engaged either directly or indirectly in interstate commerce. The act also sets a ceiling on the maximum number of hours a person can work. Finally, it also specifies that covered employees be paid a premium rate—1½ times their regular hourly rate—for all hours worked in excess of 40 per week. There is nothing in the act that limits all labor-management agreements to these exact terms. In fact, many labor agreements have significantly more generous provisions. Often, a premium is paid for excess hours worked in any one day or for work on a holiday. And some contracts specify that a standard workweek be shorter than 40 hours.

To illustrate the computation of gross pay, suppose that an hourly employee, Henry Abbott, has worked 45 hours during the weekly payroll period ended December 15. Abbott's regular hourly rate is $8, and his employer, Jones Plumbing Supply, pays time and a half for all hours worked in excess of 40 per week. His gross pay is computed as follows:

40 hours at $8	$320
5 hours at $12	60
Gross pay for the week	$380

Besides time and a half, some employees may be paid double time for work done on Sundays and holidays. For example, if a $10-per-hour worker who qualifies for double time works 8 hours a day on Monday through Friday plus 4 hours on Sunday, her gross pay would be:

40 hours at $10	$400
4 hours at $20	80
Gross pay for the week	$480

Many union contracts call for the payment of double time to specified categories of employees.

When an employee is salaried, the computations are similar once his or her hourly rate is established. To do this, the employee's salary is first converted into an annual amount that is then converted into an hourly figure. This can best be explained through an example. Suppose that Jean Larch has a monthly salary of $1,300. If her company paid her time and a half for all hours over 40, her overtime rate would be:

$$\$1,300 \times 12 \text{ months} = \$15,600 \text{ per year}$$
$$\$15,600 \div 52 \text{ weeks} = \$300 \text{ per week}$$
$$\$300 \div 40 \text{ hours} = \$7.50 \text{ per hour}$$
$$\$7.50 \times 1.5 = \$11.25 \text{ per overtime hour}$$

In most cases, a salaried employee does not get paid for overtime. If a salaried employee is compensated for overtime, however, it is often at the straight hourly rate and not at time and a half.

Some workers' pay is based on neither an hourly wage nor a salary. Piece rate workers are paid at a rate of so much per unit of production. Agricultural workers are sometimes paid by this method (X per bushel). For example, John James is a fruit picker who gets paid $.75 per bushel of fruit picked. If he picked 50 bushels of fruit in one day, he would earn $37.50 for that day (50 bushels $\times$ $.75 per bushel). Another alternative to an hourly wage or salary is a commission-based pay system. In such a case, a worker is paid a fixed percentage of sales generated. For example, an automobile salesperson might earn a 1 percent commission based on gross sales. Thus, if he or she sold a car for $9,500, he or she would earn $95 ($9,500 $\times$ 1%).

Deductions from gross pay

Employers are required by law to withhold specified amounts from every employee's gross earnings to cover the payroll taxes levied by federal, state, and local governments. These would include:

1. Federal income taxes—employee.
2. FICA taxes (social security)—employee's share.
3. State and local income taxes, where applicable—employee.

The Current Tax Payment Act of 1943 created the withholding tax. The act requires an employer to withhold an appropriate amount from each employee's paycheck for income tax. The employer is required to submit reports to the Internal Revenue Service (IRS) on a quarterly basis (Form 941) and to the employee on an annual basis (W–2 form). The Current Tax Payment Act placed federal income taxes on a pay-as-you-go basis, rather than allowing employees to pay their income taxes in a lump sum at the end of the taxable year.

Many states and some local governments also levy an income tax and have a pay-as-you-go system that requires employers to withhold a specified amount from each employee's paycheck.

The Federal Insurance Contributions Act (FICA), passed in 1935, requires that during the years of covered employment, employees, employers, and self-employed persons pay a percentage of their wages into a special fund. **FICA taxes** are used to pay retirement benefits, medicare, and disability benefits. The employer withholds FICA taxes from employees and pays them to the Internal Revenue Service.

In addition, many employers deduct amounts for such things as:

1. U.S. savings bonds or other savings plans.
2. Premiums on employee's life, health, or accidental insurance.
3. Union dues.
4. Contributions to charitable organizations.
5. Payments to pension or profit sharing funds.
6. Repayment of loans from employer or credit union.

Withholding federal income taxes

The amount of federal income tax an employer withholds from an employee's paycheck is based on (1) the employee's total earnings, (2) the number of withholding allowances, (3) the employee's marital status, and (4) the length of the employee's pay period.

Every employee is allowed to claim one withholding allowance for him- or herself, another allowance if he or she is blind or over 65, and an additional allowance for each qualifying dependent. A **withholding allowance** is a dollar amount, $1,040 for 1984, by which taxpayers may reduce their taxable income before computing their tax liability. The regulations state which household and family members qualify as **dependents.** In addition, a dependent must satisfy strict government guidelines relating to amount of support and income, form of tax return, and citizenship.

All employees must fill out an Employee's Withholding Allowance Certificate (Form W–4) and give it to their employer. A sample W–4 is shown in Illustration 6–2. Based on the information about marital status and withholding allowances contained in the W–4, the employer can compute the amount of federal income tax to withhold from the employee's paycheck.

An employer may use one of two methods to compute the required amount of income tax to withhold. The first, and probably the most

ILLUSTRATION 6–2

Form **W-4**	Department of the Treasury—Internal Revenue Service **Employee's Withholding Allowance Certificate**	OMB No. 1545-0010 Expires: 11-30-87

1 Type or print your full name
Henry William Abbott

2 Your social security number
250-80-9799

Home address (number and street or rural route)
125 Jockey Club Road

City or town, State, and ZIP code
Athens, GA 30605

3 Marital Status
☐ Single   ☒ Married
☐ Married, but withhold at higher Single rate
Note: If married, but legally separated, or spouse is a nonresident alien, check the Single box.

4 Total number of allowances you are claiming (from line F of the worksheet on page 2)   3

5 Additional amount, if any, you want deducted from each pay . . . . $ 0

6 I claim exemption from withholding because (see instructions and check boxes below that apply):

a ☐ Last year I did not owe any Federal income tax and had a right to a full refund of **ALL** income tax withheld, **AND**

b ☐ This year I do not expect to owe any Federal income tax and expect to have a right to a full refund of **ALL** income tax withheld. If both a and b apply, enter the year effective and "EXEMPT" here . . . ▶   Year

c If you entered "EXEMPT" on line 6b, are you a full-time student? . . . .   ☐Yes ☐No

Under penalties of perjury, I certify that I am entitled to the number of withholding allowances claimed on this certificate, or if claiming exemption from withholding, that I am entitled to claim the exempt status.

Employee's signature ▶ *Henry William Abbott*   Date ▶ *January 2* , 19 - -

7 Employer's name and address (**Employer: Complete 7, 8, and 9 only if sending to IRS**)   **8** Office code   **9** Employer identification number

---

common among smaller businesses, is the **wage-bracket method.** It relies on a set of withholding tables provided by the Internal Revenue Service. Each table covers a specified payroll period: daily, weekly, biweekly, semimonthly, and monthly. Within each table is a detailed breakdown both by wage bracket and by number of allowances. Since marital status is one of the determining factors, there are separate tables for single and married taxpayers.

We have included portions of the IRS's weekly tax tables for married taxpayers in Illustration 6–3 and for single taxpayers in Illustration 6–4. Since Henry Abbott is married, Illustration 6–3 is used to compute his tax liability. First find Abbott's wage range in columns 1 and 2. Because Abbott's pay for the week was $380, we look at the line labeled "At least $380 but less than $390." We then follow the line across to the column that shows the number of withholding allowances Abbott claims. Because Abbott claims three allowances, his withholding would be $39.

Gail Jones is a single employee, so we would use Illustration 6–4 to compute her income tax. Since she earned $301, we look at the line labeled "At least $300 but less than $310." We follow the line across to the column that shows the number of withholding allowances Jones claims. Since she claims two allowances, her withholding would be $37.

ILLUSTRATION 6–3

IRS Wage-Bracket Tax Table for Married Persons

MARRIED Persons—WEEKLY Payroll Period
(For Wages Paid After December 1984)

| And the wages are— | | And the number of withholding allowances claimed is— | | | | | | | | | | |
At least	But less than	0	1	2	3	4	5	6	7	8	9	10
		The amount of income tax to be withheld shall be—										
$180	$190	$17	$14	$11	$9	$6	$4	$2	$0	$0	$0	$0
190	200	18	16	13	10	8	5	3	1	0	0	0
200	210	20	17	14	11	9	6	4	2	0	0	0
210	220	21	18	16	13	10	8	5	3	1	0	0
220	230	23	20	17	14	11	9	6	4	2	0	0
230	240	24	21	18	16	13	10	8	5	3	1	0
240	250	26	23	20	17	14	11	9	6	4	2	0
250	260	28	24	21	18	16	13	10	8	5	3	1
260	270	29	26	23	20	17	14	11	9	6	4	2
270	280	31	28	24	21	18	16	13	10	8	5	3
280	290	32	29	26	23	20	17	14	11	9	6	4
290	300	34	31	28	24	21	18	16	13	10	8	5
300	310	36	32	29	26	23	20	17	14	11	9	6
310	320	38	34	31	28	24	21	18	16	13	10	8
320	330	39	36	32	29	26	23	20	17	14	11	9
330	340	41	38	34	31	28	24	21	18	16	13	10
340	350	43	39	36	32	29	26	23	20	17	14	11
350	360	45	41	38	34	31	28	24	21	18	16	13
360	370	47	43	39	36	32	29	26	23	20	17	14
370	380	48	45	41	38	34	31	28	24	21	18	16
380	390	50	47	43	39	36	32	29	26	23	20	17
390	400	52	48	45	41	38	34	31	28	24	21	18
400	410	55	50	47	43	39	36	32	29	26	23	20
410	420	57	52	48	45	41	38	34	31	28	24	21
420	430	59	55	50	47	43	39	36	32	29	26	23
430	440	61	57	52	48	45	41	38	34	31	28	24
440	450	63	59	55	50	47	43	39	36	32	29	26
450	460	66	61	57	52	48	45	41	38	34	31	28
460	470	68	63	59	55	50	47	43	39	36	32	29
470	480	70	66	61	57	52	48	45	41	38	34	31
480	490	73	68	63	59	55	50	47	43	39	36	32
490	500	75	70	66	61	57	52	48	45	41	38	34
500	510	78	73	68	63	59	55	50	47	43	39	36
510	520	80	75	70	66	61	57	52	48	45	41	38
520	530	83	78	73	68	63	59	55	50	47	43	39
530	540	85	80	75	70	66	61	57	52	48	45	41
540	550	88	83	78	73	68	63	59	55	50	47	43
550	560	90	85	80	75	70	66	61	57	52	48	45
560	570	93	88	83	78	73	68	63	59	55	50	47
570	580	95	90	85	80	75	70	66	61	57	52	48
580	590	98	93	88	83	78	73	68	63	59	55	50
590	600	101	95	90	85	80	75	70	66	61	57	52
600	610	103	98	93	88	83	78	73	68	63	59	55
610	620	106	101	95	90	85	80	75	70	66	61	57
620	630	109	103	98	93	88	83	78	73	68	63	59
630	640	112	106	101	95	90	85	80	75	70	66	61
640	650	115	109	103	98	93	88	83	78	73	68	63
650	660	117	112	106	101	95	90	85	80	75	70	66
660	670	120	115	109	103	98	93	88	83	78	73	68
670	680	123	117	112	106	101	95	90	85	80	75	70
680	690	126	120	115	109	103	98	93	88	83	78	73
690	700	129	123	117	112	106	101	95	90	85	80	75
700	710	132	126	120	115	109	103	98	93	88	83	78
710	720	136	129	123	117	112	106	101	95	90	85	80
720	730	139	132	126	120	115	109	103	98	93	88	83
730	740	142	136	129	123	117	112	106	101	95	90	85
740	750	146	139	132	126	120	115	109	103	98	93	88
750	760	149	142	136	129	123	117	112	106	101	95	90
760	770	152	146	139	132	126	120	115	109	103	98	93
770	780	155	149	142	136	129	123	117	112	106	101	95
780	790	159	152	146	139	132	126	120	115	109	103	98
790	800	162	155	149	142	136	129	123	117	112	106	101
800	810	165	159	152	146	139	132	126	120	115	109	103
810	820	169	162	155	149	142	136	129	123	117	112	106
820	830	172	165	159	152	146	139	132	126	120	115	109
830	840	175	169	162	155	149	142	136	129	123	117	112

The **percentage-rate method,** which is often used when payrolls are prepared on electronic data processing equipment, employs an estimated withholding rate. First, the employee's gross pay for the payroll period is adjusted according to the number of withholding allowances claimed. To calculate the amount to be withheld, this

ILLUSTRATION 6-4

IRS Wage-Bracket Tax Table for Single Persons

SINGLE Persons—WEEKLY Payroll Period
(For Wages Paid After December 1984)

And the wages are—		And the number of withholding allowances claimed is—										
At least	But less than	0	1	2	3	4	5	6	7	8	9	10
		The amount of income tax to be withheld shall be—										
$190	$200	$24	$21	$18	$14	$11	$9	$6	$3	$1	$0	$0
200	210	26	22	19	16	13	10	7	4	2	0	0
210	220	27	24	21	18	14	11	9	6	3	1	0
220	230	29	26	22	19	16	13	10	7	4	2	0
230	240	31	27	24	21	18	14	11	9	6	3	1
240	250	33	29	26	22	19	16	13	10	7	4	2
250	260	35	31	27	24	21	18	14	11	9	6	3
260	270	37	33	29	26	22	19	16	13	10	7	4
270	280	39	35	31	27	24	21	18	14	11	9	6
280	290	41	37	33	29	26	22	19	16	13	10	7
290	300	43	39	35	31	27	24	21	18	14	11	9
300	310	46	41	37	33	29	26	22	19	16	13	10
310	320	48	43	39	35	31	27	24	21	18	14	11
320	330	50	46	41	37	33	29	26	22	19	16	13
330	340	53	48	43	39	35	31	27	24	21	18	14
340	350	55	50	46	41	37	33	29	26	22	19	16
350	360	58	53	48	43	39	35	31	27	24	21	18
360	370	60	55	50	46	41	37	33	29	26	22	19
370	380	63	58	53	48	43	39	35	31	27	24	21
380	390	65	60	55	50	46	41	37	33	29	26	22
390	400	68	63	58	53	48	43	39	35	31	27	24
400	410	71	65	60	55	50	46	41	37	33	29	26
410	420	73	68	63	58	53	48	43	39	35	31	27
420	430	76	71	65	60	55	50	46	41	37	33	29
430	440	78	73	68	63	58	53	48	43	39	35	31
440	450	81	76	71	65	60	55	50	46	41	37	33
450	460	84	78	73	68	63	58	53	48	43	39	35
460	470	87	81	76	71	65	60	55	50	46	41	37
470	480	90	84	78	73	68	63	58	53	48	43	39
480	490	93	87	81	76	71	65	60	55	50	46	41
490	500	96	90	84	78	73	68	63	58	53	48	43
500	510	99	93	87	81	76	71	65	60	55	50	46
510	520	102	96	90	84	78	73	68	63	58	53	48
520	530	105	99	93	87	81	76	71	65	60	55	50
530	540	108	102	96	90	84	78	73	68	63	58	53
540	550	111	105	99	93	87	81	76	71	65	60	55
550	560	114	108	102	96	90	84	78	73	68	63	58
560	570	117	111	105	99	93	87	81	76	71	65	60
570	580	121	114	108	102	96	90	84	78	73	68	63
580	590	124	117	111	105	99	93	87	81	76	71	65
590	600	127	121	114	108	102	96	90	84	78	73	68
600	610	131	124	117	111	105	99	93	87	81	76	71
610	620	134	127	121	114	108	102	96	90	84	78	73
620	630	138	131	124	117	111	105	99	93	87	81	76
630	640	141	134	127	121	114	108	102	96	90	84	78
640	650	144	138	131	124	117	111	105	99	93	87	81
650	660	148	141	134	127	121	114	108	102	96	90	84
660	670	151	144	138	131	124	117	111	105	99	93	87
670	680	155	148	141	134	127	121	114	108	102	96	90
680	690	159	151	144	138	131	124	117	111	105	99	93
690	700	162	155	148	141	134	127	121	114	108	102	96
700	710	166	159	151	144	138	131	124	117	111	105	99
710	720	170	162	155	148	141	134	127	121	114	108	102
720	730	173	166	159	151	144	138	131	124	117	111	105
730	740	177	170	162	155	148	141	134	127	121	114	108
740	750	181	173	166	159	151	144	138	131	124	117	111
750	760	184	177	170	162	155	148	141	134	127	121	114
760	770	188	181	173	166	159	151	144	138	131	124	117
770	780	192	184	177	170	162	155	148	141	134	127	121

adjusted gross figure is multiplied by the appropriate percentage rate prescribed by the government. As in the wage-bracket method, the employee's marital status is considered when choosing the tax rate.

Withholding state and local taxes

Many states and an increasing number of cities have also enacted some form of income tax. While the extent of coverage and the tax rates vary widely, most require systematic withholdings from employees' paychecks that are similar to the federal plan. Due to the taxes' diversity, it is difficult to generalize about their computation. Yet most allow withholding allowances for the employee and his or her dependents, if any. Like the federal income tax, state and city taxes can be calculated using either the wage-bracket method or the percentage-rate method. The nature of the tax rate varies from a fixed percentage of gross pay to a progressive scale based on the individual's overall earnings level. Often city income taxes have different tax rates for employees who both live and work in the city and for those who only work there.

Withholding FICA taxes

Federal regulations specify both the amount of an employee's income that is subject to FICA taxes and the amount of the FICA tax rate. These figures are decided by Congress. Due to the increasing burden of social security and medicare payouts, FICA taxes can be expected to rise steadily over the coming years. In 1985, an individual was required to pay 7.05 percent in FICA taxes on the first $39,600 of his or her gross pay. Thus, Henry Abbott would be required to pay $26.79 in FICA tax on his $380 income ($380 × .0705 = $26.79). If Abbott's gross pay had exceeded $39,600, he would have already paid the maximum FICA tax required and would have no further FICA deductions taken from this and succeeding paychecks in 1985.

Miscellaneous deductions

Employees may request that additional amounts be deducted from their paychecks. The additional withholdings may be for a variety of items. Some common examples are union dues, insurance premiums, savings bonds, and charitable contributions.

All these items require specific authorization from the employees indicating the amounts to be withheld. The employer usually acts only as an intermediary between the employee and the final recipient. These payroll deduction plans are offered as a convenience to the company's employees.

The payroll records

Certain payroll records must be maintained for each employee. These payroll records not only satisfy the information needs of management but also meet the requirements of various federal and state agencies. In addition, an employer must give every employee sufficient information to complete income tax forms. The payroll records should show:

1. Each employee's name, address, and social security number.
2. The gross pay, period covered, and date paid for each payroll.
3. Each employee's cumulative gross pay since the beginning of the year.
4. The details of all taxes and other deductions withheld from each employee's paychecks.

For most businesses, regardless of size or number of employees, these requirements are met through the use of three records. They are (1) the payroll register or journal, (2) the payroll check, generally with an attached earnings statement, and (3) the earnings records of each employee on a cumulative basis. These records can be maintained manually or prepared electronically.

The payroll register *Have to be maintained for 4 yrs Others 7 years*

An example of a manually prepared **payroll register** is shown in Illustration 6–5. It summarizes the earnings and deductions for all employees for a specified period—in this case, the week ended December 15, 1985. While our example lists the employees in alphabetical order, this form is by no means universal. In fact, many businesses keep track of their employees by means of individual identification numbers: employee number, timecard number, department number,

ILLUSTRATION 6–5

PAYROLL REGISTER — For Week Ended 12-15

NAME	EMPLOYEE NO.	NO. OF EXEMPT.	MARITAL STATUS	EARNINGS REGULAR	OVER-TIME	TOTAL	CUMU-LATIVE TOTAL	TAXABLE EARNINGS UNEMP. COMP.	FICA	DEDUCTIONS FICA TAX	FED. INC. TAX	STATE TAX	CREDIT UNION	OTHER	TOTAL	DATE	NET PAY	CK. NO.
Henry Abbott	1	3	m	320 00	60 00	380 00	4820 00		380 00	26 79	39 00	3 80	2 00	SAVINGS BONDS	71 59	12-15	308 41	501
James Harrison	2	3	m	310 00		310 00	6000 00		310 00	21 85	28 00	3 10	2 00	10 00	64 95	12-15	245 05	502
Gail Jones	3	2	S	280 00	21 00	301 00	4750 00		301 00	21 22	37 00	3 01	2 00		63 23	12-15	237 77	503
James Jones	4	4	m	825 00		825 00	41250 00		0	0	146 00	8 25	10 00	10 00	174 25	12-15	650 75	504
Don Kyle	5	1	S	210 00		210 00	210 00	210 00	210 00	14 81	24 00	2 10	2 00		42 91	12-15	167 09	505
				1945 00	81 00	2026 00	89030 00	210 00	1201 00	84 67	274 00	20 26	18 00	20 00	416 93		1609 07	

or some other code. The number of columns allotted to deductions in a payroll register also varies widely. Some registers have provisions for many kinds of deductions while others rely on a Miscellaneous column for small or infrequent deductions. Of course, it is rare to find a completely manual payroll system in today's business world, but the same basic principles apply to computerized systems.

Although FICA (assuming that the employee is below the specified cutoff) and income taxes are withheld every pay period, the same may not be true for all deductions. It is not unusual to deduct the entire monthly insurance premium from the first payroll of the month. Nor is it unusual to deduct union dues or charitable contributions in a lump sum.

Looking at the first employee, Henry Abbott, we find that his gross pay for the weekly payroll period ended December 15, 1985, was $380. These earnings were based on his timecard. The amount withheld for federal income tax was based on his exemption certificate (W–4). In this example, Abbott and all other employees are subject to a state income tax equal to 1 percent of gross pay. There are no deductions for health insurance premiums because a monthly amount was withheld in the first payroll period for December. The remaining deductions are computed using the authorizations filed by each employee.

Looking at the fourth employee, James Jones, we find that his gross pay for the payroll period was $825. All the deductions except FICA were computed in the same way as were Henry Abbott's. But because Jones's gross pay exceeded the 1985 FICA ceiling of $39,600, no FICA tax was deducted.

Once all employees' names have been entered and all necessary deductions have been made, each column in the register should be footed (summed). These column totals can then be checked by cross-footing; that is, adding and subtracting the column totals across the page to ensure that everything is in balance. If all deductions have been properly subtracted and every column correctly footed, then:

Net pay column + All deductions column = Gross earnings column
$1,609.06   + $416.94   = $2,026.00

The reader should satisfy him- or herself that the column totals—net pay and deductions—crossfoot to the gross pay figure. Note also how the column totals have been ruled with single and double lines.

The required entry for the general journal can be made by using the column totals as supporting detail. For this payroll register, the following entry would be made:

GENERAL JOURNAL				PAGE	
DATE	ACCOUNT AND EXPLANATION	P.R.	DEBIT	CREDIT	
Dec. 15	Wages Expense		2026 00		
	FICA Taxes Payable			84 68	
	Employees' Fed. Income Taxes Payable			274 00	
	Employees' State Income Taxes Payable			20 26	
	Employees' Credit Union Payable			18 00	
	Employees' Savings Bonds Payable			20 00	
	Cash			1609 06	
	To record the payroll for the week ended Dec. 15.				

Companies with many employees usually use an automated payroll system to increase efficiency. These systems reduce costs and human errors. Their data output can be structured to provide more information on the breakdown and allocation of payroll expenses. The systems currently being used range from small-capacity bookkeeping machines to ultrahigh-speed electronic digital computers.

With an automated payroll system, the three basic payroll records—register, check, and earnings record—are generally prepared simultaneously. But regardless of the complexity of the system, the basic objectives remain the same as those for a manual system.

Payroll checks

Due to the special requirements of payroll procedures, several unique features usually distinguish **payroll checks** from general disbursement checks. For example, in addition to the check, the employee receives a detachable stub that contains much of the same information as the payroll register. The stub provides the employee with an **earnings statement** that includes a permanent record of gross pay and a detailed list of deductions. Before cashing the check, the employee should detach and save the stub. The kind of information found on a machine-prepared payroll check and stub is shown in Illustration 6–6. A manually prepared check would contain the same basic information.

Quite often a company maintains a separate bank account for issuing payroll checks. There are several advantages to handling payroll transactions through a specialized account. First, to provide better control over cash, the company can limit the amount of any check, perhaps for less than $500. Second, the company may think that a single-signature check gives adequate control over payroll disburse-

ILLUSTRATION 6–6

Machine-Prepared Payroll Check and Stub

PAYROLL
JONES PLUMBING SUPPLY

No. 1205

1224 West Rose Drive
Athens, Georgia 30605

DATE:

Dec. 15, 1985

PAY TO THE ORDER OF   Henry Abbott

Dollars	Cents
$308	41

Three hundred eight and 41/100 .... DOLLARS

JONES PLUMBING SUPPLY

By _____ James Jones _____

FIRST STATE BANK

Athens, Georgia 30605

1:□ 72 □ ··· □□ 6:

JONES PLUMBING SUPPLY CO.

This is a statement of your payroll payments and deductions

PLEASE DETACH FOR YOUR RECORDS

No. 1205

Home Dept. Acct.	Dist Code	Soc. Sec. No.	Employee Name	Regular Pay		O.T.		Gross Pay	
1011GH1960001	459	250-80-9799	Abbott H.	320	00	60	00	380	00

Fed. W/H		State W/H		FICA		Credit Union		Other		Net Pay	
39	00	3	80	26	79	2	00			308	41

Payment Date   Dec. 15, 1985   Pay Period Ending   Dec. 15, 1985

NOT NEGOTIABLE

ments, considering the scope of activity in this account. This would allow the company to retain a dual signature requirement on its general checking account. Third, the reconciliation procedure can generally be simplified and streamlined since the payroll account's activity is rather standardized and check volume is high.

Although our discussion has been limited to payment by check, a few businesses still pay with currency. The number of these firms, however, is small and has been declining. Under such a system, each employee's earnings are placed in an envelope that is delivered to the employee on payday. The employee is asked to sign a receipt showing that the pay envelope has been received.

Individual earnings records

An employer must keep a detailed **earnings record** that shows the gross pay, deductions, and net pay of each employee. This record is updated each payroll period, and new cumulative year-to-date totals are computed. These cumulative totals provide a signal for the employer to stop withholding the employee's share of FICA taxes.

A manually prepared employee's earnings record for Henry Abbott is presented in Illustration 6–7. Similar records would be maintained for each of the company's employees. From this example, we see that it duplicates much of the information in the payroll register. The principal difference is that the payroll register is a summary of the earnings of *all* employees for a specific pay period while the earnings records summarize the annual earnings of *each* employee.

These earnings records become the basis for the wage and tax

ILLUSTRATION 6–7

EMPLOYEE'S EARNINGS RECORD

SEX M	SEX F	DEPARTMENT	OCCUPATION	SOC. SEC. NO.	MARITAL STATUS	EXEMP-TIONS	PAY RATE	DATE OF BIRTH	DATE EMPLOYED	LAST	NAME FIRST	MIDDLE	EMP. NO.
	✓	Shipping	Loader	250-80-9799	m	3	$320 wk.	10-29-51	1-1-75	Abbott,	Henry	William	1

PERIOD END-ING	EARNINGS REGULAR	OVER-TIME	TOTAL	CUMU-LATIVE TOTAL	TAXABLE EARNINGS UNEMP. COMP.	FICA	DEDUCTIONS FICA TAX	FED. INC. TAX	STATE TAX	LIFE INS.	PRIV. HOSP. INS.	CREDIT UNION	OTHER SAVINGS BOND	TOTAL	NET PAY CK. NO.	AMOUNT
7-5	320 00		320 00	9,040 00		320 00	22 56	29 00	3 20	20 00	8 00	2 00		84 76	112	235 24
7-12	320 00		320 00	9,360 00		320 00	22 56	29 00	3 20			2 00	10 00	66 76	125	253 24
7-19	320 00	80 00	400 00	9,760 00		400 00	28 20	43 00	4 00			2 00		77 20	156	322 80
7-26	320 00		320 00	10,080 00		320 00	22 56	29 00	3 20			2 00		56 76	170	263 24
8-2	320 00		320 00	10,400 00		320 00	22 56	29 00	3 20	20 00	8 00	2 00		84 76	180	235 24
8-9	320 00		320 00	10,720 00		320 00	22 56	29 00	3 20			2 00	10 00	66 76	199	253 24
8-16	320 00		320 00	11,040 00		320 00	22 56	29 00	3 20			2 00		56 76	206	263 24
8-23	320 00		320 00	11,360 00		320 00	22 56	29 00	3 20			2 00		56 76	231	263 24
8-30	320 00		320 00	11,680 00		320 00	22 56	29 00	3 20			2 00		56 76	240	263 24
9-6	320 00	40 00	360 00	12,040 00		360 00	25 38	36 00	3 60	20 00	8 00	2 00		94 98	262	265 02
9-13	320 00		320 00	12,360 00		320 00	22 56	29 00	3 20			2 00	10 00	66 76	280	253 24
9-20	320 00		320 00	12,680 00		320 00	22 56	29 00	3 20			2 00		56 76	295	263 24
9-27	320 00		320 00	13,000 00		320 00	22 56	29 00	3 20			2 00		56 76	303	263 24
10-4	320 00	120 00	440 00	13,440 00		440 00	31 02	50 00	4 40	20 00	8 00	2 00		115 42	345	324 58
10-11	320 00		320 00	13,760 00		320 00	22 56	29 00	3 20			2 00	10 00	66 76	370	253 24
10-18	320 00	40 00	360 00	14,120 60		360 00	25 38	36 00	3 60			2 00		66 98	401	293 02
10-25	320 00		320 00	14,440 00		320 00	22 56	29 00	3 20			2 00		56 76	426	263 24

statement (Form W–2) that the employer is required to furnish employees following the end of the calendar year. This statement shows the total amount of wages paid to an employee and the amounts of federal, state, and local income taxes and FICA taxes that have been withheld from the employee's earnings. Depending on local requirements, the W–2 form should have at least four copies—two for the employee, one for the Internal Revenue Service, and one for the employer's files. If there are state or local income taxes on the employee's earnings, the number of copies increases accordingly. (Form W–2 will be discussed further in Chapter 7.)

Machine-prepared earnings records present the same information as their manually prepared counterparts. Only their method and order of presentation differ. In many electronic data processing systems, the earnings records are prepared simultaneously with the payroll register and check. Moreover, most electronic systems are programmed so that withholding of FICA taxes will cease when an employee's earnings exceed the statutory limit.

PAYROLL PREPARATION

Up to this point, the discussion has been based on an employer-operated payroll system. There are some alternatives, however. As noted earlier, there are certain advantages to using an electronic payroll system. But sometimes a company is so small that it cannot justify the purchase or rental of such a system. Increasingly, data processing services have been offered by both **service bureaus** and some *commercial* banks.

Typically, a service organization maintains a complete record of vital information for every employee: wage rate, exemptions, deductions, and so on. Each payroll period, the employer furnishes the service organization with the total hours each employee has worked plus any corrections or data needed to update the withholding and deduction information. One unique feature that is sometimes offered by bank-operated systems is to include a payroll bank account reconciliation as part of the standard service.

Recording gross pay and payroll deductions

The accounts used in accounting for payrolls range from the expense accounts charged with the gross pay to the liability accounts used to record the various deductions. It is advisable to establish separate accounts for each kind of deduction.

Wages expense

This expense account is charged with the total gross pay of all employees for each pay period. For larger payroll systems, the total expense may be broken down into several expense accounts that more fully describe the kinds of services (for example, Factory Wages Expense and Sales Salaries Expense). In addition, some systems provide separate accounts for overtime and other special premiums. Thus, charges to the account would be made in the Debit column, with the cumulative total being shown in the Debit Balance column. Using the payroll figures from Illustration 6–5, Jones Plumbing Supply's wages expense for the week ended December 15 would be shown in the ledger account as follows:

						BALANCE	
DATE		EXPLANATION	P.R.	DEBIT	CREDIT	DEBIT	CREDIT
Dec.	15	Balance				89 0 3 0 00	
	15		J25	2 0 2 6 00		91 0 5 6 00	

GENERAL LEDGER — Wages Expense — ACCT. NO. 520

The company's total wages expense for the year is now $91,056, as shown in the Debit Balance column.

FICA taxes payable

This liability account is used to record the total FICA taxes withheld from employees for each pay period. When the taxes are withheld, they are recorded as credits to the account. When the taxes are forwarded to the government, a debit is made to the account. Any outstanding balance in the account represents unremitted taxes as of that date. Again using the amounts from Illustration 6–5, here is how Jones Plumbing Supply would show the FICA taxes it withheld from employees for the pay period ended on December 15:

				GENERAL LEDGER				
		FICA Taxes Payable					ACCT. NO.	231
DATE		EXPLANATION	P.R.	DEBIT	CREDIT		BALANCE	
							DEBIT	CREDIT
Dec.	15	Balance						1 9 4 0 88
	15		J25		8 4 68			2 0 2 5 56

As of December 15, Jones Plumbing owes the government $2,025.56 in employees' FICA taxes, as shown in the Credit Balance column.

Employees' income taxes payable

Depending on the circumstances, there may be several income taxes payable accounts: federal, state, and city (where applicable). These liability accounts should be credited with the total amount withheld from employees' earnings. The account is debited whenever the taxes are remitted. Again, the balance in the account at a given time represents the unremitted portion of these taxes. Accounts for state and city income taxes withheld are handled identically. Using the amounts from Illustration 6–5, Jones Plumbing's federal income tax liability would be recorded as follows:

				GENERAL LEDGER				
		Employees' Federal Income Taxes Payable					ACCT. NO.	232
DATE		EXPLANATION	P.R.	DEBIT	CREDIT		BALANCE	
							DEBIT	CREDIT
Dec.	15	Balance						5 7 3 00
	15		J25		2 7 4 00			8 4 7 00

The balance now owed is $847.

Other payroll deductions

These liability accounts are also credited with amounts deducted from employees' earnings. Since the company is only an intermediary, it would pay these amounts to the proper organizations and debit the accounts at that time. Like the other payroll liability accounts, each balance represents collected amounts that have not yet been forwarded. For example, using the amounts in Illustration 6–5, the amount owed to the credit union would be recorded as follows:

GENERAL LEDGER							
Credit Union Payable						ACCT. NO.	236

DATE		EXPLANATION	P.R.	DEBIT	CREDIT	BALANCE	
						DEBIT	CREDIT
Dec.	15	Balance					3 6 00
	15		J25		1 8 00		5 4 00

The balance now owed to the credit union is $54.

SUMMARY

Accounting for payroll is a very significant part of the overall accounting system. Payroll transactions occur when employees are paid for their services. For the purposes of payroll accounting, it is important to distinguish between **employees** and **independent contractors.**

There are four phases in payroll accounting: (1) computation of **gross pay,** (2) calculation of all **payroll deductions** to arrive at **net pay,** (3) recording of the payroll transactions in the permanent payroll records to meet government requirements, and (4) summarization of payroll activity in the company's general records.

Most employees are paid either wages or a salary. **Wages** are usually based on an hourly pay rate, while a **salary** is customarily expressed as a monthly or yearly amount. Many companies use **timecards** to keep track of hourly workers' attendance on the job.

The computation of gross pay for certain categories of workers is governed by the **Federal Fair Labor Standards Act.** The act established a minimum wage and a ceiling on the number of hours that specified workers can work. It also established that covered employees should receive at least 1½ times their regular hourly rate for all time worked in excess of 40 hours.

An employer must withhold a portion of each employee's paycheck to pay federal taxes. The amount withheld depends on the individual's total earnings, number of **withholding allowances,** marital status, and length of pay period. The employee reports information about marital status and withholding allowances to the employer on a W–4 form. An employee may claim one withholding allowance for him- or herself, another allowance if he or she is blind or over 65, and an additional allowance for each qualifying **dependent.** Based on this information an employer computes the amount of income to withhold from each paycheck using either the **wage-bracket method** or the **percentage-rate method.**

Other payroll deductions include state and local income taxes, the employee's share of **FICA taxes,** and miscellaneous other deductions. All payroll deductions are reported to the employee on the **earnings statement** that accompanies each paycheck.

The payroll transactions are recorded in permanent records to provide information to management and to meet the requirements of federal and state agencies. Three basic components of any payroll system are the **payroll register,** the **payroll check,** and the **earnings record.**

The payroll records are used to record payroll transactions in the company's permanent records. The payroll records may be maintained by an outside data processing service, or **service bureau.** In any case, the recording of the payroll in the permanent accounting records is basically the same.

KEY TERMS

Dependent—Under the tax laws, a person for whom a taxpayer is allowed a reduction in taxable income of a specified amount. To qualify as a taxpayer's dependent, an individual must meet strict guidelines relating to support, income, relationship, citizenship, and form of tax return.

Earnings Record—A detailed record that summarizes the annual earnings of each employee. It shows the employee's gross pay, deductions, and net pay for each payroll period along with a cumulative total of gross pay.

Earnings Statement—A permanent record of an employee's gross pay and a detailed list of deductions included on the stub attached to an employee's payroll check.

Employee—An individual who is hired to provide his or her services under the direct supervision and control of an employer. The employer-employee relationship, including the payment and reporting of wages and salaries, is governed by many government laws and regulations.

Federal Fair Labor Standards Act—An act that applies to all employers engaged in interstate commerce which specifies that covered employees must be paid a minimum wage, may not work more than a specified number of hours per week, and must be paid 1½ times their regular hourly rate for all time worked in excess of 40 hours per week.

FICA Taxes—Social security taxes collected under the provisions of the Federal Insurance Contributions Act and used to pay retirement, disability, and medicare benefits to covered employees.

Gross Pay—The total amount of an employee's wages or salary before payroll deductions.

Independent Contractor—An individual who provides services to a firm but is not subject to the firm's direct supervision and control. Independent contractors receive fees for their services.

Net Pay—Gross pay minus all payroll deductions. It is the amount of pay an employee actually receives—that is, his or her take-home pay.

Payroll Accounting—The computing and recording of disbursements for wages, salaries, and related payroll taxes. It involves four phases: (1) computation of total gross pay for each employee, (2) determination of deductions for each employee, (3) recording of gross earnings and deductions in the permanent payroll records, and (4) summarization of the total payroll activity to ease recording in the company's general records.

Payroll Check—The form of check used to reimburse employees for their services. It can be distinguished from a general disbursement check by its detachable stub, which contains much the same information as the payroll register.

Payroll Deduction—An amount subtracted from an employee's gross pay before a paycheck is issued that is used by the employer to cover a specified cost.

Payroll Register (Journal)—A summary of the earnings and deductions for all employees for a specific pay period.

Percentage-Rate Method—A technique used to compute the required standard amount of income tax to withhold from an employee's pay based on an estimated withholding rate. The employee's gross pay is adjusted for the number of allowances claimed, and this adjusted gross figure is multiplied by an estimated withholding rate to obtain the required standard amount of tax to withhold.

Salary—The compensation given administrative and managerial personnel, customarily expressed as a monthly or annual amount.

Service Bureau—An organization that offers data processing services to small- and medium-sized businesses on a contract basis.

Timecard—A card used in conjunction with a time clock to provide a printed record of when each employee arrived for work and departed for the day.

Wage-Bracket Method—A technique often used by small businesses to compute the required standard amount of income to withhold from an employee's pay based on a set of withholding tables provided by the Internal Revenue Service.

Wages—The compensation given skilled and unskilled employees, usually expressed in terms of an individual hourly rate.

Withholding Allowance—A dollar amount by which taxpayers may reduce their taxable income before computing their tax liability. A taxpayer may claim one allowance for him- or herself, another allowance if he or she is blind or over 65, and an additional allowance for each qualified dependent.

QUESTIONS AND EXERCISES

1. What is the difference between an independent contractor and an employee? Give some examples of independent contractors.
2. Distinguish between salaries and wages.
3. Connie Cast works for an employer who is engaged in interstate commerce. Her regular rate of pay is $6 per hour. According to the regulations set forth in the Federal Fair Labor Standards Act, what is the minimum amount of total earnings that Connie should receive if she works 50 hours per week?
4. Nearly all employers are required to withhold part of each employee's earnings for federal income tax and for social security (FICA) taxes. Besides these required deductions, what are six other types of deductions that might be withheld from an employee's earnings?
5. What four factors must be considered in determining the amount of income tax to be withheld from an employee's earnings?
6. What three types of payroll records are usually prepared by an employer? What information can be obtained from these payroll records?

7. What is a service bureau?
8. Steve Melton receives a monthly salary of $1,080. He is entitled to overtime pay at one and one-half times his regular hourly rate for all hours worked in excess of 40 per week. How much should he be paid for each hour of overtime?
9. Sara Jones worked 44 hours during the current weekly payroll. Her regular hourly rate is $6 and she is paid time and a half for all hours worked over 40 hours a week. What would be her gross earnings for the week?
10. Marilyn Schleicher has a salary of $1,400 per month. Compute her overtime rate assuming time and a half for overtime.
11. What would be the amount of net earnings at the end of the first week in January for Matthew Thorn based on the following:
    a. He works 42 hours at $8 per hour.
    b. He receives time and a half for all time over 40 hours.
    c. FICA is 7.05%, federal withholding is $35, and state withholding $10.32.

PROBLEMS

6–1. Part A. The employees of the Perkins Company are paid time and a half for all hours worked in excess of 40 per week. For the second week in September, compute the gross earnings for each of the company's seven employees.

No.	Employee Name	Hours Worked in Second Week of September	Regular Hourly Rate
1	Collins, George	52	$5.75
2	Ferrin, Ray	46	4.50
3	Grey, Jean	50	6.00
4	Kent, Mary	42	5.00
5	Lewis, Bob	40	6.15
6	Stills, Carol	45	5.75
7	Terry, Frank	48	5.60

Part B. Four salaried employees who are entitled to time and a half for all hours worked in excess of 40 per week are also employed by the Perkins Company. Compute their gross earnings for the second week of September.

No.	Employee Name	Hours Worked in Second Week of September	Monthly Salary
8	Clark, Craig	53	$1,750
9	Holmes, Susan	50	2,200
10	Morris, John	49	1,560
11	Wells, Allen	47	2,550

6–2. The Shurfire Company pays its employees time and a half for all hours worked in excess of 40 per week. Relevant payroll information about the company's employees for the week ended July 8, is summarized on the following chart:

No.	Employee Name	Withholding Allowances Claimed	Regular Hourly Rate	M	T	W	T	F	S	Cumulative Earnings Jan. 1–July 1
1	Clay, Alex	3	$5.60	8	8	10	8	9	0	$5,600
2	Evans, Joan	1	5.90	8	0	8	8	8	4	4,500
3	French, Roy	2	5.70	10	8	8	8	7	3	5,000
4	Jones, Ann	2	5.90	8	8	8	9	8	5	5,500
5	Lentz, Lisa	4	6.00	8	8	8	9	10	0	4,650
6	Towers, Don. . . .	3	5.70	8	8	8	8	8	4	5,850
7	Troop, Dale	1	5.80	8	9	8	8	9	3	4,900
8	Vale, Karen	2	5.80	9	8	8	8	8	5	5,350

For the week ended July 8, the employees have requested the following deductions:

Clay.	$10 savings bond
Evans	15 group life insurance
French	6 private hospital insurance
Jones	10 United Fund
Lentz	15 group life insurance
Towers	10 savings bond
Troop	6 private hospital insurance
Vale	10 United Fund

Required:

For the week ended July 8, prepare a payroll register similar to the one in Illustration 6–5. Of each employee's taxable wages, 7.05 percent is to be withheld for FICA tax. All of the employees are married. To determine the amount of federal income tax to be withheld from each employee's earnings, use the weekly income tax table (Illustration 6–3).

Check nos. 378 through 385 were issued to the employees. Complete the payroll register by totaling and ruling the amount columns. Also, check the column totals by crossfooting them.

6–3. Pamela Dawn Wells is employed as a bookkeeper in the accounting department of the Henry Cole Company. Her social security number is 255-92-7689, and her employee number is 105. She is married, and she claims four withholding allowances on her income tax return. Ms. Wells's regular rate of pay is $400 per week. However, she receives time and a half for all hours worked in excess of 40 per week. Federal income taxes (See Illustration 6–3), city taxes at a 1 percent rate, and FICA taxes at a 7.05 percent rate are deducted from her paycheck every week. Also, weekly deductions of $5.00 are made for the company credit union. The first paycheck for each month contains a $25.00 deduction for life insurance and a $10 deduction for private hospital insurance. The third paycheck for each month contains a $25 deduction for savings bonds. During January, Pamela Wells worked the following number of hours:

Week ended 1/9 . . . . 50 hours
Week ended 1/16 40
Week ended 1/23 48
Week ended 1/30 52

She was issued check nos. 681, 706, 750, and 808.

Required:

Prepare an employee's earnings record like the one in Illustration 6–7 for Pamela Dawn Wells for the month of January. (Date of birth is 2/27/54, and date employed is 1/15/79.)

6–4. Jane L. Smith, an employee of Roto-Rink Company, worked 47 hours during the week of January 1–8. Her rate of pay is $7 per hour, and she gets time and a half for work in excess of 40 hours. She is married and claims three withholding allowances. Her wages are subject to the following deductions:

Federal income tax (see Illustration 6–3).
FICA tax (7.05%).
Union dues, $3.15.
Medical insurance, $27.00.

Required:

Compute regular pay, overtime pay, gross pay, and net pay.

6–5. For the following summary of columnar totals of payroll register, determine the amounts that have been omitted.

Earnings
At regular rate $22,800.00
At overtime rate . . . . . ‗‗‗‗‗‗‗‗
Total earnings . . . . ‗‗‗‗‗‗‗‗
Deductions
Income tax 3,617.53
FICA tax 1,607.40
Medical insurance . . . . . ‗‗‗‗‗‗‗‗
Union dues 500.00
Total deductions . . . 6,000.00
Net amount paid 16,800.00

6–6. The Hamrick Company pays its employees time and a half for all hours worked in excess of 40 per week. Relevant payroll information about the company's employees for the week ended March 6 is summarized on the following chart:

No.	Employee Name	Withholding Allowances	Regular Hourly Rate	Hours Worked						Cumulative Earnings Jan. 1–Feb. 28
				M	T	W	T	F	S	
1	Adams, Richard	3	$4.50	8	8	10	8	8	3	$1,600
2	Beckel, Kip	4	6.00	9	8	8	8	8	2	2,050
3	Holmes, Bill	2	5.00	10	8	10	8	0	4	1,800
4	Twomey, Claire	1	4.50	8	8	8	8	8	0	1,750

The employees have requested the following deductions for the week ended, March 6:

Adams	. . .	$ 6	group life insurance
Beckel	. . .	5	United Fund
Holmes	. . .	4	group life insurance
Twomey	. . .	23.50	savings bond

Required:

1. For the week ended March 6, prepare a payroll register similar to the one in Illustration 6–5. Of each employee's taxable wages, 7.05 percent is to be withheld for FICA tax. All of the employees are married. To determine the amount of federal income tax to be withheld from each employee's earnings, use the weekly income tax table (Illustration 6–3).

2. Check nos. 201 through 204 were issued to the employees. Complete the payroll register by totaling and ruling the amount columns. Also, check the column totals by crossfooting them.

3. Prepare the journal entry to record the payroll.

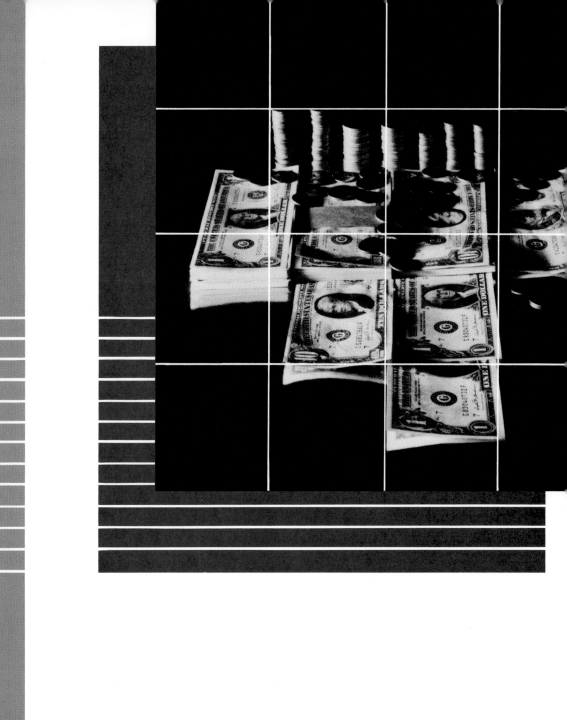

CHAPTER 7

Payroll accounting—the employer

LEARNING OBJECTIVES

In this chapter, you will continue to study the payroll records that employers must maintain on behalf of their employees. You will also learn what taxes an employer must pay on behalf of each employee. After studying this chapter, you should be able to:

1. Compute an employer's FICA tax and federal and state unemployment taxes.
2. Journalize entries to record an employer's payroll taxes.
3. Journalize the payment of taxes withheld from employees' earnings.
4. Recognize the forms used to report payroll taxes to the federal government.

EMPLOYER'S PAYROLL TAXES

In Chapter 6, we discussed the taxes that are withheld from an employee's earnings. We shall now turn our attention to payroll taxes imposed directly on an employer. Unlike the taxes explained in Chapter 6, the taxes discussed here are an additional expense to an employer for the services performed by employees. While the costs of employees' fringe benefits are also paid by the employer and likewise represent additional employment expense, only payroll taxes will be considered. These include (1) the employer's matching portion of FICA taxes, (2) the Federal Unemployment Tax Act (FUTA) tax, and, depending on local statutes, (3) a state unemployment tax.

The employer identification number

According to federal law, all employers who are required to report employment taxes or give tax statements to employees must have an **employer identification number.** The Internal Revenue Service assigns a different EIN to each employer and requires the number to be listed on all reports, and payments to the IRS and Social Security Administration. A person taking over an existing business is not permitted to use the former employer's identification number but must apply for a new one.

Payroll tax expenses

All payroll taxes imposed on an employer are considered expenses of the business and should be debited to the **Payroll Tax Expense account.** The account is debited for the employer's portion of FICA taxes as well as for state and federal unemployment taxes. Consequently, the account looks like this:

Payroll Tax Expense	
FICA (employers matching portion) Federal Unemployment Tax State Unemployment Tax	Closed at the end of the year along with all other expense accounts.

If a more detailed expense breakdown is desired, separate accounts should be established for each tax. Thus, we might have (1) FICA

ILLUSTRATION 7–1 Computing the Employer's FICA Tax	Gross Earnings	Cumulative Total	Earnings Exceeding FICA Ceiling*	Earnings Subject to FICA	FICA Rate	Employer's FICA Tax
	$ 380	$16,820	$ 0	$ 380		
	310	16,000	0	310		
	301	14,750	0	301		
	210	210	0	210		
	825	41,250	825	0		
	$2,026	$89,030	$825	$1,201	7.05%	$84.67†

* Once an employee's earnings exceed $39,600, additional earnings are not subject to FICA tax at either the employee or the employer level.
† In computing it individually on each employee's wages in Chapter 6, it came to $84.68.

Tax Expense, (2) FUTA Tax Expense, and (3) State Unemployment Tax Expense.

FICA tax—The employer's portion.   Under the Federal Insurance Contributions Act, the social security tax rate applies equally to both employee and employer. An employer must contribute an amount equal to the amount withheld from each employee's gross pay. In 1985, the FICA tax was assessed at a rate of 7.05 percent on the first $39,600 of each employee's gross pay. The ceiling amount and rate can be changed by Congress to reflect changes in the cost of living. Regardless of the rate and base, the computations are the same. Because the employer is liable for both the withheld amount and the matching liability, the amounts can be combined into a single liability account. The firm's accountant deducts the employee's share from his or her gross pay and records it in the payroll entry under FICA Tax Payable, a liability account. The employer's share is determined by multiplying the FICA tax rate times the total FICA-taxable earnings. The FICA-taxable earnings figure is taken from the payroll register. Illustration 7–1 shows the computation of the employer's FICA tax based on the Taxable Earnings columns from the payroll register first presented in Illustration 6–5 and a tax rate of 7.05 percent. Note that any employee earnings that exceed the FICA ceiling of $39,600 are deducted from gross earnings to arrive at the total subject to FICA tax ($2,026 − $825 = $1,201 × .0705 = $84.67. The journal entry to record the employer's portion of the FICA tax looks like this:

GENERAL JOURNAL				PAGE 25	
DATE	ACCOUNT AND EXPLANATION	P.R.	DEBIT	CREDIT	
Dec. 15	Payroll Taxes Expense		8 4 67		
	FICA Taxes Payable			8 4 67	
	To record the employer's share of FICA taxes				
	for payroll of week ending Dec. 15.				

And after posting, the FICA Taxes Payable account would look like this:

GENERAL LEDGER							
		FICA Taxes Payable				ACCT. NO. 231	
DATE	EXPLANATION	P.R.	DEBIT	CREDIT	BALANCE		
					DEBIT	CREDIT	
Dec. 15	Balance					1 9 4 0 88	
15	Employee			8 4 68		2 0 2 5 55	
15	Employer			8 4 68		2 1 1 0 22	

The balance of $2,110.23 includes both the FICA taxes withheld from employees and the FICA taxes owed by the employer. Some companies prefer to keep two separate FICA Taxes Payable accounts—one for the employees' share and one for the employer's share. Either a combined account or two separate accounts is acceptable.

The Federal Unemployment Tax Act (FUTA)

Originally part of the social security system, the Federal Unemployment Tax Act is now separate and affects employers only. Through FUTA, the federal government participates with the states to provide a jointly administered unemployment insurance program. The **FUTA tax** is levied only on employers who employ one or more individuals for some portion of a day in each of 20 weeks in a calendar year or who are paid $1,500 or more in wages during any quarter of the current or preceding calendar year. Certain forms of employment are exempt: agricultural labor, employees of federal and state governments, and employees of charitable and religious organizations.

In 1985, the federal unemployment tax rate was 6.2 percent of the first $7,000 paid to a covered employee during the calendar year.

ILLUSTRATION 7–2 Computing FUTA Tax Liability	Gross Earnings	Cumulative Total	Earnings Exceeding $7,000 Ceiling	Earnings Subject to FUTA	FUTA Rate	FUTA Tax
	$ 380	$16,820	$ 380	$ 0		
	310	16,000	310	0		
	301	14,750	301	0		
	210	210	0	210		
	825	41,250	825	0		
	$2,026	$89,030	$1,816	$210	.8%	$1.68

There is, however, a substantial credit against the federal tax for amounts paid into state unemployment funds. In 1985, the allowable credit for qualifying state plans is 5.4 percent of the wages taxable under the federal plan. Thus, the effective rate becomes 0.8 percent (6.2–5.4). Like FICA rates, these FUTA rates are subject to change by Congress.

Typically, the FUTA tax liability is kept in a separate account entitled FUTA Taxes Payable that is credited for the computed tax amount. The corresponding debit should be to the Payroll Tax Expense account. Payments on the tax liability should be debited to the liability account. The balance in the FUTA Taxes Payable account represents the outstanding tax liability at a point in time.

Illustration 7–2 shows how Jones Plumbing Supply's FUTA tax liability would be computed. Note that like FICA taxes, FUTA taxes are based on employees' total gross earnings for the pay period. Earnings that exceed the $7,000 per employee cumulative ceiling are deducted to arrive at the total earnings subject to FUTA. This amount is then multiplied by the FUTA tax rate to obtain the FUTA tax liability for the pay period ($2,026 − $1,816 = $210 × .008 = $1.68).

The journal entry to record the FUTA tax would be:

		GENERAL JOURNAL			PAGE 25
DATE		ACCOUNT AND EXPLANATION	P.R.	DEBIT	CREDIT
Dec.	15	Payroll Tax Expense		1 68	
		FUTA Tax Payable			1 68
		To record the employees' FUTA tax for			
		payroll of Dec. 15.			

State unemployment taxes. Every state has enacted unemployment compensation laws that provide benefits to qualified unemployed workers. These benefit programs are supported by **state unemployment taxes** paid by employers. There is some uniformity in the provisions of each state law, but there are substantial differences in coverage, tax rates, and size of benefits. The amount of employee wages subject to the state tax is the same as under the federal law.

The forms of exempt employment vary from state to state, as does the minimum number of employees. Further complications arise because some states allow employers who are subject to the federal tax to be optionally covered by the state law. So an employer must become familiar with the unemployment laws in every state in which the employer has one or more employees.

Like the federal plan, most state plans are financed entirely by taxes imposed on the employer. Although the rate structure varies among states, most have a maximum rate of less than 5.4 percent (the maximum allowable credit on the federal tax). Most states also have a **merit-rating system** under which a company's tax rate is based on its past unemployment experience. Thus, a company with a high unemployment rate will pay a higher unemployment tax rate than will a company with a low unemployment rate. As a result, companies whose workers make the most use of unemployment benefits will pay the highest tax rates.

An employer who is subject to the unemployment tax laws of several states will usually keep a separate liability account for each state. Each account is then credited with the appropriate tax liability for its state. When a tax payment is made, the liability account is then debited. The balance in the account represents the company's outstanding state unemployment tax liability at that point in time.

Illustration 7–3 shows the computation of Jones Plumbing Supply's state unemployment tax liability. Note that it is derived in the same way as the FUTA tax except that the tax rate will vary from state.

The entry to record Jones Plumbing's state unemployment tax liability is:

GENERAL JOURNAL				PAGE 25	
DATE	ACCOUNT AND EXPLANATION	P.R.	DEBIT	CREDIT	
Dec. 15	Payroll Tax Expense		11 34		
	State Unemployment Tax Payable			11 34	
	To record the employers' SUTA tax for payroll of Dec. 15.				

ILLUSTRATION 7–3 Computing State Unemployment Tax Liability	Gross Earnings	Cumulative Total	Earnings Exceeding $7,000 Ceiling	Earnings Subject to FUTA	State Unemployment Tax Rate	State Unemployment Tax Liability
	$ 380	$16,820	$ 380	$ 0		
	310	16,000	310	0		
	301	14,750	301	0		
	210	210	0	210		
	825	41,250	825	0		
	$2,026	$89,030	$1,816	$210	5.4%	$11.34

Recording the employer's payroll taxes

Technically speaking, employers are liable for payroll taxes on payrolls paid. But because paychecks may be issued in an accounting period following the one in which pay was earned, it is customary to record payroll taxes in the accounting period to which the payroll relates.

Combining the preceding individual payroll entries into one compound entry (the more usual procedure), we have:

	GENERAL JOURNAL			PAGE 25	
DATE	ACCOUNT AND EXPLANATION	P.R.	DEBIT	CREDIT	
Dec. 15	Payroll Tax Expense		97 69		
	FICA Tax Payable			84 67	
	FUTA Tax Payable			1 68	
	SUTA Tax Payable			11 34	
	To record employer's share of FICA tax and federal				
	and state unemployment tax for week ended Dec. 15.				

FILING RETURNS AND PAYING PAYROLL TAXES

All federal income taxes withheld and FICA taxes imposed on employees and an employer must be deposited with an authorized financial institution or a Federal Reserve bank. The exact schedule for making these deposits varies according to the amount of taxes due. When such a deposit is made, the FICA Taxes Payable and Employees' Federal Income Taxes Payable accounts are debited. A typical journal entry to record the deposit of federal income taxes withheld and both employees' and employer's FICA taxes would be:

GENERAL JOURNAL					
DATE	ACCOUNT AND EXPLANATION	P.R.	DEBIT		CREDIT
Nov. 14	FICA Taxes Payable		677 44		
	Employees' Federal Income Tax Payable		1096 00		
	Cash				1773 44
	To remit FICA and employees' federal tax				
	withholdings for the month of October.				

Following the end of every quarter (March 31, June 30, September 30, and December 31), an employer must file a quarterly federal tax return (Form 941) at the appropriate Internal Revenue Service Center. Form 941 summarizes the taxable wages paid to every employee during the quarter and computes the combined FICA tax liability. From this total, the employer deducts any deposits already made during the quarter. Using an extension of Jones Plumbing Supply's payroll figures from Chapter 6, Illustration 7–4 shows how a Form 941 would be prepared.

Withholding statements for employees

An employer must furnish a Form W–2 to each employee on or before January 31 of each year. The employee's individual earnings record is the source of information for completing the Form W–2. Copies of the form are given to the Social Security Administration, state, city, and local tax departments, and the employee. Illustration 7–5 shows a typical Form W–2 prepared for Henry Abbott.

The employer's annual federal income tax reports

Jones Plumbing Supply sends a copy of each employee's W–2 form to the Internal Revenue Service Center on or before January 31. The company accountant attaches these to Form W–3, the Transmittal of Income and Tax Statements. This is shown in Illustration 7–6.

In summary, at the end of each calendar year, the employer must submit: (1) Employer's Quarterly Federal Tax Return for the fourth quarter, (2) a copy of all employees' W–2 forms, and (3) Form W–3. The employer keeps copy D of the W–2 forms.

ILLUSTRATION 7–4   Form 941—Employer's Quarterly Federal Tax Return

Form **941** Department of the Treasury Internal Revenue Service	**Employer's Quarterly Federal Tax Return** ▶ For Paperwork Reduction Act Notice, see page 2.	OMB No. 1545-0029

Your name, address, employer identification number, and calendar quarter of return. (If not correct, please change.) ▶

Name (as distinguished from trade name)
James M. Jones
Trade name, if any
Jones Plumbing Supply
Address and ZIP code
1224 West Rose Drive
Athens, GA 30605

Date quarter ended
December 31, 1985
Employer identification number
64-7213412

T	
FF	
FD	
FP	
I	
T	

If address is different from prior return, check here ▶

Record of Federal Tax Liability
(Complete if line 13 is $500 or more)

See the instructions under rule 4 on page 4 for details before checking these boxes.
Check only if you made eighth-monthly deposits using the 95% rule. ▶ ☐
Check only if you are a first-time 3-banking-day depositor. ▶ ☐

If you are not liable for returns in the future, write "FINAL" ▶
Date final wages paid ▶

Complete for First Quarter Only

1 a Number of employees (except household) employed in the pay period that includes March 12th ▶
  b If you are a subsidiary corporation AND your parent corporation files a consolidated Form 1120, enter parent corporation's employer identification number (EIN) ▶

Date wages paid		Tax liability
Day		
1st-3rd	A	234.81
4th-7th	B	234.82
8th-11th	C	272.72
12th-15th	D	272.72
16th-19th	E	250.07
20th-22nd	F	250.07
23rd-25th	G	234.81
26th-last	H	234.82
I Total ▶		**1,984.84**
1st-3rd	I	241.48
4th-7th	J	241.49
8th-11th	K	241.48
12th-15th	L	241.49
16th-19th	M	279.83
20th-22nd	N	279.84
23rd-25th	O	234.81
26th-last	P	234.82
II Total ▶		**1,995.24**
1st-3rd	Q	204.61
4th-7th	R	204.62
8th-11th	S	244.67
12th-15th	T	244.67
16th-19th	U	221.67
20th-22nd	V	221.67
23rd-25th	W	221.67
26th-last	X	221.67
III Total ▶		**1,785.25**
IV Total for quarter (add lines I, II, and III)		**5,765.33**

2 Total wages and tips subject to withholding, plus other compensation ▶ | 23,100 | 00

3 a Income tax withheld from wages, tips, pensions, annuities, sick pay, gambling, etc. ▶ | 3,036 | 00
  b Backup withholding ▶
  c Total income tax withheld (add lines 3a and 3b) . | 3,036 | 00

4 Adjustment of withheld income tax for preceding quarters of calendar year:
  a From wages, tips, pensions, annuities, sick pay, gambling, etc. ▶
  b From backup withholding ▶
  c Total adjustments (add lines 4a and 4b) ▶

5 Adjusted total of income tax withheld (line 3c as adjusted by line 4c) . | 3,036 | 00

6 Taxable social security wages paid:
  $ 19,357 00 X 14.1% (.141) . | 2,729 | 33

7 a Taxable tips reported:
  $ _____ X 7.05% (.0705) .
  b Tips deemed to be wages (see instructions):
  $ _____ X 7.05% (.0705) .

8 Total social security taxes (add lines 6, 7a, and 7b) . | 2,729 | 33
9 Adjustment of social security taxes (see instructions) ▶
10 Adjusted total of social security taxes . | 2,729 | 33
11 Total taxes (add lines 5 and 10) . ▶ | 5,765 | 33
12 Advance earned income credit (EIC) payments, if any ▶
13 Net taxes (subtract line 12 from line 11). This must equal line IV (plus line IV of Schedule A (Form 941) if you have treated backup withholding as a separate liability.) ▶ | 5,765 | 33

14 Total deposits for quarter, including any overpayment applied from a prior quarter, from your records ▶ | 5,765 | 33
15 Undeposited taxes due (subtract line 14 from line 13). Enter here and pay to Internal Revenue Service ▶ | 0 |
16 If line 14 is more than line 13, enter overpayment here ▶ $ _____ and check if to be: ☐ Applied to next return, or ☐ Refunded.

Under penalties of perjury, I declare that I have examined this return, including accompanying schedules and statements, and to the best of my knowledge and belief it is true, correct, and complete.

Signature ▶ *James Jones*   Title ▶ *Owner*   Date ▶ *January 29, 1985*

Please file this form with your Internal Revenue Service Center (see instructions on "Where to File"). 　Form **941**

**ILLUSTRATION
7–5**

**Form W–2—
Wage and Tax
Statement**

1 Control number			OMB No. 1545-0008			
2 Employer's name, address, and ZIP code			3 Employer's identification number 64–7213412		4 Employer's State number 359–623	
Jones Plumbing Supply 1224 West Rose Drive Athens, GA 30605			5 Stat. employee ☐ Deceased ☐ Legal rep. ☐ 942 emp. ☐ Subtotal ☐ Void ☐			
			6 Allocated tips		7 Advance EIC payment	
8 Employee's social security number 250–80–9799		9 Federal income tax withheld $1,820.00	10 Wages, tips, other compensation $17,140.00		11 Social security tax withheld $1,208.37	
12 Employee's name, address, and ZIP code			13 Social security wages $17,140.00		14 Social security tips	
Henry William Abbott 125 Jockey Club Road Athens, GA 30605			16			
			17 State income tax $171.40	18 State wages, tips, etc. $17,140.00	19 Name of State Georgia	
			20 Local income tax	21 Local wages, tips, etc.	22 Name of locality	

Form **W-2 Wage and Tax Statement**

Copy 1 For State, City, or Local Tax Department ☐
Employee's and employer's copy compared ☐

**ILLUSTRATION
7–6**

**Form W–3—
Transmittal of
Income and
Tax
Statements**

1 Control number			OMB No. 1545-0008			
☐ Kind of Payer and Tax Statements Transmitted ▶	2 941/941E ☐ CT-1 ☐	Military ☐ 942 ☐	943 ☐ Medicare Fed. emp. ☐	3 W-2 ☐ W-2P ☐	4	5 Number of statements attached 12
6 Allocated tips	7 Advance EIC payments			8		
9 Federal income tax withheld $12,468	10 Wages, tips, and other compensation $91,056			11 Social security (FICA) tax withheld $6,244.96		
12 Employer's State number 359–623	13 Social security (FICA) wages $88,581			14 Social security (FICA) tips 0		
15 Employer's identification number — 64–7213412				16 Establishment number		
17 Employer's name Jones Plumbing Supply				18 Gross annuity, pension, etc. (Form W-2P) 0		
YOUR COPY				20 Taxable amount (Form W-2P) 0		
				21 Income tax withheld by third-party payer 0		
19 Employer's address and ZIP code						

Form **W-3 Transmittal of Income and Tax Statements**

Department of the Treasury
Internal Revenue Service

The Employer's Quarterly Federal Tax Return for the fourth quarter is shown in Illustration 7–4.

Reports and payments of federal unemployment insurance

Every employer subject to FUTA taxes must file an annual federal unemployment tax return, Form 940, on or before January 31. Like FICA taxes, the payment schedule depends on the size of the employer's tax liability. Small companies may pay FUTA taxes only once a year, while larger employers may be required to make quarterly payments. Illustration 7–7 shows a sample Employer's Annual Federal Unemployment (FUTA) Tax Return. The entry for Jones Plumbing Supply's final payment of FUTA tax for the year, in general journal form, is:

	GENERAL JOURNAL			
DATE	ACCOUNT AND EXPLANATION	P.R.	DEBIT	CREDIT
Jan. 24	Federal Unemployment Tax Payable		3 36	
	Cash			3 36
	To record the payment of federal unemployment tax.			

Jones Plumbing Supply would file a similar form and make a similar journal entry to cover its payment of state unemployment taxes.

Workers' compensation insurance

Many states require employers to provide workers' compensation insurance, either through a state-administered plan or through private insurance companies authorized by the state. **Workers' compensation insurance** guarantees that employees will continue to receive at least a portion of their pay when they are unable to work due to on-the-job injury. Generally, the employer pays the entire insurance premium, which is based on the amount of risk a job entails. Thus, the premium rate for office workers may be 0.16 percent of the payroll for office work, while the rate for labor in heavy manufacturing may be 3.2 percent of the payroll for that category.

The employer usually pays the full year's premium in advance, based on estimates of total payroll. The prepayment of the estimated premium for workers' compensation represents an asset put on deposit with the state. The account Worker's Compensation Prepaid Insurance is debited and cash is credited: At year end, when the exact

ILLUSTRATION 7-7   Form 940—Employer's Annual Federal Unemployment Tax Return

Form **940**		
Department of the Treasury Internal Revenue Service	**Employer's Annual Federal Unemployment (FUTA) Tax Return** ▶ For Paperwork Reduction Act Notice, see page 2.	OMB No. 1545-0028

	T	
	FF	
	FD	
	FP	
	I	
	T	

If incorrect, make any necessary change. ▶

Name (as distinguished from trade name)
James M. Jones
Trade name, if any
Jones Plumbing Supply
Address and ZIP code
1224 West Rose Drive
Athens, GA 30605

Calendar Year
19XX
Employer identification number
64-7213412

A Did you pay all required contributions to your state unemployment fund by the due date of Form 940? (If none required, check "No.") . . . . [X] Yes [ ] No

If you checked the "Yes" box, enter amount of contributions paid to your state unemployment fund . . . . ▶ $ _____

B Are you required to pay contributions to only one state? . . . . [X] Yes [ ] No

If you checked the "Yes" box, (1) Enter the name of the state where you are required to pay contributions . . . . ▶ Georgia

(2) Enter your state reporting number(s) as shown on state unemployment tax return . . . . ▶

Part I	**Computation of Taxable Wages and Credit Reduction (To Be Completed by All Taxpayers)**			
1	Total payments (including exempt payments) during the calendar year for services of employees	1	91,056	00
2	Exempt payments. (Explain each exemption shown, attaching additional sheets if necessary) ▶	2	Amount paid 0	
3	Payments for services of more than $7,000. Enter only the excess over the first $7,000 paid to individual employees not including exempt amounts shown on line 2. Do not use the state wage limitation	3	66,636	00
4	Total exempt payments (add lines 2 and 3)	4	66,636	00
5	**Total taxable wages** (subtract line 4 from line 1). (If any part is exempt from state contributions, see instructions) ▶	5	24,420	00

Part II	**Tax Due or Refund (Complete if You Checked the "Yes" Boxes in Both Items A and B Above)**			
1	FUTA tax. Multiply the wages in Part I, line 5, by .008 and enter here	1	195	36
2	Enter amount from Part I, line 7	2	0	
3	**Total FUTA tax** (add lines 1 and 2)	3	195	36
4	Less: Total FUTA tax deposited for the year, including any overpayment applied from a prior year (from your records) .	4	192	00
5	**Balance due** (subtract line 4 from line 3—if over $100, see Part IV instructions). Pay to IRS . . . . ▶	5	3	36
6	**Overpayment** (subtract line 3 from line 4). Check if it is to be: [ ] Applied to next return, or [ ] Refunded . . . ▶	6		

Part III	**Tax Due or Refund (Complete if You Checked the "No" Box in Either Item A or Item B Above. Also complete Part V)**			
1	Gross FUTA tax. Multiply the wages in Part I, line 5, by .062		1		
2	Maximum credit. Multiply the wages in Part I, line 5, by .054	2			
3	Enter the smaller of the amount in Part V, line 11, or Part III, line 2	3			
4	Enter amount from Part I, line 7		4		
5	**Credit allowable** (subtract line 4 from line 3) (If zero or less, enter 0.)		5		
6	Total FUTA tax (subtract line 5 from line 1)		6		
7	Less: Total FUTA tax deposited for the year, including any overpayment applied from a prior year (from your records) .		7		
8	**Balance due** (subtract line 7 from line 6—if over $100, see Part IV instructions). Pay to IRS . . . . . ▶		8		
9	**Overpayment** (subtract line 6 from line 7).Check if it is to be: [ ] Applied to next return, or [ ] Refunded . . ▶		9		

Part IV	**Record of Quarterly Federal Tax Liability for Unemployment Tax (Do not include State liability)**				
Quarter	First	Second	Third	Fourth	Total for Year
Liability for quarter	106.88	83.20	1.92	3.36	195.36

If you will not have to file returns in the future, write "Final" here (see general instruction "Who Must File") and sign the return ▶

Under penalties of perjury, I declare that I have examined this return, including accompanying schedules and statements, and to the best of my knowledge and belief, it is true, correct, and complete, and that no part of any payment made to a state unemployment fund claimed as a credit was or is to be deducted from the payments to employees.

Signature ▶ *James Jones*   Title (Owner, etc.) ▶ *Owner*   Date ▶ *Jan 24, 19XX*

Form **940**

amount of the payroll is known, the employer either pays an additional premium or receives credit for overpayment.

For example, assume a firm has three work categories: office, sales staff, and factory work. At the beginning of the year the accountant estimated the annual premium, based on the following calculations:

Classification	Estimated Payroll	Rate	Estimated Premium
Office work	$35,000	0.15%	$35,000 × 0.0015 = $ 52.50
Sales work	50,000	0.5	50,000 × 0.005 = 250.00
Factory work	10,000	2.0	10,000 × 0.02 = 200.00
Total estimated premium			$502.50

GENERAL JOURNAL

DATE		ACCOUNT AND EXPLANATION	P.R.	DEBIT	CREDIT
Jan.	15	Workers' Comp. Prepaid Insurance		502 50	
		Cash			502 50
		To record the payment of the estimated			
		workers' compensation insurance premium.			

At the end of the calendar year the actual premium is calculated.

Classification	Total Payroll	Rate	Premium
Office work	$39,280	0.15%	$ 58.92
Sales work	51,480	0.5	257.40
Factory work	11,050	2.0	221.00
Total premium . . .			$537.32

An adjusting entry is then made for the difference between the estimate and the actual premium due $537.32 − $502.50 = $34.82:

GENERAL JOURNAL

DATE		ACCOUNT AND EXPLANATION	P.R.	DEBIT	CREDIT
Dec.	31	Workers' Comp. Insurance Expense		537 32	
		Workers' Comp. Prepaid Insurance			502 50
		Workers' Comp. Insurance Payable			34 82
		To record actual expense and liability.			

The $34.82 of unpaid premium represents a liability and will be paid in January, together with the estimated premium for the next year.

SUMMARY

Accounting for payroll includes recording payroll taxes and meeting all federal, state, and local reporting requirements. According to federal law, all employers who are required to report employment taxes or give tax statements to employees must have an **employer identification number** assigned by the Internal Revenue Service. All payroll taxes imposed on an employer are considered business expenses and are recorded in the **Payroll Tax Expense account.** The employer's payroll taxes include: (1) the matching portion of FICA taxes, (2) FUTA taxes, and (3) state unemployment taxes.

The FICA tax is imposed equally on both employees and employers. The employee's share is withheld from his or her paycheck and retained by the employer until it is remitted to the federal government. The employer must pay a matching amount of FICA tax. The amount of gross pay subject to FICA taxes, as well as the amount of the FICA tax rate, is decided by Congress.

The **FUTA tax** is levied against employers only. It supports a joint unemployment insurance program with the states that provides benefits to workers who have lost their jobs. The federal government allows a credit to employers for unemployment taxes paid to state programs.

State unemployment taxes are also imposed on the employer only. Unemployment benefits, tax rates, and coverage vary from state to state. Many states have a **merit-rating system** under which a company's rate is based on its past unemployment experience.

All federal income taxes withheld and the FICA taxes imposed on both employees and the employer must be deposited with an authorized financial institution or a Federal Reserve bank. These taxes must be properly accounted for and reported to the federal government on a quarterly basis using Form 941, the Employer's Quarterly Federal Tax Return.

An employer must report total gross pay, federal income taxes withheld, FICA taxes withheld, and state and city income taxes withheld for each employee and for the company in total to the federal government annually. The employer must give each employee a Form W–2 showing individual wage and withholding information for the year and must send a copy of each W–2 and a Form W–3 showing company totals to the federal government.

Federal unemployment taxes are reported annually on Form 940. Based on the size of an employer's work force and the pay rates of its employees, FUTA tax payments may be made either quarterly or annually. State unemployment taxes are usually handled similarly.

Many states require employers to provide **workers' compensation insurance** that guarantees workers at least a portion of their pay if they are unable to work due to on-the-job injury. A company usually pays its yearly workers' compensation insurance premium in advance based on payroll estimates for the coming year. The premium is then adjusted to reflect actual payroll amounts at the end of the year.

KEY TERMS

Employer Identification Number—A number assigned to each employer by the Internal Revenue Service that must be used when submitting federal reports and payments.

FUTA Tax—A federal tax levied only on certain employers under the provisions of the Federal Unemployment Tax Act. FUTA funds are used in conjunction with state funds to support programs for unemployed workers.

Merit-Rating System—A system under which a firm's unemployment tax rate is based on its past unemployment experience. Its unemployment taxes may be reduced if it has a stable history of employment.

Payroll Tax Expense Account—A general expense account used for recording an employer's matching portion of FICA taxes, FUTA taxes, and any state unemployment taxes.

State Unemployment Tax—A state tax levied on employers whose proceeds are used to fund programs for unemployed workers. Rates, coverage, and benefits differ from state to state.

Workers' Compensation Insurance—A state-administered or privately run insurance plan that guarantees workers at least a portion of their pay if they are unable to work due to on-the-job injury; usually paid in full by the employer.

QUESTIONS AND EXERCISES

1. What payroll taxes are expenses of the employer?
2. When is the premium for workers' compensation paid and what determines the percentage rate?
3. Following are the quarterly wages subject to FUTA tax at the Braxton Book Company.

1st	$11,500	3d	$8,400
2d	11,500	4th	–0–

   Determine Braxton's tax liability based on .8 percent for each quarter, the amount deposited, and the amount owed at the end of the year.
4. The salary expense of the George Company this year was $110,000, of which $15,000 was not subject to FICA tax and $44,000 was not subject to state and federal unemployment taxes. Calculate George Company's payroll tax expense for the year, using the following rates: FICA, 7.05 percent of the first $39,600; state unemployment, 5.4 percent of first $7,000; federal unemployment, 0.8 percent of first $7,000.
5. The following information on earnings and deductions for the pay period ended December 16 is from Bell's Boat Shop's payroll records.

Name	Gross Pay	Earnings to End of Previous Pay Period
Hartwell, James S.	$520	$26,000
Masten, Ellen P.	340	17,000
Cain, Joe L.	290	14,500

   Prepare a general journal entry to record the employer's payroll taxes. Assume the following rates: FICA, 7.05 percent of the first $39,600; state unemployment tax, 5.4 percent of the first $7,000; federal unemployment, 0.8 percent of the first $7,000.
6. Assume the following end-of-the-year workers' compensation insurance information:

Total actual premium	$525.32
Less estimated premium paid	508.21
Balance of premium due	$ 17.11

   Record the adjusting entry for the actual insurance expense as well as for the additional premium due.
7. What is a merit-rating system for unemployment taxes?

8. The following information on earnings and deductions for the pay period ended December 1 is from Sarah's Florist's payroll records.

Name	Gross Pay	Earnings to End of Previous Period
James, Kay	$850	$39,700
Kite, Mary	350	15,400
Love, Rita	200	7,000
Smith, Todd	185	6,200

Prepare a general journal entry to record the employer's payroll taxes. Assume the following rates: FICA, 7.05 percent of the first $39,600; state unemployment tax, 5.4 percent of the first $7,000; federal unemployment, 0.8 percent of the first $7,000.

9. Assume the following end-of-the-year workers' compensation insurance information:

Total actual premium	$682.50
Less estimated premium paid	602.50
Balance of premium due	$ 80.00

Record the adjusting entry to reflect the insurance expense and the additional premium due.

10. Complete the following table that represents earnings for three employees for the current pay period. An employee is not subject to FICA once earnings exceed $39,600.

	Gross Earnings	Previous Periods Cumulative Total	Earnings Exceeding FICA Limit	Earnings Subject to FICA	FICA Rate	Employers' FICA Tax
	$1,800	$40,600				
	350	18,000				
	650	35,000	_____	_____		
Totals	$2,800	$93,600			7.05%	_____

PROBLEMS

7–1. The Murray Davis Company pays its employees on the 15th and the last day of the month. Each payday, the journal entry to record the payroll includes liabilities for amounts withheld from employees'

earnings. The employer's payroll tax expenses and liabilities are also
recorded each payday.

Required:

Journalize the following transactions which relate to payrolls and
payroll taxes.

1987
Jan. 15   Payroll:

Total earnings		$4,500.00
Less withholdings:		
FICA tax	$317.25	
Employee's federal income tax	600.00	917.25
Net earnings paid		$3,582.75

15   Employer's payroll taxes:

FICA tax, 7.05 percent.
State unemployment tax, 5.4 percent.
FUTA tax, 0.8 percent.

30   Paid December's payroll taxes:

FICA tax, $425.
Employees' federal income tax, $650.

30   Paid state unemployment tax for quarter
ended December 31, 1986, $70.20.

31   Paid FUTA tax for quarter ended December 31, 1986, $13.

31   Payroll:

Total earnings		$5,200.00
Less withholdings:		
FICA tax	$366.60	
Employee's federal income tax	750.00	1,116.60
Net earnings paid		$4,083.40

31   Employer's payroll taxes:

Same rates as on 15th.
All earnings are still taxable.

Feb. 13   Paid January's payroll taxes which included employees' federal income tax
withheld and both employees' and employer's share of FICA taxes.

7–2. The Harrison Company has 45 employees who earned a total of $560,000 during 1987. Twenty employees earned $13,500 each. The remainder of the payroll was divided equally among the other employees.

Required:

1. What amount did each of the remaining 25 employees earn during 1987?
2. Compute both the employees' and the employer's shares of FICA tax for 1985.
3. Compute the amounts of FUTA tax and state unemployment tax imposed on the employer during the year. The effective FUTA tax rate is 0.8 percent, and the state rate is 5.4 percent of the first $7,000.
4. What were the employer's total payroll tax expenses for 1987?

7–3. The Honeycake Food Store, operated by J. C. Honeycake, has six employees, all of whom are paid on the last day of each month. The following tax rates are effective for 1987.

FICA tax—employee	7.05 percent
FICA tax—employer	7.05
FUTA tax	0.8
State unemployment tax	5.4

Accounts related to the payroll and the payroll taxes are listed below along with their account numbers and their balances on April 1, 1987.

Account No.	Account Title	Balance
101	Cash	$32,000.00
212	FICA taxes payable	1,979.64
213	Income taxes withheld payable—federal—employee	590.00
214	Insurance premiums payable—life—employee . . .	60.00
215	Insurance premiums payable—hospital—employee . .	30.00
216	FUTA taxes payable	112.32
217	State unemployment taxes payable	758.16
502	Wages expense	14,040.00
509	Payroll tax expense . . . . : . .	1,858.30

Required:

1. Using the balance column account form, open the nine accounts listed above and enter the April 1 balances.

2. Journalize the following transactions, and post the journal entries to the ledger accounts.

3. Prepare a list of the accounts and their balances on July 1.

1987

Apr. 15 Paid insurance premiums deducted from employees' wages during March:

Life $60
Hospital 30

25 Paid payroll taxes for March:

FICA tax $1,979.64
Employees' federal income tax 590.00

26 Paid state unemployment tax for March, $758.16.
27 Paid FUTA tax for first quarter of 1987, $112.32.
30 Payroll for April:

Total earnings		$4,680.00
Less withholdings:		
FICA taxes	$ 329.94	
Employees' federal income taxes . . .	590.00	
Insurance premiums—life	60.00	
Insurance premiums—hospital . . .	30.00	1,009.94
		$3,670.06

30 Recorded employer's payroll taxes for April. All earnings were taxable for FICA, FUTA, and state unemployment taxes.

May 15 Paid insurance premiums deducted from employees' wages during April.

25 Paid FICA tax and employees' federal income tax for April.

26 Paid state unemployment tax for April.

31 Payroll for May—same as April's.

31 Recorded employer's payroll taxes for May.
All wages are taxable for FICA, $4,080 are taxable for FUTA and state unemployment.

June 15 Paid insurance premiums deducted from employees' wages during May.

25 Paid FICA tax and employees' federal income tax for May.

26 Paid state unemployment tax for May.

30 Payroll for June—same as that for April and May.

June 30   Recorded employer's payroll taxes for June. All wages are taxable for FICA, $1,680 are taxable for FUTA and state unemployment.

7–4.   James Jackson and Company had the following payroll for the week ended June 15.

Salaries		Deductions		
Sales salaries	$3,960.00	Income tax withheld . .	$580.00
Office salaries	640.00	FICA tax withheld . . .	324.30
	$4,600.00	Medical insurance . . .	300.00

Assumed tax rates are:

FICA tax, 7.05 percent (0.0705) on the first $39,600.
State unemployment tax, 5.4 percent (0.054) on the first $7,000.
Federal unemployment tax, 0.8 percent (0.008) on the first $7,000.

Required:

Record the following entries in general journal form:

1. The payroll entry as of June 15.
2. The entry to record the employer's payroll taxes as of June 15, assuming the total payroll is subject to FICA tax, and that $3,020 is subject to unemployment taxes.

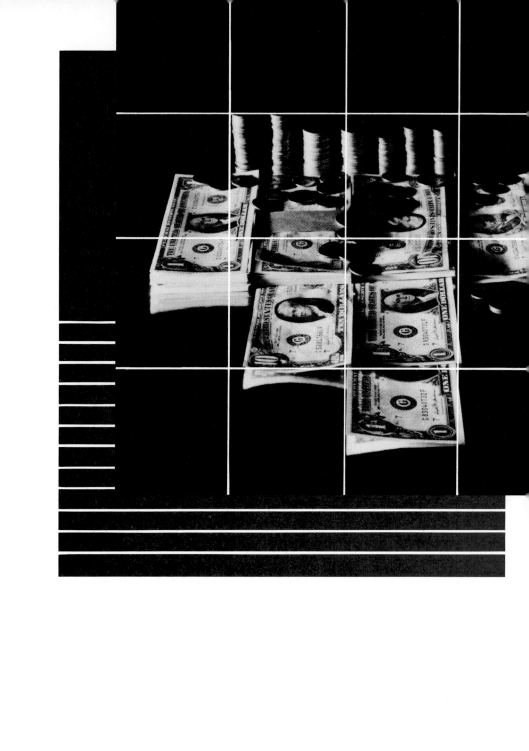

CHAPTER 8

Accounting for service enterprises—
recording transactions

LEARNING OBJECTIVES

In this chapter, we will examine the accounting process of a service company, with special focus on using a combined journal instead of a general journal. After studying this chapter, you should be able to:

1. Record transactions in a combined journal.
2. Open ledger accounts and record their balances from the previous month.
3. Post the combined journal to the ledger accounts.
4. Prepare a trial balance.

A firm is classified as a **service enterprise** if its major source of revenue is derived from services performed for customers. Common examples include professional practices, such as those of doctors, lawyers, accountants, and management consulting firms, and service businesses, such as barbershops, shoe repair shops, and real estate agencies. Some of these firms may sell a certain amount of merchandise, but their main source of revenue comes from providing a service. For example, a shoe repair shop may sell shoelaces and polish, but most of its revenue stems from the service of repairing shoes.

THE CASH BASIS OF ACCOUNTING

Service businesses frequently use the cash basis of accounting for recording revenues. A firm that uses the **cash basis of accounting** records revenue only when cash is received from a customer. Often, a firm performs services in one period but does not receive payment until a later period. Under the cash basis of accounting, the firm would record the revenue in the later period, when the cash is actually received. In a service business, the mere promise of a customer to pay is often not considered valid evidence of earned revenue because of the difficulty involved in collecting past-due accounts receivable. A merchandiser can repossess an item that has been sold, such as a washing machine or an automobile, if a buyer fails to make required payments. But a service provider cannot take back a service, such as a haircut or legal advice, once it has been performed.

Typically, when the cash basis of accounting is used to record revenues, expenses are also accounted for on a cash basis. Thus, an expense is recorded only when paid, even though it may have been incurred in a prior period. For example, if an employee is paid on the 15th of each month, the January 15 payment will cover the last half of December and the first half of January, but it will all be recorded as a January expense. Such discrepancy is of minor importance, however, because the same thing happened at the beginning of the previous year. Thus, the effect on net income is negligible. The total amount actually paid in cash and recorded as payroll expense for the year will be close to the amount actually earned by the employees. The cash basis of accounting is acceptable because most expenses tend to recur and are similar in amount from period to period.

Exceptions—supplies and depreciation

Some items that are not recurring expenses and that vary substantially in amount may cause distortion in the financial statements if they are treated on a cash basis. For example, if supplies are purchased in large quantities for cash and a large portion of them remain unused at the end of the period, it would be undesirable to treat the entire amount as an expense of the current period. When supplies are purchased, they represent an asset. As they are used to generate revenue, the amount used up is treated as an expense. Therefore, only the cost of supplies used during the period should be charged to expenses.

Another common example of a large, nonrecurring expense is the acquisition of plant assets, such as buildings and machinery. A building normally has a useful life far in excess of one year. In fact, buildings often have useful lives of 25 years or more. If such a building were purchased for cash, it would not be sound accounting practice to charge its entire cost to the year of purchase. The first year of ownership would have a very large expense for the building, and the remaining years would show no expense. This would not be a very practical way of handling the building's expense.

It is much more desirable to charge a portion of the building's total cost to each of its years of service. In this way, the cost of the building is spread over the years the business uses it. This allocation procedure is called **depreciation,** and the portion that is charged, or written off, each year by means of an adjustment is called **depreciation expense.** Depreciation expense is computed as the total cost of an asset, less what the asset can be sold for at the end of its useful life, spread in a systematic way over that life.

For example, let's assume that a building cost $85,000, was estimated to have a useful life of 25 years, and could be sold for $10,000 at the end of 25 years. To figure the depreciation expense, subtract the $10,000 you expect to recover at the end of the asset's life from your cost of $85,000. This will leave you $75,000 of cost to be spread over the 25 years of the building's useful life. By dividing $75,000 by 25 years, you arrive at $3,000—the amount to be charged off each year to depreciation expense. Different companies treat depreciation in different ways. We have only touched on the topic here in order to show that it is rarely possible to run a business on a strictly cash basis. Charging used supplies and depreciation to expense will be discussed further in Chapter 9.

CASH BASIS ACCOUNTING PROCEDURES

We will now examine the records of J. T. Adams, M.D., to demonstrate the procedures for recording business transactions on a cash basis. Dr. Adams's typical transactions for a month are presented in this chapter, and his financial statements are presented in Chapter 9. Even though unique problems arise in the operation of any enterprise, the basic principles of recording transactions and preparing financial statements remain fundamentally the same. Therefore, the system illustrated for Dr. Adams could easily be adapted to meet the needs of almost any small service or professional firm.

The chart of accounts

Dr. Adams's chart of accounts is reproduced in Illustration 8–1. Each account has been assigned a three-digit code number in which the first digit indicates the kind of account. The 100 series of accounts

ILLUSTRATION 8–1

J. T. ADAMS, M.D.
Chart of Accounts

Assets:
110 Second National Bank
120 Drugs and Medical Supplies
130 Office Equipment
140 Accumulated Depreciation—Office Equipment

Liabilities:
210 FICA Taxes Payable
220 Income Taxes Payable—Federal—Employee

Owner's Equity:
310 J. T. Adams, Capital
320 J. T. Adams, Drawing
330 Income Summary

Revenue:
410 Professional Fees

Expenses:
505 Rent Expense
510 Drugs and Medical Supplies Expense
515 Salary Expense
520 Payroll Tax Expense
525 Nonmedical Supplies Expense
530 Depreciation Expense

are assets; the 200 series are liabilities; the 300 series are owner's equity; the 400 series are revenues; and the 500 series are expenses. The second and third digits identify specific accounts. Some numbers are skipped so that accounts can be added later without disturbing the coding of the original accounts.

The books of account

Among the books used in Dr. Adams's accounting system are a combined (or combination) journal and a general ledger. Dr. Adams keeps many other records, such as a general journal, a petty cash disbursements book, detailed payroll records, drug purchase and use records (also required by state law), copies of bills sent to patients, and papers related to tax returns. These additional records are not illustrated in this chapter.

The combined journal

As one of his books of original entry, Dr. Adams uses a **combined (or combination) journal** (see Illustration 8–2). Up to this point, we have used a general journal for journalizing all transactions, but most businesses prefer a combined journal for simplicity's sake. Most routine business transactions involve the same accounts, and when a general journal is used, account titles must be written several times a day to enter debits and credits. A combined journal avoids such repetition, however, because it has separate columns for the most frequently used accounts. Since cash is normally received and paid out every day, a combined journal has both debit and credit columns for the cash account. It also has separate columns for the accounts that record the business's most common transactions. These are either debit *or* credit columns, depending on the nature of the account. Finally, a combined journal has a pair of General Debit and Credit columns for recording transactions in accounts that are not frequently used. Thus, a combined journal saves time in both recording transactions and posting to the **ledger** accounts. The Cash columns and the special columns are usually posted as a total amount at the end of *each month.* Accounts in the General columns must be posted individually, *usually weekly.* In the combined journal are recorded all day-by-day transactions. The vast majority of transactions will be for cash. End-of-period adjustments (including depreciation), and closing entries could be recorded in the "General" debit and credit

ILLUSTRATION 8–2

			SECOND NATIONAL BANK		CHECK NUMBER	PROFESSIONAL FEES CREDIT	SALARY EXPENSE DEBIT	PAYROLL DEDUCTIONS		DRUGS AND MEDICAL SUPPLIES DEBIT	GENERAL	
DATE	DESCRIPTION	P.R.	DEBIT	CREDIT				FICA CREDIT	INCOME TAXES CREDIT		DEBIT	CREDIT
			110	110		410	515	210	220	120		

COMBINED JOURNAL

columns, but Dr. Adams maintains a general journal for recording these entries. These entries will be discussed in Chapter 9.

As shown in Illustration 8–2, Dr. Adams's combined journal has the usual date, description, and Posting Reference (P.R.) columns. The next two columns provide for debits (deposits) and credits (checks issued) to the Cash account in the Second National Bank. Note the column for the check number next to the Bank Credit column. As a check is written, the check number must be recorded in this column. Five special columns provide for professional fees, salaries and the related tax withholding, and drugs and medical supplies purchased. These special columns are for Dr. Adams's most frequent transactions and thus save posting time because only the totals need to be posted to the general ledger. Finally, at the far right, the General columns provide for all other day-by-day transactions—that is, transactions that involve accounts not listed in one of the special columns. Almost every transaction will have either a debit or a credit in the Second National Bank pair of columns. The **P.R. column** is used to show the posting reference for the entries in the General columns. Dr. Adams's transactions for December are described on the following pages and entered in the combined journal, Illustrations 8–3 through 8–7. The transactions are recorded daily, while additional activities, such as summarizing and posting the transactions in the General columns to the general ledger, are performed weekly. At the end of the month, all columns are totaled, all totals (except the General pair of columns) are posted to the ledger accounts, and a trial balance is taken.

The general ledger

In Chapter 3, you were introduced to the balance column account. Remember, this form has two columns for entering debits and credits plus two columns for recording the debit or credit balance. The last two columns allow a running debit or credit balance to be maintained for the account in question. Assets, expenses, and the drawing accounts normally have debit balances, while liability, capital, and revenue accounts normally have credit balances. A typical cash account is shown below. Note that it has a debit balance, which is to be expected.

GENERAL LEDGER
Cash
ACCT. NO. 110

DATE		EXPLANATION	P.R.	DEBIT	CREDIT	BALANCE	
						DEBIT	CREDIT
1987							
May	30			2 5 0 0 00		2 5 0 0 00	
	31				3 1 0 00	2 1 9 0 00	
June	1				3 5 00	2 1 5 5 00	
	4			1 2 5 00		2 2 8 0 00	
	6				1 4 0 00	2 1 4 0 00	

A business will have a balance column account for every asset, liability, owner's equity, revenue, and expense account that it maintains. The grouping of all the balance column accounts together is called the **general ledger.**

Dr. Adams's general ledger, with the December transactions posted, is given in Illustration 8–8, beginning on page 217. Note that the balance on December 1 was entered in each account before the posting of December transactions was begun. A check mark (√) in the **P.R.** column indicates that the figure is a beginning balance.

RECORDING TRANSACTIONS IN THE COMBINED JOURNAL

We will now examine Dr. Adams's day-by-day transactions for the month of December. Individual transactions are classified and recorded in the appropriate columns of the combined journal at the end of each day. Total debits and total credits are proved at the end of each week, and items from the General columns are posted to the general ledger. Finally, at the end of the month, the figures in the Cash and special columns are summed and the totals are posted to the general ledger along with the remaining unposted items in the General columns.

Week 1 (See Illustration 8–3)

December 1

Dr. Adams received fees from patients and insurance companies totaling $3,360. This amount is first entered in the debit column of the pair of columns representing the cash in Dr. Adams's checking account at the Second National Bank. The same amount is then entered in the Professional Fees Revenue column, which represents a credit. Note that the double-entry system of accounting is used in the combined journal—each transaction results in both a debit and a credit to the appropriate account columns.

ILLUSTRATION 8–3

J. T. Adams
COMBINED JOURNAL
For Month of December 1987

DATE 1987	DESCRIPTION	P.R.	SECOND NATIONAL BANK DEBIT 110	SECOND NATIONAL BANK CREDIT 110	CHECK NUMBER	PROFESSIONAL FEES CREDIT 410
Dec. 1	Professional Fees	X	3 3 6 0 00			3 3 6 0 00
1	Medical Bldg. Inc.—Rent	505		1 5 0 0 00	481	
2	Betty Brown—Salary	X		3 2 9 07	482	
2	Carl Conner—Salary	X		3 0 8 64	483	
2	Doris Davis—Salary	X		2 3 2 45	484	
2	Payroll Tax Expense	520				
2	Quality Drug Co.—Drugs	X		1 3 5 75	485	
2	Dr. Adams—Drawing	320		1 0 0 0 00	486	
	Carried forward		3 3 6 0 00	3 5 0 5 91		3 3 6 0 00

Dr. Adams paid his December rent by issuing check no. 481 to Medical Building, Inc., for $1,500. In this case, $1,500 is entered in the credit column of the Second National Bank columns and in the debit column of the General columns. In addition, the check number is recorded in the Check Number column.

December 2

Dr. Adams issued payroll checks to his two nurses and his bookkeeper. He made a separate series of entries for each employee, showing the total amount of each check, its number, and the portions attributable to salary, FICA, and withheld income taxes. The details for these entries were based on the payroll records below.

DATE		NAME	CHECK NO.	GROSS PAY	FEDERAL INCOME TAX WITHHELD	FICA TAX WITHHELD	NET PAY
Dec.	2	Betty Brown	482	4 5 0 00	8 9 20	3 1 73	3 2 9 07
		Carl Conner	483	4 1 5 00	7 7 10	2 9 26	3 0 8 64
		Doris Davis	484	3 0 0 00	4 6 40	2 1 15	2 3 2 45
		Totals		1 1 6 5 00	2 1 2 70	8 2 14	8 7 0 16

Note that the debit for each employee's salary expense equals the credits for net pay plus FICA taxes withheld plus income taxes with-

Page 42

SALARY EXPENSE DEBIT 515	PAYROLL DEDUCTIONS		DRUGS AND MEDICAL SUPPLIES DEBIT 120	GENERAL	
	FICA CREDIT 210	INCOME TAXES CREDIT 220		DEBIT	CREDIT
				1 5 0 0 00	
4 5 0 00	3 1 73	8 9 20			
4 1 5 00	2 9 26	7 7 10			
3 0 0 00	2 1 15	4 6 40			
	8 2 14			8 2 14	
			1 3 5 75		
				1 0 0 0 00	
1 1 6 5 00	1 6 4 28	2 1 2 70	1 3 5 75	2 5 8 2 14	

held. Dr. Adams's share of FICA taxes—$82.14—must also be entered in the combined journal at this time.

Dr. Adams issued check no. 485 in the amount of $135.75 to Quality Drug Company for drugs and medical supplies to be used in the office. A credit is therefore made to the Second National Bank Cash account and a debit is recorded in the Drugs and Medical Supplies column.

Dr. Adams issued check no. 486 in the amount of $1,000 to himself for personal use. This transaction is recorded as a credit in the Second National Bank columns and as a debit in the General columns because it is a debit to the J. T. Adams Drawing account.

End of week 1

At the end of each week, it is desirable to prove the equality of debits and credits in the combined journal and to post the individual entries in the General columns. This helps to isolate any errors that may have been made and also saves posting time at the end of the period.

The equality of debits and credits is proved by (1) taking the total of each column and entering it in small figures in the column (footing), and (2) summing to see if total debits equal total credits.

At the end of the first week, the proof is:

Account Column	Debit	Credit
Second National Bank	$3,360.00	$3,505.91
Fees		3,360.00
Salary expense	1,165.00	
FICA taxes payable		164.28
Income taxes payable		212.70
Drugs and medical supplies	135.75	
General	2,582.14	
Totals	$7,242.89	$7,242.89

The posting of the individual items in the General columns can be done at any time during the period, but it should not all be postponed until the end. In Dr. Adams's case, postings are made at the end of each week. Note that the account number is entered in the P.R. column of the combined journal (Illustration 8–3) and that the page number of the combined journal is entered in the P.R. column of the ledger (Illustration 8–8). This practice indicates which items have been posted and also provides a **cross-reference system.**

An X entered in the P.R. column of the journal indicates that there is no entry in the general column on that line. Again, note that the December 1 balance of each account has been entered in the ledger before the posting started.

Since page 42 has been filled with transactions from the first week, a new page in the journal must be started. The balances determined in each column at the bottom of page 42 are entered on the first line of the new page and labeled "Balance Forward." An X is placed in the P.R. column. Balances are carried forward from page to page until the end of the month, when the column totals are posted to the ledger accounts. Remember to prove the equality of debits and credits at the end of each page before bringing the balance forward to the next page. It will help to prevent errors.

Dr. Adams's transactions for the remainder of December are described below and recorded in the combined journal pages in Illustrations 8–4 through 8–7. To fully understand the use of a combined journal, carefully compare each described transaction with its corresponding journal entries.

Week 2 (See Illustration 8-4)

December 5

Checks totaling $1,620 were received for professional fees.

December 6

Check no. 487 for $133 was issued to Physicians' Supply Company for medical supplies.

December 7

Check no. 488 for $1,475.28 was issued to deposit employees' FICA, Dr. Adams's share of FICA, and federal income taxes withheld from employees in November.

December 9

The regular weekly payroll was paid in the same amounts as last week (see transaction of December 2), using check nos. 489, 490, and 491.

Payroll tax expense of $82.14 was recorded as Dr. Adams's share of FICA taxes for his employees.

Check no. 492 for $1,100 was issued to Dr. Adams for personal use.

ILLUSTRATION 8–4

J. T. Adams
COMBINED JOURNAL
For Month of December 1987

DATE 1987	DESCRIPTION	P.R.	SECOND NATIONAL BANK DEBIT 110	SECOND NATIONAL BANK CREDIT 110	CHECK NUMBER	PROFESSIONAL FEES CREDIT 410
Dec. 2	Balance forward	X	3 3 6 0 00	3 5 0 5 91		3 3 6 0 00
5	Professional Fees	X	1 6 2 0 00			1 6 2 0 00
6	Physicians' Supply Co.	X		1 3 3 00	487	
7	Federal Govt. Withholding	220		1 4 7 5 28	488	
	FICA Taxes Payable	210				
9	Betty Brown—Salary	X		3 2 9 07	489	
	Carl Conner—Salary	X		3 0 8 64	490	
	Doris Davis—Salary	X		2 3 2 45	491	
9	Payroll Tax Expense	520				
9	Dr. Adams, Drawing	320		1 1 0 0 00	492	
	Carried forward		4 9 8 0 00	7 0 8 4 35		4 9 8 0 00

End of week 2

The equality of debits and credits in the cash journal is proved again by writing small totals in the journal and then adding to get total debits and total credits. Because page 43 of the journal is now full, the column totals are listed as beginning balances on page 44.

Account Column	Debit	Credit
Second National Bank . . .	$ 4,980.00	$ 7,084.35
Fees		4,980.00
Salary expense	2,330.00	
FICA taxes payable		328.56
Income taxes payable. . . .		425.40
Drugs and medical supplies .	268.75	
General	5,239.56	
Totals	$12,818.31	$12,818.31

Individual items from the general columns are posted to the ledger.

Week 3 (See Illustration 8–5)

December 12

Received checks for professional fees, $1,427.

December 13

Issued check no. 493 to Quality Drug Company for $427.39 for medical supplies.

Page 43

SALARY EXPENSE DEBIT 515	PAYROLL DEDUCTIONS		DRUGS AND MEDICAL SUPPLIES DEBIT 120	GENERAL	
	FICA CREDIT 210	INCOME TAXES CREDIT 220		DEBIT	CREDIT
1 1 6 5 00	1 6 4 28	2 1 2 70	1 3 5 75	2 5 8 2 14	
			1 3 3 00		
				8 5 0 80	
				6 2 4 48	
4 5 0 00	3 1 73	8 9 20			
4 1 5 00	2 9 26	7 7 10			
3 0 0 00	2 1 15	4 6 40			
	8 2 14			8 2 14	
				1 1 0 0 00	
2 3 3 0 00	3 2 8 56	4 2 5 40	2 6 8 75	5 2 3 9 56	

December 15

Issued check no. 494 to Dr. Adams for $350 for personal use.

December 16

Paid regular weekly payroll with check nos. 495, 496, and 497.

Recorded payroll tax expense of $82.14 for Dr. Adams's share of FICA taxes for his employees.

Issued check no. 498 to Medical Building Drug Store for $437 for drugs.

End of week 3

The proof of equality of debits and credits is:

Account Column	Debit	Credit
Second National Bank . . .	$ 6,407.00	$ 9,168.90
Fees		6,407.00
Salary expense	3,495.00	
FICA taxes payable		492.84
Income taxes payable. . . .		638.10
Drugs and medical supplies .	1,133.14	
General	5,671.70	
Totals	$16,706.84	$16,706.84

Individual items from the general columns are posted to the ledger.

ILLUSTRATION
8–5

J. T. Adams
COMBINED JOURNAL
For Month of December 1987

DATE 1987	DESCRIPTION	P.R.	SECOND NATIONAL BANK DEBIT 110	SECOND NATIONAL BANK CREDIT 110	CHECK NUMBER	PROFESSIONAL FEES CREDIT 410
Dec. 12	Balance forward	X	4 9 8 0 00	7 0 8 4 35		4 9 8 0 00
12	Professional Fees	X	1 4 2 7 00			1 4 2 7 00
13	Quality Drug Co.—Drugs & Med.	X		4 2 7 39	493	
15	Dr. Adams, Drawing	320		3 5 0 00	494	
16	Betty Brown—Salary	X		3 2 9 07	495	
	Carl Conner—Salary	X		3 0 8 64	496	
	Doris Davis—Salary	X		2 3 2 45	497	
16	Payroll Tax Expense	520				
16	Medical Bldg. Drug Store—Drugs	X		4 3 7 00	498	
	Carried forward		6 4 0 7 00	9 1 6 8 90		6 4 0 7 00

Week 4 (See Illustration 8–6)

December 19

Received checks totaling $3,115 for professional services.
Issued check no. 499 for office supplies in the amount of $73.50.
The check was made payable to Business Forms Supply House, Inc.

ILLUSTRATION
8–6

J. T. Adams
COMBINED JOURNAL
For Month of December 1987

DATE 1987	DESCRIPTION	P.R.	SECOND NATIONAL BANK DEBIT 110	SECOND NATIONAL BANK CREDIT 110	CHECK NUMBER	PROFESSIONAL FEES CREDIT 410
Dec. 19	Balance forward	X	6 4 0 7 00	9 1 6 8 90		6 4 0 7 00
19	Professional Fees	X	3 1 1 5 00			3 1 1 5 00
19	Business Forms Supply House	525		7 3 50	499	
20	Quality Drug Co.—Drugs & Med.	X		5 0 60	500	
21	Professional Fees	X	4 6 4 00			4 6 4 00
23	Betty Brown—Salary	X		3 2 9 07	501	
	Carl Conner—Salary	X		3 0 8 64	502	
	Doris Davis—Salary	X		2 3 2 45	503	
23	Payroll Tax Expense	520				
	Carried forward		9 9 8 6 00	1 0 1 6 3 16		9 9 8 6 00

Page **44**

SALARY EXPENSE DEBIT 515	PAYROLL DEDUCTIONS FICA CREDIT 210	INCOME TAXES CREDIT 220	DRUGS AND MEDICAL SUPPLIES DEBIT 120	GENERAL DEBIT	GENERAL CREDIT
2 3 3 0 00	3 2 8 56	4 2 5 40	2 6 8 75	5 2 3 9 56	
			4 2 7 39		
				3 5 0 00	
4 5 0 00	3 1 73	8 9 20			
4 1 5 00	2 9 26	7 7 10			
3 0 0 00	2 1 15	4 6 40			
	8 2 14			8 2 14	
			4 3 7 00		
3 4 9 5 00	4 9 2 84	6 3 8 10	1 1 3 3 14	5 6 7 1 70	

December 20

Check no. 500 was issued to Quality Drug Company for drugs and medical supplies for office use, $50.60

December 21

Checks totaling $464 were received, all from office patients for professional services.

Page **45**

SALARY EXPENSE DEBIT 515	PAYROLL DEDUCTIONS FICA CREDIT 210	INCOME TAXES CREDIT 220	DRUGS AND MEDICAL SUPPLIES DEBIT 120	GENERAL DEBIT	GENERAL CREDIT
3 4 9 5 00	4 9 2 84	6 3 8 10	1 1 3 3 14	5 6 7 1 70	
				7 3 50	
			5 0 60		
4 5 0 00	3 1 73	8 9 20			
4 1 5 00	2 9 26	7 7 10			
3 0 0 00	2 1 15	4 6 40			
	8 2 14			8 2 14	
4 6 6 0 00	6 5 7 12	8 5 0 80	1 1 8 3 74	5 8 2 7 34	

December 23

Check nos. 501, 502, and 503 were issued for the regular weekly payroll.

Recorded payroll tax expense of $82.14 for Dr. Adams's share of FICA taxes for his employees.

End of week 4

The proof of the equality of debits and credits is:

Account Column	Debit	Credit
Second National Bank . . .	$ 9,986.00	$10,163.16
Fees		9,986.00
Salary expense	4,660.00	
FICA taxes payable		657.12
Income taxes payable. . . .		850.80
Drugs and medical supplies .	1,183.74	
General	5,827.34	
Totals	$21,657.08	$21,657.08

Individual items from the general columns are posted to the ledger.

ILLUSTRATION 8–7

J. T. Adams
COMBINED JOURNAL
For Month of December 1987

DATE 1987	DESCRIPTION	P.R.	SECOND NATIONAL BANK DEBIT 110	SECOND NATIONAL BANK CREDIT 110	CHECK NUMBER	PROFESSIONAL FEES CREDIT 410
Dec. 27	Balance forward	X	9 9 8 6 00	1 0 1 6 3 16		9 9 8 6 00
27	Professional Fees	X	2 2 7 9 00			2 2 7 9 00
28	Dr. Adams, Drawing	320		4 7 5 00	504	
29	Professional Fees	X	1 6 5 0 00			1 6 5 0 00
31	Betty Brown—Salary	X		3 2 9 07	505	
	Carl Conner—Salary	X		3 0 8 64	506	
	Doris Davis—Salary	X		2 3 2 45	507	
31	Payroll Tax Expense	520				
31	Quality Drugs	X		2 1 0 00	508	
	Totals December		1 3 9 1 5 00	1 1 7 1 8 32		1 3 9 1 5 00
			(1 1 0)	(1 1 0)		(4 1 0)

Week 5 (See Illustration 8–7)

December 27

Checks totaling $2,279 were received for professional services.

December 28

Check no. 504 for $475 was written to Dr. Adams for personal use.

December 29

Checks received for professional services totaled $1,650.

December 31

Paid regular payroll with check nos. 505, 506, and 507. (December 26 was a paid holiday.)

Recorded payroll tax expense of $82.14 for Dr. Adams's share of FICA taxes for his employees.

Issued check no. 508 to Quality Drug Company for medical supplies for office use, $210.

End of the month

Since this is the last week of the month, a slightly different set of procedures is followed. The end-of-the-month procedures include

Page 46

SALARY EXPENSE DEBIT 515	PAYROLL DEDUCTIONS		DRUGS AND MEDICAL SUPPLIES DEBIT 120	GENERAL	
	FICA CREDIT 210	INCOME TAXES CREDIT 220		DEBIT	CREDIT
4 6 6 0 00	6 5 7 12	8 5 0 80	1 1 8 3 74	5 8 2 7 34	
				4 7 5 00	
4 5 0 00	3 1 73	8 9 20			
4 1 5 00	2 9 26	7 7 10			
3 0 0 00	2 1 15	4 6 40			
	8 2 14			8 2 14	
			2 1 0 00		
5 8 2 5 00	8 2 1 40	1 0 6 3 50	1 3 9 3 74	6 3 8 4 48	
(5 1 5)	(2 1 0)	(2 2 0)	(1 2 0)	(✓)	

proving the equality of debits and credits, as is done at the end of each week, plus the complete posting of all combined journal data to the ledger. No separate end-of-the-week steps are necessary because these steps are used merely to catch errors and save posting time at the end of the month. At the end of each month, each column of the combined journal is totaled and the totals are entered and ruled. Dr. Adams's final totals for December are:

Account Column	Debit	Credit
Second National Bank . . .	$13,915.00	$11,718.32
Fees		13,915.00
Salary expense	5,825.00	
FICA taxes payable		821.40
Income taxes payable. . . .		1,063.50
Drugs and medical supplies .	1,393.74	
General	6,384.48	
Totals	$27,518.22	$27,518.22

Items can now be posted from the combined journal to the general ledger. Begin with the individual items in the General pair of columns. Remember that an X in the P.R. column indicates that there is no General entry on that line. The second step is to post the total of each special column. For example, the total of $13,915 in the debit column of the Second National Bank pair of columns must be posted to the debit column of the Second National Bank account in the general ledger. This total is posted because none of the individual items of which it is composed have been posted (nor should they be posted as individual items). The account number, 110, is entered below the total in the journal to show that the total has been posted. A (√) below the general totals shows that these totals are not to be posted. (They have already been posted as individual items.) As amounts are posted to the general ledger, the P.R. column in the ledger is cross-referenced to the combined journal.

ILLUSTRATION 8–8

Second National Bank — ACCT. NO. 110

DATE		EXPLANATION	P.R.	DEBIT	CREDIT	BALANCE DEBIT	BALANCE CREDIT
1987 Dec.	1	Balance	√			17 750 86	
	31		CJ46	13 915 00		31 665 86	
	31		CJ46		11 718 32	19 947 54	

Drugs and Medical Supplies — ACCT. NO. 120

DATE		EXPLANATION	P.R.	DEBIT	CREDIT	BALANCE DEBIT	BALANCE CREDIT
1987 Dec.	1	Balance	√			17 837 10	
	31		CJ46	1 393 74		19 230 84	

Office Equipment — ACCT. NO. 130

DATE		EXPLANATION	P.R.	DEBIT	CREDIT	BALANCE DEBIT	BALANCE CREDIT
1987 Dec.	1	Balance	√			38 350 00	

FICA Taxes Payable — ACCT. NO. 210

DATE		EXPLANATION	P.R.	DEBIT	CREDIT	BALANCE DEBIT	BALANCE CREDIT
1987 Dec.	1	Balance	√				624 48
	7		CJ43	624 48			-0-
	31		CJ46		821 40		821 40

Income Taxes Payable—Federal Employee — ACCT. NO. 220

DATE		EXPLANATION	P.R.	DEBIT	CREDIT	BALANCE DEBIT	BALANCE CREDIT
1987 Dec.	1	Balance	√				850 80
	7		CJ43	850 80			-0-
	30		CJ46		1 063 50		1 063 50

J.T. Adams, Capital — ACCT. NO. 310

DATE		EXPLANATION	P.R.	DEBIT	CREDIT	BALANCE DEBIT	BALANCE CREDIT
1987 Dec.	1	Balance	√				19 702 06

ILLUSTRATION
8–8
(concluded)

Salary Expense — ACCT. NO. 515

DATE		EXPLANATION	P.R.	DEBIT	CREDIT	BALANCE DEBIT	BALANCE CREDIT
1987							
Dec.	1	Balance	√			52 725 00	
	31		CJ46	5 825 00		58 550 00	

Payroll Tax Expense — ACCT. NO. 520

DATE		EXPLANATION	P.R.	DEBIT	CREDIT	BALANCE DEBIT	BALANCE CREDIT
1987							
Dec.	1	Balance	√			3 717 11	
	2		CJ42	82 14		3 799 25	
	9		CJ43	82 14		3 881 39	
	16		CJ44	82 14		3 963 53	
	23		CJ45	82 14		4 045 67	
	31		CJ46	82 14		4 127 81	

Nonmedical Supplies Expense — ACCT. NO. 525

DATE		EXPLANATION	P.R.	DEBIT	CREDIT	BALANCE DEBIT	BALANCE CREDIT
1987							
Dec.	1	Balance	√			1 653 02	
	19		CJ45	73 50		1 726 52	

J.T. Adams, Drawing — ACCT. NO. 320

DATE		EXPLANATION	P.R.	DEBIT	CREDIT	BALANCE DEBIT	BALANCE CREDIT
1987							
Dec.	1	Balance	√			31 510 00	
	2		CJ42	1 000 00		32 510 00	
	9		CJ43	1 100 00		33 610 00	
	15		CJ44	350 00		33 960 00	
	28		CJ44	475 00		34 435 00	

Professional Fees — ACCT. NO. 410

DATE		EXPLANATION	P.R.	DEBIT	CREDIT	BALANCE DEBIT	BALANCE CREDIT
1987							
Dec.	1	Balance	√				158 865 75
	30		CJ46		13 915 00		172 780 75

Rent Expenses — ACCT. NO. 505

DATE		EXPLANATION	P.R.	DEBIT	CREDIT	BALANCE DEBIT	BALANCE CREDIT
1987							
Dec.	1	Balance	√			16 500 00	
	1		CJ42	1 500 00		18 000 00	

THE TRIAL BALANCE

The **trial balance** is the third step in Dr. Adams's accounting sequence. It is a list of all the accounts in the general ledger at the end of an accounting period and the sum of the debit or credit amounts of their balances. Debits must equal credits, otherwise, an error has occurred and must be located and corrected. The figures in the trial balance are then used in the preparation of financial statements and the closing process. The December 31 trial balance for Dr. Adams is shown in Illustration 8–9.

ILLUSTRATION 8–9

J. T. ADAMS, M.D.
Trial Balance
December 31, 1987

Account No.	Account Name	Debit	Credit
110	Second National Bank	$ 19,947.54	
120	Drugs and medical supplies	19,230.84	
130	Office equipment	38,350.00	
210	FICA taxes payable		$ 821.40
220	Income taxes payable, employee . .		1,063.50
310	J. T. Adams, capital		19,702.06
320	J. T. Adams, drawing	34,435.00	
410	Professional fees		172,780.75
505	Rent expense	18,000.00	
515	Salary expense	58,550.00	
520	Payroll tax expense	4,127.81	
525	Nonmedical supplies expense. . . .	1,726.52	
		$194,367.71	$194,367.71

SUMMARY

Service enterprises, whose primary source of revenue stems from selling services rather than products, are becoming dominant in our society. The output of service enterprises now makes up more than half of our gross national product.

Service enterprises typically use the **cash basis of accounting.** Under this system, revenue is recorded only when cash is received from a customer, and an expense is not recorded until cash is disbursed. Two items that may cause distortion in the financial statements if they are treated on a cash basis are the purchase of supplies and the acquisition of plant assets. To avoid such problems, only the cost of supplies used during the accounting period is treated as an expense, and a portion of a plant asset's cost is charged off each year of its estimated useful life. This systematic writing-off process is called **depreciation,** and the amount written off is called **depreciation expense.**

To facilitate the recording of transactions, a service organization, like all businesses, maintains a chart of accounts. Each account is assigned a number that aids in identifying its nature. Usually, accounts that start with 1 are assets; 2 represents liabilities; 3, owner's equity, 4, revenue; and 5, expenses.

To streamline the record-keeping process, many businesses use a **combined (or combination) journal.** In addition to columns for the date and a description of each transaction, a combined journal has a pair of debit and credit columns for the Cash account plus special columns that represent the accounts that record the business's most frequent transactions. For example, Dr. Adams's combined journal had columns for professional fees, salaries and related tax withholding, and drugs and medical supplies purchased. Each special column represents either debits or credits, depending on the nature of the account. The combined journal also has two General columns, one for debits and one for credits. These columns are used to record transactions in accounts that are not listed among the special columns.

When a transaction occurs, its date is entered in the date column of the combined journal, and its description is recorded. If cash is received, the amount is placed in the Cash debit column, and if cash is paid out, the amount is placed in the Cash credit column. The rest of the entry is placed either in the appropriate special column or in the General debit or credit column. At the end of each week, column totals are footed and checked to ensure that the sum of all debit columns equals the sum of all credit columns. Then the individual amounts in the General columns are posted to their **ledger** accounts. The page number is entered in the **P.R. column** of the ledger account, and the account number is entered in the P.R. column of the combined journal. This **cross-reference system** allows transactions to be traced back and forth between the combined journal and the general ledger. When a page is filled and totals are proved, the totals are carried forward to the top line of a new combined journal page.

At the end of the month, the columns in the combined journal are proved. This total is the sum of the whole month's transactions. The individual amounts in the General columns are posted to their ledger accounts for that week, while the monthly totals for the special columns are posted to their ledger accounts.

A primary benefit of the combined journal is that it saves posting time. If a general journal is used, all transactions must be posted individually to the ledger. But with a combined journal, all common transactions are listed in the special columns, totaled at the end of the month, and posted to the ledger in one step. The only transactions that must be posted individually are those recorded in the general columns.

After all posting has been completed and a balance for each account has been determined, a trial balance is prepared. A **trial balance** is a list of all the accounts in the general ledger and the sums of the debit or credit amounts of their balances. The total in all accounts with debit balances must equal the total in all accounts with credit balances.

KEY TERMS

Cash Basis of Accounting—The recording of revenue only when cash is received and the recording of expenses only when cash is paid.

Combined (or Combination) Journal—A book of original entry with special debit and/or credit columns for frequently used accounts. There are usually a pair of debit and credit columns for the Cash account, a pair of General Debit and Credit columns, and individual debit or credit columns for frequently used accounts.

Cross-Reference System—A system that allows transactions to be traced from the book of original entry to the ledger accounts or from the ledger accounts to the book of original entry. At the time of posting, the ledger account number is entered in the P.R. column of the book of original entry, and the page number of the book of original entry is entered in the P.R. column of the ledger account.

Depreciation—A systematic procedure used to allocate the cost of a plant asset to each of its years of service.

Depreciation Expense—The portion of a plant asset's cost that is charged to expense, or written off, each year. It is the total cost of the asset less the estimated cost that can be recovered at the end of the asset's useful life spread in some way over that life.

Ledger—The entire collection of the account records of a business; often referred to as the *general ledger*.

P.R. Column—In a combined journal, the column that indicates which items from the General columns have been posted and provides a cross-reference system for tracing transactions from the combined journal to the ledger accounts, or vice versa.

Service Enterprise—A firm whose major source of revenue is derived from providing services to customers. Examples would be professional practices, barbershops, and real estate agencies.

Trial Balance—A list of all the accounts in the general ledger and the sums of their debit or credit balances. Total debits must equal total credits.

QUESTIONS AND EXERCISES

1. What is a distinguishing characteristic of service enterprises? Give some examples of service enterprises.
2. How are revenues and expenses accounted for when the cash basis of accounting is used?
3. A service enterprise does not usually follow a strict cash basis of accounting. What are some exceptions to the cash basis? Why are they exceptions?
4. Why is there only a small chance of collecting a past-due account receivable in a service enterprise?
5. What procedure is followed when each page in a combined journal is filled?
6. What are the end-of-the-week procedures? What is their purpose?
7. What are end-of-the-month procedures?
8. If a company had a combined journal as shown below, which columns would be posted to the ledger:
   a. At the end of each week?
   b. At the end of the month?

Date	Description	P.R.	Cash		Check No.	Revenue	Salary Expense	General	
			Debit	Credit				Debit	Credit

PROBLEMS

8–1. Susan Carr owns and operates Suzie's Beauty Salon. Ms. Carr uses a combined journal to record all transactions. During the month of April, Ms. Carr completed the following transactions:

1987
April 1 Received $80 for beauty salon services.
     1 Issued check no. 340 for $105 to Jackson Company for beauty salon supplies.
     4 Issued check no 341 to Mary Thompson for April's rent. The amount was $175.
     5 Received $120 for beauty salon services.
     6 Received $50 for beauty salon services.
     7 Paid utility bill for March with check no. 342. The amount was $43.
     8 Received $55 for beauty salon services.
     11 Paid telephone bill for March, $27. Check no. 343.
     11 Received $30 for beauty salon services.
     13 Purchased beauty salon equipment costing $400 on account. It was bought from Salon Equipment Company.
     13 Received $45 for beauty salon services.
     14 Issued check no. 344 to Jackson Company for beauty salon supplies. The amount was $140.
     15 Received $35 for beauty salon services.
     18 Issued check no. 345 to *The Weekly Advisor* in payment for advertisement. The amount was $30.
     18 Received $40 for beauty salon services.
     20 Issued check no. 346 for $200 to Salon Equipment Company in partial payment of an account.
     21 Received $65 for beauty salon services.
     22 Issued check no. 347 for personal use. The amount was $150.
     25 Issued check no. 348 for $35 to the United Way.
     26 Received $45 for beauty salon services.
     27 Issued check no. 349 to Salon Equipment Company in payment of an account. The amount was $200.
     28 Issued check no. 350 for $175 to Jackson Company for beauty salon supplies.
     29 Received $100 for beauty salon services.

Required:

Journalize the above transactions in a combined journal. The combined journal should have columns headed Date, Description, P.R., Cash (debit and credit), Check No., Beauty Salon Revenue, Beauty Salon Supplies, and General (debit and credit). Total and rule the combined journal.

8–2. In June 1987, Joe Lasky opened a shoe repair shop. The transactions for the first month have already been recorded in the journal shown at the top of the next page. The chart of accounts is as follows:

Chart of Accounts

Account No.	Account Title
102	Cash
112	Shoe Repair Supplies
122	Repair Equipment
302	Joe Lasky, Capital
312	Joe Lasky, Drawing
402	Shoe Repair Revenue
502	Advertising Expense
512	Rent Expense
522	Utilities Expense

COMBINED JOURNAL

For the Month of June 1987   Page 4

Date	Description	P.R.	Cash Debit	Cash Credit	Check No.	Shoe Repair Revenue	Shoe Repair Supplies	General Debit	General Credit
1987 June 1	Joe Lasky, Capital		5 000 00						5 000 00
1	Repair Equipment			1 300 00	101			1 300 00	
2	Shoe Repair Supplies			450 00	102		450 00		
2	Rent Expense			150 00	103			150 00	
6	Shoe Repair Revenue		40 00			40 00			
8	Shoe Repair Revenue		55 00			55 00			
9	Advertising Expense			35 00	104			35 00	
10	Shoe Repair Revenue		70 00			70 00			
14	Shoe Repair Revenue		65 00			65 00			
15	Joe Lasky, Drawing			150 00	105			150 00	
16	Shoe Repair Revenue		80 00			80 00			
17	Shoe Repair Supplies			800 00	106		800 00		
20	Shoe Repair Revenue		50 00			50 00			
21	Utilities Expense			30 00	107			30 00	
22	Shoe Repair Revenue		65 00			65 00			
24	Repair Equipment			350 00	108			350 00	
27	Shoe Repair Revenue		80 00			80 00			
29	Shoe Repair Revenue		40 00			40 00			
30	Joe Lasky, Drawing			150 00	109			150 00	
			5 545 00	3 415 00		545 00	1 250 00	2 165 00	5 000 00

Required:

1. Open the above ledger accounts and post the appropriate journal entries and column totals for June.

2. Prepare a trial balance for June 30, 1987.

8–3.

DR. H. P. CLAXTON
Trial Balance
November 30, 1987

Account No.	Account Title	Debit	Credit
101	Cash	$15,200	
111	Petty cash	40	
121	Drugs and medical supplies	4,500	
131	Office equipment	10,000	
141	Accumulated depreciation—office equipment		$ 2,000
201	FICA taxes payable		221
211	Income taxes payable—federal— employee.		169
301	H. P. Claxton, capital		50,000
311	H. P. Claxton, drawing	15,272	
401	Professional fees		17,100
501	Rent expense	2,200	
511	Salary expense	18,700	
521	Payroll tax expense	2,662	
531	Telephone expense	150	
541	Nonmedical supplies expense	60	
551	Automobile expense	126	
561	Insurance expense.	330	
571	Miscellaneous expense	250	
		$69,490	$69,490

Required:

1. Open the above ledger accounts and record the November 30 balances.
2. Journalize the December transactions in the combined journal (column headings should be the same as those used in the J. T. Adams example in the chapter).
3. Post the journal entries to the ledger accounts.
4. Prepare a trial balance for December 31, 1987.

Dec. 1 Issued check no. 852 to Randall Drug Company for drugs and medical supplies. The total was $50.

2 Checks totaling $310 were received for professional services.

2 Issued check no. 853 for nonmedical supplies to Carry Supply Company. The amount was $20.

5 Checks totaling $400 were received for professional services.

Dec. 6 Issued and cashed check no. 854 for $21 to replenish the petty cash fund. The following expenses were compiled from the petty cash records:

Telephone expense	$ 5
Automobile expense	10
Nonmedical supplies expense	6
Total	$21

7 Issued check no. 855 for $390 for the amount of FICA and federal income taxes withheld from employees plus Dr. Claxton's share of FICA taxes.

8 Received checks totaling $250 for professional fees.

8 Issued check no. 856 to Dr. Claxton for personal use, $175.

9 Mailed check no. 857 to Independent Telephone Company for November's phone bill of $86.

9 Issued check no. 858 to Randall Drug Company for drugs. The cost was $90.

12 Received checks totaling $494 for professional services.

13 Issued check no. 859 to Helpful Insurance Company to pay premium for December. The amount was $130.

14 Issued and cashed check no. 860 to replenish petty cash fund. The expenses were:

Nonmedical supplies expense	$10
Miscellaneous expense.	15
H. P. Claxton, drawing	10
Total	$35

15 Received checks totaling $690 for professional services.

16 Issued check no. 861 for $500 to Lance Skinner in payment of December's rent.

19 Issued check no. 862 to Medic Company for medical supplies. The total cost was $50.

19 Received checks totaling $475 for professional services.

20 Issued check no. 863 to Randall Drug Company for drugs. The cost was $320.

21 Issued check no. 864 to Medic Company for medical supplies. The cost was $175.

22 Received checks totaling $1,500 for professional services.

23 Issued and cashed check no. 865 to replenish petty cash fund. The expenses were:

Automobile expense $10
Telephone expense. 5
Miscellaneous expense 5
H. P. Claxton, drawing 10
Total $30

Dec. 27 Received checks totaling $500 for professional services.

27 Issued check no. 866 to Harris Equipment Company for a new typewriter. The total cost was $300.

28 Issued check no. 867 to Carry Supply Company for non-medical supplies. The amount was $20.

29 Issued check no. 868 to the United Way for $15.

30 Received checks totaling $325 for professional services.

30 Paid the December payroll:

Total earnings. $1,700.00
    Less: FICA taxes $119.85
        Federal income taxes. . .   270.70   390.55
Net amount paid $1,309.45

Check no. 869 was issued to the payroll account.

30 Recorded the payroll tax expense for December: FICA taxes, $119.85.

30 Issued and cashed check no. 870 to replenish the petty cash fund. The expenses were:

Miscellaneous expenses. . . . $15
H. P. Claxton, drawing . . . 10
Total $25

8-4. Jimmy Carson, owner and operator of Carson's Radio Repair Shop, completed the following transactions during September, 1987:
1987

Sept. 1 Issued check no. 382 for September's rent, $125.

2 Issued check no. 383 for $25 to pay the utility bill for August.

3 Received $100 from Clyde O'Hara for radio repair revenue.

5 Paid telephone bill of $15 for August with check no. 384.

6 Received $20 from Ronnie Keats for radio repair revenue.

7 Issued check no. 385 to Bonner Supply Company for shop supplies. The total cost was $60.

8 Received $30 for radio repair revenue from Karen Kirby.

9 Issued check no. 386 to the Tinsley Company for a piece of shop equipment. The total cost was $100.

Sept. 9   Received $15 from Connie James and $25 from Debbie Butler for radio repair revenue.

13   Received $40 from Steve Melton for radio repair revenue.

14   Invested an additional $500 in the business.

15   Issued check no. 387 to Mann's Supply Company for $25 worth of shop supplies.

16   Purchased a company truck costing $4,000. Issued check no. 388 for $1,000 as a down payment. The rest will be paid on account.

17   Received $35 from Jim Kline and $45 from Bryon Wells as radio repair revenue.

19   Issued check no. 389 to the *Atlanta Journal* for newspaper advertising that cost $30.

20   Issued check no. 390 to Jimmy Carson for personal use. The amount was $25.

23   Issued check no. 391 to Bonner Supply Company for $50 worth of shop supplies.

24   Issued check no. 392 for $500 as a payment on the truck purchased on September 16.

27   Received $30 from Satish Mehra, $25 from Bobby Moore, and $60 from David Bishop for radio repair revenue.

28   Issued check no. 393 for $20 to the United Fund.

29   Issued check no. 394 for $150 to Jimmy Carson for personal use.

30   Received $25 from Ting Chan and $75 from Harvey Hightower for radio repair revenue.

Required:

Record the above transactions in a combined journal with the following column headings: Date, Description, P.R., Cash (debit and credit), Check No., Radio Repair Revenue, Shop Supplies Expense, and General (debit and credit).

8–5.   Lane Jordan is a management consultant. Jordan's transactions for the month of May have already been recorded in the combined journal which is shown on pages 232 and 233. The trial balance for April 30, 1987 is shown on the next page.

Required:

1. Open ledger accounts and post the journal entries.
2. Prepare a trial balance for May 31, 1987.

LANE JORDAN
Trial Balance
April 30, 1987

Account No.	Account Title	Debit	Credit
104	Cash	$ 1,200.00	
114	Office equipment	700.00	
124	Accumulated depreciation—office equip. .		$ 150.00
204	FICA taxes payable		21.06
214	Income taxes payable—federal— employee.		20.40
224	FUTA taxes payable.		14.40
234	State unemployment taxes payable . . .		77.76
304	Lane Jordan, capital.		4,111.90
314	Lane Jordan, drawing	4,000.00	
404	Consulting fees earned		6,500.00
504	Salary expense.	2,880.00	
514	Payroll tax expense	755.52	
524	Telephone expense	160.00	
534	Utilities expense	60.00	
544	Rent expense	800.00	
554	Postage expense	50.00	
564	Office supplies expense	200.00	
574	Miscellaneous expense	90.00	
		$10,895.52	$10,895.52

8–6. June Bennett recently graduated from law school. She decided to open her own practice in January 1987. During January, Ms. Bennett completed the following transactions:

1987
Jan. 3 Invested $2,000 cash in the law firm, June Bennett, Attorney.

4 Rented an office, and issued check no. 101 for $150 for January's rent.

4 Issued check no. 102 for $175 to purchase a typewriter.

5 Issued check no. 103 for $80 to purchase office supplies.

6 Established a petty cash fund of $30 by issuing and cashing check no. 104.

6 Issued check no. 105 to purchase office furniture costing $500.

7 Paid her two employees their weekly salaries.

Total payroll		$285.00
Less: FICA taxes	$20.09	
Federal Income taxes. . . .	33.00	53.09
Net Amount Paid		$231.91

The employees received checks nos. 106 and 107.

Jan. 7 Recorded the following payroll tax expense:

FICA taxes $20.09
FUTA taxes 2.28
State unemployment taxes. . . . 15.39

11 Received $250 from Allen Burke for legal fees.
12 Paid insurance premiums totaling $50 with check no. 108.
13 Received $150 from Mead & Sons for legal fees.
14 Issued and cashed check no. 109 to replenish the petty cash fund. Expenses were as follows:

Postage expense . . . . . . $ 5
Office supplies expense. . . . 3
Travel expense 8
Miscellaneous expense. . . . 10
Total $26

14 Paid the weekly payroll with check nos. 110 and 111. The payroll was identical to last week's.
14 Recorded the payroll tax expense which was the same as last week's.
18 Received $200 for legal fees from Don Turkey.
19 Received $85 for legal fees from Kay Carter.
20 Issued check no. 112 for $90 for office supplies.
21 Paid the weekly payroll with check nos. 113 and 114. It was the same as the previous weeks' payrolls.
21 Recorded the payroll tax expenses which were the same as last week's.
25 Received $300 for legal fees from Kurt Lewis.
26 Issued and cashed check no. 115 to replenish the petty cash fund. Expenses were as follows:

Travel expense $10
Miscellaneous expenses. . . . 12
June Bennett, drawing 5
Total $27

27 Issued check no. 116 to June Bennett for personal use. The amount was $250.
31 Received $400 for legal fees—$200 from Clay Chang and $200 from Sunit Past.
31 Paid the weekly payroll (same as before) with check nos. 117 and 118.
31 Recorded the payroll tax expenses which were the same as last week's.

CASH JOURNAL

Page 7   For Month of May 1987

Date 1987	Description	P.R.	Cash Debit	Cash Credit	Check No.	Consulting Fee Earned (Cr.)
May 3	Karen Lupe		50 00			50 00
4	Hardy Company		150 00			150 00
5	Telephone expense			50 00	298	
6	Utilities expense			15 00	299	
6	Postage expense			10 00	300	
9	Maverick Company		200 00			200 00
9	Secretary's salary			147 31	301	
9	Payroll tax expense					
10	Rent expense			200 00	302	
11	Barker Company		75 00			75 00
12	Torbert Company		150 00			150 00
13	Office equipment			300 00	303	
13	Leitch and Sons		250 00			250 00
16	Secretary's salary			147 31	304	
16	Payroll tax expense					
16	Lane Jordan, capital		900 00			
17	Office supplies expense			30 00	305	
18	Johnny Sousa		125 00			125 00
19	Miscellaneous expense			10 00	306	
20	Lennon Beadle		250 00			250 00
23	Secretary's salary			147 31	307	
23	Payroll tax expense					
24	Postage expense			20 00	308	
25	Miscellaneous expense			15 00	309	
26	Orange Company		100 00			100 00
27	Office supplies expense			25 00	310	
30	Secretary's salary			147 31	311	
30	Payroll tax expense					
31	Lane Jordan, drawing			250 00	312	
31	Membro and Sons		150 00			150 00
			2400 00	1514 24		1500 00

Payroll Deductions Page 7

Salary Expense (Dr.)	FICA Taxes Pay. (Cr.)	Income Taxes Pay. (Cr.)	FUTA Pay. (Cr.)	St. Un. Taxes Pay. (Cr.)	General Debit	General Credit
					50 00	
					15 00	
					10 00	
180 00	12 69	20 00				
	12 69		1 44	9 72	23 85	
					200 00	
					300 00	
180 00	12 69	20 00				
	12 69		1 44	9 72	23 85	
						900 00
					30 00	
					10 00	
180 00	12 69	20 00				
	12 69		1 44	9 72	23 85	
					20 00	
					15 00	
					25 00	
180 00	12 69	20 00				
	12 69		1 44	9 72	23 85	
					250 00	
720 00	101 52	80 00	5 76	38 88	1020 40	900 00

Required:

1. Open a combined journal with the following column headings:

Date
Description
P.R.
Cash—debit and credit
Check No.
Legal Fees Earned—credit
Salaries Expense—debit
Payroll Deductions:
   FICA Taxes—credit
   Income Taxes—credit
   FUTA Taxes—credit
   State Unemployment Taxes—credit
General—debit and credit

2. Record the January transactions in the combined journal.

3. Open the following ledger accounts (account numbers are in parentheses): Cash (105); Petty Cash (110); Office Equipment (115); Office Furniture (120); FICA Taxes Payable (205); Income Taxes Payable—Federal—Employee (210); FUTA Taxes Payable (215); State Unemployment Taxes Payable (220); June Bennett, Capital (305); June Bennett, Drawing (310); Legal Fees Earned (405); Salaries Expense (505); Payroll Tax Expense (510); Rent Expense (515); Office Supplies Expense (520); Postage Expense (525); Insurance Expense (530); Travel Expense (535); and Miscellaneous Expenses (540).

4. Post the journal entries to the ledger accounts.

5. Prepare a trial balance for January 31, 1987.

8–7. Michael Boyce operates a bicycle repair service. During the month of September, he completed the following transactions:

1987
Sept. 1 Issued check no. 215 to John Hull for September shop rent. The amount was $80.
    2 Received $30 for repair services.
    5 Received $50 for repair services.
    6 Issued check no. 216 to KWUE radio station for advertising. The amount was $35.
    6 Issued check no. 217 to Cycle Supply Company for repair supplies. The amount was $150.
    7 Received $65 for repair services.

Sept. 9   Issued check no. 218 for $15 for August telephone expense.
    12   Received $80 for repair services.
    13   Received $30 for repair services.
    15   Issued check no. 219 to Michael Boyce for personal use. The amount was $125.
    16   Issued check no. 220 for $100 to Cycle Supply Company for repair supplies.
    19   Received $90 for repair services.
    21   Received $50 for repair services.
    23   Issued check no. 221 for $20 to *The Downtown Daily* for advertising.
    26   Issued check no. 222 to Cycle Supply Company for repair supplies. The amount was $75.
    29   Received $130 for repair services.
    30   Issued check no. 223 to Michael Boyce for personal use. The amount was $120.

Required:

1. Journalize the above transactions in a combined journal. The journal should have the headings Date, Description, P.R., Cash (debit and credit), Check No., Repair Service Revenue, Repair Supplies, and General (debit and credit).
2. Total and rule the combined journal. Prove the equality of debits and credits.
3. Open accounts in the general ledger with the balances from the following trial balance:

MICHAEL BOYCE
Trial Balance
September 1, 1987

Account No.	Account Title	Debit	Credit
102	Cash	$ 760	
112	Repair supplies.	1,300	
122	Repair equipment.	350	
302	Michael Boyce, capital		$1,080
312	Michael Boyce, drawing.	1,750	
402	Repair service revenue		4,200
502	Telephone expense	120	
512	Rent expense	600	
522	Advertising expense	400	
		$5,280	$5,280

4. Post the journal entries for September.
5. Prepare a trial balance for September 30, 1987.

CHAPTER 9

Accounting for service enterprises—the accounting cycle

LEARNING OBJECTIVES

In Chapter 8, you learned how to record the transactions of a service enterprise in a combined journal, post the journal entries to the general ledger, and take a trial balance. In this chapter, you will study how to use a worksheet and complete the accounting cycle. After studying this chapter, you should be able to:

1. Prepare and complete a 10-column worksheet.
2. Determine which accounts need adjustment and make the adjustments on the worksheet.
3. Prepare an income statement, statement of owner's equity, and balance sheet from the information organized in the worksheet.
4. Journalize the adjusting and closing entries.
5. Post the adjusting and closing entries.
6. Prepare the ledger accounts for the new accounting period.
7. Prepare a post-closing trial balance.

The **accounting cycle** is the complete series of steps used to account for a business's financial transactions during a fiscal period. In Chapter 8, we examined the first three steps in the accounting cycle. They were:

1. Journalizing transactions
2. Posting to the ledger accounts
3. Preparing the trial balance

In this chapter, we will study the remainder of the accounting cycle, which includes:

4. Determining which accounts need adjustment
5. Completing the end-of-period worksheet
6. Preparing financial statements
7. Journalizing and posting adjusting and closing entries
8. Preparing the ledger accounts for the new accounting period
9. Preparing a post-closing trial balance

To illustrate the last six steps in the accounting cycle, we will continue with the example of J. T. Adams, M.D., begun in Chapter 8.

ACCOUNTS THAT NEED ADJUSTMENT

As mentioned in Chapter 8, certain items would cause distortion in the financial statements if they were accounted for on a purely cash basis. The most common of these are supplies and plant assets, such as buildings, machinery, and office equipment. To more accurately reflect how such items are actually used, their cost is spread out over a number of accounting periods. Consequently, at the end of each accounting period, **adjusting entries** must be made to these accounts to ensure that the financial statements will contain the correct balances. In the adjustment process, the accountant determines how much of an asset has been used up and how much remains on hand. The cost of the portion that has been used up is charged to expense.

For example, Dr. Adams has two accounts that require adjusting entries—the Drugs and Medical Supplies account and the Depreciation Expense account for office equipment. As Dr. Adams purchased the drugs and medical supplies, he recorded them as assets. Then, during the accounting period, he used some of the drugs and supplies in treating patients. The drugs and supplies he used are no longer assets; their cost must be charged to expense because they were used in generating revenue. Only the drugs and supplies that remain on hand are assets. Adjustments are first made on the end-of-period worksheet.

THE WORKSHEET

A primary objective of any accounting system is the preparation of the income statement and the balance sheet. The preparation of these statements is greatly simplified by the use of a worksheet. A **worksheet** is a working paper that aids in the preparation of adjusting entries and serves as a classification device for preparing the income statement and the balance sheet. A worksheet also helps in the early detection of errors and arranges the trial balance data in an easy-to-read form.

THE WORKSHEET FORMAT

Illustration 9–1 shows a 10-column worksheet. Note that the 10 columns are actually five pairs of columns. Each pair contains a column for debits and a column for credits.

The proper heading for a worksheet includes the name of the firm, the designation *Worksheet,* and the period of time that the transactions span ①. The Account Number ② and Account Title ③ columns are used to identify the accounts that appear on the worksheet. The account title and account number are taken from the chart of accounts. This is the same identification scheme used in recording the transactions in the books of original entry (general journal and/or combined journal) and posting to the general ledger. The account numbers and account titles from the ledger are listed in these two columns in numerical order.

The first pair of debit and credit columns is used to record the balances found in the individual ledger accounts. These are the same figures that are used to take a trial balance. Thus, these first two

ILLUSTRATION 9–1 A 10-Column Worksheet

FIRM NAME
①   **Worksheet**
For the Year Ended December 31, 1987

② ACCT. NO.	③ ACCOUNTS	④ TRIAL BALANCE		⑤ ADJUSTMENTS	
		DEBIT	CREDIT	DEBIT	CREDIT

⑥ ADJUSTED TRIAL BALANCE		⑦ INCOME STATEMENT		⑧ BALANCE SHEET	
DEBIT	CREDIT	DEBIT	CREDIT	DEBIT	CREDIT

amount columns are called the trial balance columns ④. As the account numbers and titles are entered, debit balances are placed in the Trial Balance Debit column and credit balances are transferred to the Trial Balance Credit column. The two columns should be totaled (footed) to make sure that no errors were made in transferring figures from the ledger to the worksheet. Note that, as a result of entering this information, you have prepared a trial balance. When a worksheet is used, the trial balance is taken in the first pair of columns, so a separate trial balance, as shown in Chapter 8, is unnecessary. When total debits equal total credits, a double line should be drawn under the two Trial Balance columns.

The second pair of columns is for adjustments ⑤ to bring the accounts up to date for statement preparation. In some cases, you may need to add new account numbers and titles to the worksheet to accommodate the adjustments. These are added under the trial balance totals. Adjustments are first made on the worksheet so that adjusted balances will be available for statement preparation. After all adjustments are made, the Adjustment columns should be totaled to make sure that total debits equal total credits. A double line should then be placed under the two columns.

Once adjustments have been made, the amounts in the Trial Balance columns and the Adjustments columns are combined into the Adjusted Trial Balance columns ⑥. If an account in the Trial Balance columns has a debit balance and a debit adjustment has been made to it, the two amounts are added and the total is written in the Adjusted Trial Balance Debit column. If an adjustment to a debit balance is a credit, its amount is subtracted from the original balance and the new amount is entered as a debit in the Adjusted Trial Balance columns. A similar procedure is followed for credit balances: credit adjustments are added and debit adjustments are subtracted. If there is no adjustment for an account, the amount in the Trial Balance columns is extended to the appropriate Adjusted Trial Balance column. Thus, this set of columns contains the figures from the original Trial Balance columns taken from the general ledger plus the results of any adjustments that were made. Once again the columns must be totaled to see that no errors have been made and that total debits equal total credits. A double line is then drawn under the two totals.

After the adjusted trial balance has been properly recorded on the worksheet, the accounts are sorted according to the statement in which they appear. All the dollar amounts from the revenue and expense accounts are placed in the appropriate Income Statement columns, ⑦ while the dollar amounts of the asset, liability, and owner's equity accounts are transferred to the appropriate Balance Sheet columns. ⑧ Once again, debit balances are transferred to Debit columns and credit balances are transferred to Credit columns.

PREPARING THE WORKSHEET FOR J. T. ADAMS

The first step in preparing the worksheet for J. T. Adams, M.D., is to enter the proper heading—the name of the firm, the designation *Worksheet*, and the time period of the transactions. Dr. Adams's worksheet covers the year ending December 31, 1987, as seen in Illustration 9–2.

The Trial Balance columns

In step 2, the account balances from Dr. Adams's general ledger (Illustration 8–8) are placed on the worksheet. The account numbers and titles are entered, and their respective debit or credit amounts are entered in the Trial Balance columns. The Trial Balance columns are then added. Note that the total of each column in Illustration 9–2 is $194,367.71. Debits must equal credits; otherwise, an error has occurred that must be corrected. After the totals are proved, a double line is drawn under each column.

The Adjustments columns

Any necessary adjustments are entered in the Adjustments columns, as shown in Illustration 9–3. Dr. Adams needs to make only two adjustments—one for drugs and medical supplies and one for depreciation expense on the office equipment—but other kinds of businesses may need to make many more adjustments.

To find out how much he needs to adjust the account for drugs and medical supplies, Dr. Adams counts all the drugs and supplies on hand at the end of the year. In the process, he discovers that supplies with a cost of $2,266.73 still remain. Since the asset account Drugs and Medical Supplies shows a balance of $19,230.84, and since only $2,266.73 of drugs and supplies are on hand, Dr. Adams must

ILLUSTRATION 9–2

J. T. ADAMS, M.D.
Worksheet
For the Year Ended December 31, 1987

ACCT. NO.	ACCOUNTS	TRIAL BALANCE		ADJUSTMENTS	
		DEBIT	CREDIT	DEBIT	CREDIT
110	Second National Bank	1 9 9 4 7 54			
120	Drugs and Medical Supplies	1 9 2 3 0 84			
130	Office Equipment	3 8 3 5 0 00			
210	FICA Taxes Payable		8 2 1 40		
220	Income Taxes Payable— Employee		1 0 6 3 50		
310	J. T. Adams, Capital		1 9 7 0 2 06		
320	J. T. Adams, Drawing	3 4 4 3 5 00			
410	Professional Fees		17 2 7 8 0 75		
505	Rent Expense	1 8 0 0 0 00			
515	Salary Expense	5 8 5 5 0 00			
520	Payroll Tax Expense	4 1 2 7 81			
525	Nonmedical Supplies Expense	1 7 2 6 52			
		19 4 3 6 7 71	19 4 3 6 7 71		

ADJUSTED TRIAL BALANCE		INCOME STATEMENT		BALANCE SHEET	
DEBIT	CREDIT	DEBIT	CREDIT	DEBIT	CREDIT

ILLUSTRATION 9-3

J. T. ADAMS, M.D.
Worksheet
For the Year Ended December 31, 1987

ACCT. NO	ACCOUNTS	TRIAL BALANCE		ADJUSTMENTS	
		DEBIT	CREDIT	DEBIT	CREDIT
110	Second National Bank	1 9 9 4 7 54			
120	Drugs and Medical Supplies	1 9 2 3 0 84			(a)1 6 9 6 4 11
130	Office Equipment	3 8 3 5 0 00			
210	FICA Taxes Payable		8 2 1 40		
220	Income Taxes Payable— Employee		1 0 6 3 50		
310	J. T. Adams, Capital		1 9 7 0 2 06		
320	J. T. Adams, Drawing	3 4 4 3 5 00			
410	Professional Fees		17 2 7 8 0 75		
505	Rent Expense	1 8 0 0 0 00			
515	Salary Expense	5 8 5 5 0 00			
520	Payroll Tax Expense	4 1 2 7 81			
525	Nonmedical Supplies Expense	1 7 2 6 52			
		19 4 3 6 7 71	19 4 3 6 7 71		
510	Drugs and Medical Expense			(a)1 6 9 6 4 11	
530	Depreciation Expense			(b) 3 8 3 5 00	
140	Accumulated Depre.—Off. Equip.				(b) 3 8 3 5 00
				2 0 7 9 9 11	2 0 7 9 9 11

ADJUSTED TRIAL BALANCE		INCOME STATEMENT		BALANCE SHEET	
DEBIT	CREDIT	DEBIT	CREDIT	DEBIT	CREDIT

make an adjustment for $16,964.11, the cost of the drugs and supplies used during the year ($19,230.84 − $2,266.73 = $16,964.11). He makes the adjustment by crediting the Drugs and Medical Supplies account for $16,964.11 and debiting the same amount to Drugs and Medical Supplies Expense. Thus, all drugs and supplies used during the year are charged to expense. Since the Drugs and Medical Supplies Expense account had no balance when the original trial balance was prepared, this account was not listed on the worksheet. We must write the account number and title in the worksheet on the line immediately following the totals of the trial balance columns. The number and account title is found in the chart of accounts (Illustration 8–1). In the adjustments columns, we debit this new account for $16,964.11 and credit the Drugs and Medical Supplies account for $16,964.11. We will key this entry by putting an ⓐ by both the debit and the credit amounts to show that they are related.

The other adjustment that must be made is for depreciation. As mentioned in Chapter 8, **depreciation** is the process of spreading the cost of an asset, less its salvage value, over the estimated useful life of the asset. **Salvage, or scrap, value** is an estimate of what the asset can be sold for at the end of its useful life. The **useful life** of an asset is an estimate of how long the asset will be useful to the business. For example, Dr. Adams estimates that the useful life of his office equipment is 10 years.

Depreciation is recorded by debiting an expense account, Depreciation Expense, and crediting a contra account, Accumulated Depreciation. A **contra account** is used to record deductions from a related asset account. The contra account **Accumulated Depreciation** shows the total amount of depreciation on an asset as of the date of the balance sheet. Dr. Adams's Accumulated Depreciation contra account is used to reduce the Office Equipment asset account to its book value.

Book value is the original cost of an asset minus the accumulated depreciation of that asset to date. Dr. Adams's depreciation rate for office equipment is based on an estimated life of 10 years with no salvage value remaining at that time.

An asset's depreciation expense is calculated by dividing the asset's original cost minus its salvage value by the number of years in its useful life. In our example, the office equipment's original cost is $38,350, its salvage value is $0, and its useful life is 10 years, so this year's depreciation expense would be computed as:

$$\text{(Original cost} - \text{Salvage value)} \div \begin{array}{c} \text{Estimated} \\ \text{useful} \\ \text{life} \end{array} = \begin{array}{c} \text{Depreciation} \\ \text{expense} \end{array}$$

$$(\$38{,}350 \quad - \quad \$0) \quad \div \quad 10 \quad = \quad \$3{,}835$$

In order to enter the adjustment for depreciation, two new account numbers and titles must be added to the worksheet: account number 530, Depreciation Expense, and account number 140, Accumulated Depreciation—Office Equipment. In the pair of Adjustment columns, the amount of $3,835 is then entered as a debit to Depreciation Expense and as a credit to Accumulated Depreciation—Office Equipment. We will key each of these amounts with a ⓑ to show that they are related.

After the adjustments have been entered in the Adjustments columns of the worksheet, the two columns are footed to make certain that total debits equal total credits. If any errors have occurred in the adjustment process, it is important to identify and correct them immediately. Once the Adjustments columns have been proved, a double line is placed under the two totals. In Illustration 9–3, the Adjustment columns both equal $20,799.11. We can therefore assume that no errors were made in putting the information in the Adjustments columns.

The Adjusted Trial Balance columns

The next step is to extend the trial balance amounts, plus or minus the effects of adjustments, to the Adjusted Trial Balance columns. This process is shown in Illustration 9–4. As mentioned earlier, some accounts will not be affected, some will have new balances, and some new accounts will appear that were not included in the original trial balance. In Dr. Adams's case, only one account—Drugs and Medical Supplies—has a changed balance due to adjustments. From this account's original debit balance of $19,230.84 is subtracted the credit of $16,964.11 shown in the Adjustments column. The new debit balance of $2,266.73 is then entered in the Adjusted Trial Balance Debit column. All other balances from the Trial Balance columns and the Adjustments columns are carried forward unchanged.

As before, the two new columns are footed to make certain that total debits equal total credits. In Illustration 9–4, we can see that the total of each Adjusted Trial Balance column is $198,202.71. When the columns' equality is proved, a double line is drawn under the

ILLUSTRATION 9–4

J. T. ADAMS, M.D.
Worksheet
For the Year Ended December 31, 1987

ACCT. NO.	ACCOUNTS	TRIAL BALANCE		ADJUSTMENTS	
		DEBIT	CREDIT	DEBIT	CREDIT
110	Second National Bank	1 9 9 4 7 54			
120	Drugs and Medical Supplies	1 9 2 3 0 84			(a)1 6 9 6 4 11
130	Office Equipment	3 8 3 5 0 00			
210	FICA Taxes Payable		8 2 1 40		
220	Income Taxes Payable— Employee		1 0 6 3 50		
310	J. T. Adams, Capital		1 9 7 0 2 06		
320	J. T. Adams, Drawing	3 4 4 3 5 00			
410	Professional Fees		17 2 7 8 0 75		
505	Rent Expense	1 8 0 0 0 00			
515	Salary Expense	5 8 5 5 0 00			
520	Payroll Tax Expense	4 1 2 7 81			
525	Nonmedical Supplies Expense	1 7 2 6 52			
		19 4 3 6 7 71	19 4 3 6 7 71		
510	Drugs and Medical Expense			(a)1 6 9 6 4 11	
530	Depreciation Expense			(b) 3 8 3 5 00	
140	Accumulated Depre.—Off. Equip.				(b) 3 8 3 5 00
				2 0 7 9 9 11	2 0 7 9 9 11

ADJUSTED TRIAL BALANCE				INCOME STATEMENT				BALANCE SHEET			
DEBIT		CREDIT		DEBIT		CREDIT		DEBIT		CREDIT	
1 9 9 4 7 54											
2 2 6 6 73											
3 8 3 5 0 00											
		8 2 1 40									
		1 0 6 3 50									
		1 9 7 0 2 06									
3 4 4 3 5 00											
		17 2 7 8 0 75									
1 8 0 0 0 00											
5 8 5 5 0 00											
4 1 2 7 81											
1 7 2 6 52											
1 6 9 6 4 11											
3 8 3 5 00											
		3 8 3 5 00									
19 8 2 0 2 71		19 8 2 0 2 71									

totals. The worksheet is then completed by extending the amounts in the various accounts to the appropriate financial statement columns.

The Income Statement columns

The balances in all revenue and expense accounts are entered in the appropriate Income Statement columns. Unlike the first three pairs of columns, the totals of the Income Statement columns will usually *not* be equal. If total debits equal total credits, it means that expenses equaled revenues. Thus, the firm has broken even—it has no net income and no net loss. If total debits are greater than total credits, the firm's expenses have been greater than its revenues and it has incurred a net loss. When total credits are greater than total debits, the firm has made a profit, also called net income.

Illustration 9–5 shows the filled-in Income Statement columns for J. T. Adams, M.D. The debit column totals $103,203.44. This is the sum of the expense accounts. The credit column totals $172,-780.75. This is the revenue earned. Since credits exceed debits by $69,577.31, the firm has net income of $69,577.31 for the year. To make this pair of debit and credit columns equal, the net income amount must be written in the debit column and the words *Net Income* are entered in the Accounts column. The net income of $69,577.31 is added to the total debits of $103,203.44 to make the Income Statement Debit column total $172,780.75, the same amount as the credit column. The credit total is brought down so that the bottoms of the two columns align.

The Balance Sheet columns

The Balance Sheet columns should include the balances for all asset, liability, and owner's equity accounts. According to the accounting equation, assets should equal liabilities and owner's equity. But when the figures are first transferred from the Adjusted Trial Balance columns, that is not yet the case. Note, for example, that in Illustration 9–6, the sum of the Balance Sheet Debit column is $94,999.27, while the sum of the Credit column is $25,421.96.

The inequality of the two columns can be explained by the expanded accounting equation:

$$\text{Assets} = \text{Liabilities} + \text{Owner's Equity} + \text{Revenues} - \text{Expenses}$$

So far, the Balance Sheet columns contain only the balances for assets, liabilities, and owner's capital and drawing accounts. But recall that revenues increase owner's equity while expenses decrease it. Thus, the effects of revenues and expenses must be included in the Balance Sheet columns.

The effect that revenues and expenses have on owner's equity is shown in the Income Statement columns of the worksheet. The difference between the revenue accounts and the expense accounts yields the firm's net income or net loss. This amount must be transferred to the appropriate Balance Sheet column to make the two Balance Sheet columns equal.

The Income Statement columns in Illustration 9–6 show that J. T. Adams, M.D., had a net income of $69,577.31 in 1987. To include this increase in owner's equity on the balance sheet, the net income figure of $69,577.31 must be added as a credit to the Balance Sheet columns. If the net income is added to the other figures in the credit column, the final total is $94,999.27, the same as the total of the debit column. The two Balance Sheet columns are now equal. If there had been a net loss for the year (that is, if expenses exceeded revenues), the Balance Sheet Credit column would be greater than the Debit column. The amount of the net loss would then be added to the Balance Sheet Debit column to make the two columns equal. When each pair of columns are equal, a double line is drawn under the totals of the last four columns to indicate that the worksheet is completed. Each pair of columns balances.

If the Balance Sheet columns are not equal after net income has been added, at least one error has been made. All errors must be located and corrected immediately. Once the worksheet has been corrected, the formal financial statements can be prepared directly from the data on the worksheet.

A summary of worksheet preparation

The 10-column worksheet is a useful tool for preparing adjusting entries, classifying accounts for the financial statements, and detecting errors. To prepare a 10-column worksheet:

1. Begin with the proper heading, which should include the name of the firm, the designation *Worksheet,* and the period of time that the transactions span.
2. Insert the necessary information from the chart of accounts

ILLUSTRATION 9–5

J. T. ADAMS, M.D.
Worksheet
For the Year Ended December 31, 1987

ACCT. NO.	ACCOUNTS	TRIAL BALANCE DEBIT	TRIAL BALANCE CREDIT	ADJUSTMENTS DEBIT	ADJUSTMENTS CREDIT
110	Second National Bank	1 9 9 4 7 54			
120	Drugs and Medical Supplies	1 9 2 3 0 84			(a) 1 6 9 6 4 11
130	Office Equipment	3 8 3 5 0 00			
210	FICA Taxes Payable		8 2 1 40		
220	Income Taxes Payable— Employee		1 0 6 3 50		
310	J. T. Adams, Capital		1 9 7 0 2 06		
320	J. T. Adams, Drawing	3 4 4 3 5 00			
410	Professional Fees		17 2 7 8 0 75		
505	Rent Expense	1 8 0 0 0 00			
515	Salary Expense	5 8 5 5 0 00			
520	Payroll Tax Expense	4 1 2 7 81			
525	Nonmedical Supplies Expense	1 7 2 6 52			
		19 4 3 6 7 71	19 4 3 6 7 71		
510	Drugs and Medical Expense			(a) 1 6 9 6 4 11	
530	Depreciation Expense			(b) 3 8 3 5 00	
140	Accumulated Depre.—Off. Equip.				(b) 3 8 3 5 00
				2 0 7 9 9 11	2 0 7 9 9 11
	Net Income				

ADJUSTED TRIAL BALANCE		INCOME STATEMENT		BALANCE SHEET	
DEBIT	CREDIT	DEBIT	CREDIT	DEBIT	CREDIT
1 9 9 4 7 54					
2 2 6 6 73					
3 8 3 5 0 00					
	8 2 1 40				
	1 0 6 3 50				
	1 9 7 0 2 06				
3 4 4 3 5 00					
	17 2 7 8 0 75		17 2 7 8 0 75		
1 8 0 0 0 00		1 8 0 0 0 00			
5 8 5 5 0 00		5 8 5 5 0 00			
4 1 2 7 81		4 1 2 7 81			
1 7 2 6 52		1 7 2 6 52			
1 6 9 6 4 11		1 6 9 6 4 11			
3 8 3 5 00		3 8 3 5 00			
	3 8 3 5 00				
19 8 2 0 2 71	19 8 2 0 2 71	10 3 2 0 3 44	17 2 7 8 0 75		
		6 9 5 7 7 31			
		17 2 7 8 0 75	17 2 7 8 0 75		

ILLUSTRATION 9–6

J. T. ADAMS, M.D.
Worksheet
For the Year Ended December 31, 1987

ACCT. NO.	ACCOUNTS	TRIAL BALANCE		ADJUSTMENTS	
		DEBIT	CREDIT	DEBIT	CREDIT
110	Second National Bank	1 9 9 4 7 54			
120	Drugs and Medical Supplies	1 9 2 3 0 84			(a)1 6 9 6 4 11
130	Office Equipment	3 8 3 5 0 00			
210	FICA Taxes Payable		8 2 1 40		
220	Income Taxes Payable— Employee		1 0 6 3 50		
310	J. T. Adams, Capital		1 9 7 0 2 06		
320	J. T. Adams, Drawing	3 4 4 3 5 00			
410	Professional Fees		17 2 7 8 0 75		
505	Rent Expense	1 8 0 0 0 00			
515	Salary Expense	5 8 5 5 0 00			
520	Payroll Tax Expense	4 1 2 7 81			
525	Nonmedical Supplies Expense	1 7 2 6 52			
		19 4 3 6 7 71	19 4 3 6 7 71		
510	Drugs and Medical Expense			(a)1 6 9 6 4 11	
530	Depreciation Expense			(b) 3 8 3 5 00	
140	Accumulated Depre.—Off. Equip.				(b) 3 8 3 5 00
				2 0 7 9 9 11	2 0 7 9 9 11
	Net Income				

ADJUSTED TRIAL BALANCE		INCOME STATEMENT		BALANCE SHEET	
DEBIT	CREDIT	DEBIT	CREDIT	DEBIT	CREDIT
1 9 9 4 7 54				1 9 9 4 7 54	
2 2 6 6 73				2 2 6 6 73	
3 8 3 5 0 00				3 8 3 5 0 00	
	8 2 1 40				8 2 1 40
	1 0 6 3 50				1 0 6 3 50
	1 9 7 0 2 06				1 9 7 0 2 06
3 4 4 3 5 00				3 4 4 3 5 00	
	17 2 7 8 0 75		17 2 7 8 0 75		
1 8 0 0 0 00		1 8 0 0 0 00			
5 8 5 5 0 00		5 8 5 5 0 00			
4 1 2 7 81		4 1 2 7 81			
1 7 2 6 52		1 7 2 6 52			
1 6 9 6 4 11		1 6 9 6 4 11			
3 8 3 5 00		3 8 3 5 00			
	3 8 3 5 00				3 8 3 5 00
19 8 2 0 2 71	19 8 2 0 2 71	10 3 2 0 3 44	17 2 7 8 0 75	9 4 9 9 9 27	2 5 4 2 1 96
		6 9 5 7 7 31			6 9 5 7 7 31
		17 2 7 8 0 75	17 2 7 8 0 75	9 4 9 9 9 27	9 4 9 9 9 27

and general ledger in the Account Number, Account Title, and Trial Balance columns.

3. Total the two Trial Balance columns to make sure that no errors have been made in transferring the account balances to the worksheet. Double rule the totals.

4. Determine if any accounts need adjustments to update their balances for statement preparation. Adjustments might require the creation of new ledger accounts.

5. Prepare the necessary adjusting entries in the Adjustments columns of the worksheet. Make sure to key each entry by placing a letter by each debit and credit entry.

6. Total the Adjustments columns of the worksheet to see that the debit and credit amounts are equal. Double rule the columns.

7. Combine each account's Trial Balance column amount with the amount in the Adjustments columns and place the balance in the proper Adjusted Trial Balance column.

8. Total the two Adjusted Trial Balance columns to make sure no errors have been made in combining and/or transferring the amounts. The two columns must be equal and double ruled.

9. Transfer revenue and expense amounts from the Adjusted Trial Balance columns to the appropriate Income Statement columns.

10. Transfer the dollar amounts of the asset, liability, and owner's capital and drawing accounts to the appropriate Balance Sheet columns.

11. Total the two Income Statement columns. If the total of the Income Statement Credit column exceeds the total of the Debit column, the difference is the firm's net income. The net income amount should be added to the Income Statement Debit column, and the label *Net Income* should be added in the Accounts column. If the total of the Income Statement Debit column exceeds the total of the credit column, the difference is the firm's net loss. The amount of net loss should be added to the Income Statement Credit column, and the label *Net Loss* should be added in the Accounts column.

12. Total the two Balance Sheet columns. If the firm had net income, add the amount of net income to the Balance Sheet

Credit column. If the firm had a net loss, add the amount of net loss to the Balance Sheet Debit column.

13. Total the Income Statement and Balance Sheet columns. In each pair of columns, total debits should equal total credits. Otherwise, find and correct all errors. Indicate that the worksheet is completed by placing a double rule under the last four columns.

PREPARING FINANCIAL STATEMENTS

Once the worksheet is completed, the formal financial statements can be easily prepared. The necessary information for the income statement and balance sheet can be taken directly from the completed worksheet. However, remember from Chapter 4 that the statement of owner's equity combines information from the two other statements. Thus, we must take Dr. Adams's beginning capital balance (found in the credit column of the Balance Sheet columns), the net income (found as the balancing figure in both the Income Statement and Balance Sheet columns), and subtract all withdrawals of capital (found in the debit column of the Balance Sheet columns). Once the balance of the capital account at December 31, 1987, is determined in the statement of owner's equity, only the total of $54,844.37 is shown on the balance sheet. The financial statements for J. T. Adams, M.D., are presented in Illustrations 9–7 through 9–9.

ILLUSTRATION 9–7

J. T. ADAMS, M.D.
Income Statement *listing* *totals*
For the Year Ended December 31, 1987

Revenue from professional fees		$172,780.75
Expenses:		
Rent	$18,000.00	
Drugs and medical supplies	16,964.11	
Salaries	58,550.00	
Payroll tax	4,127.81	
Nonmedical supplies.	1,726.52	
Depreciation	3,835.00	103,203.44
Net income		$ 69,577.31

ILLUSTRATION 9–8

J. T. ADAMS, M.D.
Statement of Owner's Equity
For the Year Ended December 31, 1987

J. T. Adams, capital—January 1, 1987	$19,702.06
Add net income	69,577.31
	$89,279.37
Less withdrawals	34,435.00
J. T. Adams, capital—December 31, 1987	$54,844.37

ILLUSTRATION 9–9

J. T. ADAMS, M.D.
Balance Sheet
December 31, 1987

Assets

Cash—Second National Bank		$19,947.54
Drugs and medical supplies on hand		2,266.73
Office equipment	$38,350.00	
Less: Accumulated depreciation	3,835.00	34,515.00
Total assets		$56,729.27

Liabilities

FICA taxes payable	$ 821.40	
Income taxes payable—federal—employee	1,063.50	$ 1,884.90

Owner's Equity

J. T. Adams, capital	54,844.37
Total liabilities and owner's equity	$56,729.27

ADJUSTING AND CLOSING ENTRIES

The next step in the accounting cycle is to adjust and close the appropriate accounts. First, the adjusting entries are journalized and posted so that the ledger balances will agree with the figures that appear on the financial statements. Until this point, the adjustments appear only in the Adjustments columns of the worksheet. Thus, they are not included in the company's formal records until they are journalized. In our example, there were two adjustments—one for supplies and one for depreciation. Their adjusting entries as they would appear in the general journal are shown in Illustration 9–

ILLUSTRATION 9–10

	GENERAL JOURNAL				PAGE 8	
DATE	ACCOUNT AND EXPLANATION	P.R.	DEBIT		CREDIT	
1987	Adjusting Entries					
Dec. 31	Drugs and Medical Supplies Expense	510	1 6 9 6 4 11			
	Drugs and Medical Supplies	120			1 6 9 6 4 11	
	To record drug and medical supplies used.					
31	Depreciation Expense	530	3 8 3 5 00			
	Accumulated Depreciation—Office Equip.	140			3 8 3 5 00	
	To record 1987 depreciation.					
	Closing Entries					
31	Professional Fees	410	17 2 7 8 0 75			
	Income Summary	330			17 2 7 8 0 75	
	To close the revenue account.					
31	Income Summary	330	10 3 2 0 3 44			
	Rent Expense	505			1 8 0 0 0 00	
	Drug and Medical Supplies Expense	510			1 6 9 6 4 11	
	Salary Expense	515			5 8 5 5 0 00	
	Payroll Tax Expense	520			4 1 2 7 81	
	Nonmedical Supplies Expense	525			1 7 2 6 52	
	Depreciation Expense—Office Equip.	530			3 8 3 5 00	
	To close the expense accounts.					
31	Income Summary	330	6 9 5 7 7 31			
	J. T. Adams, Capital	310			6 9 5 7 7 31	
	To close the Income Summary.					
31	J. T. Adams, Capital	310	3 4 4 3 5 00			
	J. T. Adams, Drawing	320			3 4 4 3 5 00	
	To close the drawing account.					

10. These journal entries are then posted to the ledger accounts, as shown in Illustration 9–11.

After the adjusting entries have been journalized and posted, it is time to close the books. **Closing entries** bring the capital accounts up to date and eliminate any existing balances in the expense and revenue accounts. As described in detail in Chapter 4, all temporary accounts—revenue, expense, and drawing accounts—are closed into the Owner's Capital account using closing entries. First the revenue and expense accounts are closed into the Income Summary account. Then the Income Summary and Owner's Drawing accounts are closed into the Owner's Capital account. When the closing process is completed, only asset accounts, liability accounts, and the Owner's Capital account have balances to carry forward to the next accounting period. The closing entries for J. T. Adams, M.D., are presented in Illustration 9–10.

PREPARING THE LEDGER ACCOUNTS FOR THE NEW ACCOUNTING PERIOD

Once the closing entries are journalized, they are posted to the ledger accounts (see Illustration 9–11). The revenue and expense accounts along with the Owner's Drawing account should all have zero balances after closing entries are posted. The asset, liability, and Owner's Capital accounts should all show their end-of-period balances. These accounts may be double ruled and the balance brought down to a new line. The year, month, and date of the new accounting period may be entered along with the word "Balance" and a check mark (√) in the P.R. column. All accounts are now ready to begin recording the new accounting period's transactions.

ILLUSTRATION 9–11

Second National Bank — ACCT. NO. 110

DATE		EXPLANATION	P.R.	DEBIT	CREDIT	BALANCE DEBIT	BALANCE CREDIT
1987							
Dec.	1	Balance	√			17 750 86	
	31		CJ46	13 915 00		31 665 86	
	31		CJ46		11 718 32	19 947 54	
1988							
Jan.	1	Balance	√			19 947 54	

Drugs and Medical Supplies — ACCT. NO. 120

DATE		EXPLANATION	P.R.	DEBIT	CREDIT	BALANCE DEBIT	BALANCE CREDIT
1987							
Dec.	1	Balance	√			17 837 10	
	31		CJ46	1 393 74		19 230 84	
	31		GJ8		16 964 11	2 266 73	
1988							
Jan.	1	Balance	√			2 266 73	

Office Equipment — ACCT. NO. 130

DATE		EXPLANATION	P.R.	DEBIT	CREDIT	BALANCE DEBIT	BALANCE CREDIT
1987							
Dec.	1	Balance	√			38 350 00	
1988							
Jan.	1	Balance	√			38 350 00	

ILLUSTRATION 9–11 (continued)

Accumulated Depreciation—Office Equipment   ACCT. NO. 140

DATE		EXPLANATION	P.R.	DEBIT	CREDIT	BALANCE DEBIT	BALANCE CREDIT
1987							
Dec.	31		GJ8		3 8 3 5 00		3 8 3 5 00
1988							
Jan.	1	Balance	√				3 8 3 5 00

FICA Taxes Payable   ACCT. NO. 210

DATE		EXPLANATION	P.R.	DEBIT	CREDIT	BALANCE DEBIT	BALANCE CREDIT
1987							
Dec.	1	Balance	√				6 2 4 48
	7		CJ43	6 2 4 48			- 0 -
	31		CJ46		8 2 1 40		8 2 1 40
1988							
Jan.	1	Balance	√				8 2 1 40

Income Taxes Payable—Federal Employee   ACCT. NO. 220

DATE		EXPLANATION	P.R.	DEBIT	CREDIT	BALANCE DEBIT	BALANCE CREDIT
1987							
Dec.	1	Balance	√				8 5 0 80
	7		CJ43	8 5 0 80			- 0 -
	31		CJ46		1 0 6 3 50		1 0 6 3 50
1988							
Jan.	1	Balance	√				1 0 6 3 50

J. T. Adams, Capital   ACCT. NO. 310

DATE		EXPLANATION	P.R.	DEBIT	CREDIT	BALANCE DEBIT	BALANCE CREDIT
1987							
Dec.	1	Balance	√				19 7 0 2 06
	31		CJ8		69 5 7 7 31		89 2 7 9 37
	31		CJ8	34 4 3 5 00			54 8 4 4 37
1988							
Jan.	1	Balance	√				54 8 4 4 37

**ILLUSTRATION
9–11
(continued)**

J.T. Adams, Drawing   ACCT. NO. 320

DATE		EXPLANATION	P.R.	DEBIT	CREDIT	BALANCE DEBIT	BALANCE CREDIT
1987							
Dec.	1	Balance	√			31 5 1 0 00	
	2		CJ42	1 0 0 0 00		32 5 1 0 00	
	9		CJ43	1 1 0 0 00		33 6 1 0 00	
	15		CJ44	3 5 0 00		33 9 6 0 00	
	28		CJ44	4 7 5 00		34 4 3 5 00	
	31		GJ8		34 4 3 5 00	- 0 -	

Income Summary   ACCT. NO. 330

DATE		EXPLANATION	P.R.	DEBIT	CREDIT	BALANCE DEBIT	BALANCE CREDIT
1987							
Dec.	31		GJ8		172 7 8 0 75		172 7 8 0 75
	31		GJ8	103 2 0 3 44			69 5 7 7 31
	31		GJ8	69 5 7 7 31			- 0 -

Professional Fees   ACCT. NO. 410

DATE		EXPLANATION	P.R.	DEBIT	CREDIT	BALANCE DEBIT	BALANCE CREDIT
1987							
Dec.	1	Balance	√				158 8 6 5 75
	31		CJ46		13 9 1 5 00		172 7 8 0 75
	31		GJ8	172 7 8 0 75			- 0 -

Rent Expense   ACCT. NO. 505

DATE		EXPLANATION	P.R.	DEBIT	CREDIT	BALANCE DEBIT	BALANCE CREDIT
1987							
Dec.	1		√			16 5 0 0 00	
	1		CJ42	1 5 0 0 00		18 0 0 0 00	
	31		GJ8		18 0 0 0 00	- 0 -	

**ILLUSTRATION
9–11
*(concluded)***

Drug and Medical Supplies Expense ACCT. NO. 510

DATE		EXPLANATION	P.R.	DEBIT	CREDIT	BALANCE DEBIT	BALANCE CREDIT
1987							
Dec.	31		GJ8	16 964 11		16 964 11	
	31		GJ8		16 964 11	- 0 -	

Salary Expense ACCT. NO. 515

DATE		EXPLANATION	P.R.	DEBIT	CREDIT	BALANCE DEBIT	BALANCE CREDIT
1987							
Dec.	1	Balance	√			52 725 00	
	30		CJ46	5 825 00		58 550 00	
	31		GJ8		58 550 00	- 0 -	

Payroll Tax Expense ACCT. NO. 520

DATE		EXPLANATION	P.R.	DEBIT	CREDIT	BALANCE DEBIT	BALANCE CREDIT
1987							
Dec.	1	Balance	√			3 717 11	
	2		CJ42	82 14		3 799 25	
	9		CJ43	82 14		3 881 39	
	16		CJ44	82 14		3 963 53	
	23		CJ45	82 14		4 045 67	
	31		CJ46	82 14		4 127 81	
	31		GJ8		4 127 81	- 0 -	

Nonmedical Supplies Expense ACCT. NO. 525

DATE		EXPLANATION	P.R.	DEBIT	CREDIT	BALANCE DEBIT	BALANCE CREDIT
1987							
Dec.	1	Balance	√			1 653 02	
	19		CJ45	73 50		1 726 52	
	31		GJ8		1 726 52	- 0 -	

Depreciation Expense—Office Equipment ACCT. NO.

DATE		EXPLANATION	P.R.	DEBIT	CREDIT	BALANCE DEBIT	BALANCE CREDIT
1987							
Dec.	31		GJ8	3 835 00		3 835 00	
	31		GJ8		3 835 00	- 0 -	

THE POST-CLOSING TRIAL BALANCE

To prove once again the equality of debits and credits, a **post-closing trial balance** is prepared using the final balances from the ledger accounts that remain open. This final step in the accounting cycle appears in Illustration 9–12. Note that only assets, liabilities, and the Owner's Capital account are listed in the post-closing trial balance because all revenue and expense accounts have been closed.

**ILLUSTRATION
9–12**

J. T. ADAMS, M.D.
Post-Closing Trial Balance
December 31, 1987

Account No.	Account Title	Debit	Credit
110	Second National Bank	$19,947.54	
120	Drugs and medical supplies	2,266.73	
130	Office equipment	38,350.00	
140	Accumulated depreciation—office equipment		$ 3,835.00
210	FICA taxes payable		821.40
220	Income taxes payable—federal—employee		1,063.50
310	J. T. Adams, capital		54,844.37
		$60,564.27	$60,564.27

THE ACCOUNTING CYCLE—A REVIEW

All the steps involved in recording transactions during the entire accounting period and the end-of-accounting-period procedures are referred to collectively as the accounting cycle. A complete accounting cycle for J. T. Adams, M.D., has been illustrated in Chapter 8 and in this chapter. Dr. Adams's accounting cycle is one year in length and consists of the following steps:

1. Journalize the transactions.
2. Post to the ledger.
3. Prepare a trial balance.
4. Determine the necessary adjustments.
5. Complete the worksheet.
6. Prepare the financial statements.

7. Journalize and post the adjusting and closing entries.
8. Rule the closed accounts and bring down the balance in the open accounts.
9. Prepare a post-closing trial balance.

Throughout the year, all transactions should be journalized as soon as possible after the actual event occurs, and posting should be done periodically as time permits. Steps 3 through 9 are dated the last day of the period even though they may actually be performed during the first few days or weeks of the next period. For example, it might be January 15 before the statements for Dr. Adams are actually prepared, yet they are dated December 31, which was the last day of the accounting period. It may be January 22 before the ledger is closed and the post-closing trial balance prepared. During this time, the January transactions would be recorded as usual in the journal, but could not, of course, be posted until the ledger is prepared for new entries.

SUMMARY

The **accounting cycle** is the complete series of steps used to account for a business's financial transactions during a fiscal period. Once transactions have been journalized and posted and a trial balance has been prepared, the accountant must decide which **adjusting journal entries** are required. The most common adjustments are for supplies and **depreciation. Accumulated depreciation** is a **contra account** used to reduce a related asset account. Depreciation expense is computed by subtracting an asset's **salvage value** from its original cost and dividing the result by the number of years in the asset's **useful life.** An asset's accumulated depreciation is subtracted from its original cost to arrive at the asset's **book value.**

A 10-column **worksheet** has five pairs of debit and credit columns. The first pair of columns is for the trial balance. Any adjustments required to bring the accounts up to date for statement preparation are placed in the next two columns. The amounts in the first four columns are combined into an **adjusted trial balance** in the third pair of columns. For each pair of columns, the accountant must verify that total debits equal total credits. After the Adjusted Trial Balance columns are verified, the amounts are copied into one of the last four columns. Asset, liability, and owner's capital and drawing accounts are placed in the appropriate Balance Sheet columns, while revenues and expenses are transferred to the Income Statement columns. The amount of net income or net loss determined in the Income Statement columns is transferred to the Balance Sheet columns to make them balance.

The completed worksheet is used to prepare the income statement, the statement of owner's equity, and the balance sheet. Then, the adjusting entries are recorded in the general journal and posted to the general ledger. Next, **closing entries** are recorded in the journal and posted to the ledger.

The final two steps in the accounting cycle are the preparation of the ledger for the next year and the preparation of a **post-closing trial balance.** Ledger accounts that are closed should have double lines drawn across all of their columns, and the balance of each open account should be brought down as the beginning balance of the next period. Accounts with balances are listed in the post-closing trial balance. As always, total debits must equal total credits.

KEY TERMS

Accounting Cycle—The series of steps involved in recording transactions during the entire accounting period and the end-of-period procedures. The steps are:

1. Journalize the transactions.
2. Post to the ledger.
3. Prepare a trial balance.
4. Determine the necessary adjustments.
5. Complete the worksheet.
6. Prepare the financial statements.
7. Journalize and post the adjusting and closing entries.
8. Rule the closed accounts and bring down the balance in the open accounts.
9. Prepare a post-closing trial balance.

Accumulated Depreciation Account—A contra account used to reduce a related plant asset account to its proper book value.

Adjusted Trial Balance—A trial balance taken after the adjusting entries have been made. It is the sum of the original trial balance plus the effects of the adjustments.

Adjusting Journal Entries—Journal entries made at the end of an accounting period so that the accounts will reflect the correct balances in the financial statements. These entries are necessary because some transactions have an effect on more than one accounting period, and their effects must be apportioned over the accounting periods affected.

Book Value—The original cost of an asset minus the accumulated depreciation on that asset to date.

Closing Entries—Journal entries made at the end of an accounting period to bring the equity accounts up to date and to eliminate the balances in the expense and revenue accounts.

Contra Account—An account used to record deductions from a directly related account. For example, Accumulated Depreciation—Office Equipment is the contra account to Office Equipment. Accumulated Depreciation—Office Equipment has a credit balance while Office Equipment has a debit balance.

Depreciation—The process of spreading the cost of an asset, less its salvage value, over the useful life of the asset.

Post-Closing Trial Balance—A trial balance taken after the closing journal entries have been made.

Salvage (scrap) Value—An estimate of what an asset can be sold for at the end of its useful life.

Useful Life—An estimate of how long an asset will be useful to the business.

Worksheet—A working paper that aids in the preparation of adjusting entries, serves as a classification device for preparing financial statements, and helps in the early detection of errors.

QUESTIONS AND EXERCISES

1. What is the purpose of a worksheet?
2. What is an adjusted trial balance?
3. What is the accounting cycle? Summarize the steps in the accounting cycle.
4. When are the steps in the accounting cycle performed?
5. Why are adjusting journal entries necessary?
6. An office equipment account has a balance of $16,480. The depreciation rate is based upon an estimated life of eight years with

no salvage value. What entry should be made to record one year's depreciation expense?

7. Dr. Thomas Turkey, a local optometrist, had a capital balance of $15,650 on January 1, 1987. His income statement showed net income of $16,500 for 1987. Before closing entries were made, his drawing account had a balance of $12,750. What is Dr. Turkey's capital account balance on December 31, 1987?

8. If the Office Supplies account in the trial balance has a balance of $6,350 and in counting the supplies, only $3,350 are on hand, what is the necessary adjusting entry?

9. If the following accounts are found in the adjusted trial balance on a worksheet, indicate by placing a checkmark (✓) under the remaining columns where their balance will be placed. Assume they all have their normal balance.

	Income Statement		Balance Sheet	
	Debit	Credit	Debit	Credit
Example: CASH			✓	
Service Fees				
Accounts Receivable				
FICA Taxes Payable				
Salary Expense				
Sarah Clark, Capital				
Rent Expense				
Office Equipment				
Accumulated Depreciation— Office Equipment				

10. Which of the following accounts will appear in the post-closing trial balance? Indicate by checking (✓) yes or no.

Account Title	Yes	No
Accumulated Depreciation—Office Equipment		
Cash		
Salary Expense		
Accounts Payable		
Accounts Receivable		
Don Jones, Drawing		
Income Summary		

PROBLEMS

9–1. C. H. Marlowe is an electrician. Shown below is Marlowe's December 31, 1987, trial balance.

C. H. MARLOWE
Trial Balance
December 31, 1987

Account No.	Account Title	Debit	Credit
111	Cash	$ 2,200	
121	Electrical supplies	3,750	
131	Office equipment	600	
141	Accumulated depreciation—office equipment		$ 90
151	Truck.	4,600	
161	Accumulated depreciation—truck . . .		880
211	Accounts payable.		1,200
311	C. H. Marlowe, capital		5,700
321	C. H. Marlowe, drawing	12,500	
411	Electrician revenue		17,000
511	Advertising expense	600	
541	Maintenance expense	350	
551	Miscellaneous expense	270	
		$24,870	$24,870

Required:

1. Prepare a 10-column worksheet. Use the following information for adjustments:
   a. The useful life of the office equipment is 10 years. The salvage value is zero.
   b. The useful life of the truck is 8 years. Depreciation Expense is account no. 521. The salvage value is zero.
   c. An inventory indicates that $1,350 worth of electrical supplies are on hand at the end of the year. Electrical Supplies Expense is account no. 531.
2. For the year ended December 31, 1987, prepare:
   a. An income statement.
   b. A statement of owner's equity.
   c. A balance sheet for December 31, 1987.

9–2. J. Wiley owns a health club. Shown below is Wiley's December 31, 1987, trial balance.

J. WILEY
Trial Balance
December 31, 1987

Account No.	Account Title	Debit	Credit
110	Cash.	$ 4,000	
120	Office supplies	400	
130	Exercise equipment.	70,000	
140	Accumulated depreciation—exercise equipment		$ 14,000
150	Building	80,000	
160	Accumulated depreciation—building.		12,000
210	Unearned health contracts		10,000
220	Loan payable.		65,000
310	J. Wiley, capital.		52,400
320	J. Wiley, drawing	12,000	
410	Revenue from health club contracts.		60,000
510	Utilities expense.	3,600	
520	Salaries expense.	41,600	
530	Advertising expense	1,800	
		$213,400	$213,400

Required:

1. Record the following adjustments in general journal form:
   a. The useful life is 10 years for exercise equipment. Depreciation Expense—Exercise Equipment is account no. 540. The salvage value is zero.
   b. The useful life is 20 years for the building. Depreciation Expense—Building is account no. 550. The salvage value is zero.
   c. Office supplies on hand, $180. Supplies Expense is account no. 560.

2. Prepare an adjusted trial balance for December 31, 1987.

9–3. Robert West owns and operates West's TV and Radio Repair Shop. His trial balance for December 31, 1987, is shown below:

WEST'S TV AND RADIO REPAIR SHOP
Trial Balance
December 31, 1987

Account No.	Account Title	Debit	Credit
100	Cash	$ 2,600	
120	Shop equipment	1,000	
130	Accumulated depreciation—shop equipment		$ 500
140	Truck	3,000	
150	Accumulated depreciation—truck . . .		1,200
200	Accounts payable		400
210	Employees income tax payable		120
220	FICA tax payable		80
300	Robert West, capital		5,000
310	Robert West, drawing	8,675	
400	TV repair revenue		15,000
410	Radio repair revenue		4,000
500	Salary expense	5,000	
510	Payroll tax expense	800	
520	Rent expense	2,100	
540	Shop supplies expense	3,000	
550	Miscellaneous expense	125	
		$26,300	$26,300

Required:

1. Prepare a 10-column worksheet with the following adjustments:
   a. Shop equipment 10-year useful life. The salvage value is zero.
   b. Truck, 5 year useful life. Depreciation Expense is account no. 530. The salvage value is zero.
   c. Shop supplies on hand, $1,700. Shop Supplies is account no. 110.
2. Prepare an income statement for the year ended December 31, 1987.
3. Prepare a statement of owner's equity for the year ended December 31, 1987.
4. Prepare a balance sheet for December 31, 1987.
5. Prepare the adjusting and closing entries.

9–4. The trial balance for Shermer's Hot Dog Stand for the fiscal year ended September 30, 1987 is shown below:

SHERMER'S HOT DOG STAND
Trial Balance
September 30, 1987

Account No.	Account Title	Debit	Credit
110	Cash	$ 2,500	
120	Food and beverages	400	
130	Truck	26,000	
140	Accumulated depreciation—truck		$10,400
210	Accounts payable		400
220	Loan payable		15,000
310	M. Shermer, capital		8,800
320	M. Shermer, drawing.	15,000	
410	Revenue from food sales.		9,000
420	Revenue from beverage sales		4,600
510	Food and beverage expense.	4,100	
520	Miscellaneous expense	200	
		$48,200	$48,200

Required:

1. Prepare a 10-column worksheet with the following adjustments:
   a. Truck, 10-year useful life. Depreciation Expense is account no. 530. The salvage value is zero.
   b. Food and beverages on hand, $50.
2. Prepare an income statement for the year ended September 30, 1987.
3. Prepare a statement of owner's equity for the year ended September 30, 1987.
4. Prepare a balance sheet for September 30, 1987.
5. Prepare the adjusting and closing entries.

9–5. The December 31, 1987, trial balance for Sandra Gibbs' Dance Studio is shown below:

SANDRA GIBBS' DANCE STUDIO
Trial Balance
December 31, 1987

Account No.	Account Title	Debit	Credit
107	Cash	$ 3,000	
112	Office equipment	10 600	
117	Accumulated depreciation—office equipment.		$ 240
122	Automobile	5,000	
127	Accumulated depreciation—automobile. .		1,500
207	FICA taxes payable		20
212	Employees' income taxes payable. . . .		40
307	Sandra Gibbs, capital.		4,000
312	Sandra Gibbs, drawing	10,500	
407	Dance contracts revenue.		22,500
507	Salary expense	5,600	
512	Payroll tax expense	600	
517	Advertising expense	200	
522	Automobile expense	250	
527	Rent expense	2,400	
537	Miscellaneous expense	150	
		$28,300	$28,300

Required:

1. Prepare a 10-column worksheet for the year ended December 31, 1987. Estimated useful lives are 10 years for the office equipment and 5 years for the automobile. Depreciation Expense is account no. 532. The salvage value is zero.
2. Prepare an income statement for the year ended December 31, 1987.
3. Prepare a statement of owner's equity for the year ended December 31, 1987.
4. Prepare a balance sheet for December 31, 1987.
5. Prepare adjusting and closing entries.

9–6.

M. ECKSTEIN—SOCIAL PSYCHOLOGIST
Trial Balance
December 31, 1987

Account No.	Account Title	Debit	Credit
100	Cash	$ 2,000	
110	Office supplies	300	
120	Furniture and fixtures	10,000	
130	Accumulated depreciation— furniture and fixtures		$ 3,000
200	Loan payable		5,000
300	M. Eckstein, capital		20,600
310	M. Eckstein, drawing	70,000	
400	Revenue from individual counseling. .		52,500
410	Revenue from group counseling . . .		64,000
500	Salary expense	22,000	
510	Rent expense	36,000	
530	Utilities expense	4,800	
		$145,100	$145,100

Required:

1. Prepare a 10-column worksheet with the following adjustments:
   a. Office supplies worth $100 were on hand at year-end. Supplies Expense is account no. 520.
   b. The furniture and fixtures have a useful life of 10 years. Depreciation Expense is account no. 540. The salvage value is zero.
2. Prepare an income statement for the year ended December 31, 1987.
3. Prepare a statement of owner's equity for the year ended December 31, 1987.
4. Prepare a balance sheet on December 31, 1987.

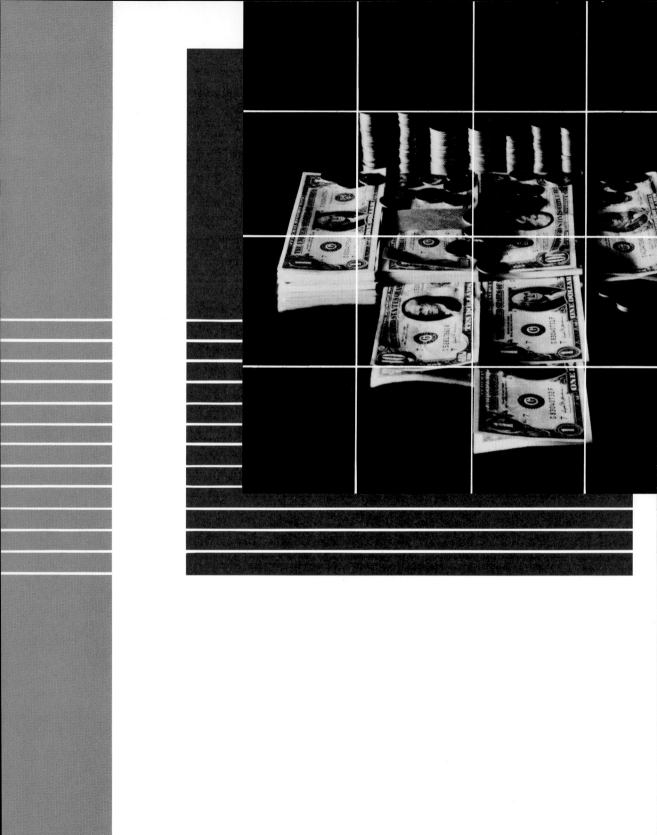

CHAPTER 10

Cash records

LEARNING OBJECTIVES

In Chapter 5, you learned how to use a checking account to control a firm's receipt and payment of cash. In this chapter, you will learn how to use special cash receipt and cash disbursement journals to facilitate the recording of cash received and paid. After studying this chapter, you should be able to:

1. Record transactions in a cash receipts journal.
2. Total and rule the cash receipts journal at the end of the month.
3. Post the cash receipts transactions to ledger accounts.
4. Record transactions in a cash disbursements journal.
5. Total and rule the cash disbursements journal at the end of the month.
6. Post the cash disbursements transactions to ledger accounts.

Chapter 5 discussed the use of cash in a business and the importance of controlling both the receipt and the disbursement, or payment, of cash. Most firms keep their cash in a checking account in a bank or a savings and loan association. The procedures for setting up such an account were also discussed in Chapter 5.

In this chapter, we will discuss how to account for both cash receipts and cash disbursements in the company journals. As an important safeguard, company policy should ensure that a person who has access to the firm's cash should not have access to any of the firm's journals. When the duties of handling cash and recording cash transactions are divided, there is less risk of cash being stolen from the firm.

CASH RECEIPTS

One means of verifying cash receipts is to have an employee who collects cash, such as a salesclerk or receptionist, make two lists of all cash receipts. One copy of the list remains with the receipts until a deposit is made. The other copy is sent to the person who records the receipts of cash in the journal. The deposit slip is verified by comparing it with the list of actual receipts. The list should include the name of the party from whom the cash was received, the date, the form (currency or check), and the amount. In addition, formal receipts can be prepared in duplicate, with the original given to the customer and the copy to the bookkeeper. When cash receipts are numerous, they may be recorded in a cash register, with the cash register tape providing the list of receipts. Regardless of the method used, the bookkeeper should not handle the cash. The temptation to steal the cash and attempt to conceal the theft by altering the accounting records may be too great.

CASH DISBURSEMENTS

A disbursement, or payment, may be made either by currency or by check. It is usually better to use checks because they can serve as receipts for payments. If currency is used, a separate receipt is an absolute necessity. Furthermore, if currency is used, the amount kept on hand may have to be very large; this increases the importance of preventing theft. There must be very tight control over the currency.

SPECIAL JOURNALS

As you will recall, a journal is the book of original entry. Up to this point, we have used two kinds of journals—the general journal and the combined journal. But a business often uses several special journals too. Normally, a given transaction is recorded in *only one journal*. If certain kinds of transactions occur frequently, a special journal may be designed to permit easy recording of them.

THE CASH RECEIPTS JOURNAL

When the volume of cash receipts is very large, a **cash receipts journal** should be used. This journal is used to record transactions that involve only the receipt of cash. The exact form of this special journal will vary according to the nature and size of a firm, but the example presented in Illustration 10–1 is typical. The number of special columns (such as Sales and Accounts Receivable) depends largely on the preference of the individual firm. If any other accounts are used frequently in cash receipts transactions, they are likely to have their own columns in the cash receipts journal.

ILLUSTRATION 10–1

CASH RECEIPTS JOURNAL									PAGE
DATE	ACCOUNT	CASH DEBIT	SALES CREDIT	ACCOUNTS RECEIVABLE CREDIT	P.R.	GENERAL	P.R.	DEBIT	CREDIT

The cash receipts journal records only transactions that involve the receipt of cash. All other transactions are recorded in the general journal or in other special journals that the firm may use. These other journals will be discussed later in this chapter and in Chapters 11 and 12.

To illustrate the use of a cash receipts journal, we will examine the cash receipt transactions of Vic's Video Supplies for the beginning of August. In summary, they were:

	Date	Transaction
	1987	
Aug.	1	Cash sales of $1,250.
	4	Acme Company paid $500 on its account.
	5	Bestever Company paid $700 on its account.
	5	Sold office equipment for $900 cash. The same equipment was purchased earlier this year for $900.
	6	Cash sales of $1,000.
	8	Sold $100 of Vic's office supplies to a firm in the next suite of offices. The supplies had cost $100.

Vic sells his supplies for cash or on account. Thus he has only three special account columns in his cash receipts journal. Cash is a debit for every transaction recorded in this journal. The Sales Credit and the Accounts Receivable Credit columns are for the two primary sources of cash. Any other transaction that involves the receipt of cash is recorded in the General Debit or Credit columns.

As shown in Illustration 10–2, Vic records the day's receipts for cash sales by placing the amount in both the Cash Debit column and Sales Credit column. The company collected $1,250 in cash sales on the first day of August. Note that the debit and the credit are

ILLUSTRATION 10–2

			CASH RECEIPTS JOURNAL						PAGE 15	
DATE 1987		ACCOUNT	CASH DEBIT	SALES CREDIT	ACCOUNTS RECEIVABLE CREDIT	P.R.	GENERAL	P.R.	DEBIT	CREDIT
➤ Aug.	1	Cash sales	1 2 5 0 00	1 2 5 0 00						

ILLUSTRATION 10–3

DATE 1987		ACCOUNT	CASH DEBIT	SALES CREDIT	ACCOUNTS RECEIVABLE CREDIT	P.R.	GENERAL	P.R.	DEBIT	CREDIT
Aug.	1	Cash sales	1 2 5 0 00	1 2 5 0 00						
	4	Acme Co.	5 0 0 00		5 0 0 00					

CASH RECEIPTS JOURNAL — PAGE 15

both written on the same line. The nature of the transaction is written in the Account column, while the titles of the accounts to debit and credit appear as separate column heads.

Illustration 10–3 shows the entry made to record that Acme Company paid $500 on its account. Accounts Receivable was debited at the time that Acme was billed for its purchase because an Account Receivable is an asset account representing a promise to pay at a later date. In the transaction on August 4, Acme Company paid part of their account. Thus, Accounts Receivable must now be credited. The company's name is written in the Account column and the amount of $500 is entered in both the Cash Debit column (to show that cash was received) and the Accounts Receivable Credit column.

Both transactions for August 5 are shown in Illustration 10–4. Bestever Company paid $700 on account, so this transaction is re-

ILLUSTRATION 10–4

DATE 1987		ACCOUNT	CASH DEBIT	SALES CREDIT	ACCOUNTS RECEIVABLE CREDIT	P.R.	GENERAL	P.R.	DEBIT	CREDIT
Aug.	1	Cash sales	1 2 5 0 00	1 2 5 0 00						
	4	Acme Co.	5 0 0 00		5 0 0 00					
	5	Bestever Co.	7 0 0 00		7 0 0 00					
	5	Sold office equipment	9 0 0 00				Office equipment			9 0 0 00

CASH RECEIPTS JOURNAL — PAGE 15

corded just like the payment from Acme Company. The sale of office equipment for $900, original cost, is handled differently, however. The explanation of the sale is written in the Account column and its sales price of $900 is placed in the Cash Debit column. Then the account title, Office Equipment, is written in the General column and the amount of $900 is placed in the General Credit column.

Illustration 10–5 shows the rest of Vic's transactions for the period. On August 6, cash sales totaled $1,000. Cash is debited for the $1,000 and Sales is credited for the same amount. On August 8, Vic helped out the firm in the next suite of offices by selling them some office supplies. The transaction's explanation is written in the Account column and the amount received, $100, is recorded as a debit to Cash. Then the account title Office Supplies is written in the General column and the $100 sale price is recorded in the General Credit column.

Illustration 10–5 is also a summary of all of Vic's transactions. In each transaction the receipt of cash was recorded by placing the amount in the Cash Debit column. When the cash was received for sales, the amount was recorded in the special Sales Credit column. When the cash received represented a collection on an account receivable, the amount was entered in the special Accounts Receivable Credit column. No special columns are included in the journal for recording the credit part of the entries for the sale of equipment or office supplies. Thus, the titles of the accounts credited were written in the column headed General. This column is used whenever an entry must be made in an account for which a special column does not exist.

Again note that the account title Cash does not have to be written in the Account column, nor do the account titles for other common

ILLUSTRATION 10–5

DATE 1987		ACCOUNT	CASH DEBIT	SALES CREDIT	ACCOUNTS RECEIVABLE CREDIT	P.R.	GENERAL	P.R.	DEBIT	CREDIT
Aug.	1	Cash sales	1 2 5 0 00	1 2 5 0 00						
	4	Acme Co.	5 0 0 00		5 0 0 00					
	5	Bestever Co.	7 0 0 00		7 0 0 00					
	5	Sold office equipment	9 0 0 00				Office equipment			9 0 0 00
	6	Cash sales	1 0 0 0 00	1 0 0 0 00						
	8	Sold office supplies	1 0 0 00				Office supplies			1 0 0 00

CASH RECEIPTS JOURNAL   PAGE 15

transactions, such as cash received from sales and collections on accounts receivable, need to be written. This can save a substantial amount of time.

The subsidiary ledger

Individual accounts must be maintained for the people who owe money as Accounts Receivable because it is important to be able to determine at any point in time how much a customer owes. Thus a subsidiary ledger entitled *Accounts Receivable* is maintained. A **subsidiary ledger** is a group of supporting records that show the details of the balance of an account in the general ledger. The balance in Accounts Receivable in the general ledger represents the total of the individual customer accounts found in the subsidiary ledger. Since it is supported by detailed information in a subsidiary ledger, Accounts Receivable is called a **control account**. At Vic's Video Supplies, the subsidiary ledger would contain detailed accounts for the Acme Company and the Bestever Company. Subsidiary ledgers will be explained in more detail in Chapter 11.

Posting the cash receipts journal

At any time during the month, the individual items in the General column may be posted to the appropriate accounts in the general ledger. At that time, the account number is written in the P.R. (Posting Reference) column of the cash receipts journal. At the same time, the page number and the journal name (CR for cash receipts journal) are placed in the P.R. column of the account to show the source of the entry. Once again the system of cross-referencing is used to allow easy tracing of entries.

At regular intervals, often daily or weekly, the individual amounts recorded in the Accounts Receivable Credit column are posted to the subsidiary ledger accounts. A check mark ($\checkmark$) is recorded in the P.R. column to indicate that the amount has been posted to the individual subsidiary account. The page number and the journal name (CR) are placed in the P.R. column of the account to show the source of the entry. For example, as shown in Illustration 10–6, $500 was posted to Acme Company's individual account in the subsidiary ledger. A check mark was then placed in the P.R. column of the cash receipts journal. CR 15 was placed in the P.R. column of the subsidiary ledger account to indicate that the posting is complete for this item.

ILLUSTRATION 10–6

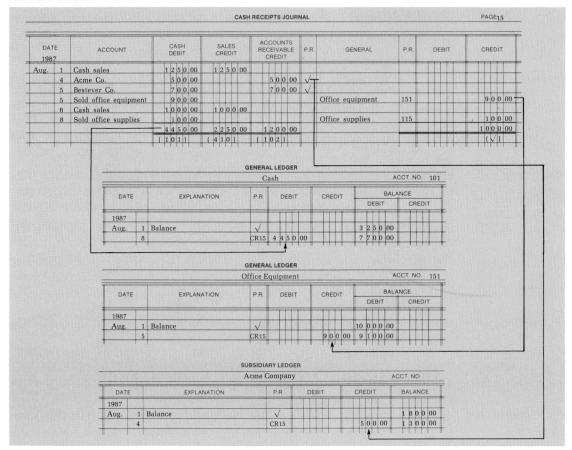

All columns are usually footed and ruled at the end of the month. Before posting, the columns should be proved to make sure that total debits equal total credits. In Illustration 10–6, the debit total is $4,450. The total of the credit columns ($2,250 + $1,200 + $1,000) equals $4,450. The totals of the special columns are posted to the appropriate general ledger accounts. For example, the total of the Accounts Receivable Credit column is posted to the general ledger account Accounts Receivable. When a column total is posted, the appropriate account number is placed below the total in that column to show that it has been posted. The journal page number and initials are placed in the posting reference column of the ledger account. As was true in the posting of the combined journal, the totals in the General columns are not posted because they do not represent a single account. The items in these columns have already been posted individually to the general ledger. A check mark under the total indicates that it is not posted as a total.

Illustration 10–6 shows how the process of posting from the cash receipts journal to some sample general ledger and subsidiary ledger accounts would look. Note the cross-referencing. The totals of the Sales and Accounts Receivable columns would be posted to the general ledger accounts. The amount of $100 for Office Supplies would be posted to the general ledger account just as the $900 was posted to Office Equipment. In the subsidiary ledger, Bestever Company would be credited for $700 as Acme Company was credited for $500. Appropriate account numbers and check marks would be recorded.

To summarize:

1. Entries from the cash receipts journal should be posted to the subsidiary ledger daily, weekly, or monthly. A check mark is placed in the P.R. column and the cash receipts journal page number and initials are written in the subsidiary account's P.R. column.

2. Entries listed in the General column are posted daily, weekly or monthly. Each general ledger account number is written in the P.R. column of the journal and the journal page number and initials are written in the P.R. column of the ledger account.

3. Columns are totaled to prove that total debits equal total credits. The columns are then ruled and double ruled.

4. Special account columns are posted in total to their respective general ledger accounts. The ledger account number is written in parentheses below the total to indicate that the total has been posted. In the ledger, the page number and initials of the journal are recorded in the P.R. column.

5. A check mark is placed under the totals in the General Debit and Credit columns to indicate that these amounts are not posted in total.

THE CASH DISBURSEMENTS JOURNAL

A firm's volume of transactions involving cash payments may dictate the need for a **cash disbursements journal.** This journal is used to record only transactions involving the disbursement of cash. As in the case of the cash receipts journal, this will save time in recording and posting. It may also allow the division of labor: one person may be responsible for recording all cash receipts, while another person may be responsible for recording all cash disbursements.

The exact form of a cash disbursements journal varies according to the size and nature of a business and its need for accounting information. The number of special columns for individual accounts in the cash disbursements journal can vary from firm to firm. Illustration 10–7 shows a page from the cash disbursements journal for Vic's Video Supplies. Note that Vic has only one special column in addition to the Cash column. In reality, most firms will usually have many more. If an account is used quite frequently in cash disbursements, it usually has its own column in the cash disbursements journal.

The cash disbursements journal records only transactions involving cash disbursements. To illustrate the use of such a journal, we will examine some typical cash disbursements for Vic's Video Supplies for the beginning of August. We will assume that all transactions are paid by check. In summary the transactions were:

Date	Check No.	Transaction
1987		
Aug. 1	302	Paid $120 for newspaper advertising.
4	303	Paid $600 to Xerxes Company for supplies purchased earlier on credit.
4	304	Paid $700 on account to Yellow Company.
8	305	Paid $3,200 for equipment.
8	306	Paid $500 on account to Zed Company.

Each transaction involves a payment of cash, so the dollar amount is recorded in the Cash Credit column. The debit portion of the entry usually involves the payment of an amount that was billed to the company at a earlier date (Accounts Payable), the incurrence of an expense, or the acquisition of an asset.

The August 1 transaction involves payment for advertising in the newspaper. Note in Illustration 10–8 that the year, month, and day are first recorded. The check no., 302, is written in the Check Number column, and the $120 payment is recorded in the Cash Credit column. The account title Advertising Expense is then entered in the General column and the dollar amount is entered in the corresponding Debit column.

Cash must be Credited

ILLUSTRATION 10–7

DATE	CHECK NO.	ACCOUNT	CASH CREDIT	ACCOUNTS PAYABLE DEBIT	P.R.	GENERAL	P.R.	DEBIT	CREDIT
CASH DISBURSEMENTS JOURNAL									PAGE

Illustration 10–9 shows the August 4 payment to Xerxes Company for supplies that were purchased on account at an earlier date. The day is written in and the name of the company being paid, Xerxes Company, is written in the Account column. The amount of $600 is written in the Cash Credit column and $600 is recorded in the Accounts Payable Debit column. The check number is recorded in the Check Number column.

The second August 4 transaction, shown in Illustration 10–10, is identical to the first August 4 transaction. This time the Yellow Company is being paid for a purchase made at an earlier date. Again the day is recorded, the name of the company is written in the Account column and the amount of $700 is entered in both the Cash Credit

ILLUSTRATION 10–8

DATE 1987	CHECK NO.	ACCOUNT	CASH CREDIT	ACCOUNTS PAYABLE DEBIT	P.R.	GENERAL	P.R.	DEBIT	CREDIT
CASH DISBURSEMENTS JOURNAL									PAGE 14
Aug. 1	302		1 2 0 00			Advertising Exp.		1 2 0 00	

ILLUSTRATION 10–9

DATE 1987		CHECK NO.	ACCOUNT	CASH CREDIT	ACCOUNTS PAYABLE DEBIT	P.R.	GENERAL	P.R.	DEBIT	CREDIT
							CASH DISBURSEMENTS JOURNAL			PAGE 14
Aug.	1	302		1 2 0 00			Advertising Exp.		1 2 0 00	
	4	303	Xerxes Co.	6 0 0 00	6 0 0 00					

column and the Accounts Payable Debit column. The check number is also entered in the appropriate column.

Store equipment was purchased on August 8. As shown in Illustration 10–11, after the day and check number are recorded, the amount of $3,200 is entered in the Cash Credit column. Then, the account to be debited, Equipment, is entered in the General column and the amount of $3,200 is entered in the General Debit column.

The last transaction shown in Illustration 10–12, is the payment to Zed Company of $500 on account. As with the payments to the Xerxes and Yellow Companies, the company name and the amount paid are entered in the appropriate columns, as are the day and check number.

Posting the cash disbursements journal

Posting the cash disbursements journal is similar to posting the cash receipts journal. At intervals during the month, the items in

ILLUSTRATION 10–10

DATE 1987		CHECK NO.	ACCOUNT	CASH CREDIT	ACCOUNTS PAYABLE DEBIT	P.R.	GENERAL	P.R.	DEBIT	CREDIT
							CASH DISBURSEMENTS JOURNAL			PAGE 14
Aug.	1	302		1 2 0 00			Advertising Exp.		1 2 0 00	
	4	303	Xerxes Co.	6 0 0 00	6 0 0 00					
	4	304	Yellow Co.	7 0 0 00	7 0 0 00					

ILLUSTRATION 10–11

					CASH DISBURSEMENTS JOURNAL					PAGE 14	
DATE 1987	CHECK NO.	ACCOUNT	CASH CREDIT	ACCOUNTS PAYABLE DEBIT	P.R.	GENERAL	P.R.	DEBIT	CREDIT		
Aug. 1	302		1 2 0 00			Advertising Exp.		1 2 0 00			
4	303	Xerxes Co.	6 0 0 00	6 0 0 00							
4	304	Yellow Co.	7 0 0 00	7 0 0 00							
8	305		3 2 0 0 00			Equipment		3 2 0 0 00			

the General accounts column are posted to the general ledger accounts. The account number of each account posted is placed in the P.R. column of the Cash Disbursements Journal after the account is posted. A coding for the appropriate journal name (CD) and the page number are placed in the P.R. column of the ledger account at the same time.

Similar to the subsidiary accounts receivable ledger, a subsidiary accounts payable ledger must be maintained. The individual amounts in the Accounts Payable Debit column are posted to the subsidiary accounts at frequent intervals, daily if possible. Frequent posting is necessary if a company wants current information about its transactions with creditors. A check is placed in the P.R. column of the journal and CD plus the page number are placed in the ledger P.R. column.

ILLUSTRATION 10–12

					CASH DISBURSEMENTS JOURNAL					PAGE 14	
DATE 1987	CHECK NO.	ACCOUNT	CASH CREDIT	ACCOUNTS PAYABLE DEBIT	P.R.	GENERAL	P.R.	DEBIT	CREDIT		
Aug. 1	302		1 2 0 00			Advertising Exp.		1 2 0 00			
4	303	Xerxes Co.	6 0 0 00	6 0 0 00							
4	304	Yellow Co.	7 0 0 00	7 0 0 00							
8	305		3 2 0 0 00			Equipment		3 2 0 0 00			
8	306	Zed Co.	5 0 0 00	5 0 0 00							

ILLUSTRATION 10–13

DATE 1987		CHECK NO.	ACCOUNT	CASH CREDIT	ACCOUNTS PAYABLE DEBIT	P.R.	GENERAL	P.R.	DEBIT	CREDIT
Aug.	1	302		1 2 0 00			Advertising Exp.		1 2 0 00	
	4	303	Xerxes Co.	6 0 0 00	6 0 0 00					
	4	304	Yellow Co.	7 0 0 00	7 0 0 00					
	8	305		3 2 0 0 00			Equipment		3 2 0 0 00	
	8	306	Zed Co.	5 0 0 00	5 0 0 00					
				5 1 2 0 00	1 8 0 0 00				3 3 2 0 00	

All columns are usually footed and ruled at the end of the month. Before posting, the columns should be proved to make sure that total debits equal total credits. In Illustration 10–13, the totals of the debit columns ($1,800 + $3,320) equal $5,120, which is the total of the one credit column, Cash, that contains a balance.

The totals of the individual special account columns are posted to their respective accounts in the ledger. As each total is posted, the account number is written below the column total. Likewise, the appropriate journal name and page number are recorded in the ledger account P.R. column. The *total* of the Accounts Payable Debit column is posted to the Accounts Payable account in the general ledger. The *totals* for the General Accounts columns are not posted; rather, the individual items are posted to the specific accounts named.

Illustration 10–14 shows the posting of Vic's Video's first two transactions for August. For the first transaction, the date is written in the Advertising Expense account in the general ledger. Next, the amount of $120 is posted in the Debit column and extended to the Debit Balance column. Then, CD 14 is written in the P.R. column to indicate that this transaction is found on page 14 of the cash disbursements journal. Finally, in the cash disbursements journal, the Advertising Expense account number, 512, is placed in the General P.R. column to indicate that the posting of this account is complete.

The payment of $600 to Xerxes Company is posted by finding Xerxes Company's account in the subsidiary accounts payable ledger. The date is written in the ledger account Date column and the $600 is posted to the Debit column. Since an account payable is a liability, this account usually has a credit balance. To compute the new balance, the $600 debit is subtracted from the $800 credit balance, and the amount owed is reduced to $200. CD 14 is placed in the P.R. column of the ledger account and a check mark (√) is placed in the P.R. column of the cash disbursements journal to indicate that posting is complete for the Xerxes Company.

Illustration 10–14 also shows how the total of $5,120 in the Cash

ILLUSTRATION 10–14

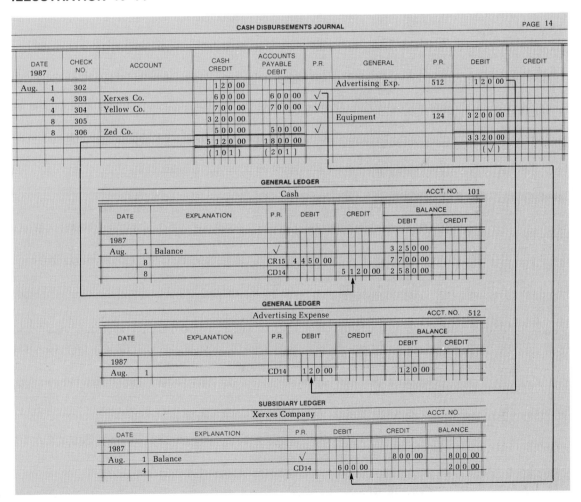

Credit column would be posted to the Cash account in the general ledger. First, the day of the posting is entered in the date column, and the total amount of cash, $5,120, is posted to the Cash Credit column. Since cash, an asset, normally has a debit balance, the $5,120 credit is subtracted from the debit balance of $7,700, leaving a debit balance of $2,580. The page number of the cash disbursements journal is written in the P.R. column of the ledger account, and the Cash account number (101) is written below the total in the Cash column in the cash disbursements journal. This indicates that this total has been posted to the proper account. The same procedure would be followed for the other ledger accounts.

SUMMARY

Special journals facilitate the recording of transactions because all transactions of a similar kind can be recorded in one place without repeatedly writing the same account titles. For example, cash receipts and cash disbursements are two kinds of transactions that occur frequently in most businesses. Therefore, a separate, special journal is often used for each.

A **cash receipts journal** can be used to record all cash coming into a business. Special columns are set up for cash debits and the most frequent sources of cash, usually from cash sales and the collection of accounts receivable. A separate pair of General Debit and Credit columns are also maintained to record the receipt of cash from transactions other than cash sales or collections on account.

The **cash disbursements journal** provides a credit column for cash since only cash disbursements are entered in this journal. A special debit column for Accounts Payable is established, and a pair of General Debit and Credit columns are maintained.

The use of these special journals eliminates the need for writing certain account titles every time cash is received or paid. The following steps should be followed in keeping these journals:

1. Enter the year, month, and day in the Date column on the first page used in each special journal for the first transaction recorded in that month. After the first transaction, enter only the day.
2. When cash is received, enter the dollar amount in the Cash

Debit column in the cash receipts journal. Then write the dollar amount on the same line in the proper credit column, depending on the source of the cash.

3. When cash is paid, enter the dollar amount in the Cash Credit column in the cash disbursements journal. Enter the amount of the debit on the same line as the cash credit in the proper debit column.

4. Daily or weekly post the individual Accounts Receivable or Accounts Payable amounts to the subsidiary ledger accounts. Place a check mark (√) in the journal P.R. column and the journal designation and page number in the P.R. column of the subsidiary account.

5. At the end of the page, or at the end of the month, foot each column to prove that the sum of the debit columns is equal to the sum of the credit columns.

6. After proving, place a double rule under the totals in the columns.

7. Post the totals of the special columns to the corresponding accounts in the general ledger. Place the general ledger account number in parentheses under the proper account title column. Then place the page number of either the cash receipts (CR) or the cash disbursements (CD) journal in the ledger account's P.R. column.

8. Post each individual amount in the General Debit and Credit columns to the appropriate ledger account. Place the ledger account number in the P.R. column. The cash receipts or cash disbursements journal page number should be listed in the P.R. column of the ledger account along with the designation of CR or CD.

9. Place a check mark (√) in parentheses under the total amounts of the General Debit and Credit columns to indicate that these amounts are not posted in total.

A **subsidiary ledger** is used to provide more detailed information about the balance of an account in the general ledger. A subsidiary ledger titled *Accounts Receivable* would contain a separate account for each customer who owes money to the company. An account that is supported by a detailed subsidiary ledger, such as Accounts Receivable, is called a **control account.** Another control account is Accounts Payable. Its subsidiary ledger would contain a separate account for each creditor to whom the company owes money.

KEY TERMS

Cash Disbursements Journal—A special journal used when the volume of cash transactions is quite large to record only transactions involving cash disbursements.

Cash Receipts Journal—A special journal used when the volume of cash transactions is quite large to record only transactions involving cash receipts.

Control Account—A general ledger account that is supported by detailed information in a subsidiary ledger.

Subsidiary Ledger—A group of supporting records that provide detailed information about the balance of a general ledger control account.

QUESTIONS AND EXERCISES

1. What is the purpose of a special journal?
2. Describe a cash receipts journal. What advantage results from using this special journal?
3. Describe a cash disbursements journal. What advantage results from using this special journal?
4. What is a control account in the general ledger?
5. What is a subsidiary ledger?
6. Explain the procedure for posting the cash receipts journal at the end of the month.
7. What does a check mark (√) beneath the totals in the General columns of the cash receipts or cash disbursements journal signify?
8. Why is a General Debit and Credit column maintained in these special journals?

PROBLEMS

10–1. B. R. Johnson Company had the following cash receipts during the month of April 1987.

1987

Apr. 1 Received a check in payment of an account from A. L. White for $1,550.

Apr. 5 Counted cash at the end of the day from the cash register for sales totaling $198.

7 B. R. Johnson put an additional $375 into the business.

10 Received a check from the Nash Company in payment of an account, $420.

16 Counted cash at the end of the day from the cash register for sales totaling $308.

23 Received a check for $770 from H. J. Smith in payment of an account.

27 Cash sales were $85.

28 Received a check for $265 from H. H. Coleson in payment of an account.

Required:

Journalize the transactions in the cash receipts journal and total and rule at the end of the month.

10–2. Wilton John's Company completed the following cash disbursements during July 1987:

Date	Check No.	Transactions	
1987			
July 1	301	Purchased a typewriter.	$ 450
3	302	Paid rent for the month	500
5	303	Purchased an office desk	300
8	304	Purchased an adding machine	125
15	305	Paid an account payable to X Co.	255
18	306	Owner withdrew cash	250
22	307	Paid for telephone	85
25	308	Paid wages.	475
29	309	Purchased a calculator	850
29	310	Paid an account payable to W Co.	1,250

Required:

Journalize the transactions in the cash disbursements journal and total and rule at the end of the month.

10–3. W. W. Thrower, contractor, began operations on June 1, 1987. On this date Thrower invested $5,000 cash in the operations. In addition to this initial investment, Thrower completed the following transactions during the month of June:

1987

June 1   Paid rent for June, $450, check no. 101.

 3   Received a check from Spots, Inc., for services rendered, $385.

 5   Paid telephone bill, $85, check no. 102.

 7   Paid utility bill, $125, check no. 103.

10   Received a check from Wonder World for services rendered, $875.

11   Withdrew $350 for personal use, check no. 104.

12   Received a check from J. D. Swift for services rendered, $1,875.

15   Paid secretary for the first half of the month, $325, check no. 105.

20   Received a check from C. O. Dunn for services rendered, $1,250.

21   Withdrew $500 for personal use, check, no. 106.

25   Paid Janitorial Service $50 for cleaning the office, check no. 107.

27   Received a check from A. B. Thompson for services rendered, $650.

29   Paid secretary's salary for the second half of the month, $325, check no. 108.

29   Withdrew $800 for personal use, check no. 109.

Thrower established a chart of accounts as follows:

Account No.	Account Title
101	Cash
310	W. W. Thrower, Capital
311	W. W. Thrower, Drawing
410	Professional Fees
510	Utilities Expense
515	Telephone Expense
520	Rent Expense
525	Salary Expense
530	Miscellaneous Expense

Required:

1. Journalize the above transactions in the proper journal, using a cash receipts and cash disbursements journal.

2. Total and rule each column.

3. Open ledger accounts and post the journal entries.

4. Prepare a trial balance.

 10–4. T. S. Hill invested $7,000 in his new counseling practice on August 1, 1987. As well as making this investment, Hill completed the following transactions during August:

1987

Aug. 1   Paid rent for August, $385, check no. 101.

3   Received $160 from C. R. Cross for services rendered.

4   Paid $55 for miscellaneous supplies, check no. 102.

10   Received $145 from J. L. Home for services rendered.

12   Withdrew $500 for personal use, check no. 103.

15   Paid receptionist's salary, $280, check no. 104.

15   Paid telephone bill for July, $75, check no. 105.

18   Received a check, $120, from Jack Cole for services rendered.

21   Received $130 from B. H. Hunter for services rendered.

22   Paid water bill, $15, check no. 106.

23   Received for services, $75 cash.

25   Received a check from R. L. Brown, $85 for services rendered.

27   Paid $30 for temporary office help, check no. 107.

28   Received $135 from B. R. Frank for services rendered.

30   Paid the receptionist's salary, $280, check no. 108.

30   Paid the electricity bill, $98, check no. 109.

Hill's ledger included the following accounts:

Account No.	Account Title
101	Cash
310	T. S. Hill, Capital
320	T. S. Hill, Drawing
401	Fees Earned
501	Rent Expense
505	Salaries Expense
511	Telephone Expense
515	Utilities Expense
521	Miscellaneous Expense

Required:

1. Journalize the above transactions in either the cash receipts or cash disbursements journal.

2. Total and rule each column.

3. Open ledger accounts and post the journal entries.

4. Prepare a trial balance.

10–5. Frances Thorne, a consulting forester, invested $8,000 cash in the operations of a new business. In addition to this initial investment, Thorne completed the following transactions during the month of September:

1987

Sept. 1 Paid the September rent, $480, check no. 101.

2 Received a check for services rendered, $125.

4 Purchased office supplies, $85, check no. 102.

7 Received a check from G. H. Hunter for services rendered, $275.

10 Withdrew $200 for personal use, check no. 103.

12 Received a check from A. D. Easley for services rendered, $130.

15 Paid part-time secretary's salary for first half of the month, $260, check no. 104.

17 Paid water bill, $18, check no. 105.

18 Received a check for services rendered, $85.

20 Paid telephone bill, $75, check no. 106.

22 Received check from Nathan Allen for services rendered, $350.

23 Paid utility bill, $120, check no. 107.

30 Paid part-time secretary's salary for last half of the month, $260, check no. 108.

30 Withdrew $1,000 for personal use, check no. 109.

Thorne established a chart of accounts as follows:

Account No.	Account Title
101	Cash
310	F. Thorne, Capital
320	F. Thorne, Drawing
401	Professional Fees
501	Rent Expense
503	Salaries Expense
508	Telephone Expense
509	Utilities Expense
511	Office Supplies Expense

Required:

1. Journalize the above transactions in either the cash receipts or cash disbursements journal.
2. Total and rule each column.
3. Open ledger accounts and post the journal entries.
4. Prepare a trial balance.

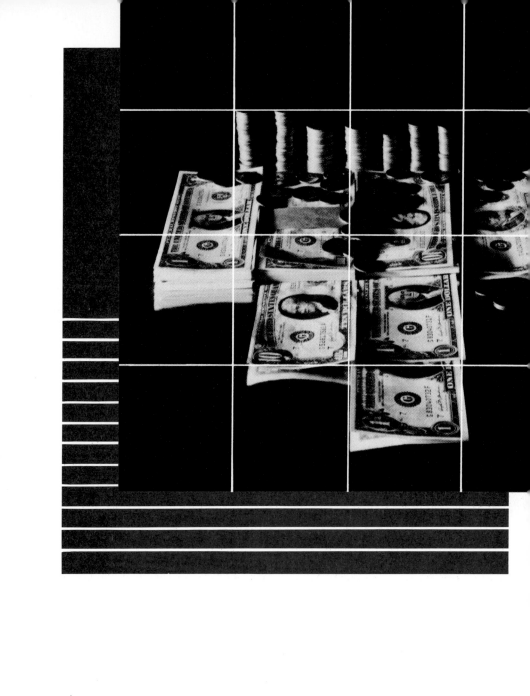

CHAPTER 11

Accounting for merchandise—purchases

LEARNING OBJECTIVES

Wise purchasing practices are an important key to success in merchandising. In this chapter, you will learn the basic terminology of purchasing as well as how purchases are made and accounted for. After studying this chapter, you should be able to:

1. Identify and complete some common purchasing documents.
2. Compute and record two kinds of purchase discounts.
3. Define the terms and abbreviations that are commonly used on invoices.
4. Account for purchases using a purchases journal.
5. Use an invoice register to record all purchases on account.
6. Post purchasing transactions to the general ledger.

In Chapters 8 through 10, we examined the accounting procedures used in service enterprises. Now, in Chapters 11 through 14, we will discuss the accounting practices commonly followed by merchandising firms. A **merchandising** firm derives most of its revenue from selling goods to customers. This is in contrast to a service enterprise, which derives most of its revenue from selling services. An important difference between merchandisers and service providers is that merchandisers must usually stock a large inventory of items for resale in the future. The purchase, storing, and resale of this merchandise inventory call for different, and more complex, accounting procedures. Central to merchandising is the purchase of goods, which is the focus of this chapter.

Before a merchandising firm can make a sale, it must first have something to sell. The items a merchandiser buys for resale to customers are called **purchases.** The procedures followed in making purchases depend on the type and size of the business enterprise. For example, in a small retail store, the owner may do all the purchasing, or only one employee may devote part of his or her time to purchasing. In larger firms, a separate department usually handles all purchasing for the entire firm. Regardless of type or size, most businesses use the terminology and procedures presented in this chapter to make their purchasing activities efficient and effective.

PURCHASING DOCUMENTS

Purchase requisitions

Any department within an enterprise may request the purchasing department to purchase merchandise or other items (such as office supplies) by submitting a form called a **purchase requisition.** Purchase requisitions are generally prenumbered consecutively to prevent their misuse or loss. The requisitions are prepared in duplicate with the original going to the purchasing department and the duplicate being retained by the department preparing the requisition.

Illustration 11-1 presents an example of a purchase requisition. The requisition shows merchandise requested by Department A and originates with the head of the department. Upon approval, the purchasing agent placed an order with General Supply Corporation,

ILLUSTRATION 11–1

Purchase Requisition

```
Adams Office Supplies          PURCHASE REQUISITION
415 Concord Lane                          Requisition No.  B-114
Atlanta, Georgia 30312


Required for  Department A              Date issued  June 10, 1987

Advise  Mr. Adams        on delivery   Date required  June 30, 1987


    Quantity                      Description


    100 dz.      Item 1374—No. 2 Lead pencil
    100 dz.      Item 4856—Black, fine point, ball-point pens
     45 rms.     Item 7420—8 1/2 x 11 Erasable bond typing paper




Approved by B. R. Jacobs       Requisition placed by T. C. Adams
                  Purchasing Agent's Memorandum

Purchase Order No.  179              Issued to: General Supply Corp.
                                                115 Berkley Dr.
Date  June 10, 1987                             Nashville, Tenn. 37214
```

as indicated by the purchasing agent's memorandum. The approved purchase requisition is the purchasing department's authorization to order the requested merchandise.

Purchase orders

A **purchase order** is a buyer's formal order for the merchandise requested on a purchase requisition. Purchase orders are usually prepared on specially designed forms, but they may be written on a printed stock form or on forms provided by the seller or supplier. Purchase orders are prepared in multiple copies and are numbered consecutively. Generally, but not always, the original copy goes to the supplier from whom the goods are ordered. In addition, it is common practice to send a duplicate copy to the supplier. The duplicate copy is an **acknowledgment copy** that the supplier signs to indicate acceptance of the order. This creates a formal contract. The signed acknowledgment copy is then returned to the ordering firm.

How the remaining copies of a purchase order are distributed varies from firm to firm. Usually, the department that originated the pur-

ILLUSTRATION 11–2

Purchase Order

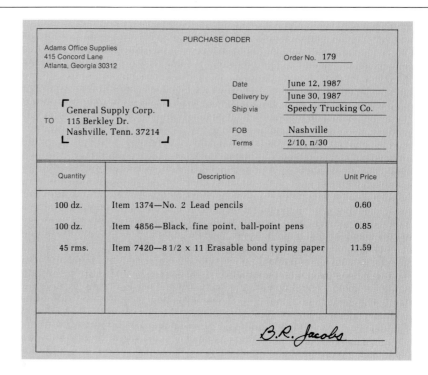

chase will receive a copy, the receiving department will get a copy, and/or the accounting department will get a copy. The distribution of copies depends on the company's rules for requisitioning, purchasing, receiving, recording, and paying for merchandise.

Illustration 11–2 shows an example of a purchase order. This document contains the same information as the purchase requisition in Illustration 11–1. In addition, the purchase order shows the unit prices that have been quoted by the supplier.

Purchase invoices

A **purchase invoice** is a document that the seller sends to the buyer to record a purchase transaction. The purchase invoice contains such information as the seller's name, the date of purchase, the invoice number, the method of shipment, the terms of the purchase order, and the kind and quantity of goods ordered and shipped. While the buyer considers this document to be a purchase invoice, the seller considers it a sales invoice.

Usually, the buyer receives the purchase invoice before the shipment arrives. Upon receipt, the invoice is numbered (consecutively) and compared with a copy of the purchase order to ensure that quantities, prices, descriptions, and terms are correct and that the delivery date and method of shipment meet the buyer's specifications. A separate form may be used to verify this information, or a rubber stamp may be used to indicate approval. If a separate form is used, it must be attached to the invoice. The invoice in Illustration 11–3 was approved using a rubber stamp.

When the purchases arrive, the recipient can either prepare a separate **receiving report** listing the merchandise that was received or compare the contents of the shipment with a copy of the purchase order. When items are compared to the purchase order, the receiving personnel should initial each item as it is verified (see Illustration 11–3). If a receiving report is prepared, someone in either the accounting or the purchasing department must compare the purchase order with the receiving report to verify the quantity received and the prices charged.

Back orders

Often a supplier is unable to fill a complete order at the time requested and must **back order** the items not shipped. In such a case, the supplier may ship a partial order and send the invoice for the complete order, indicating what has been back ordered and when it will be shipped.

Trade discounts

Manufacturers and wholesalers of certain kinds of merchandise often quote list prices in their catalogs that are subject to substantial reductions known as **trade discounts.** This allows the seller to revise prices without going through the costly process of revising the catalogs. It also enables the seller to offer different prices to various categories of customers.

A trade discount is generally shown on the face of the invoice as a deduction from the invoice total. If the invoice in Illustration 11–3 had been subject to a trade discount of 15 percent, the discount

**ILLUSTRATION
11–3**

**Purchase
Invoice**

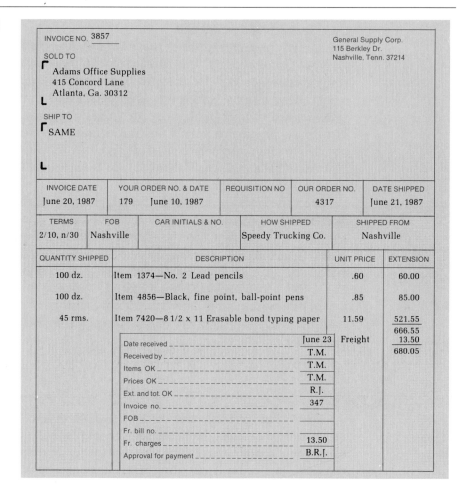

INVOICE NO. 3857

General Supply Corp.
115 Berkley Dr.
Nashville, Tenn. 37214

SOLD TO

Adams Office Supplies
415 Concord Lane
Atlanta, Ga. 30312

SHIP TO

SAME

INVOICE DATE	YOUR ORDER NO. & DATE	REQUISITION NO	OUR ORDER NO.	DATE SHIPPED
June 20, 1987	179 June 10, 1987		4317	June 21, 1987

TERMS	FOB	CAR INITIALS & NO.	HOW SHIPPED	SHIPPED FROM
2/10, n/30	Nashville		Speedy Trucking Co.	Nashville

QUANTITY SHIPPED	DESCRIPTION	UNIT PRICE	EXTENSION
100 dz.	Item 1374—No. 2 Lead pencils	.60	60.00
100 dz.	Item 4856—Black, fine point, ball-point pens	.85	85.00
45 rms.	Item 7420—8 1/2 x 11 Erasable bond typing paper	11.59	521.55
			666.55
		Freight	13.50
			680.05

Date received _____ June 23
Received by _____ T.M.
Items OK _____ T.M.
Prices OK _____ T.M.
Ext. and tot. OK _____ R.J.
Invoice no. _____ 347
FOB _____
Fr. bill no. _____
Fr. charges _____ 13.50
Approval for payment _____ B.R.J.

would be stated in the body of the invoice, as shown in Illustration 11–4.

When the invoice is recorded, it is entered at the net amount after deducting the trade discount. Since trade discounts are merely price reductions, they are not entered in either the buyer's or seller's books.

It is not uncommon to find more than one trade discount allowed on the same invoice. For example an invoice may be subject to a chain discount of 20, 15, and 5 percent. In computing the net invoice amount, the discounts are computed individually on the successive

ILLUSTRATION 11–4

QUANTITY SHIPPED	DESCRIPTION	UNIT PRICE	EXTENSION
100 dz.	Item 1374—No. 2 Lead pencils	0.60	$ 60.00
100 dz.	Item 4856—Black, fine point, ball-point pens	0.85	85.00
45 rms.	Item 7420—8 1/2 x 11 Erasable bond typing paper	11.59	521.55
			666.55
		Less 15% discount	99.98
			$566.57

net invoice amounts. To illustrate, assume that an invoice subject to trade discounts of 20, 15 and 5 percent has a gross amount of $500. The net invoice amount is computed as follows:

Gross invoice amount.	$500
Less 20% (20% × $500)	100
Balance	$400
Less 15% (15% × $400)	60
Balance	$340
Less 5% (5% × $340).	17
Net invoice amount	$323

Again, when the invoice is recorded, only the net amount, $323, is to be entered.

Cash discounts

While trade discounts are used to offer different prices to different classes of customers and to avoid catalog revisions, **cash discounts** are used primarily to encourage customers to pay promptly. The payment terms are clearly stated on the face of the invoice. Note, for example, that on the invoice in Illustration 11–3, the terms are clearly stated as "2/10, n/30." This means that if the invoice is paid within 10 days from the invoice date (June 20), a discount of 2 percent will be allowed. Hence, should the invoice be paid on or before June 30, the buyer may deduct a discount of $13.33 (0.02 × $666.55) from the invoice amount. *Notice that the discount is NOT allowed on freight charges.* The freight charges have been prepaid by the seller for the convenience of the buyer and must be repaid in full. Thus in this example, assuming that the invoice is paid during the discount period, the amount paid to the vendor is

$666.72 [$666.55 − $13.33 (discount) + $13.50 (freight)]. If the invoice is not paid within the discount period, the total invoice price plus freight ($680.05) must be paid not later than July 20, which is 30 days after the invoice date.

There are two acceptable methods for recording purchases that are subject to cash discounts. Purchases can be recorded at the total invoice price or net of the cash discount. When purchases are recorded at the total invoice price *(gross method),* the cash discount is ignored until the time of payment. If payment is made within the discount period, the amount of the discount is deducted and a check issued for the net amount. When the check is recorded, the discount will be credited to a **Purchases Discount account.** At the end of the accounting period, the total credit balance of the Purchases Discount account is shown as a deduction from purchases.

Purchases can be recorded net of the cash discount *(net method),* assuming that all discounts will be taken. Failure to take a cash discount is considered inefficient. If payment is made after the discount period, the total invoice price must be paid and the amount of the discount not taken is debited to a **Purchases Discount Lost account.** At the end of the accounting period, the balance of the Purchases Discount Lost account is included with other administrative expenses. Assuming a purchase invoice of $500 with terms of 2/10, n/30, here are examples of the two alternative treatments.

	Gross Method			*Net Method*		
	Purchases Recorded at Total Invoice Price			Purchases Recorded at Net of Cash Discount		
Receipt of invoice	Purchases	500		Purchases...............	490	
	Accounts Payable		500	Accounts Payable........		490
Payment within	Accounts Payable	500		Accounts Payable	490	
discount period	Purchases Discount		10	Cash		490
	Cash		490			
Payment after	Accounts Payable	500		Accounts Payable	490	
discount period	Cash		500	Purchases Discount Lost......	10	
				Cash		500

Occasionally, an invoice is subject to both cash and trade discounts. Then the trade discounts are deducted from the gross amount of the invoice before the cash discount is applied. For example, assume that an invoice with a gross amount of $1,375 had trade discounts of 25, 10, and 5 percent and the terms were 2/10, n/30. The net amount payable within 10 days of the invoice is computed as follows:

Gross invoice amount	$1,375.00
Less 25% (25% × $1,375)	343.75
Balance	$1,031.25
Less 10% (10% × $1,031.25)	103.12
Balance	$ 928.13
Less 5% (5% × $928.13)	46.41
Amount subject to cash discount	$ 881.72
Less 2% cash discount: (2% × $881.72)	17.63
Net amount payable	$ 864.09

While most vendors require that an invoice be paid in full within the specified time period in order to obtain the cash discount, some vendors allow the discount on a partial payment. To illustrate, assume that an invoice totaling $1,500 with terms 2/10, n/30 is received. Under the gross method, the original entry would be a debit to Purchases for $1,500 and a credit to Accounts Payable for $1,500.

GENERAL JOURNAL

DATE	ACCOUNT AND EXPLANATION	P.R.	DEBIT	CREDIT
	Purchases		1 5 0 0 00	
	Accounts Payable			1 5 0 0 00
	To record purchase of merchandise.			

If a discount is allowed on a partial payment and a payment of $980 is made within the discount period, the amount of the discount would be computed as:

$$100 \text{ percent} = \text{Amount for which customer should receive credit}$$
$$100 \text{ percent} - 2 \text{ percent} = 98 \text{ percent}$$
$$98 \text{ percent} = \$980$$
$$\$980 \div 98 \text{ percent} = \$1,000$$
$$\$1,000 - \$980 = \$20 \text{ discount}$$

To record this transaction, the buyer would debit Accounts Payable for $1,000, credit Purchases Discounts for $20, and credit Cash for $980.

GENERAL JOURNAL

DATE	ACCOUNT AND EXPLANATION	P.R.	DEBIT	CREDIT
	Accounts Payable		1 0 0 0 00	
	Purchases Discount			2 0 00
	Cash			9 8 0 00
	To record payment on merchandise within the			
	discount period.			

To record the payment of the remaining $500 after the discount period, the buyer would debit Accounts Payable for $500 and credit Cash for $500. The invoice is now paid in full.

		GENERAL JOURNAL			
DATE		ACCOUNT AND EXPLANATION	P.R.	DEBIT	CREDIT
		Accounts Payable		500 00	
		Cash			500 00
		To pay off account after discount period.			

If the net method of accounting for purchases is used for the same invoice, the following entries would be required:

1. To record the $1,500 invoice net of the 2 percent cash discount ($30):

		GENERAL JOURNAL			
DATE		ACCOUNT AND EXPLANATION	P.R.	DEBIT	CREDIT
		Purchases		1470 00	
		Accounts Payable			1470 00
		To record $1,500 invoice net of 2% cash discount.			

2. To record a partial payment of $980 within the discount period:

		GENERAL JOURNAL			
DATE		ACCOUNT AND EXPLANATION	P.R.	DEBIT	CREDIT
		Accounts Payable		980 00	
		Cash			980 00
		To record partial payment within the discount period.			

Notice that with the net method it is not necessary to figure the discount for the partial payment.

3. To record payment of the remainder of the bill after the discount period, we must show both the amount paid and the amount of the lost discount. The amount in the Accounts Payable account that remains to be paid is $490 ($1,470 —

$980). The computation of the amount of the discount lost is as follows:

$$100\% - 2\% = 98\% \text{ (Full price less 2\% discount)}$$
$$\$490 \div 98\% = \$500$$
$$\$500 - \$490 = \$10 \text{ discount lost}$$

The entry to record the payment would be:

	GENERAL JOURNAL			
DATE	ACCOUNT AND EXPLANATION	P.R.	DEBIT	CREDIT
	Accounts Payable		490 00	
	Purchases Discount Lost		10 00	
	Cash			500 00
	To record payment of remainder after the			
	discount period.			

PURCHASE INVOICE TERMS

Here are some terms commonly used on invoices:

2/10, n/30 This is read as "two ten, net thirty" and means that a 2 percent discount (2 percent of the gross invoice price of the merchandise) is allowed if payment is made within 10 days after the invoice date, and the gross invoice price is due 30 days from the invoice date.

2/EOM, n/60 This is read as "two EOM, net sixty" and means a 2 percent discount may be deducted if the invoice is paid by the end of the month. The discount may not be taken after the end of the month, and payment is due 60 days from the invoice date.

2/10/EOM, n/60 This is read as "two ten EOM, net sixty" and means that a 2 percent discount may be deducted if the invoice is paid by the 10th of the following month. No discount is allowed after that date, and the gross invoice amount is due 60 days from the invoice date.

f.o.b. destination This means "free on board at destination." The seller has agreed to be ultimately responsible for all transportation costs and to assume all responsibility for the merchandise until it reaches the buyer's destination.

f.o.b. shipping point This stands for "free on board at shipping point." The buyer has agreed to be ultimately responsible for the freight charges and to assume all risks until the time the merchandise is accepted for shipment by the carrier.

Freight collect This term means that the buyer is to pay the freight when the merchandise arrives. If terms are f.o.b. destination, the buyer will be able to deduct the cost of the freight when paying the invoice.

Freight prepaid This means that the seller has paid the freight on the goods at the time of shipment. If the terms are f.o.b. shipping point, the seller will be able to collect the cost of the freight from the buyer.

OTHER PURCHASING FORMS

Sometimes the purchase of merchandise and other property involves the use of some additional forms and procedures. We will now discuss the most common of these.

Bills of lading

A **bill of lading** is a receipt given to a shipper when merchandise is shipped by airfreight, highway freight, or railroad. The bill of lading is prepared in triplicate (original, shipping order, and memorandum). All three copies are signed by the freight agent, who returns the original and memorandum copies to the shipper and retains the shipping copy for his or her records.

When it comes to the description and quantity of merchandise, a bill of lading may differ from its corresponding purchase invoice. This may occur because the merchandise is grouped together and shipped in large crates, cartons, and other packages rather than in individual containers. The total number of packages and total weight are indicated on the bill of lading. Freight charges are based on the total weight of the merchandise, the type of merchandise, and the distance it is being shipped. A bill of lading is shown in Illustration 11–5.

**ILLUSTRATION
11–5**

STRAIGHT BILL OF LADING
ORIGINAL — NOT NEGOTIABLE
CAROLINA FREIGHT CARRIERS CORP.
(NAME OF CARRIER)

SHIPPER NO. 4380
CARRIER NO. 7145
DATE 7/6/87

TO:
CONSIGNEE Smith Bros.
STREET 105 Georgetown Drive
DESTINATION Albany, Georgia   ZIP CODE 31700
ROUTE:

FROM:
SHIPPER Jones, Inc.
STREET 4481 Elm Street
ORIGIN Atlanta, Georgia   ZIP CODE 30303
VEHICLE NUMBER

NO. SHIPPING UNITS	KIND OF PACKAGING, DESCRIPTION OF ARTICLES, SPECIAL MARKS AND EXCEPTIONS	WEIGHT (SUBJECT TO CORR.)	RATE	CHARGES (FOR CARRIER USE ONLY)
1	1 Carton Redwood Stain	45 lbs.		

REMIT C.O.D.
TO

ADDRESS

NOTE—Where the rate is dependent on value, shippers are required to state specifically in writing the agreed or declared value of the property.
The agreed or declared value of the property is hereby specifically stated by the shipper to be not exceeding.

$_____ per _____

COD AMT: $

Subject to Section 7 of the conditions, if this shipment is to be delivered to the consignee without recourse on the consignor, the consignor shall sign the following statement:
    The carrier shall not make delivery of this shipment without payment of freight and all other lawful charges.

_____
(Signature of Consignor)

C.O.D. FEE
PREPAID ☐ $
COLLECT ☐

TOTAL CHARGES $

FREIGHT CHARGES:
FREIGHT PREPAID   Check box except when if charges are box at right to be is charged   ☐ collect

RECEIVED, subject to the classifications and tariffs in effect on the date of the issue of this Bill of Lading, the property described above in apparent good order, except as noted (contents and condition of contents of packages unknown), marked, consigned, and destined as indicated above which said carrier (the word carrier being understood throughout this contract as meaning any person or corporation in possession of the property under the contract) agrees to carry to its usual place of delivery at said destination, if on its route, otherwise to deliver to another carrier on the route to said destination. It is mutually agreed as to each carrier of all or any of said property over all or any portion of said route to destination and as to each party at any time interested in all or any of said property, that every service to be performed hereunder shall be subject to all the bill of lading terms and conditions in the governing classification on the date of shipment.
Shipper hereby certifies that he is familiar with all the bill of lading terms and conditions in the governing classification and the said terms and conditions are hereby agreed to by the shipper and accepted for himself and his assigns.

SHIPPER

PER

CARRIER
CAROLINA FREIGHT CARRIERS CORP. Agent

PER David C. Bailey
DATE 7/6/87

COD

Merchandise is often purchased under terms that require payment on delivery. This is known as collect on delivery, or cash on delivery **(COD).** At the time of delivery, the cost of the merchandise, transportation, and COD charges must be paid by the recipient. When COD shipments are made by highway freight, the bill of lading specifies the amount to be collected by the transportation company. The transportation company then collects this amount plus a COD charge and sends the transportation charges to the shipper.

Freight and drayage

When a transportation company receives merchandise for shipment, its agent prepares a **waybill.** This document describes the merchandise being shipped, shows the point of origin and destination, and indicates special handling requirements, if any. The original is forwarded to the transportation company's office at the point of destination. The agent also prepares a **freight bill,** which is a bill for the transportation charges. The freight bill is similar in content to the bill of lading; however, in addition to the description of the shipment, freight charges are shown.

If the buyer must hire a trucking company or delivery service to move the merchandise from the freight office to the buyer's location, additional costs known as **drayage** will be incurred. In this case, the trucking company will prepare and submit a drayage bill to the buyer.

Debit and credit memoranda

Merchandise is not always received in satisfactory condition or according to previously agreed-on terms. The shipment may be damaged, contain the wrong merchandise, or arrive too late. In such cases, the buyer may either return the shipment to the seller or agree to keep the shipment if granted an allowance.

For example, let's assume that a buyer has purchased 12 office chairs for resale and that 6 of these arrive slightly damaged. Rather than return the damaged chairs, the buyer might request that an allowance be granted. Thus, a debit memorandum would be prepared as shown in Illustration 11–6. A **debit memorandum** is used by a buyer to notify a seller that the seller's Account Payable account on the buyer's books is being debited due to an error or an allowance for damaged merchandise.

After deciding that the amount of the adjustment is reasonable, General Supply Corporation would send a **credit memorandum** similar to the one in Illustration 11–7. The credit memorandum would inform the buyer that the buyer's Account Receivable account on the seller's books has been credited to reflect the allowance.

Occasionally, merchandise is received in such condition that it cannot be sold and must be returned. Upon notification and receipt of the merchandise, the vendor will issue a credit memorandum similar to the one shown in Illustration 11–8.

Sometimes it is difficult to recall which party issues which kind of memorandum. Remember, a *credit memorandum* is issued by the *selling company* to notify a buyer that his accounts receivable balance has been reduced (credited). Conversely, a *debit memorandum* is

ILLUSTRATION 11–6

Debit Memorandum

Adams Office Supplies
415 Concord Lane
Atlanta, Georgia 30312

Debit Memorandum No. 24
Date 8/6/87

TO: General Supply Corp.
115 Berkley Dr.
Nashville, Tenn. 37214

Your account has been debited as follows:

In reference to your Invoice No. 4752 dated 8/3/87, six chairs arrived slightly damaged and must be sold as seconds. We believe we can sell the chairs at a satisfactory profit margin and will accept them if an allowance of $120 is granted. We believe this difference should be credited to our account.

issued by the *buyer* to notify a seller that his accounts payable balance is being reduced (debited). The document in Illustration 11–8 is called a credit memorandum because General Supply Corporation (the seller) is notifying the buyer (Adams Office Supplies) that credit for the return of 100 dozen pencils is being given. Thus, General Supply Corporation has credited Adam's Accounts Receivable account for the amount of the returned merchandise, $60.

ILLUSTRATION 11–7

Credit Memorandum Showing an Allowance for Damaged Goods

General Supply Corp.
115 Berkley Dr.
Nashville, Tenn. 37214

Credit Memorandum No. 75

TO: Adams Office Supplies
415 Concord Lane
Atlanta, Georgia 30312

Your account has been credited for $120 pertaining to Invoice No. 4752.

We regret the inconvenience that the receipt of damaged merchandise may have caused you. Your effort to sell the merchandise rather than returning it to us is greatly appreciated.

ILLUSTRATION 11–8

Credit Memorandum Showing a Return of Goods

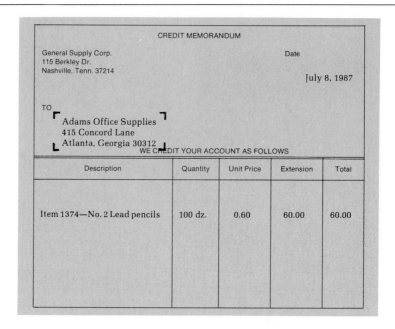

CREDIT MEMORANDUM

General Supply Corp.
115 Berkley Dr.
Nashville, Tenn. 37214

Date

July 8, 1987

TO
Adams Office Supplies
415 Concord Lane
Atlanta, Georgia 30312

WE CREDIT YOUR ACCOUNT AS FOLLOWS

Description	Quantity	Unit Price	Extension	Total
Item 1374—No. 2 Lead pencils	100 dz.	0.60	60.00	60.00

MERCHANDISE INVENTORY

A merchandising firm buys goods for resale to its customers. To ensure that it will have enough goods to meet customer demand, a merchandiser must maintain a stock of goods on hand and available for sale. These purchases are called **merchandise inventory.** Although a service enterprise also purchases supplies and similar items, such items are not held for resale and would not be classified as purchases or as merchandise inventory. In order to calculate net income, a merchandiser needs to know the value of the goods in merchandise inventory. This value is usually determined in one of two ways.

Inventory methods

A merchandising firm may use either a periodic inventory system or a perpetual inventory system. With a **periodic system,** inventory is counted only at the close of each accounting period. The general ledger account, Merchandise Inventory, contains only the beginning balance in inventory—what was on hand at the beginning of the period. Inventory purchases for the period are recorded in a separate ledger account, Purchases. In contrast, with a **perpetual inventory system,** a merchandiser maintains a running total of inventory quantities and values. Instead of recording each purchase in a Purchases account, a debit is made to the Merchandise Inventory account. In the perpetual inventory system, no Purchases account is maintained. All examples in this chapter are based on a periodic inventory system.

ACCOUNTING FOR PURCHASES

The Purchases account

Purchases of merchandise during the current period are entered in an account entitled Purchases. All merchandise purchases, whether for cash or on credit, are debited to Purchases. This account is considered a temporary owner's equity account and is closed out at the end of the accounting period.

To illustrate the use of the Purchases account, suppose that on October 14, the Alpha Company purchases $254 of merchandise on account. This transaction would require a debit to Purchases with an offsetting credit to Accounts Payable. (Recall that Accounts Payable is a liability account and represents the amount due to creditors.) Likewise, if the company purchases $38 of merchandise on October 17 for cash, Purchases is debited for $38, while Cash is credited for the same amount. After these two transactions, the Purchases account will look as follows:

	GENERAL LEDGER						
	Purchases					ACCT. NO.	510
						BALANCE	
DATE	EXPLANATION	P.R.	DEBIT	CREDIT	DEBIT	CREDIT	
1987							
Oct. 14		GJ8	2 5 4 00		2 5 4 00		
17		CD6	3 8 00		2 9 2 00		

In addition to the cost of the merchandise itself, sometimes there are other expenses, such as transportation charges and insurance costs, that also could be debited to the Purchases account. If such expenses are common and their amounts are significant, separate ledger accounts should be established for them.

The Purchases Returns and Allowances account

It is not unusual for a business to occasionally receive merchandise that either was not ordered or was in excess of the requested amount. Likewise, the merchandise may be damaged in some way that would reduce its resale value. As mentioned earlier, when this occurs, the purchaser has two options. First, the goods can be returned. Second, the merchandise can be kept and a deduction from the regular price can be accepted. Either way, an adjustment must be made to the buyer's account. If the purchase was on account, the buyer's account must be credited. If the purchase was paid for in cash, a refund must be given.

The refund or allowance can be credited either to the Purchases account or to a separate account, Purchases Returns and Allowances, which is also a temporary owner's equity account. When a separate account is used, the total amount of returns and allowances for the period are readily available. Should this total be large or show a significant increase within a period, it may indicate problems in purchasing procedures. Since the costs of handling and accounting for returned merchandise are likely to be high, a rise in returned goods would call for investigation and correction.

To demonstrate the operations of the Purchase Returns and Allowances account, assume that in its October 17 shipment, the Alpha company received $54 worth of goods that it never ordered. These items were returned to the seller, which resulted in a credit to the Purchase Returns and Allowances account and a matching debit to Accounts Payable. Then, on October 31, the company received some slightly damaged merchandise. The seller and Alpha agreed that the price of the 100 damaged units should be reduced by $50. Consequently, Alpha credited its Purchase Returns and Allowances account for $50 and entered an offsetting debit to Accounts Payable. After recording these transactions, Alpha's Purchase Returns and Allowances account would appear as follows:

GENERAL LEDGER

Purchase Returns and Allowances   ACCT. NO. 511

DATE		EXPLANATION	P.R.	DEBIT	CREDIT	BALANCE	
						DEBIT	CREDIT
1987							
Oct.	17		GJ8		54 00		54 00
	31		GJ8		50 00		1 04 00

The Purchase Returns and Allowances account is a reduction in the recorded cost of purchases and will be shown accordingly in the income statement.

The purchases journal

Thus far we have assumed that all purchases were recorded in the general journal. In a larger business, however, purchase transactions occur frequently, and recording them individually in the general journal becomes time-consuming and leads to many postings to the ledger accounts. For this reason, most companies use a special journal called a **purchases journal** to record all purchases made on credit. Purchases for cash are recorded with the other cash disbursements.

The purchases journal is arranged so that a single entry suffices for both the debit to Purchases and the offsetting credit to Accounts Payable. Using this compact format, only one summary posting is made to the general ledger accounts each month. An example of a purchases journal is shown in Illustration 11–9. The columns in the purchases journal are self-explanatory except for the Terms column. In this column, the payment terms from each invoice are entered. In Illustration 11–9, the first invoice is listed as net 10, which means that it should be paid within 10 days after its invoice date. Since each creditor sets his or her own terms of sale, the entries in this column will vary considerably. Often, a creditor will offer a cash discount to encourage rapid payment of an invoice, as explained earlier, and these discounts should be taken advantage of.

ILLUSTRATION 11–9

PURCHASES JOURNAL PAGE 5

DATE		TERMS	INVOICE NO.	CREDITOR	PURCHASES DR. ACC. PAY. CR. AMOUNT	P.R.
1987						
Oct.	5	Net 10	973	Lash Distributors	2 3 7 44	√
	7	Net 30	1243	Midwest Carpet Co.	1 5 6 7 40	√
	14	Net 20	47	White Installation Service	1 1 3 00	√
	20	Net 10	3743	Armstrong Brothers	9 8 5 21	√
	28	Net 30	6771	Central Specialty	4 6 1 35	√
	31				3 3 6 4 40	
					(5 1 0 / 250)	

At the end of the month, the Amount column is totaled and ruled as shown. This total then becomes the basis for a **summary posting** to the Purchases and Accounts Payable accounts in the general ledger. The entries would be:

1. Debit Purchases for $3,364.40.
2. Credit Accounts Payable for $3,364.40.

When posting these amounts, P5 should be placed in the Posting Reference column of each ledger account to indicate that the posting source is page 5 of the purchases journal. The summary postings to the Accounts Payable and Purchases accounts from the purchases journal are illustrated below:

GENERAL LEDGER

Accounts Payable   ACCT. NO. 250

| DATE | | EXPLANATION | P.R. | DEBIT | CREDIT | BALANCE | |
						DEBIT	CREDIT
1987							
Oct.	31		P5		3 3 6 4 40		3 3 6 4 40

GENERAL LEDGER

Purchases   ACCT. NO. 510

| DATE | | EXPLANATION | P.R. | DEBIT | CREDIT | BALANCE | |
						DEBIT	CREDIT
1987							
Oct.	31		P5	3 3 6 4 40		3 3 6 4 40	

Accounts Payable

As mentioned earlier, the **Accounts Payable** ledger account is classified as a *liability* account because its balance represents the amounts due to creditors. The credit balance in the account represents the total amount owed by the company for merchandise purchases.

Because the account shows only the total liability to all vendors, a more detailed subsidiary record is needed for each creditor. These supporting records should show the outstanding balance owed to a particular creditor. The sum of these supporting records should equal the Accounts Payable controlling account balance. Basically, there are two accounting methods used to maintain supporting records.

The ledger account system. With the **ledger account system,** it is customary to maintain a separate ledger account for each creditor.

These subsidiary accounts are not maintained in the general ledger but instead are kept in alphabetical order in a ledger for subsidiary payable records. When a purchase on account is made, the supporting invoice becomes the basis for the credit to the particular creditor's ledger account. A P and the page number of the purchases journal should be recorded in the Posting Reference column of the subsidiary ledger account. A check ($\sqrt{}$) should be placed in the Posting Reference column of the purchases journal to indicate that the amount has been posted to the subsidiary account (see Illustration 11–9).

When a payment is made, it is debited to the appropriate creditor's account. Most payments cover the entire amount of the invoice. A credit balance in any subsidiary account represents the unpaid amount of that particular creditor. By totaling all the account balances in the subsidiary ledger, we should arrive at the Accounts Payable control total.

The invoice method.   Under the **invoice method,** all unpaid invoices are kept in an open file according to their due dates. This ensures their being paid when they become due. When an invoice is paid in full, it is removed from the open file and placed in a paid file according to vendor name. However, if only a partial payment is made, then an appropriate notation should be made on the invoice explaining the amounts paid, and the invoice should be retained in the open file. This open file may be as simple as a single manila folder or as complex as a magnetic computer tape. At any point in time, the total of open invoices should agree with the Accounts Payable control account balance.

INVOICE REGISTERS

An **invoice register** is a book of original entry that is used to record *all* invoices for purchases on account, whether the purchases involve merchandise, supplies, or other items. Thus, it differs from a purchases journal, which is used to record only merchandise bought on credit. A separate invoice register may be set up for each department in a company in order to provide more information and better control.

Generally, items purchased fall into one of three categories: (1) merchandise for resale, (2) supplies for use in the course of business, or (3) equipment (plant assets) for use in operating the business.

Therefore, an invoice register is set up to handle these kinds of transactions.

When an invoice register is used to record all incoming purchase invoices, adequate provision should be made for proper classification of debits and credits. As shown in Illustration 11–10, debits are recorded on the left side of the register, and credits are recorded on the right. On the debit side is a separate column for purchases plus a General Ledger section that is used to record debits to other accounts, such as Office Supplies, Office Equipment, and Transportation-In. The Account Number column is used to record the account numbers for the entries in the General column.

In the center of the invoice register, the accountant records the day of the month, the date of the invoice, the invoice number, and the name of the supplier that issued the invoice.

On the credit side of the invoice register are an Accounts Payable column and a General Ledger section. This General Ledger section is used to record credits to any accounts other than Accounts Payable.

We will now examine a series of purchase transactions for Jones and Hicks, a retail plumbing supply business in Greenville, South Carolina. As each invoice is received, the information it contains is

ILLUSTRATION 11–10   Jones and Hicks Invoice Register

MONTH OF July 1987 — INVOICE REGISTER — PAGE 7

PURCHASES	ACCT. NO.	AMOUNT	√	DAY	DATE OF INVOICE	INV. NO.	NAME	ACCOUNTS PAYABLE	√	ACCT. NO.	AMOUNT	√
1875 00	530	54 75	√	1	6/29	178	Plumb. Fixtures, Inc.	1929 75	√			
	143	118 50	√	2	7/2	179	Smith Office Supp. Co.	118 50	√			
956 00	530	27 60	√	2	6/30	180	Lincoln Lavatories	983 60	√			
	151	475 00	√	5	7/2	181	Business Machines	475 00	√			
2540 00	530	114 85	√	6	7/5	182	Thompson Metals	2654 85	√			
348 50				9	7/8	184	Plumbing Parts	348 50	√			
60 00				12	7/3	182	Thompson Metals (corrected invoice)	60 00	√			
	260	25 00	√	12	6/30	178	Plumb. Fixtures, Inc. (corrected invoice)			501	25 00	√
5779 50		815 70						6570 20			25 00	
(501)		(√)						(260)			(√)	

recorded in the invoice register. Here are the account names and numbers that Jones and Hicks uses to record items bought on credit:

501   Purchases
502   Purchase Discounts
503   Purchase Returns and Allowances
530   Transportation-In
143   Office Supplies
151   Office Equipment
260   Accounts Payable

Here are Jones and Hicks's purchase transactions for the first 12 days of July. Note how this information is recorded in the invoice register in Illustration 11–10.

JONES AND HICKS
Description of Purchase Transactions
July 1–12, 1987

Date
1987
July 1   Received Purchase Invoice No. 178 from Plumbing Fixtures, Inc., Atlanta, Ga.: bathtubs, $1,875; terms, June 29—2/10, n/30; freight prepaid and added to invoice, $54.75.

Beginning on the first line of the invoice register, the cost of the bathtubs, $1,875.00, is recorded in the Purchases column. The freight cost of $54.75 is entered in the General Ledger column along with the account number, 530, which corresponds to the Transportation-In account. The day of the month is entered in the Day column, while the date and number of the invoice are written in the next two columns. Next, the name of the creditor, Plumbing Fixtures, Inc., is recorded in the Name column. Finally, the total amount owed for goods and shipping ($1,875.00 + $54.75 = $1,929.75) is entered in the Accounts Payable Credit column.

2   Received Purchase Invoice No. 179 from Smith Office Supply Company, Greenville: office supplies, $118.50; terms, July 2—net 30.

In this case, there is no entry in the Purchases column because only goods intended for resale are classified as purchases. The office supplies will be used by company employees in the course of business, so their cost is entered in the General column and charged to account number 143, Office Supplies. The Day, Date, and other columns are completed in the same way as before.

As you read the rest of Jones and Hick's transactions, match them to the entries in Illustration 11–10.

July 2 Received Purchase Invoice No. 180 from Lincoln Lavatories, Winston Salem: lavatories, $956; terms, June 30—2/10, n/30; freight prepaid and added to invoice, $27.60.

5 Received Purchase Invoice No. 181 from Business Machines, Raleigh: typewriter, $450; terms, July 2—net 30; freight prepaid and added to invoice, $25.

6 Received Purchase Invoice No. 182 from Thompson Metals, Asheville: metal piping, $2,540; terms, July 5—2/10, n/30; freight prepaid and added to invoice, $114.85.

9 Received Purchase Invoice No. 183 from Plumbing Parts, Atlanta, Ga.: chrome faucets, $348.50; terms, July 8—2/20, n/30; freight collect.

12 Received a corrected invoice from Thompson Metals, $2,600, excluding freight. See Invoice No. 182.

12 Received a corrected invoice from Plumbing Fixtures, Inc., $1,850, excluding freight. See Invoice No. 178.

Corrected purchase invoices

Often, an incorrect invoice will be received. Then, at a later date, another purchase invoice will be received to correct the initial invoice. If the corrected purchase invoice is received before the initial invoice has been entered in the invoice register, the initial invoice may be discarded and the corrected invoice may be entered. If the initial invoice has already been entered in the invoice register when the corrected invoice is received, however, only the difference between the two invoices is recorded. If the corrected invoice is for a greater amount than the initial invoice, the difference is debited to the proper account and credited to accounts payable. (See Invoice No. 182.) This amount is also posted to the proper creditor's account in the accounts payable subsidiary ledger.

If the amount of the corrected invoice is less than the amount of the initial invoice, the difference (a decrease) is debited to Accounts Payable and credited to the proper account. The amount is also posted to the proper creditor's account in the accounts payable subsidiary ledger. (See Invoice No. 178.) Also, the corrected invoice should be attached to the initial invoice.

Proving the invoice register

At any time, the invoice register may be proved by footing (totaling) the columns and checking to see that total debits equal total credits.

The two usual times to prove the register are when it is posted at the end of the month and when a register page is completed. Jones and Hicks's invoice register was proved in the following manner on July 12, when page 7 was completed:

Account Column	Debit	Credit
Purchases	$5,779.50	
General ledger	815.70	
Accounts payable		$6,570.20
General ledger		25.00
Totals	$6,595.20	$6,595.20

Posting procedures

Transactions are posted to both the general ledger and the accounts payable subsidiary ledger. This includes both summary posting and individual transaction posting. The ledgers used in the Jones and Hicks example include the general ledger in Illustration 11–11 and the accounts payable subsidiary ledger in Illustration 11–12. Upon entering each purchase invoice in the invoice register, the invoice was used to post to the proper creditor's account in the accounts payable subsidiary ledger. The invoice number is placed in the P.R. column in the accounts payable subsidiary ledger.

Posting to creditors' accounts directly from the invoice provides certain advantages over posting from the invoice register (which is also permissible). The invoice provides all the necessary information for proper posting, whereas additional information would have to be entered in the invoice register before it could be used for posting. For example, the invoice register does not contain the terms of a purchase invoice. In addition, certain errors can be eliminated. If an error is made in entering an invoice in the invoice register and posting to the accounts payable subsidiary ledger is done from the invoices, the same error is not likely to be made in the accounts payable subsidiary ledger. However, if the invoice register is used for posting to the accounts payable subsidiary ledger, an error in the invoice register will carry through to the accounts payable subsidiary ledger.

Posting directly to creditors' accounts from the invoices provides efficiency and a method of internal control. One person may enter the invoices in the invoice register and post from the invoice register to the general ledger, while another person may post from the invoices

ILLUSTRATION 11–11

Jones and Hicks General Ledger (Partial)

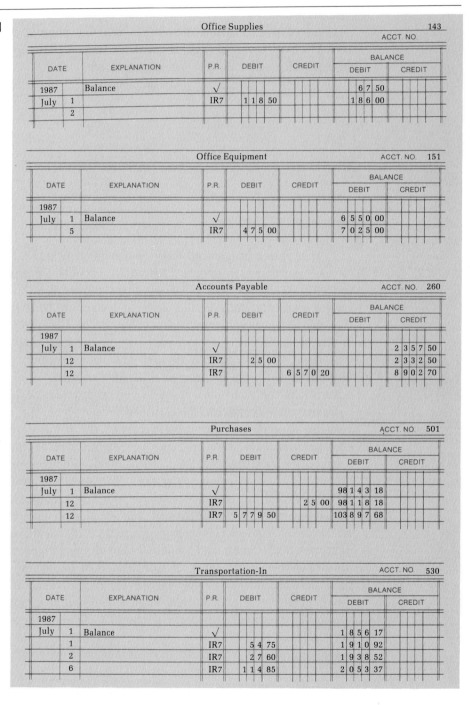

Office Supplies   ACCT. NO. 143

DATE		EXPLANATION	P.R.	DEBIT	CREDIT	BALANCE DEBIT	BALANCE CREDIT
1987		Balance	√			67 50	
July	1		IR7	118 50		186 00	
	2						

Office Equipment   ACCT. NO. 151

DATE		EXPLANATION	P.R.	DEBIT	CREDIT	BALANCE DEBIT	BALANCE CREDIT
1987							
July	1	Balance	√			6 550 00	
	5		IR7	475 00		7 025 00	

Accounts Payable   ACCT. NO. 260

DATE		EXPLANATION	P.R.	DEBIT	CREDIT	BALANCE DEBIT	BALANCE CREDIT
1987							
July	1	Balance	√				2 357 50
	12		IR7	25 00			2 332 50
	12		IR7		6 570 20		8 902 70

Purchases   ACCT. NO. 501

DATE		EXPLANATION	P.R.	DEBIT	CREDIT	BALANCE DEBIT	BALANCE CREDIT
1987							
July	1	Balance	√			98 143 18	
	12		IR7		25 00	98 118 18	
	12		IR7	5 779 50		103 897 68	

Transportation-In   ACCT. NO. 530

DATE		EXPLANATION	P.R.	DEBIT	CREDIT	BALANCE DEBIT	BALANCE CREDIT
1987							
July	1	Balance	√			1 856 17	
	1		IR7	54 75		1 910 92	
	2		IR7	27 60		1 938 52	
	6		IR7	114 85		2 053 37	

to creditors' accounts in the accounts payable subsidiary ledger. This creates a separation of duties, and a check on accuracy can be obtained at any time by comparing the total of the accounts payable subsidiary ledger with the balance of the Accounts Payable control account maintained in the general ledger.

ILLUSTRATION 11–12

Jones and Hicks Accounts Payable Subsidiary Ledger (Partial)

Business Machines

DATE		EXPLANATION	INV. NO.	P.R.	DEBIT	CREDIT	BALANCE
1987							
July	5	7/2—net 30	181			4 5 0 00	4 5 0 00
	5	Freight prepaid	181			2 5 00	4 7 5 00

Lincoln Lavatories

DATE		EXPLANATION	INV. NO.	P.R.	DEBIT	CREDIT	BALANCE
1987							
July	1	Balance	√				1 2 7 5 00
	2	6/30—2/10, n/30	180			9 5 6 00	2 2 3 1 00
	2	Freight prepaid	180			2 7 60	2 2 5 8 60

Plumbing Fixtures, Inc.

DATE		EXPLANATION	INV. NO.	P.R.	DEBIT	CREDIT	BALANCE
1987							
July	1	6/29—2/10, n/30	178			1 8 7 5 00	1 8 7 5 00
	1	Freight prepaid	178			5 4 75	1 9 2 9 75
	12	Corrected invoice	178		2 5 00		1 9 0 4 75

Plumbing Parts

DATE		EXPLANATION	INV. NO.	P.R.	DEBIT	CREDIT	BALANCE
1987							
July	1	Balance	√				4 0 7 25
	9	7/8—2/10, n/30	184			3 4 8 50	7 5 5 75

**ILLUSTRATION
11–12
(concluded)**

Smith Office Supply Company

DATE		EXPLANATION	INV. NO.	P.R.	DEBIT	CREDIT	BALANCE
1987							
July	1	Balance		√			2 4 8 65
	2	7/2—net 30	179			1 1 8 50	3 6 7 15

Thompson Metals

DATE		EXPLANATION	INV. NO.	P.R.	DEBIT	CREDIT	BALANCE
1987							
July	1	Balance		√			1 1 4 6 50
	6	7/5—2/10, net 30	182			2 5 4 0 00	3 6 8 6 50
	6	Freight prepaid	182			1 1 4 85	3 8 0 1 35
	12	Corrected invoice	182			6 0 00	3 8 6 1 35

Summary posting

Summary posting from the invoice register to the general ledger is normally performed at the end of the month. To keep our example simple, however, we will do a summary posting of Jones and Hicks's invoice register as of July 12. The total of the column headed Purchases is debited to Purchases, Account No. 501, in the general ledger. The total of the column headed Accounts Payable is credited to Accounts Payable, Account No. 260, in the general ledger. When the total of each of these columns is posted, the account number is written in parentheses below the total in the invoice register to indicate that posting is complete. The page number of the invoice register is entered in the P.R. column of the general ledger as a cross-reference. A check mark is placed below the totals of the other columns of the invoice register to indicate that these totals were not posted as a total.

Individual posting

Every invoice entered in the Accounts Payable column of the invoice register must be posted to the proper creditor's account in the accounts payable subsidiary ledger. If transportation charges are prepaid and stated separately, they must be posted separately from the merchandise or other property purchased. This procedure is necessary since discounts are not allowed on transportation charges.

In addition, it is necessary to individually post each item entered in the General Ledger debit and credit columns of the invoice register. This posting is generally performed daily, and a check mark is placed in the Check column beside the amount posted. The invoice number is entered in the P.R. column of the subsidiary ledger account to which the amount is posted. (See the ledgers for Jones and Hicks, Illustration 11–11 and 11–12.)

Cash and COD purchases

Cash and COD purchases are not usually entered in the invoice register. Instead, they are recorded in the cash disbursements journal. (Cash purchases may be recorded in the same manner as purchases on accounts, however.) If cash purchases are recorded in the cash disbursements journal, no entry is made in the individual creditor's accounts. The cost of property purchased under COD terms is the total amount paid, including COD charges and any transportation costs. Payment must be made prior to receipt of the property; hence, the COD purchase is essentially treated as a cash purchase. The cash disbursements journal is used for the initial recording, and the proper account is debited for the total cost, including transportation and COD charges, and cash is credited for the same amount.

Transportation costs

In discussing purchase invoice terms on pages 313 and 314, we mentioned that shipping charges may be prepaid by the seller or paid by the buyer at the time of delivery. The merchandise may be delivered to the buyer or may be delivered to a freight office where the buyer obtains the merchandise or incurs the additional cost of having it delivered.

Freight prepaid. If the shipper pays the transportation charges (freight prepaid), the amount may or may not be added to the invoice, depending on the terms of the sale. If the terms are f.o.b. shipping point, it is understood that the buyer will pay the shipping costs in addition to the invoice price. If the terms are f.o.b. destination, it is understood that the invoice price includes the shipping costs and the buyer is obligated to pay only the invoice price.

Freight collect. If merchandise is shipped f.o.b. shipping point, freight collect, the buyer must pay the shipping charges before obtaining possession of the merchandise. The method of recording these shipping charges is the same as for recording shipping charges prepaid by the seller and added to the invoice.

If merchandise is shipped f.o.b. destination, freight collect, the buyer must pay the shipping charges before obtaining possession of the merchandise; however, the buyer deducts the transportation charges from the invoice amount when paying the creditor.

Recording transportation charges. Transportation charges may be recorded as a debit to Purchases. However, a more common practice is to record the transportation charges on incoming merchandise in a separate account titled **Transportation-In.** This account is treated as an extension of the Purchases account.

In the Jones and Hicks illustration, the shipping charges are recorded as a separate item in a Transportation-In account. The only transportation charges reflected in the invoice register are those that have been prepaid by the seller and added to the invoice. All other transportation costs on merchandise purchased will be recorded in the cash disbursements journal.

Transportation costs on plant assets, such as office and delivery equipment, should be treated as part of the cost of the asset. (See Invoice No. 181 in the Jones and Hicks illustration.) It does not matter if the freight is prepaid or collect. The amount of freight is still recorded as a part of the asset cost in the asset account.

Insurance on merchandise. Generally, merchandise shipped by parcel post mail is insured against loss or damage in transit. These insurance charges are rarely recorded as a separate item. Usually, they are either charged directly to the Purchases account or included with transportation costs in the Transportation-In account.

If the purchaser does not want merchandise insured, he or she assumes the risk of loss or damage in transit, since title to merchandise shipped by parcel post mail ordinarily passes to the purchaser when it is placed in the hands of the post office for delivery.

AUTOMATED ACCOUNTING SYSTEMS

The purchasing process involves a number of steps including:

1. Requisitioning.
2. Issuing purchase orders.
3. Receiving and inspection.
4. Storing.
5. Checking accuracy of vendors' invoices with respect to prices and totals.
6. Processing returns and allowances.
7. Maintaining adequate accounts payable records.
8. Making payments to vendors.

If a firm has a large volume of purchases, it may use an automated purchasing system. Data may be keypunched on cards or paper tapes or recorded on magnetic tapes, so that computers can be used to process the data and produce the desired records. Also, since purchases are directly related to inventories and cash disbursements, the automated accounting system might be designed to include cash disbursements and account for transactions including merchandise inventory.

SUMMARY

A **merchandising firm** derives most of its revenue from selling goods to customers. Before a merchandising firm can make a sale, it must first have something to sell. Items of merchandise bought for resale to customers are called **purchases.** Any department within a company may request the purchasing department to buy merchandise by submitting a **purchase requisition.** When the purchase requisition is approved, an order is placed with the supplier. This order, known as a **purchase order,** is the buyer's written order for merchandise or other items recorded on the purchase requisition. When the purchase order is sent to the supplier, it is often accompanied by a duplicate **acknowledgment copy,** which must be signed and returned to the buyer.

A **purchase invoice** is a document that the buyer receives from the seller to record the purchase transaction. The purchase invoice contains such information as the seller's name, the date of purchase, the invoice number, the method of shipment, the terms of the purchase, and the kind and quantity of goods ordered. When purchases arrive, the recipient may check their correctness against the purchase invoice or may prepare a separate **receiving report.** Often a supplier is unable to fill a complete order at the time requested and will notify the buyer that the remaining goods will be sent on **back order.**

Suppliers may offer purchasers two kinds of discounts. A **trade discount** is usually shown on the face of the invoice as a deduction from the total price. A **cash discount** is usually used to encourage customers to pay promptly. To qualify for a cash discount, a customer must pay the supplier within a specified period of time. There are two methods of recording purchases that are subject to cash discounts. With the gross method, purchases are recorded at the total invoice price, and the discount is ignored until the time of payment. Then the discount is credited to the **Purchases Discounts account.** With the net method, purchases are recorded net of the cash discount. If the discount isn't taken, its amount is recorded in the **Purchases Discounts Lost account.**

A number of terms and abbreviations are used on invoices. Among the most common are those that state the terms of payment, such as 2/10, n/30 or 2/EOM, n/60, and those that describe shipping terms and charges, such as **f.o.b. destination, f.o.b. shipping point, freight collect,** and **freight prepaid.** A buyer may also incur **drayage** charges in moving the merchandise from the freight office to the buyer's office. Buyers who prefer to postpone payment until the goods are received will order merchandise **COD.**

Merchandise is not always received in satisfactory condition or according to previously agreed-on terms. In such a case, the buyer uses a **debit memorandum** to notify the seller that the buyer's books have been adjusted accordingly. If the seller agrees that the adjustment is reasonable, he will send the buyer a **credit memorandum** to indicate that the seller's books have also been adjusted.

The purchase of merchandise and other property may involve a number of other forms, including **bills of lading, waybills,** and **freight bills.**

A merchandising firm may use either a **periodic inventory system** or a **perpetual inventory system** to keep track of its merchandise inventory. With a periodic system, inventory is counted only at the close of an accounting period. In contrast, with a perpetual inventory system, a running total of inventory quantities and values is maintained.

Under the periodic method, purchases of merchandise during the current period are recorded in the Purchases account. Occasionally, a business may receive merchandise that was not ordered or is in excess of the requested amount. Likewise, the merchandise may be damaged. Under these situations, the purchasing firm makes an adjustment to the Purchases Returns and Allowances account. This account is deducted from the Purchases account at the end of the period to arrive at net purchases.

When a firm is large, a separate journal, the **purchases journal,** is used to record purchases on credit. The purchases journal is arranged so that a single entry suffices for both the debit to Purchases and the offsetting credit to Accounts Payable. At the end of the month, the Amount column is totaled and used as a **summary posting** to the general ledger.

The **Accounts Payable account** is classified as a liability because the balance in the account represents amounts due to creditors. The credit balance in the account represents the total amount owed by the company for merchandise purchases. There are two methods of supporting the Accounts Payable ledger account, the **ledger account system** and the **invoice method.**

The **invoice register,** unlike the purchases journal, is a book of original entry in which *all* invoices dealing with purchases on account—whether merchandise, supplies, or other items—are entered.

In summary, the purchasing process involves a number of steps including: (1) requisitioning, (2) issuing purchase orders, (3) receiving and inspecting, (4) storing, (5) checking the accuracy of the vendor's invoice with respect to individual and total prices, (6) processing returns and allowances, (7) maintaining adequate accounts payable records, and (8) making payments to vendors.

KEY TERMS

Accounts Payable Account—A liability account used to keep record of amounts due to creditors.

Acknowledgment Copy—Duplicate copy of the purchase order signed by the supplier to indicate acceptance of the order.

Back Order—An order or part of an order that cannot be filled at the time requested but will be shipped at a later date.

Bill of Lading—A receipt given to a shipper when merchandise is shipped by air freight, highway freight, or rail. It indicates the total number of packages, the total weight, and a description of the packages.

Cash Discount—A means of encouraging prompt payment by allowing customers to take a deduction from the gross invoice amount if they pay the invoice within a specified time period. It is a sales discount to the seller and a purchases discount to the buyer.

COD—Collect on delivery, or cash on delivery, meaning that payment is required at the time the merchandise is delivered.

Credit Memorandum—A document that a seller uses to inform a buyer that the buyer's Accounts Receivable account on the seller's books has been credited due to errors, returns, or allowances.

Debit Memorandum—A document that a buyer uses to inform a seller that the seller's Accounts Payable account on the buyer's books is being debited due to an error or an allowance for damaged merchandise.

Drayage—Additional costs incurred when a buyer hires a trucking company or delivery service to move merchandise from the freight office to the buyer's location.

f.o.b. Destination—Free on board at destination. Freight terms which indicate that the seller has agreed to be ultimately responsible for all transportation costs and to assume all responsibility for the merchandise until it reaches the buyer.

f.o.b. Shipping Point—Free on board at shipping point. Freight terms which indicate that the buyer has agreed to be ultimately responsible for the freight charges and to assume all risks at the time the merchandise is accepted for shipment by the carrier.

Freight Bill—A bill for transportation charges similar in content to a bill of lading, except that it shows the freight charges in addition to a description of the shipment.

Freight Collect—Terms indicating that the buyer is to pay the freight changes when the merchandise arrives. If terms are f.o.b. destination, the buyer will be able to deduct the amount of the freight when paying the invoice.

Freight Prepaid—Terms indicating that the seller has paid the freight on the goods at the time of shipment. If the terms are f.o.b. shipping point, the seller will be able to collect the amount of the freight from the buyer.

Invoice Register—A book of original entry in which all invoices dealing with purchases on account, whether the purchases involve merchandise, supplies, or other items, are recorded.

Invoice System—A subsidiary record system used to support the Accounts Payable control account. All unpaid invoices are kept in an open file according to their due dates. When an invoice is paid in full, it is removed from the open file and placed in the paid file.

Ledger Account System—A subsidiary record system used to support the Accounts Payable control account in which a separate subsidiary ledger account is maintained for each creditor.

Merchandise Inventory—The amount of goods on hand and available for sale at a particular point in time.

Merchandising Firm—A business enterprise that derives most of its revenue from selling goods to customers.

Periodic Inventory System—A system of accounting for merchandise when inventory is counted only at the close of an accounting period. The general ledger account Merchandise Inventory contains only the beginning balance in inventory, while inventory purchases for the period are recorded in a separate ledger account, Purchases.

Perpetual Inventory System—A system of accounting for merchandise in which a running total of inventory quantities and values are maintained in the Merchandise Inventory account.

Purchase Invoice—A document that the seller sends to the buyer to record a purchase transaction. It includes all details of the purchase, such as a description of the merchandise, price, terms of sale, and method of shipment.

Purchase Order—A document that the buyer sends the seller as a formal order for merchandise.

Purchase Requisition—A document that is submitted to the purchasing department as a formal request to purchase merchandise or other items.

Purchases—Items of merchandise bought for resale to customers.

Purchases Discounts Account—An account in which the amount of cash discounts taken is recorded. At the end of the accounting period, its balance is shown as a deduction from purchases.

Purchases Discounts Lost Account—An account used to record cash discounts lost due to payments made after the discount period has expired.

Purchases Journal—A special journal in which all purchases of merchandise on account are recorded.

Receiving Report—A report prepared by the receiving personnel listing the merchandise received. It should be compared with the purchase order.

Summary Posting—The posting of total credit purchases for the month from the purchases journal to the Purchases and Accounts Payable ledger accounts.

Trade Discount—A reduction in the list price of merchandise. It enables a seller to offer different prices to various categories of customers and to revise prices without going through the costly process of revising the catalogs.

Transportation-In Account—An account in which transportation charges on incoming merchandise are recorded. It is an extension of the Purchases account.

Waybill—A document prepared by an agent of the transportation company when merchandise is received for shipment. It describes the merchandise being shipped, shows points of origin and destination, and indicates any special handling requirements.

QUESTIONS AND EXERCISES

1. Distinguish among a purchase requisition, a purchase order, and a purchase invoice.
2. What is a purchase invoice? What type of information is found on the face of the invoice?
3. Distinguish between trade discounts and cash discounts.
4. What is meant by the following terms?
   a. 1/20, n/30.
   b. 2/EOM, n/60.
   c. 2/10/EOM, n/60.
5. Define the following terms:
   a. f.o.b. destination.
   b. f.o.b. shipping point.
   c. Freight collect.
   d. Freight prepaid.

6. What is a bill of lading? Why might the quantity specified on the bill of lading differ from the quantity shown on the purchase invoice?
7. Define the following terms:
   a. Waybill.
   b. Drayage.
8. How does a periodic inventory system operate?
9. What types of transactions are recorded in a Purchase Returns and Allowances account?
10. Describe a purchases journal.
11. What two accounting methods are used to maintain supporting records for Accounts Payable? Describe both methods.
12. How are transportation charges commonly recorded on (a) merchandise purchases and (b) plant assets?
13. What factors should be considered when computing the freight charges on a shipment of merchandise?
14. What eight steps are involved in the purchasing process?
15. Ruth Hines purchased some lamps for resale in her decorating business. The total of the invoice is $750, and it is subject to trade discounts of 10, 15, and 5 percent. Compute the amount she will pay for the lamps. (Round to the nearest dollars.)
16. Roy Zuckerman buys $3,000 of merchandise subject to a 2 percent cash discount if paid within 10 days of the invoice date.
    a. Compute the amount he will owe if he pays within the discount period.
    b. Compute the amount he will owe if he does not pay within the discount period.

PROBLEMS

11-1. Part A: Cassie's Boutique ordered the following merchandise from the Casual Fashion Garment Corporation:

Item	Quantity	Unit Price
Jeans.	30	$14.00
Skirts	15	16.50
Blouses	20	9.25
T-shirts	50	4.75

The gross invoice amount is subject to a trade discount of 10 percent. Shipping terms are f.o.b. shipping point and the freight charges of

$20 were prepaid by the Casual Fashion Garment Corporation. Cassie's Boutique does not maintain an invoice register.

Required:

Prepare a general journal entry to record receipt of the merchandise.

Part B: Assume that Cassie's Boutique purchased the merchandise listed in Part A under the following conditions.

1. The gross invoice price was subject to a chain discount of 20, 10, and 5 percent.
2. Shipping terms were f.o.b. destination.
3. Cassie's Boutique paid the freight charges ($20) when the merchandise arrived.

Required:

Prepare general journal entries to record the receipt of the merchandise and the payment of the freight charges.

11–2.   The Cowboy Shop ordered the following items from the Ranchers Company:

Item	Quantity	Unit Price
Boots.	25 pairs	$30.00
Spurs.	40 pairs	9.50
Chaps	32 pairs	28.00
Western shirts. . . .	50 each	20.00
Jeans.	70 pairs	12.00

The gross amount of the invoice is subject to trade discounts of 25, 10, and 5 percent, and the payment terms are 2/10, n/30. The invoice date is April 15.

Required:

1. Compute the following items:
   a. Gross invoice amount.
   b. Amount subject to cash discount.
   c. Net amount payable within ten days of invoice date.
2. Make the general journal entry to record the receipt of the purchase invoice (gross method).
3. Make the general journal entry to record payment for the merchandise if the payment is made on April 24.
4. Make the general journal entry to record payment for the merchandise if the payment is made on May 10.

5. Repeat requirements 2, 3, and 4 assuming purchases are accounted for by the net method.

11–3. The Collegiate Bookstore ordered the following calculators from the Flagstone Electronics Corporation for resale:

Model	Quantity	Unit Price
FE 1001—Bookkeeper.	10	$ 27.00
FE 1205—Accountant.	8	65.00
FE 1551—Engineer	5	89.00
FE 1812—Scientific	5	101.00
FE 2001—Programmable.	2	185.00

The gross amount of the invoice is subject to trade discounts of 20, 15, and 5 percent, and the payment terms are 2/10/EOM, n/60. The invoice date is June 5.

Required:

1. Compute the following:
   a. Gross invoice amount.
   b. Amount subject to cash discount.
   c. Net amount payable within the discount period.
2. Make the general journal entry to record the receipt of the merchandise (gross method).
3. Make the general journal entry to record payment for the merchandise on July 5.
4. Make the general journal entry to record payment for the merchandise on August 1.
5. Repeat requirements 2, 3, and 4 assuming purchases are accounted for by the net method.

11–4. The Coaster Store ordered merchandise from the Carson Wholesale Company at a gross invoice amount of $3,600. This amount ($3,600) is subject to trade discounts of 20, 10, and 5 percent, and the payment terms are 2/10, n/60. The Carson Wholesale Company allows a discount to be taken when partial payment is made during the discount period.

Required:

1. Make the journal entry to record the receipt of the purchase invoice (gross method).
2. Make the journal entry to record payment for the entire shipment of merchandise during the discount period.

3. Make a journal entry to record a partial payment of $1,800 during the discount period.
4. Make a journal entry to record payment for the merchandise 30 days after the invoice date.
5. Repeat requirements 1, 2, and 4 assuming purchases are accounted for using the net method.
6. Make a journal entry to record a partial payment of $1,800 during the discount period assuming the purchase was originally accounted for using the net method.
7. Make a journal entry to record payment of the remaining amount due after the discount period.

11–5. The King and Cole Sporting Goods Store completed the following purchase transactions during the month of May 1987:

1987
May 3 Received Purchase Invoice No. 201 from Roberts Wholesale for baseball equipment, $900; terms, May 1—2/10, n/30; freight prepaid and added to invoice, $45.50.

6 Received Purchase Invoice No. 202 from Novak, Incorporated, for tennis equipment, $425; terms, May 1—2/10, n/30; freight collect.

10 Received Purchase Invoice No. 203 from Palmer Golf Company for golf equipment, $1,080; terms, May 5—2/10, n/60; freight collect.

13 Received Purchase Invoice No. 204 from Bradley Milton Company for indoor and outdoor games, $575; terms, May 10—2/10, n/30; freight prepaid and added to invoice, $32.

17 Received Purchase Invoice No. 205 from Hargrove Supply Company for office supplies, $280; terms, May 14—2/10, n/60; freight collect.

20 Received Purchase Invoice No. 206 from Flemmen & Sons for store equipment, $650; terms, May 15—n/60; freight prepaid and added to invoice, $85.

24 Received a corrected purchase invoice from Palmer Golf Company for $1,028. (See Invoice No. 203.)

Required:

Record each of the invoices in an invoice register like the one shown in Illustration 11–10. The following account numbers may be used:

160   Office Supplies
180   Store Equipment
210   Accounts Payable
510   Purchases
515   Transportation-In

11–6. The Printer's Shop is a retail store which sells books, office supplies, and school supplies. During the month of August, the following selected transactions occurred:

1987

Aug. 2   Received Purchase Invoice No. 410 from Reading, Incorporated, for reference books, $800; terms, July 28—2/10, n/30; freight collect.

    6   Received Purchase Invoice No. 411 from Kano Supply Company for school supplies, $500; terms, August 3—n/30; freight collect.

    9   Received Purchase Invoice No. 412 from Daze & Son for store equipment, $350; terms, August 4—2/10, n/60; freight prepaid and added to invoice, $43.

    13   Received Purchase Invoice No. 413 from Joe's Autos for a delivery car, $5,000; Terms, August 10—2/10, n/60; freight prepaid and added to invoice, $185.

    16   Received a corrected purchase invoice from Kano Supply Company for $550. (See Invoice No. 411.)

    20   Received Purchase Invoice No. 414 from Reading, Incorporated, for educational books, $600; terms, August 16—2/10, n/30; freight collect.

    23   Received Purchase Invoice No. 415 from Haas Supply Company for office supplies for resale, $489; terms, August 21—n/30; freight prepaid and added to invoice, $36.

    27   Received Purchase Invoice No. 416 from Odell Printing Company for Bibles and other religious books, $750; terms, August 23—2/10, n/60; freight prepaid and added to invoice, $62.

    30   Received a corrected purchase invoice from Haas Supply Company for $469 plus $36 freight charges. (See Invoice No. 415.)

Required:

1. Record each of the invoices in an invoice register like the one shown in Illustration 11–10, and post the invoice amount directly to the creditor's account in a subsidiary accounts payable ledger. (See balances below.)

2. Make the necessary individual postings and summary postings to the following accounts in the general ledger.

Account No.	Account Title	Balance July 31, 1987
148	Store Equipment	$ 400
149	Delivery Car	0
221	Accounts Payable.	10,000
511	Purchases	21,000
518	Transportation-In	580

Subsidiary Accounts Payable Balances (Partial)
August 1, 1987

Daze & Son	$200
Haas Supply Company	150
Joe's Autos.	0
Kano Supply Company.	120
Odell Printing Company	500
Reading, Incorporated	200

11–7. The Snow Hardware Company has just completed its first month in business. During this month, the following purchases were made:

1987

Jan. 3 Received Purchase Invoice No. 10 from Abby's Wholesale for radios, $450; terms, December 29—2/10, n/30; freight prepaid and added to invoice, $18.

8 Received Purchase Invoice No. 11 from Cook's Appliances for appliances, $1,200; terms, January 3—2/10, n/60; freight collect.

10 Received Purchase Invoice No. 12 from Hansel Company for watches and clocks, $380; terms, January 7—2/10/ EOM, n/60; freight collect.

14 Received Purchase Invoice No. 13 from Cobra Wholesale for athletic equipment, $950; terms, January 10—2/10, n/30; freight prepaid and added to invoice, $84.

17 Received Purchase Invoice No. 14 from Abby's Wholesale for toys and games, $620; terms, January 15—2/10, n/30; freight prepaid and added to invoice, $25.

19 Received a corrected purchase invoice from Cook's Appliances for $1,120. (See Invoice No. 11.)

21 Received Purchase Invoice No. 15 from King Supply Company for office supplies, $200, and store supplies, $500; terms, January 17—2/10, n/30; freight collect.

1987

Jan. 24 Received Purchase Invoice No. 16 from Florida Equipment Company for office equipment, $600; terms, January 16—2/10/EOM, n/60; freight prepaid and added to invoice, $45.

24 Received a corrected purchase invoice from Abby's Wholesale for $602 plus freight (No. 14).

24 Received Purchase Invoice No. 17 from Cobra Wholesale for guns and knives, $800; terms, January 20—2/10, n/30; freight prepaid and added to invoice, $80.

28 Received Purchase Invoice No. 18 from Brooks Manufacturing Company for hand tools and power tools, $960; terms, January 22—2/10, n/60; freight collect.

29 Received Purchase Invoice No. 19 from Byron's Bikes for bicycles, tricycles, and unicycles, $1,000; terms, January 22—2/10, n/60; freight prepaid and added to invoice, $125.

Required:

1. Record each of the invoices in an invoice register like the one shown in Illustration 11–10, and post the invoice amount directly to the creditor's account in a subsidiary accounts payable ledger.

2. Make the necessary individual and summary postings to the following accounts in the general ledger:

Account No.	Account Title
130	Office Supplies
131	Store Supplies
140	Office Equipment
212	Accounts Payable
401	Purchases
404	Transportation-In

11–8. During the month of June, Crawford's Sporting Goods conducted the following purchase transactions:

1987

June 2 Received Purchase Invoice No. 652 from Court King, Inc., for tennis rackets, $380; terms, June 1—2/10, n/30; freight prepaid and added to invoice, $19.

4 Received Purchase Invoice No. 653 from Aqua-Master Corporation for scuba equipment, $1,160; terms, June 2—2/EOM, n/60; freight collect.

7 Received Purchase Invoice No. 654 from The Snow Snake

Ski Company for skis, bindings, and poles, $740; terms, June 4—2/10, n/30; freight collect.

June 11 Received a corrected Purchase Invoice from Aqua-Master Corporation for $1,060. (See Invoice No. 653).

14 Received Purchase Invoice No. 655 from Trail-Rite Outfitters for backpacking equipment for $590; terms, June 11—2/10/EOM, n/60; freight collect.

15 Received a corrected invoice from Court King, Inc., for $308 plus freight. (See Invoice No. 652.)

17 Received Purchase Invoice No. 656 from Long Drive Golf Club Company for clubs and irons, $620; terms, June 14—2/10, n/30; freight collect.

18 Received Purchase Invoice No. 657 from Fast Wheels Corporation for skateboards, $190; terms, June 16—2/10, n/30; freight prepaid and added to invoice, $17.

20 Received Purchase Invoice No. 658 from Neat Duds Company for sportswear, $810; terms, June 18—2/10/EOM, n/60; freight collect.

20 Received a corrected purchase invoice from Trail-Rite Outfitters for $560. (See Invoice No. 655.)

22 Received Purchase Invoice No. 659 from Sharp-Cast Tackle Company for rods and reels, $848; terms, June 21—2/10, n/30; freight prepaid and added to invoice, $36.

23 Received Purchase Invoice No. 660 from Split-Second Chronograph Corporation for stopwatches, $444; terms, June 20—2/10, n/30; freight collect.

25 Received Purchase Invoice No. 661 from Triple Threat Athletic Supply Company for football, baseball, and hockey equipment, $1,781; terms, June 23—2/EOM, n/60; freight prepaid and added to invoice, $42.

27 Received Purchase Invoice No. 662 from Baxter Equipment Company for display racks, $220; terms, June 24—2/10, n/30; freight collect.

29 Received a corrected purchase invoice from Split-Second Chronograph Corporation for $484. (See Invoice No. 660.)

Required:

1. Record each of the invoices in an invoice register like the one shown in Illustration 11–10, and post the invoice amount directly to the creditor's account in the subsidiary accounts payable ledger.

2. Make the necessary individual and summary postings to the following accounts in the general ledger:

Account No.	Account Title
150	Store Equipment
222	Accounts Payable
501	Purchases
502	Transportation-In

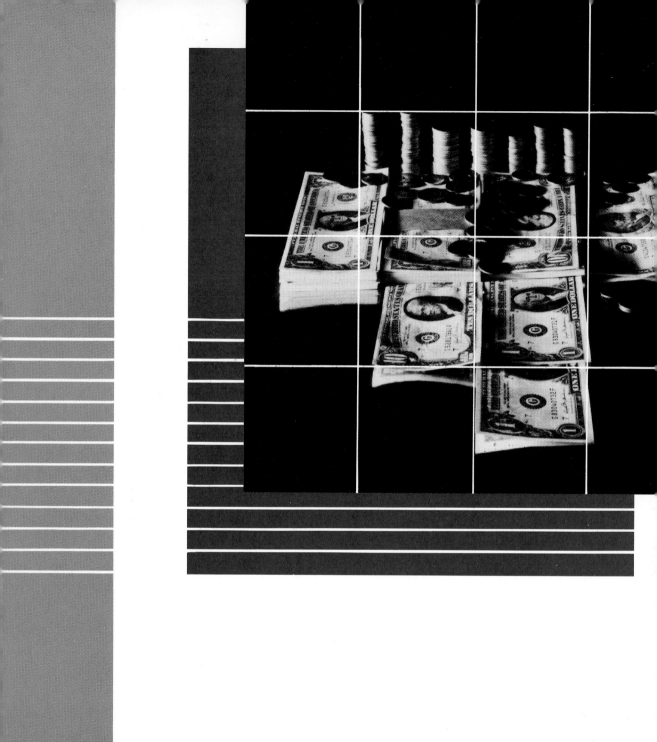

Cost of goods sold
Beginning inventory
+ Net Purchases
- Ending inventory (Count)
= Cost of Goods Sold

Mdse available for sale
Sales
- C.G.S
Gross margin
- expense
= net income

CHAPTER **12**

Accounting for merchandise—sales

Revenue
C.O.G.S
Expenses

LEARNING OBJECTIVES

In this chapter, you will learn how to account for sales in a merchandising firm. After reading this chapter, you should be able to:

1. Identify various types of sales.
2. Handle incoming purchase orders.
3. Record transactions in a sales journal.
4. Maintain an Accounts Receivable control account and subsidiary ledger.
5. Record transactions in a sales register.

ACCOUNTING FOR SALES

The procedures used in accounting for sales depend on several factors including the kind of business, the organization of the sales department, the goods sold, the volume of sales, the method of selling, and the sales terms.

There are a number of steps in the accounting cycle for sales transactions. First, when the orders are received, they are examined for acceptability. Next, the selling terms are determined and credit is approved. From the order approval, a sales invoice is prepared. Along with preparing the sales invoice, the merchandise is packed and shipped or delivered. Finally, to complete the sales cycle, collection of payment is made. An important factor for both the buyer and the seller are the terms of sale.

KINDS OF SALES

Sales for cash

While some businesses sell for both cash and credit, others sell for cash only. In a **sale for cash,** the seller exchanges merchandise for cash only. No other form of payment is accepted. Examples include snack shops, newsstands, food stores, and some gas stations. Various procedures are used to handle cash sales. When cash sales are numerous, one or more kinds of cash registers are likely to be used. Sales may be accumulated on the cash register in several ways. Some registers can accumulate various subtotals in addition to the total sales amount. Depending on the keys punched, subtotals may be accumulated by department, by type of merchandise, or by salesperson. If a sales tax is required, it is usually recorded separately. Sales tickets are normally prepared in duplicate form. One copy is given to the customer as a receipt, and the second copy is retained in the register and later removed by a person in the accounting department who will analyze and record the sales. The cash register provides a means of internal control since the total cash sales for the day should be reconciled to the cash in the register drawer. If more than one person operates the register, each operator should have a separate register drawer. Such internal control allows a firm to protect its assets from waste and theft, evaluate employee performance, promote operational efficiency, and guarantee compliance with company policies.

Sales on credit

Sales on credit are often referred to as *sales on account* or *charge sales.* In such a sales transaction, the seller exchanges merchandise for the buyer's promise to pay at a later date. A credit sale is recorded by debiting or charging Accounts Receivable and by crediting the Sales account. The balance owed by each individual customer will be recorded in an accounts receivable subsidiary ledger. Most wholesale sales and a significant portion of retail sales are now made on credit. Since a business that sells on account assumes some risk that all debts will not be repaid, it should investigate the financial condition of its buyers. Larger businesses often have a credit department that establishes credit policies and approves or disapproves individual credit sales. Experienced credit managers have learned to establish credit policies that will neither be so tight as to reduce sales nor so loose as to create excessive losses due to bad debts.

Salesclerks should be careful not to sell on credit to anyone who is not an approved credit customer. The problem is significantly lessened by providing established credit customers with charge cards. Not only do the cards provide evidence that the buyer has an account, but they can be used in a mechanical device to print the customer's name, address, and account number on the sales ticket. In a wholesale business, where a large portion of the sales orders are received by phone or mail, credit sales are approved in a routine manner before the goods are released. Credit sales orders received by phone or mail need not be processed immediately since the buyer is not physically present and waiting for the order.

Salesclerks should remember that a charge card may not necessarily belong to the person who presents it. To make sure the card belongs to the holder, a salesclerk may request further identification or may compare the signature on the charge card with the one on the sales ticket.

Bank credit cards

The use of **bank credit cards** has become very common in retail merchandising. Such cards are issued through financial institutions and can be used to purchase merchandise worldwide. Two well-known bank credit cards are VISA and MasterCard. Many retail businesses use this form of credit exclusively; therefore, they do not bear the risk of uncollectible accounts receivable. Credit card transactions can be accounted for in nearly the same manner as cash sales.

When goods are sold to customers using bank credit cards, the merchant's copies of the sales tickets are taken to the bank like a deposit. The company debits Cash for the total amount of the tickets and credits Sales. If at this time the bank charges a service fee for the credit sales, the company debits Cash for the amount of the tickets minus the fee. For example, if a store's total receipts from VISA are $9,000 and the bank charges a fee of $270, the store would debit its Cash account for $8,730, debit Bank Credit Card Expense for $270, and credit Sales for $9,000. The journal entry would be:

		GENERAL JOURNAL			
DATE		ACCOUNT AND EXPLANATION	P.R.	DEBIT	CREDIT
	15	Cash		8 7 3 0 00	
		Bank Credit Card expense—VISA		2 7 0 00	
		Sales			9 0 0 0 00
		To record the deposit of VISA sales tickets.			

Another way of handling bank credit card transactions is to deposit the VISA tickets with each day's deposits of checks, currency, and coin. Cash is debited and Sales is credited for the amount of the sales by VISA. At the end of the month, the bank will figure the fee on the total tickets for the month and notify the merchant of the amount. Then the merchant can debit the Bank Credit Card Expense—VISA account and credit the Cash account for the appropriate amount. This is the usual procedure for handling bank credit card transactions. The fee the bank charges represents its charge for collecting the amount of a sale at a later date, while the merchant receives credit for the sale amount on the day of the sale.

Sales on approval

A **sale on approval** gives the customer the right to return the goods within a specified time period. Therefore, the sale is not final until the customer's intentions are known. Mail-order businesses that sell stamps, coins, or books are examples of businesses that sell on approval. When approval sales are handled as charge sales, returns can be treated as ordinary sales returns. When approval sales are handled as cash sales, a record is kept until it is known that the customer will keep the goods. By a specified date, the customer must either pay for the goods or return them. The accountant may wait until payment is received and then record the transaction as a cash sale.

Layaway sales

Sales on approval should not be confused with layaway, or "will call," sales. With **layaway sales,** the buyer agrees to purchase the goods with the understanding that they will be picked up and paid for in full at a later date. When the goods are purchased, a deposit is usually made. The transaction is then recorded as a debit to Cash for the amount of the deposit, a debit to Accounts Receivable for the remaining amount that is owed, and a credit to Sales for the total amount of the sale.

COD sales

Merchandise may be sold for **cash on delivery (COD).** Such terms call for the buyer to pay for the goods when they are delivered. The delivery and collection agent may be the seller's employee, the post office, an express company, a trucking company, a railroad, a steamship company, or any other common carrier.

Cash on delivery sales made by a retail business are usually recorded as cash sales. Upon approval, a sales ticket is prepared and listed on a COD list for control purposes. The merchandise is delivered, and the sales price is collected. At the end of each day, the delivery agent returns the COD sales tickets and the money collected. These tickets are compared with the COD list, and the sale is recorded in the same manner used for a cash sale. If the customer refuses the merchandise, it is returned to the stock room, and no sale is recorded.

Sales on consignment

Sometimes a business will make **sales on consignment.** When sold on consignment, merchandise is shipped to an agent dealer with the agreement that payment is not required unless the goods are sold. Under such a method of selling, title to the consigned goods is retained by the shipper until the goods are sold by the agent dealer. The owner of the goods shipped on consignment is referred to as the **consignor.** The agent dealer is called the **consignee.** When the goods are shipped, a shipment invoice is prepared. The shipment invoice should not be confused with a sales invoice because a consignment shipment is not a sale. The shipment invoice is used merely to inform the consignee of the goods shipped. Many types of goods, such as livestock, vegetables, radios and televisions, garden equipment, power tools, and other products are often marketed on a consignment basis.

Installment sales

Computers, appliances, stereo equipment, furniture, clothes, automobiles, real estate, and many other kinds of merchandise may be sold on an installment basis. In an **installment sale,** the seller agrees to give the buyer physical possession of the goods in exchange for a promise to make payments periodically over a specified period of time. The agreement between the buyer and seller is referred to in legal terms as a conditional sales contract. Quite often a down payment is required. The sales contract will specify that the seller will retain title to the property until payment is made in full. The contract may also state that the full sales price will become due immediately should the buyer default in making payment. Because the terms of an installment sale may vary from contract to contract, a buyer should carefully read and understand the contract terms before signing the agreement.

Since the buyer does not receive title to the property until full payment is made, a business can be more lenient in extending credit to customers who buy on installment. A higher price is usually charged for goods sold on installment to offset the added risk imposed on the seller for waiting to collect payments and the additional record-keeping expenses involved.

HANDLING INCOMING PURCHASE ORDERS

Some merchants receive sales orders by telephone, mail, or telegram. Purchase orders may be written on the buyer's purchase order form, letterhead, or other stationery, or on the seller's order blank. Orders received over the telephone should be carefully recorded on prepared forms. In handling purchase orders, it is important that well-organized procedures be established and followed. Such procedures should increase efficiency and help to prevent clerical mistakes. The following steps will help assure that purchase orders are properly handled.

Examination

As each purchase order is received, it should be examined. The customer's identity should be determined, and the description and quantities of goods ordered should be reviewed. Sometimes merchandise is ordered by name, inventory number, or special code word. The person examining the purchase orders should make sure the inventory number or code word agrees with the merchandise description. Abbreviated inventory names and titles along with code words should be carefully checked. Particular attention should be given to unit prices and total prices. Inaccurate pricing will result in incorrect billing as well as unnecessary customer ill will.

Credit approval

Part of the examination process should include the separation of orders involving credit from all other incoming orders. The credit orders should be sent to the credit department for approval before any billing or shipping takes place. COD orders should also be approved by the credit department. If a customer does not accept a COD order, the seller will have to bear the additional shipping charges when the order is returned. Thus, if a customer abuses the COD privilege, he or she may be asked to make full or partial payment before the order is shipped. It is not uncommon for sellers to require a partial cash prepayment to accompany all COD orders.

Transportation

As each order is processed, it is necessary to determine how the order will be shipped and who will bear the transportation expenses. Orders may be shipped by parcel post, express, rail, or by the firm's own delivery trucks. Orders transported by a common carrier are usually insured. Express orders will go by rail or air, while freight shipments may be delivered by truck, rail, air, or water.

When shipments are sent by parcel post, the transportation charges must be prepaid by the seller. The amount paid is added to the amount that the buyer owes the seller. The seller will make the following entry when he prepays the postage:

	GENERAL JOURNAL			
DATE	ACCOUNT AND EXPLANATION	P.R	DEBIT	CREDIT
	Postage Expense		1 00	
	Cash			1 00
	Postage on sale.			

When the goods are shipped, the seller debits Accounts Receivable and credits Sales and Postage Expense. For example, assume that office supplies of $25 are ordered by a customer. The postage charged to mail them is $1. The entry would be recorded as follows:

	GENERAL JOURNAL			
DATE	ACCOUNT AND EXPLANATION	P.R	DEBIT	CREDIT
	Accounts Receivable		2 6 00	
	Sales			2 5 00
	Postage Expense			1 00
	To record sale and prepaid postage.			

The effect of the two entries posted to the account Postage Expense is a zero balance in the account. The seller is not responsible for the expense, the buyer is. Therefore, the seller should not show any dollar amount of expense for the period. He will collect it from the buyer.

Express or freight transportation charges may be paid by the seller or by the purchaser upon receipt of the goods. If the transportation charges are prepaid, the inclusion or exclusion of shipping charges on the invoice will depend on whether the invoice price was quoted as f.o.b. destination or f.o.b. shipping point. As discussed in Chapter 11, the term *f.o.b. destination* means the seller is responsible for paying the shipping charges. The term *f.o.b. shipping point* means the buyer is responsible for paying the shipping charges.

Billing

After a purchase order is examined and approved for credit and the method of shipping is determined, a bill, or **sales invoice,** is

**ILLUSTRATION
12–1**

**Purchase
Order
Received**

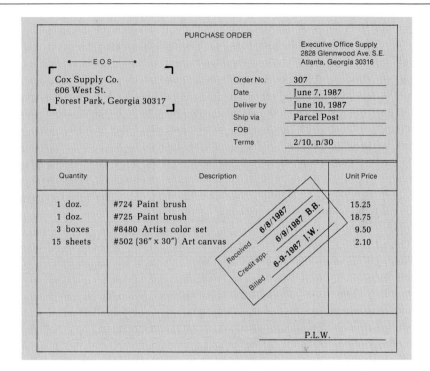

prepared. Illustration 12–1 shows a purchase order that the Cox Supply Company received from the Executive Office Supply Company. When the purchase order was received, it was rubber stamped, and the date of receipt was recorded in the space provided. Later, the date and initials of the persons responsible for credit approval and billing were recorded in the appropriate spaces. When the billing was completed, the purchase order was filed alphabetically by customer name—Executive Office Supply Company—for future reference.

Several copies of a sales invoice are normally prepared. This may be done through the use of carbon paper, no-carbon-required invoice forms, or some type of duplicating device. At least three copies are required. The original copy is sent to the customer, a copy is sent to the accounting department, and a copy is used to authorize the shipment of the merchandise. The sales invoice shown in Illustration 12–2 was prepared for the purchase order presented in Illustration 12–1. For control purposes, sales invoices should be prenumbered

ILLUSTRATION 12–2

Customer Copy of Sales Invoice

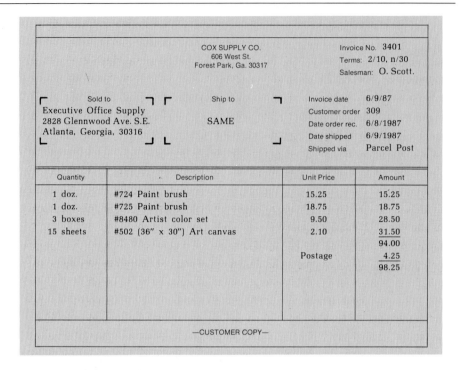

COX SUPPLY CO.
606 West St.
Forest Park, Ga. 30317

Invoice No. 3401

Terms: 2/10, n/30

Salesman: O. Scott.

Sold to
Executive Office Supply
2828 Glennwood Ave. S.E.
Atlanta, Georgia, 30316

Ship to
SAME

Invoice date 6/9/87
Customer order 309
Date order rec. 6/8/1987
Date shipped 6/9/1987
Shipped via Parcel Post

Quantity	Description	Unit Price	Amount
1 doz.	#724 Paint brush	15.25	15.25
1 doz.	#725 Paint brush	18.75	18.75
3 boxes	#8480 Artist color set	9.50	28.50
15 sheets	#502 (36" x 30") Art canvas	2.10	31.50
			94.00
		Postage	4.25
			98.25

—CUSTOMER COPY—

in consecutive order. When the tickets are sorted by number, management can determine the quantity, kinds, and amounts of sales made by each salesperson.

In addition to the usual three sales invoice copies, other copies may be prepared. When the sale is made by a branch office, a copy may be forwarded to that office. Another copy may be sent to the salesperson making the sale. To make sure shipments are properly addressed, a copy may be sent to the shipping department. In such cases, the buyer's address may be separated from the sales invoice and used as a shipping label.

ACCOUNTING FOR SALES

The terms and concepts introduced thus far form the foundation for recording sales activities of a merchandising business. To actually record the sales transactions, certain accounting procedures must be followed. These procedures include establishing accounts for sales, sales tax payable, sales discounts, and sales returns and allowances. Likewise, most merchandising firms use a sales journal to record sales, whether for cash or on credit.

The Sales account

Merchandise sales for the period are recorded in the **Sales account.** Since sales are applicable to a specific accounting period, the Sales account is a revenue, or temporary owner's equity, account. Thus, it will be closed out at the end of every accounting period. We will have more to say on closing procedures in subsequent chapters. For the present time, it is sufficient to note that the balance in the Sales account at any point in time represents the cumulative sales from the beginning of the accounting period.

For example, assume that during the week ending October 7 a company sold $127.50 of merchandise on account. When this transaction was recorded in the general journal, it required a credit to Sales with a matching debit to Accounts Receivable. Remember, Accounts Receivable is an account established when a person buys goods with a promise to pay for them at a later date. Also, suppose that during the same week, the company sold $48.27 of merchandise for cash. This was journalized in a cash receipts journal by crediting Sales and debiting Cash for the sales amount. The company's Sales account would appear as follows:

GENERAL LEDGER								
		Sales					ACCT. NO. 410	
DATE	EXPLANATION	P.R.	DEBIT	CREDIT		BALANCE		
						DEBIT	CREDIT	
1987								
Oct. 7		GJ12		1 2 7 50			1 2 7 50	
9		CR20		4 8 27			1 7 5 77	

Remember that sales increase owner's equity. Since owner's equity is increased by credits, the Sales account is also increased by credits and will have a credit balance. This company's cumulative sales for the accounting period total $175.77 as of October 9.

Retail sales tax

Many businesses are required by state or city law to collect a **retail sales tax** from their customers. Such a tax is usually levied on the gross sales price of retail merchandise. It may apply only to specific items, such as automobiles, televisions, radios, and selected appliances, or it may be imposed on all merchandise. Some states, such as Florida, exclude prescription drugs and food products from the retail sales tax.

To minimize the computations on smaller amounts, it is customary for the taxing authority to provide a sales tax schedule. One such schedule for the 7 percent retail sales tax imposed by Illinois is given in Illustration 12–3.

Under many tax laws, nonprofit organizations are exempt from paying sales tax on their purchases. Consequently, a merchandiser must devise some procedure that enables exempt sales to be excluded from the sales tax liability computation. Sales returns and allowance also affect sales tax accounting.

A merchandiser's sales tax liability is accumulated in a liability account called **Sales Tax Payable.** This account is credited for the amount of sales taxes collected and debited for the amount of taxes paid to the taxing authorities. An example of the Sales Tax Payable account is shown below.

GENERAL LEDGER

Sales Tax Payable — ACCT. NO. 253

DATE	EXPLANATION	P.R.	DEBIT	CREDIT	BALANCE DEBIT	BALANCE CREDIT
	Sales tax collected on sales			2 26		2 26
	Sales tax remitted to state		2 26			00

A company can compute its tax liability using the actual amounts from all invoices, or once a month the company can compute its total liability based on its taxable sales for the period. The method selected will depend on the governing statutes or the business's preference.

To illustrate how sales tax would be recorded, assume that a company operating in a state with a 4 percent sales tax sold $56.39 of merchandise to a customer. The amount of sales tax credited to the Sales Tax Payable account would be $2.26 ($56.39 × .04). When the taxes are remitted to the taxing authorities, the account would

ILLUSTRATION 12–3 State Retail Sales Tax (7 Percent)

Amount of Sale	Tax
.08 thru .21	.01
.22 " .35	.02
.36 " .49	.03
.50 " .64	.04
.65 " .78	.05
.79 " .92	.06
.93 " 1.07	.07
1.08 " 1.21	.08
1.22 " 1.35	.09
1.36 " 1.49	.10
1.50 " 1.64	.11
1.65 " 1.78	.12
1.79 " 1.92	.13
1.93 " 2.07	.14
2.08 " 2.21	.15
2.22 " 2.35	.16
2.36 " 2.49	.17
2.50 " 2.64	.18
2.65 " 2.78	.19
2.79 " 2.92	.20
2.93 " 3.07	.21
3.08 " 3.21	.22
3.22 " 3.35	.23
3.36 " 3.49	.24
3.50 " 3.64	.25
3.65 " 3.78	.26
3.79 " 3.92	.27
3.93 " 4.07	.28
4.08 " 4.21	.29
4.22 " 4.35	.30
4.36 " 4.49	.31
4.50 " 4.64	.32
4.65 " 4.78	.33
4.79 " 4.92	.34
4.93 " 5.07	.35
5.08 " 5.21	.36
5.22 " 5.35	.37
5.36 " 5.49	.38
5.50 " 5.64	.39
5.65 " 5.78	.40
5.79 " 5.92	.41
5.93 " 6.07	.42
6.08 " 6.21	.43
6.22 " 6.35	.44
6.36 " 6.49	.45
6.50 " 6.64	.46
6.65 " 6.78	.47
6.79 " 6.92	.48
6.93 " 7.07	.49
7.08 " 7.21	.50
7.22 " 7.35	.51
7.36 " 7.49	.52
7.50 " 7.64	.53
7.65 " 7.78	.54
7.79 " 7.92	.55
7.93 " 8.07	.56
8.08 " 8.21	.57
8.22 " 8.35	.58
8.36 " 8.49	.59
8.50 " 8.64	.60
8.65 " 8.78	.61
8.79 " 8.92	.62
8.93 " 9.07	.63

Amount of Sale	Tax
9.08 " 9.21	.64
9.22 " 9.35	.65
9.36 " 9.49	.66
9.50 " 9.64	.67
9.65 " 9.78	.68
9.79 " 9.92	.69
9.93 " 10.07	.70
10.08 " 10.21	.71
10.22 " 10.35	.72
10.36 " 10.49	.73
10.50 " 10.64	.74
10.65 " 10.78	.75
10.79 " 10.92	.76
10.93 " 11.07	.77
11.08 " 11.21	.78
11.22 " 11.35	.79
11.36 " 11.49	.80
11.50 " 11.64	.81
11.65 " 11.78	.82
11.79 " 11.92	.83
11.93 " 12.07	.84
12.08 " 12.21	.85
12.22 " 12.35	.86
12.36 " 12.49	.87
12.50 " 12.64	.88
12.65 " 12.78	.89
12.79 " 12.92	.90
12.93 " 13.07	.91
13.08 " 13.21	.92
13.22 " 13.35	.93
13.36 " 13.49	.94
13.50 " 13.64	.95
13.65 " 13.78	.96
13.79 " 13.92	.97
13.93 " 14.07	.98
14.08 " 14.21	.99
14.22 " 14.35	1.00
14.36 " 14.49	1.01
14.50 " 14.64	1.02
14.65 " 14.78	1.03
14.79 " 14.92	1.04
14.93 " 15.07	1.05
15.08 " 15.21	1.06
15.22 " 15.35	1.07
15.36 " 15.49	1.08
15.50 " 15.64	1.09
15.65 " 15.78	1.10
15.79 " 15.92	1.11
15.93 " 16.07	1.12
16.08 " 16.21	1.13
16.22 " 16.35	1.14
16.36 " 16.49	1.15
16.50 " 16.64	1.16
16.65 " 16.78	1.17
16.79 " 16.92	1.18
16.93 " 17.07	1.19
17.08 " 17.21	1.20
17.22 " 17.35	1.21
17.36 " 17.49	1.22
17.50 " 17.64	1.23
17.65 " 17.78	1.24
17.79 " 17.92	1.25
17.93 " 18.07	1.26

Amount of Sale	Tax
18.08 " 18.21	1.27
18.22 " 18.35	1.28
18.36 " 18.49	1.29
18.50 " 18.64	1.30
18.65 " 18.78	1.31
18.79 " 18.92	1.32
18.93 " 19.07	1.33
19.08 " 19.21	1.34
19.22 " 19.35	1.35
19.36 " 19.49	1.36
19.50 " 19.64	1.37
19.65 " 19.78	1.38
19.79 " 19.92	1.39
19.93 " 20.07	1.40
20.08 " 20.21	1.41
20.22 " 20.35	1.42
20.36 " 20.49	1.43
20.50 " 20.64	1.44
20.65 " 20.78	1.45
20.79 " 20.92	1.46
20.93 " 21.07	1.47
21.08 " 21.21	1.48
21.22 " 21.35	1.49
21.36 " 21.49	1.50
21.50 " 21.64	1.51
21.65 " 21.78	1.52
21.79 " 21.92	1.53
21.93 " 22.07	1.54
22.08 " 22.21	1.55
22.22 " 22.35	1.56
22.36 " 22.49	1.57
22.50 " 22.64	1.58
22.65 " 22.78	1.59
22.79 " 22.92	1.60
22.93 " 23.07	1.61
23.08 " 23.21	1.62
23.22 " 23.35	1.63
23.36 " 23.49	1.64
23.50 " 23.64	1.65
23.65 " 23.78	1.66
23.79 " 23.92	1.67
23.93 " 24.07	1.68
24.08 " 24.21	1.69
24.22 " 24.35	1.70
24.36 " 24.49	1.71
24.50 " 24.64	1.72
24.65 " 24.78	1.73
24.79 " 24.92	1.74
24.93 " 25.07	1.75
25.08 " 25.21	1.76
25.22 " 25.35	1.77
25.36 " 25.49	1.78
25.50 " 25.64	1.79
25.65 " 25.78	1.80
25.79 " 25.92	1.81
25.93 " 26.07	1.82
26.08 " 26.21	1.83
26.22 " 26.35	1.84
26.36 " 26.49	1.85
26.50 " 26.64	1.86
26.65 " 26.78	1.87
26.79 " 26.92	1.88
26.93 " 27.07	1.89

Amount of Sale	Tax
27.08 " 27.21	1.90
27.22 " 27.35	1.91
27.36 " 27.49	1.92
27.50 " 27.64	1.93
27.65 " 27.78	1.94
27.79 " 27.92	1.95
27.93 " 28.07	1.96
28.08 " 28.21	1.97
28.22 " 28.35	1.98
28.36 " 28.49	1.99
28.50 " 28.64	2.00
28.65 " 28.78	2.01
28.79 " 28.92	2.02
28.93 " 29.07	2.03
29.08 " 29.21	2.04
29.22 " 29.35	2.05
29.36 " 29.49	2.06
29.50 " 29.64	2.07
29.65 " 29.78	2.08
29.79 " 29.92	2.09
29.93 " 30.07	2.10
30.08 " 30.21	2.11
30.22 " 30.35	2.12
30.36 " 30.49	2.13
30.50 " 30.64	2.14
30.65 " 30.78	2.15
30.79 " 30.92	2.16
30.93 " 31.07	2.17
31.08 " 31.21	2.18
31.22 " 31.35	2.19
31.36 " 31.49	2.20
31.50 " 31.64	2.21
31.65 " 31.78	2.22
31.79 " 31.92	2.23
31.93 " 32.07	2.24
32.08 " 32.21	2.25
32.22 " 32.35	2.26
32.36 " 32.49	2.27
32.50 " 32.64	2.28
32.65 " 32.78	2.29
32.79 " 32.92	2.30
32.93 " 33.07	2.31
33.08 " 33.21	2.32
33.22 " 33.35	2.33
33.36 " 33.49	2.34
33.50 " 33.64	2.35
33.65 " 33.78	2.36
33.79 " 33.92	2.37
33.93 " 34.07	2.38
34.08 " 34.21	2.39
34.22 " 34.35	2.40
34.36 " 34.49	2.41
34.50 " 34.64	2.42
34.65 " 34.78	2.43

Amount of Sale	Tax
34.79 " 34.92	2.44
34.93 " 35.07	2.45
35.08 " 35.21	2.46
35.22 " 35.35	2.47
35.36 " 35.49	2.48
35.50 " 35.64	2.49
35.65 " 35.78	2.50
35.79 " 35.92	2.51
35.93 " 36.07	2.52
36.08 " 36.21	2.53
36.22 " 36.35	2.54
36.36 " 36.49	2.55
36.50 " 36.64	2.56
36.65 " 36.78	2.57
36.79 " 36.92	2.58
36.93 " 37.07	2.59
37.08 " 37.21	2.60
37.22 " 37.35	2.61
37.36 " 37.49	2.62
37.50 " 37.64	2.63
37.65 " 37.78	2.64
37.79 " 37.92	2.65
37.93 " 38.07	2.66
38.08 " 38.21	2.67
38.22 " 38.35	2.68
38.36 " 38.49	2.69
38.50 " 38.64	2.70
38.65 " 38.78	2.71
38.79 " 38.92	2.72
38.93 " 39.07	2.73
39.08 " 39.21	2.74
39.22 " 39.35	2.75
39.36 " 39.49	2.76
39.50 " 39.64	2.77
39.65 " 39.78	2.78
39.79 " 39.92	2.79
39.93 " 40.07	2.80
40.08 " 40.21	2.81
40.22 " 40.35	2.82
40.36 " 40.49	2.83
40.50 " 40.64	2.84
40.65 " 40.78	2.85
40.79 " 40.92	2.86
40.93 " 41.07	2.87
41.08 " 41.21	2.88
41.22 " 41.35	2.89
41.36 " 41.49	2.90
41.50 " 41.64	2.91
41.65 " 41.78	2.92
41.79 " 41.92	2.93
41.93 " 42.07	2.94
42.08 " 42.21	2.95
42.22 " 42.35	2.96
42.36 " 42.49	2.97

Amount of Sale	Tax
42.50 " 42.64	2.98
42.65 " 42.78	2.99
42.79 " 42.92	3.00
42.93 " 43.07	3.01
43.08 " 43.21	3.02
43.22 " 43.35	3.03
43.36 " 43.49	3.04
43.50 " 43.64	3.05
43.65 " 43.78	3.06
43.79 " 43.92	3.07
43.93 " 44.07	3.08
44.08 " 44.21	3.09
44.22 " 44.35	3.10
44.36 " 44.49	3.11
44.50 " 44.64	3.12
44.65 " 44.78	3.13
44.79 " 44.92	3.14
44.93 " 45.07	3.15
45.08 " 45.21	3.16
45.22 " 45.35	3.17
45.36 " 45.49	3.18
45.50 " 45.64	3.19
45.65 " 45.78	3.20
45.79 " 45.92	3.21
45.93 " 46.07	3.22
46.08 " 46.21	3.23
46.22 " 46.35	3.24
46.36 " 46.49	3.25
46.50 " 46.64	3.26
46.65 " 46.78	3.27
46.79 " 46.92	3.28
46.93 " 47.07	3.29
47.08 " 47.21	3.30
47.22 " 47.35	3.31
47.36 " 47.49	3.32
47.50 " 47.64	3.33
47.65 " 47.78	3.34
47.79 " 47.92	3.35
47.93 " 48.07	3.36
48.08 " 48.21	3.37
48.22 " 48.35	3.38
48.36 " 48.49	3.39
48.50 " 48.64	3.40
48.65 " 48.78	3.41
48.79 " 48.92	3.42
50.00 —	3.50
60.00 —	4.20
70.00 —	4.90
75.00 —	5.25
80.00 —	5.60
85.00 —	5.95
90.00 —	6.30
95.00 —	6.65
100.00 —	7.00

7% ILLINOIS SALES TAX CHART

be debited for $2.26. The balance in the account at any point in time represents the total of the unremitted taxes.

Trade and sales discounts

As discussed in Chapter 11, manufacturers and wholesalers of certain types of merchandise often quote list prices that are subject to substantial reductions known as **trade discounts.** Trade discounts provide a means of revising prices without revising catalogs, and they allow the seller to offer different prices to various categories of customers. Such discounts are normally shown as a reduction in the total sales invoice amount. Trade discounts should not be reflected in the seller's accounts since they are simply reductions in the selling price of the merchandise.

To encourage buyers to pay promptly, sellers may also offer a **cash discount** that allows a deduction from the gross invoice amount if the invoice is paid within a specified period of time. When a cash discount is offered, it should be clearly noted in the terms of the sale. At the time of sale, the seller has no way of knowing if the discount will be taken. Therefore, the cash discount should be ignored when recording the sale. If the discount is taken, it may be treated as either an expense or a reduction in sales. Most commonly, cash discounts taken by customers are recorded in the **Sales Discounts account.** The total in this account is then deducted from gross sales on the income statement.

Sales returns and allowances

Occasionally a customer will receive a larger quantity of an item than originally ordered or an incorrect item, style, or color. In other cases, merchandise may arrive damaged or spoiled. When this happens, the seller can request that the merchandise be returned, usually at the seller's expense, and a credit will be recorded in the customer's account. If the sale was for cash or if the customer has already paid the account, the seller will give a cash refund. Some buyers may prefer to keep the merchandise provided they receive a reduction in price. Like a merchandise return, this entitles the customer to a cash refund or a credit that reduces his or her account balance. A seller gives credit for returns or allowances by issuing a credit memorandum.

As mentioned in Chapter 11, a **credit memorandum** is a form that a seller uses to notify a buyer that the buyer's account is being reduced due to an error, return, or allowance. A sample credit memorandum is shown in Illustration 12–4. Remember that a credit memorandum reduces (credits) the customer's account receivable balance held on the selling company's book.

Since both returns and allowances reduce the total sales for the period, they could be debited directly to the Sales account. Yet there are several reasons for recording these items in a separate contra account called **Sales Returns and Allowances.** For instance, a large balance in Sales Returns and Allowances may indicate inadequate ordering, packing, or shipping procedures. In addition, any unusual fluctuations in the account will be readily apparent. When computing the net sales for the period, the balance of the Sales Returns and Allowances account must be deducted from the Sales account. The company's sales tax liability should also be calculated after the Sales account has been adjusted for returns and allowances.

For example, assume that a customer has informed a seller that $67 worth of merchandise was being returned because the style was incorrect. The buyer would debit Sales Returns and Allowances for $67 and credit Accounts Receivable for a matching amount. Had the original transaction been for cash, a cash refund would be made.

ILLUSTRATION 12–4

A Credit Memorandum

Credit Memorandum No. 45

Howard Building Supplies
19 North Avenie
Summerville, TN 37914

TO: Omega Retailers
813 First Street
Jefferson, SC 26314

Your account has been credited for $80 pertaining to Invoice No. 11249.
We are sorry for any inconvenience these damaged goods caused.
Thank you for notifying us of the situation.

Howard Building Supplies

The journal entry would be the same, except that the credit would be to Cash, not to Accounts Receivable.

To illustrate an allowance, assume that a buyer has informed a seller that slightly damaged merchandise had been received. The buyer agreed, however, to keep the item in return for an allowance of 20 percent on the $180 purchase price. The seller would debit Sales Returns and Allowances for $36 (20% × $180) and credit Accounts Receivable for the same amount. Had the original transaction been for cash, a cash refund would be made. The entry would be the same, except that the credit would be to Cash, not to Accounts Receivable.

ACCOUNTS RECEIVABLE

A company must keep a record of amounts due from its customers. This asset account—**Accounts Receivable**—must reflect credit-granting activity for the period and indicate the unpaid balances at any point in time.

As first discussed in Chapter 10, a company must not only know the total but also have a detailed breakdown of the amount each customer owes. One alternative would be to have a separate account in the general ledger for each customer. If the number of customers is large, this is cumbersome and awkward. For this reason, a single general ledger account—Accounts Receivable—is often used for *all* customers. This account is the **control account.** Supporting this account is a group of detailed records, called a **subsidiary ledger,** which discloses the balance owed by each individual customer. The total of the accounts in the subsidiary ledger should equal the control account balance.

Individual ledger accounts

A company that uses the subsidiary ledger system maintains a separate account for each customer. These are filed in alphabetical order. Whenever a sale is made, the amount is first journalized and then posted to the appropriate customer's subsidiary ledger account. Posting is done on a daily or weekly basis. Any payments discounts taken or allowances are also posted as a credit to the subsidiary accounts. Thus the account balance will represent only the unpaid amount. At the end of the month, if all individual balances are totaled, they should equal the amount found in the control account in the general ledger—Accounts Receivable. The final section of this chapter presents an example of this method.

The sales invoice method

If a company does not maintain a subsidiary ledger, it will use the **sales invoice method** to keep track of accounts receivable. Under this system, all unpaid sales invoices are kept in a file organized by customer name. Any allowances or partial payments are noted on the face of the invoice, but every invoice is retained in the open file until the total amount is paid. By adding up a customer's invoices, the receivable balance can be readily determined. The total of all customers' receivable balances should equal the balance in the control account—Accounts Receivable.

THE SALES JOURNAL

All credit sales of merchandise could initially be recorded in the general journal. In many businesses, however, the volume of credit sales transactions is sufficiently large to require a special **sales journal.** This journal can have either one or three columns depending on whether the company is subject to a sales tax. If the company is not subject to a sales tax, there will be a single column representing the credit to Sales and the debit to Accounts Receivable. Otherwise, there will be three columns: Accounts Receivable—a debit, Sales— a credit, and Sales Tax Payable—a credit. Cash sales are not entered in the sales journal but rather in the cash receipts journal.

A sample one-column sales journal is given in Illustration 12–5. When using a sales journal like the one in Illustration 12–5, a single line is sufficient to record a transaction. If more detail is desired, all required information is readily available from the sales invoice.

In a company that uses the sales invoice method, every invoice is filed by customer name immediately after the transaction is recorded

**ILLUSTRATION
12–5**

DATE		SOLD TO	INVOICE NO.	ACCTS. REC. DR. SALES, CR. AMOUNT	P.R.
1987					
Oct.	3	Dr. Jones	7837	1 2 7 13	√
	6	Kamins Mfg. Co.	7838	6 3 7 20	√
	8	L. Dunn	7839	4 2 73	√
	13	S. Mair	7840	6 1 20	√
	17	Beer's Drug Store	7841	1 4 2 50	√
	19	H. Smith	7842	2 3 15	√
	24	L. Howard	7843	1 3 70	√
	26	Midwest Specialty	7844	1 4 7 88	√
				1 1 9 5 49	
				(1 1 5 / 4 10)	

SALES JOURNAL — Page 8

in the sales journal. In a company that maintains a separate account for each customer in a subsidiary ledger, each sales invoice is posted to the appropriate customer's account before being filed. The posting could be made from the sales journal. However, it is preferable for the posting to be made from the invoice because it provides efficiency and accuracy. After the invoice is posted, an S and the page number of the sales journal are entered in the Posting Reference column of the subsidiary ledger account and a check is made in the far right column of the sales journal. Note that this posting is to customer accounts found in the subsidiary accounts receivable ledger, not the control Accounts Receivable account found in the general ledger. Here is how a posting in a subsidiary accounts receivable ledger would look:

Dr. Harvey Jones

Date	Explanation	P.R.	Debit	Credit	Balance
1987 Oct. 3	Sale	S8	127.13		127.13

At the end of the month, the single column of the sales journal is footed and ruled, as shown in Illustration 12–5. The total is posted

ILLUSTRATION 12–6

	SALES JOURNAL							Page 8
DATE	SOLD TO	INVOICE NO.	ACCOUNTS RECEIVABLE DEBIT	SALES CREDIT	SALES TAX PAYABLE CREDIT	P.R.
1987						
Oct. 3	D. Jones	7837	1 3 0 95	1 2 7 13	3 81	√
6	Kamins Mfg. Co.	7838	6 5 6 32	6 3 7 20	1 9 12	√
8	L. Dunn	7839	4 4 02	4 2 73	1 28	√
13	S. Mair	7840	6 3 04	6 1 20	1 84	√
17	Beer's Drug Store	7841	1 4 6 78	1 4 2 50	4 28	√
19	H. Smith	7842	2 3 85	2 3 15	69	√
24	L. Howard	7843	1 4 12	1 3 70	41	√
26	Midwest Specialty	7844	1 5 2 32	1 4 7 88	4 44	√
			1 2 3 1 40	1 1 9 5 49	3 5 87	
			(1 1 5)	(4 1 0)	(2 4 0)	

to the general ledger. In our example, the required entries would be:

1. Debit Accounts Receivable for $1,195.49.
2. Credit Sales for $1,195.49.

To provide a cross-reference in the general ledger, the source for the entry should be indicated in the Posting Reference column of the affected accounts. This is best done by using an S to indicate sales journal, followed by the page number. In our illustration, the notation would be S8.

A company that is subject to retail sales tax would maintain a three-column sales journal like the one in Illustration 12–6. Here, using the information from Illustration 12–5, we assumed that the company must pay a 3 percent sales tax. As a result, the customer would have to pay 3 percent more.

Given this situation, let's assume that Midwest Specialty returned merchandise of $103 from Invoice No. 7844. The entry would be made in the general journal (page 8). Accounts Receivable would be credited for $103, Sales Tax Payable would be debited for $3, and Sales Returns and Allowances would be debited for $100.

At the end of the month, the columns would be footed and the totals posted to the proper accounts in the general ledger as follows:

Accounts Receivable — ACCT. NO. 115

DATE		EXPLANATION	INV. NO.	P.R.	DEBIT	CREDIT	BALANCE DEBIT	BALANCE CREDIT
1987								
Oct.	31			S8	1 2 3 1 40		1 2 3 1 40	
	31			GJ8		1 0 3 00	1 1 2 8 40	

Sales — ACCT. NO. 410

DATE		EXPLANATION	INV. NO.	P.R.	DEBIT	CREDIT	BALANCE DEBIT	BALANCE CREDIT
1987								
Oct.	31			S8		1 1 9 5 49		1 1 9 5 49

Sales Tax Payable — ACCT. NO. 240

DATE		EXPLANATION	INV. NO.	P.R.	DEBIT	CREDIT	BALANCE DEBIT	BALANCE CREDIT
1987								
Oct.	31			S8		3 5 91		3 5 91
	31			GJ8	3 00			3 2 91

Sales Returns and Allowances — ACCT. NO. 411

DATE		EXPLANATION	INV. NO.	P.R.	DEBIT	CREDIT	BALANCE DEBIT	BALANCE CREDIT
1987								
Oct.	31			GJ8	1 0 0 00		1 0 0 00	

The posting reference S8 refers to page 8 of the sales journal. GJ8 refers to page 8 in the general journal. This cross-referencing of the general ledger postings to the sales journal and the general journal is necessary so that the accounting records can be checked to see that they agree.

ACCOUNTING FOR SALES: AN EXAMPLE

The Cox Supply Company is a wholesaler of office and art supplies. Sales in the Office and Art departments are recorded in separate accounts. Each charge sale is entered in a sales register. A **sales register** is a book of original entry that is used to record credit (and sometimes cash) sales. As shown in Illustration 12–7, debits are recorded on the left side of the register, and credits are recorded on the right. On the debit side is a separate column for Accounts Receivable plus a General Ledger section that is used to record debits to other accounts, such as Sales Returns and Allowances. The Account Number column is used to record the account numbers for the entries in the General column. In the center of the register, the accountant records the day of the month, the name of the customer, and the invoice number.

On the credit side of the sales register are two Sales columns—one for the Office Department and one for the Art Department—plus a General Ledger section that is used to record credits to any accounts other than the sales accounts.

We will now use some transactions from the Cox Supply Company to illustrate how to record charge sales on a departmental basis. Here are the accounts and account numbers that Cox uses to record items sold on credit:

120	Accounts Receivable
510	Sales—Office Department
511	Sales Returns and Allowances—Office Department
520	Sales—Art Department
521	Sales Returns and Allowances—Art Department
685	Postage Expense

Large orders involving considerable weight are usually sent by express or freight. When such shipments occur, the transportation charges are handled on a collect basis and thus are not recorded in Cox's books. Postage charges for sales sent by parcel post are simply added to the invoice price. The prepaid postage is credited to Postage Expense, account number 685, in the General Ledger column, when the invoice is entered in the general ledger. Some local customers prefer to avoid transportation and postage charges by picking up their merchandise themselves.

Here are the Cox Supply Company's credit sales for the first six days in August. Note how the information is recorded in the sales register in Illustration 12–7. The source for each entry is the sales invoice.

ILLUSTRATION 12–7

MONTH OF August 1987						SALES REGISTER						PAGE 33	
DEBIT								CREDIT					
GENERAL LEDGER			ACCTS. REC'BLE	√	DAY	NAME	SALE NO.	SALES		GENERAL LEDGER			
ACCT. NO.	AMOUNT	√						OFFICE DEPT.	ART DEPT.	ACCT. NO.	AMOUNT	√	
			73 18	√	1	The Paint Brush	807		66 75	685	6 43	√	
			693 18	√	1	Baker Office Supply	808	693 18					
			138 12	√	1	Standard Stationeries	809	125 44		685	12 68	√	
			54 92	√	1	The Art Shop	810		54 92				
511	5 08	√	39 80	√	2	Alexander's	811	44 88					
			248 52	√	3	Henson Office Supply	812	248 52					
			164 25	√	3	The Gallery	813		164 25				
			5 25	√	4	Baker Office Supply	814	5 25					
520	10 00	√			5	The Paint Brush	815			120	10 00	√	
			75 15	√	6	The Paint Brush	816		75 15				
			112 26	√	6	Standard Stationeries	817	108 91		685	3 35	√	
			1043 19	√	6	Baker Office Supply	818	1043 19					
			476 65	√	6	The Paint Brush	819		444 70	685	31 95	√	
	15 08		3124 47					2269 37	805 77		64 41		
	(√)		(120)					(510)	(520)		(√)		

COX SUPPLY COMPANY
Description of Sales Transactions
August 1–6, 1987

August 1

Made the following charge sales:

No. 807: The Paint Brush, art supplies, $66.75; postage of $6.43 added to invoice.

Let's look at the first credit sale on August 1—Invoice No. 807. Beginning on the first line of Illustration 12–7, the total amount billed to The Paint Brush is entered in the Accounts Receivable column. Next, the date of the sale, the name of the buyer, and the invoice number are recorded. The selling price of the goods is then recorded as a credit to the Art Department's Sales account. Finally, the cost of the postage is entered in the General Ledger section, along with the account number 685, to indicate a credit to the Postage Expense account. Note that the amount credited to Sales—Art Department ($66.75) plus the amount credited to Postage Expense ($6.43) equal the total debited to Accounts Receivable ($73.18).

August 1

No. 808: Baker Office Supply, office supplies, $693.18; express collect.

Now let's consider the second sale—Invoice No. 808. In this case, as before, the selling price of the supplies is debited to Accounts Receivable. But this time the credit is made to Sales—Office Department. Note that because the goods are being shipped express collect, no postage or transportation charge is recorded.

As you read the rest of Cox Supply's sales transactions, match them to the sales register in Illustration 12–7.

No. 809: Standard Stationeries, office supplies, $125.44; insured parcel post, $12.68.

No. 810: The Art Shop, art supplies, $54.92; to be picked up.

August 2

Made the following charge sale:

No. 811: Alexander's, office supplies, $44.88; less credit of $5.08 for defective pencils which were returned. Accounts Receivable was debited for net amount. To be picked up.

August 3

Made the following charge sales:

No. 812: Henson Office Supply, office supplies, $248.52; to be picked up.

No. 813: The Gallery, art supplies, $164.25, to be picked up.

August 4

Sent Baker Office Supply a corrected invoice for the August 1 purchase of office supplies. The original invoice (No. 808) was for $693.18. The corrected invoice (No. 814) amounted to $698.43.

August 5

Sent the Paint Brush a corrected invoice for the August 1 purchase of art supplies. The original invoice (No. 807) was for $66.75. The corrected invoice (No. 815) amounted to $56.75. Postage charges remained the same.

August 6

Made the following charge sales:

No. 816: The Paint Brush, art supplies, $75.15; to be picked up.

No. 817: Standard Stationeries, office supplies; $108.91; postage of $3.35 added to invoice.

No. 818: Baker Office Supply, office supplies, $1,043.19; freight collect.

No. 819: The Paint Brush, art supplies, $444.70; postage of $31.95 added to invoice.

Sales invoice corrections. Since no system is error-free, every company has set procedures for correcting errors when they occur. If an error is discovered before it is entered in the sales register, a corrected invoice is prepared. The new invoice is entered in the sales register in the usual manner, and the original invoice is canceled. If the error is discovered after the original invoice has been entered and the postings completed, a corrected invoice is prepared. When the corrected invoice is more than the original invoice, the increase is recorded in the sales register by debiting Accounts Receivable and by crediting the appropriate sales account (see Invoice No. 814). The amount of increase should be posted as a debit to the customer's account in the accounts receivable subsidiary ledger.

The reverse procedure is used when the corrected invoice amount is less than the original invoice amount. The decrease is recorded by debiting the appropriate sales account and by crediting Accounts Receivable (see Invoice No. 815). The amount of decrease should be posted as a credit to the customer's account in the accounts receivable subsidiary ledger.

For future reference, a copy of the corrected invoice should be filed with the original invoice. A copy of the corrected invoice should be promptly forwarded to the customer.

Proving the sales register. The sales register of Cox Supply Company is normally proved at the end of each month when the register is posted. However, when a page is completed, the register should be proved before proceeding to the next page. The register may be proved at any time by footing the columns and comparing the sum of the debit footings with the sum of the credit footings. The following schedule was prepared to prove the sales register of Cox Supply on August 6, when p. 33 was full:

Account Column	Debit	Credit
General ledger	$ 15.08	
Accounts receivable	3,124.47	
Sales—office department . . .		$2,269.37
Sales—art department		805.77
General ledger		64.41
Totals	$3,139.55	$3,139.55

Posting procedures

Sales transactions are posted to both the general ledger and the accounts receivable subsidiary ledger. This includes both individual and summary postings. The general ledger accounts that Cox uses to record sales transactions are shown in Illustration 12–8, and the accounts in the accounts receivable subsidiary ledger are presented in Illustration 12–9.

After each sales transaction is recorded in the sales register, it is posted to the appropriate customer account in the accounts receivable subsidiary ledger. Debits may be the result of charge sales or invoice corrections, while credits may result from invoice corrections or sales returns and allowances. When payment is received, the invoice is pulled and its amount is compared with the cash received.

Individual postings are also required for items recorded in the General Ledger debit and credit columns of the sales register. Such postings are normally performed daily or as the items are recorded. Since the account number is given in the entry as a means of indicating whether the amounts have been posted, a check mark is placed in the check column as the items are posted. To cross-reference the posting, the page number of the sales register is entered in the P.R. column of the affected general ledger or subsidiary ledger account.

Posting summary. Cox Supply Company usually does its summary posting from the sales register to the general ledger at the end of the month. To keep our example simple, however, we will do a summary posting as of August 6. The procedure would be:

1. The Accounts Receivable column total is posted as a debit to Accounts Receivable, account no. 120, in the general ledger.
2. The Sales—Office Department column total is posted as a credit to Sales—Office Department, account no. 510, in the general ledger.
3. The Sales—Art Department column total is posted as a credit to Sales—Art Department, account no. 520, in the general ledger.

As each column total is posted, the account number of the account being posted is recorded below the column total. To cross-reference the posting, the page number of the sales register is entered in the P.R. column of the general ledger account. To indicate that the General Ledger debit and credit columns are not to be posted, a check mark is placed below those column totals.

**ILLUSTRATION
12–8**

**Cox Supply
Company
General
Ledger (Partial)**

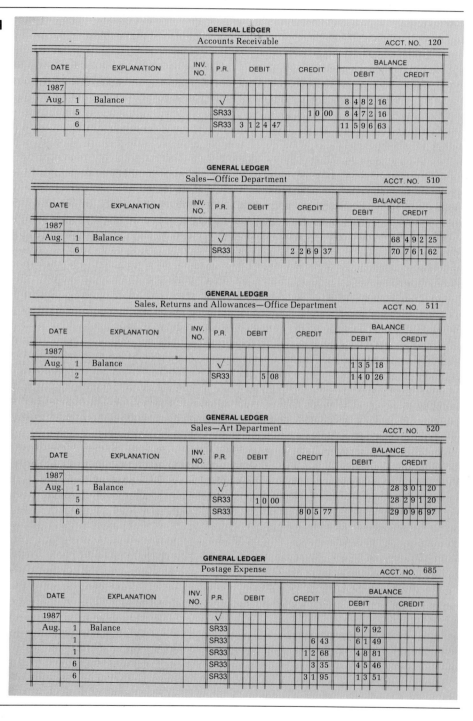

GENERAL LEDGER

Accounts Receivable   ACCT. NO. 120

DATE		EXPLANATION	INV. NO.	P.R.	DEBIT	CREDIT	BALANCE DEBIT	BALANCE CREDIT
1987								
Aug.	1	Balance		√			8 482 16	
	5			SR33		1 0 00	8 472 16	
	6			SR33	3 1 2 4 47		11 596 63	

GENERAL LEDGER

Sales—Office Department   ACCT. NO. 510

DATE		EXPLANATION	INV. NO.	P.R.	DEBIT	CREDIT	BALANCE DEBIT	BALANCE CREDIT
1987								
Aug.	1	Balance		√				68 492 25
	6			SR33		2 2 6 9 37		70 761 62

GENERAL LEDGER

Sales, Returns and Allowances—Office Department   ACCT. NO. 511

DATE		EXPLANATION	INV. NO.	P.R.	DEBIT	CREDIT	BALANCE DEBIT	BALANCE CREDIT
1987								
Aug.	1	Balance		√			1 3 5 18	
	2			SR33	5 08		1 4 0 26	

GENERAL LEDGER

Sales—Art Department   ACCT. NO. 520

DATE		EXPLANATION	INV. NO.	P.R.	DEBIT	CREDIT	BALANCE DEBIT	BALANCE CREDIT
1987								
Aug.	1	Balance		√				28 301 20
	5			SR33	1 0 00			28 291 20
	6			SR33		8 0 5 77		29 096 97

GENERAL LEDGER

Postage Expense   ACCT. NO. 685

DATE		EXPLANATION	INV. NO.	P.R.	DEBIT	CREDIT	BALANCE DEBIT	BALANCE CREDIT
1987								
Aug.	1	Balance		√ SR33			6 7 92	
	1			SR33		6 43	6 1 49	
	1			SR33		1 2 68	4 8 81	
	6			SR33		3 35	4 5 46	
	6			SR33		3 1 95	1 3 51	

**ILLUSTRATION
12–9**

**Accounts
Receivable
Subsidiary
Ledger (Partial)**

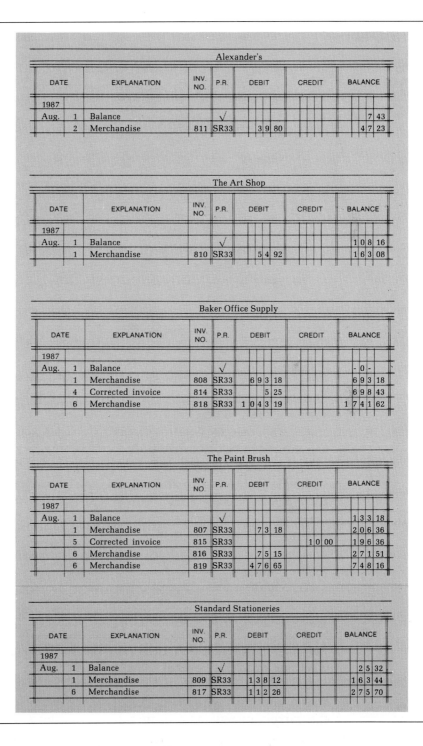

Alexander's

DATE		EXPLANATION	INV. NO.	P.R.	DEBIT	CREDIT	BALANCE
1987							
Aug.	1	Balance		√			7 43
	2	Merchandise	811	SR33	3 9 80		4 7 23

The Art Shop

DATE		EXPLANATION	INV. NO.	P.R.	DEBIT	CREDIT	BALANCE
1987							
Aug.	1	Balance		√			1 0 8 16
	1	Merchandise	810	SR33	5 4 92		1 6 3 08

Baker Office Supply

DATE		EXPLANATION	INV. NO.	P.R.	DEBIT	CREDIT	BALANCE
1987							
Aug.	1	Balance		√			- 0 -
	1	Merchandise	808	SR33	6 9 3 18		6 9 3 18
	4	Corrected invoice	814	SR33	5 25		6 9 8 43
	6	Merchandise	818	SR33	1 0 4 3 19		1 7 4 1 62

The Paint Brush

DATE		EXPLANATION	INV. NO.	P.R.	DEBIT	CREDIT	BALANCE
1987							
Aug.	1	Balance		√			1 3 3 18
	1	Merchandise	807	SR33	7 3 18		2 0 6 36
	5	Corrected invoice	815	SR33		1 0 00	1 9 6 36
	6	Merchandise	816	SR33	7 5 15		2 7 1 51
	6	Merchandise	819	SR33	4 7 6 65		7 4 8 16

Standard Stationeries

DATE		EXPLANATION	INV. NO.	P.R.	DEBIT	CREDIT	BALANCE
1987							
Aug.	1	Balance		√			2 5 32
	1	Merchandise	809	SR33	1 3 8 12		1 6 3 44
	6	Merchandise	817	SR33	1 1 2 26		2 7 5 70

ILLUSTRATION 12-9 (concluded)

The Gallery

DATE		EXPLANATION	INV. NO.	P.R.	DEBIT	CREDIT	BALANCE
1987							
Aug.	1	Balance		√			2 0 6 75
	3	Merchandise	813	SR33	1 6 4 25		3 7 1 00

Henson Office Supply

DATE		EXPLANATION	INV. NO.	P.R.	DEBIT	CREDIT	BALANCE
1987							
Aug.	1	Balance		√			- 0 -
	3	Merchandise	812	SR33	2 4 8 52		2 4 8 52

Cash sales

Since Cox Supply Company is a wholesale business, most of its sales are made on account. Although the practice will vary from firm to firm, Cox Supply Company only records credit sales in the sales register. When cash sales occur, they are recorded in the cash receipts journal by debiting the bank or cash account and by crediting the appropriate sales account. Entries may be made in the cash receipts journal as each cash sale is made or through the use of a summary entry at the end of each business day or other designated time period. Because no receivable arises from a cash sale, it is not necessary to post the sales transactions to individual customer accounts. The use of a cash receipts journal is illustrated in Chapter 10.

COD sales

Cox Supply Company accounts for COD sales in the same manner they do for charge sales. As with ordinary credit sales, several days may pass before a payment is received from an out-of-town customer who has ordered on COD terms. Under such a system, COD sales orders are entered in the sales register in the same manner as ordinary credit sales. As explained earlier in the chapter, the customer pays the carrying agent who in turn forwards the remittance to the seller.

Upon receipt, the remittance is recorded in the cash receipts record. Also, as individual payments are received, they should be posted to the accounts receivable subsidiary ledger.

Sales returns and allowances

As mentioned earlier in this chapter, sales returns and allowances usually result from damaged or defective merchandise or from shipments that do not satisfy the customer's needs. Upon request, Cox Supply Company will issue a credit memorandum to the buyer for the adjustment. The credit memo is recorded by debiting the appropriate sales returns and allowances account and by crediting Accounts Receivable. The adjustment is also posted to the customer's account in the accounts receivable subsidiary ledger.

For example, assume that The Paint Brush requested an allowance on an order of drawing paper that was damaged during shipment. In response to the request, Cox Supply Company issued a credit memorandum for $41.52. The following general journal entry was used to record the allowance:

	GENERAL JOURNAL						
DATE	ACCOUNT AND EXPLANATION	P.R.	DEBIT		CREDIT		
	Sales Return and Allowances—Art Department		41 52				
	Accounts Receivable—The Paint Brush				41 52		
	Credit Memorandum No. 67 issued to						
	The Paint Brush.						

After the entry was recorded in the general journal, the amount of the allowance was posted to the The Paint Brush's account in the accounts receivable subsidiary ledger.

Shipping charges

When shipments are sent by parcel post, the postage charges and any related insurance charges must be prepaid. If the buyer is to bear these charges, they should be added to the invoice. Unless the customer requests otherwise, Cox Supply Company sends all express and freight shipments on a transportation-charges collect basis. When express and freight charges are prepaid, the charges are recorded by debiting the **Transportation-Out account** and by crediting the bank account. When the sale and related shipping charges are recorded in the sales register, the Transportation-Out account is credited for shipping charges. If all shipping charges were charged to the customers, the Transportation-Out account should have a zero balance at the end of the month. However, when shipments are made f.o.b. destination, the seller bears the shipping charges. In such a case, the Transportation-Out account will have a debit balance. The debit balance will represent the amount of selling expense incurred from the seller's bearing of shipping charges.

If a company prepays a significant amount of shipping charges, it may keep a special credit column in the sales register to record the charges that are to be added to the customer's sales invoice. When postings are made, the column total is posted in summary as a credit to Transportation-Out.

Automated processing of sales transactions

Businesses with a large volume of sales transactions may find it advisable to install a more advanced system to handle sales. The extent of automation will vary depending on the system needed to satisfy the user's needs. Throughout the sales cycle, a number of transactions must be performed involving different business documents. The more advanced systems will permit purchase order data to be punched on cards, recorded on magnetic tape, or entered through a computer terminal. With proper programming, the system will analyze the purchase order for completeness, perform a credit check, prepare a sales invoice, issue shipping orders, adjust inventory levels, keep an accounts receivable subsidiary ledger, and make the necessary individual and summary postings to related accounts. Most systems with such capabilities will also be programmed to prepare customers' monthly statements and assist in the preparation of monthly reports.

SUMMARY

The procedures used in accounting for sales depend on several factors, including the kind of business, the organization of the sales department, the goods sold, the volume of sales, the method of selling, and the sales terms.

There are several kinds of sales transactions. **Sales for cash** can be handled in various ways. When cash sales are numerous, one or more cash registers are used to ensure internal control. In a **sale**

on credit, also referred to as a *sale on account* or a *charge sale,* the seller exchanges merchandise for the buyer's promise to pay at a later date. When a bank **credit card** is used, a financial institution assumes responsibility for collecting the resulting account receivables. A **sale on approval** means that the customer has the right to return the goods within a specified time period. With **layaway sales,** the buyer agrees to purchase the goods with the understanding that they will be picked up and paid for in full at a later date. A deposit is usually made to hold goods on layaway. **Cash on delivery (COD) sales** call for the buyer to pay when the goods are delivered. Sometimes a business will market goods on **consignment.** In such cases, the owner **(consignor)** ships the merchandise to an agent dealer **(consignee)** with the agreement that the consignee is not required to pay for the goods unless they are sold. Property such as computers, appliances, furniture, clothes, automobiles, and real estate may be sold **on installment.** Under such a plan, the seller agrees to give the buyer physical possession of the goods in exchange for a promise to make payment periodically over a specified time interval. Usually, title to the goods does not pass to the buyer until payment is made in full.

Well-organized procedures must be established for the handling of purchase orders, and these procedures must be closely followed. When a purchase order arrives, it is closely examined to determine the buyer's identity and the description and quantity of the goods ordered. In addition, all credit orders are checked for the credit department's approval. Each purchase order should also be checked for the accuracy of its unit prices, additions, and total price. Finally, as each order is processed, it is necessary to determine how the order will be shipped and who will bear the transportation expenses.

After the purchase order has been examined, a bill, or **sales invoice,** should be prepared. Sales invoices are normally prepared in multicopy form. The original copy is sent to the customer, a copy is sent to the accounting department, and a copy is used to authorize the shipment of the merchandise.

Merchandise sales for the period are recorded in the **Sales account.** The balance in this revenue, or temporary owner's equity, account at any point in time represents the cumulative sales from the beginning of the period.

Many business enterprises are required by state or city law to collect a **retail sales tax** from their customers. The tax is usually levied on the gross sales price of retail merchandise. Sales taxes collected are credited to the **Sales Tax Payable account.**

Manufacturers and wholesalers often quote list prices that are subject to substantial reductions known as **trade discounts.** Trade discounts enable a seller to revise prices without revising catalogs and to offer different prices to different categories of customers. A merchandiser may also offer a **cash discount** to encourage customers to pay promptly. Cash discounts taken are accumulated in the **Sales Discounts account** and subtracted from gross sales on the income statement.

Sales returns and allowances reduce total sales for the period and are granted for various reasons. For example, the buyer may receive the incorrect item, style, or color. Likewise, the merchandise may be damaged or spoiled. To notify a buyer that his or her account is being credited due to a sales return or allowance, the seller issues a **credit memorandum.** The balance in the **Sales Returns and Allowances account** is deducted from the Sales account to determine net sales for the period.

During the accounting period, a company must keep a record of the amounts due from its customers. This asset account, **Accounts Receivable,** must reflect credit-granting activity for the period and indicate the unpaid balances due from customers at any point in time. The Accounts Receivable account in the general ledger is a **control account** that reflects the balance owed by all customers. It is supported by a **subsidiary ledger** of detailed accounts for each credit customer. Companies that don't use a subsidiary ledger will use the **sales invoice method** to keep track of accounts receivable.

All credit sales of merchandise are initially recorded in the **sales journal.** This journal can have either one or three columns depending on whether the company is subject to a sales tax. If the company is not subject to a sales tax, there will be a single column representing the credit to Sales and the debit to Accounts Receivable. Otherwise, there will be three columns: Accounts Receivable, a debit; Sales, a credit; and Sales Tax Payable, a credit.

A **sales register** is a book of original entry in which credit (and sometimes cash) sales transactions are recorded. It increases efficiency because similar transactions can be listed together by department and totaled for summary posting.

KEY TERMS

Accounts Receivable Account—An asset account that is used to record amounts due from customers.

Bank Credit Card—A charge card, issued through a financial institution, that can be used to purchase merchandise worldwide.

Cash Discount—A means of encouraging customers to pay promptly by allowing a deduction from the gross invoice amount if the invoice is paid within a specified time period.

COD Sale (cash on delivery sale)—A sales transaction in which the buyer pays for the goods when they are delivered.

Consignee—An agent dealer who is not required to pay for goods unless they are sold.

Consignor—The owner of goods shipped on consignment. The consignor retains title to the consigned goods until they are sold by the consignee.

Control Account—A general ledger account that is supported by detailed information in a subsidiary ledger.

Credit Memorandum—A document that a seller uses to inform a buyer that the buyer's Account Receivable account on the seller's books has been credited due to errors, returns, or allowances.

Installment Sale—A method of selling whereby the seller agrees to give the buyer physical possession of the goods in exchange for a promise to make payments periodically over a specified time interval. Usually, title to the goods does not pass to the buyer until payment is made in full.

Layaway Sale—A sales transaction in which the buyer agrees to purchase goods with the understanding that they will be picked up and paid for at a later date.

Retail Sales Tax—A tax that is levied on the gross sales price of retail merchandise.

Sale for Cash—A sales transaction in which the seller exchanges merchandise for cash only. No other form of payment is accepted.

Sale on Approval—Sale that gives the customer the right to return the goods within a specified time period. Sales on approval can be handled either as credit sales or as cash sales.

Sale on Consignment—A sales transaction in which merchandise is shipped from a consignor to an agent dealer, or consignee, with the agreement that the consignee is not required to pay for the goods unless they are sold.

Sale on Credit—A sales transaction in which the seller exchanges merchandise for the buyer's promise to pay at a later date. Also referred to as *sales on account* or *charge sales*.

Sales Account—A revenue, or temporary owner's equity account that is credited for merchandise sales during the current period. The balance in the account at any point in time represents the cumulative sales from the beginning of the accounting period.

Sales Discounts Account—An account in which cash discounts taken by customers are recorded. The balance in the account is subtracted from gross sales on the income statement.

Sales Invoice—A document prepared by the seller that states the items shipped, the cost of the merchandise, and the method of shipment. It is a purchase invoice to the buyer.

Sales Invoice Method—One of two basic accounting methods used to maintain supporting records for control accounts. Under the sales invoice method, all sales invoices are kept in an open file organized by customer name until paid. Under the purchases invoice method, all unpaid invoices are kept in an open file according to their due dates. Under both methods, allowances or partial payments are noted on the face of the invoice, but the invoice is retained in the open file until the total amount is paid.

Sales Journal—A special journal in which all credit sales are recorded.

Sales Register—A book of original entry in which credit sales (and sometimes cash sales) transactions are recorded.

Sales Returns and Allowances Account—An account in which the selling price of returned merchandise and allowances (deductions from sales prices) granted to customers because of unsatisfactory merchandise is recorded. Its balance is shown as a deduction from sales on the income statement.

Sales Tax Payable Account—A liability account that is credited for the amount of sales taxes collected from customers because of state or municipal statutes.

Subsidiary Ledger—A group of supporting records that provide detailed information about the balance in a corresponding control account in the general ledger.

Trade Discount—A reduction in the list price of merchandise.

Transportation-Out Account—An account that is debited when the seller prepays the express and freight charges and that is credited when the sale and related shipping charges are recorded in the sales register. A debit balance in the account represents the amount of selling expenses incurred from the seller's bearing of shipping charges.

QUESTIONS AND EXERCISES

1. What are some of the factors that must be considered when an accountant is trying to establish procedures to account for sales transactions?
2. List the steps that should be followed to account for sales transactions.
3. Identify (a) sales on credit and (b) sales on approval.
4. Explain how goods are sold on a consignment basis.
5. Identify the following terms:
   a. Consignor.
   b. Consignee.
   c. Invoice of shipment.
6. What is an installment sale? Name some goods that are sold on an installment basis.
7. Why is it better to record sales returns and allowances in a separate account rather than to debit them to the Sales account?
8. Describe a sales journal.
9. Why should postings to individual customer accounts be made directly from the sales invoice instead of from the sales register?
10. Why are shipping charges recorded separately from the amount of merchandise purchased?
11. How are bank credit card sales recorded on the sellers books?
12. If the retail sales tax is 4 percent, what is the amount that will be credited to Sales Tax Payable if the amount of the sale is $75?
13. If a customer received damaged merchandise of $200 and is given a 20 percent allowance on the purchase, what amount should be debited to Sales Returns and Allowances?

PROBLEMS

12–1. R. E. Sigmon is a wholesale distributor of chemical supplies and pool supplies. Sigmon keeps merchandise accounts on a departmental basis. During January 1987, Sigmon made the following charge sales:

1987
Jan. 5 No. 100: Aldridge & Sons, chemical supplies, $250.
      7 No. 101: Holton and Pope, pool supplies, $560.

1987

Jan. 9 No. 102: Frost Company, chemical supplies, $100, and pool supplies, $300.

10 No. 103: Starnes and Staton, pool supplies, $150.

15 No. 104: Hope Hunt Company, chemical supplies, $680.

15 No. 105: Lindsey Brothers, chemical supplies, $490.

17 No. 106: Sundry Supply Incorporated, pool supplies, $280.

19 No. 107: Aldridge & Sons, chemical supplies, $305.

22 No. 108: Bill Weiss, pool supplies, $195.

22 No. 109: Oscar's Place, pool supplies, $308.

24 No. 110: Frost Company, chemical supplies, $200.

29 No. 111: Bill Weiss, pool supplies, $240.

29 No. 112: Gray and White, chemical supplies, $306.

31 No. 113: Wells and Wilson, pool supplies, $250, and chemical supplies, $485.

Required:

1. Record the above charge sales in a sales register like the one in Illustration 12–6.

2. Foot and rule the sales register on January 31, 1987.

12–2. Richard Benton and Elane Kitchens own and operate a wholesale store that sells farm and garden supplies, tools, and equipment. The store is divided into two departments—the Farm Department and the Garden Department. During May, the following charge sales were made:

1987

May 3 No. 303: Anderson & Sons, farm tools, $450; postage of $7 added to invoice.

4 No. 304: Bailey Brothers, farm equipment, $950; express collect.

6 No. 305: Canning Company, garden supplies, $308; postage of $6 added to invoice.

7 No. 306: Duckworth and Drane, garden equipment, $609; freight collect.

9 No. 307: Estes Equipment Company, garden equipment, $498; farm equipment, $809; freight collect.

10 No. 308; Franklin's Hardware Store, garden tools and supplies, $305; postage of $5 added to invoice.

13 No. 309: Gilbert's Shop, garden tools, $205; to be picked up.

1987

May 18   No. 310: Highland Company, garden equipment, $568; freight collect.

     20   No. 311: Anderson & Sons, garden supplies, $195; to be picked up.

     21   No. 312: Ingram House, farm equipment, $558; express collect.

     23   No. 313: Jackson Brothers, garden tools, $150, and farm tools, $380; to be picked up.

     25   No. 314: Kevin's Supply Store, farm supplies, $286; postage of $4 added to invoice.

     28   No. 315: Lee and Lee, farm tools, $580; to be picked up.

     31   No. 316: Morris & Sons, farm equipment, $650; freight collect.

Required:

1. Record the above transactions in a sales register like the one in Illustration 12–6. All prepaid postage should be credited to Postage Expense, account no. 685. Other accounts that might be needed are as follows:

505   Sales—Garden
506   Sales Returns and Allowances—Garden
510   Sales—Farm
511   Sales Returns and Allowances—Farm
112   Accounts Receivable

2. Foot and rule the sales register on May 31, 1987.

12–3. Ronald Akers and Daniel Ruffin operate a wholesale plumbing and electrical supplies store. The following charge sales were made during August, 1987:

1987

Aug. 2   No. 721: Ralph Baker, plumbing supplies, $106; to be picked up.

     4   No. 722: Bruce Hill, electrical supplies, $96; to be picked up.

     5   No. 723: Diana Moore, plumbing supplies, $290; postage of $6 added to invoice.

     9   No. 724: Reed and Reagan, electrical supplies, $560; express collect.

     11   No. 725: Barker and Britt, plumbing supplies, $300, and electrical supplies, $350; freight collect.

1987
Aug. 13 No. 726: Bradley Gable, electrical supplies, $255; postage of $3 added to invoice.

16 No. 727: Ralph Baker, plumbing supplies, $85; to be picked up.

18 No. 728: Taylor Company, plumbing supplies, $116; postage of $5 added to invoice.

23 No. 729: Filbert and Ward, plumbing supplies, $78; to be picked up.

25 No. 730: Bruce Hill, electrical supplies, $110; to be picked up.

27 No. 731: Hilda Wesley, electrical supplies, $75, and plumbing supplies, $130; postage of $6 added to invoice.

30 No. 732: Carey Edenfield, plumbing supplies, $103; to be picked up.

31 No. 733: Lorenson Company, plumbing supplies, $450; freight collect.

Required:

1. Record the above charge sales in a sales register like the one in Illustration 12–6. All prepaid postage should be credited to Postage Expense, account no. 666.

Other relevant accounts are as follows:

122 Accounts Receivable
510 Sales—Plumbing
511 Sales Returns and Allowances—Plumbing
520 Sales—Electrical
521 Sales Returns and Allowances—Electrical

2. Foot and rule the sales register on August 31, 1987.

3. Assuming that all postings, both individual and summary, have been completed, make the necessary check marks and other notations in the sales register.

12–4. L. White is a wholesaler of television and radio parts and supplies. White keeps merchandise accounts on a departmental basis and sells only to retailers. During November 1987, White made the following charge sales:

1987
Nov. 1 No. 946: Corporal Company, television parts, $542; express collect.

1987

Nov. 2   No. 947: Callaway Brothers, radio parts, $165; postage of $5 should be added to invoice.

3   No. 948: H. C. Allen & Sons, television parts, $250; to be picked up.

4   No. 949: Freeman and Oakley, radio supplies, $92; less credit of $8 for defective earphones which were returned. Accounts Receivable should be debited for the net amount. To be picked up.

5   No. 950: Homrich Brothers, television parts, $385; freight collect.

9   No. 951: Callaway Brothers, radio parts, $105; postage of $3 should be added to invoice.

10   No. 952: Wall's, television parts, $400, and radio parts, $275; express collect.

11   No. 953: Todd Wells, radio parts, $133; postage of $4 should be added to invoice.

12   No. 954: Freeman and Oakley, radio supplies, $104; to be picked up.

15   No. 955: Ramsey and Ray, television parts, $198; freight collect.

16   No. 956: Callaway Brothers, radio parts, $123; less credit of $45 for defective parts which were returned; postage of $3 should be added to invoice. Accounts Receivable should be debited for net amount.

17   No. 957: H. C. Allen & Sons, television supplies, $111; to be picked up.

19   No. 958: Homrich Brothers, television supplies, $163; postage of $5 should be added to invoice.

22   No. 959: Triplex Company, radio parts, $675; express collect.

23   No. 960: Ramsey and Ray, television parts, $221; to be picked up.

24   No. 961: Walls's, television supplies, $175, and radio supplies, $75; postage of $10 should be added to invoice.

25   No. 962: Freeman and Oakley, radio supplies, $86; to be picked up.

29   No. 963: H. C. Allen & Sons, television parts, $395; express collect.

30   No. 964: Ramsey and Ray, television supplies, $113; to be picked up.

Required:

1. Open the following general ledger accounts and insert the November 1, 1987, balances:

Account No.	Account Title	Balance
113	Accounts Receivable	$ 637
505	Sales—Television	28,000
506	Sales Returns and Allowances—Television	420
510	Sales—Radio	15,600
511	Sales Returns and Allowances—Radio . .	240
648	Postage Expense	75

2. Open the following subsidiary accounts receivable ledger accounts and insert the November 1, 1987, balances:

H. C. Allen & Sons	$ 62
Callaway Brothers	106
Corporal Company	55
Freeman and Oakley. . . .	22
Homrich Brothers	103
Ramsey and Ray	66
Todd Wells	45
Triplex Company	76
Wall's	102

3. Record the charge sales listed above in a sales register like the one shown in Illustration 12–6. Prepaid postage should be credited to account no. 648. Post the charge sales directly to the customers' accounts in the subsidiary ledger.
4. Foot and rule the sales register on November 30, 1987.
5. Make the individual and summary postings to the general ledger accounts.

12–5. The Hitchcock Wholesale Company is divided into two departments—Department A and Department B. The following charge sales were made during June 1987.

1987

June 1 No. 646: Medley Company, Department A, $350; postage of $8.50 should be added to invoice.

2 No. 647: Pathak and Patwardhan, Department A, $480, and Department B, $295; freight collect.

3 No. 648: Walbro, Department B, $260; to be picked up.

4 No. 649: Webb-Wax Company, Department A, $175, and Department B, $320; freight collect.

1987

June 8 No. 650: Yang Company, Department B, $406; express collect.

10 No. 651: Walbro, Department A, $296; to be picked up.

11 No. 652: Kelley's Store, Department B, $323; postage of $10 should be added to invoice.

15 No. 653: Medley Company, Department B, $206; postage of $6.50 should be added to invoice.

16 No. 654: Webb-Wax Company, Department A, $116; postage of $5 should be added to invoice.

17 No. 655: Yang Company, Department B, $358; less credit of $85 for unacceptable merchandise which was returned. Accounts Receivable should be debited for the net amount; freight collect.

22 No. 656: Pathak and Patwardhan, Department B, $198; to be picked up.

23 No. 657: Kelley's Store, Department A, $265; postage of $7 should be added to invoice.

25 No. 658: Walbro, Department B, $195; to be picked up.

29 No. 659: Yang Company, Department A, $260; postage of $5 should be added to invoice.

Required:

1. Open the following general ledger accounts, and insert the June 1, 1987, balances:

Account No.	Account Title	Balance
115	Accounts Receivable.	$ 968
501	Sales—Department A	15,500
502	Sales Returns and Allowances—Dept. A . .	250
507	Sales—Department B	18,900
508	Sales Returns and Allowances—Dept. B . .	475
655	Postage Expense	80

2. Open a subsidiary ledger of accounts receivable and insert the June 1, 1987, balances:

Kelley's Store	$225
Medley Company.	56
Pathak and Patwardhan. . . .	304
Walbro	74
Webb-Wax Company	106
Yang Company	203

3. Record the charge sales for June in a sales register like the one in Illustration 12–6. Post directly to the customer's account in the subsidiary ledger.

4. Foot and rule the sales register on June 30, 1987.

5. Make the individual and summary postings to the general ledger accounts.

12–6. Jabro's Wholesale Clothing Store is divided into two departments—Men's and Women's. The following charge sales were made during February 1987:

1987

Feb. 2 No. 344: Marshall Brothers, Men's, $458; to be picked up.

3 No. 345: Delilah's Fashion Boutique, Women's, $696; freight collect.

4 No. 346: Hooper-Hayes, Men's, $590; Women's, $665; express collect.

5 No. 347: Weldon's Men's Shop, Men's, $378; to be picked up.

7 No. 348: Potter-Lind Company, Men's, $360, Women's, $480; express collect.

7 No. 349: A. B. Smith & Sons, Women's, $403; to be picked up.

11 No. 350: Wallace and Valenti, Men's, $665, Women's, $420; express collect.

12 No. 351: Oscar George Company, Women's, $596; less credit of $116 for unacceptable defective garments which were returned. Accounts Receivable should be debited for the net amount; express collect.

12 No. 352: Weldon's Men's Shop, Men's, $422; to be picked up.

14 No. 353: Rigsby-Teaford Company, Men's, $360, Women's, $489; freight collect.

16 No. 354: Potter-Lind Company, Men's, $486; less credit for $120 for defective merchandise which was returned. Accounts Receivable should be debited for the net amount; to be picked up.

17 No. 355: Delilah's Fashion Boutique, Women's, $367; freight collect.

18 No. 356: A. B. Smith & Sons, Women's, $412; express collect.

21 No. 357: Marshall Brothers, Men's, $508; freight collect.

1987
Feb. 24   No. 358: Wallace and Valenti, Men's, $498; express collect.
　　25   No. 359: Rigsby-Teaford Company, Women's, $562; less credit of $82 for defective garments which were returned. Accounts Receivable should be debited for the net amount; freight collect.
　　26   No. 360: Oscar George Company, Women's, $667; express collect.
　　26   No. 361: Hooper-Hayes, Men's, $498, Women's, $575; freight collect.

Required:

1. Open the following general ledger accounts, and insert the February 1, 1987, balances:

Account No.	Account Title	Balance
125	Accounts Receivable	$1,984
510	Sales—Men's	6,800
511	Sales Returns and Allowances—Men's . . .	250
520	Sales—Women's	7,900
521	Sales Returns and Allowances—Women's . .	485

2. Open a subsidiary ledger of accounts receivable and insert the February 1, 1987, balances:

Delilah's Fashion Boutique . . .	$408
Hooper-Hayes	230
Marshall Brothers	360
Oscar George Company	105
Potter-Lind Company.	120
Rigsby-Teaford Company . . .	206
A. B. Smith & Sons	309
Wallace and Valenti	144
Weldon's Men's Shop.	102

3. Record the charge sales for February in a sales register like the one in Illustration 12–6. Post directly to the customers' accounts in the subsidiary ledger.
4. Foot and rule the sales register on February 28, 1987.
5. Make the individual and summary postings to the general ledger accounts.

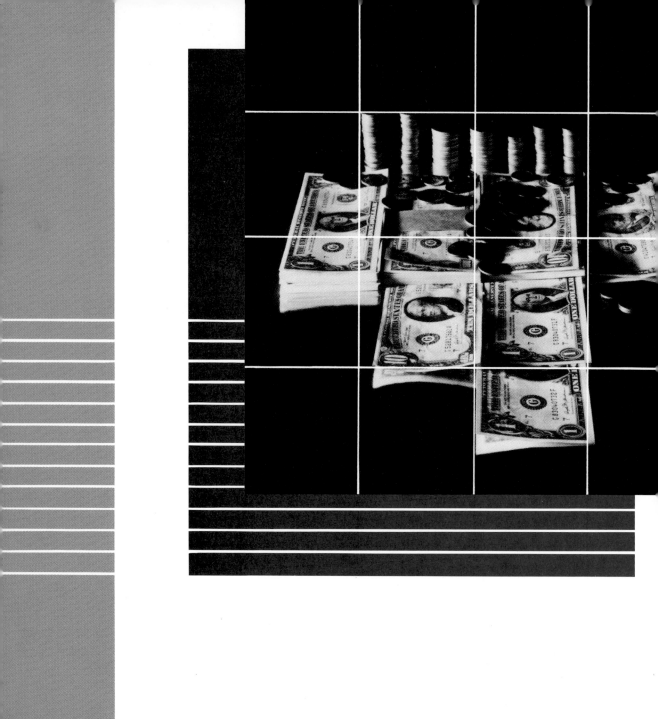

CHAPTER 13

Accounting for merchandise—accrual accounting and record-keeping

LEARNING OBJECTIVES

In this chapter, you will learn some important differences between the cash and the accrual bases of accounting and how to use the accrual basis to account for transactions in a merchandising firm. After studying this chapter, you should be able to:

1. Distinguish between the cash and the accrual bases of accounting.
2. Account for bad debts using three different methods: direct write-off, allowance method based on sales, and the allowance method based on the aging of accounts receivable.
3. Compute gross margin and cost of goods sold.
4. Record merchandising transactions in a general journal and in special journals for cash receipts, cash disbursements, sales, and purchases.
5. Post merchandising transactions to the general and subsidiary ledgers.
6. Prepare a schedule of accounts receivable and a schedule of accounts payable.

THE CASH BASIS VERSUS THE ACCRUAL BASIS OF ACCOUNTING

A merchandising firm derives most of its revenues from selling goods to customers. Accounting for a merchandising firm is based on the fundamental concepts that have been presented in Chapters 11 and 12. But certain characteristics of a merchandising firm require additional techniques for accumulating and presenting accounting data.

In Chapter 8 (Accounting for Service Enterprises—Recording Transactions), we presented an example of a service enterprise using the **cash basis of accounting.** When accounting records are kept on a cash basis, revenues are recorded when cash is received, expenses are recorded when cash is paid out. However, cash-basis accounting violates an important principle of accounting called the **matching concept.** According to the matching concept, net income for a given period should include only the revenue earned during the period and the various expenses that were necessary to generate the earned revenue. To implement the matching concept correctly, the **accrual basis of accounting** is generally used for merchandising enterprises. When accounting records are kept on an accrual basis, revenues are recorded in the period in which they are earned, and expenses are recorded in the period in which they cause revenues to be earned. Thus, many items that affect net income are recorded before or after the receipt or payment of cash. The **adjusting journal entries** for supplies and depreciation discussed in Chapter 9 were based on accrual accounting. Through them, the cash-basis records were adjusted to reflect the matching concept. They were necessary because the transactions involving supplies and office equipment affected more than one accounting period and their effects had to be apportioned accordingly. To follow the matching concept, records kept on the accrual basis will also need adjusting entries.

In a merchandising firm, sales of goods are the principal means of earning revenue. The revenue is recorded at the *time of sale* even though a large portion of the sales may be on credit. This system of recognizing revenue differs from the system used with the cash basis of accounting in Chapter 8. In accrual accounting, the point of sale is considered to be the appropriate time to recognize revenue because the sale is the critical event in the earning of revenue. Once the sale is made and the revenue is recognized, the expenses incurred to generate the revenue must also be recorded. It is in recognizing these associated expenses that most adjusting entries occur.

To determine net income for a merchandising firm using accural accounting, it is necessary to make adjusting entries. The most common adjustments are for depreciation, use of supplies, and bad debts. Since depreciation and supplies were discussed in Chapter 9, we will not repeat their explanation. Instead, we will focus on accounting for bad debts.

ACCOUNTING FOR BAD DEBTS

When a company makes a sale for credit, the amount of the sale is debited to the Accounts Receivable asset account. But each time a company grants credit, it runs the risk that the customer will fail to pay his or her account. When nonpayment occurs, the firm incurs a loss that is charged to **bad debt expense.** If a company could determine in advance which customers would not pay their accounts, it could refuse to grant them credit and bad debt expense could be avoided. This, however, is impossible. It is only after credit has been granted and some time has passed that the probability of nonpayment becomes apparent. Once an account is known to be uncollectible, it should no longer be considered an asset since no future payment is expected. There are three methods of accounting for bad debts.

The direct write-off method

When the **direct write-off method of accounting for bad debts** is used the accountant debits the amount of the unpaid account to Bad Debt Expense and credits Accounts Receivable for the same amount. Thus, if John Jones failed to pay his account for $150, the journal entry would look like this:

GENERAL JOURNAL					
DATE 1987		ACCOUNT AND EXPLANATION	P.R.	DEBIT	CREDIT
Dec.	31	Bad Debt Expense		150 00	
		Accounts Receivable, John Jones			150 00
		To record account written off.			

The credit would be posted both to the Accounts Receivable account in the general ledger and to John Jones's account in the subsidiary ledger. This method is convenient because it is so simple, but it is not entirely consistent with the principles of the accrual basis of accounting. In accrual accounting, revenue is usually recorded in the period in which the sale is made. However, the uncollectibility of an account does not usually become apparent until a later date, which may be in the next accounting period. Thus, a sale's revenue is recognized in one period, and its related bad debt expense is recognized in another, which violates the matching concept.

If a firm's total amount of bad debts is quite small, the direct write-off approach is acceptable. For example, since most small service businesses use the cash basis of accounting and seldom sell services or merchandise on credit, they can use the direct write-off method. However, this method is not recommended for firms that sell much of their merchandise on credit.

The allowance method based on sales

Firms that make many sales on credit commonly use the **allowance method based on sales** to **account for bad debts.** They prefer this method because the expense of the bad debts is matched with the revenue generated by their sales. Also, their accounts receivable are shown on the balance sheet at the amount that is expected to be collected in cash, called the *net realizable value.*

When the allowance method is used, an *estimate* is made of the total dollar value of receivables that are expected to be uncollectible from the current period's sales. This amount is then debited to the Bad Debts Expense account and credited to the **Allowance for Doubtful Accounts** account, which is a contra asset account used to reduce Accounts Receivable. When individual customer accounts become uncollectible, the allowance account is debited, and the Accounts Receivable account is credited. A credit is also posted to the subsidiary ledger account.

The estimate of bad debts is based on the expected collectibility of a period's sales. It is typically derived from previous experience. If a firm's credit policy has not changed a great deal, past experience is usually a good basis for a period's estimate.

For example, Jeb Barnard owns the High-Fi Stereo Store in Tampa, Florida. The store carries top-quality merchandise and has produced a loyal following of customers. In 1987, High-Fi's sales were $1,200,000. Jeb's past experience has shown that 1½ percent of his gross sales become uncollectible even though he always makes credit checks on all his customers. To compute his 1987 allowance for doubtful accounts, at the end of the year, Jeb would multiply his total annual sales ($1,200,000) by his usual percentage of uncollectible sales (1.5 percent or .015) to arrive at $18,000. He would then record this amount as a debit to Bad Debt Expense and a credit to Allowance for Doubtful Accounts, as follows:

GENERAL JOURNAL

DATE		ACCOUNT AND EXPLANATION	P.R.	DEBIT	CREDIT
1987					
Dec.	31	Bad Debt Expense		18000 00	
		Allowance for Doubtful Accounts			18000 00
		To record estimated bad debts.			

On his balance sheet, Jeb would deduct the balance in his allowance for doubtful accounts from his accounts receivable balance as of December 31 to arrive at the adjusted balance. His accounts receivable balance at the end of the year was $160,000, so the balance sheet would show:

Accounts receivable $160,000
Less allowance for doubtful accounts . . .   18,000 $142,000

Finally, on his income statement, Jeb would treat his bad debt expense as an operating expense which would reduce income for the period. As a result of this method of recognizing bad debts, revenues and expenses would be appropriately matched for the year 1987.

During the year, when it is determined that an individual account has become uncollectible, it should be written off as a debit to Allowance for Doubtful Accounts and a credit to Accounts Receivable. Thus, if on April 1, 1988, Jeb discovered that three accounts were uncollectible, he would make the following journal entry:

GENERAL JOURNAL

DATE 1988		ACCOUNT AND EXPLANATION	P.R.	DEBIT	CREDIT
April	1	Allowance for Doubtful Accounts		2100 00	
		Accounts Receivable—Joe Black			900 00
		Accounts Receivable—Sue Blue			800 00
		Accounts Receivable—Bob White			400 00
		To write off uncollectible accounts.			

Aging of accounts receivable

Another way to determine bad debts expense using the allowance account is by **aging the accounts receivable.** Under this approach, a chart is made in which accounts are classified according to the length of time they have been owed to the company. Estimates are made on what percentage of the accounts will prove uncollectible, based on the age group to which they belong. The estimated uncollectible amounts from each category are then totaled to determine what amount should be carried in the Allowance for Doubtful Accounts account. The amount of bad debts expense is then determined in relationship to the amount currently carried in the allowance account. Depending on this amount, either a debit or a credit will be needed to bring the total in the allowances account to the amount determined by aging. Here is the 1987 Accounts Receivable aging chart for the High-Fi Stereo Store:

HIGH-FI STEREO STORE
Accounts Receivable Aging Chart
December 31, 1987

Customer's Name	Net Due	1 to 30 Days Past Due	31 to 60 Days Past Due	61 to 90 Days Past Due
Fran Aaron	35 00			
Joe Black			50 00	
Sue Blue				25 00
Tom Harrell		60 00		
Rod Myers		40 00		
Jan Ryan			25 00	
Todd Smith	20 00			
Bob White	15 00			
Total	70 00	100 00	75 00	25 00

Based on experience, Jeb assumes that the following percentages of each category will prove uncollectible:

Not due 1%
1 to 30 days past due . . . 3
31 to 60 days past due . . . 6
61 to 90 days past due . . . 10

So Jeb would estimate the following amounts as uncollectible: ($70 × 0.01) + ($100 × 0.03) + ($75 × 0.06) + ($25 × 0.10) = $0.70 + $3.00 + $4.50 + $2.50 = $10.70. Assuming that the Allowance for Doubtful Accounts account currently had a credit balance of $5.00, the following entry would be necessary:

	GENERAL JOURNAL			
DATE	ACCOUNT AND EXPLANATION	P.R.	DEBIT	CREDIT
1987				
Dec. 31	Bad Debt Expense		5 70	
	Allowance for Doubtful Accounts			5 70
	To record estimated uncollectible accounts.			

The entry for $5.70 plus the $5.00 balance already there will now give the desired ending balance of $10.70.

Bad debt recoveries

Sometimes an account that has been written off will be paid. In such a case, the account receivable should be reinstated, and the payment should then be recorded in the usual manner. The reinstatement of the account is a reversal of the entry made to write off the account. The entry to record the payment is the same as if the account had not been written off.

For example, assume that in 1987, Jeb wrote off Jill Hamnik's account as uncollectible. In March 1988, to everyone's surprise, Jill sent a check for the payment of her account. Depending on the write-off method, the entries necessary to record the recovery are as follows:

Direct Write-Off Method

	GENERAL JOURNAL			
DATE	ACCOUNT AND EXPLANATION	P.R.	DEBIT	CREDIT
1988				
Mar. 1	Accounts Receivable—Jill Hamnik		2 0 0 00	
	Bad Debts Expense			2 0 0 00
	To record the rein. of acc. write off.			
1	Cash		2 0 0 00	
	Accounts Receivable—Jill Hamnik			2 0 0 00
	To record receipt on account.			

Allowance Method

		GENERAL JOURNAL			
DATE		ACCOUNT AND EXPLANATION	P.R	DEBIT	CREDIT
1988					
Mar.	1	Accounts Receivable—Jill Hamnik		2 0 0 00	
		Allowance for Doubtful Accounts			2 0 0 00
		To record the rein. of acc. write off.			
	1	Cash		2 0 0 00	
		Accounts Receivable—Jill Hamnik			2 0 0 00
		To record receipt on account.			

At the end of the year, Jeb would also make adjusting entries to record his depreciation expense and the value of the supplies he used. The procedures used to make these adjustments were explained in Chapter 9.

COST OF GOODS SOLD AND GROSS MARGIN

A merchandising firm, unlike a service firm, has a product cost, or cost of goods sold. The **cost of goods sold** is a very important figure because it tells how much the products bought for resale cost the seller. The selling price of merchandise must be set high enough to cover cost of goods sold *and* operating expenses if a merchandising firm is to earn a profit.

Another important figure for a merchandiser is **gross margin,** or **gross profit.** This is the merchandiser's profit before operating expenses and other items are deducted. In order to calculate gross margin, a merchandiser must first know the period's net sales, net purchases, and cost of goods sold.

A period's **net sales** are calculated as follows:

$$\text{Net sales} = \text{Total sales} - \text{Sales returns and allowances} - \text{Sales discounts}$$

The figures for total sales, sales returns and allowances, and sales discounts can be found in the general ledger.

Net purchases are computed as:

$$\text{Net purchases} = \text{Total purchases} - \text{Purchase returns and allowances} - \text{Purchases discounts}$$

Cost of Goods Sold

ILLUSTRATION 13–1	Revenue:				
	Sales				$110,000
	Less: Sales returns and				
	allowances		$3,500		
	Sales discounts		500		4,000
	Net sales			①	$106,000
	Cost of goods sold:				
	Merchandise inventory, beginning				
	of period.			$10,700	
	Purchases		$85,500		
	Less: Purchase returns and				
	allowances	$1,700			
	Purchase discounts . . .	400	2,100		
	Add: New purchases.		②	83,400	
	Cost of goods available for sale . .			$94,100	
	Merchandise inventory, end of				
	period.			12,300	
	Cost of goods sold			③	81,800
	Gross margin on sales			④	$ 24,200

The necessary figures for this calculation can also be found in the general ledger.

Cost of goods sold is determined as follows:

Cost of goods sold = Beginning merchandise inventory + Net purchases − Ending merchandise inventory

To determine the value of the merchandise inventory, a physical count of goods on hand must be taken at the end of the accounting period. The quantity of inventory is then multiplied by its unit cost to arrive at a dollar value. The ending inventory of one period is the beginning inventory of the next period, so inventory needs to be counted only once—at the end of the accounting period.

The calculation of net sales, cost of goods sold, and gross margin is shown in Illustration 13–1. Note that the format is similar to that of the income statement. Also note how the calculations are based on the formulas just introduced:

1. Net sales = Total sales − Sales returns and allowances − Sales discounts
   Net sales = $110,000 − $3,500 − $500
   Net sales = $106,000

   2. Net purchases = Total purchases − Purchases returns and allowances − Purchase discounts
     Net purchases = $85,500 − $1,700 − $400
     Net purchases = $83,400
   3. Cost of goods sold = Beginning merchandise inventory + Net purchases − Ending merchandise inventory
     Cost of goods sold = $10,700 + $83,400 − $12,300
     Cost of goods sold = $81,800
   4. Gross margin = Net sales − Cost of goods sold
     Gross margin = $106,000 − $81,800
     Gross margin = $24,200

To arrive at net income, the company would then deduct operating expenses and other items from the gross margin.

ACCOUNTING PROCEDURES—A SMALL MERCHANDISING BUSINESS

The transactions of a merchandising business are recorded in much the same way as those of any other enterprise. If the number of transactions is small, the only book of original entry will be a standard two-column general journal or a combined journal. As the volume of activity increases, however, the company is likely to use a combination of special journals including:

   1. A purchase journal (see Chapter 11).
   2. A sales journal (see Chapter 12).
   3. A cash receipts journal (see Chapter 10).
   4. A cash disbursements journal (see Chapter 10).
   5. A general journal.

At the end of every month, these special journals will be summarized, and postings will be made to the appropriate general ledger accounts. Posting to the subsidiary accounts should be done daily or weekly.

A trial balance of all accounts in the general ledger should be made at the end of every month. Its purpose is to prove the equality of the debit and credit account balances. At the same time the Accounts Receivable control account balance from the general ledger should be reconciled to the total of the amounts in the supporting subsidiary records. A detailed listing of customer balances is often prepared for this purpose. Likewise, the balance in the Accounts

Payable control account should be reconciled to a list of amounts owed to suppliers in the subsidiary Account Payable ledger accounts.

To illustrate these accounting procedures, we will (1) record selected transactions from a representative month in the applicable journals, (2) post amounts to subsidiary Account Receivable or Accounts Payable ledgers, (3) post all required entries to the general ledger accounts, (4) prepare a schedule of accounts receivable balances, and (5) prepare a similar schedule of accounts payable balances. Since the accounts we are concerned with are only one segment of the total general ledger, we will not prepare a trial balance.

The High-Fi Stereo Store uses a purchases journal, a sales journal, separate journals for cash receipts and disbursements, and a general journal. The company maintains an unpaid invoice file as supporting detail for its accounts payable. For accounts receivable, however, an individual subsidiary ledger account is maintained for each customer. The company is not subject to a retail sales tax. Neither sales or purchase discounts are offered.

Here is a chart of accounts listing only the account names and numbers affected by our selected transactions:

Chart of Accounts (Partial)

Assets:	*Revenues:*
110 Cash	410 Sales
115 Accounts Receivable	411 Sales Returns and Allowances
Liabilities:	*Cost of Goods Sold:*
250 Accounts Payable	510 Purchases
	511 Purchase Returns and Allowances

Explanation of transactions

1987

Nov. 1 Received Invoice No. 6734 from Xenith for merchandise purchased at a cost of $374.51. Terms are 10 days net.

2 Sold merchandise on account to Sue Blue for $38.50. Sales Invoice No. 7881.

3 Purchased merchandise on account from Magnabox, $132.18. Terms are 20 days net. Invoice No. 13838.

4 Sold merchandise on account to Jan Ryan for $17.45. Sales Invoice No. 7882.

4 Issued check no. 282 to Pitachi for payment on account of $482.91. (This would be recorded in the cash disbursement journal.)

Nov. 5 Purchased $78 of merchandise from Tobert Brothers Company with check no. 283.

7 Counted cash sales from the totals on the cash register tape of $347.81. These totals represent all cash sales made during the week through closing time on Saturday. (The totals should be recorded in the cash receipts journal by debiting Cash and crediting Sales. Cash sales would not be recorded in the sales journal because it is used only for sales on account.)

8 Received $73 from Todd Smith for payment on account.

9 Sold merchandise on account to Tom Harrell for $318. Sales Invoice No. 7883.

11 Paid account with Xenith for $374.51. Check no. 284.

12 Received $38.50 from Sue Blue as payment on account.

15 Cash sales for the week were $451.37.

18 Issued a credit for $13.50 to Tom Harrell for merchandise returned.

19 Received Invoice No. 913 from United Electric for merchandise purchases of $148.91. Terms, net 10 days.

22 Received a purchase allowance of $21 from United Electric for damaged merchandise in the November 19 shipment.

24 Received Invoice No. 67742 from Bitushi for merchandise purchases of $210. Terms, net 20 days.

25 Issued check no. 285 to United Electric for $127.91. This represents the original purchase of $148.91 less the allowance of $21.00 received on November 22.

26 Cash sales for the week were $462.43.

30 Received $304.50 from Tom Harrell for payment on account. This covers the sale of November 9 for $318 less $13.50 for merchandise returned on November 18.

30 Cash sales for November 29 and 30 were $56.70.

Recording the transactions

High-Fi's November transactions were recorded in the applicable journals, as shown in Illustrations 13–2, 13–3, and 13–4. The purchases and sales journals (Illustration 13–4) include all transactions for the month, and the amount columns foot to the illustrated totals. Since the company maintains individual accounts for each customer, these were posted on a daily basis (Illustration 13–5). Note that parentheses are used to indicate a debit balance in an account that

ILLUSTRATION 13–2

Cash Receipts Journal

CASH DR.	DATE	DESCRIPTION	SALES CR.	ACCOUNTS RECEIVABLE, CR.			SUNDRY ACCOUNTS, CR.		
				AMOUNT	√	ACCT. NO.	AMOUNT	√	

CASH RECEIPTS JOURNAL — PAGE 8

CASH DR.	DATE	DESCRIPTION	SALES CR.	AMOUNT	√	ACCT. NO.	AMOUNT	√
	1987							
347 81	Nov. 7	Cash Sales	347 81					
73 00	8	Todd Smith		73 00	√			
38 50	12	Sue Blue		38 50	√			
451 37	15	Cash Sales	451 37					
462 43	26	Cash Sales	462 43					
304 50	30	Tom Harrell		304 50	√			
56 70	30	Cash Sales	56 70					
1734 31	30		1318 31	416 00				
(110)			(410)	(115)				

ILLUSTRATION 13–3

Cash Disbursements Journal

CASH DISBURSEMENTS JOURNAL — PAGE 9

ACCOUNTS PAYABLE, DR.		SUNDRY ACCOUNTS, DR.			DATE	DESCRIPTION	CHECK NO.	CASH CR.
AMOUNT	√	ACCT. NO	AMOUNT	√				
					1987			
482 91					Nov. 4	Pitachi Company	282	482 91
		510	78 00		5	Tobert Brothers Company	283	78 00
374 51					11	Xenith Company	284	374 51
127 91					25	United Electric	285	127 91
985 33			78 00					1063 33
(250)			(√)					(110)

ILLUSTRATION 13–4

Purchases, Sales, and General Journals

PURCHASES JOURNAL — PAGE 6

DATE	TERMS	INVOICE NO.	CREDITOR	PURCHASES, DR. ACC. PAY., CR. AMOUNT	P.R.
1987					
Nov. 1	Net 10 days	6734	Xenith Company	374 51	
3	Net 20 days	13838	Magnabox	132 18	
19	Net 10 days	913	United Electric	148 91	
24	Net 20 days	67742	Bitushi	210 00	
				865 60	
				(510 / 250)	

**ILLUSTRATION
13–4
(concluded)**

SALES JOURNAL				PAGE 5	
DATE	SOLD TO	INVOICE NO.	ACCTS. REC., DR. SALES, CR. AMOUNT	P.R.	
1987					
Nov. 2	Sue Blue	7881	3 8 50	√	
4	Jan Ryan	7882	1 7 45	√	
9	Tom Harrell	7883	3 1 8 00	√	
			3 7 3 95		
			(1 1 5 / 4 10)		

GENERAL JOURNAL				PAGE 6
DATE	ACCOUNT AND EXPLANATION	P.R.	DEBIT	CREDIT
1987				
Nov. 18	Sales Returns and Allowances	411	1 3 50	
	Accounts Receivable—Tom Harrell	115 √		1 3 50
	To record credit issued for returned merchandise.			
22	Accounts Payable—United Electric	250 √	2 1 00	
	Purchases Returns and Allowances	511		2 1 00
	To record purchase allowance from United Electric.			

normally has a credit balance, such as Accounts Payable (Illustration 13–6). Likewise, parentheses are used to indicate a credit balance in an account that normally has a debit balance, such as Cash. See account numbers 115 and 250 in Illustration 13–6 for examples of such **negative account balances.**

Posting

Only those general ledger accounts affected by the selected transactions are shown. Since High-Fi has been in operation some time, some

ILLUSTRATION 13–5

Accounts Receivable Subsidiary Ledger

Sue Blue

DATE		EXPLANATION	P.R.	DEBIT	CREDIT	BALANCE
1987						
Nov.	2		S5	38 50		38 50
	12		CR8		38 50	-0-

Tom Harrell

DATE		EXPLANATION	P.R.	DEBIT	CREDIT	BALANCE
1987						
Nov.	9		S5	318 00		318 00
	18		GJ6		13 50	304 50
	30		CR8		304 50	-0-

Jan Ryan

DATE		EXPLANATION	P.R.	DEBIT	CREDIT	BALANCE
1987						
Nov.	1	Balance	√			20 00
	4		S5	17 45		37 45

Todd Smith

DATE		EXPLANATION	P.R.	DEBIT	CREDIT	BALANCE
1987						
Nov.	1	Balance	√			73 00
	8		CR8		73 00	-0-

accounts have a balance carried forward from the previous month. For accounts receivable, any customer account with an unpaid balance as of November 1 is shown in the subsidiary ledger. Amounts for the month were posted to the subsidiary ledger on a daily basis.

The order of posting to the general ledger accounts was (1) general journal, (2) sales journal, (3) purchases journal, (4) cash receipts journal, and (5) cash disbursements journal. For each of these, the columns were footed and ruled as indicated. While the Sundry Accounts columns in the cash journals are totaled, this is for crossfooting purposes only. Each item in these columns must be posted individually since a number of different ledger accounts are involved.

Posting is indicated by a check mark. The other column totals are posted directly to their respective ledger accounts. Note that the ledger account number is shown below or next to its corresponding total to indicate posting.

When a company uses a number of special journals, the source

ILLUSTRATION 13–6

General Ledger (Partial)

GENERAL LEDGER

Cash — ACCT. NO. 110

DATE		EXPLANATION	P.R.	DEBIT	CREDIT	BALANCE DEBIT	BALANCE CREDIT
1987							
Nov.	1	Balance	√			1 741 50	
	30		CR8	1 734 31		3 475 81	
	30		CD9		1 063 33	2 412 48	

GENERAL LEDGER

Accounts Receivable — ACCT. NO. 115

DATE		EXPLANATION	P.R.	DEBIT	CREDIT	BALANCE DEBIT	BALANCE CREDIT
1987							
Nov.	1	Balance	√			93 00	
	18		GJ6		13 50	79 50	
	30		CR8		4 16 00	(3 36 50)	
	30		S5	3 73 95		37 45	

GENERAL LEDGER

Accounts Payable — ACCT. NO. 250

DATE		EXPLANATION	P.R.	DEBIT	CREDIT	BALANCE DEBIT	BALANCE CREDIT
1987							
Nov.	1	Balance	√				4 82 91
	22		GJ6	21 00			4 61 91
	30		CD9	9 85 33			(5 23 42)
	30		P6		8 65 60		3 42 18

GENERAL LEDGER

Sales — ACCT. NO. 410

DATE		EXPLANATION	P.R.	DEBIT	CREDIT	BALANCE DEBIT	BALANCE CREDIT
1987							
Nov.	1	Balance	√				28 147 23
	30		CR8		1 318 31		29 465 54
	30		S5		3 73 95		29 839 49

**ILLUSTRATION
13–6
(concluded)**

GENERAL LEDGER

Sales Returns and Allowances — ACCT. NO. 411

DATE		EXPLANATION	P.R.	DEBIT	CREDIT	BALANCE DEBIT	BALANCE CREDIT
1987							
Nov.	1	Balance	√			3 13 10	
	18		GJ6	1 3 50		3 26 60	

GENERAL LEDGER

Purchases — ACCT. NO. 510

DATE		EXPLANATION	P.R.	DEBIT	CREDIT	BALANCE DEBIT	BALANCE CREDIT
1987							
Nov.	1	Balance	√			16 4 33 66	
	5		CD9	7 8 00		16 5 11 66	
	30		P6	8 65 60		17 3 77 26	

GENERAL LEDGER

Purchases Returns and Allowances — ACCT. NO. 511

DATE		EXPLANATION	P.R.	DEBIT	CREDIT	BALANCE DEBIT	BALANCE CREDIT
1987							
Nov.	1	Balance	√				4 13 09
	22		GJ6		2 1 00		4 34 09

of each entry in the general ledger should be indicated. For our example, this was done using the following code:

CR = Cash receipts journal
CD = Cash disbursements journal
S = Sales journal
P = Purchases journal
GJ = General journal

These initials are followed by the page number of the journal.

The schedule of accounts receivable

At the end of each month, a merchandiser should compile a list of the amounts due from all credit customers. This **schedule of accounts receivable** can be readily prepared using the balances from the individual ledger accounts. If this total does not agree with the balance in the Accounts Receivable control account from the general ledger, the reason for this difference must be determined. The schedule of accounts receivable for High-Fi Stereo Store as of November 30, 1987, is:

HIGH-FI STEREO STORE
Schedule of Accounts Receivable
November 30, 1987

Jan Ryan $37.45

The schedule of accounts payable

A detailed list of the amounts owed to all creditors should also be prepared at the end of the month. This **schedule of accounts payable** is compiled from the file of unpaid invoices. Again, the schedule total should agree with the balance in the Accounts Payable control account from the general ledger. Should these amounts differ, postings to the Accounts Payable control account and invoices in the unpaid file must be rechecked until the error is found. The schedule of accounts payable for High-Fi Stereo Store as of November 30, 1987, is:

HIGH-FI STEREO STORE
Schedule of Accounts Payable
November 30, 1987

Bitushi $210.00
Magnabox 132.18
$342.18

SUMMARY

Until this chapter, we have focused primarily on the **cash basis of accounting,** under which revenues are recorded only when cash is received and expenses are recorded only when cash is paid. But this method of accounting ignores an important principle of accounting—the **matching concept**—which states that net income for a given period should include only the revenue earned during the period and the various expenses that were necessary to generate the earned revenues. To implement the matching concept correctly, merchandising firms use the **accrual basis of accounting.** With accrual accounting, revenues are recorded in the period in which they are earned, and expenses are recorded in the period in which they help revenues to be earned.

When granting credit, a company always runs the risk that the customer will not pay. If this happens, the firm incurs a loss that must be charged to **bad debt expense.** There are three methods of accounting for bad debts using **adjusting journal entries:** (1) the **direct write-off method,** (2) the **allowance method based on sales,** and (3) the allowance method based on the **aging of accounts receivable.** Both allowance methods require an estimated amount to be credited to a contra account called **Allowances for Doubtful Accounts.**

A merchandising firm, unlike a service firm, has a product cost, or **cost of goods sold.** This figure tells how much the products purchased for resale cost the seller during a specified accounting period. Cost of goods sold = Beginning merchandise inventory + **Net purchases** − Ending merchandise inventory. The difference between **net sales** for the period and the cost of goods sold is called the **gross margin,** or **gross profit.** Gross profit is the merchandiser's profit before operating expenses and other items are deducted.

Depending on its number of transactions, a merchandising firm may use only one book of original entry or an assortment that includes a general journal plus special journals for purchases, sales, cash receipts, and cash disbursements. The journalizing and posting processes are similar to those discussed in earlier chapters. In posting to the ledger accounts, care must be taken to use parentheses to note any **negative account balances.**

At the end of each month, a merchandiser should prepare a **schedule of accounts receivable,** which is a detailed list of amounts due from all credit customers, and a **schedule of accounts payable,** which is a detailed list of the amounts due to all creditors.

KEY TERMS

Accrual Basis of Accounting—The recording of revenues in the period in which they are earned and the recording of expenses in the period in which they help revenues to be earned. Thus, many items will be recorded before or after cash is actually received or paid.

Adjusting Journal Entries—Journal entries made at the end of an accounting period so that the accounts will reflect the correct balances in the financial statements. These entries are necessary because some transactions have an effect on more than one accounting period, and their effects must be apportioned accordingly.

Aging of Accounts Receivable—Preparation of a schedule in which the accounts receivable are listed and categorized according to length of time outstanding.

Allowance for Doubtful Accounts Account—A contra asset account used to reduce Accounts Receivable to its estimated collectible amount.

Allowance Method of Accounting for Bad Debts Based on Sales—A method of accounting for bad debts that matches the expense of the bad debt with the revenue generated by the sale. An estimate is made of the total dollar value of receivables that are expected to be uncollectible from the current period's sales. This amount is debited to Bad Debts Expense and credited to the Allowance for Doubtful Accounts. When individual accounts become uncollectible, the allowance account is debited and the Accounts Receivable account is credited.

Bad Debt Expense—An expense incurred by a business when it grants credit to a customer who fails to pay his or her account.

Cash Basis of Accounting—The recording of revenue only when cash is received and the recording of expenses only when cash is paid.

Cost of Goods Sold—The cost of the products sold by a company. It is computed as Merchandise inventory (beginning of period) + Net Purchases − Merchandise inventory (end of period).

Direct Write-off Method of Accounting for Bad Debts—A method commonly used by small businesses to account for bad debts. When an individual account receivable becomes uncollectible, it is written off by debiting Bad Debts Expense and crediting Accounts Receivable.

Gross Margin (or Gross Profit)—A merchandiser's profit before operating expenses and other items are deducted; it is the difference between net sales for the period and the cost of goods sold.

Matching Concept—An accounting concept which states that net income for a given accounting period should include only the revenue earned during the period and the various expenses that were necessary to generate the earned revenue.

Negative Account Balances—Credit balances in accounts that normally have debit balances or debit balances in accounts that normally have credit balances.

Net Purchases—Total purchases − Purchase returns and allowances − Purchases discounts.

Net Sales—Total sales − Sales returns and allowances − Sales discounts.

Schedule of Accounts Payable—A detailed list of the amounts owed to all creditors, usually prepared monthly.

Schedule of Accounts Receivable—A detailed list of the amounts due from all credit customers, usually prepared monthly.

QUESTIONS AND EXERCISES

1. What is the accrual basis of accounting? Why is it generally used for merchandising enterprises?
2. What is the matching principle?
3. What are the adjusting entries? Why are they necessary?
4. Describe the three methods of accounting for bad debts.
5. The Blue Tube Company wrote off a $500 account receivable which was owed by the Greenway Company. Six months later, the account was paid. What entries should be made to record the payment of the account using (a) the direct write-off method and (b) the allowance method?
6. Use equations to define the following terms:
   a. Net sales.
   b. Net purchases.
   c. Cost of goods sold.
   d. Gross margin.
7. The Caldwell Company has two sales departments. In 1987, Department A had sales of $208,000 and sales returns and allowances of $5,820, and Department B had sales of $109,600 and sales returns and allowances of $1,860. At December 31, 1987, the sales discounts account had a balance of $5,900 which is to be divided between the two departments in relationship of their respective gross sales to total gross sales. Prepare the sales section of the income statement for the Caldwell Company for the year ended December 31, 1987.
8. What is the schedule of accounts receivable? Why is it prepared? When is it prepared?
9. What is the schedule of accounts payable? Why is it prepared? When is it prepared?

10. Compute cost of goods sold using the following figures:

Beginning merchandise inventory. . . .	$ 30,000
Purchases	200,000
Purchase returns and allowances	5,000
Purchase discounts	10,000
Ending merchandise inventory	25,000

11. Compute the gross margin using the following figures:

Sales	$50,000
Sales returns and allowances	5,000
Sales discounts	1,000
Beginning merchandise inventory. . . .	8,000
Purchases	20,000
Purchase returns and allowances	3,000
Purchase discounts	1,000
Ending merchandise inventory	10,000

PROBLEMS

These problems will require the student to refer to Chapters 11 and 12 in addition to this chapter.

13–1. Frank Hughes has decided to open a hardware store. He uses the following books of original entry: a cash receipts journal, a cash disbursements journal, a purchases journal, a sales journal, and a general journal. This problem, however, relates only to the cash receipts and cash disbursements journals, the purchases journal, and the general journal. Hughes completed the following transactions during August 1987:

1987
Aug. 1 Invested $10,000 in the new hardware store.
    2 Purchased display equipment for $900 from Collier Display.
    3 Purchased merchandise for cash, $300. Check No. 101.
    6 Received Invoice No. 1002 dated August 2, 1987, from Halsey Company for merchandise purchased, $450. Terms, net 20.
    6 Purchased office furniture on account, $650, from ABC Office Supply.
    8 Received Invoice No. 227 from Grant Brothers dated August 3, 1987, for merchandise purchased, $250. Terms, net 30.

1987

Aug. 9 Received Invoice No. 750 dated August 3, 1987, from Joyce Suppliers, Inc., for merchandise purchased, $550. Terms, net 10.

10 Paid $450 on account for display equipment purchased on August 2. Check No. 102.

13 Paid Joyce Suppliers, Inc., in full for Invoice No. 750 dated August 3. Check No. 103.

15 Returned defective merchandise to Halsey Company, $150.

16 Received Invoice No. 175 dated August 9, 1987, from Royston Company for merchandise purchased, $375. Terms, net 20.

17 Purchased merchandise for cash, $125. Check No. 104.

20 Paid $450 on account for display equipment purchased August 2. Check No. 105.

22 Received Invoice No. 837 dated August 17, 1987, from Grant Brothers for merchandise purchased, $670. Terms, net 15.

22 Paid Halsey Company the full amount owed to them. Check No. 106.

23 Returned defective merchandise to Grant Brothers, $170.

24 Paid Royston Company in full the amount owed to them. Check No. 107.

26 Paid $500 on office furniture purchased on August 6. Check No. 108.

29 Received Invoice No. 217 dated August 24, 1987, from Chaise Company for merchandise purchased, $300. Terms, net 20.

Required:

1. Record the above transactions in the appropriate journal. Use the following accounts:

111   Cash
121   Office Equipment
131   Display Equipment
211   Accounts Payable
311   Frank Hughes, Capital
511   Purchases
512   Purchases Returns and Allowances

2. Open the above accounts and post the journal entries for August.

3. Prepare a trial balance for August 31, 1987. ₭ 11,520

13–2.   B. A. Ganton has decided to open an appliance store. During the month of April 1987, the following selected transactions were completed:

1987

Apr. 1 Invested $12,000 in Ganton's Appliances.

2 Sold merchandise to Bryan Holman on account, $35, Invoice No. 101.

4 Sold merchandise on account to Bill Shane, $70, Invoice No. 102.

9 Received $35 from Bryan Holman in payment of his account.

11 Sold merchandise to Sheila Newman on account, $125, Invoice No. 103.

13 Sold merchandise on account to Sam Hill, $75, Invoice No. 104.

16 Bill Shane returned merchandise for credit, $40.

16 Received $100 from Sheila Newman in partial payment of her account.

18 Sam Hill returned merchandise for credit, $35.

21 Received $30 from Bill Shane in payment of his account.

23 Sold merchandise to Brenda Clinton on account, $200, Invoice No. 105.

25 Received $25 from Sheila Newman in payment of her account.

27 A customer returned merchandise that had been purchased for cash and received a cash refund of $30.

30 Cash sales for April, $2,200.

Required:

1. Record the above transactions in the appropriate journals. (Assume that Ganton uses a sales journal, a cash receipts journal, a cash disbursements journal, and a general journal.) Use the following accounts:

111   Cash
121   Accounts Receivable
311   B. A. Ganton, Capital

411 Sales
416 Sales Returns and Allowances

2. Open the above accounts and post the journal entries for April.

3. Prepare a trial balance for April 30, 1987.

13–3. S. G. Coleman had decided to open a furniture store. Coleman's books of original entry include a purchases journal, a sales journal, a cash receipts journal, a cash disbursements journal, and a general journal. During the month of February 1987, Coleman completed the following transactions:

1987

Feb. 2 Invested $12,000 in Coleman's Furniture Store.

3 Received Invoice No. 818 dated January 27 from Haven Brothers for merchandise purchased, $2,000. Terms, net 30.

4 Paid rent expense for February, $250.

5 Purchased office equipment for cash, $550.

7 Received Invoice No. 601 dated January 31 from Maddox and Sons, $750. Terms, net 20.

9 Sold merchandise to Michael Cook on account, $250, sales Invoice No. 10.

10 Returned defective merchandise to Haven Brothers, $500.

11 Received Invoice No. 690 dated February 7 from Joplin Company, $1,000. Terms, net 10.

12 Sold merchandise to Mary Myers on account, $150, sales Invoice No. 11.

14 Sold merchandise to Bruce Cooper on account, $50, sales Invoice No. 12.

16 Paid $50 to the local newspaper for advertising.

17 Michael Cook paid $150 on his account.

18 Mary Myers returned a defective chair for credit, $75.

19 Sold merchandise to Bill Groover on account, $200, sales Invoice No. 13.

21 Paid Joplin Company in full for Invoice No. 690 dated February 7.

23 Michael Cook paid $100 on his account.

24 Mary Myers paid her account in full, $75.

25 Received Invoice No. 109 dated February 21 from Gresham's Store for merchandise purchased, $750. Terms, net 20.

26 Paid Maddox & Sons in full for Invoice No. 601 dated January 31.

28 Cash sales for February, $700.

Required:

1. Record the above transactions in the appropriate journals.
2. Open the following accounts and post the journal entries for February:

110   Cash
120   Accounts Receivable
130   Office Equipment
210   Accounts Payable
310   S. G. Coleman, Capital
410   Sales
415   Sales Returns and Allowances
510   Purchases
515   Purchase Returns and Allowances
520   Rent Expense
530   Advertising Expense

3. Prepare a trial balance for February 28, 1987.

13–4. Martha Stone operates a clothing store called Stone's. Four books of original entry are kept—a sales journal, a purchases journal, a cash receipts journal, and a cash disbursements journal. This problem involves only the sales journal. All sales are subject to a 3 percent retail sales tax which is computed on each invoice. During the first half of December 1987, Stone completed the following selected transactions:

1987
Dec.   1 Sold merchandise to Joan Wilson on account, $55, plus sales tax $1.65. Invoice No. 803.

2 Sold merchandise to Albert Boggs on account, $15, plus sales tax $0.45. Invoice No. 804.

3 Sold merchandise to Lewis Tummins on account, $80, plus sales tax $2.40. Invoice No. 805.

5 Sold merchandise to Beverly Scoggins on account, $33, plus sales tax $0.99. Invoice No. 806.

6 Sold merchandise to Charlotte Buchanan on account, $27, plus sales tax $0.81. Invoice No. 807.

7 Sold merchandise to Linda Merley on account, $14, plus sales tax $0.42. Invoice No. 808.

8 Sold merchandise to Russ Hilley on account, $39, plus sales tax $1.17. Invoice No. 809.

1987

Dec. 9 Sold merchandise to Dan Kelly on account, $48, plus sales tax $1.44. Invoice No. 810.

10 Sold merchandise to Linda Merley on account, $28, plus sales tax $0.84. Invoice No. 811.

12 Sold merchandise to Albert Boggs on account, $26, plus sales tax $0.78. Invoice No. 812.

13 Sold merchandise to Beverly Scoggins on account, $16, plus sales tax $0.48. Invoice No. 813.

14 Sold merchandise to Joan Wilson on account, $18, plus sales tax $0.54. Invoice No. 814.

15 Sold merchandise to Charlotte Buchanan on account, $26, plus sales tax $0.78. Invoice No. 815.

Required:

1. Open the following general ledger accounts and record the December 1, 1987, balances:

Account No.	Account Title	Balance 12/1/87
116	Accounts Receivable	$ 600
216	Sales Tax Payable	56
403	Sales	9,800

2. Open a subsidiary ledger for individual accounts receivable. The accounts had the following balances on December 1, 1987:

Albert Boggs.	$ 25
Charlotte Buchanan	80
Russ Hilley	105
Dan Kelly.	65
Linda Merley	96
Beverly Scoggins	82
Lewis Tummins.	76
Joan Wilson	71

3. Record the transactions in the sales journal and post to the individual customer's accounts.

4. Foot the sales journal and post the totals to the general ledger accounts.

5. Prepare a schedule of accounts receivable as of December 15, 1987.

13–5.

THE INDIA STORE
Trial Balance
December 31, 1987

Account No.	Account Title	Debit	Credit
101	Cash	$ 5,000	
111	Accounts receivable	1,500	
121	Merchandise inventory, 1/1/87	4,000	
131	Office supplies.	500	
141	Office equipment	3,000	
151	Accum. depreciation—office equip..		$ 600
201	Accounts payable.		800
301	Thota Hamsa, capital		20,000
311	Thota Hamsa, drawing.	12,000	
401	Sales		51,600
411	Sales returns and allowances	200	
501	Purchases	35,000	
511	Purchase returns and allowances		300
521	Salaries expense	9,000	
531	Rent expense	1,800	
541	Insurance expense	600	
551	Advertising expense	200	
561	Utilities expense	500	
		$73,300	$73,300

Merchandise inventory, 12/31/87, is $5,000.

Required:

Compute (1) cost of goods sold and (2) gross margin on sales.

13–6. Tony Partridge has decided to open a retail store called The Partridge Shop. He keeps a sales journal, a purchases journal, a cash receipts journal, a cash disbursements journal, and a general journal as books of original entry. During the month of August, the following transactions were completed:

1987
Aug. 2 Invested $10,000 in The Partridge Shop.
   3 Received Invoice No. 182 dated July 30 from Sportsco for merchandise purchased, $300. Terms are 10 days net.
   4 Paid rent for August with Check No. 101, $800.
   5 Received Invoice No. 102 dated August 2 from Corbin Brothers for merchandise purchased, $450. Terms, net 10.
   6 Purchased office equipment from Drake Equipment Company on account, $1,500.

1987

Aug. 8 Paid Sportsco the full amount of Invoice No. 182, $300. Check no. 102.

9 Sold merchandise to Kathy Mason on account, $75. Sales Invoice No. 10.

10 Sold merchandise to Della Swan on account, $155. Sales Invoice No. 11.

11 Received Invoice No. 95 dated August 7 from Ramsey Company for merchandise purchased, $400. Terms, net 10.

12 Paid Corbin Brothers the full amount of Invoice No. 102, $450. Check No. 103.

13 Sold merchandise to Ronnie Akins on account, $125. Sales Invoice No. 12.

15 Received Invoice No. 316 dated August 11 from Sportsco for merchandise purchased, $200. Terms, net 10.

15 Withdrew $300 for personal use. Check no. 104.

16 Allowed a credit of $35 to Ronnie Akins for merchandise returned.

16 Sold merchandise to Ravi Jain on account, $80. Sales Invoice No. 13.

17 Kathy Mason paid her account in full, $75.

17 Paid Ramsey Company the full amount of Invoice No. 95, $400. Check no. 105.

18 Returned unacceptable merchandise to Sportco, $75.

19 Sold merchandise to Glenn Hawkins on account, $165. Sales Invoice No. 14.

19 Paid $130 for newspaper advertising. Check no. 106.

20 Received Invoice No. 168 dated August 17 from Corbin Brothers for merchandise purchased, $175. Terms, net 20.

22 Paid Drake Equipment Company for part of the office equipment purchased on the 6th, $500. Check no. 107.

23 Della Swan paid her account in full, $155.

23 Sold merchandise to Kathy Mason on account, $95. Sales Invoice No. 15.

24 Ronnie Akins paid his account in full, $90.

24 Paid Sportsco the full amount owed on Invoice No. 316, $125. Check No. 108.

25 Purchased office supplies on account from Ace Supply Company, $150.

26 Kathy Mason returned defective merchandise that cost $55.

1987

Aug. 27 Paid Drake Equipment Company $1,000 for office equipment purchased on the 6th. Check no. 109.

     29 Sold merchandise to Ronnie Akins on account, $50. Sales Invoice No. 16.

     29 Received Invoice No. 155 dated August 26 from Ramsey Company, $200. Terms, net 10.

     30 Withdrew $300 for personal use. Check no. 110.

     31 Returned defective merchandise to Ramsey Company, $80.

     31 Cash sales for August, $2,500.

Required:

1. Using the following accounts and account numbers, record each of the above transactions in the appropriate journal:

101	Cash
111	Accounts Receivable
121	Office Equipment
201	Accounts Payable
301	Tony Partridge, Capital
311	Tony Partridge, Drawing
401	Sales
411	Sales Returns and Allowances
501	Purchases
511	Purchase Returns and Allowances
521	Rent Expense
531	Advertising Expense
541	Office Supplies Expense

2. Open a general ledger that contains the foregoing accounts and open subsidiary ledgers for individual accounts receivable and accounts payable.

3. Post the transactions that occurred during August.

4. Prepare a trial balance for August 31, 1987.

5. Prepare a schedule of accounts receivable and a schedule of accounts payable as of August 31, 1987.

13–7. The Spiral Department Store sold $2,000,000 worth of merchandise during 1987. At the end of 1987, the Allowance for Doubtful Accounts had a balance of $5,500. Past experience has shown that 1½ percent of sales become uncollectible.

Required:

1. Make the journal entry to record the allowance for doubtful accounts for 1987.

2. Record the following events which occurred in 1988 using the allowance method based on a percentage of sales.
   a. Wrote off the following accounts with a compound entry: James Kaminsky, $1,000; Jerry Nutting, $225; and Alice Stone, $75.
   b. Reinstated and recorded the collection of Marshall Babcock's account, $250.
   c. Wrote off the account of Charles Welch, $1,500.
   d. The allowance was increased by 1½ percent of sales for 1988. Sales for 1988 were $1,750,000.
3. Record entries given in 2(a), (b), and (c) using the direct write-off method.

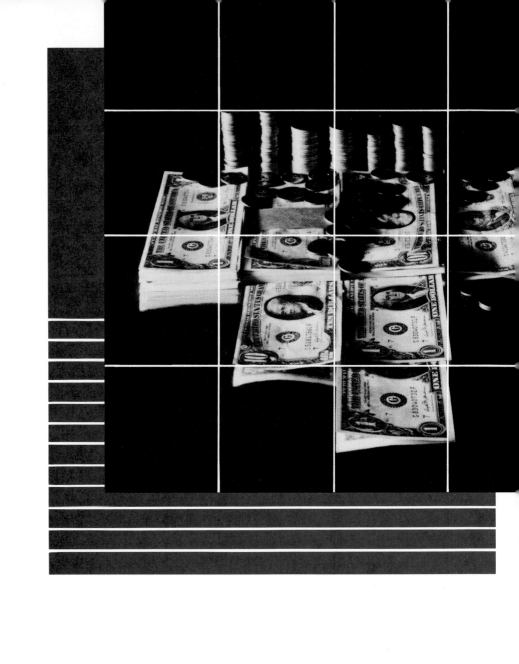

CHAPTER 14

Accounting for merchandise—end-of-period procedures

LEARNING OBJECTIVES

In this chapter, you will learn how to complete the accounting cycle in a merchandising firm. After studying this chapter, you should be able to:

1. Prepare the adjusting entries a merchandiser needs to make at the end of each period to account for inventory, prepaid expenses, and accrued salaries payable.
2. Complete a worksheet for a merchandising firm.
3. Prepare a merchandiser's income statement and balance sheet.
4. Journalize and post a merchandising firm's adjusting and closing entries.
5. Prepare a post-closing trial balance for a merchandising firm.

The three previous chapters introduced some basic information about accounting in a merchandising firm. In addition, Chapter 13 explained the accumulation of accounting data by showing selected transactions from the High-Fi Stereo Store for the month of November. These transactions dealt with the purchase and sale of merchandise, the return of merchandise, cash collections from customers, and cash payments to suppliers. Other transactions, such as the payment of salaries and the purchase of office supplies, were not shown. These transactions would be recorded as described in Chapters 6 through 10.

At the end of each accounting period, a merchandising firm follows procedures that are very similar to those used in a service enterprise. To illustrate these end-of-period procedures, we will continue our example of the High-Fi Stereo Store. We will review some of the adjustments presented in Chapter 9, and we will also show how to deal with accounts such as Merchandise Inventory, Sales, Sales Returns and Allowances, Purchases, and Purchase Returns and Allowances. We will then examine the financial statements and look at some key relationships within the statements.

THE ACCOUNTING CYCLE

The **accounting cycle**—the complete series of steps used to account for a business's financial transactions—is the same for both service and merchandising firms. As discussed in Chapter 9, the steps in the accounting cycle are:

1. Journalize the transactions.
2. Post to the ledger.
3. Prepare a trial balance.
4. Determine the necessary adjustments.
5. Complete the worksheet.
6. Prepare the financial statements.
7. Journalize and post the adjusting and closing entries.
8. Rule the closed accounts and bring down the balances in the open accounts.
9. Prepare a post-closing trial balance.

So far, we have covered Steps 1 and 2 for the High-Fi Stereo Store. Our sample transactions ended on November 30, which is the end of High-Fi's financial reporting period. Thus, High-Fi's accounting year runs from December 1 through November 30. A 12-month financial reporting period such as this, which begins on any date other than January 1, is called a **fiscal year.** A 12-month financial reporting period that *does* begin on January 1 is called a **calendar year.** With all of High-Fi's transactions for the year journalized and posted, we can now proceed with the rest of the accounting cycle.

THE TRIAL BALANCE

At this point, it is important to take a trial balance in order to find any errors that may have occurred as quickly as possible. In this case, we will take our trial balance on the worksheet. The worksheet facilitates the preparation of financial statements and provides a check against errors before the formal financial statements are prepared. Recall that worksheets were first introduced in Chapter 9. Thus, although we will do some reviewing, we will focus primarily on some new aspects of the worksheet as they apply to merchandising.

The first step in completing the worksheet is to enter the end-of-period account balances in the first pair of debit and credit columns, which are labeled Trial Balance. The account balances are taken directly from High-Fi's general ledger. The trial balance that is taken at this time is referred to as the *unadjusted trial balance.* It is shown in the first pair of columns in Illustration 14–1.

ADJUSTMENTS

The next step is to make the necessary adjustments in the second pair of columns. The information needed to make the adjustments can be found in various company records. For example, the information necessary to adjust the asset account Prepaid Insurance would come from the insurance policy itself. The adjustment for depreciation on office equipment is based on previously determined information: the cost of the equipment, its expected useful life, and its salvage value. Each adjustment is based on information that the firm already has.

ILLUSTRATION 14-1

HIGH-FI STEREO STORE
Worksheet
For the Year Ended November 30, 1987

ACCOUNTS	TRIAL BALANCE DEBIT	TRIAL BALANCE CREDIT	ADJUSTMENTS DEBIT	ADJUSTMENTS CREDIT
Cash	1 3 4 0 00			
Accounts Receivable	5 3 6 00			
Allowance for Doubtful Accounts		5 0 00		c 1 5 2 81
Merchandise Inventory	7 2 2 0 00		b 9 6 4 0 00	a 7 2 2 0 00
Prepaid Insurance	2 4 0 00			d 2 0 00
Prepaid Rent	1 8 0 0 00			e 3 0 0 00
Office Equipment	6 0 0 0 00			
Accumulated Depreciation—Off. Equip.		1 5 0 0 00		f 5 0 0 00
Accounts Payable		1 8 8 1 40		
Jeb Barnard, Capital		1 5 9 5 1 88		
Jeb Barnard, Drawing	5 2 1 7 50			
Sales		3 0 8 8 8 89		
Sales Returns and Allowances	3 2 6 60			
Purchases	1 8 0 9 6 16			
Purchase Returns and Allowances		4 3 4 09		
Advertising Expense	6 0 0 00			
Delivery Expense	9 0 0 00			
Rent Expense	1 4 0 0 00		e 3 0 0 00	
Repair and Maintenance Expense	2 5 5 00			
Salaries Expense	6 5 0 0 00		g 8 0 0 00	
Utilities Expense	2 7 5 00			
	5 0 7 0 6 26	5 0 7 0 6 26		
Income Summary			a 7 2 2 0 00	b 9 6 4 0 00
Bad Debt Expense			c 1 5 2 81	
Insurance Expense			d 2 0 00	
Depreciation Expense—Office Equip.			f 5 0 0 00	
Salaries Payable				g 8 0 0 00
			1 8 6 3 2 81	1 8 6 3 2 81
Net Income				

ADJUSTED TRIAL BALANCE		INCOME STATEMENT		BALANCE SHEET	
DEBIT	CREDIT	DEBIT	CREDIT	DEBIT	CREDIT
1 3 4 0 00				1 3 4 0 00	
5 3 6 00				5 3 6 00	
	2 0 2 81				2 0 2 81
9 6 4 0 00				9 6 4 0 00	
2 2 0 00				2 2 0 00	
1 5 0 0 00				1 5 0 0 00	
6 0 0 0 00				6 0 0 0 00	
	2 0 0 0 00				2 0 0 0 00
	1 8 8 1 40				1 8 8 1 40
	1 5 9 5 1 88				1 5 9 5 1 88
5 2 1 7 50				5 2 1 7 50	
	3 0 8 8 8 89		3 0 8 8 8 89		
3 2 6 60		3 2 6 60			
1 8 0 9 6 16		1 8 0 9 6 16			
	4 3 4 09		4 3 4 09		
6 0 0 00		6 0 0 00			
9 0 0 00		9 0 0 00			
1 7 0 0 00		1 7 0 0 00			
2 5 5 00		2 5 5 00			
7 3 0 0 00		7 3 0 0 00			
2 7 5 00		2 7 5 00			
7 2 2 0 00	9 6 4 0 00	7 2 2 0 00	9 6 4 0 00		
1 5 2 81		1 5 2 81			
2 0 00		2 0 00			
5 0 0 00		5 0 0 00			
	8 0 0 00				8 0 0 00
6 1 7 9 9 07	6 1 7 9 9 07	3 7 3 4 5 57	4 0 9 6 2 98	2 4 4 5 3 50	2 0 8 3 6 09
		3 6 1 7 41			3 6 1 7 41
		4 0 9 6 2 98	4 0 9 6 2 98	2 4 4 5 3 50	2 4 4 5 3 50

Below is a list of adjustments that are common in a merchandising firm. Included is all the information necessary to make each adjustment. If you were an accountant employed by a merchandising firm, you would have to secure this information on your own before you could proceed.

1. A physical count of the merchandise inventory at the end of the period indicates that the ending balance is $9,640.
2. Past experience has shown that 0.5 percent of net sales will be uncollectible.
3. On November 1, 1987, High-Fi purchased a 12-month fire insurance policy for $240 covering a period of one year from that date. This figure was recorded in the Prepaid Insurance account.
4. On October 1, 1987, High-Fi paid $1,800 for the next 12 months' rent. This figure was recorded in the Prepaid Rent account.
5. High-Fi's office equipment was purchased three years ago for $6,000. The equipment has an estimated useful life of 12 years with no salvage value anticipated.
6. As of November 30, salaries of $800 have been earned but will not be paid until December 15, 1987.

These adjustments appear in the Adjustments column of the worksheet in Illustration 14–1. Since several accounts involved in the adjustments had no previous balance, they are not listed in the Trial Balance columns. Their account names and account balances have been added following the trial balance accounts. The adjustments are keyed with a small letter to identify which debit and which credit go together. This system can be very helpful if there are many adjustments and an error is made. A quick check of each set of entries will usually locate the error.

We will now briefly discuss each adjustment on High-Fi's worksheet. Most have already been explained in detail in earlier chapters.

Adjustments *a* and *b*—income summary

1. A physical count of the merchandise inventory at the end of the period indicates that the ending balance is $9,640.

The first two adjustments are unique to merchandising firms. They deal with the product cost portion of the income statement and are necessary in order to calculate the cost of goods sold for a firm that uses a periodic inventory system. Both the beginning and ending balances of merchandise inventory enter into the calculation of cost of goods sold, so their balances should appear on the income statement. This is accomplished in the Adjustment columns of the worksheet as follows:

a. Debit Income Summary and credit Merchandise Inventory for the dollar amount of the beginning inventory:

Entry a Income Summary 7,220
           Merchandise Inventory   7,220

b. Debit Merchandise Inventory and credit Income Summary for the dollar amount of the ending inventory:

Entry b Merchandise Inventory. 9,640
           Income Summary   9,640

Adjustment *a* reduces the balance in the Merchandise Inventory account to zero and adds the beginning inventory balance to the Income Summary account. (Note that $7,220 is the amount shown for Merchandise Inventory in the unadjusted trial balance.) This entry is appropriate because the balance in the Merchandise Inventory account is correct only at the beginning of the period. (Recall that no running record is kept of an inventory account's balance during the period if a periodic inventory system is used.) As explained in Chapter 13, the starting point for calculating Cost of Goods Sold is the beginning inventory of the period. Thus, the beginning inventory balance needs to be a debit in the Income Summary account.

Adjustment *b* creates the correct balance in the inventory account by debiting the Merchandise Inventory account for the ending balance, which would have been calculated at the end of the period. Since the first entry left the Merchandise Inventory account with a zero balance, the second entry places the appropriate balance in the account for the end of the period.

The second half of Adjustment *b* has the effect of subtracting the ending inventory in computing cost of goods sold in the income statement. This is appropriate because the cost of inventory on hand cannot be part of the cost of the merchandise sold. The credit in the Income Summary account has the ultimate effect of reducing cost of goods sold.

Adjustment *c*—bad debts expense

2. Past experience has shown that 0.5 percent of net sales will be uncollectible.

The third adjustment is made to account for bad debts. This year, the High-Fi Stereo Store has decided to change the way it computes its allowance for doubtful accounts. In Chapter 13, High-Fi computed its allowance based on gross sales, but its accountant believes that a figure based on net sales would be more accurate. Based on past data, she estimates that 0.5 percent of High-Fi's net sales will probably be uncollectible. Thus, the calculation of High-Fi's bad debts expense based on net sales is:

$$(\text{Sales} - \text{Sales returns and allowances}) \times 0.005$$
$$(\$30{,}888.89 - \$326.60) \times 0.005 = \$152.81$$

The entry is a debit to Bad Debts Expense and a credit to Allowance for Doubtful Accounts, which is an accounts receivable contra account. Added to the Adjustments column of the worksheet is:

c. Bad Debts Expense 152.81
    Allowance for Doubtful Accounts 152.81

For a review of accounting for bad debts, see Chapter 13.

Adjustment d—the expiration of an asset (prepaid insurance)

3. On November 1, 1987, High-Fi purchased a 12-month fire insurance policy for $240 covering a period of one year from that date. This figure was recorded in the Prepaid Insurance account.

The fourth adjustment deals with the expiration of an asset. An asset must have future economic value to the firm. When any part of that value expires, the expired portion should be charged off as a current expense, leaving only the unexpired portion remaining as an asset. This represents a prepayment of an expense for a future period. In the fourth adjustment, a portion of the fire insurance policy that was purchased on November 1 has expired. The cost of the one month of protection that is gone is charged off with a debit to Insurance Expense and a credit to Prepaid Insurance. The amount to be charged off is $\frac{1}{12} \times \$240$, or $20:

d. Insurance Expense 20
    Prepaid Insurance   20

This reduces the Prepaid Insurance account to its appropriate remaining value and matches the expense of fire insurance protection for the period with the revenue generated in the period. Prepaid insurance is a **prepaid expense.** That is, it is an asset that represents an expense that has already been paid but not consumed during the current period.

Adjustment *e*—the expiration of an asset (prepaid rent)

4. On October 1, 1987, High-Fi paid $1,800 for the next 12 months' rent. This figure was recorded in the Prepaid Rent account.

The adjustment for prepaid rent is very similar to the adjustment for prepaid insurance. The portion of the rent that has been used is charged to the Rent Expense account, and the unexpired portion remains an asset recorded in the Prepaid Rent account. The entry is a debit to Rent Expense and a credit to Prepaid Rent for $300 ($\frac{2}{12} \times \$1,800 = \$300$):

e. Rent Expense	300	
Prepaid Rent		300

Adjustment *f*—depreciation

5. High-Fi's office equipment was purchased three years ago for $6,000. The equipment has an estimated useful life of 12 years with no salvage value anticipated.

The sixth adjustment is necessary to spread the cost of the office equipment over its entire useful life. As explained in Chapter 9, this apportioned cost is called *depreciation expense.* The office equipment has a cost of $6,000, a 12-year useful life, and no salvage value. Therefore, the calculation of the annual depreciation charge is:

$$\frac{\text{Cost} - \text{Salvage value}}{\text{Useful life}} = \frac{\$6,000 - \$0}{12} = \$500$$

The entry is a debit to Depreciation Expense—Office Equipment and a credit to Accumulated Depreciation—Office Equipment, a contra asset account:

f. Depreciation Expense—Office Equipment	500	
Accumulated Depreciation—Office Equipment. . . .		500

If the purpose of the entries *d, e,* and *f* is not clear, you should review the sections entitled "Accounts That Need Adjustment" and "The Adjustments Columns."

Adjustment *g*—the accrual of salaries

6. As of November 30, salaries of $800 have been earned but will not be paid until December 15, 1987.

The last adjustment is for the accrual of salaries earned but unpaid at the end of the period. A firm may have more than one accrued expense at the end of the period. In this case, however, salaries is the only accrued expense. The entry is a debit for $800 to Salaries Expense and a credit of the same amount to **Accrued Salaries Payable,** a liability account that reflects the firm's obligation to pay the salaries in the future:

g. Salaries Expense 800
   Salaries Payable   800

Whenever an account is labeled *Accrued,* it means that the expense has been recorded but has not yet been paid. In this case, the expense of $800 relates to November but will not be paid until December. Due to the matching concept and accrual accounting, the expense must be recorded. The accrual of expenses will always involve an expense account and a liability account. An **accrued liability** is an obligation that exists at the end of an accounting period but is not recorded until adjusting entries are made. When salaries are paid in December, the liability account will be reduced to zero.

The adjustments we have presented here are examples of some very common adjustments. A firm may have many more adjustments. But regardless of their number, adjustments should be handled in the same general way that you have just learned.

After the adjustments have been entered on the worksheet, the two Adjustment columns should be footed to prove the equality of the debits and credits. If an error has been made, it is much better to identify it now than to have to search for it later. Our Adjustment columns balance at $18,632.81 in debits and credits.

COMPLETING THE WORKSHEET

The adjusted trial balance

Next, the trial balance plus the effects of the adjustments are entered in the Adjusted Trial Balance columns. Once again, our primary objective with the adjusted trial balance is to locate any errors that might have been made in adjusting the unadjusted trial balance. In the example, the Adjusted Trial Balance columns balance at $61,799.07.

The Balance Sheet and Income Statement columns

The asset, liability, permanent owner's equity, and owner's drawing account balances are then transferred to the Balance Sheet columns. All the revenue and expense accounts are placed in the Income Statement columns. These columns will not balance unless no net income or net loss resulted during the period. If the credit column is greater than the debit column, net income has been earned. A net debit balance would indicate a net loss. In our example, High-Fi had net income of $3,617.41.

This amount is then transferred to the Balance Sheet credit column because income increases the owner's equity account. Remember that owner's equity increases with credits and decreases with debits. Had a net loss occurred, it would have been transferred to the debit column of the balance sheet.

The two Balance Sheet columns balance at $24,453.50. If the two had not balanced, a search would be made to locate the error. After the net income is added to the Income Statement debit column, the two Income Statement columns will also balance. In our example, they balance at $40,962.98

THE FINANCIAL STATEMENTS

Once the worksheet has been completed, the financial statements are easy to prepare. Sometimes the term classified financial statements is used because financial statements are often prepared with the accounts grouped into classifications that make the information more meaningful. While the specific classifications in financial statements may vary, the general classifications tend to be standard.

The income statement

As shown in Illustration 14–2, the income statement of a merchandising firm has three basic classifications: (1) the revenue section showing net sales, (2) the product cost section showing the cost of goods sold, and (3) the operating expense section. The revenue section consists of the Sales account, which is usually reduced by a Sales Returns and Allowances account. Sometimes a firm will grant a cash discount if payment is received within a specified period of time.

**ILLUSTRATION
14–2**

HIGH-FI STEREO STORE
Income Statement
For the Year Ended November 30, 1987

Revenue:			
Sales		$30,888.89	
Less: Sales returns and allowances		326.60	
Net sales			$30,562.29
Cost of goods sold:			
Merchandise inventory, December 1, 1986		$ 7,220.00	
Purchases	$18,096.16		
Less: Purchase returns and allowances	434.09		
Net purchases		17,662.07	
Goods available for sale		$24,882.07	
Merchandise inventory, November 30, 1987		9,640.00	
Cost of goods sold			15,242.07
Gross margin from sales			$15,320.22
Operating expenses:			
Advertising expense		$ 600.00	
Bad debts expense		152.81	
Delivery expense		900.00	
Depreciation expense—office equipment		500.00	
Insurance expense		20.00	
Rent expense		1,700.00	
Repairs and maintenance expense		255.00	
Salaries expense		7,300.00	
Utilities expense		275.00	
Total operating expenses			11,702.81
Net income			$ 3,617.41

This discount is usually recorded in the Sales Discount account. The Sales Returns and Allowances and Sales Discounts accounts are subtracted from the Sales account to calculate net sales.

The cost of goods sold section is used to show the product cost of goods sold during the period. This is what the firm had to pay for the merchandise that it sold during the period. The High-Fi Stereo Store uses the periodic inventory technique. In such a case, as shown in Illustration 14–2, the cost of goods sold is subtracted from the net sales to compute gross margin on sales, sometimes called *gross profit.*

The operating expenses must be subtracted from gross margin before the net income or net loss can be determined. Thus, a merchandis-

Classified Balance Sheet

ILLUSTRATION 14–3

HIGH-FI STEREO STORE
Balance Sheet
November 30, 1987

Assets

Current assets:

Cash		$1,340.00
Accounts receivable	$536.00	
Less: Allowance for doubtful accounts . .	202.81	333.19 *net receivables*
Merchandise inventory		9,640.00
Prepaid insurance		220.00
Prepaid rent		1,500.00
Total current assets		$13,033.19

Plant assets:

Office equipment	$6,000.00	
Less: Accumulated depreciation— office equipment	2,000.00	
Total plant assets		4,000.00
Total assets		$17,033.19

Liabilities

Current liabilities:

Accounts payable	$1,881.40	
Salaries payable	800.00	
Total current liabilities		$ 2,681.40

Owner's Equity

Jeb Barnard, Capital—November 30, 1987 . .	14,351.79
Total liabilities and owner's equity	$17,033.19

Capital 6000—
net income 33080—
withdrawals 10,000   23080
29080

ing firm must sell its merchandise for a price that will cover both the product cost and the operating costs if it is to make a profit. Operating expenses, also known as *selling and administrative expenses,* may be broken into a number of different categories.

The balance sheet

We already know that the balance sheet consists of assets, liabilities, and owner's equity. Nonetheless, it is often clearer to divide these broad classifications more specifically, as shown in Illustration 14–3.

Assets. The first classification in the asset section is current assets. **A current asset** is any asset that is expected to expire or be converted into cash within one year or one operating cycle, whichever is longer.

Some common examples are cash, accounts receivable, merchandise inventory, and prepaid assets. Because current assets are the most liquid of a firm's assets, they are very important to creditors and others who are interested in a company's financial health. Liquid assets can be converted to cash easier than other kinds of assets. Cash, of course, is the most liquid asset.

Usually, the next classification of assets is **long-term investments,** which consists of stocks, bonds, and other investments that will be held for a number of accounting periods. Investments that will be held for only a short period of time should be classified as current assets. Note that according to Illustration 14–3, the High-Fi Stereo Store has no long-term investments. If High-Fi had long-term investments, they would be listed between current assets and plant assets.

The **plant asset** section of the balance sheet includes such items as equipment, buildings, and land. A plant asset has a relatively long useful life and is used in the normal operation of the firm instead of being held for resale. All plant assets except land are subject to depreciation. The High-Fi Stereo Store has only one plant asset—office equipment. In Illustration 14–3, note that the **net book value** of High-Fi's office equipment is the cost of the asset minus the accumulated depreciation as of November 30, 1987. The net book amount of an asset is also known as the **carrying value.**

Intangible assets are usually presented after plant assets. **Intangible assets** have value but lack physical form. For example, patents, copyrights, and trademarks are all intangible assets. The High-Fi Stereo Store has no assets that would be classified as intangible.

Liabilities. The first classification in the liabilities section of the balance sheet is **current liabilities,** which are obligations that must be paid within a year. Accounts payable, accrued taxes payable, and accrued salaries payable are current liabilities.

An obligation that extends beyond one year is a **long-term liability.** For example, a mortgage is a long-term liability. High-Fi Stereo has no long-term liabilities.

Jeb Barnard runs High-Fi Stereo as a sole proprietorship. A **sole proprietorship** is a business that is owned and operated by one person. The owner's equity section of the balance sheet reflects only the proprietor's capital account. In a separate *statement of owner's equity,* Jeb would show the balance in the capital account at the beginning of the year, add the net income, and subtract all owner's withdrawals to arrive at the balance in the account at the end of the year. High-Fi's formal statement of owner's equity is presented in Illustration 14–4.

ILLUSTRATION 14–4

HIGH-FI STEREO STORE
Statement of Owner's Equity
For the Year Ended November 30, 1987

Jeb Barnard, capital—December 1, 1986		$15,951.88
Net income	$3,617.41	
Less: Withdrawals	5,217.50	(1,600.09)
Jeb Barnard, capital—November 30, 1987		$14,351.79

Note that Jeb withdrew more money than the income earned, thus the net effect is a substraction from beginning capital.

COMPLETING THE ACCOUNTING CYCLE

Once the formal financial statements are prepared, the adjusting entries should be journalized and posted. So far, the adjustments have only appeared on the worksheet. They have not yet been journalized.

ILLUSTRATION 14–5

High-Fi Stereo's Adjusting Journal Entries

GENERAL JOURNAL   PAGE 7

DATE		ACCOUNT AND EXPLANATION	P.R.	DEBIT	CREDIT
1987					
Nov.	30	Income Summary	590	7 2 2 0 00	
		Merchandise Inventory	120		7 2 2 0 00
		To reverse beginning inventory.			
	30	Merchandise Inventory	120	9 6 4 0 00	
		Income Summary	590		9 6 4 0 00
		To record ending inventory.			
	30	Bad Debt Expense	520	1 5 2 81	
		Allowance for Doubtful Accounts	116		1 5 2 81
		To record adj. to allowance acct.			
	30	Insurance Expense	525	2 0 00	
		Prepaid Insurance	125		2 0 00
		To record Nov. insurance expense.			
	30	Rent Expense	545	3 0 0 00	
		Prepaid Rent	130		3 0 0 00
		To record Oct. and Nov. rent exp.			
	30	Depreciation Expense—Office Eqpt.	530	5 0 0 00	
		Accumulated Depreciation—Office Eqpt.	141		5 0 0 00
		Depre. expense for 1987.			
	30	Salaries Expense	525	8 0 0 00	
		Salaries Payable	260		8 0 0 00
		To record Nov. salaries.			

The journal entries will be the same as the entries made in the Adjustments column of the worksheet. After the adjusting entries are journalized, they will be posted to the ledger accounts. The journal entries are shown in Illustration 14–5.

The closing entries are made after the adjusting entries have been posted. Once again, the necessary information is available from the worksheet. All revenue and expense accounts in the Income Statement columns will be closed. Also, the Drawing account that appears in the Balance Sheet debit column will be closed. After the closing entries are journalized and posted, the post-closing trial balance will be prepared to ensure that the records are ready for the next accounting period. High-Fi's closing entries are shown in Illustration 14–6, while its ledger accounts are reproduced in Illustration 14–7. Finally, the company's post-closing trial balance is shown in Illustration 14–8.

ILLUSTRATION 14–6

High-Fi Stereo's Closing Journal Entries

GENERAL JOURNAL PAGE 8

DATE		ACCOUNT AND EXPLANATION	P.R.	DEBIT	CREDIT
Nov.	30	Sales	410	3 0 8 8 8 89	
		Purchases Returns and Allowances	511	4 3 4 09	
		Income Summary	590		3 1 3 2 2 98
		To close accounts with credit balances.			
	30	Income Summary	590	3 0 1 2 5 57	
		Sales Returns and Allowances	411		3 2 6 60
		Purchases	510		1 8 0 9 6 16
		Advertising Expense	535		6 0 0 00
		Delivery Expense	540		9 0 0 00
		Rent Expense	545		1 7 0 0 00
		Repair and Maintenance Expense	550		2 5 5 00
		Salaries Expense	555		7 3 0 0 00
		Utilities Expense	560		2 7 5 00
		Bad Debt Expense	520		1 5 2 81
		Insurance Expense	525		2 0 00
		Depreciation Expense	530		5 0 0 00
		To close accounts with debit balances.			
	30	Income Summary	590	3 6 1 7 41	
		Jeb Barnard, Capital	320		3 6 1 7 41
		To close Income Summary.			
	30	Jeb Barnard, Capital	320	5 2 1 7 50	
		Jeb Barnard, Drawing	350		5 2 1 7 50
		To close the Drawing Account.			

ILLUSTRATION 14–7

High-Fi Stereo's Ledger Accounts, Year-End 1987

Cash — ACCT. NO. 110

DATE		EXPLANATION	P.R.	DEBIT	CREDIT	BALANCE DEBIT	BALANCE CREDIT
1987							
Nov.	30	Balance	√			1 3 4 0 00	

Accounts Receivable — ACCT. NO. 115

DATE		EXPLANATION	P.R.	DEBIT	CREDIT	BALANCE DEBIT	BALANCE CREDIT
1987							
Nov.	30	Balance	√			5 3 6 00	

Allowance for Doubtful Accounts — ACCT. NO. 116

DATE		EXPLANATION	P.R.	DEBIT	CREDIT	BALANCE DEBIT	BALANCE CREDIT
1987							
Nov.	30	Balance	√				5 0 00
	30	Adjusting entry	GJ7		1 5 2 81		2 0 2 81

Merchandise Inventory — ACCT. NO. 120

DATE		EXPLANATION	P.R.	DEBIT	CREDIT	BALANCE DEBIT	BALANCE CREDIT
1987							
Nov.	30	Balance	√			7 2 2 0 00	
	30	Adjusting entry	GJ7		7 2 2 0 00	- 0 -	
	30	Adjusting entry	GJ7	9 6 4 0 00		9 6 4 0 00	

Prepaid Insurance — ACCT. NO. 125

DATE		EXPLANATION	P.R.	DEBIT	CREDIT	BALANCE DEBIT	BALANCE CREDIT
1987							
Nov.	30	Balance	√			2 4 0 00	
	30	Adjusting entry	GJ7		2 0 00	2 2 0 00	

Prepaid Rent — ACCT. NO. 130

DATE		EXPLANATION	P.R.	DEBIT	CREDIT	BALANCE DEBIT	BALANCE CREDIT
1987							
Nov.	30	Balance	√			1 8 0 0 00	
	30	Adjusting entry	GJ7		3 0 0 00	1 5 0 0 00	

**ILLUSTRATION
14–7
(continued)**

Office Equipment — ACCT. NO. 140

DATE		EXPLANATION	P.R.	DEBIT	CREDIT	BALANCE DEBIT	BALANCE CREDIT
1987							
Nov.	30	Balance	√			6 0 0 0 00	

Accumulated Depreciation—Office Equipment — ACCT. NO. 141

DATE		EXPLANATION	P.R.	DEBIT	CREDIT	BALANCE DEBIT	BALANCE CREDIT
1987							
Nov.	30	Balance	√				1 5 0 0 00
	30	Adjusting entry	GJ7		5 0 0 00		2 0 0 0 00

Accounts Payable — ACCT. NO. 250

DATE		EXPLANATION	P.R.	DEBIT	CREDIT	BALANCE DEBIT	BALANCE CREDIT
1987							
Nov.	30	Balance	√				1 8 8 1 40

Salaries Payable — ACCT. NO. 260

DATE		EXPLANATION	P.R.	DEBIT	CREDIT	BALANCE DEBIT	BALANCE CREDIT
1987							
Nov.	30	Adjusting entry	GJ7		8 0 0 00		8 0 0 00

Jeb Barnard—Capital — ACCT. NO. 320

DATE		EXPLANATION	P.R.	DEBIT	CREDIT	BALANCE DEBIT	BALANCE CREDIT
1987							
Nov.	30	Balance	√				15 9 5 1 88
	30	Closing entry	GJ8		3 6 1 7 41		19 5 6 9 29
	30	Closing entry	GJ8	5 2 1 7 50			14 3 5 1 79

**ILLUSTRATION
14–7
(continued)**

Jeb Barnard

Drawing
ACCT. NO. 350

DATE		EXPLANATION	P.R.	DEBIT	CREDIT	BALANCE DEBIT	BALANCE CREDIT
1987							
Nov.	30	Balance	√			5 2 1 7 50	
	30	Closing entry	GJ8		5 2 1 7 50	- 0 -	

Sales
ACCT. NO. 410

DATE		EXPLANATION	P.R.	DEBIT	CREDIT	BALANCE DEBIT	BALANCE CREDIT
1987							
Nov.	30	Balance	√				30 8 8 8 89
	30	Closing entry	GJ8	30 8 8 8 89			- 0 -

Sales Returns and Allowances
ACCT. NO. 411

DATE		EXPLANATION	P.R.	DEBIT	CREDIT	BALANCE DEBIT	BALANCE CREDIT
1987							
Nov.	30	Balance	√			3 2 6 60	
	30	Closing entry	GJ8		3 2 6 60	- 0 -	

Purchases
ACCT. NO. 510

DATE		EXPLANATION	P.R.	DEBIT	CREDIT	BALANCE DEBIT	BALANCE CREDIT
1987							
Nov.	30	Balance	√			18 0 9 6 16	
	30	Closing entry	GJ8		18 0 9 6 16	- 0 -	

Purchase Returns and Allowances
ACCT. NO. 511

DATE		EXPLANATION	P.R.	DEBIT	CREDIT	BALANCE DEBIT	BALANCE CREDIT
1987							
Nov.	30	Balance	√				4 3 4 09
	30	Closing entry	GJ8	4 3 4 09			- 0 -

Bad Debts Expense
ACCT. NO. 520

DATE		EXPLANATION	P.R.	DEBIT	CREDIT	BALANCE DEBIT	BALANCE CREDIT
1987							
Nov.	30	Adjusting entry	GJ7	1 5 2 81		1 5 2 81	
	30	Closing entry	GJ8		1 5 2 81	- 0 -	

**ILLUSTRATION
14–7
(continued)**

Insurance Expense — ACCT. NO. 525

DATE		EXPLANATION	P.R.	DEBIT	CREDIT	BALANCE DEBIT	BALANCE CREDIT
1987							
Nov.	30	Adjusting entry	GJ7	2 0 00		2 0 00	
	30	Closing entry	GJ8		2 0 00	- 0 -	

Depreciation Expense — ACCT. NO. 530

DATE		EXPLANATION	P.R.	DEBIT	CREDIT	BALANCE DEBIT	BALANCE CREDIT
1987							
Nov.	30	Adjusting entry	GJ7	5 0 0 00		5 0 0 00	
	30	Closing entry	GJ8		5 0 0 00	- 0 -	

Advertising Expense — ACCT. NO. 535

DATE		EXPLANATION	P.R.	DEBIT	CREDIT	BALANCE DEBIT	BALANCE CREDIT
1987							
Nov.	30	Balance				6 0 0 00	
	30	Closing entry	GJ8		6 0 0 00	- 0 -	

Delivery Expense — ACCT. NO. 540

DATE		EXPLANATION	P.R.	DEBIT	CREDIT	BALANCE DEBIT	BALANCE CREDIT
1987							
Nov.	30	Balance	√			9 0 0 00	
	30	Closing entry	GJ8		9 0 0 00	- 0 -	

Rent Expense — ACCT. NO. 545

DATE		EXPLANATION	P.R.	DEBIT	CREDIT	BALANCE DEBIT	BALANCE CREDIT
1987							
Nov.	30	Balance	√			1 4 0 0 00	
	30	Adjusting entry	GJ7	3 0 0 00		1 7 0 0 00	
	30	Closing entry	GJ8		1 7 0 0 00	- 0 -	

Repair and Maintenance Expense — ACCT. NO. 550

DATE		EXPLANATION	P.R.	DEBIT	CREDIT	BALANCE DEBIT	BALANCE CREDIT
1987							
Nov.	30	Balance	√			2 5 5 00	
	30	Closing entry	GJ8		2 5 5 00	- 0 -	

**ILLUSTRATION
14–7
(concluded)**

		Salaries Expense				ACCT. NO. 555	
DATE	EXPLANATION	P.R.	DEBIT	CREDIT	BALANCE		
					DEBIT	CREDIT	
1987							
Nov. 30	Balance	√			6 5 0 0 00		
30	Adjusting entry	GJ7	8 0 0 00		7 3 0 0 00		
30	Closing entry	GJ8		7 3 0 0 00	- 0 -		

		Utilities Expense				ACCT. NO. 560	
DATE	EXPLANATION	P.R.	DEBIT	CREDIT	BALANCE		
					DEBIT	CREDIT	
1987							
Nov. 30	Balance	√			2 7 5 00		
30	Closing entry	GJ8		2 7 5 00	- 0 -		

		Income Summary				ACCT. NO. 590	
DATE	EXPLANATION	P.R.	DEBIT	CREDIT	BALANCE		
					DEBIT	CREDIT	
1987							
Nov. 30	Adjusting entry	GJ7	7 2 2 0 00		7 2 2 0 00		
30	Adjusting entry	GJ7		9 6 4 0 00		2 4 2 0 00	
30	Closing entry	GJ8		31 3 2 2 98		33 7 4 2 98	
30	Closing entry	GJ8	30 1 2 5 57			3 6 1 7 41	
30	Closing entry	GJ8	3 6 1 7 41			- 0 -	

**ILLUSTRATION
14–8**

HIGH-FI STEREO STORE
Post-Closing Trial Balance
November 30, 1987

	Debits	Credits
Cash	$ 1,340.00	
Accounts receivable	536.00	
Allowance for doubtful accounts		$ 202.81
Merchandise inventory	9,640.00	
Prepaid insurance	220.00	
Prepaid rent	1,500.00	
Office equipment	6,000.00	
Accumulated depreciation—office equipment		2,000.00
Accounts payable		1,881.40
Salaries payable		800.00
Jeb Barnard, capital		14,351.79
	$19,236.00	$19,236.00

SUMMARY

This chapter illustrated the end-of-period accounting procedures that are used in a merchandising firm. The **accounting cycle** is the same for both merchandising and service enterprises. And both types of businesses may choose either a **calendar year** or a **fiscal year** as their basic reporting period.

The worksheet in a merchandising enterprise performs the same functions that it does in a service enterprise. It facilitates the preparation of financial statements and provides a check against errors before formal financial statements are prepared.

Special attention must be paid to the Adjustments column of a worksheet. As each adjustment is made, it should be keyed with a small letter to indicate which debit and which credit go together. Among the most common adjusting entries for a merchandiser are those related to merchandise inventory, bad debts expense, **prepaid expenses,** depreciation, and **accrued liabilities,** such as **accrued salaries payable.**

Once the worksheet has been completed, the financial statements can easily be prepared. In **classified financial statements,** accounts are grouped into categories that make information more meaningful.

The income statement of a merchandising firm has three basic classifications: (1) the revenue section, which shows net sales, (2) the product cost section, which shows the cost of goods sold, and (3) the operating expense section.

The balance sheet lists assets, liabilities, and owner's equity. These broad classifications are often divided into more specific categories.

The first category in the asset section is usually **current assets.** Common examples of current assets are cash, accounts receivable, inventory, and prepaid expenses. The next classification is **long-term investments.** This section lists all stocks, bonds, and other investments that will be held for more than one accounting period. The **plant asset** section is usually next. It lists the **net book values** of such items as equipment and buildings. Finally comes the list of **intangible assets,** such as patents, copyrights, and trademarks.

The first classification in the liabilities section of the balance sheet is **current liabilities.** These are obligations that must be paid within one year. Accounts payable and accrued salaries payable are examples of current liabilities. An obligation that extends beyond one year, such as a mortgage, is a **long-term liability.** Long-term liabilities are presented after current liabilities.

The owner's equity section of the balance sheet shows all accounts related to owner's equity. In a **sole proprietorship,** the owner's equity section need only show the year-end balance in the owner's capital account.

Once the formal financial statements are prepared, the adjusting entries should be journalized and posted. Then the closing entries are made, so that all revenue and expense accounts, as well as the owner's drawing account, will have zero balances. After the closing entries are journalized and posted, the post-closing trial balance is prepared. The books are then ready to begin the new accounting period.

KEY TERMS

Accounting Cycle—The complete series of steps used to account for a business's financial transactions during an accounting period.

Accrued Liability—An obligation that exists at the end of an accounting period but is not recorded until adjusting entries are made. An example is accrued salaries payable.

Accrued Salaries Payable—A liability account that reflects an obligation to pay salaries, it results from the adjusting entry to record salaries expense.

Calendar Year—A 12-month financial reporting period that begins on January 1 and closes on December 31.

Classified Financial Statement—A financial statement that groups the accounts into classifications in order to present more meaningful information.

Current Asset—An asset that will expire or be converted into cash within one year or one operating cycle, whichever is longer. Examples are cash, accounts receivable, prepaid expenses, and inventory.

Current Liability—An obligation that must be paid within one year. Accounts payable and accrued salaries payable are current liabilities.

Fiscal Year—A 12-month accounting period that begins on a date other than January 1.

Intangible Asset—An asset that has value but lacks physical form, such as a patent, copyright, or trademark.

Long-term Investment—A stock, bond, or other investment that will be held for a number of accounting periods.

Long-term Liability—An obligation that extends beyond one year.

Net Book Value (carrying value)—The cost of a plant asset minus accumulated depreciation.

Plant Asset—An asset that has a relatively long useful life and is used in the normal operation of the firm instead of being held for resale.

Prepaid Expense—A current asset that represents an expense that has already been paid but not consumed during the current period. Prepaid rent and prepaid insurance are examples of prepaid expenses.

Sole Proprietorship—A business that is owned and operated by one person.

QUESTIONS AND EXERCISES

1. What is the function of a worksheet in a merchandising enterprise?
2. What three basic classifications are found on an income statement for a merchandising enterprise?
3. Name four classifications found in the asset section of the balance sheet. Specifically, what assets would be found under each classification?
4. Distinguish between current liabilities and long-term liabilities. Give examples of each type.
5. What steps must be followed to complete a worksheet?
6. Given the following information concerning operations for 1987, compute Holly Pyle's capital balance on December 31, 1987:

   Net income $4,606
   Withdrawals 1,700
   Holly Pyle, capital, 1/1/87. . . . 6,505

7. On August 1, 1987, the Harley Company paid $2,400 for the next 12 months rent. It was recorded in the Prepaid Rent account. What adjustment is necessary on December 31, 1987?
8. Office equipment costing $9,000 was purchased four years ago. The equipment has an estimated useful life of 10 years with no salvage value anticipated. What adjusting journal entry is needed to record the annual depreciation charge?

9. Sales and sales returns and allowances had the following balances on December 31, 1987:

Sales $99,000
Sales returns and allowances . . .   8,000

Past experience has shown that 0.5 percent of net sales will be uncollectible. What adjusting entry should be made to record bad debts expense for 1987?

10. The $3,600 premium on a three-year insurance policy is paid on January 1, 1987. It is recorded in Prepaid Insurance. What adjusting entry is necessary at December 31, 1987?

11. Office supplies of $4,000 were purchased and recorded in the asset account, Office Supplies. At the end of the period a count is made and only $800 of the supplies are still on hand. What adjusting entry is necessary?

PROBLEMS

14–1. The Johnson Shoe Store has just completed its fiscal year ending July 31, 1987. From the following information, prepare the adjusting entries that are required at the end of the year.

a. The Merchandise Inventory account had a balance of $13,400 on August 1, 1986. A physical count of the merchandise inventory on July 31, 1987, indicates that the ending balance is $12,700.

b. On April 1, 1987, the firm paid $480 for a fire insurance policy for 12 months coverage. The payment was recorded in the Prepaid Insurance account.

c. Display equipment had been purchased two years ago for $12,000. It is expected to last eight years with no salvage value anticipated.

d. As of July 31, 1987, salaries of $200 have been earned but will not be paid until August 10, 1987.

14–2. The Anderson Appliance Store has just completed its fiscal year ending March 31, 1987. Given the following information, prepare the adjusting entries that are required at the end of the year.

a. The Merchandise Inventory account had a balance of $31,500 on April 1, 1986. A physical count of the merchandise inventory on March 31, 1987, indicated that the ending inventory is $40,000. 1987, indicated that the ending inventory is $40,000.

b. At the end of the fiscal year, salaries of $800 have been earned but will not be paid until April 15, 1987.

c. On January 1, 1987, the firm paid $1,500 for the next 12 months rent. The payment was recorded in the Prepaid Rent account.

d. On October 1, 1986, the firm purchased a 12-month fire insurance policy for $300. The payment was recorded in the Prepaid Insurance account.

e. Store equipment costing $15,000 was purchased four years ago. The expected useful life is 12 years, and no salvage value is anticipated.

f. Office equipment was purchased five years ago at a cost of $5,000. Its expected useful life is 10 years with no salvage value anticipated.

g. At the end of the fiscal year, the Office Supplies account had a balance of $500. A physical count revealed that $200 worth of office supplies were on hand on March 31, 1987.

14–3.

RHODEN'S MUSIC STORE
Trial Balance
July 31, 1987

Account Title	Debit	Credit
Cash	$ 12,390	
Accounts receivable	2,500	
Allowance for doubtful accounts		$ 200
Merchandise inventory	15,700	
Prepaid insurance	600	
Prepaid rent	4,800	
Office equipment	6,000	
Accumulated depreciation—office equipment		2,250
Accounts payable		4,000
Clyde Rhoden, capital		6,000
Clyde Rhoden, drawing	10,000	
Sales		152,640
Sales returns and allowances	500	
Purchases	99,600	
Purchase returns and allowances		700
Advertising expense	500	
Rent expense	900	
Salaries expense	11,600	
Utilities expense	700	
	$165,790	$165,790

C. R. Rhoden has prepared the foregoing trial balance for Rhoden's Music Store. The following information was gathered which will be used to prepare adjusting entries:

a. A physical count of the merchandise inventory at the end of the period indicates that the ending balance is $13,200.

b. Past experience has shown that 0.4 percent of net sales will be uncollectible. Round to the nearest $10.

c. On April 1, 1987, a 12-month fire insurance policy was purchased for $600. Coverage began on April 1, 1987.

d. On February 1, 1987, Nixon paid $4,800 for the next 12 months rent. The payment was recorded in the Prepaid Rent account.

e. The office equipment was purchased four years ago for a cost of $6,000. The equipment has an estimated useful life of eight years with no salvage value anticipated.

Required:

1. Prepare a worksheet for Rhoden's Music Store for the fiscal year ended July 31, 1987.
2. Prepare an income statement for the fiscal year ended July 31, 1987.
3. Prepare a balance sheet for July 31, 1987.

14–4. The trial balance of the Marvel Book Store for December 31, 1987, is shown below:

MARVEL BOOK STORE
Trial Balance
December 31, 1987

Account Title	Debit	Credit
Cash	$ 20,000	
Accounts receivable	6,304	
Allowance for doubtful accounts		$ 300
Merchandise inventory	20,243	
Store supplies	845	
Office supplies	636	
Prepaid insurance	432	
Prepaid rent	1,620	
Office equipment	4,000	
Accumulated depreciation—office equipment		800
Store equipment	9,100	
Accumulated depreciation—store equipment		4,200
Accounts payable		6,280
Beth Marvel, capital		45,000
Beth Marvel, drawing	20,000	
Sales		109,000
Sales returns and allowances	2,200	
Purchases	65,500	
Purchase returns and allowances		2,500
Advertising expense	600	
Rent expense	800	
Salaries expense	15,000	
Utilities expense	800	
	$168,080	$168,080

Required:

1. Prepare a worksheet for the year ended December 31, 1987. The following information will be needed for adjustments:
   a. Merchandise inventory, December 31, 1987, $17,980.
   b. Store supplies on hand at December 31, 1987, $150.
   c. Office supplies on hand at December 31, 1987, $200.
   d. Prepaid insurance, December 31, 1987, $288.
   e. Prepaid rent, December 31, 1987, $1,080.
   f. Bad debts expense for 1987, $354.
   g. Depreciation expense for 1987:

Office equipment	$800
Store equipment	700

2. Prepare an income statement for the year ended December 31, 1987.
3. Prepare a balance sheet for December 31, 1987.

14–5. The trial balance for the Burger Carpet Shop for December 31, 1987, is shown below:

BURGER CARPET SHOP
Trial Balance
December 31, 1987

Account Title	Debit	Credit
Cash	$ 15,000	
Accounts receivable	6,500	
Allowance for doubtful accounts		$ 200
Merchandise inventory	30,600	
Office equipment	1,500	
Accumulated depreciation—office equipment		750
Delivery equipment	6,000	
Accumulated depreciation—delivery equipment		3,000
Accounts payable		20,700
Elmo Burger, capital		39,000
Elmo Burger, drawing.	12,000	
Sales		95,000
Sales returns and allowances	1,500	
Purchases	78,700	
Purchase returns and allowances		2,450
Advertising expense	600	
Insurance expense	480	
Miscellaneous expense.	120	
Rent expense.	1,740	
Salaries expense .	5,720	
Utilities expense.	640	
	$161,100	$161,100

Required:

1. Prepare a worksheet for the year ended December 31, 1987. Use the following information to make adjustments:
   a. Merchandise inventory at the end of the year, $36,850.
   b. Prepaid rent, December 31, 1987, $348.
   c. Prepaid insurance, December 31, 1987, $96.
   d. Bad debts expense has been estimated to be 0.4 percent of net sales.
   e. Depreciation expense for 1987:

Office equipment	$ 250
Delivery equipment	1,000

2. Prepare an income statement for the year ended December 31, 1987.
3. Prepare a balance sheet for December 31, 1987.
4. Prepare adjusting and closing journal entries.

14–6. The trial balance for the Beckel Store for December 31, 1987, is shown below:

BECKEL STORE
Trial Balance
December 31, 1987

Account Title	Debit	Credit
Cash	$ 3,815	
Accounts receivable	4,200	
Allowance for doubtful accounts		$ 110
Merchandise inventory	14,580	
Office equipment	350	
Store supplies	500	
Prepaid insurance	540	
Prepaid rent	4,320	
Office equipment	2,500	
Accumulated depreciation—office equipment		500
Store equipment	5,000	
Accumulated depreciation—store equipment		625
Delivery equipment	8,400	
Accumulated depreciation—delivery equipment		2,100
Accounts payable		6,000
Rudolph Beckel, capital		52,100
Rudolph Beckel, drawing	10,500	
Sales		130,545
Sales returns and allowances	2,985	
Purchases	90,320	
Purchase returns and allowances		3,450

Trial Balance (*concluded*)

Account Title	Debit	Credit
Advertising expense	480	
Miscellaneous expense.	240	
Payroll taxes expense	4,200	
Salaries expense	41,600	
Utilities expense.	900	
	$195,430	$195,430

Required:

1. Prepare a worksheet for the year ended December 31, 1987. Use the following information to make adjustments:
   a. Merchandise inventory, December 31, 1987, $12,250.
   b. Office supplies on hand, December 31, 1987, $50.
   c. Store supplies on hand, December 31, 1987, $125.
   d. Expired insurance, $360.
   e. Expired rent, $2,160.
   f. Bad debts expense for 1987, $450.
   g. Depreciation expense for 1987:

Office equipment.	$ 500
Store equipment	625
Delivery equipment. . . .	2,100

2. Prepare an income statement for the year ended December 31, 1987.
3. Prepare a balance sheet for December 31, 1987.
4. Prepare the adjusting and closing journal entries.
5. Prepare a post-closing trial balance.

14–7. The trial balance for the Wilkes Store on December 31, 1987, is shown below:

WILKES STORE
Trial Balance
December 31, 1987

Account Title	Debit	Credit
Cash	$ 4,800	
Accounts receivable	14,250	
Allowance for doubtful accounts		$ 400
Merchandise inventory	16,100	
Office equipment	650	
Store supplies	1,200	
Prepaid rent	1,800	

Trial Balance *(concluded)*

Account Title	Debit	Credit
Prepaid insurance	480	
Office equipment	3,000	
Accumulated depreciation—office equipment		300
Display equipment	5,400	
Accumulated depreciation—display equipment		1,800
Delivery equipment	6,000	
Accumulated depreciation—delivery equipment		1,500
Accounts payable		5,200
A. J. Wilkes, capital		31,150
A. J. Wilkes, drawing	10,000	
Sales		120,500
Sales returns and allowances	4,500	
Purchases	85,000	
Purchase returns and allowances		3,000
Advertising expense	650	
Miscellaneous expense	320	
Payroll taxes expense	500	
Salaries expense	8,500	
Utilities expense	700	
	$163,850	$163,850

Required:

1. Prepare a work sheet for the year ended December 31, 1987. Use the following information to make adjustments:
   a. Merchandise inventory, December 31, 1987, $12,300.
   b. Office supplies on hand, December 31, 1987, $150.
   c. Store supplies on hand, December 31, 1987, $350.
   d. Expired rent, $600.
   e. Expired insurance, $240.
   f. Bad debts expense for 1987, $400.
   g. Depreciation expense for 1987:

Office equipment	$ 300
Display equipment	900
Delivery equipment	1,500

2. Prepare an income statement for the year ended December 31, 1987.
3. Prepare a balance sheet for December 31, 1987.
4. Prepare the adjusting and closing journal entries.
5. Prepare a post-closing trial balance.

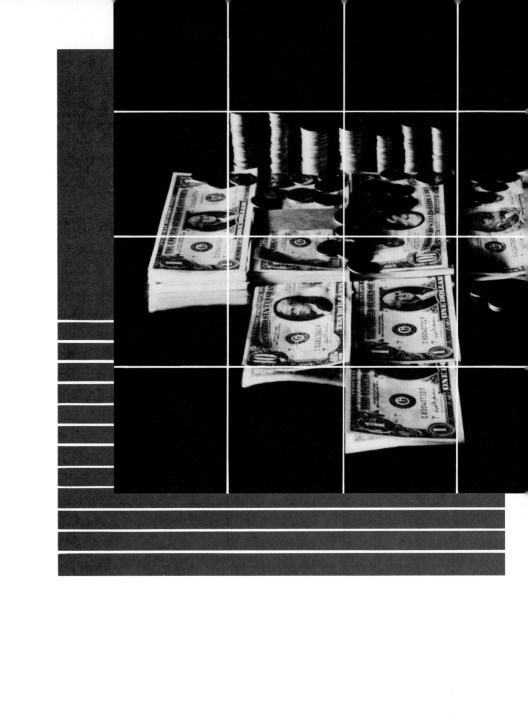

Interest expense always has to be debited
Interest expense always has to be credited

CHAPTER 15

Accounting for notes and interest

You never show interest until its recieved or paid
Whenever you debit or credit notes receivable it has to be for the note amount. Interest can not be included
Interest revenue is always a credit balance

LEARNING OBJECTIVES *Cash can have principal + interest*

The extensive use of credit in commercial buying and selling has made it necessary to account for credit transactions in a detailed manner. A study of this chapter will provide an understanding of the accounting procedures used for notes receivable and notes payable. After studying this chapter, you should be able to:

1. Calculate interest on notes receivable and payable.
2. Discount notes receivable.
3. Record transactions relative to notes including receipt, discounting, and a dishonored note.

Notes payable you issue a note (liability)

Cash
*   Notes Payable*
*   Borrow*

Notes Payable
Interest Exp.
*   Cash*

Purchases
*   Notes Payable*
*   Get merchandise*

Accounts Payable
*   Notes Payable*
*   Extension of time*

457

The extensive use of credit has become a characteristic of modern business. Individuals, as well as business organizations, use credit. Millions of credit transactions occur daily that involve the exchange of goods and services for promises to pay at later dates. The terms *on credit, on account,* and *charge* are commonly used to describe credit sales. Although some credit transactions involve a written promise to pay, most credit sales simply involve a buyer's signature on a sales receipt to acknowledge the receipt of the goods or services. This type of credit arrangement is called an *open account.* Other kinds of credit devices commonly used are the *credit card* and the *promissory note.*

Promissory notes are used in several different types of transactions. A promise to repay borrowed cash usually takes the form of a note. Promises for later payment other than for borrowed cash sometimes take the form of a note, especially when credit is extended for periods of more than 60 days or when large sums of money are involved.

The characteristics associated with a promissory note make it a negotiable instrument (in other words, it can be legally transferred from one person to another). Such notes must have the following legal attributes:

1. Unconditional promise to pay a specified sum of money.
2. Payable either at a fixed future time or on demand.
3. Payable to a specified person, a firm, or the bearer of the note.
4. Must be signed by the person or the firm making the promise.

The promissory note in Illustration 15–1 has all the required legal characteristics. Tom Jones, the person to whom the amount of money will be paid, is called the **payee.** The promissory note is a *note receivable* (that is, an asset) to the payee. Ed Wheeler, the person who promises to pay money, is known as the **maker** of the note. The promissory note is a *note payable* (that is, a liability) to the maker.

The note in Illustration 15–1 is interest bearing. At the maturity (or due) date, the maker of the note will repay the face amount plus **interest** at 12 percent. A noninterest-bearing note would not show an interest rate on its face. Instead, the interest amount is part of the face amount of the note. Noninterest-bearing notes are issued at a **discount.** The maker of the note receives an amount less than the face amount that he or she promises to repay. The difference between the amount received by the maker and the face amount equals the amount of the discount. The discount amount is equal

**ILLUSTRATION
15–1**

**Promissory
Note**

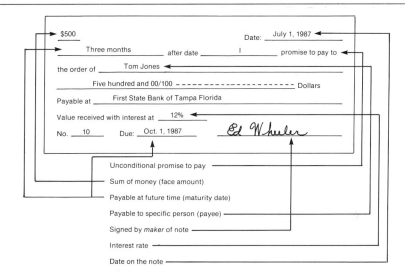

to the **amount of total interest expense at maturity.** For example, a borrower (the maker) gives a $500 note payable in 90 days to a bank (the payee) in return for **cash of $485.00.** The $15.00, difference between the face amount of the note and the amount received by the borrower, is **equal to the interest expense** at the maturity date. Note that both interest-bearing and noninterest-bearing notes involve interest expense for the maker and interest revenue for the payee.

COMPUTING INTEREST

There are three factors to consider when computing interest: (1) principal, (2) interest rate, and (3) time period. The **principal** is the amount of money borrowed. The amount of interest is based on this figure.

The interest rate is usually given on the face of the note. **If the** note is interest bearing and the interest rate is not given on the face of the note, the legal rate must be used. The legal rate varies among the different states. The interest rate shown on the face of the note is always an annual percentage rate unless stated otherwise. For example, 12 percent is assumed to be an annual percentage rate unless otherwise stated. Twelve percent is equivalent to 1 percent per month.

The time period of the note is the number of days or months

from the date of the note (the date the note is issued) until the date of maturity. Interest computations are based on this time period. When the maturity date is specified in months, the fraction of the year the months represent is used to calculate interest. For example, if a note spefecies maturity in four months, interest is calculated for $\frac{4}{12}$, or $\frac{1}{3}$, of the year. If maturity is specified in days, interest is calculated based on the fraction of the year those days represent. Three hundred sixty days is usually used as the number of days in a year. For example, if a note matures in 60 days, interest is based on $\frac{60}{360}$, or $\frac{1}{6}$, of a year. Some institutions such as banks or governmental agencies may use 365 days as the base in computing daily interest. For example, if the annual percentage rate is 12 percent, the daily interest rate is $\frac{12}{365}$ or .0329 percent.

If the due date is specified on a note, the exact number of days from the date of the note through the due date or maturity date must be determined. For example, if a note is issued on January 2 and is due on March 18, the time period is computed as follows:

Days in January	31
Date of note, January 2	2
Days remaining in January	29
Days in February.	28
Days in March	18
Time period in days	75

Notice in the above computation that the date of maturity is included but the date of the note is excluded.

After determining the proper factors, interest is calculated using the following formula:

Principal × Rate × Time Period = Amount of Interest

Remember, the time period is usually a fraction of a 360-day year.

To illustrate the application of the formula, the note in Illustration 15–1 is used. The principal amount is $500; the interest rate is 12 percent; the time period is three months. The interest payable is $15, computed as follows:

$$\$500 \times 12\% \times \frac{3}{12} = \$15 \text{ interest}$$

Assume the same facts as in the above example except that the note matures 90 days after issuance instead of three months. The interest is $15, computed as follows:

$$\$500 \times 12\% \times \frac{90}{360} = \$15 \text{ interest}$$

Normally interest is computed based on the number of days involved instead of using months or fractions of a month. Computing interest on a per-day basis results in a more precise amount which is essential in the business world. The difference that would result in using the exact number of days versus the number of months could be substantial when dealing with the large principal amounts that arise in business transactions.

For example, the following would have resulted if the actual number of days in the three-month period, July through September, had been used in the calculation of interest:

$$\$500 \times 12\% \times \frac{92}{360} = \$15.33$$

or

$$\$500 \times 12\% \times \frac{92}{365} = \$15.12$$

The number of days, 92, was determined by:

Days in July	31
Day of note, July 1.	1
Days remaining in July	30
Days in August	31
Days in September	30
Days in October.	1
Time period in days	92

There is a slight difference in the interest calculated depending on whether a customary 360-day year or a 365-day banker's year is used.

Present value

The **present value of a note** increases as the number of days to maturity decreases. The value increases because interest is accruing on the note. The present value of an interest-bearing note is equal to the face amount of the note plus accrued interest. If the note is noninterest bearing, the present value is computed by subtracting from the face amount the remaining balance of the original discount.

If the payee exchanges the note at the bank for cash, the present value is equal to the maturity value less the bank's discount. The **maturity value** is the amount the payee would receive on the maturity date.

The present value of a note must be determined if the note is exchanged for credit or for cash. For example, the original payee may endorse the note and use it to buy goods and services, or the payee may exchange the note at the bank for cash. Consider these situations involving the interest-bearing note in Illustration 15–1.

1. On August 1 (one month after the date of note), Tom Jones exchanges the note for merchandise at McKinney Wholesale. McKinney agrees to allow Jones merchandise worth the present value of the note.

   The present value, $505, is calculated as follows:

   $$\text{Present value} = \text{Principal} + \text{Accrued interest}$$

   Principal = $500
   Accrued interest = Principal × Rate × Length of time payee has held note = $500 × 0.12 × $\frac{1}{12}$ = $5
   Present value = $500 + $5 = $505

2. Tom Jones decides to exchange the note at the bank for cash. The bank will buy the note if it is discounted at 15 percent. The following steps are necessary to compute the discount.
   a. Determine the maturity value of the note. The maturity value is the sum of the principal and interest:

   $$\text{Interest} = \text{Principal} \times \text{Rate} \times \text{Time}$$
   $$\text{Interest} = \$500 \times 12\% \times \tfrac{3}{12} = \$15$$
   $$\text{Maturity value} = \text{Principal} + \text{Interest}$$
   $$\text{Maturity value} = \$500 + \$15 = \$515$$

   b. Determine the discount time or discount period (the length of time from the date of discount to the date of maturity):

   $$3 \text{ months} - 1 \text{ month} = 2 \text{ months}$$

   Two months is the remaining life of the note on August 1, the date on which the note is discounted.

   c. Calculate the amount of discount charged by the bank:

   $$\text{Discount} = \text{Maturity value} \times \text{Discount rate} \times \text{Discount period}$$

Discount $= \$515 \times 15\% \times \frac{2}{12}$
Discount $= \$12.88$

Now the present value, of the note can be computed as follows:

Present value $=$ Maturity value $-$ Discount
Present value $= \$515 - \$12.88$
Present value $= \$502.12$

It is customary for banks to calculate the discount on the value of the note at the maturity date. The present value of the note is equal to the maturity value of the note less the discount.

3. Let's assume the same basic facts as illustrated in the previous example, a $500, 12 percent note dated July 1, 1987. However, assume that the note is a 90-day note rather than a three-month note. Tom Jones will discount the note at the bank on July 10.

   a. Determine the maturity date of the note. The time period is computed as follows:

   Days in July. 31
   Date of note, July 1 1
   Days remaining in July 30
   Days in August 31
   Number of days in September needed to equal term of note. . 29
   Term of note 90

   Thus, September 29 is the maturity date of the note.

   b. Determine the maturity value of the note. The maturity value is the sum of principal and interest:

   Interest $=$ Principal $\times$ Rate $\times$ Time
   Interest $= \$500 \times 12\% \times \frac{90}{360} = \$15$
   Maturity value $=$ Principal $+$ Interest
   Maturity value $= \$500 + \$15 = \$515$

   c. Determine the discount time or discount period:

   Days in July. 31
   Date of note, July 1 1
   Days remaining in July 30
   Discount date, July 10 10
   Days in discount period in July 20
   Days in August 31
   Days in September until maturity date. . . 29
   Discount period . . . . 80 days

The discount period includes the remaining 20 days in July, plus all of August and the 29 days in September.

d. Calculate the amount of discount charged by the bank:

Discount = Maturity   value × Discount   rate × Discount period
Discount = $515 × 15\% × ^{80}\!/_{360}$
Discount = \$17.17

Now the present value of the note can be computed as follows:

Present value = Maturity value − Discount
Present value = \$515 − \$17.17
Present value = \$497.83

The party discounting a note (also called exchanging a note) is usually responsible for paying its maturity value in the event that the maker defaults (does not pay) at the maturity date. This possible future liability is known as a **contingent liability.**

Notice in the past illustrations that accrued interest is computed using the principal of the note as a base, while the discount is computed using the maturity value of the note as a base.

In summary:

Principal × Rate × Time period = Interest
Principal + Interest = Maturity value
Maturity value × Discount rate
× Discount period = Discount
Maturity value − Discount = Present value (of discounted note receivable)
Principal + Accrued interest = Present value (interest-bearing note)
Face amount − Discount = Present value (noninterest-bearing note)

The 60-day, 6 percent method

When a 360-day year is used to calculate interest, the 60-day, 6 percent method can be used as a shortcut. The interest amount for the period is determined by taking 1 percent of the principal. The 1 percent is determined in the following manner:

Factors:
   1. Interest rate—6 percent, or $^6\!/_{100}$.
   2. Time period—60 days.

Calculation:

$$\frac{6}{100} \times \frac{60}{360} = \frac{6}{100} \times \frac{1}{6} = \frac{1}{100} \text{ or } 1\%$$

Thus, the interest of $445 for 60 days at 6 percent annual interest is $4.45. You simply move the decimal two places to the left—this represents interest of 6 percent for 60 days.

The 60-day, 6 percent method can now be used to calculate interest when the time period is *greater or less than 60 days.* For example:

1. The interest on a $500 note for 30 days at 6 percent is $2.50, calculated as follows:
   a. 1% × 500 = $5 interest for 60 days.
   b. 30 days = One half of 60 days.
   c. One half of $5 = $2.50, interest for 30 days.
2. The interest on a $4,000 note for 120 days at 6 percent is $80, calculated as follows:
   a. 1% × $4,000 = $40, interest for 60 days.
   b. 120 days = 2 × 60 days.
   c. 2 × $40 = $80, interest for 120 days.

When the *interest rate is not 6 percent,* the 60-day, 6 percent method is used as illustrated below:

1. The interest on a $2,600 note for 60 days at 9 percent is $39, computed as follows:
   a. $2,600 × 1% = $26, interest at 6%.
   b. 9% = 1½ × 6%.
   c. 1½ × $26 = $39, interest at 9%.
2. The interest on a $2,600 note for 60 days at 12 percent is $52, computed as follows:
   a. $2,600 × 1% = $26, interest at 6%.
   b. 12% = 2 × 6%.
   c. 2 × $26 = $52, interest at 12%.

When interest is not 6 percent and the number of days is not 60, the amount of interest is calculated in the following manner:

1. The interest on a $3,000 note for 30 days at 9 percent is $22.50.
   a. $3,000 × 1% = $30, interest at 6% for 60 days.
   b. One half of $30 = $15, interest at 6% for 30 days.
   c. 1½ × $15 = $22.50, interest at 9% for 30 days.

2. The interest on a $4,600 note for 120 days at 10 percent is $153.34.

    a. $4,600 $\times$ 1% = $46, interest at 6% for 60 days.

    b. 2 $\times$ $46 = $92, interest at 6% for 120 days.

    c. $1\frac{2}{3}$ $\times$ $92 = $153.34, interest at 10% for 120 days.

ACCOUNTING FOR NOTES RECEIVABLE *Customer*

Notes are received in several types of transactions. The most common transactions are notes exchanged for (1) cash loans, (2) goods and services, and (3) extensions of payment time on a previous obligation.

Note received for a cash loan

First National Bank received a note from John Martin in exchange for a loan of $800. The bank records the note receivable as indicated by the following general journal entry:

		GENERAL JOURNAL			
DATE		ACCOUNT AND EXPLANATION	P.R.	DEBIT	CREDIT
Jan.	1	Notes Receivable		8 0 0 00	
		Cash			8 0 0 00
		Loaned John Martin $800.			

Note received in exchange for goods and services

SGA Wholesale Company received a note from Ken Baker in exchange for merchandise valued at $375. The general journal entry for SGA Wholesale Company is the following:

		GENERAL JOURNAL			
DATE		ACCOUNT AND EXPLANATION	P.R.	DEBIT	CREDIT
Feb.	1	Notes Receivable		3 7 5 00	
		Sales			3 7 5 00
		Sale of merchandise to Ken Baker.			

Note received for an extension of payment time on a previous obligation

Earl Rogers requested a time extension on $200 due William's Department Store. William's agreed to the time extension in exchange for a note from Rogers. The general journal entry for William's Department Store is the following:

		GENERAL JOURNAL			
DATE		ACCOUNT AND EXPLANATION	P.R.	DEBIT	CREDIT
March	3	Notes Receivable		2 0 0 00	
		Accounts Receivable—Earl Rogers			2 0 0 00
		Note from Earl Rogers.			

Extension of time

Accounts Receivable is credited, therefore, balancing the account receivable account of Earl Rogers to zero.

Assume the same facts except Rogers makes a partial payment of $50 on the account receivable balance due and issues a note for the $150 remaining balance. The general journal entry on the books of William's Department Store is:

		GENERAL JOURNAL			
DATE		ACCOUNT AND EXPLANATION	P.R.	DEBIT	CREDIT
March	3	Cash		5 0 00	
		Notes Receivable		1 5 0 00	
		Accounts Receivable—Earl Rogers			2 0 0 00
		Note from Earl Rogers.			

Again the Accounts Receivable is credited for $200 to remove the previous $200 debit balance from the books.

NOTE DISCOUNTED BEFORE MATURITY

As previously illustrated, notes are often discounted before their maturity dates. Instead of issuing a promissory note of his or her own, a person could **discount notes receivable** to obtain cash. For example, on April 2, Tom Odom issues a $600 face amount, 12 percent note due in 90 days to Thompson Company in exchange for merchandise. Thompson Company discounts the note at Citizens Bank at 15 percent on April 4. The proceeds from the note equal the present value of the discounted note receivable. The present value of the note discounted at 15 percent is calculated as follows:

1. $600 \times 12\% \times {}^{90}\!/_{360} = \$18$, accrued interest at maturity date.
2. $\$600 + \$18 = \$618$, value of note at maturity date.
3. Term of note, 90 days, less 2 days held by Thompson (April 4, discount date—April 2, date of note) = 88 days in discount period.
4. $\$618 \times 15\% \times {}^{88}\!/_{360} = \$22.67$, discount on maturity value of the note.
5. $\$618 - \$22.67 = \$595.33$, present value of the note discounted at 15%.

The following is the general journal entry to record the note discounted before maturity date on the books of the Thompson Company:

DATE		ACCOUNT AND EXPLANATION	P.R.	DEBIT	CREDIT
April	4	Cash		595 33	
		Interest Expense		4 67	
		Notes Receivable			600 00
		Discounted Tom Odom's note at bank.			

GENERAL JOURNAL

Notice that the $4.67 difference between the face value of the note and the cash proceeds from discounting the note is interest expense. However, if the cash proceeds from discounting the note are greater than the face amount, then the difference is accounted for as interest revenue. For example, assume the same facts as the previous problem except Thompson Company does not discount the note at Citizens Bank until May 2. The present value of the note discounted at 15 percent is:

1. $\$600 \times 12\% = {}^{90}\!/_{360} = \$18$, accrued interest at maturity date.

2. $600 + $18 = $618, value of note at maturity date.

3. $618 \times 15\% \times {}^{60}\!/_{360} = $15.45, discount on maturity value of the note.

4. $618 - $15.45 = $602.55, present value of the note discounted at 15 percent.

The following is the general journal entry on Thompson's books:

		GENERAL JOURNAL							
DATE		ACCOUNT AND EXPLANATION	P.R.	DEBIT			CREDIT		
May	2	Cash		6 0 2	55				
		Notes Receivable					6 0 0	00	
		Interest Revenue						2	55
		Discounted Tom Odom's note at bank.							

REPORTING A CONTINGENT LIABILITY

As previously explained, the person discounting a note is guaranteeing that the note will be paid. If the maker fails to pay the note when due, the holder of the note can collect from the person who discounted the note. For example, if Cox Corporation discounts a $3,000 note received from Tom Wilkes at First National Bank, Cox Corporation must report a contingent liability for the discounted note until the note is paid.

The contingent liability generally is disclosed in a footnote to the balance sheet. If Cox Corporation has other notes receivable of $10,000 that are not discounted, the balance sheet would have the following disclosure:

Current Assets:
Notes receivable (see Note No. 1) $10,000
Note No. 1: Contingent liability on notes receivable discounted $3,000.

COLLECTION OF A NOTE AT MATURITY

When a note matures, the holder usually collects the maturity value. If the maker directly pays the payee at the due date of the note, the payee records the transaction in the following manner. Assume that Tat Thompson pays a $400 note plus $6 of interest directly to Cooper's Wholesale on the maturity date:

GENERAL JOURNAL					
DATE	ACCOUNT AND EXPLANATION	P.R.	DEBIT		CREDIT
July 10	Cash		406 00		
	Notes Receivable				400 00
	Interest Revenue				6 00
	Tat Thompson paid $400 note plus $6 interest.				

Occasionally, the holder may want to turn the note over to a bank for collection because it is inconvenient to collect the note personally. If it collects the note, the bank charges a fee for this service and notifies the holder that the note was collected and credited to his or her account. The bank uses a credit advice similar to the one in Illustration 15–2 to notify the holder of collection.

ILLUSTRATION 15–2

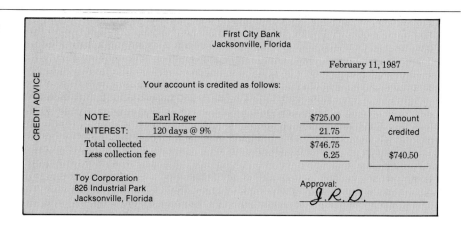

The entry on Toy Corporation's (the holder) books after the bank's collection of Earl Roger's (the maker) note is the following:

GENERAL JOURNAL														
DATE		ACCOUNT AND EXPLANATION	P.R.	DEBIT					CREDIT					
Feb.	11	Cash			7	4	0	50						
		Collection Expense					6	25						
		Notes Receivable								7	2	5	00	
		Interest Revenue									2	1	75	
		Bank collection of Earl Roger's note plus interest.												

RENEWAL OF A NOTE AT MATURITY

The payee may permit the maker of a note to renew all or part of the note at the maturity date if the maker is unable to pay.

For example, assume that Tat Thompson, a customer, is granted a renewal of his note for $400 but he pays the interest accrued to date. Cooper's Wholesale, the payee, would make the following general journal entry:

GENERAL JOURNAL														
DATE		ACCOUNT AND EXPLANATION	P.R.	DEBIT					CREDIT					
July	10	Cash				6	00							
		Notes Receivable (new note)			4	0	0	00						
		Interest Revenue										6	00	
		Notes Receivable (old note)								4	0	0	00	
		Tat Thompsom renewed note for $400 and												
		paid accrued interest.												

DISHONORED NOTES

If a maker fails to pay a note when it becomes due and the note is not renewed, the note is said to be dishonored. The note is no longer negotiable and must be removed from the payee's books. Assume that Thompson from the previous example defaulted in payment, instead of renewing the note. The following general journal entry would be made on Cooper's books:

Dishonored

		GENERAL JOURNAL			
DATE		ACCOUNT AND EXPLANATION	P.R.	DEBIT	CREDIT
July	10	Accounts Receivable—Tat Thompson		4 0 6 00	
		Interest Revenue			6 00
		Notes Receivable			4 0 0 00
		Dishonored note and interest.			

If Cooper's Wholesale had discounted Thompson's note at the bank and Thompson then dishonored it, Cooper's Wholesale is liable to the bank for the maturity value. Cooper's journal entry for its payment to the bank would be as follows:

		GENERAL JOURNAL			
DATE		ACCOUNT AND EXPLANATION	P.R.	DEBIT	CREDIT
July	20	Accounts Receivable—Tat Thompson		4 0 6 00	
		Cash			4 0 6 00
		Discounted note dishonored.			

The bank may charge the payee a service fee because of the default. The payee would collect the service charge from the maker, along with the maturity valuc. If in the case of Thompson's defaulted note the bank charged Cooper a $5 service charge, Cooper's entry would be for $411 rather than $406.

		GENERAL JOURNAL			
DATE		ACCOUNT AND EXPLANATION	P.R.	DEBIT	CREDIT
July	10	Accounts Receivable—Tat Thompson		4 1 1 00	
		Cash			4 1 1 00
		Discounted note dishonored with service fee attached.			

The amount transferred to Accounts Receivable remains on the books until it is paid or the payee determines that the obligation will not be paid. If Cooper makes that determination, Allowance for Doubtful Accounts will be debited and Accounts Receivable will be credited.

ILLUSTRATION 15–3

B. E. Camp Co.

								INTEREST		DISCOUNTED			
DATE	NO.	NAME	WHERE PAYABLE	DATE MADE	TIME PE-RIOD	MA-TURITY DATE	AMOUNT	RATE-	AMOUNT	BANK	DATE	DATE PAID	REMARKS
2/1/87	1	Becker Co.	First Nat./ Tampa	2/1/87	90 days	5/2/87	6 0 0 00	12 %	1 8 00			5/2/87	
2/3/87	2	J. D. Nelton	First Nat./ Pensacola	2/3/87	60 days	4/4/87	4 0 0 00	10 %	6 67			4/4/87	
2/6/87	3	Harry Smith	First Nat./ Tampa	2/6/87	90 days	5/7/87	2 5 0 00	10 %	1 8 75	First Nat.	3/7/87		
2/9/87	4	David Jones	Second Nat./ Miami	2/9/87	60 days	4/10/87	5 4 5 00	9 %	8 18			4/8/87	
2/14/87	5	Donna Clay	Second Nat./ Miami	2/14/87	90 days	5/15/87	6 1 5 00	12 %	1 8 45				
2/16/87	6	Rogers Co.	First Nat./ Tampa	2/16/87	90 days	5/17/87	4 3 0 00	10 %	1 0 75	First Nat.	2/23/87		
2/21/87	7	Grimm Co.	First Nat./ Pensacola	2/21/87	30 days	3/23/87	3 0 0 00	10 %	2 50	First Nat.	3/23/87		

NOTES RECEIVABLE REGISTER

NOTES RECEIVABLE REGISTER

A business firm should keep a separate record of each note receivable. This record is commonly called a **notes receivable register.** Illustration 15–3 indicates one form of the notes receivable register used by the B. E. Camp Company.

Although most of the information recorded in the register comes directly from the face of the note, other information is also reported. The total amount of interest is calculated; if the note is discounted, the name of the bank that bought the note is recorded and the date the note is paid is recorded.

NOTES RECEIVABLE ACCOUNT

The Notes Receivable account shown in Illustration 15–4 should agree with the notes recorded in the register. Notice that the amounts in the account are cross-referenced to the register by using the numbers of the notes. The debit in the Notes Receivable account represents the original face value of the note. The credit represents the part of the face amount that has been paid. Thus the balance represents the uncollected amount. The balance in the account can be determined easily, as shown in Illustration 15–4.

The notes receivable register and the Notes Receivable account are periodically compared to prove the accuracy of the account. This comparison usually is made monthly. In the above example, only note No. 5 is uncollected.

ILLUSTRATION 15–4

Notes Receivable			Account No. 120
No. 1	600	No. 6	430
No. 2	400	No. 3	750
No. 3	750	No. 7	300
No. 4	545	No. 2	400
No. 5	615	No. 4	545
No. 6	430	No. 1	600
No. 7	300		
Balance	615		

The purpose of maintaining a Notes Receivable account separate from a notes receivable register is to ensure proper internal control. The account and register are maintained by different people. This will help reduce errors in the accounting records and will possibly discourage fraud.

ENDORSEMENT OF NOTES

Before a note can be transferred to another party, the holder must endorse the note unless it is a bearer note (a note payable to the bearer of the note). Even though it is not required, a bearer note should also be endorsed. The two most important forms of endorsements are the **blank endorsement** and the **special endorsement** (see Illustration 15–5). The payee makes a blank endorsement when only his or her name is signed on the back of the note. If the payee signs "Pay to the order of" followed by someone's name, a special endorsement is made. Under both types of endorsements, the endorser becomes contingently liable for the note in the event the maker is

**ILLUSTRATION
15–5**

**Note
Endorsements**

Blank
endorsement ──────► Rob Willis

Special
endorsement ──────► Pay to the Order of
Frank Griffin
John Jones

unable to pay at maturity. The blank endorsement makes the note payable to the bearer of the note, while the special endorsement specifies to whom payment is to be made.

ACCOUNTING FOR NOTES PAYABLE

When notes payable are issued, the same kinds of transactions occur that are common with notes receivable. The common transactions involve: (1) cash loan, (2) exchange for goods and services, (3) extension of payment time on a previous obligation, (4) payment at maturity, and (5) renewal at maturity.

NOTES ISSUED FOR A CASH LOAN

Many companies experience periods when they need more cash than they can raise in the course of normal business operations. For example, during periods of inventory buildup, cash from within the business may be inadequate to purchase additional goods or materials. The business may then issue a promissory note (either interest-bearing or noninterest-bearing) to a bank in exchange for a cash loan. For example, assume that Martin Company issues an interest-bearing note to Peoples Bank in exchange for a loan of $1,000 for 90 days at 15 percent. Martin's general journal entry would be:

	GENERAL JOURNAL				
DATE	ACCOUNT AND EXPLANATION	P.R.	DEBIT	CREDIT	
April 25	Cash		1 0 0 0 00		
	Notes Payable			1 0 0 0 00	
	Issuance of $1,000 note to Peoples Bank.				

The principal is equal to the face value of the note. Martin will record interest expense of $37.50 ($1,000 × $^{90}/_{360}$ × 15%) when it repays the loan. Therefore, the maturity value is $1,037.50, which is the face value plus the interest.

If the note is noninterest-bearing, the difference between the cash received and the face value of the note is accounted for as interest expense. Assume that Martin Company issued a noninterest-bearing note for $1,000 for 90 days and Peoples Bank discounted the note at 15 percent. Martin Company's general journal entry is as follows:

	GENERAL JOURNAL				
DATE	ACCOUNT AND EXPLANATION	P.R.	DEBIT	CREDIT	
April 25	Cash		9 6 2 50		
	Interest Expense		3 7 50		
	Notes Payable			1 0 0 0 00	
	Issued noninterest-bearing note to Peoples Bank				
	for 90 days discounted at 15 percent.				

In this case, the principal is $962.50, which is the amount of cash received. Martin will repay $1,000 at the maturity date. Therefore, the maturity value is equal to the face value for a noninterest-bearing note.

For both of these notes, the stated interest rate is 15 percent. However, the notes involve different costs. With the interest-bearing note Martin may borrow $1,000 at a cost of $37.50, making the actual interest rate 15 percent ($37.50 ÷ $1,000 = 3.75% for 90 days; 15% for 360 days). With the noninterest-bearing note Martin will pay $37.50 in interest to borrow $962.50, making the actual cost higher than for the interest-bearing note. The effective rate of interest for the noninterest-bearing note is about 15.6 percent ($37.50 ÷ $962.50 = 3.9% for 90 days; 15.6% for 360 days).

Note issued in exchange for goods and services

Ken Baker issued a $400 note for 60 days at 12 percent to Wayne Company in exchange for merchandise. Baker makes the following general journal entry:

		GENERAL JOURNAL			
DATE		ACCOUNT AND EXPLANATION	P.R.	DEBIT	CREDIT
May	12	Purchases		4 0 0 00	
		Notes Payable			4 0 0 00
		Issued 60-day, 12 percent note to Wayne Company.			

Note issued for extension of payment time on a previous obligation

K. C. Roberts Company owes a $200 accounts payable to Glenn Company. Glenn agrees to accept a 12 percent note in exchange for an extension of 60 days. Robert's general journal entry is:

		GENERAL JOURNAL			
DATE		ACCOUNT AND EXPLANATION	P.R.	DEBIT	CREDIT
Sept.	13	Accounts Payable—Glenn Company		2 0 0 00	
		Notes Payable			2 0 0 00
		Issued 60-day, 12 percent note to Glenn Company.			

If Roberts made a partial payment of $50 and issued a note for the balance, the following general journal entry would be made:

		GENERAL JOURNAL			
DATE		ACCOUNT AND EXPLANATION	P.R.	DEBIT	CREDIT
Sept.	13	Accounts Payable—Glenn Company		2 0 0 00	
		Cash			5 0 00
		Notes Payable			1 5 0 00
		Issued 60-day, 12 percent note to Glenn Company.			

In both cases, the remaining balance for Robert's accounts payable to Glenn Company is zero.

Payment of a note at maturity

The maker of a note may pay the payee directly or the payee may choose to have a bank collect the payment. A bank will always send the maker a notice similar to the one in Illustration 15–6 notifying him or her that the note is due.

In either case, Bill Brown's general journal entry is:

	GENERAL JOURNAL				
DATE	ACCOUNT AND EXPLANATION	P.R.	DEBIT	CREDIT	
	Notes Payable		5 0 0 00		
	Interest Expense		3 4 15		
	Cash			5 3 4 15	
	Payment of note plus interest.				

Renewal of a note at maturity

If the payee agrees, the maker may renew the note at maturity for all or part of the amount. For example, Joan Miller agrees to renew an $800 note of Lynn Drake, but Drake must pay accrued interest of $40. Drake's general journal entry is:

	GENERAL JOURNAL				
DATE	ACCOUNT AND EXPLANATION	P.R.	DEBIT	CREDIT	
March 5	Notes Payable (old note)		8 0 0 00		
	Interest Expense		4 0 00		
	Cash			4 0 00	
	Notes Payable (new note)			8 0 0 00	
	Note to Joan Miller renewed, accrued interest is paid.				

NOTES PAYABLE REGISTER

A company should record notes payable in a separate register from the general journal record. All information shown on the face of the note is recorded. In addition, the amount of interest payable at

ILLUSTRATION 15–6

	First State Bank			
Maker	Number	Date Due		
Bill Brown	40-125	8/31/87	Principal	$500.00
			Interest	34.15
			Total	$534.15
	To: Bill Brown 1235 Main Street Jacksonville, Florida 40572			

maturity is recorded. The **notes payable register** is shown in Illustration 15–7.

NOTES PAYABLE ACCOUNT

The amounts recorded in the Notes Payable account (illustrated on page 480) agree with amounts shown in the notes payable register and are cross-referenced by the number of the note. The credit amounts represent the amount owed. The debit amounts represent the amount that has been paid. The balance in the account is found by taking the difference between debits and credits, as shown in the illustration.

ILLUSTRATION 15–7

								INTEREST		
DATE	NO.	PAYABLE TO WHOM	WHERE PAYABLE	DATE MADE	TIME PERIOD	WHEN DUE	AMOUNT	RATE AMOUNT	DATE PAID	REMARKS
1/3/87	1	Ross Bros.	First State Bank	1/3/87	90 days	4/3/87	1 000 00	12% 30 00		
1/4/87	2	Robb Co.	Peoples Bank	1/4/87	15 days	1/19/87	3 000 00	12% 15 00	1/19/87	
1/5/87	3	Martin Co.	First State Bank	1/5/87	15 days	1/20/87	2 00 00	10% 0 83	1/20/87	
1/18/87	4	Harris Bros.	Second National Bank	1/18/87	30 days	2/17/87	4 00 00	12% 4 00		
1/21/87	5	Harvey Co.	First State Bank	1/21/87	60 days	3/22/87	5 00 00	12% 10 00		

NOTES PAYABLE REGISTER

		Notes Payable	Account No. 230
No. 2	3,000	No. 1	1,000
No. 3	200	No. 2	3,000
		No. 3	200
		No. 4	400
		No. 5	500
		Balance	1,900

The notes payable register and the Notes Payable account are kept separately by different people within the firm. This provides better internal control, and greater reliance can thus be placed on the accounting records. The register and account are periodically compared to indicate the accuracy of the records. This comparison is usually made monthly or annually, depending on the needs of a particular firm. A schedule of outstanding notes payable is usually prepared, similar to the one below:

Notes payable at January 31, 1987

No. 1 . . . . $1,000
No. 4 400
No. 5 500
Total $1,900

ACCRUAL OF INTEREST RECEIVABLE

If any interest-bearing notes receivable are outstanding at the end of an accounting period, it is necessary to account for the interest that accrues until the last day of the period. Because interest accrues on a day-to-day basis, net income would be understated and current assets would be understated if the accrued interest adjustment were not made. It is necessary to debit Accrued Interest Receivable and credit Interest Revenue to adjust for the interest at the end of the period.

To illustrate the problem, assume that Baker Company has three interest-bearing notes receivable outstanding at its March 31 fiscal year-end. The schedule in Illustration 15–8 would be prepared from

ILLUSTRATION 15–8

NOTE NO.	PRINCIPAL	ISSUE DATE	INTEREST RATE	DAYS OUTSTANDING	ACCRUED INTEREST
\multicolumn{6}{c}{Accrued interest on outstanding notes receivable on March 31, 1987}
3	$ 500	Dec. 31, 1986	10%	90	$12.50
4	400	Jan. 10, 1987	12	80	10.67
7	1,000	Mar. 1, 1987	12	30	10.00
		Total accrued interest			$33.17

information obtained from the face of the notes or from the notes receivable register.

The following journal entry is made on Baker's books:

GENERAL JOURNAL

DATE	ACCOUNT AND EXPLANATION	P.R.	DEBIT	CREDIT
1987				
March 31	Accrued Interest Receivable		33 17	
	Interest Revenue			33 17
	Accrued interest earned on notes receivable.			

Accrued interest receivable is shown as a current asset in the balance sheet. Interest revenue is shown in the income statement, thus increasing net income.

ACCRUAL OF INTEREST PAYABLE

If interest-bearing notes payable are outstanding at the close of a fiscal period, an adjusting entry must be made by debiting Interest Expense and crediting Accrued Interest Payable. If the entry is not made, net income will be overstated, and current liabilities in the balance sheet will be understated. The calculation for accrued interest payable is just like that for accrued interest receivable. Assume that Baker Company in the last example has accrued interest payable of $33.17. The following journal entry is made at the close of the fiscal year:

GENERAL JOURNAL					
DATE	ACCOUNT AND EXPLANATION	P.R.	DEBIT	CREDIT	
1987					
March 31	Interest Expense		3 3 17		
	Accrued Interest Payable			3 3 17	
	Accrued interest owed on notes payable.				

Accrued interest payable is shown as a current liability in the balance sheet. Interest expense is shown in the income statement, thus decreasing net income.

SUMMARY

The use of credit is an integral part of modern business. The most common forms of credit are open accounts, credit cards, and promissory notes.

Promissory notes can be used in many situations. If a **promissory note** has the following characteristics, it is a negotiable instrument:

1. Unconditional promise to pay a specified sum of money.
2. Payable either at a fixed future time or on demand.
3. Payable to a specified person, a firm, or the bearer of the note.
4. Must be signed by the person or firm making the promise.

A promissory note is a note receivable to the payee and a note payable to the maker. The note can be either interest-bearing or noninterest-bearing. Noninterest-bearing notes are issued at a **discount.**

Three factors must be considered when computing **interest:** (1) principal, (2) interest rate, and (3) time period. The interest amount is the product of these three factors. A shortcut method of computing interest is the 60-day, 6 percent method.

Notes receivable arise when notes are exchanged for cash loans, goods and services, and extensions of payment time on previous obligations. A note receivable may be discounted before its maturity. If it is discounted, the person discounting the note is still contingently liable for the face amount of the note.

At maturity, a note may be collected, renewed, or dishonored. Each outcome requires a different accounting treatment.

A separate notes receivable ledger should be maintained. This subsidiary ledger supplies necessary information and must agree with the general ledger control account.

The holder of a note can transfer it to another party by endorsing the note. Two forms of endorsement are the **blank endorsement** and the **special endorsement.**

Notes payable are the converse of notes receivable. The same basic principles apply. A **notes payable register** should be maintained which has all the essential information regarding the notes and agrees with the amount in the general ledger control account.

Interest should be accrued at the close of a fiscal period for both notes receivable and notes payable.

KEY TERMS

Blank Endorsement—The payee's signature on the back of a note making the note payable to the bearer of the note.

Contingent Liability—A possible future liability or obligation that can materialize if certain events occur. For example, a person who discounts a note has an obligation to pay the note if the maker does not pay.

Discount (on a Noninterest-Bearing Note)—The difference between the face amount of a note and the amount of cash received by the maker.

Discounting Notes Receivable—Exchanging a note at the bank for cash and being held liable for its maturity value if the maker defaults. The amount of cash received from the bank will be equal to the maturity value of the note less a discount computed with the maturity value as a base.

Dishonored Note—A note which the maker failed to pay at the due date. It is no longer negotiable.

Endorsing a Payment—Recording on the back of a note the amount of a partial payment and the date on which it was made.

Interest—Money paid for the use of money; it is equal to the Principal × Interest rate × Time period. The time period is usually a fraction of a 360-day year.

Maker—The person who promises to pay money by signing his or her name on the face of a note.

Maturity Value—The principal plus interest accrued until the due date; the amount which the holder of a note should receive on the due date.

Notes Payable Register—A record separate from the general ledger which contains detailed information about each note payable—the date made, date due, to whom payable, when payable, time period covered, face amount of note, interest, and date paid.

Notes Receivable Register—A separate record in which detailed information is recorded about each note receivable—date made, date due, by whom payable, when payable, time period covered, face amount of note, interest, bank at which discounted, date of discount, and date paid.

Payee—The person to whom the amount of money specified on a note will be paid.

Present Value (of a Note)—Face amount or principal of the note plus accrued interest for an interest-bearing note; face amount less a discount for a noninterest-bearing note; maturity value less a discount for a note discounted at the bank.

Principal—The amount of money borrowed or the face amount of a note which must be paid on the maturity date.

Promissory Note—A negotiable instrument which has the following legal attributes: (1) unconditional promise to pay a specified sum of money, (2) payable at a fixed future time or on demand, (3) payable to a specific person, to a firm or to bearer, and (4) signed by the person or firm making the promise.

Special Endorsement—An endorsement which specifies to whom payment is to be made. The payee signs "pay to the order of" followed by someone else's name and the payee's signature.

QUESTIONS AND EXERCISES

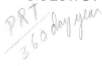

Assume a 360-day year in these questions and exercises.

1. What amount of interest is due at maturity on a $800 note at 12 percent for 90 days?
2. On March 1, Leigh Peaks issued a 90-day, 15 percent note for $1,200. What is the present value of the note on March 31?
3. Eva Brown issued a 15 percent, $350 promissory note to Coyle

Construction Company for materials on April 15. The maturity date of the note is November 1.

   a. How much interest will Eva have to pay at maturity?
   b. What general journal entries would Coyle have to make on April 15 and November 1?

4. On April 1, John Garrett issued a promissory note in satisfaction of an account payable of $3,700 to Johnson Services, Inc. The terms of the note are as follows:

Interest rate: 11%
Maturity date: . . . .   October 1

   a. How much interest will John have to pay at maturity?
   b. What general journal entries would Garret and Johnson have to make on April 1 and October 1?

5. How is a contingent liability from a discounted note reported in the financial statements?

6. What is the present value on May 15 of a 120-day note issued on March 1 at 12 percent for $5,000?

7. Geary Company has an interest-bearing note receivable from Hardy for $500 at 12 percent for four months. First Financial Bank collected the note and interest at maturity for Geary and charged a $5 service charge. What general journal entry would Geary make to record the transaction after receiving notification of collection?

8. Metz Manufacturing Company has a noninterest-bearing note receivable for $850 from Meyer Distributors, Inc. Meyer failed to pay the note at maturity. What is Metz's journal entry to record this transaction?

9. On June 1, Tim Craven issues a 60-day, 12 percent, $750 promissory note to Crawford Company for landscaping a piece of property. On June 11, Crawford discounts the note at Miami Federal Bank at 15 percent.

   a. What is Crawford's general journal entry at date of discount?
   b. What is Tim Craven's general journal entry at date of maturity?
   c. What is Crawford's general journal entry if Craven dishonors the note?

10. On June 1, Milford's Wood, Inc., issued a six-month, 18 percent, $5,000 note to Miegel Equipment Company for several chain saws.

a. What general journal entries would Milford's Wood, Inc., make on June 1 and also at maturity?

b. What general journal entries would Miegel make on June 1 and also at maturity?

11. On April 30, Aiken Company issues a $1,200 note at 14 percent interest for three months to the Bank of Key Largo for a cash loan. After paying the accrued interest, Aiken renews the note on July 31. What is Aiken's general journal entry on July 31 for this transaction?

12. What is the purpose of maintaining a separate register and ledger account for both notes receivable and notes payable?

PROBLEMS

15–1. Use the 60-day, 6 percent method to calculate the interest amount on each of the following notes. Assume a 360-day year. Show computations.

a. $5,350 note for 60 days at 6 percent.

b. $755 note for 60 days at 6 percent.

c. $1,200 note for 20 days at 6 percent. 4.00

d. $3,500 note for 120 days at 6 percent. 70

e. $900 note for 60 days at 10 percent. 15 -

f. $650 note for 60 days at 4 percent. 4.33

g. $2,600 note for 40 days at 9 percent. 26 -

h. $7,800 note for 90 days at 12 percent. 234 -

15–2. Part A: On June 13, 1987, Jeff Dentler requested a time extension on $750 owed to Pine Lumber Company. The time extension was granted to Dentler in exchange for a 30 day, 12 percent, $750 note. On June 14, 1987, Pine Lumber Company exchanged the note at the bank for cash. The note was discounted at 15 percent.

Required:

On the books of the Pine Lumber Company, make the journal entries to record: (1) the receipt of the note, (2) the discounting of the note, and (3) the dishonor of the note by Dentler.

Part B: On April 27, 1987, Laura Hayes issued a note to Nu-Craft, Inc., for merchandise valued at $325. The $325 note was for 60 days at 12 percent interest. Nu-Craft, Inc., sent the note to a bank for collection. On June 30, 1987, Nu-Craft, Inc., was notified that the note had been collected on June 26, 1987. Nu-Craft's bank account was credited for the amount of the note plus interest less a $2.25 collection fee.

Required:

On the books of Nu-Craft, Inc., record (1) the receipt of the note and (2) the collection of the note.

15–3. Reece Wholesale Company often accepts notes in exchange for merchandise and for extension of payment time on previous obligations.

Required:

Record the following transactions related to notes receivable.

1987

Jan. 15 Accepted a 60-day, 12 percent note for $500 from Hugh Nail. The note was dated January 15 and is payable at First National Bank, Forsyth. Mr. Nail issued the note for $500 worth of merchandise.

Feb. 19 Accepted a 90-day, 10 percent note for $650 from Pat Bailey. The note was dated February 17 and is payable at Farmer's Bank, Thomaston. Ms. Bailey received extension of payment time on a previous obligation.

Mar. 16 Renewed Hugh Nail's 60-day, 12 percent note for $500. Received interest that was due on the original note.

Apr. 19 Discounted Pat Bailey's note at 14 percent at the First National Bank, Forsyth.

May 15 Received a check from Hugh Nail in payment of his note plus interest.

18 Notified that Pat Bailey's note has been dishonored. First National Bank requests payment.

July 8 Accepted a 90-day, 12 percent note for $800 from Ray Malone in exchange for merchandise. The note was dated July 6 and is payable at County Bank, Woodland. This note was turned over to a bank for collection.

Sept. 24 Accepted a 120-day, 15 percent note for $300 from Tina Evans. The note was dated September 22 and is payable at Farmer's Bank, Thomaston. Ms. Evans received extension of payment time on a previous obligation.

Oct. 6 Received a memo stating that the company's bank account

1987

Oct. 6   had been credited for the amount of Ray Malone's note plus interest less a collection fee of $10.

Dec. 31   Recorded the interest that had accrued on Tina Evans's note.

15–4. D. M. Blum, owner and operator of Blum's Department Store, often finds it necessary to issue notes in exchange for cash loans, for goods and services, or for an extension of payment time on a previous obligation. During 1987, Blum was engaged in the following notes payable transactions:

1987

Jan. 15   Issued a $500, 30-day, 10 percent note to Cotton Wholesale Company in exchange for merchandise.

Feb. 14   Issued a check to Cotton Wholesale Company in payment of the note plus interest.

Mar. 1   Issued a note to Merchant's Bank in exchange for a loan of $800 for 90 days at 15 percent.

Apr. 19   Issued a $450, 60-day, 12 percent note to Hair Brothers in exchange for merchandise.

May 30   Issued a check to Merchant's Bank in payment of the note plus interest.

June 18   Renewed note issued to Hair Brothers for 60 days and paid accrued interest.

July 16   Issued a $300, 90-day, 10 percent note to Tejero Company for an extension of payment time on a previous obligation.

Aug. 17   Issued a check to Hair Brothers in payment of the note plus interest.

Oct. 14   Issued a check to Tejero Company in payment of the note plus interest.

Nov. 11   Issued a $700, 90-day, 12 percent note to Gable & Sons, Inc., in exchange for merchandise.

Dec. 31   Recorded the interest that had accrued on the note issued to Gable & Sons, Inc.

Required:

Record the above transactions in general journal form.

15–5. J. D. Shea operates a furniture and appliance store. Sometimes Shea accepts notes from customers and extends their payment time on accounts that are due. During 1987, Shea was involved in the following notes receivable transactions:

1987

Jan. 15 Received a 90-day, 12 percent note for $300 from Abe Lewis. The note was dated January 12 and is payable at Corpus State Bank, Atoka.

Feb. 5 Received a 60-day, 12 percent note for $500 from Bill Nelson. The note was dated February 4 and is payable at First City Bank, Hachita.

Mar. 14 Received a 120-day, 12 percent note for $800 from Candy Olsen. The note was dated March 11 and is payable at First National Bank, Berino.

Apr. 5 Received a check from Bill Nelson in payment of his note plus interest.

12 Received a check from Abe Lewis in payment of his note plus interest.

May 10 Discounted Candy Olsen's note at 15 percent at First National Bank, Berino. *find maturity value & due date*

July 12 Received a 60-day, 12 percent note for $400 from Dawn Pelt. The note was dated July 12 and is payable at Corpus State Bank, Atoka.

Sept. 10 Dawn Pelt was granted a renewal of her note for $400. She also paid the interest due on the old note.

Nov. 9 Received a check from Dawn Pelt in payment of her note plus interest.

Dec. 5 Received a 90-day, 12 percent note for $700 from Elaine Quartz. The note was dated December 1 and is payable at First National Bank, Berino.

31 Made an adjusting entry to record accrued interest on notes receivable.

Required:

1. Record the transactions in the general journal.
2. Prepare a notes receivable register to serve as a detailed record of notes received by Shea.

15–6. Christina Rosado owns and operates Rosado's Furniture Store. Occasionally she issues notes in exchange for cash loans, for goods and services, or for an extension of payment time on a previous obligation. During 1987, Ms. Rosado was involved in the following notes payable transactions:

1987

Jan. 28 Issued a $1,000, 90-day, 10 percent note to First National Bank in exchange for a $1,000 loan.

1987

Mar. 11 Issued a $550, 60-day, 9 percent note to Akruk Wholesale Company in exchange for merchandise.

Apr. 28 Issued a check to First National Bank in payment of the note plus interest.

May 10 Renewed note issued to Akruk Wholesale Company and paid accrued interest.

June 14 Issued a $740, 90-day, 12 percent note to Chang Equipment Company for office equipment costing $740.

July 9 Issued a check to Akruk Wholesale Company in payment of the note plus interest.

Sept. 12 Issued a check to Chang Equipment Company in payment of the note plus interest.

Oct. 5 Issued a $300, 30-day, 10 percent note to the Sigalos Company for an extension of payment time on a previous obligation.

Nov. 4 Issued a check to the Sigalos Company in payment of the note plus interest.

16 Issued a $360, 30-day, 10 percent note to First National Bank in exchange for a $360 loan.

Dec. 10 Issued a $405, 60-day, 10 percent note to Korker Manufacturing Company for merchandise.

16 Renewed note issued to First National Bank and paid accrued interest.

31 Recorded the interest that had accrued on the notes issued to First National Bank and Korker Manufacturing Company.

Required:

1. Record the above transactions in the general journal.
2. Prepare a notes payable register to serve as a detailed record of notes issued by Ms. Rosado. (All notes are payable at the First National Bank.)

 15–7. B. G. Franklin operates a hardware and building supplies store, Franklin Hardware. During the normal course of business Franklin accepts notes from customers and extends their payment time on accounts that are due, and occasionally issues notes in exchange for cash, goods and services, or extension of a previous obligation. During 1987, Franklin was involved in the following transactions:

1987

Jan. 10 Received a 60-day, 12 percent note for $200 from Gary

1987

Pratt. The note was dated January 10 and is payable at First City Bank, Hachita.

Jan. 14 Issued a $480, 120-day, 10 percent note to Craig Equipment Company for warehouse equipment.

Feb. 17 Received a 90-day, 12 percent note for $900 from Sherry Lane. The note was dated February 15 and is payable at Corpus State Bank, Atoka.

28 Issued a $350, 60-day, 9 percent note to Maple Supply Company in exchange for merchandise.

Mar. 11 Gary Pratt was granted a renewal of his old note for $200. Pratt paid the interest due on the old note.

17 Discounted Sherry Lane's note at 15 percent at The Corpus State Bank, Atoka.

Apr. 1 Issued a $1,000, 180-day, 10 percent note to First City Bank in exchange for a $1,000 loan.

23 Received a 90-day, 12 percent note for $450 from Josh Parker. The note was dated April 21 and is payable at First National Bank, Berino.

29 Renewed note issued to Maple Supply Company and paid accrued interest.

May 10 Received check from Gary Pratt in payment of his note plus interest.

14 Issued a check to Craig Equipment Company in payment of note plus interest.

31 Received a 60-day, 10 percent note for $690 from Jill Hart. The note was dated May 31 and is payable at First City Bank, Hachita.

June 28 Issued a check to Maple Supply Company in payment of note plus interest.

30 Made adjusting entries to record accrued interest on notes payable and notes receivable (end of fiscal year).

Required:

1. Record the transactions in general journal form.
2. Prepare a notes receivable register to serve as a detailed record of notes received by Franklin.
3. Prepare a notes payable register to serve as a detailed record of notes issued by Franklin.
(All notes are payable at First City Bank.)

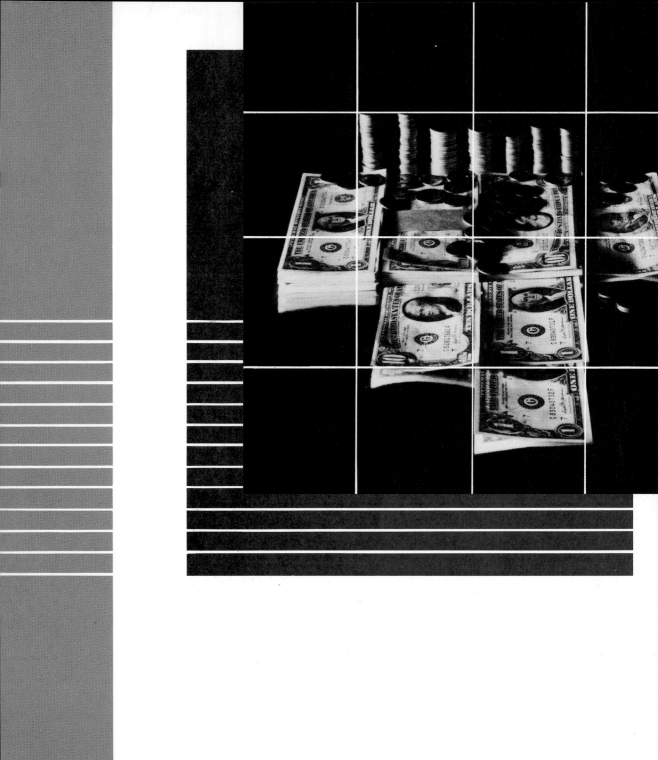

CHAPTER 16

Merchandise inventory

[handwritten:] ↑ FIFO first in can't be used
↓ LIFO
weighted average

LEARNING OBJECTIVES

Merchandise inventories are frequently a major portion of a merchant's current assets. A thorough study of this chapter will provide an understanding of the accounting procedures used for inventory. After studying this chapter, you should be able to:

1. Compute the merchandise inventory on hand at the end of the period using the following cost methods:
   a. FIFO.
   b. LIFO.
   c. Weighted average.
2. Calculate the cost of goods sold.
3. Calculate the inventory at the lower of cost or market.
4. Use the gross profit method to estimate the amount of inventory.
5. Compute the inventory on hand using the retail inventory method.

[handwritten:] Gross Profit 30% of sales
Co Goods 70%

Begin inv. 10,000
Purchases + 4000
mdse avail f sale 14000
Cost of Goods S. - 4200
9800

net sales
6000 X 70%

Inventories have value because they are assets that will provide future benefits to their owner. In fact, expected future use and earning power are the factors from which all assets receive their value. Since merchandise inventories normally will benefit their owner in the coming accounting period or business operating cycle, they are reported in the Current asset section of the balance sheet. Often the dollar value of merchandise inventories represents a major part of a business's assets. Unless inventories are properly reported, periodic net income will be improperly stated. For these reasons, it is important that proper records be kept.

MERCHANDISE INVENTORY

Not all inventories of a business are included in the balance sheet under **merchandise inventory.** As the title suggests, only items that will be resold are properly included. Inventories of office supplies, custodial supplies, and other items not held for resale are not included in merchandise inventory. They will be discussed in the next chapter since they are prepaid expenses. Merchandise inventory includes only items that the firm normally will sell in the ordinary course of business.

Purpose of taking periodic inventory counts

There are a number of reasons for keeping an accurate record of merchandise inventories. The most important reason is that unless a firm keeps satisfactory accounting records, its periodic net income will be misstated. Remember that in computing cost of goods sold, a major expense of a business, both beginning and ending merchandise inventory are used in the calculation. In Illustration 16–1, we see that the correct amount of ending inventory is $7,000. If in counting inventories we were to fail to include $3,000 of the inventory in our count due to overlooking these items, our ending inventory would only be $4,000. This means the understatement of the ending inventory causes the overstatement of cost of goods sold and then income is understated by the $3,000 error. The opposite effect on income is true if ending inventory is overstated. Assume that we double-counted some of the items and listed $10,000 as merchandise inventory rather than $7,000. Illustration 16–1 shows the effect of cost of goods sold being overstated and understated and net income understated and overstated by the $3,000 error.

ILLUSTRATION 16–1

	Ending Inventory		
	Correctly Stated	Understated	Overstated
Sales	$100,000	$100,000	$100,000
Beginning inventory .	$ 5,000	$ 5,000	$ 5,000
Purchases	50,000	50,000	50,000
Goods available . . .	$55,000	$55,000	$55,000
Ending inventory . .	7,000	4,000	10,000
Cost of goods sold . .	48,000	51,000	45,000
Gross margin (profit) .	$ 52,000	$ 49,000	$ 55,000
Operating expenses. .	30,000	30,000	30,000
Net income	$ 22,000	$ 19,000	$ 25,000

One of management's duties is to make sure that assets are safeguarded. Managers must take necessary steps to prevent theft, spoilage, and excessive waste. Since inventories represent a relatively large asset, taking inventory and keeping adequate records are ways of fulfilling this duty. Another reason for keeping accurate inventory records is that purchases should be made according to business needs. Without proper records, inventories may be overstocked, resulting in an unnecessary investment of funds that might be better used in other ways. Alternatively, inventories may run out, causing lost sales and ill will among customers.

Taking inventory

The key to a successful inventory count is preplanning. Determining the proper date to take inventory is especially important. Often inventory taking will be a sizable job. For this reason, a date should be selected when inventories are at their lowest. This usually coincides with a time when business operations are at a low point. This low point varies from business to business and is referred to as the end of the natural business year. Often, a business will select this natural business year as its fiscal year for reporting purposes.

To ensure a proper count, inventory is often taken after business hours or while the business is closed for a few days. Without advance planning, taking inventory during working hours can cause problems. It may be necessary to hire additional help in order to take inventory in as short a time as possible. Also, if inventory is taken during working hours, steps must be taken to assure that inventory items are not double-counted or omitted. An inventory count should include only company property. Goods waiting shipment on which title has passed to the buyer should not be included. In addition, control should be maintained over inventory, and a record should be kept of any movement of goods such as "rush" or "special" orders. Professional inventory firms are sometimes hired to take inventory.

On the day(s) inventory is taken, information is recorded on forms known as inventory sheets. During the inventory count, inventory takers work in pairs. One person counts the inventory and calls out the count to a partner who records the amount on the inventory sheet. On the prenumbered sheets are spaces for date, description, quantity, and initials of persons calling, recording, pricing, extending, and examining the sheets. Illustration 16–2 shows a typical inventory sheet for a hardware store.

After the inventory takers have recorded the counts, unit costs are recorded by a different person. Then, a fourth person multiplies the units by the appropriate unit cost. As a final check, a fifth individual examines the inventory sheets for accuracy and completeness.

Valuation of inventory

The assignment of a cost to inventories is not always simple. If the costing of each inventory item or specific identification is possible,

ILLUSTRATION 16–2

Inventory Sheet

INVENTORY SHEET

Called by _BRW._

Recorded by _D. L. W._

Costed by _HLR_

Extended by _A.R.U._

Checked by _DAW_

Store __Hill Hardware Co.__

June __30__ 19 __87__ Page __1__

Sheet No. __1__

Department __B__

Location __Warehouse__

Description	Quantity	Unit	Unit Cost	Extension
Power drills	11	each	$15.75	$173.25
Hammers	36	each	3.90	140.40
Tape measures	24	each	2.25	54.00
Tool boxes	10	each	9.50	95.00
Miter boxes	7	each	4.75	33.25
Total				$495.90

then it is a simple procedure to add up the costs to arrive at the total cost of the inventory. However, often the cost of a particular item is not known. This is particularly true if inventory consists of many similar items which were purchased at different times and at different prices. Not only will the quantity of inventory affect inventory cost and periodic net income, but the cost of inventory items will also affect net income. To help solve the problem of inventory costing when specific identification costing is not possible, various methods of valuation have been developed. Three of the most popular methods are: (1) first-in, first-out (FIFO); (2) last-in, first-out (LIFO); and (3) weighted-average.

To illustrate methods of inventory valuation, the following data from the Hardin Company will be used:

Inventory at start of period	200 units at $5 each	$1,000
Purchases during period:		
First	300 units at $6 each	1,800
Second	250 units at $7 each	1,750
Third	200 units at $8 each	1,600
Fourth	50 units at $9 each	450
Total	1,000	
Total cost of units available for sale . .		$6,600

Ending inventory of 275 units.

Specific identification costing.

Specific identification costing is an inventory valuation method that assigns a known actual cost to a specific product. The specific identification costing method requires that each item sold and each item remaining in inventory be specifically identified so that its purchase price can be properly assigned to the balance sheet as inventory or to the income statement as cost of goods sold. This method is feasible for a business which has a relatively low sales volume, where the inventory consists of items with relatively high unit values, and where the inventory items can be distinguished easily from each other. A good example is an automobile dealership. To illustrate how this method works using the data for the Hardin Company, which is really too low in terms of dollar amounts but will illustrate the method, assume that the 725 items sold were the 200 units on hand at the beginning of the period, 250 units from the first purchase, 150 units from the second purchase, 100 units from the third purchase, and 25 units from the fourth purchase. The cost assigned to the 275 units of inventory is determined as follows:

300–250 = 50 units at $6 each . . .	$ 300	
250–150 = 100 units at $7 each . . .	700	
200–100 = 100 units at $8 each . . .	800	
50– 25 = 25 units at $9 each . . .	225	
	$2,025	

First-in, first-out.   **First-in, first-out,** commonly known as the FIFO method, is the most widely used of the three methods. FIFO assumes that the first items purchased are the first ones sold. Therefore, the goods on hand at any point in time represent the most recent purchases. This method is most appropriate for goods that have a short life and are apt to spoil. In such cases, the latest purchases are placed at the back of existing stock so that the oldest inventory will be sold first, as is done with milk and dairy products in a store.

Assuming that the first units purchased are the first ones sold, the ending inventory of 275 units for the Hardin Company will be priced as follows, starting with the most recent purchase:

Most recent purchase	50 units at $9 each	$ 450
Next most recent purchase	200 units at $8 each	1,600
Next most recent purchase	25 units at $7 each	175
	275 units	
Cost assigned to ending inventory . .		$2,225

FIFO is widely used for three reasons: (1) it represents the physical movement of the items sold, (2) it results in the most current costs being assigned to inventory as shown on the balance sheet, and (3) it has been used for a long time and business persons are reluctant to change. When valuation methods are changed, records are less comparable and consistency is destroyed. Business executives rely on consistent, comparable records in making economic decisions.

Last-in, first-out.   **Last-in, first-out,** known as LIFO, is the opposite of FIFO. LIFO assumes that the most recent purchases are sold first. Using LIFO and the data given for the Hardin Company, the following cost will be assigned to the 275 units in ending inventory:

Inventory on hand at beginning of period . .	200 units at $5 each	$1,000
First purchase	75 units at $6 each	450
	275 units	
Cost assigned to ending inventory . .		$1,450

Some defenders of LIFO claim that LIFO represents the movement of goods in a business, but this is seldom the case. Probably a more convincing argument is that **LIFO** results in the most recent costs being matched with a period's revenues. This produces net income that is neither inflated nor deflated by price changes. Furthermore, when prices are rising, LIFO results in a lower net income figure because the higher, most recent costs are assigned to cost of goods sold. This lower net income figure results in lower income taxes.

Although arguments exist in favor of using LIFO, it is a weak valuation method for at least two reasons. First, LIFO does not normally represent the physical flow of goods. Second, and more important, LIFO does not result in a meaningful inventory figure on the balance sheet. In certain businesses where prices have steadily increased and inventories are material in amount, the use of LIFO will result in a significant understatement of current assets.

Weighted average.   The third method used to value inventory is the **weighted-average method.** In calculating the weighted average, all of the units available for sale in a period are multiplied by their respective costs. The amounts are then added and divided by the total units. This figure represents the weighted average cost per unit during the period. Note that weighted average cost is an average of units multiplied by costs and is not a simple average of various unit costs during the period. Referring to the data for the Hardin Company, the weighted average ending inventory (275 units) is assigned a value of $1,815.

> Unit cost ($6,600 ÷ 1,000 units) . . $6.60
> Value of ending inventory
>   (275 units × $6.60). $1,815

FIFO, LIFO, and weighted average are usually referred to as methods of inventory valuation, but they are actually methods of cost assignment. The cost that is calculated will be assigned either to the cost of goods actually sold or to the cost of goods that are not sold (inventory). It is important that all costs be assigned so that the income statement and the balance sheet will be presented fairly.

Lower of cost or market.   The **lower-of-cost-or-market method** is a combination method of inventory valuation. First, a cost is assigned to the inventory using its FIFO value or its weighted average value, whichever is lower. (The tax law does not permit the use of LIFO when valuing inventories at lower of cost or market.) Then market value is considered. *Market value* is the replacement cost of the inventory in terms of the quantity usually purchased. The lower of the two amounts is then assigned to the inventory for valuation purposes.

For example, assume that the Hardin Company has the following items on hand at December 31:

	FIFO Cost	Weighted-Average Cost	Market
Item A . . .	$1,000	$ 750	$ 800
Item B . . .	575	225	200
Item C . . .	650	840	700
Total	$2,225	$1,815	$1,700

Using the lower-of-cost-or-market method applied to total inventory, the value assigned to inventory will be $1,700.

Comparison of valuation methods. To compare the results of using LIFO, FIFO, and the lower of cost or market, refer to the data for the Hardin Company. Keep in mind that the example given in Illustration 16–3 is based on a period in which prices are rising. If prices are falling, the cost of goods sold under LIFO will be lower

---

ILLUSTRATION 16–3

	FIFO		Weighted-Average		LIFO	
Sales		$10,000		$10,000		$10,000
Goods available for sale	$6,600		$6,600		$6,600	
Valuation of ending inventory	2,225		1,815		1,450	
Cost of goods sold		4,375		4,785		5,150
Gross margin (profit)		$ 5,625		$ 5,215		$ 4,850
Operating expenses.		2,000		2,000		2,000
Net income		$ 3,625		$ 3,215		$ 2,850

	FIFO	Weighted-Average	Market	Lower of Cost or Market	Units		Amount
Fourth purchase	$9	$6.60	$6	$6	× 50	=	$ 300
Third purchase	8	6.60	6	6	× 200	=	1,200
Second purchase	7	6.60	6	6	× 25	=	150
					275		
Amount assigned to inventory of 275 units.							$1,650

than under FIFO. In that case, net income under LIFO will be higher than net income under FIFO.

When compared with FIFO and weighted average, the lower-of-cost-or-market method results in a lower valuation of inventory. The arguments for using lower of cost or market are based on the fact that recording inventories at a lower value will result in a no-less-than reasonable return on sales in the next accounting period.

Purchases discounts and shipping charges.   The cost of a unit of inventory is not always the invoice price. Purchase discounts, if taken, should be deducted from the invoice price. It is not necessary to adjust each item of inventory for purchases discounts. If the purchases for the period are $10,000 and discounts amount to $125, then the discounts represent 1¼ (1.25) percent of purchases. Assuming an ending inventory of $2,000, the adjustment for discounts will equal $25 (1.25 percent of $2,000). Thus, the ending inventory will be valued at $1,975 ($2,000 less 1.25 percent of $2,000). The above example is based on a FIFO method of valuation. If the lower-of-cost-or-market method is applied, the $1,975 inventory figure will be used unless the replacement (market) cost is lower.

The shipping charges of inventory units are a final point to consider in valuing inventory. Since goods are only useful to the buyer when received, the shipping charges are properly included as an inventory cost. In fact, reasonable and necessary expenditures incurred to place any asset in condition and position for use are a part of an asset's cost. Often the shipping charges are an important part of the inventory cost, especially if long distances and/or special handling are involved.

Maintaining inventory records

It is important to know the cost of inventory on hand. Just taking a physical inventory once a year to help determine periodic net income is not enough. If the quantity of inventory on hand is not known at all times, inventories may run short, thus hindering production or sales. On the other hand, inadequate records may result in excessive purchases that raise storage costs and tie up cash. To help keep abreast of inventory quantities and values, three methods are often used. They are (1) the gross profit method, (2) the retail method, and (3) the perpetual method. The first two methods aid in determining inventory cost, whereas the perpetual method is used to calculate both cost and quantity of items. All three methods are useful in preparing interim reports.

Gross profit method. The **gross profit method** involves reducing the sales figure by the normal gross profit percentage. This figure represents the cost of goods sold. This amount is subtracted from the cost of goods available for sale to provide an estimation of the ending inventory. As an illustration, assume a gross profit percentage of 40 percent. Beginning inventory is $20,000, and purchases to date amount to $80,000. Sales to date have been recorded at $125,000. Cost of goods sold for the period is assumed to be 60 percent of sales (Sales 100 percent − 40 percent gross profit = 60 percent cost of goods sold).

Beginning inventory	$ 20,000
Purchases	80,000
Goods available for sale	$100,000
Less: Cost of goods sold.	75,000
Estimated ending inventory	$ 25,000

Therefore the cost of goods sold amounts to $75,000 (Sales $125,000 × 60 percent). Since cost of goods available for sale is $100,000, the ending inventory is $25,000. Total goods available for sale must either be sold or be in ending inventory.

The gross profit method has other uses that make it a valuable tool. When inventory is physically taken, the gross profit method can be used to test the reasonableness of inventory amounts. The gross profit method can also be used when inventories have been destroyed. Should such an occasion arise, the calculation will be helpful in trying to negotiate an insurance settlement.

Although the gross profit method is a useful accounting tool, it does have weaknesses. The most obvious drawback is that the calculation will be accurate only if the gross profit percentage has been fairly constant in the past and is expected to remain so in the future. It should be remembered that, at best, calculations made using this method are only reasonable estimates and should not be relied on as exact figures.

Retail method. In calculating the cost of goods sold and ending inventory, a variation of the gross profit method is often used. The **retail method** involves keeping records that show both costs and retail prices of purchases on a current basis. With this information, it is possible to calculate the ratio between the cost and retail selling price. First, the period's sales are subtracted from the retail value of the ending inventory. Then the value of inventory at retail prices is multiplied by the ratio of cost to retail to obtain an estimate of the cost of ending inventory. An example of the retail method is shown in Illustration 16–4.

An advantage of the retail method is that the cost per unit of each inventory item need not be recorded. Only the aggregate cost of beginning inventory and purchases need be recorded for future reference. This makes it easier to take inventory once the goods have been priced at retail. By properly using the cost-retail ratio, a reasonable estimation of inventory cost can be obtained. The retail method can also be used to estimate losses from theft.

Perpetual method. Depending on the nature of their inventory, some firms find it easier to keep records on a perpetual basis. The **perpetual inventory method** involves keeping a running total of inventory quantities and aggregate value. The system works in a manner similar to an individual's checkbook or savings account. Each time purchases are made a debit is made to the Merchandise Inventory account and a credit is made to either Cash or Accounts Payable. As sales are made, two entries are recorded: (1) a debit is made to Cost of Goods Sold and a credit is made to Merchandise Inventory, and (2) a debit is made to Cash or Accounts Receivable along with a credit to the Sales account. The Merchandise Inventory account shows the amount of merchandise that should be on hand.

Keeping inventory with the perpetual method does not eliminate the need for a periodic physical inventory count. There is always the possibility of human error or loss from theft. Taking a **periodic inventory** will help assure that the amounts determined on the perpet-

ILLUSTRATION 16–4		Cost	Retail
Inventory, beginning of period		$27,000	$35,000
Purchases during period (net)		33,000	45,000
Goods available for sale		$60,000	$80,000
Deduct sales of period			50,000
Ending inventory at retail			$30,000
Ratio of cost to retail ($60,000 ÷ $80,000)			75%
Estimated ending inventory at cost ($30,000 × 0.75)		$22,500	

ual basis are reasonable. In addition, a physical inventory count will allow differences between actual and recorded amounts to be corrected.

A perpetual inventory system may not be appropriate for all businesses. Stores with low-cost, high-volume goods (such as grocery stores) would not find it desirable to keep a perpetual inventory because it would be very expensive and time consuming to try to maintain all the necessary records. On the other hand, a firm with high-cost items (such as a furniture store or automobile dealer) would find it both convenient and economical to keep a perpetual inventory. Instead of using the perpetual system as a central method of keeping inventory records, many firms use it as a supplementary system for determining when to make purchases.

Although the perpetual method has not been widely used in certain situations, there is increasing evidence that this will soon change. Technology is rapidly advancing, and retail stores are already installing electronic sensing devices at the point of sale. These sensors record the retail price as well as the stock number of the item being sold. Such information is then fed into a central system that maintains inventory records, sales, cost of sales, and signals for reorder. Such devices can be expected to change the procedures used to maintain inventory records in the future.

SUMMARY

Merchandise inventory consists of items held for resale. To ensure that the accounting records and financial statements reflect the proper value of goods on hand, a **periodic inventory** count should be taken. The inventory count should be carefully planned to be as efficient as possible.

Values must be placed on the inventory. Three of the most widely used inventory valuation methods are (1) **first-in, first-out (FIFO),** (2) **last-in, first-out (LIFO),** and (3) **weighted average.** A combination method of valuation is the **lower-of-cost-or-market method.**

Inventory records must be maintained to keep abreast of inventory quantities and values. Three methods used are the **gross profit method,** the **retail method,** and the **perpetual inventory method.** The gross profit method is based on the gross profit rate experienced in the past. The retail method requires that purchases be maintained at both cost and retail values. These two methods give a reasonable estimate of the inventory values.

The **perpetual inventory method** gives an accurate value of inventory that should be on hand at any point in time. All purchases, purchase returns, sales, and sales returns are indicated in the records. Normally, only companies with high-cost items maintain a perpetual inventory system.

KEY TERMS

First-in, First-out (FIFO)—The most widely used inventory valuation method. It assumes that the first items purchased are the first ones sold. Thus, it assigns the most recent costs to merchandise inventory as shown on the balance sheet.

Gross Profit Method—A method used to estimate the value of inventory. It involves the reduction of the sales figure by the normal gross profit percentage. This figure then represents the cost of goods sold which is subtracted from the cost of goods available for sale resulting in an estimation of ending inventory.

Last-in, First-out (LIFO)—An inventory valuation method which assumes that sales during the period consist of the most recent purchases. Thus, the earliest costs are assigned to merchandise inventory as shown on the balance sheet.

Lower-of-Cost-or-Market Method—An inventory valuation method which involves the assignment of cost, calculated on the FIFO or weighted average basis, or market value, whichever is lower, to the inventory units.

Merchandise Inventory—The amount of items on hand and available for resale.

Periodic Inventory Method—A procedure by which the cost of merchandise sold and the cost of merchandise on hand at the end of the period is determined by taking a physical count of the inventory units in stock.

Perpetual Inventory Method—A procedure for keeping a running total of inventory quantities and aggregate values.

Retail Method—A method for estimating the value of inventory which involves maintaining records showing both costs and retail prices of purchases. A ratio is calculated between the cost and retail selling price. The period's sales are subtracted from the retail value of the goods available for sale which results in an estimate of the retail value of ending inventory. An estimate of the ending inventory cost is obtained by multiplying the retail value of inventory by the ratio of cost to retail.

Specific Identification Costing—An inventory valuation method that assigns a known actual cost to a specific product.

Weighted-Average Method—An inventory valuation method. All the units available for sale in a period are multiplied by their respective costs. The amounts are summed and divided by the total number of units. This figure is the weighted cost per unit. It is multiplied by the number of units in ending inventory to obtain a valuation for ending inventory.

QUESTIONS AND EXERCISES

1. Calculate the change in net income for the Zero Company when the ending inventory is understated by $15,000 and when it is overstated by $25,000. The following data shows the correct inventory value:

Sales		$750,000
Beginning inventory	$ 25,000	
Purchases	491,250	
Goods available	$516,250	
Ending inventory	67,000	
Cost of goods sold		449,250
Gross margin (profit). . . .		$300,750
Operating expenses		257,000
Net Income		$ 43,750

(handwritten notations beside Ending inventory: 52,000   92,000)

2. What is specific identification costing?

3. Give an example of when specific identification costing could be used.

4. What are the three methods of inventory valuation? What assumptions are made when using each method?

5. Give three reasons for the widespread use of FIFO.

6. How can one justify the use of LIFO? What are the weaknesses in this method?
7. How is the weighted-average unit cost computed?
8. What is the lower-of-cost-or-market method?
9. How are purchases discounts and shipping charges accounted for?
10. How can a reasonable inventory cost figure be derived without taking a physical inventory?
11. The Kurtz Company wants to estimate the amount of inventory on hand as of June 30, 1987, without taking a physical inventory. Beginning inventory on January 1, 1987, is $15,000, and purchases from January 1 to June 30 amount to $30,000. Sales to date are $50,000. The normal gross profit percentage is 45 percent. Compute the estimated amount of inventory on hand at June 30.
12. The Stocking Company has just completed its first year of business. Its records reveal the following purchases:

First . . . . . 5,000 units @ $5   25000
Second . . . . 1,000 units @ 4
Third . . . . . 2,000 units @ 6

At the end of the year, 1,000 units are on hand. Calculate three different possible costs for the ending inventory.
13. What is the perpetual inventory method? When is this method appropriate to use? What entries are made when goods are purchased or sold?

PROBLEMS

FIFO   14ᵗ   LIFO14.50

16–1. Lybrand Corporation is in the wholesale electrical fixtures business. Stock records are kept on all merchandise handled. With respect to Item 43, data was assembled from the stock records and appeared as follows:

Quantity on hand at beginning of period . . . 500 units
First purchase during period . . . . 750 units @ $15
Second purchase during period . . . . . . 550 units @   13
Third purchase during period . . . . . . 650 units @   18
Final purchase during period . . . . 600 units @   16
Quantity on hand at end of period . . . . . 625 units

Required:

Compute (1) the total cost of units on hand at the end of the period and (2) the total cost of the units sold during the period under (a) the FIFO method and (b) the LIFO method. Assume that the units on hand at the beginning of the period were assigned a cost of $14 under the FIFO method and $14.50 under the LIFO method.

16–2. Shuman Brothers, Inc., is a wholesale appliance company with stock records kept on all merchandise handled. Data assembled from the stock records with regard to Item X appeared as follows:

Inventory at beginning of period. . . .	800 units @ $52.00
First purchase during period	200 units @ 56.00
Second purchase during period	760 units @ 50.00
Third purchase during period.	890 units @ 55.00
Fourth purchase during period	950 units @ 58.00
Final purchase during period.	650 units @ 57.50
Inventory at end of period.	1,050 units

Required:

Compute (1) the total cost of the ending inventory and (2) the total cost of units sold during the period under (a) the weighted-average method and (b) the LIFO method of cost assignment.

16–3. The following data is from the records of the Mitchell Furniture Company:

Item	Number	Cost per Unit	Market Value per Unit
Tables . .	60	$60	$62
Chairs . .	210	35	35
Desks . . .	50	95	97
Lamps . .	150	17	15

Required:

Compute the inventory value using the lower-of-cost-or-market method applied to:

1. Each class in the inventory.
2. Total inventory.

16–4. The Blue Sea Company sells three special types of aquariums—A, B, and C. The stock records reveal the following information on December 31, 1987:

Type of Aquarium	Amount on Hand	FIFO	Cost Weighted Average	Cost to Replace	Selling Price
A	500	$7.00	$6.50	$8.00	$15.00
B	600	6.00	6.75	6.50	11.00
C	1,000	5.00	4.25	3.50	8.00

Required:

Compute the total value of the inventory using:

1. FIFO.
2. Weighted average.
3. Market.
4. Lower-of-cost-or-market as applied to each individual category.
5. Lower-of-cost-or-market as applied to total inventory.

16–5. For the past six years, the Whatley Farms has maintained a gross profit percentage of 35 percent of sales. The following information is available for 1987:

Merchandise inventory, January 1	$ 26,000
Purchases	280,000
Sales	380,000

Required:

Use the gross profit method to estimate (1) cost of goods sold and (2) ending merchandise inventory for 1987.

16–6. The Garrison Company values its inventory at retail. Given the following information from the Garrison Company's records, compute the cost of the ending inventory.

	Cost	Retail
Inventory, beginning of period	$ 54,000	$ 72,000
Purchases during period (net)	356,000	543,000
Sales during period		405,000

16–7. Part A. The Duncan Berry Company values its inventory at retail. Given the following information from the Duncan Berry Company's records, compute the cost of the ending inventory.

	Cost	Retail
Inventory, beginning of period	$ 25,000	$ 50,000
Purchases during period (net)	312,500	700,000
Sales during period		710,000

Part B. For the past several years, the Callaway Company has maintained a gross profit percentage of 45 percent of sales. The following information is available for 1987:

Merchandise inventory, January 1 . . . $ 42,000
Purchases 368,000
Sales 590,000

Required:

Use the gross profit method to estimate (1) cost of goods sold and (2) ending merchandise inventory for 1987.

1. Cost of Goods sold = 590,000 × 55% = 324,500

2. Mdse Inv 1/1   42,000
   Purchases   368,000
   Cost of G avail Sale   410,000
   Cost of G sold   324 500
   mdse Inv   85,500

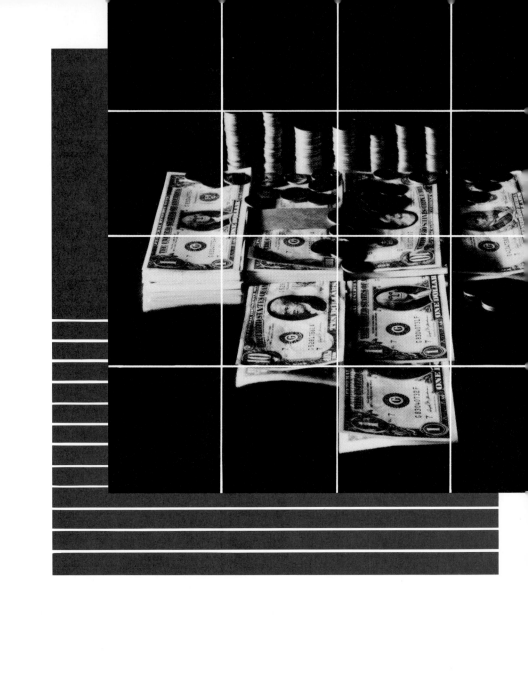

CHAPTER 17

Prepaid expenses

LEARNING OBJECTIVES

Prepaid expenses are current assets that were not wholly consumed during the current period and should provide benefits in the near future. In this chapter you will learn the kinds of prepaid expenses and the difference between the asset and the expense methods of accounting for prepaid expenses. After studying this chapter, you should be able to:

1. Record transactions relating to prepaid expenses.
2. Journalize adjusting entries to bring the prepaid expense accounts up to date.
3. Post to the ledger accounts.
4. Prepare an insurance register to account for prepaid insurance.

In a typical business, the balance sheet will report certain prepaid expenses as current assets. These assets are business expenses that are not wholly consumed (used) during the current period and are expected to provide benefits in the near future. Examples of **prepaid expenses** are rent, interest, and insurance paid in advance; office and store supplies that are not consumed at the end of the period; and advertising expenditures incurred to benefit present as well as future periods. It is necessary to adjust the various prepaid expense accounts to recognize amounts that should be expensed in order to determine net income for the period.

ACCOUNTING FOR PREPAYMENTS

Prepayments are recorded by using either the asset or the expense method. Under the asset method, prepayments are originally recorded as assets. At the end of the period, the accountant must determine how much of each asset was consumed during the period. The amount consumed is reported as an expense on the income statement.

Under the expense method, prepayments are originally recorded as expenses. At the end of the period, the part of each expense that was not consumed will be transferred to an asset account. This method will require another adjustment at the beginning of the next period, which will be discussed later.

Asset method - *Left only*

The **asset method** is normally used when it is expected that an asset will not be completely consumed during the period. If it is reasonably certain that an asset will be completely consumed during the period, then the expense method should be used.

Advertising.   Advertising supplies and services is an example of a prepaid expense. Often a firm will design catalogs and purchase advertising supplies that are expected to benefit more than one period. In this case, the purchase results in a debit to Advertising Supplies and a credit to either Accounts Payable or Cash, depending on whether the purchase was made on account or for cash.

When the period ends, the supplies are counted. The amount of supplies on hand is then subtracted from the amount recorded in the Advertising Supplies account to determine the advertising expense of the period.

For example, assume that on January 2, Rachel's Clothing Store purchased Advertising Supplies at a cost of $450. Using the asset method, the following entry was made on January 2:

GENERAL JOURNAL					
DATE 1987		ACCOUNT AND EXPLANATION	P.R.	DEBIT	CREDIT
Jan.	2	Advertising Supplies		450 00	
		Cash			450 00
		To record purchase of advertising supplies.			

On December 31 the advertising supplies are counted, and it is found that $175 worth of materials are still on hand. Therefore, $275 ($450 − $175) worth of supplies have been consumed and must be shown as an expense for the period. To show this expense, the following entry must be made:

GENERAL JOURNAL					
DATE 1987		ACCOUNT AND EXPLANATION	P.R.	DEBIT	CREDIT
Dec.	31	Advertising Supplies Expense		275 00	
		Advertising Supplies			275 00
		Amount of advertising supplies consumed			
		during period.			

After the Advertising Supplies account has been adjusted, the account will have a $175 balance. This balance will be reported on the balance sheet as a current asset. The expense of $275 will be shown as an operating expense on the income statement.

Rents.   At year's end, it is not unusual to find prepaid rents in the current asset section of the balance sheet. Rents are normally paid in advance, and rents that have not been consumed in the current period are deferred to the next period through the use of the Prepaid Rent account. Rents are consumed over time, requiring the calculation of consumed rents at the period's end.

Assume that on November 1, Rachel's Clothing Store paid the rent for the next six months. Rent is $200 per month. Therefore, the following entry was made on November 1:

		GENERAL JOURNAL			
DATE 1987		ACCOUNT AND EXPLANATION	P.R.	DEBIT	CREDIT
Nov.	1	Prepaid Rent		1 2 0 0 00	
		Cash			1 2 0 0 00
		To record payment of 6 months' rent in advance			
		(6 months × $200 per month).			

On December 31, two months' rent has been used. An expense for rents consumed of $400 (2 months × $200 per month) must be recorded so that the current period's income will be correct. The rent expense will be recorded in the following manner:

		GENERAL JOURNAL			
DATE 1987		ACCOUNT AND EXPLANATION	P.R.	DEBIT	CREDIT
Dec.	31	Rent Expense		4 0 0 00	
		Prepaid Rent			4 0 0 00
		To record rent expenses for November and December.			

After the December 31 entry has been made, the Prepaid Rent account will have a balance of $800 (4 months × $200 per month). The $800 debit balance is for prepaid rents for January, February, March, and April of the next year.

Office supplies. During the year, various office supplies such as paper, typewriter ribbons, ink, pencils, rubber bands, paper clips, carbon paper, envelopes, and the like are purchased and consumed. Not all of the supplies will be completely consumed at the year's end. For this reason, it is necessary to determine the amount of supplies on hand at December 31. This amount is then subtracted from the amount of supplies purchased during the year. Under the asset method of recording prepaid expenses, the amount purchased is represented by the debit balance in the Office Supplies account.

Assume that Rachel's Clothing Store bought $500 worth of supplies on January 2. The following entry was made when the supplies were bought:

GENERAL JOURNAL

DATE 1987		ACCOUNT AND EXPLANATION	P.R.	DEBIT	CREDIT
Jan.	2	Office Supplies		500 00	
		Cash			500 00
		To record purchase of office supplies.			

On December 31, the quantity of office supplies is counted, and it is found that $175 worth of supplies are on hand. Therefore, $325 ($500 − $175) worth of supplies were used and must be shown as an expense for the period. To show this expense, the following entry must be made:

GENERAL JOURNAL

DATE 1987		ACCOUNT AND EXPLANATION	P.R.	DEBIT	CREDIT
Dec.	31	Office Supplies Expense		325 00	
		Office Supplies			325 00
		To record office supplies consumed during the year.			

After making the above entry, the Office Supplies account will have a balance of $175 which is the supplies on hand at year's end. The $325 expense will be reported on the income statement as an operating expense.

Store supplies. Store supplies are accounted for in the same manner as office supplies. Items such as paper bags, wrapping paper, tape, string, cleaning supplies, and the like are classified as store supplies. When supplies are purchased, they are debited to Store Supplies, and a credit is made either to Accounts Payable or to Cash. The procedure used in calculating store supplies expense is the same as that used in determining office supplies expense.

Interest. As with prepaid rent, prepayments of interest expire over time. When interest paid in advance does not expire in the current period, it is necessary to make an adjusting entry. Since the prepaid interest remaining at the end of the current period is expected to benefit the next period, it is classified as a current asset on the balance sheet.

For example, assume that on December 1 Rachel's Clothing Store borrowed $2,000 from First National Bank. The bank was given a 90-day, 12 percent note. Therefore, the total interest that must be paid on the note is $60 ($2,000 $\times$ .12 $\times$ 90/360). The bank required Rachel's Clothing Store to pay the entire amount of interest in advance. Therefore, the following entry was made on December 1 when the interest was paid to the bank:

GENERAL JOURNAL

DATE 1987		ACCOUNT AND EXPLANATION	P.R.	DEBIT	CREDIT
Dec.	1	Prepaid Interest		60 00	
		Cash			60 00
		To record interest paid on 90-day, 12 percent note.			

On December 31, 30 days have passed since the note was issued. Therefore, one third of the interest expense has expired. To account for the expiration of interest, the following entry is made on December 31:

GENERAL JOURNAL

DATE 1987		ACCOUNT AND EXPLANATION	P.R.	DEBIT	CREDIT
Dec.	31	Interest Expense		20 00	
		Prepaid Interest			20 00
		Recording of expired amount of prepaid interest.			

After making the adjusting entry, the Prepaid Interest account will have a debit balance of $40, which is the unexpired portion of prepaid interest. In the next period, an entry will be made debiting Interest Expense for $40 and crediting Prepaid Interest. By making the adjusting entry on December 31 and the entry in the next period, the expired interest will be recorded in the period receiving the benefit. Without these entries, the reported income of both periods will be incorrect.

Insurance. In addition to business risks, a company faces other risks, such as the risk of loss due to fire, water, theft, wind, and other physical damage. To protect against such losses, most businesses take out a contract with an insurance company. The contract is known as an insurance policy. The insurance company is the insurer and the person or business signing the contract is the insured. In exchange for protection in the event of loss, the insured agrees to make payments, commonly known as premiums, to the insurer. Premium payments are charged at a specific rate per $1,000 of insurance and are *payable in advance.* Since an insurance policy often covers more than one period, its premiums are debited to the Prepaid Insurance account. This account is reported in the current asset section of the balance sheet.

Like interest and rent, prepaid insurance expires over time. In effect, a portion of the premium expires daily. Making daily adjusting entries for expired insurance is unnecessary and time consuming. Adjusting entries are usually made on a monthly or yearly basis. For a large business that may have several hundred policies, making monthly adjustments may still be a time-consuming task. Such firms normally use an **insurance register** to simplify the task. The register provides an organized record of policies and shows at a glance which policies will terminate and require renewal during the period.

The register has columns for the date a policy was issued, the policy number, the insurer, the property insured, the amount of insurance, the length of the policy, the expiration date, and the amount of unexpired premium at the beginning of the period. In addition, columns are provided for the amount of premiums expiring each month, and a final column shows the amount of unexpired premiums at the period's end. An example of an insurance register is shown in Illustration 17–1.

The amount of premium that expires each period is calculated by dividing the total premium payments by the term or length of coverage. Thus, if the premium is $60 and the length of the policy is one year, then $5 will be the monthly insurance expense. In reference to policy No. 60206 issued on March 1, 1987, the premium payment is $126 and the length of the policy is one year. Therefore, $10.50 will be recorded as expense each month. When the policy was issued, the insured debited Prepaid Insurance for $126 and credited Cash. If No. 60206 is the only policy, then the Prepaid Insurance account will have a debit balance of $21 on December 31.

If a company has several policies, the monthly or yearly expense

ILLUSTRATION 17-1

				INSURANCE REGISTER 1987				
DATE OF POLICY	POLICY NO.	INSURER	PROPERTY INSURED	AMOUNT	TERM	TOTAL PREMIUM	EXPIRATION DATE	UNEXPIRED PREMIUM 1/1/87
8/1/86	70423	Midstate Insurance Co.	Office Equipment	10,000	1	102.00	8/1/87	59.50
10/2/84	22204	Southern Fire & Casualty	Building	40,000	5	900.00	10/2/89	495.00
3/1/87	60206	Freedom Insurance Co.	Merchandise	30,000	1	126.00	3/1/88	—
4/4/84	11104	Atlantic Fire & Casualty	Public Liability	200,000	3	405.00	4/4/87	33.75
8/1/87	89765	Midstate Insurance Co.	Office Equipment	12,000	1	108.00	8/1/88	—
4/1/87	77706	Nationwide Insurance Co.	Public Liability	200,000	3	432.00	4/1/90	—
								588.25

is determined by adding up the premiums expiring each month. Assuming that adjustments are made on a monthly basis, the following entry is made in July:

		GENERAL JOURNAL						
DATE 1987		ACCOUNT AND EXPLANATION	P.R.		DEBIT		CREDIT	
July	31	Insurance Expense—Office Equipment			8 50			
		Insurance Expense—Building			15 00			
		Insurance Expense—Merchandise			10 50			
		Insurance Expense—Public Liability			12 00			
		Prepaid Insurance					46 00	
		To record expiration of insurance during July.						

If the only adjusting entry is made at year-end, the amounts shown in the total column will be used. As the policies are issued, they are all debited to the Prepaid Insurance account. However, when the entries are made for monthly or yearly expense, separate expense accounts are used for each insured item. This is done so that expenses may be charged to the various segments of a business for planning and control purposes.

At the end of each year, a new register is made containing only the policies that are in force on December 31. Management must protect the firm's assets. Buying insurance against possible loss is a justifiable means of fulfilling this duty. Keeping an insurance register

**ILLUSTRATION
17-1**
(*concluded*)

						EXPIRING PREMIUM							
JAN.	FEB.	MAR.	APR.	MAY	JUNE	JULY	AUG.	SEPT.	OCT.	NOV.	DEC.	TOTAL	UNEXPIRED PREMIUM 12/31/87
8.50	8.50	8.50	8.50	8.50	8.50	8.50						59.50	
15.00	15.00	15.00	15.00	15.00	15.00	15.00	15.00	15.00	15.00	15.00	15.00	180.00	315.00
		10.50	10.50	10.50	10.50	10.50	10.50	10.50	10.50	10.50	10.50	105.00	21.00
11.25	11.25	11.25										33.75	
							9.00	9.00	9.00	9.00	9.00	45.00	63.00
		12.00	12.00	12.00	12.00	12.00	12.00	12.00	12.00	12.00	12.00	108.00	324.00
34.75	34.75	45.25	46.00	46.00	46.00	46.00	46.50	46.50	46.50	46.50	46.50	531.25	723.00

helps management to be sure that the firm's assets are effectively protected.

Expense method - *Used*

Prepayments can be recorded as expenses instead of assets. The **expense method** is most useful when the items or services purchased are expected to be wholly consumed during the period. If prepaid expenses have been completely consumed during the period, no adjusting entry is required under the expense method. To illustrate, assume that during the period, $25 was spent for postage stamps and that at the end of the period no stamps were left. Using the expense method, the following entry was made at the time of purchase:

		GENERAL JOURNAL				
DATE 1987		ACCOUNT AND EXPLANATION	P.R.	DEBIT	CREDIT	
Dec.	1	Postage Expense		25 00		
		Cash			25 00	
		To record purchase of postage stamps.				

No adjusting entry is required at the end of the period because all the stamps were used. Postage expense for the period is $25, as the Postage Expense account shows.

Now assume the same entry was made when the stamps were purchased, but $4 worth of stamps are on hand at December 31. This means that only $21 worth of stamps were used during the period and postage expense should be $21 instead of $25. The amount of stamps on hand must be transferred to an asset account. The following entry must be made on December 31:

		GENERAL JOURNAL			
DATE 1987		ACCOUNT AND EXPLANATION	P.R.	DEBIT	CREDIT
Dec.	31	Postage Stamps		4 00	
		Postage Expense			4 00
		Postage stamps on hand.			

Notice that this entry sets up an asset account (Postage Stamps) that records the $4 in unused stamps. These stamps will be expensed in the period they are used. The entry also reduces the Postage Expense account by $4, bringing the account to its proper balance of $21.

If the expense method is used, the adjusting entry must be reversed in the next period (January 1). The **reversing entry** is as follows:

		GENERAL JOURNAL			
DATE 1988		ACCOUNT AND EXPLANATION	P.R.	DEBIT	CREDIT
Jan.	1	Postage Expense		4 00	
		Postage Stamps			4 00
		To record reversal of December 31 adjusting entry.			

If the reversal is not made, the asset method will be in use in the next period to account for the $4 of unused stamps, while the expense method is used for new purchases of stamps. A special adjusting entry will be necessary to record the expense when the $4 of stamps are finally used. Reversing entries avoid this problem. They enable the accountant to record all prepayments and adjustments in the same way from period to period. Reversals are usually made on the first day of the next accounting period.

Comparison of asset and expense methods

If all prepayments expire during the period, the expense method results in fewer entries than the asset method. This is because prepayments are recorded initially as expenses. However, since it is hard to predict whether prepayments will all expire during the period, time should not be spent trying to decide which method will result in fewer entries. Both methods require about the same amount of work and achieve the same result. Firms should select the method that is more convenient to them under existing circumstances. Once a method is chosen it should be used consistently, thereby lessening any chance of error from switching from one method to the other.

The following example illustrates that similar results are achieved under each method. Assume that advertising supplies amounting to $400 are purchased on August 12 on account. On December 31 the supplies are counted and $125 worth remain on hand.

GENERAL JOURNAL						
DATE 1987		ACCOUNT AND EXPLANATION	P.R.	DEBIT	CREDIT	
		Asset Method				
Aug.	12	Advertising Supplies		400 00		
		Accounts Payable			400 00	
		Purchased advertising supplies.				
Dec.	31	Advertising Expense		275 00		
		Advertising Supplies			275 00	
		Advertising supplies consumed during period.				
		Expense Method				
Aug.	12	Advertising Expense		400 00		
		Accounts Payable			400 00	
		Purchased supplies.				
Dec.	31	Advertising Supplies		125 00		
		Advertising Expense			125 00	
		Advertising supplies on hand.				

Asset Method

Advertising Supplies				Advertising Expense	
Aug. 12	400	Dec. 31	275	Dec. 21	275
Dec. 31 Balance	125				

Expense Method

Advertising Supplies			Advertising Expense		
Dec. 31	125		Aug. 12	400	Dec. 31	125
			Dec. 31 Balance	275	

Both methods lead to an Advertising Supplies balance of $125 and an Advertising Expense balance of $275, so the final results are the same. Under the expense method, the December 31 adjusting entry must be reversed the next day if the expense method is to be continued in the new year. The reversing entry is made by debiting Advertising Expense for $125 and crediting Advertising Supplies for $125. Then all purchases of advertising supplies in the new year are debited to the Advertising Expense account.

SUMMARY

Prepaid expenses are current assets that are not wholly consumed during the current period and should provide benefits in the near future. Some of the most common prepaid expenses are rent, interest, and insurance paid in advance; office and store supplies that remain at the end of the period; and advertising expenditures incurred to benefit present as well as future periods.

Prepayments can be recorded by using the **asset method** or the **expense method.** Under the asset method, prepayments are recorded as assets when funds are disbursed. At the end of the fiscal period, an expense is recorded to reflect the amount consumed during the period and the asset account is reduced by the same amount. Under the expense method, prepayments are recorded initially as expenses.

At the end of the period, the expense account is adjusted by transferring the amount not consumed to an asset account. The adjusting entry is reversed at the beginning of the new period.

A company should determine which method is more convenient under existing circumstances. Once a method is chosen, it should be used consistently.

KEY TERMS

Asset Method (of Accounting for Prepayments)—Recording prepayments as assets and making calculations at the end of the period to determine the portion of the asset that was consumed during the period.

Expense Method (of Accounting for Prepayments)—Recording advance payments as expenses and, at the end of the period, transferring the portion of expense that was not consumed to an asset account.

Insurance Register—An organized record of insurance policies indicating the date the policy was issued, the policy number, the insurer, the property insured, the amount of insurance, the length of the policy, the expiration date, the amount of unexpired premium at the beginning of the period, the amount of premiums expiring each month, and the amount of unexpired premiums at the period's end.

Prepaid Expenses—Business expenses that were not wholly consumed during the current period. They will provide benefits in the near future. Examples are prepaid rent and office supplies on hand.

Reversing Entry—An entry that reverses the adjustment that was made at the end of a period to record the asset portion of advance payments.

QUESTIONS AND EXERCISES

1. Name some common prepaid expenses.
2. What are the two methods of accounting for prepaid expenses?

Explain how prepaid expenses are recorded under each method. When should each method be used?

3. On May 1, 1987, Robert's Repair Shop paid rent for the next two years. Rent is $250 per month. The original entry was to Prepaid Rent. How much should be charged to Rent Expense on December 31, 1987?

4. On December 31, 1987, the accountant for Tucker Inn made the following entry on the books:

Advertising Supplies Expense . . .   300
    Advertising Supplies   300

What method did the accountant use in originally recording prepaid expenses? If $750 worth of advertising supplies had been purchased on March 1, 1987, what entry would the accountant have made?

5. When the Payne Company purchases office supplies, the Office Supplies account is debited. On December 31, 1987, the balance in the Office Supplies account is $8,000. A physical inventory of the supplies shows that $500 worth are on hand at December 31. What adjusting entry should the accountant make? If all purchases had originally been debited to Office Supplies Expense, what adjusting entry would the accountant have to make?

6. The Balsur Company debits the Advertising Expense account when it negotiates an advertising contract. On December 31, 1987, the balance in Advertising Expense was $7,500. However, only $2,500 of the contracts applied to advertising services for 1987. What adjusting entry should the accountant make?

7. Under which method of accounting for prepaid expenses would reversing entries normally occur? Why is this the case?

8. How do companies insure against losses due to fire, water, theft, wind, and other physical damages? Define the terms *insurer* and *insured.*

9. How are insurance premiums determined and when are they usually paid?

10. Explain how an insurance register is used.

11. The Fairfax Company uses the expense method of recording prepaid expenses.

The following entry was made on December 31, 1987:

Postage Stamps   10
    Postage Expense. . . .   10

Why must the accountant reverse this entry on January 1, 1988?

PROBLEMS

17–1. The J and J Company is a retail store that provides both over-the-counter and mail-order services. Metered postage is used on all items except general postage on which stamps are used. All postage is initially charged to Prepaid Postage, account no. 173, and the account is adjusted periodically to charge the postage used to the following expense accounts:

708 General Postage Expense
741 Parcel Post Expense
763 Advertising Postage Expense

On July 31, before adjusting entries were made, the Prepaid Postage account had a debit balance of $2,560. During the month of July, postage used on parcel post amounted to $1,250 and on advertising, $675. The unused metered postage on July 31 was $325, and unused stamps on hand amounted to $87.

Required:

1. Open the necessary T accounts and enter the prepaid postage balance before adjustment.
2. Make the necessary journal entry to record all postage expense for the month and post to the accounts.
3. Balance and rule the Prepaid Postage account and bring down the balance as of August 1.

17–2. The Hardman Ton Company uses the asset method to account for prepayments. The relevant asset accounts had the following balances at the end of the year:

Prepaid rent	$12,000
Prepaid insurance	1,500
Office supplies	4,000
Advertising supplies	2,500
Store supplies.	5,000

During the year, $6,000 of rent and $500 of insurance had expired. At the end of the year, physical inventories revealed that the following amounts of supplies were on hand:

Office supplies	$1,500
Advertising supplies . . .	300
Store supplies	3,500

Required:

Make the journal entries to adjust the accounts at the end of the year.

17–3. The Bridge Box Company uses the expense method to record prepaid expenses. On December 31, 1987, the relevant expense accounts had the following balances:

Rent expense	$14,000
Insurance expense	4,000
Office supplies expense	7,500
Advertising supplies expense . . .	3,800
Postage expense	2,600

On December 31, 1987, $6,800 of rent and $1,000 of insurance had not expired. The following amounts of supplies were on hand at December 31, 1987:

Office supplies	$2,500
Advertising supplies . . .	600
Postage stamps	150

Required:

Prepare journal entries to adjust the accounts at the end of the year.

17–4. The Billingsley Company uses the asset method to account for prepayments. The relevant asset accounts had the following balances at the end of the year:

Prepaid rent	$9,000
Prepaid insurance	2,000
Office supplies	6,800
Advertising supplies	900
Store supplies	4,200
Postage stamps	3,900

During the year, $7,200 of rent and $1,800 of insurance had expired. At the end of the year, physical inventories revealed that the following amounts of supplies were on hand:

Office supplies	$1,100
Advertising supplies . . .	150
Store supplies	600
Postage stamps	950

Required:

Prepare journal entries to adjust the accounts at the end of the year.

17–5. The Domansky Company borrowed $7,500 from the Third National Bank on August 1, 1987. The bank was given a 60-day, 10 percent note. The bank required that the total amount of interest be paid in advance. The Domansky Company's year end is on August 31.

Required:

Prepare the journal entries for August 1 and August 31 under both the asset method and expense method. Only those entries which relate to the interest payment and interest expense need be given.

17–6. The Forbes Wholesale Company has several insurance policies to protect against loss due to fire, water, theft, wind, and other physical damages as well as liability damages. During 1987 the following policies were in force:

Policy no. 64646 with Fidelity Insurance Company covering office equipment for $12,000 with a total premium of $235.20 and a term of May 1, 1985, to May 1, 1987.

Policy no. 83538 with Dartmouth Insurance Company covering warehouse equipment for $24,000 with a total premium of $396 and a term of October 1, 1985, to October 1, 1987.

Policy no. 39281 with Franklin Insurance Company covering public liability for $500,000 with a total premium of $612 and a term of February 1, 1986, to February 1, 1989.

Policy no. 19870 with Eastern Insurance Company covering merchandise for $40,000 with a total premium of $495 and a term of August 1, 1986, to August 1, 1989.

Policy no. 21177 with Pratt Fire and Casualty covering buildings for $90,000 with a total premium of $1,320 and a term of November 1, 1986, to November 1, 1991.

Policy no. 69321 with Fidelity Insurance Company covering office equipment for $15,000 with a total premium of $288 and a term of May 1, 1987, to May 1, 1989.

Policy no. 89654 with Dartmouth Insurance Company covering automobiles for $27,000 with a total premium of $439.20 and a term of October 1, 1987, to October 1, 1989.

Required:

1. Complete the Forbes Wholesale Company's insurance register for 1987. (See Illustration 17–1.)
2. Determine (a) the total insurance expense for 1987 and (b) the amount of Prepaid Insurance to be carried on the December 31, 1987, Balance Sheet.
3. Prepare a journal entry to record the expiration of insurance during June 1987, assuming Prepaid Insurance was debited when the premiums were paid.

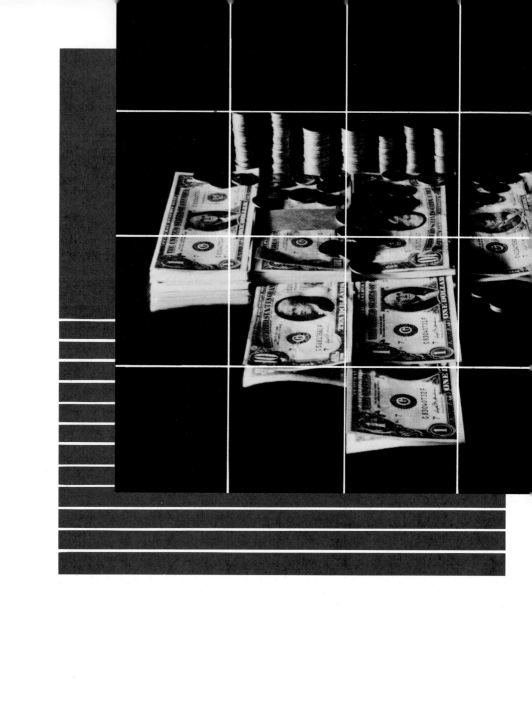

CHAPTER 18

Plant assets

LEARNING OBJECTIVES

Many businesses spend significant amounts of cash for plant assets. Such investments have lasting effects on a firm's income. This chapter will discuss the procedures used in accounting for plant assets. After studying this chapter, you should be able to:

1. Prepare entries to record the purchase and use of plant assets.
2. Calculate depreciation expense using the following methods:
   a. Straight-line.
   b. Units of production.
   c. Sum-of-the-years'-digits.
   d. Declining-balance.
3. Prepare a schedule of depreciation expense.
4. Prepare entries to dispose of plant assets.
5. Prepare entries for wasting assets and calculate depletion expense.
6. Record the purchase of intangible assets and compute amortization expense.

As a basis for operations, most businesses buy assets that they expect to provide benefits for current and future periods. Assets that last several periods are called **plant assets.** They are also known as long-lived assets, fixed assets, or capital assets. Plant assets can be classified on the basis of (1) legal characteristics, (2) physical characteristics, and (3) accounting treatment characteristics.

Legally, plant assets are classed as either real property or personal property. **Real property** is land and anything that is attached to the land. **Personal property** is defined as all assets other than real property. In most cases, real property is classified as a plant asset. Personal property may also be classified as a plant asset if it is expected to last several periods. Equipment, trucks, patents, copyrights, and office furniture are examples of personal property owned by a business.

A second way of classifying assets is by physical properties. Assets that can be seen and touched are **tangible assets,** while those that cannot be seen and touched are **intangible assets.** Both real and personal property can be tangible assets. Although they do not exist physically, intangible assets do exist in a legal or economic sense; that is, they usually represent a legal right that the company owns. Examples of intangibles are patents, leases, copyrights, trademarks, and business goodwill. Often, businesses will invest in stocks or bonds of another company. Based on classification by physical properties, it would seem that these investments should be classified as intangibles. However, because of the nature of such assets, they are normally reported as either current assets or investments on the balance sheet depending on how long the business expects to hold them.

It is the third method of asset classification that will be discussed in this chapter. Classification by accounting treatment is a common way of reporting plant assets. Since accounting records are usually based on historical cost, an asset is recorded on the books by debiting a particular asset account for the cost and crediting Cash or a liability account. Because the accounting process attempts to match period benefits (revenues) with period sacrifices (expenses), the portion of a plant asset's cost that is used in the period should be recorded as a period expense. Tangible plant assets are said to depreciate during the asset's life. Not all plant assets are depreciated. At present, land is the only tangible asset that is not depreciated. Since land does not normally deteriorate, a portion of its cost is not expensed each period. Examples of depreciable tangible plant assets are buildings, machinery, equipment, and furniture. Expensing of intangible assets is called **amortization.**

In contrast to tangible plant assets, which are depreciated over time, some assets are actually consumed or used up over time. Examples of such assets are oil wells, mines, and timber. These assets are called **wasting assets.** The expensing of these assets is called **depletion.**

The terms *depreciation, amortization,* and *depletion* make it easier to understand what form of asset is being expensed. This chapter is primarily concerned with accounting for the more common tangible plant assets, such as land, buildings, and machinery. Accounting for intangible and wasting assets will be discussed at the end of the chapter.

DEPRECIATION

Accounting attempts to record revenues in the period in which they are earned and expenses in the period that benefits from the expenditures. Plant assets benefit more than one period. Therefore, the cost of such assets must be spread across the periods that receive the benefit so that periodic net income will be correct. The process of spreading asset costs across periods is called **depreciation.**

Depreciation, or the loss of usefulness of an asset, may be the result of physical and/or functional depreciation. **Physical depreciation** is the decline in usefulness of an asset due to physical wear and tear. Various factors determine how fast an asset deteriorates. Much physical deterioration depends on how regularly an asset is used. Also, the amount of maintenance will greatly affect the length of an asset's life. Another factor that affects physical depreciation is the environment in which the asset is used. A forklift truck that is used outdoors will deteriorate faster than one that is used indoors.

Functional depreciation is the loss in usefulness of an asset due to inadequacy or obsolescence. In certain situations, functional depreciation may be as important or more important than physical depreciation in determining the useful life of an asset. For example, changing technology in the computer industry is causing older computers to be worthless. An asset may still have several years of useful physical life but be almost worthless due to obsolescence.

Determining depreciation expense

Spreading the cost of an asset over the periods expected to benefit from its use involves at least two basic problems. First, only the net cost of an asset is expensed over its useful life. **Net cost** is the cost of an asset less any salvage or scrap value it may have after it has served its purpose. **Salvage value** is the expected value of an asset at the end of its useful life. Determining the salvage value of an asset is not easy. If an asset has a relatively short life and has been replaced often in the past, its salvage value can be estimated from experience. But, if an asset is expected to last 15 to 20 years, it may be very difficult to determine future salvage value.

A second problem involves determining an asset's useful life. As already mentioned, an asset may become obsolete due to changes in demand or technology. Predicting the future is difficult, if not impossible, and it is not easy to decide the number of years an asset will last.

In trying to determine an asset's salvage value or useful life, an accountant can use several sources of information. First, the accountant can rely on past experience. For example, if most of the company's machines have had a useful life of 15 years, the accountant may be able to determine that a similar new machine will have the same useful life. If the company has no experience with such machines, the accountant may rely on the past experience of other companies that are familiar with the situation.

Often statistical information can be obtained from industry trade associations and government agencies. For unusual or highly specialized equipment, engineers and appraisers may be helpful. Although past experience may be useful, it is not always the best guide. Estimates from the past may be reliable, but estimates about the future should always be made with care.

There are many ways to calculate depreciation. The method a company selects should be both appropriate and reasonable under the circumstances. We will discuss four depreciation methods in this chapter.

1. Straight-line method.
2. Declining-balance method.
3. Sum-of-the-years'-digits method.
4. Units-of-production method. - *Wasting assets*

Since depreciation is only an estimate, there is no single best method. However, one method may well be better than another under specific circumstances. Although some firms find it convenient to use the same depreciation method for both business and tax purposes, they are not required to do so. The tax law requires the accelerated cost recovery system to be used for tax purposes, for assets placed in service after December 31, 1980.

Straight-line method. The straight-line method is the easiest way to calculate depreciation expense. As the name suggests, the straight-line method allocates an equal amount of an asset's net cost to each period of its useful life. For example, assume that an asset has a cost of $2,500 and is expected to last five years. Its estimated salvage value is $250. Using the straight-line method, the yearly depreciation expense is computed as follows:

$$\frac{\$2,500 - \$250}{5} = \$450$$

Cost - salvage value ÷ # of years

Under the straight-line method, each year of an asset's life will be charged with an equal amount of depreciation expense. When shown on a graph (see Illustration 18–1), the method results in a straight line, which is how the method got its name. At any time during an asset's life, the book value of the asset is equal to the cost of the asset less accumulated depreciation. **Accumulated depreciation** is the total depreciation taken on an asset to date. For example, if a machine was bought five years ago and the annual depreciation is $1,000, the accumulated depreciation is $5,000 ($1,000 per year

ILLUSTRATION 18–1

Annual Depreciation Expense

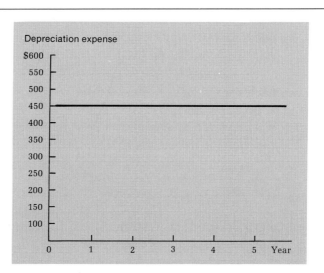

× 5 years). The **book value** is the part of the asset's cost that has not yet been depreciated. Book value is not the same as market value.

Although an asset depreciates daily, depreciation expense is normally recorded only once a year and is calculated to the nearest whole month. Accountants use the rule that assets purchased before the 15th of the month are considered to have been owned for a full month. Those purchased after the 15th are treated as if they had been purchased on the first of the following month. For example, if an asset is purchased on March 24 and depreciation for the year is calculated on December 31, depreciation expense will be charged for nine months (April through December). Since the asset was purchased after March 15, no depreciation is computed for March.

Since the usefulness of many assets declines evenly, the straight-line method is favored because it closely resembles reality. Another advantage is that it is simple. Some experts say that, since all depreciation calculations are estimates, more complicated and time-consuming methods are unnecessary.

Declining-balance method.   The straight-line method assumes that repairs will be made evenly and that the asset will steadily decline in value over its life. However, repairs will probably be more frequent in later years. Also, some experts argue that an asset is most useful when it is new and should be depreciated at a faster rate in its earlier years. The declining-balance method takes these considerations into account. Under this method, depreciation expense is larger in the early years of an asset's life and smaller in the later years. The method gets its name from the fact that depreciation expense declines each year. This is because depreciation expense for each year is computed by multiplying the asset's book value, which is declining, by a fixed percentage rate. Salvage value is ignored in the computation because it is already included in the fixed percentage rate. Normally, a percentage rate of twice the straight-line percentage rate is used. (Hence, this method is commonly called the double-declining-balance method.) If the asset is expected to last five years, the depreciation rate using the straight-line method would be 20 percent (100 percent ÷ 5 years). The declining balance method would double the straight-line rate, resulting in a declining-balance rate of 40 percent. For example, if an asset cost $800 and a declining-balance rate of 40 percent is used, the following expenses and book values will be shown at the end of each year:

Year	Depreciation Expense	Accumulated Depreciation	Book Value
0			$800.00
1	$320.00	$320.00	480.00
2	192.00	512.00	288.00
3	115.20	627.20	172.80
4	69.12	696.32	103.68
5	41.47	737.79	62.21

The amount of depreciation expense is determined by multiplying the 40 percent times the asset's book value at the beginning of the year. Thus for year one the depreciation expense is $320 (40% × $800). At the beginning of the second year, the book value is $480 ($800 cost − $320 accumulated depreciation). When this book value is multiplied by 40 percent (40% × $480), the depreciation expense is $192.

The formula for calculating the depreciation under the double-declining-balance method is:

Depreciation expense per year

$$= (2) \left(\frac{100 \text{ percent}}{N} \right) \left(\begin{array}{l} \text{Book value of the asset at} \\ \text{the beginning of the year} \end{array} \right)$$

where N = number of years in the asset's expected useful life.

Sum-of-the-years'-digits method. Instead of using the declining-balance method to obtain smaller amounts of depreciation each year, some companies choose the sum-of-the-years'-digits method. Depreciation calculations using the sum-of-the-years'-digits method take salvage value into account. The calculations are based on the asset's net cost (cost less salvage value). The asset's book value at the end of its useful life is equal to the salvage value. Depreciation expense is determined each year by multiplying the asset's net cost by a declining fraction. The denominator of the fraction is the same each year and is the sum of the years of the asset's expected life. The numerator of the fraction changes each year and is the number of expected years of service left in the asset at the beginning of the accounting period. The complete fraction is therefore smaller each year.

For example, assume that an asset costing $2,000 is purchased. Salvage value is estimated to be $200 at the end of a useful life of five years. The fraction's denominator is determined by computing the sum of the years' digits, which is $5 + 4 + 3 + 2 + 1 = 15$. For the first year, $\frac{5}{15}$ of the net cost would be recorded as depreciation expense. The second year's depreciation expense would be $\frac{4}{15}$ of the asset's net cost; the third, $\frac{3}{15}$; the fourth, $\frac{2}{15}$; and the fifth, $\frac{1}{15}$. The following table illustrates the year-end results of the calculations for each of the five years:

Year		Depreciation Expense	Accumulated Depreciation	Book Value
0				$2,000
1	$\frac{5}{15} \times \$1,800$	$600	$ 600	1,400
2	$\frac{4}{15} \times 1,800$	480	1,080	920
3	$\frac{3}{15} \times 1,800$	360	1,440	560
4	$\frac{2}{15} \times 1,800$	240	1,680	320
5	$\frac{1}{15} \times 1,800$	120	1,800	200

When using the sum-of-the-years'-digits method, finding the sum of the years to use in the fraction's denominator may be time consuming. For example, an asset with a life of 25 years would require the addition of the digits 1 through 25. In order to save time, the following formula is often used:

$$\text{Denominator} = (N) \left(\frac{N+1}{2}\right)$$

where N = Number of years in the asset's expected useful life. For an asset with a useful life of 25 years, the calculation is:

$$\text{Denominator} = 25 \left(\frac{(25+1)}{2}\right) = 325$$

Depreciation expense is then calculated with the following formula:

$$\text{Depreciation expense for the year} = \left(\frac{\text{Remaining years of life at the beginning of the year}}{\text{Sum of the years' digits}}\right) \left(\frac{\text{Net}}{\text{cost}}\right)$$

Units-of-production method. With the straight-line, declining-balance, and sum-of-the-years'-digits methods, depreciation expense can be determined ahead of time. This is not the case when the units-of-production method is used. With this method, the depreciation expense for each period is determined by the number of units produced, and depreciation is recorded only when an asset is used. Sometimes it is possible to estimate the total number of units that an asset will produce during its useful life. When this can be done, the net cost of the asset can be allocated to each unit by dividing the net cost by the total number of units expected to be produced.

The units-of-production method cannot be used for all assets. It can only be used if the asset being depreciated produces goods or services that can be measured in units. For example, a machine that makes parts for cars can be depreciated this way, but an office building cannot. Some experts think this method is preferable because depreciation is recorded only in the periods that receive benefits and only to the degree that benefits are realized.

For example, assume that a machine is purchased and is expected to produce 400,000 units during its lifetime. The machine cost $35,000 and after 400,000 units of production it is expected to have a trade-in value of $3,000. If the machine produced 45,000 units during the first year, the depreciation expense for the year is computed as follows:

$$\text{Depreciation expense} = \left(\frac{\text{Cost of asset} - \text{Salvage value}}{\text{Total estimated units of production}}\right)$$

$$\times \left(\begin{array}{c}\text{Units produced in the}\\ \text{current period}\end{array}\right)$$

$$= \left(\frac{\$35,000 - \$3,000}{400,000 \text{ units}}\right) \times (45,000 \text{ units})$$

$$= \$3,600$$

Comparison of methods. Only the straight-line, declining-balance, and sum-of-the-years'-digits methods can be accurately compared. The units-of-production method is not comparable because it is based on a variable (production) and is not calculated in advance by using a formula. The table and graph in Illustration 18–2 show the results achieved under each of the three methods. Calculations are based on an asset costing $1,000 with an expected salvage of $100 at the end of five years.

Note that the straight-line method results in a straight horizontal line. This occurs because equal amounts of depreciation expense are recorded each year.

The declining-balance method results in a curved line. The line is curved because the depreciation charge each year is determined by multiplying the book value by 40 percent (twice the straight-line rate of 20 percent). When the declining-balance method is used, the salvage value at the end of five years is $77.76. To make the salvage

ILLUSTRATION 18–2

Year	Straight-Line Method		Declining-Balance Method		Sum-of-the-Years'-Digits Method	
	Depreciation Expense	Book Value	Depreciation Expense	Book Value	Depreciation Expense	Book Value
0		$1,000.00		$1,000.00		$1,000.00
1	$180.00	820.00	$400.00	600.00	$300.00	700.00
2	180.00	640.00	240.00	360.00	240.00	460.00
3	180.00	460.00	144.00	216.00	180.00	280.00
4	180.00	280.00	86.40	129.60	120.00	160.00
5	180.00	100.00	51.84	77.76	60.00	100.00

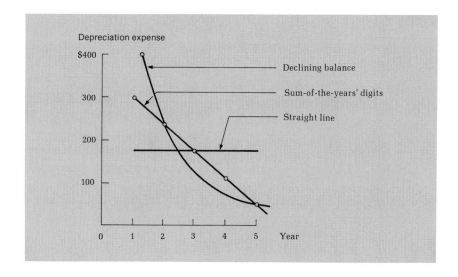

value equal $100, the depreciation charges for the later years should be reduced. For example, the depreciation expense for year 5 should be only $29.60 so that a $100 salvage value will remain. Since the declining-balance method multiplies an asset's book value each year by a fixed percentage, the book value will never equal zero and will seldom equal the salvage value at the end of the asset's life. For this reason, depreciation charges must usually be adjusted in the asset's later years.

The sum-of-the-years'-digits method results in a straight line that decreases by a fixed amount each year. In our example, the depreciation expense declines by $60 each year. Notice that this is $\frac{1}{15}$ of the asset's net cost ($\frac{1}{15} \times \$900$). Since each year's fraction decreases by $\frac{1}{15}$, the depreciation charges produce a downward sloping straight line.

ACCOUNTING FOR PLANT ASSETS

The accounting system used to record the acquisition, depreciation, and disposal of tangible plant assets will depend on the size of the business. If only a few plant assets exist, a separate account for each will be kept in the general ledger along with the asset's accumulated depreciation account (except for land, which is not depreciated). Since each asset is accounted for separately, the periodic depreciation charge for each asset will be individually calculated.

If there are many plant assets, the general ledger will not include separate accounts for each asset. Instead, a control account will be used in the general ledger for each class of assets, and individual accounts for each asset will be recorded in a subsidiary ledger. The subsidiary records are often kept on cards or sheets with spaces for recording the asset's acquisition, depreciation, and final disposition. By using the asset record cards, the accountant can quickly see an asset's past and present accounting status. Asset record cards will be discussed later in the chapter after we have studied the basic journal entries used in accounting for tangible plant assets.

PURCHASE OF ASSETS

Accounting for the purchase of an asset is relatively simple. Accountants record assets at their cost. The purchase is recorded by debiting the asset account for the cost of the asset and crediting either Cash or a payable or both. Both Cash and a payable are credited when an asset is purchased by making a partial cash payment and promising to pay the balance later. Payment may also be made by exchanging an existing asset other than cash. Then the asset traded will be credited instead of Cash or a payable.

For example, assume that Jim's Printing Shop purchased a printing press for $15,000 cash on January 5. The machine is expected to have a salvage value of $1,000 at the end of 10 years. To record the purchase, the following general journal entry is required.

		GENERAL JOURNAL				
DATE 1987		ACCOUNT AND EXPLANATION	P.R.	DEBIT	CREDIT	
Jan.	5	Printing Press		1 5 0 0 0 00		
		Cash			1 5 0 0 0 00	
		Purchase of printing press for $15,000 cash.				

If Jim's Printing Shop had not paid cash, a different account, usually either another asset or a liability account, would have been credited.

DEPRECIATION OF ASSETS

A depreciation schedule is prepared at least annually and includes the following:

1. Description of the asset.
2. Depreciation method used.
3. Useful life of the asset.
4. Salvage value of the asset, if applicable.
5. Accumulated depreciation as of the beginning of the accounting period.
6. The current period depreciation expense.
7. Accumulated depreciation as of the end of the accounting period.

A schedule is usually maintained for each plant asset account in the general ledger. Once depreciation schedules have been prepared, the monthly or yearly depreciation charges are easy to make. Assume that Jim's Printing Shop records depreciation expense at the end of each year and uses the straight-line method. The following general journal entry is made at the end of each of the 10 years:

		GENERAL JOURNAL				
DATE		ACCOUNT AND EXPLANATION	P.R.	DEBIT	CREDIT	
1987						
Dec.	31	Depreciation Expense—Printing Press		1 4 0 0 00		
		Accumulated Depreciation—Printing Press			1 4 0 0 00	
		To record depreciation on Printing Press				
		No. 60423.				

Because Jim's Printing Shop is a small company and has few assets, the accountant makes individual entries for each asset. In a larger firm, depreciation charges would be summarized in the subsidiary records, and an entry would be made in the general journal for each class of assets. The number of entries made will depend on the detail desired in the general journal and periodic statements.

As noted earlier, an asset's cost less the accumulated depreciation to date is the asset's book value. Whenever an asset is disposed of, the depreciation must be brought up to date to the nearest full month. Unless the depreciation is adjusted before the asset's disposal, the calculation of the gain or loss on disposal will be incorrect.

DISPOSAL OF ASSETS

An asset is normally disposed of in one of three ways:

1. Disposal through sale.
2. Disposal through exchange.
3. Disposal by retiring or discarding.

These are **voluntary disposals** made in the ordinary course of business. A fourth possibility for disposal exists when assets are destroyed by natural disaster or stolen. This is known as an **involuntary disposal.** The discussion in this chapter will focus on accounting for voluntary disposals.

Disposal through sale

As previously mentioned, it is necessary to know an asset's book value in order to determine the proper gain or loss on its sale. The difference between an asset's cost and the depreciation recorded to date is the asset's book value.

Assume that Jim's Printing Shop bought a typewriter for $500 on January 4, 1984. The machine is depreciated at 10 percent per year. On July 1, 1987, the company sold the machine. Before the entry is made to dispose of the typewriter, depreciation must be recorded to the date of sale. If the company records depreciation on December 31 of each year, depreciation expense for the period January 1, 1987, through June 30, 1987, must be recorded. Depreciation expense must be updated because the last depreciation entry was made on December 31, 1986. Therefore, the following journal entry is made:

GENERAL JOURNAL					
DATE 1987	ACCOUNT AND EXPLANATION	P.R.	DEBIT	CREDIT	
June 30	Depreciation Expense—Typewriter		2 5 00		
	Accumulated Depreciation—Typewriter			2 5 00	
	To record depreciation for one-half year				
	($500 × .10 × ½).				

No matter how the asset is disposed of, the depreciation charges must first be brought up to date. The following discussion will assume that depreciation has been recorded to the date of sale.

After Jim's Printing Shop records the depreciation for January 1 through June 30, the typewriter has a book value of $325. The book value is computed as follows:

$500   Cost
- (150)   Depreciation for January 1, 1984, to December 31, 1986
       (500 × .10 × 3)
- (25)   Depreciation for January 1, 1987, through June 30, 1987
$325   Book value

If the asset is sold for $325, there is no gain or loss because the book value equals the sales price. If the typewriter is sold for cash, the following journal entry is made:

GENERAL JOURNAL					
DATE 1987	ACCOUNT AND EXPLANATION	P.R.	DEBIT	CREDIT	
July 1	Cash		3 2 5 00		
	Accumulated Depreciation—Typewriter		1 7 5 00		
	Typewriter			5 0 0 00	
	To record sale of typewriter.				

If the typewriter is sold for $425, a gain of $100 must be recorded. The gain is the excess of the sales price over the asset's book value, calculated as follows:

$425   Sales price
−325   Book value
$100   Gain on sale

The sale of the typewriter for $425 requires the following general journal entry:

		GENERAL JOURNAL						
DATE 1987		ACCOUNT AND EXPLANATION	P.R.	DEBIT	CREDIT
July	1	Cash		425 00	
		Accumulated Depreciation—Typewriter		175 00	
		Typewriter			500 00
		Gain on sale of Typewriter			100 00
		To record sale of typewriter.			

If the typewriter is sold for $200, there is a loss of $125, calculated as follows:

$$\begin{array}{ll} \$325 & \text{Book value} \\ -200 & \text{Sales price} \\ \hline \$125 & \text{Loss on sale} \end{array}$$

The sale of the typewriter for $200 requires the following entry:

		GENERAL JOURNAL						
DATE 1987		ACCOUNT AND EXPLANATION	P.R.	DEBIT	CREDIT
July	1	Cash		200 00	
		Accumulated Depreciation—Typewriter		175 00	
		Loss on Sale of Typewriter		125 00	
		Typewriter			500 00
		To record sale of typewriter.			

In all of the preceding entries, it is important to note that (1) the asset is removed by crediting the particular asset account; (2) the accumulated depreciation account is debited, thus eliminating depreciation charges to date for the disposed asset; (3) cash is debited for the sales price of the asset; and (4) the difference between the debits and credits is the gain or loss on disposal and is recorded as either a debit (loss) or a credit (gain). If the entry is properly made, it has the effect of completely removing the asset and the related accumulated depreciation account from the books. This is desirable because the asset has been removed from the business.

Disposal through exchange

When new equipment is purchased, the asset being replaced is frequently traded as part of the payment. The difference between the sales price and the trade-in allowance of the old asset is referred to as **boot** (the balance owed). If the trade-in allowance is less than the old asset's book value, there is a loss; if it is greater than the book value, there is a gain. However, according to *APB Opinion No. 29,* gains on the exchange of similar assets are not recognized on a firm's books.

The asset being traded is often similar to the asset being bought. The income tax laws state that if assets are traded for similar assets, there will be no gain or loss recorded. In such situations, the cost of the new asset is adjusted for any gain or loss resulting from the exchange.

For example, assume that on January 2, 1985, Jim's Printing Shop bought a truck that cost $15,000. On January 2, 1987, the company decides to trade in the old truck for a new one. Total depreciation taken to date is $5,000. Therefore, the book value of the truck is $10,000 ($15,000 − $5,000). The company is given a trade-in allowance of $12,000 in exchange for a new truck costing $18,000. Therefore, the boot, or cash, that Jim's Printing Shop must pay is $6,000 ($18,000 − $12,000). Because similar assets are being exchanged, no gain or loss is recorded. The basis, or cost, of the new asset is $16,000 ($10,000 book value + $6,000 boot given). The general journal entry to record the exchange is as follows:

		GENERAL JOURNAL			
DATE		ACCOUNT AND EXPLANATION	P.R.	DEBIT	CREDIT
1987					
Jan.	2	Truck (new)		16 0 0 0 00	
		Accumulated Depreciation—Truck		5 0 0 0 00	
		Truck (old)			15 0 0 0 00
		Cash			6 0 0 0 00
		To record exchange of old truck for new truck.			

When dissimilar assets are exchanged, gains and losses are recorded. For example, assume that a car is traded for a tractor. The car originally cost $10,000, and after recording depreciation to date, it has a book value of $4,000 ($10,000 cost − $6,000 accumulated depreciation). The new tractor costs $16,000. A trade-in allowance of $11,000 is given for the car, so a cash payment of $5,000 ($16,000 − $11,000) is required. The gain to be recorded is $7,000, which represents the difference between the book value of the car ($4,000) and the trade-in allowance ($11,000). The transaction is recorded with the following general journal entry:

GENERAL JOURNAL

DATE 1987		ACCOUNT AND EXPLANATION	P.R.	DEBIT	CREDIT
May	1	Tractor		16 0 0 0 00	
		Accumulated Depreciation—Car		6 0 0 0 00	
		Car			10 0 0 0 00
		Gain on exchange of Car			7 0 0 0 00
		Cash			5 0 0 0 00
		To record exchange of car for tractor.			

If the trade-in allowance had been less than the $4,000 book value of the car, there would have been a loss as a result of the exchange. It should be noted that when assets are exchanged, it is as if the old assets were sold and the new assets were purchased in separate transactions. If two entries were made, the net effect would be the same as the entry shown above.

Disposal by retiring or discarding

Sometimes assets are thrown away. In such cases the recording of a loss depends on whether the asset has been fully depreciated. If the discarded asset has not been fully depreciated, the loss will equal the book value. For assets that have no book value, there will be no loss. The asset will be eliminated from the accounts by debiting the accumulated depreciation account and crediting the asset account for the cost of the asset.

Assume that an office desk costing $250 is discarded when it has a book value of $35. The following general journal entry shows the disposal and loss of $35:

GENERAL JOURNAL

DATE 1987		ACCOUNT AND EXPLANATION	P.R.	DEBIT	CREDIT
Dec.	31	Accumulated Depreciation—Office Desk		2 1 5 00	
		Loss on Disposal of Desk		3 5 00	
		Office Desk			2 5 0 00
		Disposal of office desk.			

In summary, every time a tangible plant asset is disposed of (through sale, exchange, or retirement), two important steps must be taken.

1. The depreciation account must first be brought up to date.
2. The asset and related accumulated depreciation account must be removed from the books.

ASSETS IN FINANCIAL STATEMENTS

The way in which a company shows assets and their depreciation in its financial statements depends on the amount of detail desired. Depreciation expense is usually classified as an operating expense on the income statement. Depreciation of assets used in selling may be classified as selling expenses, while depreciation of assets used for administrative purposes (desks, chairs, and office equipment) may be classified as general and administrative expenses.

Because the accumulated depreciation accounts are closely related to the corresponding asset accounts, accumulated depreciation is shown as a deduction from the cost of the asset on the balance sheet. The net figure represents the asset's book value.

Although the net amount (cost   accumulated depreciation) is referred to as the asset's book value, it is not the asset's market value. The net amount is not expected to equal the market value. The amount that an asset might be sold for has no effect on its book value. The book value should be viewed only as the portion of an asset's cost that has not been charged to operations.

ASSET RECORDS

For tracking purposes, information about each asset is usually kept on asset record cards or sheets. The record cards describe the assets and give necessary information so that depreciation charges can be calculated. The following notes are descriptions of the information recorded on the asset record card shown in Illustration 18–3.

ILLUSTRATION 18–3

Asset Record Card

ASSET RECORD							
Description Riding lawn mower				Account Yard equipment			
Estimated life 4 years				Annual depreciation rate 25%			
Estimated salvage value $200				Annual depreciation $200			

Cost				Depreciation			
Date Purchased		Description	Amount	Year	Rate	Amount	Total to Date
July 1984	1	Riding lawn mower (Lazy Garden Shop)	1,000 00	1984	25%	100 00	100 00
				1985	25%	200 00	300 00
Date Sold				1986	25%	200 00	500 00
				1987	25%	100 00	600 00
June 1987	30	Sold mower for $450 Cash gain of $50					

1984

July   1   Purchased a riding lawn mower from the Lazy Garden Shop for $1,000 with an estimated life of 4 years and estimated salvage value of $200.

Dec. 31   Annual depreciation of $100 (25 percent rate).

1985

Dec. 31   Annual depreciation of $200 (25 percent rate).

1986

Dec. 31   Annual depreciation of $200 (25 percent rate).

1987

June 30   Annual depreciation of $100 (25 percent rate).

     30   Sold mower for $450 cash.

The entry to bring depreciation up to date for the year 1987 is:

	GENERAL JOURNAL					
DATE		ACCOUNT AND EXPLANATION	P.R.	DEBIT		CREDIT
1987						
June	30	Depreciation Expense		1 0 0 00		
		Accumulated Depreciation—Yard Equipment.				1 0 0 00
		To bring depreciation up to date.				

The following general journal entry is made to record the sale:

		GENERAL JOURNAL			
DATE		ACCOUNT AND EXPLANATION	P.R.	DEBIT	CREDIT
1987					
June	30	Cash		4 5 0 00	
		Accumulated Depreciation—Yard Equipment		6 0 0 00	
		Yard Equipment			1 0 0 0 00
		Gain on sale of Mower			5 0 00
		To record sale of mower.			

The use of asset record cards is most helpful when there are a large number of assets. Once the card is established, it provides the accountant with a simple method of keeping track of an asset's history and current status. In addition, it aids in recording periodic depreciation charges.

INTANGIBLE ASSETS

As a class, intangible assets represent certain legal or economic rights a firm may obtain in the course of business. Included among intangible assets are patents, leases, copyrights, trademarks, and goodwill. Assets in this category have relatively long lives and have no physical substance beyond the certificates or other documents relating to them. Note that intangible assets, as the term is used in accounting, do not include items such as bank accounts, prepaid insurance, or accounts receivable.

In accounting, the treatment of intangible assets is the same as the treatment of tangible assets. The cost of the asset is spread over the time the asset has value to the company. However, the expensing of intangible assets is called *amortization* instead of depreciation. Also, the way the amortization is recorded and shown in the accounts is different from the method used for depreciation.

Patents.   Patents are granted by the federal government and give inventors the exclusive right to produce and sell their inventions for 17 years. Companies that incur research and development costs must expense these costs as they occur. If the research leads to the development of an item that can be patented, however, the cost incurred in applying for the patent is charged to the Patents account.

If a patent is purchased from its owner, the purchase price is debited to the Patents account. Costs incurred in a lawsuit to defend a patent are also debited to the Patents account.

For expensing purposes, it should not automatically be assumed that a patent's useful life will be the entire 17-year period of the patent rights. Rapid development in a field may lead to obsolescence before the 17 years pass.

For example, assume that a firm has purchased a patent for a total cost of $16,000. It is estimated that the patent has a remaining useful life of eight years. Using the straight-line method, the annual amortization cost for the patent would be $2,000 ($16,000 ÷ 8). The following journal entry illustrates how the amortization expense is recorded:

		GENERAL JOURNAL			
DATE 1987		ACCOUNT AND EXPLANATION	P.R.	DEBIT	CREDIT
Dec.	31	Amortization Expense		2 0 0 0 00	
		Patents			2 0 0 0 00
		Amortization of patents.			

Note that no Accumulated Amortization account is credited in the above entry. The credit is made directly to the Patents account. As a result, the amount of the Patents account appears on the balance sheet at its current book value. This method of crediting amortization directly to the asset account is used for most intangible assets.

Copyrights. A copyright is similar in many ways to a patent. It is a grant by the federal government of the exclusive right to reproduce and sell material for publication of a musical, artistic, or literary composition. Copyrights are issued for the life of the creator plus 50 years. Copyrights are rarely useful for that amount of time, and their estimated useful lives are usually much shorter.

The cost of obtaining a copyright may be small and, therefore, may be charged as a current expense. However, if the cost of purchasing a copyright is material in amount, the Copyrights account is debited. Amortization expense must be recorded periodically in the same manner as amortization expense for patents.

Assume that the Stratford Company has spent $20,000 to obtain several copyrights that have a useful life of 20 years. Computing amortization expense using the straight-line method, the annual amount is $1,000 ($20,000 ÷ 20 years). The entry to record the amortization is as follows:

		GENERAL JOURNAL			
DATE 1987		ACCOUNT AND EXPLANATION	P.R.	DEBIT	CREDIT
Dec.	31	Amortization Expense		1 0 0 0 00	
		Copyrights			1 0 0 0 00
		Amortization of copyrights.			

Trademarks.   To protect the unique means by which it identifies its products, a company often registers its trademarks and trade names in the United States Patent Office. This action, along with the continuous use of the trademark or trade name, protects the company from infringement by others.

The cost of buying the sole rights to use a trademark may range from a small amount to a material amount of money. Also, the life of a trademark may be estimated to extend indefinitely. These factors make it difficult to determine the amount of amortization expense that should be recorded each period. Normally, however, the cost of protecting a trademark should be expensed over a few years.

For example, assume that The Alford Company spends $12,000 to buy a trademark. The company decides to amortize the cost over a period of 12 years, thus expensing $1,000 ($12,000 ÷ 12 years) per year. The following entry shows how the expense is recorded:

		GENERAL JOURNAL			
DATE 1987		ACCOUNT AND EXPLANATION	P.R.	DEBIT	CREDIT
Dec.	31	Amortization Expense		1 0 0 0 00	
		Trademarks			1 0 0 0 00
		Amortization of trademarks.			

The amortization period for the cost of an intangible asset should not be longer than the legal life of the asset. Accounting pronouncements have limited the amortization period to a maximum of 40 years, even if the legal life of the asset is longer.

WASTING ASSETS

Wasting assets are real property that is consumed during production. Natural resources such as timber, oil and gas wells, and mines are wasting assets. The term *wasting* is used because it is expected that such valuable resources will eventually be completely exhausted. In some cases, such as oil and gas wells, only the resources below the surfaces are owned and not the actual land surface.

The expensing of wasting assets is called *depletion,* because that term best describes the manner in which the assets are consumed. Charges for depletion of wasting assets are similar to depreciation as calculated under the units-of-production method. The net cost of the property is determined by subtracting the expected salvage value from the property's cost. The net cost is then divided by the estimated number of units the property contains. The division results in the depletion expense per unit. Multiplying the unit expense by the number of units removed results in the depletion expense for the period.

Assume that the rights to drill for oil are acquired by the Maxwell Drilling Company for $1,000,000. It is estimated that there are 4,000,000 barrels of oil available for pumping. The first year resulted in the production of 900,000 barrels of oil. Depletion expense is computed as follows:

$$\frac{\text{Cost of oil pumping rights, } \$1,000,000}{\text{Expected number of barrels of oil, } 4,000,000} = 25¢ \text{ depletion expense per barrel}$$

Production of first year	900,000.00
	× 0.25
First year depletion expense . . .	$225,000.00

The following general journal entry reflects the first year's depletion expense:

GENERAL JOURNAL

DATE 1987		ACCOUNT AND EXPLANATION	P.R.	DEBIT	CREDIT
Dec.	31	Depletion Expense		22 5 0 0 0 00	
		Accumulated Depletion—Oil Well			22 5 0 0 0 00
		Depletion of 900,000 barrels at 25 cents per			
		barrel.			

The difference between the cost of the oil well rights and the accumulated depletion is the book value of the asset:

Cost of oil well rights.	$1,000,000
Less: Accumulated depletion. . . .	225,000
Book value of oil rights	$ 775,000

The depletion expense is reported as an operating expense on the income statement, and the asset and related accumulated depletion accounts are reported on the balance sheet.

Because the number of units to be produced is an estimate and changes from time to time, it is occasionally necessary to revise the per unit depletion expense. It is not necessary to adjust previous depletion charges. Instead, a new per unit depletion expense is calculated based on the asset's book value and the remaining estimated units to be produced. Assume that the oil well mentioned previously yields 1,100,000 barrels of oil the second year. At the end of the year, it is estimated that there are 1,400,000 barrels of oil remaining. The revised depletion expense would be calculated as follows:

$$\frac{\text{Book value of oil rights at beginning of year}}{\text{Production this year} + \text{Expected production}}$$

$$= \frac{\$775,000}{1,100,000 + 1,400,000} = 31\cent$$

Depletion charges on the current year's production would be $341,000 (1,100,000 barrels × 31 cents per barrel).

SUMMARY

Plant assets remain useful for several periods. They are also called long-lived assets, fixed assets, and capital assets. These assets can be classified in three ways: (1) by legal characteristics as either **real** or **personal property,** (2) by physical characteristics as either **tangible** or **intangible,** and (3) by accounting treatment characteristics. Using accounting treatment characteristics, plant assets are classified by whether they are depreciated, amortized, or depleted.

Depreciation reflects an asset's loss of usefulness as a result of physical and/or functional deterioration. An asset's **physical depreciation** is its decline in usefulness due to physical wear and tear. **Func-**

tional depreciation is loss of usefulness stemming from inadequacy or obsolescence.

To calculate depreciation expense, the **net cost, salvage value,** and useful life of an asset must be determined. An asset's salvage value and useful life are hard to determine because they are based on unknown future events.

There are four basic methods of calculating depreciation: (1) the straight-line method; (2) the declining-balance method; (3) the sum-of-the-years'-digits method; and (4) the units-of-production method. The method chosen should be based on the nature of the assets and the business operations involved.

A subsidiary ledger is normally kept to record the acquisition, depreciation, and disposal of tangible plant assets. A depreciation schedule is prepared periodically.

An asset is normally disposed of in one of three ways: (1) through sale, (2) through exchange, or (3) through retiring or discarding. When an asset is disposed of, the depreciation records should be updated and the asset and accumulated depreciation accounts should be removed from the books.

Intangible assets represent legal or economic rights obtained in the course of business. The cost of such assets is expensed through amortization. Intangible assets include patents, leases, copyrights, trademarks, and goodwill.

Wasting assets are real property that is consumed during production. They include natural resources such as timber, oil and gas wells, and mines. The expensing of the cost of such assets is called **depletion.**

KEY TERMS

Accumulated Depreciation—The total depreciation expense taken to date on an asset.

Amortization—The expensing of intangible assets.

Book Value (of Plant Asset)—Cost of the asset less accumulated depreciation or accumulated depletion.

Boot—The amount of cash paid when an old asset is exchanged for a new asset. It is equal to the difference between the sales price of the new asset and the trade-in allowance of the old asset.

Depletion—The expensing of wasting assets such as natural resources which are consumed or exhausted during production. Depletion expense is calculated by dividing the net cost (cost less salvage value) of the property by the estimated number of units the property contains. This results in the depletion expense per unit which is multiplied by the number of units removed to obtain the depletion expense for the period.

Depreciation—An estimate of the amount of a plant asset's cost that expires during a period. The periodic expense can be calculated using one of several different methods. The straight-line method allocates an equal amount of an asset's net cost to each period during its useful life. The declining-balance method applies a fixed percentage rate to the asset's book value each year. The result is a lower depreciation charge for each succeeding year. Using the sum-of-the-year's-digits method, depreciation expense is determined by multiplying the asset's net cost by a fraction. The denominator of the fraction is the sum of the years of the asset's expected life. The numerator is the expected number of years of service left in the asset at the beginning of the accounting period.

Functional Depreciation—The loss of usefulness of an asset because of inadequacy or obsolescence.

Intangible Assets—Assets which cannot be seen or touched but which do exist in a legal or economic sense. Patents, leases, copyrights, trademarks, and business goodwill are examples of intangible assets.

Involuntary Disposal—Assets are destroyed by natural disasters or stolen.

Net Cost—An asset's cost less any salvage or scrap value it may have after it has served its purpose.

Personal Property—All assets owned other than real property. Examples include equipment, trucks, patents, copyrights, office furniture, machinery, and tools.

Physical Depreciation—An asset's decline in usefulness because of physical wear and tear.

Plant Assets—Assets whose useful lives extend over several periods. The cost of such assets must be allocated to periods receiving benefits to determine proper periodic net income. Also referred to as long-lived assets, fixed assets, or capital assets.

Real Property—Land and anything that is attached to the land. It includes buildings, parking lots, loading docks, fences, and sidewalks.

Salvage Value—The expected value of an asset at the end of its useful life.

Tangible Assets—Assets which can be seen and touched. Buildings, land, and equipment are examples of tangible plant assets.

Voluntary Disposal—Assets are disposed of through sale, through exchange, or by retiring or discarding.

Wasting Assets—Real property which is consumed or used over time. Examples are natural resources such as timber, oil wells, gas wells, and mines.

QUESTIONS AND EXERCISES

1. What is the difference between real and personal property? Give three examples of each.
2. What is the difference between physical and functional depreciation? Name the factors influencing each.
3. What are two estimates that are used in calculating depreciation expense?
4. The Burr Company paid $9,000 cash for a car that has a five-year useful life and a $1,000 salvage value. What general journal entries should be made to record the purchase and the first year's depreciation expense using the straight-line method?
5. What is the reason for using the declining-balance method of depreciation?
6. The Talbot Corporation purchased a machine for $10,000. The machine is estimated to have a five-year useful life and the sum-of-the-years'-digits method for depreciation is to be used. What is the amount of depreciation expense for the first year assuming the machine was purchased at the beginning of the year? (Round to the nearest $.)
7. When can the units-of-production method be used to determine depreciation?
8. Name three ways to dispose of an asset voluntarily.
9. A tractor that originally cost $12,000 was sold for $5,000. The related accumulated depreciation account had a balance of $7,400

on the date of sale. What general journal entry should be made to record the sale?

10. What are wasting assets? Give some examples.

11. The Eddis Corporation paid $100,000 for rights to drill for oil. The well is expected to produce 400,000 barrels of oil. What is the depletion expense per barrel?

12. What is the book value of a coal mine that originally cost $2,000,000 and now has an accumulated depletion account balance of $500,000?

13. Define intangible assets and list three examples.

PROBLEMS

18–1. On January 3, 1987, the Reeves Company purchased a forklift for $33,700. The forklift is expected to have a useful life of eight years. The company plans to sell the forklift for $1,700 at the end of this period. Calculate the annual depreciation expense using the straight-line method.

18–2. The Angle Corporation purchased a machine on April 1, 1985, for $71,500. It has been estimated that the machine will produce 220,000 units during its entire useful life and that it will have no salvage value. Calculate the depreciation expense for 1985, 1986, and 1987, using the units-of-production method and the following information.

Year	Number of Units Produced
1985	40,000
1986	58,000
1987	49,000

18–3. The Bobco Manufacturing Company installed a computer on January 3, 1985. Given the following information about the computer, calculate the depreciation expense and book value for each of the five years of its estimated useful life and give the general journal entry to record the expense in 1987.

Cost: $500,000
Salvage value: 0
Depreciation method: Double-declining balance

18–4. The Jones Manufacturing Company purchased factory equipment costing $440,000. The equipment has a six-year useful life and a

$20,000 salvage value. Using the sum-of-the-years'-digits method, calculate the depreciation expense for each of the six years.

18–5. Give the general journal entries to record the following transactions for the Betagam Company.

1987

Jan. 3 Purchased land costing $40,000 and a building costing $125,000. Paid $50,000 cash and charged the rest to accounts payable. The building has a 40-year useful life and no salvage value.

Feb. 1 Purchased typewriter on account for $550. The typewriter has an estimated useful life of five years with an expected salvage value of $50.

Mar. 2 Purchased office desk for cash. The cost of the desk was $900, and it has an estimated useful life of eight years with an expected salvage value of $100.

Apr. 11 Purchased electronic desk calculator on account. The calculator cost $450 and has a $50 salvage value and an estimated useful life of five years.

May 2 Purchased on account a delivery truck costing $12,000. The truck has an expected useful life of eight years and a $2,000 salvage value.

Dec. 31 Record the depreciation expense for the year using the straight-line method for each item. (Make one compound general journal entry.) Compute depreciation to the nearest month.

18–6. Given below are three assets which the Yeagle Company owns:

Asset	Cost	Date of Purchase	Esti- mated Useful Life	Sal- vage Value	Depreciation Method
Truck	$12,500	June 30, 1981	8 years	$ 500	Straight-line
Machine	75,000	January 30, 1982	20 years	1,300	Units-of-production
Car	6,000	January 6, 1985	4 years	300	Sum-of-the years' digits

The machine produced the following number of units each year. It was expected to produce a total of 368,500 units during its entire useful life.

Year	Number of Units Produced
1982	25,000
1983	15,000
1984	27,000
1985	35,000
1986	40,000
1987	18,000

Required:

1. Complete the following schedule showing the depreciation expense for each asset for each of the years 1981–87.

Depreciation Expense Schedule
1981–1987

Years	Truck	Machine	Car	Annual Depreciation Expense
1981		—	—	
1982			—	
1983			—	
1984			—	
1985				
1986				
1987				
Accumulated depreciation as of December 31, 1987				

2. Total the rows to find the annual depreciation expense for each year and sum the columns to compute the accumulated depreciation account balances as of December 31, 1987.
3. Make the general journal entries to dispose of the assets on January 2, 1988, under the following circumstances:
   a. The truck was sold for $600.
   b. The machine became obsolete and was retired from service.
   c. The old car was exchanged for a new car that had an invoice price of $7,500. A $500 trade-in allowance was received on the exchange. (No gain or loss was to be recognized on the exchange.)

18–7. On February 27, 1986, the Minor Company acquired a coal mine at a cost of $1,200,000. It has been estimated that the mine contains

2,400,000 tons of coal. In 1986, 50,000 tons were mined, and 65,000 tons were mined in 1987.

Required:

1. Calculate the depletion expense per ton.
2. Make the general journal entries to record the depletion expense for 1986 and 1987.
3. Calculate the book value of the coal mine as of December 31, 1987.

18–8. Askan Corporation purchased a patent from a research company on April 30, 1987. The purchase price was $25,000. Askan Corporation estimated that the patent would have a useful life of 10 years. On July 1, 1987, the firm obtained a copyright for a professional manual. The costs involved in obtaining the copyright amounted to $12,000 and it was estimated that the useful life would be eight years.

Required:

1. Using the straight-line method, calculate amortization expense for both assets for 1987.
2. Record the 1987 entries in a general journal.

CHAPTER 19

Voucher system

LEARNING OBJECTIVES

Control over cash disbursements is an important function of any business. The contents and use of a voucher system is studied. After studying this chapter, you should be able to:

1. Record transactions in a voucher register.
2. Record transactions in a check register.
3. Foot and rule the registers.
4. Post to the Vouchers Payable account.
5. Prepare a schedule of unpaid vouchers.

Many companies use a voucher system to handle cash and control expenditures. A **voucher system** is a very important part of the overall accounting system because it provides documentation and control of the disbursement process. If a voucher system is used and is working properly, it is not easy for a person to embezzle company funds because functions are divided among different people. Before a cash payment can be made, written approval must be obtained. Corporate officers are authorized to approve specific expenditures, and a cashier is authorized to issue checks for approved payments. Without a voucher system, it is virtually impossible to control cash disbursements properly. A voucher system usually includes:

1. Vouchers.
2. A voucher register.
3. A Vouchers Payable account (general ledger).
4. Voucher checks.
5. A check register.

Voucher systems may be used for materials, payrolls, supplies, taxes, interest, payables, and other expenditures. Although voucher systems are quite flexible and can be used in most situations involving cash expenditures, these systems are not appropriate under all circumstances. Voucher systems are best used when one or more of the following conditions exist:

1. Invoices are paid in full when due rather than in partial payments.
2. Controls over expenditures are needed because there is a large number of transactions.
3. It is desirable to record invoices when received rather than when payment is made.

THE PURCHASING PROCESS

A voucher system for purchasing goods consists of several documents which are accumulated through a lengthy process. When a company purchases goods from a vendor, several steps must be performed. For illustration purposes, assume that the Star Manufacturing Company, an organization in the home building and repair business, needs certain items in its home repairs department. First, the department that needs the goods sends a purchase request to the purchasing department. An example of the requisition is shown in Illustration 19–1. The purchasing agent, after approving the purchase request, sends a purchase order to the vendor. The purchasing agent is an employee who is responsible for issuing purchase orders. The agent keeps a copy of the purchase order on file. See Illustration 19–2 for an example of a purchase order. When the company receives the goods from the vendor, the receiving clerk prepares a receiving report. The receiving report contains a description of the nature, quantity, and condition of the goods received. One copy of the receiving report is sent to the purchasing agent and another copy is sent to the accounting department. The purchasing agent compares the receiving report with the purchase order to make sure that the correct goods were received. Illustration 19–3 presents a diagram of the purchasing process.

When the goods are shipped, the vendor sends a **purchase invoice** to the purchaser's accounting department. The purchase invoice is

ILLUSTRATION 19–1

Purchase Requisition

Purchase Requisition No. __4706__

The STAR Manufacturing Co.
228 Cherry St.
Macon, Georgia 31204

Order from:

Southern Supply, Inc.
6103 Broad Street S.E.
Atlanta, Georgia 30303

Date Issued __February 12, 1987__
Date Required __March 5, 1987__
Deliver to __Jon Lattimer__
Requisitioning Department __Home repair__

Quantity	Description
25 gal.	Glue-it glue
20 gross	Brass screws
10 doz.	Hinges
15 boxes	Staples

Requisitioned by _Terry Carlson_
Approved by _Mary Harrison_
Purchase order __#105__

ILLUSTRATION 19–2

Purchase Order

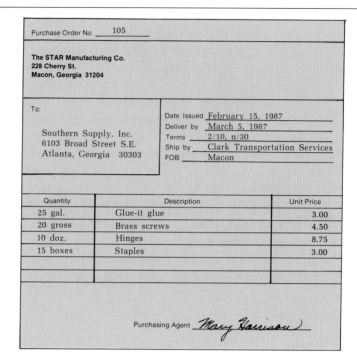

the bill for the goods supplied. Invoices may be received for purchases of materials, supplies, services, inventories, or plant assets.

The accounting department performs three functions in the purchasing process: (1) it verifies all extensions and additions; (2) it compares the purchase invoice with the **receiving report** to make

ILLUSTRATION 19–3

Purchasing Process

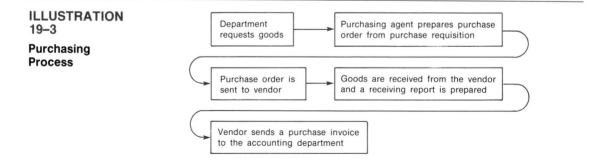

**ILLUSTRATION
19–4**

**Purchase
Invoice**

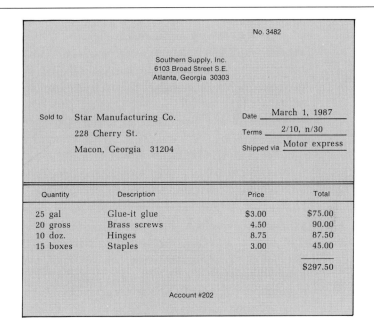

No. 3482

Southern Supply, Inc.
6103 Broad Street S.E.
Atlanta, Georgia 30303

Sold to   Star Manufacturing Co.

228 Cherry St.

Macon, Georgia   31204

Date _March 1, 1987_

Terms _2/10, n/30_

Shipped via _Motor express_

Quantity	Description	Price	Total
25 gal	Glue-it glue	$3.00	$75.00
20 gross	Brass screws	4.50	90.00
10 doz.	Hinges	8.75	87.50
15 boxes	Staples	3.00	45.00
			$297.50

Account #202

sure that the company is being billed for goods actually received; and (3) it indicates the account or accounts to be charged after invoice amounts are judged correct. Invoices for services are usually verified by the department that received the service.

Illustration 19–4 shows an invoice received by the Star Manufacturing Company from Southern Supply, Inc., for materials purchased on account. The receiving clerk prepared the receiving report for the materials. The prices and quantities were verified by the purchasing agent. The accounting department checked the extensions and compared the purchase invoice with the receiving report. Extensions are the amounts payable on the invoice that are calculated by multiplying the quantities of goods ordered and delivered by the unit prices charged by the vendor. The individual extensions are then added together (footed) to arrive at the total invoice amount.

VOUCHER PREPARATION

A **voucher** is a document used to record information about the purchase of goods or services. A voucher usually contains spaces for accounts to be charged, dollar amounts, approval, and authorization of payment along with other details. The purchase order, receiving report, and purchase invoice contain the information necessary to prepare the voucher. The voucher must then be authorized so that payments can be made for goods and services. Illustration 19–5 presents a diagram of the purchasing process when vouchers are used.

Vouchers are prepared for each invoice received except for minor expenses. (Such expenses are usually paid out of a petty cash fund.) The form of the voucher varies from business to business and depends upon the nature of the business, the accounts involved, and the voucher's routing through the business system. After a purchase invoice has been verified, the voucher clerk or other authorized person will prepare a voucher. The purchase invoice is attached to the voucher and sent to the accounting department. The accounting department compares the voucher with the verified invoice and related receiving report to make sure the voucher is complete and correct before making payment. The back of each voucher contains a payment summary. The date of payment, amount, and check number are recorded in the spaces provided.

The front and back of the voucher used by the Star Manufacturing Company are shown in Illustration 19–6. The voucher information was taken from the invoice shown in Illustration 19–4.

ILLUSTRATION 19–5   The Purchasing Process Using a Voucher System

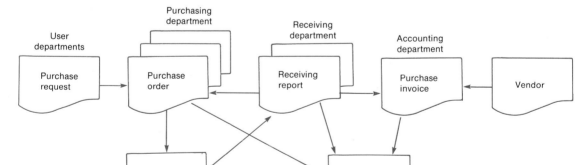

ILLUSTRATION 19–6

Voucher— Face

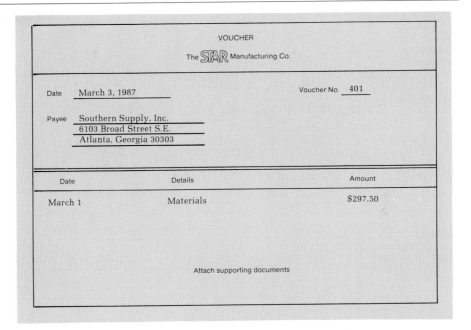

Voucher— Back

VOUCHER

The STAR Manufacturing Co.

| Date | March 3, 1987 | Voucher No. | 401 |

Payee Southern Supply, Inc.
6103 Broad Street S.E.
Atlanta, Georgia 30303

Date	Details	Amount
March 1	Materials	$297.50

Attach supporting documents

DISTRIBUTION

Materials	Manufacturing Expense		Operating Expenses		Sundry Accounts	
	Acct. No.	Amount	Acct. No.	Amount	Acct. No.	Amount
297 50						

Voucher Summary		Payment Summary	
Amount	297.50	Date	
Adjustment		Amount	
Discount	5.95	Check No.	
Net	291.55	Approved	Treasurer
Approved *D. L. W.*	Controller	Recorded	
Recorded *J. J.*			

miscellaneous

ILLUSTRATION 19–7

Voucher Register

DAY	VCHR. NO.	PAYEE	SUNDRY ACCOUNTS CR.			VOUCHERS PAYABLE CR.	PAID	
			ACCT. NO.	AMOUNT	√		DATE	CK. NO.
3	401	Southern Supply, Inc.				2 9 7 50	3/7	304
3	402	Butler Supply				1 8 08	3/16	309
4	403	Riverside Truck Co.				5 8 4 2 88		
5	404	Mid-South Lumber Co.				1 0 5 2 25	3/11	305
7	405	Sharp Suppliers				4 5 05	3/14	306
7	406	National Fire and Casualty Co.				1 6 5 00		
8	407	Tri-State Power Co.				4 0 8 19	3/15	307
15	432	Payroll (March 1-15)	404	2 9 5 51	√	3 3 6 7 37	3/15	308
			407	5 2 8 75	√			

individual posting   *total posting*

RECORDING VOUCHERS

When the voucher, invoice, and receiving report are complete and in agreement, the voucher is recorded in the **voucher register.** Since the voucher register is used to record the purchase of assets and services, it can be thought of as an enlarged purchases journal; it is also similar to an invoice register. The number and kinds of columns in the register depend on the nature of the business and the classification of accounts. For example, a manufacturing firm does not make the same kinds of purchases as a service business.

The Star Manufacturing Company uses the form of voucher register shown in Illustration 19–7. Voucher no. 401 (Illustration 19–6) is the first entry in the register. The voucher was recorded by debiting Materials Inventory, account no. 202, and crediting **Vouchers Payable** for $297.50.

Here is a summary of some vouchers that were recorded in the register for March 1 through March 15:

1987
Mar. 3   No. 401: Southern Supply, Inc., 6103 Broad Street, S.E., Atlanta; Materials, account no. 202; terms, March 1–2/10, n/30, $297.50.

3   No. 402: Butler Supply, 2020 Hawkins Ave; Office Supplies, account no. 208; terms, March 2–n/30, $18.08.

MATERIAL PURCHASES, DR.	MANUFACTURING EXP. DR.			OPERATING EXPENSE, DR.			SUNDRY ACCOUNTS, DR.		
	ACCT. NO.	AMOUNT	√	ACCT. NO.	AMOUNT	√	ACCT. NO.	AMOUNT	√
297.50									
							208	18 08	√
							303	5 842 88	√
1052.25									
	6402	45 05	√						
							210	165 00	√
	7410	408 19	√						
	6019	683 75	√	7403	543 18	√	601	888 18	√
				7404	1 328 02	√			
				7405	748 50	√			

individual posting

1987
Mar. 4 No. 403: Riverside Truck Company, 5340 Riverside Dr.; Delivery Truck, account no. 303; terms, March 3–n/30, $5,842.88. Charge to Delivery Equipment.

5 No. 404: Mid-South Lumber Company, 304 First Street, Dalton: Materials, account no. 202; terms, March 3–2/10, n/30, $1,052.25.

7 No. 405: Sharp Suppliers, 1010 Oak Rd; Factory Supplies, account no. 6402; terms, March 7–2/10, n/30, $45.05.

7 No. 406: National Fire and Casualty Company, 101 Courtland Ave; factory insurance premium, account no. 210; terms, March 5–n/60, $165.

8 No. 407: Tri-State Power Company, 1084 Jackson Street; factory power bill, account no. 7410; terms, March 6–n/10, $408.19.

15 No. 432; Payroll, March 1–15. Distributed as follows: Office Salaries Expense, account no. 7403, $543.18; Officers' Salaries Expense, account no. 7404, $1,328.02; Sales Salaries Expense, account no. 7405, $748.50; Direct Labor, account no. 601, $888.18; Indirect Labor, account no. 6019, $683.75; Taxes Withheld; FICA Taxes Payable, account no. 404, $295.51; Employees' Income Taxes Payable, account no. 407, $528.75.

It should be noted that some of the voucher entries do not have a date paid and a check number. Not all vouchers are paid immediately. The blank lines indicate that a voucher is outstanding and must be paid at a later date.

The total payroll entry can be handled by the voucher system in the same way as any other payment. The payroll distribution detail is included on the voucher to record the payroll transaction properly. Voucher no. 432 is based on a payroll schedule prepared by the payroll clerk. The amount payable is determined by deducting the taxes withheld. Wages and salaries earned, during the March 1–15 period amount to $4,191.63. The total is based on the following payroll amounts:

Distribution	Amount
Office salaries	$ 543.18
Officers' salaries	1,328.02
Sales salaries	748.50
Direct labor	888.18
Indirect labor	683.75
Total	$4,191.63

In order to record voucher no. 432, three lines are used in the voucher register. This is because three separate labor accounts in the operating expense ledger are involved. To meet legal requirements, it is necessary to record the payroll taxes that the employer must pay. The general journal entry used to record these taxes is shown below:

GENERAL JOURNAL

DATE		ACCOUNT AND EXPLANATION	P.R.	DEBIT	CREDIT
1987					
Mar.	15	Operating Expenses		347 11	
		Manufacturing Expenses		208 28	
		FICA Taxes Payable			295 51
		FUTA Taxes Payable			33 53
		State Unemployment Taxes Payable			226 35
		To record employer's payroll tax expense.			

Note that the tax liabilities are debited to general ledger accounts (Operating Expenses and Manufacturing Expenses). Because the amounts are debited to control accounts, it is also necessary to record the amounts in detail in the subsidiary ledgers. The debit of $347.11 to Operating Expenses is recorded in the subsidiary operating expense ledger by debiting Payroll Taxes—Administrative, account no. 7418, for $247.93 and by debiting Payroll Taxes—Sales, account no. 7427, for $99.18. The debit of $208.28 to Manufacturing Expenses is recorded in the subsidiary manufacturing expenses ledger by debiting Payroll Taxes—Factory, account no. 6023, for $208.28.

The Star Manufacturing Company uses the following procedure to record the payroll expenses and related tax liabilities:

1. Employee timecards are checked for completeness and reasonableness. After recorded hours are shown to be correct, the gross earnings are determined for each employee. A payroll clerk then prepares a payroll summary report showing:
   a. Classification of wages earned (classification usually determines the accounts to be charged).
   b. Total earnings to be charged to each account.
   c. Total deductions (taxes, insurance).
   d. Net amount of wages payable.
2. A voucher is prepared to record the payroll and is entered in the voucher register. The voucher includes debits to the proper labor accounts and credits to the related tax liability accounts and a credit to Vouchers Payable for the net amount of wages payable.
3. After the payroll voucher is prepared and approved, the treasurer or other authorized officer issues a check in payment of the payroll voucher. The check is made payable to Payroll. The check can then be used to meet the payroll in one or more of the following ways:
   a. The check is cashed at the bank and funds are obtained in proper denominations to pay employees in cash.
   b. The check is cashed and funds are deposited directly in employees' bank accounts.
   c. Individual payroll checks are drawn after the check has been deposited in a special payroll checking account. The check issued for the net amount of the payroll is recorded by debiting Vouchers Payable and crediting the proper bank account.
4. A general journal entry is made to record the employer's liability for payroll taxes. Payroll taxes that the employer must pay may be recorded each payday or at the end of each month.

Regardless of whether the payroll taxes are recorded each payday or at the end of each month, a voucher should be prepared when such taxes become due. After the voucher has been authorized, it is recorded in the voucher register by debiting the appropriate liability accounts and crediting Vouchers Payable. When the taxes are paid, payment is recorded by debiting Vouchers Payable and crediting the proper bank account.

The number of accounts that are debited in recording the payroll taxes depends on the kind of business and the detail desired in the accounting records. A manufacturing business may wish to separate expenses related to factory wages, administrative salaries, and sales salaries. In that case, separate expense accounts for taxes are kept for each category of wages. Note from the earlier discussion that the Star Manufacturing Company uses separate expense accounts for payroll taxes for the factory, administrative, and sales departments.

The voucher register is proved by footing each column in the register. The sum of the debits is compared with the sum of the credits to make sure that they are equal. The register should be proved before carrying footings forward to the next page and before making summary postings.

FILING UNPAID VOUCHERS

There is no set procedure for filing **unpaid vouchers.** Once the vouchers are recorded in the register, they may be filed alphabetically or numerically by date due. When the vouchers are filed numerically by date due only the vouchers at the front of the file need to be examined to determine which ones are due. Regardless of the method of filing, the invoices represented by the vouchers should be paid according to their terms. Late payments not only result in lost discounts but may also damage a company's credit rating.

POSTING THE VOUCHER REGISTER

Amounts in the voucher register are posted both individually and in summary. Items in the Manufacturing Expenses debit column are posted individually to the proper accounts in the manufacturing expense subsidiary ledger. In addition, amounts in the Operating Expense debit column are posted to the operating expense subsidiary ledger. Individual items in the Sundry Accounts debit and credit columns are posted to the designated accounts in the general ledger. As each item is posted, a check mark ($\sqrt{}$) is made in the voucher register's check mark column. Also, the page number of the voucher register should be entered in the P.R. column of the ledger account being posted. Illustration 19–7 shows the results of the posting process.

At the end of each month or other specified period, the following summary postings are made from the voucher register:

1. The Materials Purchases debit column total is posted as a debit to the Materials Purchases account in the general ledger.
2. The Manufacturing Expense debit column total is posted as a debit to the Manufacturing Expense account in the general ledger.
3. The Operating Expense debit column total is posted as a debit to the Operating Expense account in the general ledger.
4. The Vouchers Payable credit column total is posted as a credit to the Vouchers Payable account in the general ledger.

Note that each posting is made to a control account in the general ledger. As each column total is posted, the number of the account used is recorded below the column total. The page number of the voucher register is recorded in the P.R. column of the ledger account to which the voucher is posted. Individual items in the manufacturing expense and operating expense columns are also posted to individual accounts in the appropriate subsidiary ledgers. Thus, the manufacturing and operating expenses are posted in total to the control accounts in the general ledger and also as individual items in the subsidiary ledgers. To avoid posting the totals of the Sundry Accounts debit and credit columns, it is a common practice to place a check mark ($\sqrt{}$) below these column totals. This serves as an indication that these column totals should not be posted in summary because they have been posted as individual amounts. Totals in Illustration 19–7 are not posted because it is not the end of the month.

VOUCHER PAYMENTS

As already emphasized, a voucher system is used to control expenditures. When payment is due, or shortly before, the treasurer or other authorized person must approve the expenditure. After approval,

ILLUSTRATION 19–8

Voucher Check

Last National Bank			66-101 2304

Date __March 7, 1987__   No. __304__

Pay to the order of __Southern Supply Inc.__ $ __291.55__

__Two hundred ninety one and 55/100__   Dollars

The STAR Manufacturing Co.

__Dwight Matthews__ Treasurer

- -

Detach statement before depositing check

THE STAR MANUFACTURING CO.

Attached check is for full settlement of the following   Date __March 7, 1987__

Invoice		Details	Invoice Amount	Deductions	Net Amount
Date	Number				
March 1	3482	Materials	297 50	5 95 (discount)	291 55

the voucher is delivered to the proper disbursing officer for payment. Payment may be made by an ordinary check, or by a special form of check called a **voucher check.** A voucher check has space for recording information from the invoice being paid. The form of voucher check used by the Star Manufacturing Company is shown in Illustration 19–8. The check was issued to Southern Supply, Inc., in payment of its March 1 invoice. The statement attached to the check describes the items purchased, date of invoice, invoice number, invoice amount, any deductions, and the net amount. Voucher checks are used to identify the items covered by the payment. This is helpful to the payee.

FILING PAID VOUCHERS

Paid vouchers may be filed in any convenient manner. The chosen method should permit easy access to the vouchers for later reference.

This is often accomplished by filing either numerically by voucher number or alphabetically by creditor. Quite often the canceled check or a copy of the canceled check is filed with the voucher.

RECORDING VOUCHER CHECKS

All checks issued by the Star Manufacturing Company are recorded in the check register shown in Illustration 19–9. It is not necessary to identify the accounts to be charged in the **check register** because this has already been done in the voucher register. However, quite often the check register will include a column for recording deductions made at the time of a payment. Note that the check register in Illustration 19–9 contains a column for purchases discount deductions. As checks are written and recorded in the check register, appropriate notation should also be made in the voucher register. When a check is issued, the date and number of the check are recorded in the voucher register to indicate that the voucher has been paid.

Here is a summary of the information shown in the check register in Illustration 19–9:

1987
Mar. 7 No. 304; Southern Supply, Inc., $291.55, in payment of voucher no. 401 for $297.50 less 2 percent discount.

11 No. 305: Mid-South Lumber Company, $1,031.21, in payment of voucher no. 404 for $1,052.25 less 2 percent discount.

14 No. 306: Sharp Suppliers, $44.15, in payment of voucher no. 405 for $45.05 less 2 percent discount.

15 No. 307: Tri-State Power Company, $408.19, in payment of voucher no. 407.

15 No. 308: Payroll, $3,367.37, in payment of voucher no. 432.

16 No. 309: Butler Supply, $18.08, in payment of voucher no. 402.

The check register is proved by footing the columns and determining that the Vouchers Payable debit column total is equal to the sum of the Purchases Discount credit and Bank credit column totals. The check register should be proved before making the summary postings and before column totals are carried forward to the next page. Illustration 19–10 shows a footed check register.

post total

ILLUSTRATION 19–9

Check Register

MONTH OF March 1987			CHECK REGISTER			PAGE 3	
VOUCHERS PAYABLE, DR.		DAY	PAYEE	PURCHASES DISCOUNT CR.	BANK, CR.		
NO.	AMOUNT				CK. NO.	AMOUNT	
401	297 50	7	Southern Supply, Inc.	5 95	304	291 55	
404	1052 25	11	Mid-South Lumber Co.	21 04	305	1031 21	
405	45 05	14	Sharp Suppliers	0 90	306	44 15	
407	408 19	15	Tri-State Power Co.		307	408 19	
432	3367 37	15	Payroll		308	3367 37	
402	18 08	16	Butler Supply		309	18 08	

ILLUSTRATION 19–10

Footed Check Register

MONTH OF March 1987			CHECK REGISTER			PAGE 3	
VOUCHERS PAYABLE, DR.		DAY	PAYEE	PURCHASES DISCOUNT CR.	BANK, CR.		
NO.	AMOUNT				CK. NO.	AMOUNT	
401	297 50	7	Southern Supply, Inc.	5 95	304	291 55	
404	1052 25	11	Mid-South Lumber Co.	21 04	305	1031 21	
405	45 05	14	Sharp Suppliers	0 90	306	44 15	
407	408 19	15	Tri-State Power Co.		307	408 19	
432	3367 37	15	Payroll		308	3367 37	
402	18 08	16	Butler Supply		309	18 08	
	5188 44			27 89		5160 55	
	(201)			(503)		(101)	

CHECK REGISTER POSTING

Since the check register involves only three general ledger accounts, no individual postings are necessary. At the end of each month or period, the check register is proved, and the column footings are posted.

The following posting procedures are used when making the summary postings from the check register:

1. The Vouchers Payable debit column total is posted as a debit to the Vouchers Payable account in the general ledger.
2. The Purchases Discount credit column total is posted as a credit to the Purchases Discount account in the general ledger.
3. The Bank credit column total is posted as a credit to the Bank account in the general ledger.

As the column totals are posted, the number of the account used is recorded below the column total. Illustration 19–10 shows that the check register has been posted. The page number of the check register is recorded in the P.R. column of the general ledger account.

VERIFYING VOUCHERS PAYABLE

Before a trial balance is taken, the Vouchers Payable account balance should be verified. This can be done by preparing a list of all unpaid vouchers. The total of unpaid vouchers should equal the balance of the general ledger Vouchers Payable account.

FRACTIONAL PAYMENTS

When a voucher system is used, full rather than partial payments should be made. A voucher system is generally not suitable when a business makes many partial payments. However, partial payments may sometimes occur in a business that uses a voucher system. In such cases special handling is required, and separate vouchers should be prepared for each intended payment.

If partial payments are to be made on a voucher that has already been prepared, it is best to cancel the original voucher and prepare two or more new ones. The sum of the new vouchers should equal the amount of the old voucher. When recording the new vouchers in the register, the debit may be to Vouchers Payable. This will offset the credit made to Vouchers Payable in recording the original invoice. The accounts debited in recording the original voucher will remain from the old voucher.

The following general journal entries illustrate the procedures that may be used when new vouchers are prepared to replace an old one:

GENERAL JOURNAL

DATE 1987		ACCOUNT AND EXPLANATION	P.R.	DEBIT	CREDIT
March	13	Materials		2 0 0 0 00	
		Vouchers Payable			2 0 0 0 00
		Original voucher prepared for purchase of			
		materials amounting to $2,000.			
		Vouchers Payable		2 0 0 0 00	
		Vouchers Payable			1 0 0 0 00
		Vouchers Payable			7 5 0 00
		Vouchers Payable			2 5 0 00
		Entry used to cancel original voucher and to			
		record new vouchers representing the fractional			
		payments to be made in the amounts of $1,000,			
		$750, and $250.			

Appropriate notation should be made in the voucher register to indicate that the original voucher has been canceled and to show the numbers of the new vouchers issued. Later payments for the new vouchers will be recorded in the usual manner.

TEMPORARY VOUCHER SETTLEMENT

A business may give a note in temporary settlement of a voucher that is due. Such a settlement may be recorded by debiting Vouchers Payable and crediting Notes Payable. Notation should be made on the original voucher and in the voucher register indicating that the voucher has been settled temporarily with a note. For example, assume that voucher no. 403 from the earlier illustrations is settled temporarily with a note. The following journal entry is made:

GENERAL JOURNAL

DATE		ACCOUNT AND EXPLANATION	P.R.	DEBIT	CREDIT
1987					
Mar.	21	Vouchers Payable		5 8 4 2 88	
		Notes Payable			5 8 4 2 88
		To record the temporary settlement of			
		voucher no. 403.			

A notation in the voucher register is also required, as shown below:

| | | | SUNDRY ACCOUNTS CR. | | | VOUCHERS | PAID | |
DAY	VCHR. NO.	PAYEE	ACCT. NO.	AMOUNT	√	PAYABLE CR.	DATE	CK. NO.
4	403	Riverside Truck Co.				5 8 4 2 88	Settled temporarily by a note 3-21-87	

VOUCHER REGISTER

A new voucher is authorized when the note becomes due. The new voucher is recorded in the voucher register. The entry in the voucher register is a debit to Notes Payable for the amount of the note, a debit to Interest Expense for the interest on the note, and a credit to Vouchers Payable for the amount of the voucher check (which includes principal and interest).

If a new note is issued in settlement of an old note and accrued interest, the entry may be a debit to Notes Payable for the amount of the old note, a debit to Interest Expense for the accrued interest on the old note, and a credit to Notes Payable for the amount of the new note. A voucher is prepared in the usual way when the new note becomes due. For example, assume that the note issued for voucher no. 403 is a 90-day, 11 percent note issued on March 21, 1987. When the note is due on June 19, 1987, a new note is issued in settlement. The following journal entry is made on June 19, 1987:

GENERAL JOURNAL

DATE		ACCOUNT AND EXPLANATION	P.R.	DEBIT	CREDIT
1987					
June	19	Notes Payable (old note)		5 8 4 2 88	
		Interest Expense		1 6 0 68	
		Notes Payable (new note)			6 0 0 3 56
		To record the note given in settlement of the 90			
		day, 11% note issued on 3-21-87.			

Interest expense is calculated as follows:

$$\$5,842.88 \times 11\% \times 90/360 = \$160.68$$

Sometimes a check is issued in payment of interest and in partial payment of the principal or an outstanding note. In this situation, a new note is issued for the balance of the principal and a voucher is prepared for the amount to be paid in cash. The voucher is recorded in the voucher register by debiting Notes Payable for the principal paid, debiting Interest Expense for the accrued interest, and crediting Vouchers Payable for the total amount paid. The voucher is then paid in the usual manner. The new note is issued for the remaining portion of the original note and is recorded in the general journal by debiting Notes Payable (old) and crediting Notes Payable (new) for the face amount of the new note. This entry effectively cancels the old note and records the new one. When the new note is due, a voucher is prepared, recorded, and paid in the usual manner. For example, assume that instead of issuing a new note for the old note and accrued interest as illustrated above, the accrued interest and $2,842.88 of the principal are paid. At the same time, a new 60-day, 11 percent note is issued for the remaining $3,000 of principal. The following entry is made in the voucher register:

MONTH OF June, 1987

VOUCHER REGISTER

| DAY | VCHR. NO. | PAYEE | SUNDRY ACCOUNTS CR. | | | VOUCHERS PAYABLE CR. | PAID | |
			ACCT. NO.	AMOUNT	√		DATE	CK. NO.
15	602	Riverside Truck Co.				3 0 0 3 56	6/19	566

The entry in the check register is as follows:

MONTH OF June 1987   **CHECK REGISTER**   PAGE 5

| VOUCHERS PAYABLE, DR. | | DAY | PAYEE | PURCHASES DISCOUNT CR. | BANK, CR. | |
NO.	AMOUNT				CK. NO.	AMOUNT
602	3 0 0 3 56	19	Riverside Truck Co.		566	3 0 0 3 56

An entry is also made in the general journal:

GENERAL JOURNAL

DATE		ACCOUNT AND EXPLANATION	P.R.	DEBIT	CREDIT
1987					
June	19	Notes Payable (old note)		3 0 0 0 00	
		Notes Payable (new note)			3 0 0 0 00
		To record the settlement of the 90 day, 11%			
		note issued 3-21-84 and the issuance of a new			
		60 day, 11 % note.			

PURCHASE RETURNS AND ALLOWANCES

The use of a voucher system will not prevent purchase returns and allowances. The effect of such transactions must be reflected in the voucher register and related accounts. If a credit memo is received for returned merchandise, the Vouchers Payable balance should be reduced.

MATERIAL PURCHASES. DR.	MANUFACTURING EXP. DR.			OPERATING EXPENSE. DR.			SUNDRY ACCOUNTS. DR.		
	ACCT. NO.	AMOUNT	√	ACCT. NO.	AMOUNT	√	ACCT. NO.	AMOUNT	√
				6501	1 6 0 68		210	2 8 4 2 80	

Returns and allowances may be recorded in several ways. If the return or allowance is related to a voucher that has been recorded in the current month, a correction can be made in the voucher register. If the return involves an item in the Operating Expense debit column, the correction can be made by recording the adjustment above the amount in question and also above the related amount in the Vouchers Payable credit column. To draw attention, the adjustment is usually circled or made in a different color ink. The correction should also be noted on the voucher itself. If the corrections are separately totaled for the Materials debit and Vouchers Payable credit columns, the materials total can be posted as a credit to the material Purchase Returns and Allowances account, and the total of the vouchers payable adjustments can be posted as a debit to Vouchers Payable. Keep in mind that this adjustment procedure can be used only in the same month that the voucher was recorded and before any summary postings involving the adjusted purchases have been made. Adjustments involving manufacturing expense, operating expense, or sundry account purchases must be posted individually.

If the return or allowance involves a voucher recorded in a previous month, the old voucher should be canceled and the adjustment recorded in the general journal. A new voucher is then prepared for the adjusted amount. Appropriate notation concerning the canceled voucher should be made in the register. Some accountants do not approve of the correction procedure described in the preceding paragraph and recommend that all returns and allowances be handled by canceling the old voucher and preparing a new one. That is the procedure used in large, complex businesses.

A procedure that is often used to record returns and allowances involves (1) noting the adjustment on the voucher, and attaching the credit memo to the voucher; (2) recording the correction in the voucher register beside the voucher being reduced; and (3) recording a general journal entry to reflect the transaction. The general journal entry involves a debit to Vouchers Payable and a credit to the account charged for the purchase (Purchase Returns and Allowances if for materials).

To illustrate the treatment of a purchase return, assume that the goods covered by voucher no. 406 from prior illustrations were returned to the vendor in April. The transactions for March have already been posted. Therefore, the voucher must be canceled. The following journal entry is made:

	GENERAL JOURNAL			
DATE	ACCOUNT AND EXPLANATION	P.R.	DEBIT	CREDIT
1987				
April 6	Vouchers Payable		2 9 7 50	
	Purchase Returns and Allowances			2 9 7 50
	To record the return of goods purchased.			

A notation is also made in the voucher register to indicate that voucher no. 406 has been canceled.

INVOICE CORRECTIONS

Because of mistakes in billing, a corrected invoice may be received after the original invoice has been recorded in the voucher register. The correction may either increase or decrease the amount of the original voucher. A general journal entry should be made to reflect the change in the original voucher. An explanation should be noted on the original voucher, and the corrected invoice should be attached to the original invoice and voucher. As with purchase returns and allowances, some accountants prefer to cancel the original voucher and prepare a new one.

VOUCHERS PAYABLE SUBSIDIARY LEDGER

A voucher system makes it unnecessary to keep a subsidiary accounts payable ledger. The Vouchers Payable account balance is supported by the unpaid voucher file. The voucher register also provides support because each blank line in the Paid column indicates an unpaid voucher.

If a subsidiary accounts payable ledger is not kept and unpaid vouchers are filed by date due, there is no way of rapidly determining the amount owed to a particular creditor. Such detailed information may not be important because most business executives are more concerned with the total amount payable rather than the amounts owed to individual creditors. If specific creditor information is desired, a subsidiary creditors' ledger may be kept by filing copies of vouchers by creditor.

VOUCHER SYSTEM AND THE PETTY CASH FUND

A petty cash fund eliminates the need to write checks for small cash payments. A petty cash fund may be kept by either an imprest or a journal method. The imprest method was discussed in Chapter 5. It requires that cash on hand plus disbursements equal the balance of the petty cash fund in the general ledger.

The journal method differs from the imprest method because disbursements are recorded in a journal as they are made. Under this method, each payment is recorded by debiting the proper account and crediting Petty Cash. Postings to the accounts involved are made directly from the journal. Under the imprest method, a journal entry is prepared from the information summarized in the petty cash disbursements record, and posting is done from this entry.

A voucher system does not affect the manner in which a petty cash fund is operated. The only difference is that a voucher must be prepared when the fund is replenished. These vouchers are recorded in the voucher register in the usual manner. When the imprest method is used, a voucher is prepared to create the fund, debiting Petty Cash and crediting Vouchers Payable. Subsequent replenishment of the fund is accomplished by preparing vouchers, debiting the proper accounts, and crediting Vouchers Payable. Under the journal method, vouchers issued for the petty cash fund are recorded by debiting Petty Cash and crediting Vouchers Payable.

Checks issued to petty cash under both methods are recorded by debiting Vouchers Payable and crediting the Bank account.

SUMMARY

A **voucher system** is used to handle cash and control expenditures; it usually includes the following:

1. Vouchers.
2. A voucher register.
3. A **Vouchers Payable account** (general ledger).
4. Voucher checks.
5. A check register.

A voucher system can be used in some but not all circumstances. Vouchers are best used when one of the following conditions exists:

1. Invoices are paid in full when due rather than in partial payments.
2. Controls over expenditures are needed because there is a large number of transactions.
3. It is desirable to record invoices when received rather than when payment is made.

The purchasing process generates several documents, including a purchase request, a purchase order, a receiving report, and a **purchase invoice.** The documents are compared and checked before a voucher is prepared.

A **voucher** is a document which contains all the necessary information for an employee to obtain authorization to pay invoices. A voucher normally contains spaces for accounts to be charged, dollar amounts, approval, and authorization of payment. The information needed to prepare a voucher is obtained from the purchase order, the receiving report, and the purchase invoice.

After a voucher is prepared, it is recorded in the **voucher register.** The amounts in the register are posted periodically both individually and in summary to the general ledger.

When vouchers are paid, a **voucher check** is issued. Voucher checks are entered into a check register. Periodically the **check register** is posted in summary to the appropriate general ledger accounts.

A voucher system should not be used in a business that often makes partial payments. If an occasional partial payment occurs, the original voucher should be canceled and a new voucher prepared. Vouchers may have to be canceled if a note is given to the vendor in temporary settlement of a voucher. When the note becomes due, a new voucher is prepared.

Invoice corrections can be handled by correcting the voucher and voucher register if the register has not been posted. If the register has already been posted, the voucher should be canceled and a new voucher issued.

Purchase returns and allowances also require special treatment. As with invoice correction, the purchase return and allowance can be made by adjusting the voucher register if the register has not yet been posted. Otherwise, the original voucher should be canceled and a new voucher issued.

A voucher system may also be used for reimbursements of a petty cash fund. The voucher does not affect the way the petty cash fund operates.

KEY TERMS

Check Register—A special register in which all checks written are recorded in numerical order.

Paid Voucher File—A permanent file in which vouchers that have been paid may be filed in any convenient manner, such as alphabetically or numerically.

Purchase Invoice—A document prepared by the seller that states the items shipped, the cost of the merchandise, and the method of shipment.

Receiving Report—A report that describes the nature, quantity, and condition of goods received.

Unpaid Vouchers File—A file in which unpaid vouchers may be filed either alphabetically or numerically by date due.

Voucher—A form which records information about the liability being incurred. It also has spaces for approval signatures, the date of the check used for payment, and the check number.

Voucher Checks—Checks that are issued in payment of vouchers. The canceled check or a copy of the canceled check is filed with the voucher in the paid voucher file.

Voucher Register—A journal in which prenumbered vouchers are recorded in numerical sequence.

Vouchers Payable Account—Similar to an Accounts Payable account, it is used when a voucher system is maintained.

Voucher System—A system that provides tight internal control over all cash disbursements.

QUESTIONS AND EXERCISES

1. What items are usually included in a voucher system?
2. Name some conditions under which it would be appropriate to use a voucher system.
3. Describe the functions of the accounting department in the purchasing process.
4. What is a voucher?
5. Why should vouchers be paid according to their terms?
6. How can the Vouchers Payable account balance be verified?
7. On May 1, a voucher was prepared for the purchase of a truck costing $8,000. On May 16, the company decided to make partial payments of $4,000, $2,500, and $1,500. What general journal entries are required to record (1) the purchase of the truck and (2) the decision to make partial payments?

8. What journal entry should be made when a note is issued in temporary settlement of a voucher that is due? What voucher register entry should be made when the note becomes due?

9. What, if anything, should be done to the voucher register when a voucher payment is entered in the check register?

10. What is the best way to handle partial payments of a voucher?

11. What correction should be made in the voucher register if a return of office supplies is related to a voucher that has been recorded in the current month?

12. What correction procedure is necessary if a purchase return or allowance involves a voucher recorded in the previous month?

13. What effect does a voucher system have on the petty cash fund?

PROBLEMS

19-1. Grayson Manufacturing, Inc., uses a voucher register like the one shown in Illustration 19-7. Vouchers are recorded in the register at their gross amounts. During the first half of February 1987, the following purchase invoices were received:

1987

Feb. 1 No. 412: Haley Suppliers, 207 Jocylin Ave; Materials, account no. 125; terms, January 30—2/10, n/30, $600.

2 No. 413: Royce Equipment Co., 1400 Perry St.; Factory Equipment, account no. 180; terms, February 1—2/10, n/60, $950.

3 No. 414: Regional Power Suppliers, 100 Second Ave.; Factory Power Bill, account no. 6122; terms, February 2—n/20, $215.

4 No. 415: Clay's, Inc., 1273 Pontiac Trail; Office Equipment, account no. 170; terms, February 2—2/10, n/30, $320.

5 No. 416: City Press, 111 Huron Ave.; Advertising, account no. 570; terms, February 1—n/10, $69.

7 No. 417: Maxey's Supply Company, 218 Saginaw Street; Materials, account no. 125; terms, February 5—2/10, n/30, $750.

8 No. 418: Hal's Repair Service, 7200 Telegraph Blvd.; Repairs to Factory Equipment, account no. 6217; terms, February 8—2/10, n/30, $125.

9 No. 419: Rayson & Holt, 690 Halsted; Factory Supplies, account no. 6271; terms, February 8—2/10, n/60, $210.

1987

Feb. 10 No. 420: Caldwell Motor Sales, 2000 Main St.; Delivery Truck, account no. 186; terms, February 10—2/20, n/60, $7,250.

11 No. 421: Simm's Insurance Agency, 1040 Wide Track; Office Equipment Insurance Premium, account no. 140; terms, February 11—n/30, $75.

12 No. 422: Basil's Material Supply, 2101 Sycamore Ave.; Materials, account no. 125; terms, February 10—2/10, n/30, $600.

14 No. 423: Jayne's, Inc., 2111 Angle Ave; Repairs to Delivery Truck, account no. 555; terms, February 14—net 20, $200.

Required:

1. Record the invoices in a voucher register. Assume the voucher number is the same as the invoice number.

2. Foot the amount columns of the voucher register.

19–2. Hamilton's Store maintains a check register like the one in Illustration 19–9. During the first two weeks of September, the following checks were issued in payment of vouchers:

1987

Sept. 1 No. 510: Hugh Company, $695.80, in payment of voucher no. 408 for $710 less 2 percent discount.

2 No. 511: Arnold's Supply Company, $260, in payment of voucher no. 409 for $260.

3 No. 512: Carson's Manufacturers, $656.60, in payment of voucher no. 418 for $670 less 2 percent discount.

5 No. 513: State Power Company, $160, in payment of voucher no. 416 for $160.

6 No. 514: Vale and Sons, $245, in payment of voucher no. 415 for $250 less 2 percent discount.

7 No. 515: Harrison's, Inc., $421.40, in payment of voucher no. 417 for $430 less 2 percent discount.

8 No. 516: Kane and Wolf, $85, in payment of voucher no. 422 for $85.

9 No. 517: Sharren Company, $607.60, in payment of voucher no. 424 for $620 less 2 percent discount.

10 No. 518: National Telephone Company, $63, in payment of voucher no. 425 for $63.

1987

Sept. 12   No. 519: Royston Company, $147, in payment of voucher no. 427 for $150 less 2 percent discount.

　　　13   No. 520: Clarkston and Clark, $215.60, in payment of voucher no. 426 for $220 less 2 percent discount.

　　　14   No. 521: Herron Suppliers, $300, in payment of voucher no. 430 for $300.

Required:

1. Record the checks in a check register.

2. Foot the amount columns of the check register.

19–3.   Tiffin and Till is a wholesale store that sells a variety of merchandise to retailers. A voucher register is one of the accounting records used by Tiffin and Till. The voucher register contains debit columns for purchases, operating expenses, and sundry accounts and credit columns for vouchers payable and sundry accounts. During July 1987 the following transactions relating to vouchers occurred:

1987

July 1   Received an invoice for $400 from Coolidge Realtors, 617 Jordan Avenue, for rent, account no. 536.

　　　2   Received a telephone bill for $75 from Franklin Telephone Company, 2110 Lancelot Place (account no. 544).

　　　2   Received an invoice for $500 from Stonehead Manufacturing Company, 692 Cherokee Avenue, Charlotte, for merchandise purchases; terms, July 1—2/10, n/30.

　　　5   Received an invoice for $150 from Cal's Supply Company, 1020 Kingston Road, for office supplies, account no. 540; terms, July 5—net 20.

　　　6   Received an invoice for $650 from Stewart's Distributors, 540 Pope Street, Kansas City, for merchandise purchases; terms, July 2—2/10, n/30.

　　　7   Received an invoice for $350 from Galahad Equipment Company, 418 Buckhead Road, Montgomery, for office equipment, account no. 145; terms, July 5—2/10, n/30.

　　　8   Received an invoice for $125 from Farmington Advertising Company, 598 Christmas Lane, for advertising, account no. 542.

　　　9   Received an invoice for $860 from Stomper-Tack Manufacturers, 302 South Green Street, Augusta, for merchandise purchases; terms, July 7—2/10, n/30.

1987

July 12 Received an invoice for $250 from Kersey Suppliers, 198 Woodlake Plaza, for store supplies, account no. 538; terms, July 12—net 20.

13 Received an invoice for $45 from Lane's Repair Shop, 211 Scott Road, for repairs to office equipment, account no. 552; terms, July 13—net 5.

15 Prepared a voucher for the payroll. Payroll was distributed as follows: Office Salaries Expense, account no. 524, $525; Officers' Salaries Expense, account no. 525, $890; Sales Salaries Expense, account no. 526, $1,250; FICA Taxes Payable, account no. 205, $173; Employees' Income Taxes Payable, account no. 206, $465.

19 Received an invoice for $50 from the *Concord Times,* 111 North Avenue, for advertising, account no. 542.

20 Received an invoice for $680 from Twin Equipment Company, 984 Parkview Square, for store equipment, account no. 155; terms, July 20—n/30.

21 Received an invoice for $55 from Cal's Supply Company, 1020 Kingston Road, for office supplies, account no. 540; terms, July 20—net 20.

22 Received an invoice for $750 from Johnson and Myers Company, 2666 Briarcliff Avenue, Albany, for merchandise purchases; terms, July 19—2/10, n/30.

23 Received an invoice for $380 from Williams Brothers, 505 Kings Road, for merchandise purchases; terms, July 23—2/10, n/20.

26 Prepared a voucher for $75 to establish a petty cash fund, account no. 105.

27 Prepared a voucher for $30 to purchase postage stamps, account no. 546.

28 Received an invoice for $75 from Fox Insurance Agency, 888 Freeport Drive, for insurance, account no. 534.

29 Received an invoice for $250 from Bond-Patton Equipment Company, 4849 Peach Avenue, Birmingham, for office equipment, account no. 145; terms, July 27—2/10, n/30.

30 Received an invoice for $485 from Stewart's Distributors, 540 Pope Street, Kansas City, for merchandise purchases; terms, July 27—2/10, n/30.

30 Prepared a voucher for the payroll. Payroll was distributed as follows: Office Salaries Expense, account no. 524, $650;

1987

July   Officers' Salaries Expense, account no. 525, $780; Sales Salaries Expense, account no. 526, $1,400; FICA Taxes Payable, account no. 205, $184; Employees' Income Taxes Payable, account no. 206, $485.

Required:

Record the transactions in a voucher register; foot and rule the voucher register. Number the vouchers consecutively, beginning with no. 82.

19–4. The Spring Store's treasurer issued the following checks during the month of May 1987:

1987

May 2   Check no. 546 to Kent Lane Realty Company in payment of voucher no. 483, $250.

3   Check no. 547 to Corporal Telephone Company in payment of voucher no. 486, $45.

4   Check no. 548 to Leitch Supply Company in payment of voucher no. 475, $150.

5   Check no. 549 for $352.80 to Carrel Distributors in payment of voucher no. 476, $360 less 2 percent discount.

6   Check no. 550 for $573.30 to Morris Manufacturers in payment of voucher no. 478, $585 less 2 percent discount.

7   Check no. 551 for $637 to Simmons Manufacturing Company in payment of voucher no. 480, $650 less 2 percent discount.

9   Check No. 552 to Alamo Newspaper in payment of voucher no. 492, $65.

10   Check no. 553 to Seabrook Power Company in payment of voucher no. 493, $105.

11   Check no. 554 for $182.28 to King Brothers in payment of voucher no. 482, $186 less 2 percent discount.

12   Check no. 555 to Bluff Suppliers in payment of voucher no. 484, $135.

13   Check no. 556 to Allen's Equipment Company in payment of voucher no. 469, $502.

14   Check no. 557 for $456.68 to Davenport Company in payment of voucher no. 488, $466 less 2 percent discount.

16   Check no. 558 to Payroll in payment of voucher no. 498, $6,500.

1987

May 17   Check no. 559 to Cliburn Brothers in payment of voucher no. 490, $59.

18   Check no. 560 to Buffington Cleaners in payment of voucher no. 497, $42.

19   Check no. 561 to Mason and Dixon in payment of voucher no. 491, $163.

20   Check no. 562 for $377.30 to Warren Hart Manufacturing Company in payment of voucher no. 489, $385 less 2 percent discount.

21   Check no. 563 for $523.80 to Hodges Manufacturers in payment of voucher no. 494, $540 less 3 percent discount.

23   Check no. 564 to Carter's Repair Shop in payment of voucher no. 496, $86.

24   Check no. 565 to WKZK Radio Station in payment of voucher no. 499, $94.

25   Check no. 566 for $592.90 to Elmo Manufacturing Company in payment of voucher no. 495, $605 less 2 percent discount.

26   Check no. 567 to Petty Cash in payment of voucher no. 506, $100.

27   Check no. 568 for $317.52 to Carrel Distributors in payment of voucher no. 550, $324 less 2 percent discount.

28   Check no. 569 to Bates Supply Company in payment of voucher no. 487, $175.

30   Check no. 570 for $761.46 to Hamby Manufacturers in payment of voucher no. 501, $777 less 2 percent discount.

31   Check no. 571 to Payroll in payment of voucher no. 512, $6,650.

Required:

1. Record the issuance of the checks in a check register like the one shown in Illustration 19–9.

2. Foot and rule the check register on May 31, 1987.

19–5.   The Arbor Dell Manufacturing Corporation was granted its charter in January 1987. It began operating on February 2. The following selected transactions occurred during the first month of operations:

1987

Feb. 2   Received an invoice for $600 from Cobbler Company, 4593 Bender Road, for materials; terms, January 30—2/10, n/30.

1987

Feb. 3 Received an invoice for $800 from Ellis Realtors, 502 Parkway Drive, for rent, account no. 5162. Issued check no. 101 in payment of the rent.

4 Received an invoice for $250 from Brownlee Suppliers, account no. 5166; terms, February 4—n/30.

5 Received an invoice for $5,000 from Norton Equipment Company, 1050 Eagle Drive, Griffin, for factory equipment, account no. 140; terms, February 3—n/30.

5 Received an invoice for $1,500 from Porter Equipment Company, 5194 Cherokee Road, Miami, for office equipment, account no. 150; terms, February 3—n/30.

7 A voucher was prepared to establish a petty cash fund of $150. Check no. 102 was cashed for that amount. (Petty Cash is account no. 105.)

7 Received an invoice for $550 from Beck Supply Company, 811 Wildwood Place, for factory supplies, account no. 6142; terms, February 7—n/30.

9 Issued check no. 103 to Cobbler Company in payment of voucher no. 1 less 2 percent discount.

10 Received an invoice for $1,380 from Harding Steel Company, 301 Pinecrest Drive, Atlanta, for materials; terms, February 9—2/10, n/30.

11 Received an invoice for $820 from Hancock, Incorporated, 4133 Cascade Road, Dublin, for materials; terms, February 9—2/10, n/30.

12 Issued check no. 104 to Brownlee Suppliers in payment of voucher no. 3.

12 Received an invoice for $75 from WFDT Radio Station, 611 Church Street, for advertising, account no. 5172; terms, February 12—n/5.

14 Issued check no. 105 to WFDT Radio Station in payment of voucher no. 10.

14 Decided to pay Norton Equipment Company with fractional payments of $1,500, $1,500, and $2,000 instead of $5,000 as noted on voucher no. 4. Canceled voucher no. 4 and issued three new vouchers for $1,500, $1,500, and $2,000.

16 Issued check no. 106 to Norton Equipment Company in payment of voucher no. 11.

17 Received an invoice for $650 from Robert Newman, Attor-

1987

ney, 6109 Fairfax Parkway, Atlanta, for legal fees, account no. 5175.

Feb. 18 Issued check no. 107 to Harding Steel Company in payment of voucher no. 8 less 2 percent discount.

18 Issued check no. 108 to Hancock, Incorporated, in payment of voucher no. 9 less 2 percent discount.

19 Received an invoice for $150 from Smith Supply Store, 420 Fifth Avenue, for office supplies, account no. 5166; terms, February 19—n/10.

19 Issued check no. 109 to Robert Newman, attorney, in payment of voucher no. 14.

21 Received an invoice for $580 from Cobbler Company, 4593 Bender Road, for materials; terms, February 19—2/10, n/30.

23 Issued check no. 110 to Porter Equipment Company in payment of voucher no. 5.

24 Received an invoice for $50 from T-*Town Press,* 4119 Goshen Road, for newspaper advertising, account no. 5172; terms, February 23—n/5.

25 Issued check no. 111 to Beck Supply Company in payment of voucher no. 7.

26 Issued check no. 112 to T-*Town Press* in payment of voucher no. 17.

26 Issued check no. 113 to Cobbler Company in payment of voucher no. 16 less 2 percent discount.

28 Issued check no. 114 to Smith Supply Store in payment of voucher no. 15.

Required:

1. Record the transactions in the voucher register or check register, whichever is appropriate. Number the vouchers consecutively beginning with No. 1.

2. Foot and rule the registers on February 28, 1987. (Note: Vouchers Payable is account no. 250.)

 19–6. Jefferson Footwears, Incorporated, is a new wholesale shoe store which has just opened in Griffin, Georgia. During the first month of business, the following selected transactions occurred:

1987

Jan. 5 Received an invoice for $750 from Silva Manufacturers, 217 Forest Avenue, Columbus, for shoes; terms, January 2—2/10, n/30.

1987

Jan. 6 Received a bill for $300 from Hunt Realty Company, 185 East Road, for rent, account no. 532; terms, January 6—n/5.

8 Received an invoice for $570 from Morgan's Shoes, 901 Woodland Drive, Atlanta, for shoes; terms, January 7—2/10, n/30.

8 Issued check no. 101 to Hunt Realty Company in payment of voucher no. 2.

10 Received an invoice for $960 from Bluster Shoe Company, 105 Chalfont Avenue, Albany, for shoes; terms, January 8—2/10, n/30.

10 Received an invoice for $200 from Kevin's Supply Store, 359 Hilton Street, for office supplies, account no. 536; terms, January 10—n/10.

10 Issued check no. 102 to Silva Manufacturers in payment of voucher no. 1 less 2 percent discount.

12 Received an invoice for $6,000 from Kody Motor Company, 191 Carter Drive, for a delivery truck, account no. 160; terms, January 9—n/60. Fractional payments of $2,000 each are to be made three times. 3 voucher

13 Received a bill for $75 from WKRX-TV, 408 Lakewood Plaza, for advertising, account no. 542; terms, January 12—n/5.

15 Received an invoice for $500 from Kenton Equipment Company, 104 Whitehall Road, for office equipment, account no. 150; terms, January 14—n/30.

15 Issued check no. 103 to WKRX-TV in payment of voucher no. 9.

15 Issued check no. 104 to Morgan's Shoes in payment of voucher no. 3 less 2 percent discount.

17 Issued check no. 105 to Bluster Shoe Company in payment of voucher no. 4 less 2 percent discount.

19 Received an invoice for $450 from Silva Manufacturers, 217 Forest Avenue, Columbus, for shoes; terms, January 15—2/10, n/30.

20 Issued check no. 106 to Kevin's Supply Store in payment of voucher no. 5.

22 Received an invoice for $1,200 from Kinsaul Shoe Manufacturers, 650 Greenwood Road, Chicago, for shoes; terms, January 17—2/10, n/30.

22 Received an invoice for $550 from Hasty Shoe Company,

1987

122 Spring Road, Athens, for shoes; terms, January 22—2/10, n/30.

Jan. 24   Issued check no. 107 to Silva Manufacturers in payment of voucher no. 11 less 2 percent discount.

26   Issued check no. 108 to Kinsaul Shoe Manufacturers in payment of voucher no. 12 less 2 percent discount.

27   Received an invoice for $250 from Dorsey Suppliers, 206 Avalon Way, for store supplies, account no. 538; terms, January 27—n/10.

29   Issued check no. 109 to Kody Motor Company in payment of voucher no. 6 ($2,000).

29   Issued check no. 110 to Hasty Shoe Company in payment of voucher no. 13 less 2 percent discount.

29   Received an invoice for $80 from Griffin Free Press, 120 Granger Drive, for advertising, account no. 542; terms, July 29—n/5.

31   Received an invoice for $680 from Morgan's Shoes, 901 Woodland Drive, Atlanta, for shoes; terms, January 29—2/10, n/30.

Required:

1. Record the transactions in a voucher register or check register, whichever is appropriate. The check register should look like the one in Illustration 19–9, and the voucher register will be similar to the one in Illustration 19–7 except there will be no need for a Manufacturing Expense column. The first column should be labeled Purchases. Vouchers should be numbered consecutively beginning with no. 1.

2. Foot and rule the voucher register and the check register.

3. Post the footings of the Vouchers Payable columns in each register to the Vouchers Payable account (account no. 230).

4. Prepare a schedule of unpaid vouchers as of January 31, 1987, and compare the total to the Vouchers Payable account balance.

19–7. The Roman Products Company completed the following selected transactions during the month of July, 1987:

1987

July 2   Received an invoice for $750 from Gordon Manufacturers, 712 Bunker Way, for materials, account no. 125; terms, June 27—2/10, n/30 (voucher no. 308).

1987

July 5 Issued check no. 214 for $343 to Solar Peripherals, Inc., in payment of voucher no. 296 for $350 less 2 percent discount.

7 Issued check no. 215 for $620 to Ramsey, Inc., in payment of voucher no. 298 for $620.

9 Received an invoice for $250 from Hammon Suppliers, 101 Park Drive, for office equipment, account no. 150; terms, July 7—n/30 (voucher no. 309).

9 Received an invoice for $70 from State Power company, 1127 Maine, for June power bill, account no. 6120; terms, July 8—n/15 (voucher no. 310).

11 Issued check no. 216 for $784 to Bowen Company in payment of voucher no. 300 for $800 less 2 percent discount.

12 Received an invoice for $110 from the Mooney Company, 6125 Power Ave., for office supplies, account no. 112; terms, July 9—2/10, n/30 (voucher no. 311).

13 Received an invoice for $690 from Grayson Products Company, 7000 Homer Road, for materials, account no. 125; terms, July 10—2/10, n/60 (voucher no. 312).

13 Issued check no. 217 for $70 to State Power Company in payment of voucher no. 310 for $70.

16 Issued check no. 218 for $750 in payment of voucher no. 308.

20 Received an invoice for $390 from Rose Manufacturing Company, 2900 Blackbird Street, for materials, account no. 125; terms, July 19—2/20, n/60 (voucher no. 313).

27 Issued check no. 219 to Hammon Suppliers for $250 in payment of voucher no. 309.

Required:

1. Record the transactions in a voucher register or check register, whichever is appropriate.

2. Foot and rule the registers on July 31, 1987.

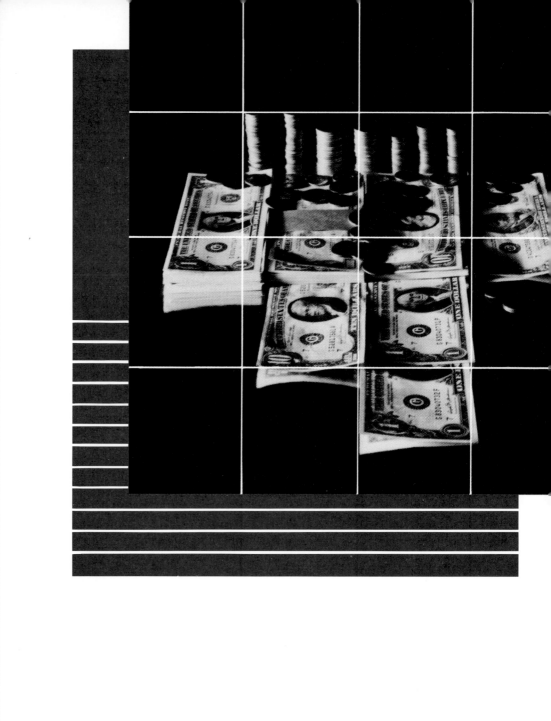

CHAPTER 20

Accounting for proprietorships and partnerships

LEARNING OBJECTIVES

Partnerships and proprietorships are two common forms of business organizations. Although similar in some respects, there are differences in accounting for partnerships and proprietorships. This chapter considers the differences between accounting for a partnership and accounting for a proprietorship. After studying this chapter, you should be able to:

1. Record transactions for a sole proprietorship.
2. Record closing entries for a sole proprietorship.
3. Prepare a statement of owner's equity for a sole proprietorship.
4. Record transactions for a partnership, using both the bonus and goodwill methods for initial contributions.
5. Distribute profits and losses among the partners.
6. Prepare a balance sheet and an income statement for a partnership.
7. Record journal entries for the liquidation of a partnership.
8. Prepare a statement of liquidation.

Whether a business is operating as a proprietorship with a single owner or as a partnership with multiple owners, its assets are usually subject to the claims of several parties. Liabilities on a firm's balance sheet represent the creditors' claims on the assets. The difference between assets and liabilities is the amount of owner's equity. Owner's equity represents the owner's claim to the firm's assets. Owner's equity is an important part of the accounting equation and should be accounted for properly.

PROPRIETORSHIPS

A **proprietorship** is a business that is owned by a single person. Even though creditors have claims to a proprietorship's assets, the owner actually has exclusive title to business assets. The owner is personally liable for creditors' claims. The amount of owner's equity (Assets — Liabilities) on a proprietorship's balance sheet is sometimes referred to as the net worth, net assets, or capital of the proprietorship. To identify the net amount of the owner's investment (or equity), the term *capital* usually follows the name of the owner in the owner's equity section of the balance sheet. Illustration 20–1 illustrates the owner's equity of Jim's Sporting Goods.

The proprietorship form of business is most common in small merchandising and personal service companies. For example, proprietorships are common in the medical and dental professions, although there is a noticeable trend toward professional corporations. An obvi-

ILLUSTRATION 20–1

JIM'S SPORTING GOODS
Balance Sheet
December 31, 1987

Assets		Liabilities and Owner's Equity	
Cash	$ 800	Liabilities:	
Accounts receivable	4,500	Accounts payable	$ 8,750
Inventory	14,500	Accrued salaries	1,500
Building and equipment		Total liabilities	$ 10,250
(Net of accumulated		Owner's equity:	
depreciation)	85,000	Jim Jackson, capital	$ 94,550
		Total liabilities and	
Total assets	$104,800	owner's equity	$104,800

ous reason for choosing the proprietorship form is the simplicity of operating as sole owner. Since the proprietor is both manager and owner, he or she does not need to enter into legal agreements with others for decisions on ownership and business conduct. Compliance with state and local laws is all that is necessary to operate a single proprietorship.

Organization of a proprietorship

Since the proprietor is the only investor, he or she alone decides the forms and amount of assets that will be invested in the business. The initial investment may consist of cash only or of cash along with other assets, such as office and store equipment, buildings, land, and merchandise. For record-keeping purposes, a proprietor should keep the property invested in the business separate from any other properties he or she owns. An individual may invest in several businesses, operating each as a separate proprietorship. The individual may find that it is easier to manage each proprietorship by keeping separate books for each.

A sole proprietorship has several distinct advantages compared with other forms of business organizations, including:

1. Organizational simplicity.
2. Independence in making business decisions.
3. Reduced reporting requirements and government control.

It also has the following disadvantages:

1. Limited capital.
2. Proprietorship's sole responsibility for business debt.
3. Limited business knowledge and experience.
4. Limited life.

Accounting in a proprietorship

Accounting procedures for ordinary business transactions do not vary with a firm's organizational structure. Differences in the legal structure of proprietorships, partnerships, and corporations have little effect on routine transactions. The main differences among the three forms of organization are in the owner's equity section of the balance sheet.

Initial entries of a proprietorship.   The accounts needed to open the books of a proprietorship depend on the kinds of assets transferred to the business. The owner may invest cash as well as other types of assets. If the assets transferred include real or personal property that has not been paid for, the related liabilities may also be transferred. For the individual who makes an initial investment consisting only of cash, the opening entry is simply a debit to Cash and a credit to Capital. For example, if A. B. Campbell invests $2,000 to start a business, the following entry is made:

GENERAL JOURNAL

DATE		ACCOUNT AND EXPLANATION	P.R.	DEBIT	CREDIT
1987					
June	1	Cash		2 0 0 0 00	
		A.B. Campbell, Capital			2 0 0 0 00
		To record initial investment in the business.			

If other assets along with cash are transferred to the new business, the entry includes debits to Cash and other asset accounts for the amounts transferred and a credit to the Capital account for the total amount invested. If liabilities are attached to the assets, the liabilities will be recorded as credits in the opening entry. The liability accounts credited may include Accounts Payable, Mortgages Payable, Notes Payable, or other accounts to record the liabilities incurred to obtain the assets. When liabilities are recorded in the opening entry, the Capital account is credited only for the difference between the amount of assets invested and the amount of liabilities recorded. For example if Ms. Campbell in the previous illustration had purchased items on account which she placed in the business, the initial entry would be as follows:

GENERAL JOURNAL

DATE		ACCOUNT AND EXPLANATION	P.R.	DEBIT	CREDIT
1987					
June	1	Cash		2 0 0 0 00	
		Office Equipment		9 5 0 00	
		Accounts Payable			5 0 0 00
		A.B. Campbell, Capital			2 4 5 0 00
		To record initial investment in the business.			

To illustrate a complete opening entry for the proprietorship, assume that A. B. Campbell transfers the following assets and liabilities: cash amounting to $2,000, delivery equipment worth $5,000, and office equipment worth $3,500. Campbell owes $500 on the office equipment and has a $1,000 note payable on the delivery equipment. Since all cash of the business is assumed to be deposited immediately in the bank, Cash in Bank will be debited for the cash transferred. To open the books of A. B. Campbell, the following general journal entry is used:

			GENERAL JOURNAL				
DATE			ACCOUNT AND EXPLANATION	P.R.	DEBIT	CREDIT	
1987							
June	1		Cash in bank		2 0 0 0 00		
			Office Equipment		3 5 0 0 00		
			Delivery Equipment		5 0 0 0 00		
			Accounts Payable			5 0 0 00	
			Notes Payable			1 0 0 0 00	
			A.B. Campbell, Capital			9 0 0 0 00	
			To record investment in business.				

Many small businesses operate with little or no record-keeping. The only daily records they keep may be those on check stubs. Accounts receivable and accounts payable are not organized into the formal records that are part of the double-entry system. In such cases, rough calculations and estimates must be made in order to prepare an income statement. Statements prepared in such a haphazard manner are often incorrect because calculation errors and information oversights are likely to occur. For accuracy, records should be made soon after a transaction has taken place. In addition, using double-entry accounting makes it possible to check the mathematical accuracy of records as they are made.

A small business may soon discover that its record-keeping system is inadequate. It is therefore best to begin with a record-keeping system that will allow for growth. An owner who decides to use a double-entry system must prepare a balance sheet that will be used in making the opening entry.

Assume that T. M. Selick is the single proprietor of a small janitorial business. Because he lacks good records, Selick is finding it difficult to keep track of receivables and payables. As a result, he has had

**ILLUSTRATION
20–2**

T. M. SELICK
Balance Sheet
December 31, 1987

Assets

Cash in bank.		$ 1,750
Accounts receivable	$4,850	
Less: Allowance for doubtful accounts	700	4,150
Cleaning supplies		1,200
Service equipment	$6,000	
Less: Accumulated depreciation	1,250	4,750
Total Assets		$11,850

Liabilities

Accounts payable	$1,100	
Notes payable	500	
Total Liabilities		$ 1,600

Owner's Equity

T. M. Selick, Capital		10,250
Total Liabilities and Owner's Equity.		$11,850

difficulty in determining business income. To set up a double-entry system, Selick and his accountant prepared the balance sheet shown in Illustration 20–2.

After all asset, liability, and owner's equity amounts have been determined as shown in the balance sheet, the following general journal entry is used to open the general ledger:

GENERAL JOURNAL

DATE		ACCOUNT AND EXPLANATION	P.R.	DEBIT	CREDIT
1987					
Dec.	31	Cash in bank		1750 00	
		Accounts Receivable		4850 00	
		Cleaning Supplies		1200 00	
		Service Equipment		6000 00	
		Accounts Payable			1100 00
		Notes Payable			500 00
		Allowance for Doubtful Accounts			700 00
		Accumulated Depreciation—Service Equipment			1250 00
		T.M. Selick, Capital			10250 00
		To open general ledger.			

After the general journal has been opened, the debits and credits in the opening entry are posted to the proper accounts in the general ledger. Each asset account is debited for the proper amount. Each liability and contra asset account (Allowance for Doubtful Accounts and Accumulated Depreciation) is credited for the right amount. The Capital account of T. M. Selick is credited for Selick's equity. Balances for the Accounts Receivable and Accounts Payable ledger accounts can be taken from the schedules of accounts receivable and accounts payable, respectively.

Notice that Accounts Receivable and Accounts Payable are controlling accounts. A record is kept in a subsidiary ledger for each customer and creditor. At any time, the balance of the Accounts Receivable general ledger account should equal the sum of the individual customers' balances in the accounts receivable subsidiary ledger. The same is true for the accounts payable ledger.

Equity accounts. The owner's equity section of a single proprietorship contains two kinds of accounts. First, there are accounts that remain from period to period. Second, there are temporary accounts that are closed out at the end of each accounting period.

In a single proprietorship, the only permanent equity account is the Capital account. As indicated earlier, the owner's equity in the business is identified by the owner's name followed by the term *capital,* such as Selick, Capital.

The temporary owner's equity accounts summarize the transactions of the period that affect owner's equity. Since the capital account is regarded as a permanent account, it is not adjusted for revenues, expenses, and cash withdrawals on a daily basis. Instead, a **summary account** is maintained for revenues and expenses, and a drawing account is used to record cash withdrawals by the owner. At the end of the accounting period, these temporary accounts are closed out to the capital account. The number of summary accounts will depend on the kind of business operation. An account called Income Summary may be the only summary account for a service proprietorship. If the proprietorship is a merchandising or manufacturing business, an account called Cost of Goods Sold may also be used.

Owner's equity transactions during the period. Transactions that affect the owner's drawing account or capital account are called

owner's equity transactions. Appearing below is a list of typical owner's equity transactions and journal entries:

1. Additional cash investment in the business increasing owner's equity:

Cash 10,000
  T. M. Selick, Capital 10,000

2. Reduction of cash with the intention of reducing owner's equity:

T. M. Selick, Capital 5,000
  Cash 5,000

3. Payment of nonbusiness debts with business cash:

T. M. Selick, Drawing 2,500
  Cash 2,500

4. Withdrawal of cash for personal use:

T. M. Selick, Drawing 2,500
  Cash 2,500

Because the owner is the only person responsible for the firm's debts, he or she is free to increase or decrease personal investment in the business. When the owner makes withdrawals that are intended to be permanent decreases in owner's equity, the amounts should be charged (debited) to the owner's Capital account. If investments of cash are intended to increase equity permanently, the owner's Capital account should be credited.

Periodically, an owner may withdraw cash for personal use or to pay nonbusiness debts. In such cases, the owner's drawing account, and not a business expense account, should be charged for the withdrawal. Although a cash withdrawal may be for the owner's salary, it should not be treated as a business expense because a proprietorship's income is considered personal income for tax purposes. A proprietor reports business income on his or her personal income tax return. Frequently, an owner pays personal debts out of the same bank checking account that is used for business debts. In that case, the owner should make sure that payments for business debts are charged to the proper business expense accounts and that payments for personal debts are charged to the owner's drawing account.

Transactions in temporary owner's equity accounts. Not all transactions affecting owner's equity are recorded directly in the owner's equity account. The revenue and expenses of the business are recorded in separate accounts so that information can be gathered to prepare an income statement. Below is a list of typical transactions and journal entries:

1. Sale of goods to customers for cash:

Cash. 1,000
    Sales 1,000

2. Sale of goods to customers on account:

Accounts Receivable 750
    Sales 750

3. Payment of operating expenses:

General Expenses 950
    Cash 950

4. Accrual of salaries for employees:

Salaries Expense. 1,200
    Accrued Salaries Payable 1,200

As mentioned earlier in the chapter, if the business is a merchandising or a manufacturing operation, a Cost of Goods Sold account may be used to account for the cost of inventory items sold to customers.

At the end of the accounting period, the Income Summary account is debited for the beginning inventory and is credited for the merchandise inventory existing at the end of the period. In addition, all other expenses and revenues are transferred to the Income Summary account. A debit balance in the Income Summary account will represent a net loss, while a credit balance will represent net income for the period. The Income Summary account is used only to close the books at the end of the period. The Income Summary account and the owner's drawing account are closed to the permanent owner's equity account (the Capital account). All accounts which have been closed will have a zero balance.

Closing the Income Summary account. The Income Summary account is a temporary account that is opened and closed out at the end of each accounting period. The result of business operations is shown by a debit (loss), or a credit (income) balance in the account. To summarize a business's income or loss, the balance in the Income Summary account is closed to the Capital account. The balance in the Drawing account is then closed to the Capital account.

For example, assume that before closing, the Income Summary account of the T. M. Selick proprietorship has a credit balance of $25,000. The owner's Drawing account has a debit balance of $23,500, and the owner's Capital account has a credit balance of $11,750. The following entries in general journal form are used to close the Income Summary and Drawing accounts:

		GENERAL JOURNAL			
DATE		ACCOUNT AND EXPLANATION	P.R.	DEBIT	CREDIT
1987					
Dec.	31	Income Summary		2 5 0 0 0 00	
		T. M. Selick, Capital			2 5 0 0 0 00
		To close the Income Summary account.			
		T. M. Selick, Capital		2 3 5 0 0 00	
		T. M. Selick, Drawing			2 3 5 0 0 00
		To close the Drawing account.			

As a result of these entries, the Income Summary and Drawing accounts have a zero balance and the capital account shows a balance of $13,250 ($11,750 + $25,000 − $23,500). This represents the owner's interest in the assets of the company.

Presentation of owner's equity in the balance sheet. The account titles used in financial statements vary from business to business. But the balance sheet should report (1) business assets, (2) business liabilities, and (3) owner's equity. To give proper information, the owner's equity section, or a separate statement of owner's equity, should report the owner's capital balance at the beginning of the year, business net income or loss, withdrawals, and the owner's capital balance at the end of the accounting period. The following presentation of owner's equity is based on the operations of T. M. Selick as discussed above, assuming there were no investments or withdrawals of equity during the period.

Owner's Equity		
T. M. Selick, Capital, January 1, 1987		$11,750
Net income	$25,000	
Less: Withdrawals	23,500	1,500
T. M. Selick, Capital, December 31, 1987		$13,250

PARTNERSHIPS

A **partnership** is a business firm in which two or more individuals have invested assets for a common business purpose. Partnerships are found in all kinds of businesses. The partnership form is especially common in service organizations, such as medical, legal, and accounting firms.

Partnership organization

To help regulate the formation and operation of partnerships, many states have adopted the **Uniform Partnership Act.** The act defines a partnership as "an association of two or more persons who carry on, as co-owners, a business for profit." Although many partnerships operate under an implied or oral agreement, it is preferable to have a written and signed contract. This agreement is usually referred to as the articles of copartnership.

Although some states seek to control the formation and operation of partnerships, there is no standard form of **partnership agreement.** Nonetheless, since the articles of copartnership describe how a partnership will operate, they should include:

1. Date of agreement and how long the partnership is expected to last.
2. Names and signatures of partners.
3. Nature, scope, and location of business.
4. Initial investments of each partner.
5. Method of dividing profits and losses.
6. Rights, duties, and responsibilities of each partner.
7. Method of liquidation.
8. Salary, drawing, and interest on owner's equity to be allowed.
9. Any other special agreements between the partners.

Except where otherwise agreed, each partner is personally liable for all business debts, as is a single proprietor. Partnerships in which all partners have unlimited liability are called **general partnerships.** Some states allow one or more partners to possess limited liability, but at least one partner must be a general partner with unlimited liability. Such a partnership is known as a **limited partnership.**

Advantages and disadvantages of a partnership

Compared with a single proprietorship, a partnership has both advantages and disadvantages. A great advantage is that the business may gain from the combined resources, experience, and talents of the partners. In addition, because of the unlimited liability of each general partner, the partnership may be able to obtain larger amounts of credit.

A partnership also has several disadvantages. One is that all general partners have unlimited liability. Each general partner is personally liable for all business debts. Also, a partner cannot transfer his or her interest in the partnership to a new partner without the consent of the other partners. In addition, if a partner goes bankrupt, dies, or commits an illegal act, the partnership is automatically dissolved.

Individuals should consider both the advantages and disadvantages of a partnership before entering into an agreement. If it is decided to form a partnership, the partners should make sure that the partnership agreement is drafted appropriately.

Accounting for a partnership

Except for the division of profits and losses among partners, accounting for a partnership is similar to accounting for a single proprietorship. Separate owner's capital and drawing accounts are kept for each partner. The main problems in partnership accounting are (1) the protection of each partner's interests when partners are admitted or withdrawn and (2) the division of partnership profits and losses.

Initial partnership entry.   Just like a single owner, partners may invest cash or cash and other property in their business. If liabilities are attached to contributed assets, the partnership may agree to take them over. For each partner, the opening entry includes debits to asset accounts for the assets transferred, credits to liability accounts for the liabilities assumed, and a credit to the partner's capital account for the difference between assets and liabilities.

Assume that J. D. Holly and E. O. Green agree to form a partnership. Each is to contribute $10,000, as stated in the articles of copartnership. The opening entries in general journal form are as follows:

GENERAL JOURNAL

DATE		ACCOUNT AND EXPLANATION	P.R.	DEBIT	CREDIT
1987					
Jan.	1	Cash in Bank		1 0 0 0 0 00	
		J.D. Holly, Capital			1 0 0 0 0 00
		Investment in partnership.			
		Cash in Bank		1 0 0 0 0 00	
		E.O. Green, Capital			1 0 0 0 0 00
		Investment in partnership.			

The partnership entered into by Holly and Green is the simplest kind. Each partner simply contributes agreed-upon amounts of cash. In other cases, partners usually contribute cash and other assets or just other assets. Assume that in the above example, Holly had contributed cash of $1,000, office equipment amounting to $10,000, and a truck valued at $4,000. In addition, the partnership is to assume a mortgage on the truck of $2,000 and note payable of $3,000 on the office equipment. To record Holly's investment, the following general journal entry is used:

GENERAL JOURNAL

DATE		ACCOUNT AND EXPLANATION	P.R.	DEBIT	CREDIT
1987					
Jan.	1	Cash in Bank		1 0 0 0 00	
		Office Equipment		1 0 0 0 0 00	
		Truck		4 0 0 0 00	
		Notes Payable			3 0 0 0 00
		Mortgage Payable			2 0 0 0 00
		J.D. Holly, Capital			1 0 0 0 0 00
		Investment in partnership.			

Combination of existing businesses. To benefit from the advantages of a partnership, two or more individuals who already have businesses may decide to join forces. For the protection of each individual's interest, the partners must agree on the valuation of assets and the amount of liabilities to be assumed by the partnership. Assume that on January 1, O. C. Black and J. L. Taylor will enter into a partnership agreement. Both agree that assets will be contributed and liabilities assumed as reported on each partner's balance sheet. Profits and losses will be shared equally, and liquidation will result in distribution of assets in relation to each partner's capital at the time of liquidation. Each partner will receive credit for their interest equal to the amount of net assets contributed. In other words, each owner's capital account will be the same as it was in the single proprietorship. Illustration 20–3 shows the balance sheets that Black and Taylor will use to record the opening entries and to establish each partner's capital.

Instead of reporting the plant assets at their cost and showing the accumulated depreciation to date, the balance sheet reports the assets transferred at their book values. The delivery equipment contributed by Black is recorded at $4,000 (cost of $5,000 less accumulated depreciation of $1,000). The office equipment contributed by Taylor is valued in the same way.

Accounts receivable of each partner also can be contributed to the partnership. If the partners know which accounts receivable are in fact uncollectible, the accounts receivable balance is adjusted before the partnership's opening entries are made. When the collectibility of the accounts is not known, the accounts receivable balance is recorded as a debit along with the appropriate credit to allowance for doubtful accounts.

The entries in general journal form to open the books of the Black and Taylor partnership are shown in Illustration 20–4. The amounts are taken directly from the balance sheets for the separate proprietorships of Black and Taylor. That is not always the case, however. Assume that after examining Taylor's merchandise inventory, both partners agreed that the current market value was only $4,000. In that case, the merchandise inventory would be reduced by $300 and Taylor's capital would be $10,300 ($10,600 − $300). Regardless of the values of the assets and liabilities before the partnership is formed, the partners must examine each account and determine the amount at which it is to be recorded on the partnership books.

Black and Taylor have agreed to share profits and losses equally. Notice that this ratio is not related to their owner's capital balance ($12,500 versus $10,600). This is not unusual because the method of distributing profits and losses in a partnership need not be based

**ILLUSTRATION
20–3**

O. C. BLACK
Balance Sheet
January 1, 1987

Assets

Cash in bank		$ 5,000
Accounts receivable.	$4,000	
Less: Allowance for doubtful accounts	200	3,800
Supplies		1,500
Delivery equipment.	$5,000	
Less: Accumulated depreciation.	1,000	4,000
Total assets		$14,300

Liabilities

Accounts payable	$1,200	
Notes payable	600	
Total liabilities		$ 1,800

Owner's Equity

O. C. Black, capital		12,500
Total liabilities and owner's equity		$14,300

J. L. TAYLOR
Balance Sheet
January 1, 1987

Assets

Cash in bank		$ 2,000
Accounts receivable.	$3,500	
Less: Allowance for doubtful accounts	100	3,400
Merchandise		4,300
Office equipment.	$6,300	
Less: Accumulated depreciation.	1,200	5,100
Total assets		$14,800

Liabilities

Accounts payable	$2,000	
Notes payable	2,200	
Total liabilities		$ 4,200

Owner's Equity

J. L. Taylor capital		10,600
Total liabilities and owner's equity		$14,800

on the capital ratios. It is quite common to find one partner who invests most of the assets and spends little time working, while the second partner invests a small amount of assets and devotes full time to the business. Partners are free to decide how they wish to distribute profits and losses and it is the duty of the accountant to

**ILLUSTRATION
20–4**

		GENERAL JOURNAL			
DATE		ACCOUNT AND EXPLANATION	P.R.	DEBIT	CREDIT
1987					
Jan.	1	Cash in Bank		5 0 0 0 00	
		Accounts Receivable		4 0 0 0 00	
		Supplies		1 5 0 0 00	
		Delivery Equipment		4 0 0 0 00	
		Accounts Payable			1 2 0 0 00
		Notes Payable			6 0 0 00
		Allowance for Dbt. Accounts			2 0 0 00
		O.C. Black, Capital			1 2 5 0 0 00
		Investment of Black in partnership.			
	1	Cash in Bank		2 0 0 0 00	
		Accounts Receivable		3 5 0 0 00	
		Merchandise		4 3 0 0 00	
		Office Equipment		5 1 0 0 00	
		Accounts Payable			2 0 0 0 00
		Notes Payable			2 2 0 0 00
		Allowance for Dbt. Accounts			1 0 0 00
		J.L. Taylor, Capital			1 0 6 0 0 00
		Investment of Taylor in partnership.			

follow the partners' intentions as stated in the articles of copartnership.

Partner's compensation.   As already mentioned, partners may receive varying amounts of compensation, depending on their partnership agreement. They may receive compensation in the form of salaries, interest on capital, interest on loans, royalties, and bonuses. Because of the income tax laws, salaries generally are not considered a business expense. Assigning salaries is just one method of distributing the profits based on each partner's contribution to the enterprise. The dollar amounts assigned as salary, along with all other partnership income are reported on the individual partners' tax returns as taxable income.

A drawing account is kept for each partner. All withdrawals are debited to the drawing account when the partner is paid. After the profit or loss has been allocated to each partner's capital account, the balance in the drawing account is closed to the respective partner's capital account.

Partnership profits and losses.   At the end of each accounting period, all partnership profits and losses must be divided among the partners as stated in the partnership agreement. If **profit and loss ratios** have not been established, profits and losses are shared equally regardless of the amount of each partner's equity. When the partners have agreed to distribute profits but not losses, losses are distributed in the same ratio as profits.

After all expense and revenue accounts have been closed to the Income Summary account, the summary account will have a debit balance (loss), a credit balance (net income), or possibly a zero balance (breakeven). Whatever the balance, it is allocated to the partners' capital accounts as agreed. For example, assume that after one year of operating as a partnership, Black and Taylor have income of $78,000. All expense and revenue accounts have been closed to the Income Summary account, which now has a credit balance of $78,000. The partnership agreement states that the partners will share profits equally. The journal entry required to distribute the income to the owner's equity accounts is:

Income Summary	78,000	
O. C. Black, Capital		39,000
J. L. Taylor, Capital		39,000

Notice that the distribution of income *increases* the capital accounts. If the partnership had operated at a loss, the Income Summary account would have a debit balance and the Owners' Capital accounts would decrease when closing the summary account:

O. C. Black, Capital	39,000	
J. L. Taylor, Capital	39,000	
Income Summary		78,000

After closing the summary account to the partners' capital accounts, the drawing accounts are closed to the capital accounts. The balance in a partner's drawing account decreases (debit balance) that partner's capital account. Debits in the drawing accounts result from payments made to the partner. If the capital account is not adjusted for withdrawals during the accounting period, the balance transferred from the drawing account to the capital account reflects the net result of the partner's withdrawals.

Partnership balance sheet: Owner's equity.   The owner's equity section of a partnership's balance sheet is the same as for a sole

ILLUSTRATION 20–5

Owner's Equity

O. C. Black, Capital, January 1, 1987		$12,500	
Income (½ of $78,000)	$39,000		
Less: Withdrawals	21,500	17,500	
O. C. Black, Capital, December 31, 1987			$30,000
J. L. Taylor, Capital, January 1, 1987		$10,600	
Income (½ of $78,000)	$39,000		
Less: Withdrawals	19,600	19,400	
J. L. Taylor, Capital, December 31, 1987			30,000
Total Owner's Equity			$60,000

proprietorship except that separate capital accounts are shown for each partner. The owner's equity section of the Black and Taylor partnership's balance sheet is shown in Illustration 20–5. As with a single proprietorship, incomes increase the capital balances and withdrawals decrease the capital balances.

Admission of a new partner. Whenever a new partner is admitted or an existing partner withdraws, the partnership agreement is voided and a new agreement must be drafted and accepted by the remaining partners. A new partner may be admitted only if all remaining partners agree to it. Under the Uniform Partnership Act, a partner can transfer his or her interest and right to income without the consent of the other partners. But the new person cannot have an actual voice in the business unless admitted into the partnership by the consent of all partners.

An individual may acquire equity in a partnership either by purchasing a share of existing partners' capital or by contributing assets to the partnership. To buy a share of existing partners' capital, the incoming partner simply pays the partners. The only entry required on the partnership books is to transfer capital from the existing partners to the new partner.

For example, O. C. Black and J. L. Taylor each have capital balances of $30,000 in their partnership. To keep all capital balances equal, they agree to sell D. E. Land, a new partner, one third of their capital. After the sale, each partner has a capital balance of $20,000. The entry in general journal form to record the purchase is:

		GENERAL JOURNAL			
DATE		ACCOUNT AND EXPLANATION	P.R.	DEBIT	CREDIT
1987					
June	1	O.C. Black, Capital		1 0 0 0 0 00	
		J.L. Taylor, Capital		1 0 0 0 0 00	
		D.E. Land, Capital			2 0 0 0 0 00
		Transfer of capital to Land.			

If Black and Taylor agree to sell Land one third of their capital, the above entry is made regardless of the actual dollar amounts paid to Black and Taylor. The payments they receive do not affect the partnership; only the transferred capital is recorded. For example, Land might be willing to pay $25,000 for a $20,000 share in the equity of the partnership. In that case, the $5,000 difference between Land's payment and the value of her equity in the partnership would not be recorded in the partnership's books.

Instead of purchasing existing capital, a new partner may contribute cash or cash and other assets in exchange for new capital in the partnership. The new partner then receives capital equal to the assets contributed. With this method of adding a partner, the partnership's total capital increases. For example, assume that Land contributes $30,000 of cash to the Black and Taylor partnership as new capital. The entry in general journal form to record the transaction is:

		GENERAL JOURNAL			
DATE		ACCOUNT AND EXPLANATION	P.R.	DEBIT	CREDIT
1987					
June	1	Cash		3 0 0 0 0 00	
		D.E. Land, Capital			3 0 0 0 0 00
		To record the admission of Land.			

This entry increases the total owner's equity to $90,000: $30,000 for Black, $30,000 for Taylor, and $30,000 for Land.

In many cases, the existing partners agree to give the new partner an amount of capital greater than the amount of assets contributed. (This may be done if they expect to receive increased income as a result of the new partner's admission.) If so, an additional account must be debited so that the entry will balance. Since the expectation of future income is an intangible asset, the additional debit is usually made to an intangible asset account called **Goodwill.** For instance, assume that D. E. Land contributes $20,000 cash in exchange for capital of $30,000. Using the intangible asset account Goodwill, the following general journal entry is made to record Land's admission:

GENERAL JOURNAL					
DATE		ACCOUNT AND EXPLANATION	P.R.	DEBIT	CREDIT
1987					
June	1	Cash in Bank		2 0 0 0 0 00	
		Goodwill		1 0 0 0 0 00	
		D.E. Land, Capital			3 0 0 0 0 00
		To record admission of Land.			

Although the goodwill method is used, accountants often prefer to avoid recording goodwill because it involves assumptions about the future. As an alternative, the existing partners may transfer part of their capital to the new partner. This method is called the bonus method because the existing partners actually give a bonus (equity) to the new partner. The bonus results in a reduction of the old partners' capital accounts. This reduction is allocated between the old partners according to the profit and loss ratio existing before the new partner is admitted. For example, assuming that O. C. Black and J. L. Taylor share profits and losses equally, the general journal entry to record Land's admission is:

GENERAL JOURNAL					
DATE		ACCOUNT AND EXPLANATION	P.R.	DEBIT	CREDIT
1987					
June	1	Cash in Bank		2 0 0 0 0 00	
		O. C. Black, Capital		5 0 0 0 00	
		J. L. Taylor, Capital		5 0 0 0 00	
		D. E. Land, Capital			3 0 0 0 0 00
		To record admission of Land.			

In other cases, a new partner may be willing to receive an amount of capital that is less than the assets he or she contributes. The new partner may do this with the expectation of benefiting financially from association with the partnership. In such situations, the bonus method should be used. For example, assume once again that Land is to be admitted to the partnership of Black and Taylor who share profits and losses equally. Land is to receive capital of $30,000 for a cash contribution of $40,000. In this case, Land agrees to pay a bonus to the existing partners in order to be admitted. The general journal entry to record Land's admission is:

		GENERAL JOURNAL			
DATE		ACCOUNT AND EXPLANATION	P.R.	DEBIT	CREDIT
1987					
June	1	Cash in Bank		4 0 0 0 0 00	
		O.C. Black, Capital			5 0 0 0 00
		J.L. Taylor, Capital			5 0 0 0 00
		D.E. Land, Capital			3 0 0 0 0 00
		To record admission of Land.			

Withdrawal of a partner. The procedures used in accounting for the withdrawal of a partner are the opposite of those used when a partner is admitted. Dissolution of the partnership may result from a partner's death or from the partnership's bankruptcy. As with the admission of a new partner, the partners review the asset and capital accounts to make sure that each partner's capital account is properly stated before the entry is made to record the withdrawal. Withdrawal is similar to admission in that the partner may receive assets that are either more or less than his or her capital. Again, both the goodwill and the bonus methods can be used to account for the difference, but the bonus method is preferable.

Assume that after two years of being a partner with Black and Taylor, Land decides to withdraw. At the time of the withdrawal the partnership has the following capital balances: O. C. Black, $69,000; J. L. Taylor, $53,500; and D. E. Land, $60,000. Also assume that Land will be paid in cash for the full amount of her capital. To record the withdrawal, the following general journal entry is needed:

		GENERAL JOURNAL			
DATE		ACCOUNT AND EXPLANATION	P.R.	DEBIT	CREDIT
1989					
June	1	D.E. Land, Capital		6 0 0 0 0 00	
		Cash in Bank			6 0 0 0 0 00
		To record withdrawal of Land.			

If Land is paid only $50,000 for her capital, she will be giving a bonus to Black and Taylor. Assuming that the partners share profits and losses equally, the following general journal entry is required:

			GENERAL JOURNAL					
DATE			ACCOUNT AND EXPLANATION	P.R.	DEBIT		CREDIT	
1989								
June	1		D.E. Land, Capital		6 0 0 0 0 00			
			O.C. Black, Capital				5 0 0 0 00	
			J.L. Taylor, Capital				5 0 0 0 00	
			Cash in Bank				5 0 0 0 0 00	
			To record withdrawal of Land.					

The payment to Land of an amount less than her capital may have resulted from an overvaluation of partnership assets. If so, the overvalued assets are decreased and the remaining partners do not receive a bonus. In situations where the payment to the withdrawing partner is more than his or her capital balance, the bonus method is generally used because accountants are reluctant to write up assets.

Liquidation of partnership.   The mechanics of a liquidation vary depending upon the agreement between the partners. But, regardless of how the assets are to be divided, several procedures are the same for all partnership liquidations. First, all creditors are paid by setting aside certain assets. After the creditors are paid, the remaining assets are either sold or valued for distribution to the partners. Before the assets are distributed, the gains and losses resulting from the sale and valuation of assets are allocated to the partners according to their profit and loss ratios. After all creditors have been satisfied and gains and losses have been allocated to the partners, the remaining assets are distributed in the amounts indicated by the partners' capital balances. Illustration 20–6 shows the liquidation of the Baker and Duncan partnership.

As shown in the illustration, immediately before the liquidation began the partnership had $27,000 in assets: $15,000 in cash and $12,000 in other assets. On March 5, $3,500 in cash was paid to creditors to satisfy their claims to partnership assets. The other assets were then sold for $9,000 which resulted in a $3,000 loss, ($9,000 cash received − $12,000 basis of assets = $3,000 loss). The loss was allocated to the partners to reduce their capital balances. At this point, all that remained in the partnership was $20,500 in cash to

ILLUSTRATION 20–6   **BAKER AND DUNCAN PARTNERSHIP**
Statement of Liquidation—Complete
March 1–March 31, 1987

Profit and Loss Ratio 50:50	Assets		Accounts Payable	Capital	
	Cash	Other than Cash		Baker	Duncan
March 1—balance	$ 15,000	$ 12,000	$ 3,500	$ 11,500	$ 12,000
March 5—payment of accounts payable	(3,500)		(3,500)		
Balance	$ 11,500	$ 12,000	–0–	$ 11,500	$ 12,000
March 25—sales of assets for $9,000 and allocation of loss between partners	9,000	(12,000) *book value*		(1,500)	(1,500)
Balance	$ 20,500	–0–		$ 10,000	$ 10,500
March 31—distribution of cash	(20,500)			(10,000)	(10,500)
Balance	–0–	–0–	–0–	–0–	–0–

cover the capital balances of Baker ($10,000) and Duncan ($10,500). The liquidation was completed by the distribution of cash to the partners.

The following journal entries reflect the partnership's liquidation:

		GENERAL JOURNAL			
DATE 1987		ACCOUNT AND EXPLANATION	P.R.	DEBIT	CREDIT
Mar.	5	Accounts Payable		3 500 00	
		Cash			3 500 00
		Paid creditors.			
	25	Cash		9 000 00	
		Baker, Capital		1 500 00	
		Duncan, Capital		1 500 00	
		Assets (other than Cash)			12 000 00
		Sale of assets for $9,000 and allocation of loss between partners.			
	31	Baker, Capital		10 000 00	
		Duncan, Capital		10 500 00	
		Cash			20 500 00
		Distribution of cash.			

SUMMARY

Owner's equity represents the owner's claim to the assets of the business. It is the difference between the assets and the liabilities on the balance sheet.

A **proprietorship** is a business owned by one person. Some of the advantages of this form of business are organizational simplicity, independence in making business decisions, and reduced reporting requirements and governmental control. Some disadvantages are limited capital, sole responsibility for business debts, limited business knowledge and experience, and limited life.

The owner's equity account is affected by additional contributions of capital, the results of operations, and the owner's drawings. The **owner's equity transactions** are reflected in the owner's equity section of the balance sheet.

The results of operations are also reported on the income statement. This shows the total revenue earned and the total expenses incurred. The revenue and expense accounts are closed out each period.

A **partnership** is a form of business owned by two or more individuals. This form of business is governed by the **Uniform Partnership Act.** To control the formation and operation of the business, the owners should develop a written **partnership agreement.** The agreement should state:

1. The date of the agreement and how long the partnership is expected to last.
2. The names and signatures of the partners.
3. The nature, scope, and location of the business.
4. The initial investment of each partner.
5. The method of dividing profits and losses.
6. The rights, duties, and responsibilities of each partner.
7. The method of liquidation.
8. The salary, drawing, and interest on owner's equity to be allowed.
9. Any special agreements between partners.

A partnership has many of the same basic advantages and disadvantages as a proprietorship. In a **general partnership,** each general partner is liable for all business debts; that is, each partner is bound by the actions of the other partners. Also, a partnership terminates if a partner goes bankrupt, dies, or commits an illegal act.

The unique feature of the accounting process for partnerships is the allocation of profits and losses. Profits and losses are allocated as agreed in the partnership agreement. If the agreement is silent on this point, the partners share equally in profits and losses.

When a new partner is admitted to a partnership, the owner's equity changes. The new partner may contribute assets to the business to increase the partnership's capital in exchange for a share of the existing partnership capital. If a new partner receives a partnership interest that is greater than the value of the assets he or she has contributed, the difference can be recorded using either the **goodwill** method or the bonus method. If the new partnership interest is less than the assets contributed, the difference is treated as a bonus to existing partners. These methods may also be used when a partner withdraws from the business.

The liquidation of a partnership is governed by the partnership agreement or, in its absence, by the Uniform Partnership Act. First, all creditors are paid. Then the remaining assets are liquidated and distributed. When the assets are liquidated, any gains or losses recognized are allocated to the partners in accordance with the **profit and loss ratios.** The remaining assets are then distributed to the partners based on their capital account balances.

KEY TERMS

Contra Accounts—Accounts that are used to record subtractions from related accounts which have positive balances. Examples of contra accounts include Allowance for Doubtful Accounts, Purchase Returns and Allowances, and Accumulated Depreciation.

Controlling Accounts—General ledger accounts that are supported by detailed information in subsidiary ledgers.

General Partnership—A partnership in which all the partners have unlimited liability.

Goodwill—An intangible asset that results primarily from the expectation that the entity has the ability to produce an above-average rate of income compared to similar entities in the same industry.

Limited Partnership—A partnership in which one or more partners possess a limited liability but at least one partner is a general partner with unlimited liability.

Owner's Equity Transaction—A transaction that affects the owner's drawing account or capital account.

Partnership—A business in which two or more individuals have invested assets for a common business purpose.

Partnership Agreement—An agreement among the partners that states the basis and conditions upon which the partnership is formed and operated (also referred to as Articles of Copartnership).

Profit and Loss Ratios—The percentage established in the partnership agreement which determines how partners share profits and losses.

Proprietorship—A business organization owned by one person.

Summary Account—A temporary account maintained for revenues and expenses of a sole proprietorship or partnership. It is normally closed to the Capital account(s) at the end of the accounting period.

Uniform Partnership Act—A law intended to govern the formation and operation of a partnership. It establishes guidelines for matters not made clear in the partnership agreement.

QUESTIONS AND EXERCISES

1. What is a proprietorship and in what type of business is it most common?
2. List three advantages and three disadvantages of the proprietorship form of an organization.
3. Dr. B. T. Wilson's professional practice contains business assets of $75,000 and business liabilities of $20,000. What is the amount of Dr. Wilson's owner's equity?
4. List four types of owner's equity transactions.
5. J. E. Brown opened a dry cleaning service in 1987. Brown's initial investment in the business consisted of $20,000 cash and a new delivery truck that cost $12,000. What journal entry should

be made to record the formation of Brown's Dry Cleaning Service?

6. What are some typical transactions that affect the temporary owner's equity accounts?

7. Before the Income Summary is closed at the end of the year, what does its balance reflect?

8. What is a partnership? Give some typical examples.

9. Describe the articles of copartnership. What type information does it contain?

10. List three advantages and three disadvantages of the partnership form of organization.

11. Bill Atlas and Bob World have agreed to form the Atlas-World Partnership. Bill will contribute $15,000 cash and a truck worth $9,000. The partnership will assume a $3,000 mortgage on the truck. Bob will contribute $18,000 cash and office furniture worth $3,000. What general journal entries should be made to record each partner's initial investment?

12. In addition to a share of the profits, what other types of compensation might a partner receive?

13. Ed Write has decided to sell his $50,000 partnership interest to Tom Read. Read has agreed to pay Write $55,000 for his interest. What general journal entry should be made on the partnership's books to record the transaction between Read and Write?

PROBLEMS

20–1. On April 20, 1987, J. C. Hill opened a grocery store in Highland. Hill initially invested $15,000 cash, a delivery truck valued at $9,600, and a building valued at $62,400. There was a $30,000 mortgage on the building. On December 31, 1987, after the Expense and Revenue accounts were closed, the Income Summary account had a $32,400 credit balance, and the Drawing account had a $11,400 debit balance. *profit*

Required:

1. Make the general journal entry to record Hill's initial investment.
2. Close the Income Summary account and the Drawing account.

3. Prepare a statement of owner's equity for the year ended, December 31, 1987.

20–2.

JAMES BUTLER
Adjusted Trial Balance
December 31, 1987

Account Title	Balance	
	Debit	Credit
Cash.	$ 10,500	
Accounts receivable.	6,000	
Prepaid rent	2,700	
Prepaid insurance	1,650	
Office equipment.	18,000	
Accumulated depreciation—		
office equipment		$ 5,400
Office furniture	22,500	
Accumulated depreciation—		
office furniture		11,250
Accounts payable		12,750
James Butler, capital,		
January 1, 1987		11,400
James Butler, drawing	25,500	
Professional fees		73,500
Rent expense	3,600	
Insurance expense	2,250	
Advertising expense	1,800	
Depreciation expense	4,050	
Salaries expense	15,750	
	$114,300	$114,300

Required:

1. Journalize the closing entries.
2. Prepare an income statement.
3. Prepare a balance sheet.

20–3. Two dentists, Dr. Gum and Dr. Teeth, have decided to combine their practices into a partnership. Each dentist is to receive an interest in the partnership equal to the amount of net assets contributed. Using their balance sheets, make the necessary journal entries to record the formation of the partnership.

Get all debits & credits together
allow for doubt acct
Dental equip 44,000—

DR. GUM
Balance Sheet
September 14, 1987

Assets

Cash		$22,000
Accounts receivable	$13,200	
Less: Allowance for doubtful accounts	1,100	12,100
Dental supplies		1,760
Dental equipment	$66,000	
Less: Accumulated depreciation	22,000	44,000
Total assets		$79,860

Liabilities

Accounts payable	$ 4,400	
Notes payable	2,200	
Total liabilities		$ 6,600

Owner's Equity

Dr. Gum, capital		73,260
Total liabilities and owner's equity		$79,860

DR. TEETH
Balance Sheet
September 14, 1987

Assets

Cash		$13,200
Accounts receivable	$ 6,600	
Less: Allowance for doubtful accounts	220	6,380
Dental supplies		1,100
Dental equipment	$22,000	
Less: Accumulated depreciation	4,400	17,600
Total assets		$38,280

Liabilities

Accounts payable	$ 1,100	
Notes payable	4,400	
Total liabilities		$ 5,500

Owner's Equity

Dr. Teeth, capital		32,780
Total liabilities and owner's equity		$38,280

20–4. Baker, Carter, and Masche are all general partners in the BCM Company. Given the following independent assumptions (a) and (b), complete the chart below showing the distribution of income and loss for 1985, 1986, and 1987.

  a. The partnership agreement does not specify how profits and losses are to be distributed.
  b. The partnership agreement states that the profit and loss sharing ratio for Baker, Carter, and Masche is 50:40:10.

Assumption	Year	Net Income (Loss)	Distribution of Partnership Profits and Losses		
			Baker	Carter	Masche
a.	1985	$36,000			
	1986	(9,900)			
	1987	4,500			
b.	1985	36,000			
	1986	(9,900)			
	1987	4,500			

20–5. P. T. Bone and M. E. Debs each have $70,000 interest in the Epitome Company. They have recently decided to admit a third partner, A. S. Samson. What journal entry should be made to record the admission of Samson under each of the following unrelated assumptions?

  a. Samson pays each partner $16,800 for one fifth of his interest.
  b. Samson contributes $14,000 cash to the partnership and receives capital equal to the value of the asset contributed.
  c. Samson contributes $14,000 cash in exchange for capital of $12,600.
  d. Samson contributes $14,000 cash in exchange for capital of $21,000:
    1. Goodwill method.
    2. Bonus method.

Chapter 13 & 14

20–6.

THE JORCON HARDWARE STORE
Adjusted Trial Balance
December 31, 1987

Account Title	Debit	Credit
	Balance	
Cash.	$ 7,000	
Accounts receivable	20,000	
Allowance for doubtful accounts		$ 1,500
Inventory	50,000	
Prepaid insurance	1,000	
Office supplies	500	
Building	40,000	
Accumulated depreciation—building		10,000
Office equipment.	5,000	
Accumulated depreciation— office equipment		1,500
Delivery equipment.	10,000	
Accumulated depreciation— delivery equipment		2,000
Service equipment	15,000	
Accumulated depreciation— service equipment		5,000
Accounts payable		8,000
Interest payable		100
Notes payable		10,000
Mortgage payable		20,000
L. J. Jordan, capital		40,200
K. B. Conner, capital		44,000
L. J. Jordan, drawing	10,000	
K. B. Conner, drawing	9,000	
Sales.		150,000
Cost of goods sold *Expense*	100,000	
Depreciation expense	7,500	
Wages expense	14,000	
Insurance expense	1,200	
Office supplies expense.	700	
Bad debts expense	300	
Other expense	1,100	
	$292,300	$292,300

Inc statement
Rev - COS = gross margin
- expenses = net margin

Required:

1. Prepare the necessary closing entries. (Jordan and Conner share profits and losses equally.)
2. Prepare an income statement for the year ended December 31, 1987.
3. Prepare a balance sheet as of December 31, 1987. *p 620*

Begin + purchases.   *COGS*

25,200 net income

20–7. On January 1, 1987, Sue Collins decides to withdraw from the partnership she has been operating along with Julian Peek and Leigh Raney. Their capital balances are as follows: Collins, $22,000; Peek, $20,000; and Raney, $25,000. What journal entry should be made to record the withdrawal of Collins under each of the following unrelated assumptions?

a. Collins is paid in cash for the full amount of her capital.
b. Collins is paid $18,000 for her capital and Peek and Raney share profits and losses equally. (Use the preferable method of recording a withdrawal.)

20–8. On June 15, 1987, P. R. Reeves and C. N. Orlens decide to liquidate their business, the R&O Partnership. On that date, the partnership had $15,600 in Cash and other assets totaling $35,100. It also had Accounts Payable of $9,750. The capital balances of Reeves and Orlens were $22,100 and $18,850, respectively. They share profits and losses equally.

On June 20, 1987, the creditors were paid in full. On June 27, the assets were sold for $27,950. On June 30, 1987, the Cash was distributed between the partners.

Required:

1. Prepare a statement of liquidation from the above information.
2. Prepare the general journal entries to record the liquidation.

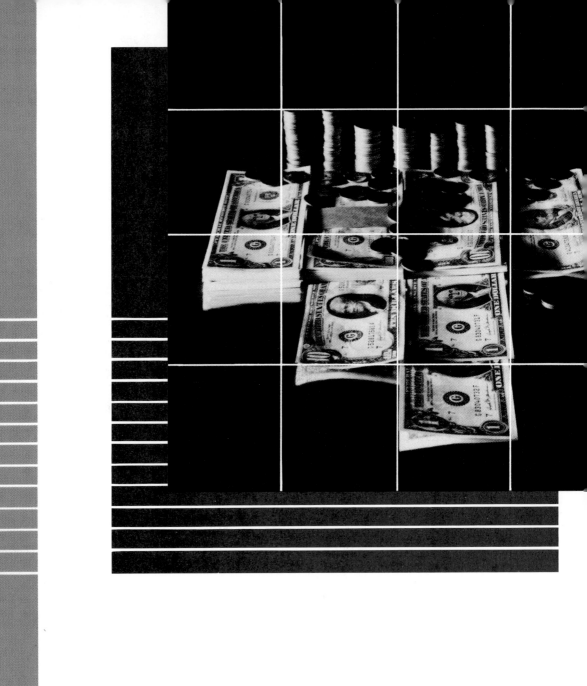

Owners Equity section

read the glossary
key terms
questions
exclude participating
preferred ↑

CHAPTER **21**

Accounting for corporations—organization and capital stock

LEARNING OBJECTIVES

The corporation is a third form of business organization. There are certain legal rights and responsibilities that exist with this form of doing business that do not exist with a partnership or a sole proprietorship. After studying this chapter, you should be able to:

1. Record transactions for a corporate form of business.
2. Prepare the stockholder's equity section of the balance sheet.
3. Prepare a balance sheet for the corporation.
4. Compute the book value per share of each class of stock.

Par value is what you deal with in debits & credits

A **corporation,** unlike a proprietorship or a partnership, is created by law and is separate from its owners. Although the owners, referred to as **stockholders** or **shareholders,** own the corporation, they are not the corporation. Chief Justice Marshall in the *Dartmouth College* case stated: "A corporation is an artifical being, invisible, intangible, and existing only in contemplation of the law." Since a corporation is a separate legal entity, it can own property, sue and be sued, and enter into legal contracts. In short, a corporation has all the rights and responsibilities of an individual except the right to vote and to marry.

Although there are more proprietorships and partnerships than corporations, the dollar amount of business transacted by corporations is much larger than that of proprietorships and partnerships. When compared to the forms of business discussed in the preceding chapter, the corporate form of business has a number of advantages as well as some distinct disadvantages.

ADVANTAGES OF INCORPORATION

A corporation has the following advantages:

1. Limited liability of owners.   Since a corporation is a legal entity separate from its owners, its stockholders are not personally liable for its debts. Each stockholder's liability is limited to the amount of his or her investment. A shareholder does not have unlimited liability for corporate debts or other shareholders' obligations. On the other hand, sole proprietors and general partners have unlimited personal liability for all the debts of their businesses. The limited liability feature is an important advantage of the corporation.

2. Continuity of life.   A corporation continues either forever or for the length of time stated in its charter. A corporation's life is not related to its owners' lives, as is the case with proprietorships and partnerships.

3. Ease of raising equity capital.   A corporation can obtain large amounts of capital by issuing stock. The ownership of a corporation is often divided among thousands of individual stockholders. Sole proprietorships and partnerships have only one or a few owners.

4. Ease of transferring ownership.   Ownership in a corporation is represented by shares of stock. A stockholder can transfer his or her stock to another person without the consent of the other stockholders. In a partnership, a partner must obtain permission from the other partners in order to transfer his or her interest to another person.

5. No mutual agency.   An individual stockholder has no power to bind the corporation or other stockholders to contracts and legal obligations. Because a stockholder is not bound by the acts of the corporation or fellow stockholders, investment in a corporation can be made with less consideration than would be necessary when investing in a partnership. Greater care must be taken when selecting partners because each partner is an agent of the partnership.

DISADVANTAGES OF INCORPORATION

A corporation also has several disadvantages when compared with sole proprietorships and partnerships.

1. Government regulation.   Because corporations are created by state law, states exercise more control and supervision over corporations than over proprietorships and partnerships. Corporate laws vary from state to state, so the laws of the state where the business becomes a corporation must be carefully studied.

2. Double taxation of corporate income.   Because a corporation is a separate legal entity, it must pay income taxes. In effect, corporate income is taxed twice. First, a corporation must pay taxes on its income before any of the income is distributed to stockholders as dividends, and second, stockholders must pay taxes on the dividends they receive. Sole proprietorships and partnerships do not pay income taxes. The individual proprietor or the partners are taxed for the income of these businesses. The double taxation of income is considered the major disadvantage of corporations.

3. Limited ability to borrow money.   Stockholders' limited liability is both an advantage and disadvantage of the corporate form of business. For a small corporation, limited liability is a disadvantage because only the corporation's assets can be used to pay creditors if the firm goes bankrupt. Usually, a partnership can borrow more money than a corporation of equal size because each general partner is personally liable for the partnership's debts. This disadvantage is often avoided if a stockholder personally signs for corporate notes and obligations. Of course, any stockholder who cosigns corporate obligations must pay the debts personally if the corporation is unable to do so.

CORPORATE ORGANIZATION

As mentioned earlier, the laws of the state in which incorporation takes place must be carefully studied. The corporation is legally formed when the state issues a **corporate charter.** The persons applying for incorporation are known as the **incorporators.** The incorporators must draft a proposed charter, called the **articles of incorporation,** showing:

1. The name of the proposed corporation.
2. The address of the corporation.
3. The purpose of corporate organization.
4. The limitations, qualifications, restrictions, and rights of each class of stock, if more than one class is to be issued.
5. The amounts of authorized stock.
6. The name, address, occupation, number of shares held, and amount paid for shares of each of the incorporators.
7. The names, addresses, and length of appointment for the original directors and trustees.

All the incorporators must sign the charter. After the charter has been filed and incorporation fees have been paid, the charter is examined by state officials. If all requirements have been fulfilled, a charter or certificate of incorporation is issued.

Once the charter has been issued, the corporation becomes a legal body. Although the charter contains basic information about the organization of the corporation, a set of **bylaws** governing the actions of the directors and officers is adopted at the first stockholders' meeting. The bylaws contain the following information:

1. The number of directors as well as their duties, qualifications, and terms of office.

2. The duties, authority, and terms of office for corporate officers other than directors.
3. Rules and regulations governing corporate officers and rules governing the election of directors and the appointment of officers.

Because the corporate charter is the basic legal document of the corporation, the bylaws must not contradict or violate the charter. At all times the directors and officers must carry out their duties in accordance with the charter and the bylaws.

CORPORATE MANAGEMENT

Since the stockholders are the owners of the corporation, they have ultimate control. The stockholders of most large corporations, however, are spread out across the country. In addition, many shareholders lack the knowledge and ability needed to run a large corporation. Therefore, the stockholders elect a board of directors to provide professional management. Stockholders' voting rights are based on the number of shares they hold. They elect the directors according to the corporate bylaws.

The board of directors is responsible for managing the corporation and is accountable to the stockholders. The directors, and not the stockholders, are the legal agents of the corporation. The board of directors consists of three or more persons, who may or may not be stockholders. If a large number of directors are elected, an executive committee is appointed and given authority to manage the corporation.

After election by the stockholders, the board of directors appoints the corporate officers. The corporate officers normally include a president, vice president, secretary, and treasurer. In a large corporation a different individual will be appointed for each executive office. In a small corporation it is common to find the same person holding two positions, such as secretary and treasurer. The officers are directly responsible to the board of directors and receive their instructions from them. They have only the authority that the board gives them to carry out specified duties. Officers must perform their duties as outlined in the bylaws; they are liable for fraud and for actions that exceed the duties and authority given in the bylaws. The difference between the board of directors and the corporate officers is that the

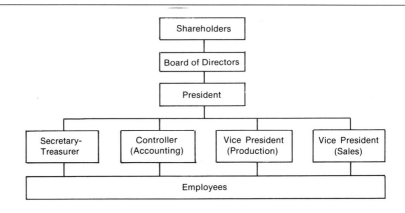

**ILLUSTRATION
21–1**

**Corporate
Organization
Chart**

directors make company plans and policies while the officers carry out the plans in accordance with company policies.

Illustration 21–1 shows a typical corporate organization chart. Note the relationships between stockholders, directors, officers, and company employees.

COSTS OF ORGANIZATION

Costs such as state incorporation fees, attorney's fees, promotional expense, and the cost of printing stock certificates must be incurred to organize a corporation. Such costs are paid only once, but they benefit the corporation during its entire lifetime. Since organization costs benefit more than one period, they should not be expensed completely during the first accounting period. They should be debited to an intangible asset account called Organization Costs and then amortized to expense over a period of 40 years or less. Income tax laws allow organization costs to be amortized over five or more years.

CORPORATE RECORDS

Corporations use many records that are similar to those used by proprietorships and partnerships. However, the following records are unique to the corporate form of organization:

1. Subscriptions records. When a corporation is formed, the incorporators and others who wish to become owners subscribe for a certain number of shares of stock at a specified price per share. A subscription for stock is an agreement to buy shares of a corporation's stock. The shares of stock covered by subscriptions are called subscribed stock. The subscription price is the price specified in the subscription agreement. Subscribers may pay for the stock by transferring cash or other assets or by providing services to the corporation. Stock subscriptions may be made before or after incorporation. Before incorporation, the subscription is actually an agreement to subscribe for stock. Since the corporation does not exist until after incorporation, a subscription made before incorporation is an agreement between the incorporators and the subscribers and not between the corporation and the subscribers.

The amount due from the subscribers is debited to a Subscriptions Receivable account in the general ledger. An account for each subscriber may be kept in a subsidiary ledger or stock payment record. The total amount due from subscribers according to the subscription ledger should equal the balance in the Subscriptions Receivable control account.

2. Stock certificate book. The corporation issues a stock certificate to each subscriber who has fully paid for his or her stock. The certificate identifies the issuing company, the subscriber, the date issued, and the number of shares held. The company officers sign the certificate, which may also be impressed with the company seal. The blank stock certificates often have stubs attached and are bound in a *stock certificate book.* When a stock certificate is issued, the following information should be entered on the stub: the name and address of the stockholder, the number of shares issued, and the date of issuance. Both the certificates and the stubs should be numbered consecutively.

Stockholders who transfer their stock to someone else must return their stock certificates to the corporation. The corporation cancels the old stock certificates and issues one or more new stock certificates to the new stockholders. This procedure is necessary to maintain an up-to-date record of stockholders and the number of shares each holds. Such information is required for voting and dividend purposes.

3. Stockholders' ledger. The **stockholders' ledger** contains an account for each stockholder that shows the number of shares owned as of a particular date. These accounts do not contain dollar amounts.

4. Minutes book. The minutes of stockholders' meetings and board of directors' meetings are recorded in the corporation's **minutes book.** The minutes book contains a detailed narrative record of the proceedings of stockholders' and directors' meetings. It should contain information about decisions related to purchasing and selling plant assets, borrowing money, declaring dividends, issuing bonds, and adopting or amending the bylaws.

CAPITAL STOCK

The division of a corporation's capital into shares of capital stock makes it possible for many people to have equity in the company. Authorized capital stock is the maximum amount of capital stock that a corporation can legally issue, as specified in the corporate charter. It is illegal to issue any stock in excess of the authorized amount. When a corporation sells capital stock and delivers certificates to its stockholders, the stock is said to be issued. Not all of a corporation's authorized stock must be issued; a corporation often has issued and unissued stock. The number of shares outstanding is equal to the number of shares issued less the number of shares reacquired by the corporation either by purchase or donation. Reacquired stock is known as **treasury stock.** Treasury stock is discussed in greater detail in Chapter 22.

Common stock

If a corporation issues only one kind of stock, the stockholders are owners "in common" and the stock is called common stock. Owners of common stock generally have four basic rights:

1. The right to vote for corporate directors and on other issues that are put to a stockholder vote.
2. The right to share in distributions of earnings (dividends) declared by the board of directors.
3. The right to subscribe to additional shares of stock that the corporation may issue, in proportion to their present holdings. This right is referred to as the **preemptive right.** It allows each stockholder to maintain a proportionate share in the corporation's equity if desired.
4. The right to share in distributions of company assets resulting from liquidation of the corporation.

No matter what kind of stock a person owns, his or her rights are always in direct proportion to the number of shares held. This is quite different from a partnership, in which distributions are made in accordance with the articles of copartnership and not in accordance with the amount of each partner's equity or capital.

Preferred stock

Some corporations issue more than one class of stock. Owners of different classes of stock have different rights. Besides common stock, a corporation may issue one or more classes of preferred stock. Preferred stock entitles the owner to certain rights and preferences over common stockholders. Preferred stockholders may have special claims to dividends, assets, or both. Holders of stock with dividend preference have the right to receive a fixed amount of dividends before common stockholders receive any distributions. Holders of stock with preference to assets have the right upon liquidation to receive a certain amount of any remaining company assets before the common stockholders are considered. Preferred stock will usually have a stated liquidation value and a stated dividend rate. Liquidation value is an amount per share that preferred stockholders will receive if the corporation liquidates. In most cases, preferred stockholders do not have voting rights. Preferred stock may be cumulative or noncumulative and participating or nonparticipating.

Cumulative and noncumulative preferred stock. **Cumulative preferred stock** is preferred stock on which dividends accumulate from year to year if they are not paid. A corporation does not have to pay dividends every year. It is only legally obligated to pay a dividend if the board of directors decides to distribute earnings and declares the dividend. All undeclared prior years' dividends on cumulative preferred stock are called **dividends in arrears.** The current year's dividend plus all dividends in arrears must be paid before the common stockholders receive any dividends. Most preferred stock is cumulative. For example, assume that Ramon Products, Inc., a corporation, has cumulative preferred stock outstanding. The stock has a $1.25 per share dividend rate, no dividends have been paid for three years, and 10,000 shares have been outstanding for the past five years. If any dividends are declared, the preferred stockholders must be paid $37,500 (10,000 × $1.25 × 3 years) for dividends in arrears and $12,500 in current dividends (10,000 × $1.25) before any dividends can be paid to common stockholders.

Noncumulative preferred stock is preferred stock on which dividends do not accumulate. A dividend not paid in one year is lost forever. Only the current year's dividend must be paid before common stockholders can receive a dividend.

Participating and nonparticipating preferred stock. **Participating preferred stock** is preferred stock that is allowed to receive dividends in excess of the fixed dividend rate. Participating preferred stockholders receive their regular fixed dividend first. Then the common stockholders receive a certain amount of dividends. Then the preferred stockholders share with the common stockholders in any additional earnings distributions. **Nonparticipating preferred stock** is preferred stock that is entitled to receive only the stated amount of dividends. Most preferred stock is nonparticipating.

Convertible preferred stock. If preferred stock is exchangeable for another class of stock, it is called **convertible stock.** Convertible stock may be exchanged for other shares of stock (usually common stock) on a specified date and in a specified ratio. For example, one share of convertible preferred stock may be exchanged for three shares of common stock. The conversion feature is an advantage when the market value of the common shares has become greater than the market value of the preferred shares.

Callable preferred stock. Callable preferred stock can be bought back from the stockholders at the option of the corporation. The price at which the shares can be called is usually a little higher than the par value. The difference between the call price and the par value is known as the **call premium.**

Par value

Par value is usually the least amount of money for which a corporation may sell a share of stock when the stock is first issued. Some states allow corporations to sell new stock for amounts below par value. If a subscriber buys stock at less than par value when the stock is first issued, he or she incurs a discount liability (excess of par value over selling price) to the corporation or to the corporation's creditors upon liquidation. In other words, if the corporation is liquidated and is unable to settle its debts, stockholders who have bought newly issued stock at below par value are liable for the debts to the extent of the discount.

The par value can be any amount chosen by the incorporators. Par values of $1, $10, and $25 are often used. The par value should be stated in the articles of incorporation and should be printed on each stock certificate. The **authorized capital** of the corporation is equal to the par value per share times the number of shares authorized. Stock is usually issued at or above par value when a firm becomes a corporation.

Par value is a legal notion and has little practical significance. It is not directly related to market value per share. Par value is also called *face value*.

No-par stock and stated value

Stock that does not have a par value is referred to as **no-par stock.** No-par stock can be issued at any amount without any discount liability. Holders of no-par stock cannot be misled into thinking that the value of the stock is equal to its par value.

When no-par stock is issued, there is less temptation to overvalue noncash assets received in exchange for the stock. Directors of a corporation have the power to place a value on noncash assets received in exchange for stock. In the case of par value stock, directors often have overstated the value of the assets received so that the stock will be considered paid for in full and the stockholders will have no discount liability.

The laws permitting no-par stock often require the stock to be assigned a stated value that is similar to par value. The directors usually assign a low value, such as $1. The **legal capital** of the corporation is equal to the par or stated value per share times the number of shares issued. A corporation's legal capital is the amount of capital that must be kept and not distributed to shareholders.

Book value per share is the amount of owner's equity represented by one share of stock. The book value per share of common stock for a company that has only one class of stock is equal to total owner's equity divided by the number of shares outstanding. As with sole proprietorships and partnerships, the owners' equity of a corporation is determined by subtracting total liabilities from total assets. If preferred stock is also outstanding, book value per common share does not include the capital that would be allocated to preferred stockholders at liquidation. The **liquidation value** of the preferred stock is subtracted from total owner's equity, and the resulting figure is divided by the number of outstanding shares of common stock to determine book value per common share. The liquidation value represents preferred's book value per share. For example, assume that A Company has 1,000 shares of preferred stock outstanding with a liquidation value of $105 per share. It also has 10,000 shares of common stock outstanding. The company's balance sheet is as shown in Illustration 21–2.

ILLUSTRATION 21–2

A COMPANY
Balance Sheet
December 31, 1987

Assets

Cash	$ 72,500
Accounts receivable	108,500
Plant, Property, and Equipment	
(net of accumulated depreciation)	327,250
Other assets	120,000
Total assets	$628,250

Liabilities

Accounts payable	$ 27,500
Notes payable	103,000
Other liabilities	16,500
Total liabilities	$147,000

Owner's Equity

6% Preferred stock, $100 par value	
(1,000 shares authorized and outstanding	
with a liquidation value of $105)	$100,000
Common stock, $10 par value (10,000 shares authorized and issued) . .	100,000
Premium on common stock	150,000
Retained earnings	131,250
Total owner's equity	$481,250
Total liabilities and owner's equity	$628,250

Book value of common stock would be computed as follows:

Total owner's equity	$481,250
Less: Liquidation value of preferred stock	105,000
Owner's equity of common stockholders	$376,250

$$\frac{\$376,250}{10,000} = \$37.625 \text{ book value per share}$$

The book value per share of stock is not expected to be the same as the market value per share which is discussed next.

Market value

The **market value** of a share of stock is the price at which it can be bought and sold at a particular time. If the stock is actively traded on a stock exchange, its quoted price is a fair representation of its market value. If an unlisted stock has been bought or sold recently, the purchase or selling price may be used as an estimate of current market value.

Market value per share is influenced by several factors. Probably the most important influence is the expected success of the company in the future. If higher earnings are expected, the market price will probably increase. If lower earnings are expected, the market price will probably decrease. Other contributing factors include past and present earnings and dividends, financial position, general economic conditions, and the effectiveness of management. Par value or stated value, book value, and market value will usually be three different amounts.

ACCOUNTING FOR CAPITAL STOCK TRANSACTIONS

The procedures used to account for a corporation's assets, liabilities, revenues, and expenses are generally the same as those used for sole proprietorships and partnerships. The main differences are in accounting for owner's equity.

In accounting for the owner's equity of a corporation (also known as stockholders' equity), the corporation's earnings are kept separate from the amounts invested by the stockholders. Thus, the owner's equity is composed of two amounts—the equity invested by the stockholders (paid-in capital) and the equity resulting from profitable operations (retained earnings). Keeping invested equity separate from retained earnings is quite different from the system used for sole proprietorships or partnerships in which invested amounts and earnings are combined in owner's capital accounts.

Issuance of stock at par

The basic entry in accounting for owner's equity is recording the issuance of stock. When stock is sold at par value, the proper account is debited for cash and/or other assets received, and the stock account is credited. Noncash assets, such as buildings and equipment, should be recorded at their fair market values. If more than one class of stock exists, a separate account is used for each class.

To illustrate, assume that the Stanley Corporation is authorized to issue 5,000 shares of $100 par value 9% preferred stock and 50,000 shares of $10 stated value common stock. On November 1, 1987, Stanley issues 2,000 shares of preferred stock at par for cash and 10,000 shares of common stock at par for cash. The entry to record this transaction is:

		GENERAL JOURNAL			
DATE		ACCOUNT AND EXPLANATION	P.R.	DEBIT	CREDIT
1987					
Nov.	1	Cash		30 0 0 0 0 00	
		9% Preferred Stock			20 0 0 0 0 00
		Common Stock			10 0 0 0 0 00
		Issued 2,000 shares of 9% preferred stock and			
		10,000 shares of common stock at par.			

To continue the illustration, assume that on November 15, Stanley issued 5,000 shares of common stock for land with a market value of $10,000 and a building with a market value of $40,000. The entry to record this transaction is:

		GENERAL JOURNAL			
DATE		ACCOUNT AND EXPLANATION	P.R.	DEBIT	CREDIT
1987					
Nov.	15	Land		1 0 0 0 0 00	
		Building		4 0 0 0 0 00	
		Common Stock			5 0 0 0 0 00
		Issued 5,000 shares of common stock for			
		land and a building.			

Issuance of stock at a premium or a discount

Original issues of capital stock are often sold at par. However, shares are sometimes sold at prices above par and, if permitted by state law, at prices below par.

If more than the par value is paid for stock, the difference is credited to Premium on Common Stock. As an example, assume that 100 shares of common stock with a par value of $25 are sold for $30 per share. The entry in general journal form is:

			GENERAL JOURNAL								
DATE			ACCOUNT AND EXPLANATION	P.R.	DEBIT		CREDIT	
1987								
Nov.	16	Cash			3 0 0 0 00			
			Common Stock				2 5 0 0 00	
			Premium on Common Stock				5 0 0 00	
			To record sale of stock at a premium.					

If stock is sold for less than its par value, the difference between the par value and the price of the stock is debited to Discount on Common Stock. To illustrate, assume that 200 shares of common stock with a par value of $10 are sold for $8 per share. The journal entry is:

			GENERAL JOURNAL								
DATE			ACCOUNT AND EXPLANATION	P.R.	DEBIT		CREDIT	
1987								
Nov.	16	Cash			1 6 0 0 00			
			Discount on Common Stock			4 0 0 00		
			Common Stock				2 0 0 0 00	
			To record sale of stock at a discount.					

The premium account is an owner's equity account whereas the discount account is a contra owner's equity account because it reduces owner's equity. Some states do not permit the issuance of stock at a discount. Other states allow stock to be issued at a discount only under certain conditions. As already discussed, in some states, stockholders who purchase stock at a discount are held personally liable for the amount of the discount. If the corporation liquidates and is unable to pay its creditors in full, stockholders can be forced to contribute amounts up to the amount of the discount.

Issuance of stated value stock

Not all states require stock to have a par value. Many states allow the issuance of no-par stock, but some states require it to be assigned a stated value. Stated value is an arbitrary amount assigned by the board of directors to each share of stock. Generally, the stated value represents the corporation's legal capital, which cannot be withdrawn by stockholders.

Accounting for stated value stock is similar to accounting for par value stock. If stock is sold for its stated value, Cash is debited and the capital stock account is credited. If stock is sold for more than its stated value, Cash is debited for the amount received, the capital stock account is credited for the stated value, and an account called Paid-in Capital in Excess of Stated Value is credited for the difference between the selling price and the stated value. The Paid-in Capital in Excess of Stated Value account is comparable to the Premium on Stock account used for par value stock.

To illustrate, assume that the Felix Corporation issues 2,000 shares of $10 stated value common stock for $22,000. In addition, the corporation issues 500 shares to its organizers in return for services provided. The stock has a market value of $11 per share according to the stock market quotations. The journal entries to record these transactions are:

GENERAL JOURNAL

DATE		ACCOUNT AND EXPLANATION	P.R.	DEBIT	CREDIT
1987					
Nov.	18	Cash		2 2 0 0 0 00	
		Common Stock			2 0 0 0 0 00
		Paid-in Cap. in Excess Std. Value			2 0 0 0 00
		To record issuance of 2,000 shares at $11.			
	18	Organization Costs		5 5 0 0 00	
		Common Stock			5 0 0 0 00
		Paid-in Cap. in Excess Std. Value			5 0 0 00
		To record issuance of 500 shares to			
		corporation's organizers.			

Issuance of no-par stock

Accounting for no-par stock without a stated value is simpler than accounting for par value or stated value stock. When no-par stock is issued, the capital stock account is credited for the amount of cash or market value of other assets received. There is no premium or discount on no-par stock. For example, assume that Caleb Corporation issues 5,000 shares of no-par common stock for $20,000 cash. The journal entry is:

	GENERAL JOURNAL			
DATE	ACCOUNT AND EXPLANATION	P.R.	DEBIT	CREDIT
1987				
Nov. 19	Cash		20000 00	
	Common Stock			20000 00
	To record issuance of no-par stock.			

Accounting for stock subscriptions

As discussed earlier, a corporation may obtain subscriptions for its stock. In a stock subscription, the subscriber agrees to buy a certain number of shares at a specified price called the **subscription price.** The subscriber also agrees to pay for the shares either all at one time or in installments over a predetermined length of time. When shares are subscribed to, the transaction is recorded by debiting Subscriptions Receivable and crediting *Common Stock Subscribed* (assuming that the subscription is for par value). To illustrate, assume that a subscription is received for 50 shares of common stock at $15. The shares have a $10 par value. The general journal entry to record the subscription is:

	GENERAL JOURNAL			
DATE	ACCOUNT AND EXPLANATION	P.R.	DEBIT	CREDIT
1987				
Nov. 20	Subscriptions Receivable		750 00	
	Common Stock Subscribed			500 00
	Premium on Common Stock			250 00
	To record stock subscriptions for 50 shares.			

Payments on the subscription should be debited to Cash (or other asset received) and credited to Subscriptions Receivable. It is important to note that the stock is not issued until payment has been made in full for the subscription. If payment is made in installments, the Subscriptions Receivable account is reduced by the amount of each payment, and the stock is issued when subscriptions have been paid in full. Based on the information given in the previous entry, assume that a cash payment is made for the full subscription price. The entries to record the receipt of cash and issuance of stock in general journal form are as follows:

					GENERAL JOURNAL				
DATE		ACCOUNT AND EXPLANATION	P.R.	DEBIT		CREDIT	
1987							
Nov.	30	Cash		7 5 0 00			
		Subscription Receivable				7 5 0 00	
		To record the payment on Subscriptions					
		Receivable.					
	30	Common Stock Subcribed		5 0 0 00			
		Common Stock				5 0 0 00	
		To record issuance of stock.					

If a balance sheet is constructed on a date when subscriptions have not been paid in full, the Subscriptions Receivable account is reported in the current assets section. The Common Stock Subscribed account is shown in the owner's equity section of the balance sheet and represents the amount of equity that will eventually be added to common stock. The Premium on Common Stock account is also shown in the owner's equity section.

Illustration of a corporation's balance sheet

Several new balance sheet accounts have been introduced in this chapter. A corporation's balance sheet containing these new accounts is shown in Illustration 21–3. The new accounts are:

Current Assets   Subscriptions Receivable, 8% Preferred Stock ①
                     Subscriptions Receivable, Common Stock ②
Intangible Assets   Organization Costs ③
Owner's Equity   8% Preferred Stock ④
                     Preferred Stock Subscribed ⑤
                     Premium on Preferred Stock ⑥
                     Common Stock ⑦
                     Common Stock Subscribed ⑧
                     Paid-in Capital in Excess of Stated Value ⑨
                     Retained Earnings ⑩

ILLUSTRATION 21–3

BOATSMAN CORPORATION
Balance Sheet
December 31, 1987

Assets

Current assets:

Cash		$ 12,000
Notes receivable		10,000
Interest receivable		200
Accounts receivable	$80,000	
Less: Allowance for doubtful accounts	1,000	79,000
① Subscriptions receivable, 8% preferred stock		2,600
② Subscriptions receivable, common stock		7,500
Merchandise inventory and supplies		131,000
Prepaid insurance		1,000
Total current assets		$243,300

Plant assets:

Office equipment	$42,000		
Less: Accumulated depreciation	16,800	$ 25,200	
Store equipment	$80,000		
Less: Accumulated depreciation	20,000	60,000	
Total plant assets			85,200

Intangible assets:

③ Organization costs	10,000
Total assets	$338,500

Liabilities and Owner's Equity

Liabilities:

Current liabilities:

Notes payable	$ 20,000	
Accounts payable	100,000	
Accrued salaries payable	5,000	
Accrued interest payable	1,000	
Total liabilities		$126,000

Owner's equity:

Paid-in capital:

④ 8% Preferred stock, $50 par value (1,000 shares authorized; 800 shares issued)	$40,000		
⑤ Preferred stock subscribed (100 shares)	5,000		
⑥ Premium on preferred stock	1,800	$ 46,800	
⑦ Common stock, $10 stated value (10,000 shares authorized; 6,000 shares issued)	$60,000		
⑧ Common stock subscribed (1,000 shares)	10,000		
⑨ Paid-in capital in excess of stated value	35,000	105,000	
Total paid-in capital		$151,800	
⑩ Retained earnings		60,700	
Total owner's equity			212,500
Total liabilities and owner's equity			$338,500

As discussed in previous chapters, owner's equity is the difference between total assets and total liabilities. Owner's equity in a corporation comes from two sources—(1) investments by stockholders, called **paid-in capital** or *contributed capital,* and (2) retained earnings. The owner's equity section of the balance sheet varies for different corporations depending on the classes of stock and the amounts paid for each.

SUMMARY

A **corporation** is a legal entity separate from its owners and creditors. The owners of a corporation are called **stockholders** or **shareholders.** Among the advantages of doing business as a corporation are:

1. Limited liability.
2. Continuous existence.
3. Procurement of capital through stock issuance.
4. Ease of transferring ownership.
5. Owner's inability to legally bind the corporation and the corporation's inability to legally bind the owners.

Some of the disadvantages are:

1. Strict state regulation.
2. Double taxation.
3. Limited ability to borrow funds.

A corporation is legally formed when a **corporate charter** is issued. Before incorporation, the incorporators draft a proposed charter known as the **articles of incorporation.** After the corporate charter is issued, a set of **bylaws** governing the corporation and its officers is adopted.

The owners of the corporation do not directly manage its day-to-day operations. Instead, they elect a **board of directors** to perform the management functions. The board of directors appoints the corporate officers.

When a corporation is being organized, costs are incurred, such as state incorporation fees, attorney's fees, promotional expenses, and stock certificate printing costs. These expenses are recorded as an intangible asset of the corporation, **Organization Costs.**

A corporation must keep permanent records, including a **subscriptions ledger,** stock certificate books, a **stockholders' ledger,** and a corporate minutes book.

Corporate ownership is evidenced by **stock certificates.** Upon incorporation, a corporation is authorized to issue a specified amount of stock that is known as the **authorized capital** stock. There are two basic classes of stock: common and preferred. The various kinds of stock are accounted for based on the proceeds received.

If only one class of stock is issued, it is **common stock.** It is called common stock because the stockholders are owners "in common." Common stockholders have four basic rights:

1. The right to vote for corporate directors.
2. The right to share in distributions of earnings declared by the board of directors.
3. The right to subscribe to additional shares that the corporation may issue, in proportion to their present holdings (the **preemptive right**).
4. The right to share in the distribution of the company's assets resulting from a liquidation of the corporation.

Preferred stock is another class of stock that is sometimes issued. It is called preferred stock because its owners are entitled to certain rights and preferences over common stockholders. Preferred stock can be **cumulative** or **noncumulative** and **participating** or **nonparticipating.** Special kinds of preferred stock may be issued, such as convertible preferred stock and callable preferred stock. Convertible preferred stock can be exchanged for common stock. Callable preferred stock can be bought back from the stockholder at the corporation's option.

Accounting for stock transactions and owner's equity requires the use of special accounts. Some of these are:

1. Subscriptions Receivable.
2. Organization Costs.
3. Preferred Stock.
4. Preferred Stock Subscribed.
5. Premium on Preferred Stock.
6. Common Stock.
7. Common Stock Subscribed.
8. Paid-in Capital in Excess of Stated Value.
9. Retained Earnings.

KEY TERMS

Articles of Incorporation—A document submitted to the state by persons wishing to form a corporation. It contains significant information about the proposed corporation.

Authorized Capital—The *par* value of shares times the number of shares authorized.

Board of Directors—A group of persons elected by the stockholders of a corporation. They are given responsibility for directing the affairs of the corporation.

Book Value—The proceeds that each stockholder of a corporation would receive if all the corporation's assets were liquidated at amounts stated on the books and all its debts and obligations were paid.

Bylaws—A set of rules and regulations adopted by the stockholders of a corporation to govern the conduct of the affairs of the corporation within the general laws of the state and the policies and purposes found in the corporate charter.

Call Premium—With regard to callable preferred stock, it is the difference between the call price and the par value of the stock.

Capital Stock Authorized—The class or classes and amount of capital stock that a corporation may issue as specified in the corporate charter.

Common Stock—The residual equity of a corporation. Common stockholders have voting privileges and receive assets and dividends only after preferred stockholders have been paid.

Corporate Charter—A document granted by the state that acknowledges a corporation's legal existence.

Corporation—A business organization created by law. It is viewed as a legal entity separate from its owners and creditors. Ownership in a corporation is usually shown by shares of capital stock.

Cumulative Preferred Stock—Preferred stock on which dividends accumulate each year if they are not declared.

Discount on Stock—The amount by which the par value exceeds the selling price of newly issued stock.

Dividends in Arrears—All undeclared prior years' dividends on cumulative preferred stock.

Double Taxation—The process of taxing corporate earnings twice—first at the corporate level before distribution and again at the individual level after the earnings are distributed to the stockholders.

Incorporators—The persons who apply for incorporation of an organization.

Issued Stock—Stock that has been delivered to stockholders.

Legal Capital—The minimum amount of paid-in capital that a corporation must maintain. It is the par or stated value times the number of shares issued. It cannot be withdrawn by stockholders.

Liquidation Value—The amount per share that will be paid to preferred stockholders upon liquidation of the corporation.

Market Value—The price at which shares of stock can be bought and sold at a particular time.

Noncumulative Preferred Stock—Preferred stock on which dividends not declared in one year are lost forever.

Nonparticipating Preferred Stock—Preferred stock that is entitled to receive only the stated amount of dividends.

No-Par Stock—Stock that does not have a par value; it may or may not have a stated value.

Organization Costs—Costs incurred to organize a corporation, such as attorneys' fees, incorporation fees, promotional expense, and costs of printing stock certificates. They are an intangible asset.

Outstanding Stock—Stock which has been issued and is still in the hands of stockholders; issued stock minus treasury stock.

Paid-in Capital—Amounts invested by stockholders.

Participating Preferred Stock—Preferred stock that is allowed to receive dividends in excess of the fixed dividend rate.

Par Value (or Face Value)—An arbitrary amount assigned to each share of capital stock of a given class and printed on the stock certificate. It represents the legal capital of the corporation.

Determined by whoever does the incorporation

Preemptive Right—A stockholder's right to subscribe to additional issuances of stock in proportion to his or her present holdings so that the stockholder can maintain proportionate ownership of the corporation.

Preferred Stock—A class of corporate capital stock which carries certain privileges and rights not given to all outstanding shares of stock. Holders of preferred stock are usually entitled to a specified dividend before any dividend payment may be made on common stock. Preferred stockholders usually have no voting rights.

Premium on Stock—The amount by which the selling price of newly issued stock exceeds its par value.

Retained earnings — profit or loss

Shareholders (or Stockholders)—Basically, the owners of a corporation.

Stated Value—An arbitrary amount assigned to each share of no-par stock by the board of directors. It represents the legal capital of the corporation.

Stock Certificate—A document that shows proof of ownership in a corporation.

Stockholders' Ledger—A subsidiary ledger that contains an account for each stockholder showing the number of shares owned as of a particular date. A stockholders' ledger does not contain dollar amounts.

Stock Payment Record—A record kept for each stock subscriber showing the amount owed for subscriptions to stock.

Subscribed Stock—Stock that individuals have agreed to purchase but for which stock certificates have not yet been issued.

Subscriber—A person who agrees to purchase shares of a corporation's stock.

Subscription—An agreement to purchase shares of a corporation's stock.

Subscription Ledger—A subsidiary ledger that contains an account for each stock subscriber showing the amount owed for subscriptions to stock.

Subscription Price—The price a subscriber agrees to pay for shares of stock in a subscription contract.

Subscriptions Receivable—A control account showing the total amount owed by stock subscribers.

Treasury Stock—Stock that has been issued and reacquired by the issuing corporation but has not been canceled. *Deduction from owners equity*

QUESTIONS AND EXERCISES

1. Discuss the advantages and disadvantages of the corporate form of organization.
2. What items are contained in a corporation's charter? In its by-laws?
3. Describe the organizational chart of a corporation. What is the difference between directors and officers?

4. What are the normal costs that are incurred to organize a corporation? How are such costs expensed?

5. What are the four basic rights of common stockholders?

6. How does preferred stock differ from common stock? What is meant by each of the following terms associated with preferred stock?

   a. Cumulative.
   b. Noncumulative.
   c. Participating.
   d. Nonparticipating.

7. Distinguish among par value, book value, and market value of common stock.

8. What are the two components of owner's equity?

9. How does the owner's equity section of a corporation's balance sheet differ from the owner's equity section of a proprietorship or partnership's balance sheet?

10. The Milton Hart Corporation has the following amounts of capital stock outstanding:

    4,000 shares of 7% preferred stock, $100 par value, $105 liquidation value.

    12,000 shares of common stock, $10 stated value.

    The corporation has total owner's equity of $854,000. Compute the book value per share of common stock. (All current year dividends on preferred stock have been paid.)

11. The Quarterman Corporation was organized on March 3, 1987, and was authorized to issue 7,500 shares of 9% cumulative preferred stock with a $100 par value and 75,000 shares of $10 par value common stock. Record the following selected transactions which occurred during 1987.

    Mar. 4 Sold 7,500 shares of common stock at par for cash.
          5 Issued 150 shares of common stock to Charles Sanders in exchange for legal services connected with incorporation. Mr. Sander's bill amounted to $1,500.
    Apr. 10 Sold for cash 1,500 shares of preferred stock at $103 per share.
    May 15   Issued 7,500 shares of common stock for a building and tract of land. The building and land have market values of $67,500 and $15,000, respectively.

12. John Miller subscribed to 80 shares of Slimey Corporation stock on May 1. The stock has a par value of $10, but John agreed

to pay $17 per share. He paid for the stock on June 1, and Slimey Corporation issued the stock upon the receipt of the cash. What general journal entries should be made to record the subscription, the receipt of cash, and the issuance of the stock?

13. The Hurley Corporation is authorized to issue 10,000 shares of $25 par value 8% preferred stock and 100,000 shares of $10 par value common stock. Given the following account balances as of December 31, 1987, prepare the owners' equity section of the corporation's December 31, 1987, balance sheet.

	Debits	Credits
Discount on preferred stock	$6,400	
Common stock		$560,000
Premium on common stock		480,000
Preferred stock subscribed		10,000
8% preferred stock		80,000
Common stock subscribed		40,000
Retained earnings		348,800

PROBLEMS

21–1. The Blakely Company applied for and received a charter from the state of Vermont that authorized it to issue 30,000 shares of common stock with a $60 par value.

Required:

Prepare journal entries to record the following owner's equity transactions.

1987
Jan. 20   Received cash and issued 5,000 shares at par.
Mar. 15   Received subscriptions for 6,000 shares at $100 per share. A $40 per share down payment accompanied the subscriptions.
Apr. 30   Received the balance due on the March 15 subscriptions and issued the stock.
July 10   Issued 2,000 shares in exchange for a building valued at $100,000 and land valued at $30,000.
Sept. 20   Issued 8,000 shares for $470,000 cash.

21-2. When the Moore Corporation was organized, it was authorized to issue 40,000 shares of $10 par value common stock and 10,000 shares of $20 par value preferred stock. The preferred stock has a liquidation value of $25 per share. The following owners' equity section appeared on the Moore Corporation's balance sheet on December 31, 1987.

Owner's Equity

Preferred stock, $20 par, 8,000 shares issued	$160,000
Common stock, $10 par, 30,000 shares issued	300,000
Retained earnings	500,000
Total owner's equity	$960,000

Required:

Compute the book value per share for each class of stock.

21-3. The Sterling Corporation has been granted a charter and has been authorized to issue 10,000 shares of $10 par value preferred stock and 50,000 shares of $20 par value common stock.

1987

Jan. 5 Sold and issued 5,000 shares of preferred at par.
  11 Received subscriptions to 3,000 shares of common at $25 per share.
Feb. 11 Received a $15 per share payment on all January 11 subscriptions.
Mar. 11 Received balance due on January 11 subscriptions and issued the stock certificates.
June 18 Received subscriptions to 1,000 shares of preferred at $20 per share.
July 3 Sold and issued 4,000 shares of common at par.
  19 Received payment for June 18 subscriptions and issued the stock.
Aug. 14 Sold and issued 2,000 shares of common at $50 per share.

Required:

1. Record the above transactions in general journal form.
2. Prepare the owner's equity section of the Sterling Corporation's balance sheet as it would appear on December 31, 1987. (Assume retained earnings are $40,000 at December 31, 1987.)

21-4. The Tanner Corporation was organized on September 5, 1987, and was authorized to issue 2,000 shares of 7½% preferred stock with a $50 par value and 50,000 shares of no-par common stock with a $5 stated value. During 1987, the Tanner Corporation completed the following owners' equity transactions:

1987

Sept. 6 Received subscriptions to 6,000 shares of common stock at $8 per share and collected 20 percent of the subscription price.

8 Issued 500 shares of common stock to the original promoters of the corporation for services valued at $4,000.

Oct. 10 Received balance due on the September 6 subscriptions and issued the stock.

12 Sold and issued 1,500 shares of preferred stock at $51 per share.

Nov. 3 Sold and issued 7,500 shares of common stock at $10 per share.

17 Issued 1,000 shares of common stock for land valued at $11,000.

Dec. 2 Received subscriptions to 5,000 shares of common stock at $12 per share and collected one third of the subscription price.

10 Received subscriptions to 200 shares of preferred stock at $54 per share and collected one half of the subscription price.

Required:

1. Record the above transactions in general journal form.

2. Prepare the owners' equity section of the Tanner Corporation's balance sheet as it would appear on December 31, 1987. (Assume retained earnings are $86,000 at December 31, 1987.)

21–5. The Morse Company has been granted a charter and has been authorized to issue 5,000 shares of preferred stock with a par value of $25 per share and 15,000 shares of no-par common stock. The following owners' equity transactions took place during the company's first year of operation.

1987

Jan. 10 Sold and issued 2,000 shares of preferred at par.

20 Received subscriptions to 4,000 shares of common at $35 per share. Received $15 of the price of each share.

Feb. 21 Received balance due on January 20 subscriptions and issued the stock.

Aug. 3   Sold and issued 7,000 shares of common stock at $30 per share.

Oct. 12   Received subscriptions for 1,000 shares of preferred at $40 per share.

Nov. 12   Received payment for October 12 subscriptions and issued stock.

     15   Sold and issued 1,500 shares of preferred at $45 per share.

Dec. 10   Sold and issued 3,200 shares of common at $25 per share.

Required:

1. Record the above transactions in general journal form.
2. Prepare the owners' equity section of the Morse Company's balance sheet as it would appear on December 31, 1987. (Assume retained earnings are $36,000 at December 31, 1987.)

21–6. The Branan Corporation is authorized to issue 5,000 shares of 8% preferred stock with a $100 par value and 100,000 shares of no-par common stock with a stated value of $20. The worksheet for the corporation shows the following account balances in the Balance Sheet columns at December 31, 1987:

Subscriptions receivable—common	$ 90,000
Cash	13,500
Accounts payable	99,000
Building	441,000
Equipment	153,000
Common stock	540,000
Preferred stock	180,000
Accumulated depreciation, building	44,100
Allowance for doubtful accounts	2,700
Merchandise inventory	225,000
Land	27,000
Premium on preferred stock	3,600
Accumulated depreciation, equipment	72,000
Retained earnings	72,000
Organization costs	10,800
Notes payable	9,000
Paid-in capital in excess of stated value	90,900
Common stock subscribed	18,000
Accounts receivable	171,000

Required:

Prepare a balance sheet as of December 31, 1987.

21–7. The Hecht Corporation is authorized to issue 20,000 shares of 7% preferred stock with a $50 par value and 500,000 shares of common stock with a $10 par value. The worksheet for the corporation shows the following account balances in the Balance Sheet columns at December 31, 1987:

Allowance for doubtful accounts	$ 15,000
Interest receivable	2,000
Common stock	2,400,000
Accounts payable.	500,000
Cash .	51,000
7% preferred stock	600,000
Subscriptions receivable—preferred.	50,000
Accrued salaries payable	30,000
Notes receivable	50,000
Mortgage note payable, due 1990	300,000
Accumulated depreciation, buildings	380,000
Accumulated depreciation, equipment.	96,000
Discount on preferred stock	60,000
Premium on common stock	1,300,000
Land .	500,000
Retained earnings	1,500,000
Subscriptions receivable—common .	150,000
Preferred stock subscribed.	100,000
Equipment .	1,200,000
Buildings	3,800,000
Organization costs	100,000
Accounts receivable .	600,000
Prepaid insurance	50,000
Merchandise inventory .	850,000
Common stock subscribed.	200,000
Accrued interest payable	2,000
Short-term notes payable	40,000

Required:

Prepare a balance sheet for December 31, 1987.

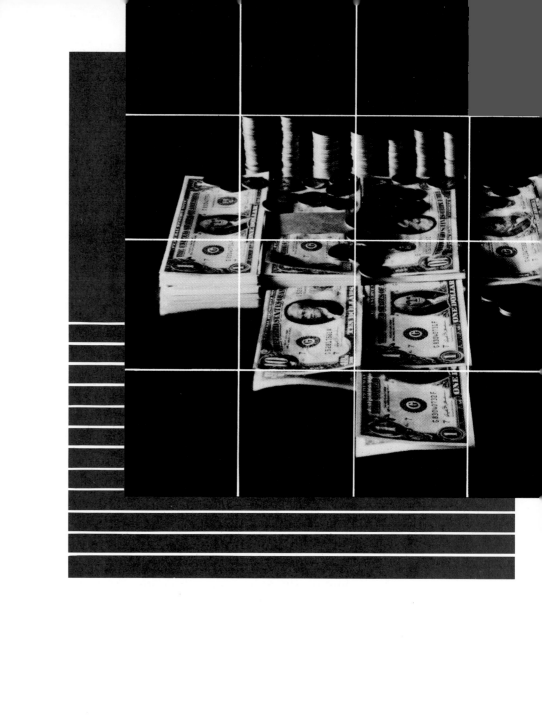

CHAPTER 22

Accounting for corporations—income taxes, retained earnings, dividends, and treasury stock

---

LEARNING OBJECTIVES

Owner's equity is affected by much more than the transactions discussed in Chapter 21. The results of a corporation's operations have a significant effect on the owner's equity. Chapter 22 increases your understanding of accounting for a corporation's transactions after its formation and issuance of capital stock. After studying this chapter, you should be able to:

1. Compute the estimated federal income tax a corporation must pay.
2. Compute the actual federal income tax a corporation must pay.
3. Prepare journal entries that record the declaration and payment of both cash and stock dividends.
4. Record both the purchase and sale of treasury stock.
5. Record donations of assets and stock to the corporation.
6. Record the entry for retiring stock.
7. Prepare the closing entries for the corporate form of business.
8. Prepare the following statements for the corporation:
   a. Income statement.
   b. Statement of retained earnings.
   c. Balance sheet.

669

Chapter 21 described the organization of a corporation and the accounting entries required to record the original issuance of capital stock. This chapter concentrates on the year-end accounting procedures followed by a corporation, and the accounting entries used to record dividend and treasury stock transactions.

DETERMINING CORPORATE NET INCOME AND INCOME TAXES

In most respects a corporation's net income is computed in the same way as the net income of a proprietorship or partnership. It is determined by subtracting total expenses from total revenues. The only difference is that corporations are subject to federal income taxes, and sometimes state and local taxes, while a sole proprietorship's income is taxed to the proprietor. A partnership's income is taxed to the individual partners. As forms of organization, corporations pay income taxes but partnerships and proprietorships do not. Thus, a corporation's income statement may show income tax expense and a corporation's balance sheet may show prepaid income taxes or income tax payable.

Corporations are required to estimate the amount of federal income taxes they will have to pay for the coming year. Then they must pay the estimated taxes in four equal installments during the year. Each payment is recorded by a debit to Income Taxes and a credit to Cash.

At the end of the year, the corporation computes its income before tax and determines its actual tax liability. If the actual tax liability is less than the amount paid, the corporation debits the overpayment to Prepaid Income Taxes or Income Taxes Paid in Advance, a current asset account, and credits Income Tax. If the actual tax liability is greater than the amount paid, the corporation debits Income Tax and credits Income Tax Payable, a current liability account, for the amount of the underpayment. The liability can be paid in two equal installments which are recorded by debits to Income Tax Payable and credits to Cash.

Accounting for income taxes

To illustrate accounting for income taxes, assume that the Biltweed Corporation, on January 3, 1987, estimates its 1987 income before tax to be $600,000. The corporate tax rates are:[1]

---

[1] These tax rates are in effect as of 1984. However, tax rates are subject to change by congressional action.

15 percent of the first $25,000 of income
18 percent of the second $25,000 of income
30 percent of the third $25,000 of income
40 percent of the fourth $25,000 of income
46 percent of all income in excess of $100,000

Thus, the corporation estimates its federal income tax for 1987 to be $255,750, computed as follows:

15 percent of $25,000 = $ 3,750	
18 percent of $25,000 = 4,500	
30 percent of $25,000 = 7,500	
40 percent of $25,000 = 10,000	
46 percent of $500,000 = 230,000	
Estimated tax liability $255,750	

The corporation pays the estimated taxes in four installments of $63,937.50 each on April 15, June 15, September 15, and December 15. The following journal entry is required to record the payment of each installment:

GENERAL JOURNAL

DATE	ACCOUNT AND EXPLANATION	P.R.	DEBIT	CREDIT
1987				
	Income Tax		6 3 9 3 7 50	
	Cash			6 3 9 3 7 50
	To record quarterly installment payment of			
	federal income taxes.			

On December 31, 1987, Biltweed Corporation computes its income before tax for the year to be $650,000. Thus, its actual tax liability for 1987 is $278,750:

15 percent of $25,000 = $ 3,750	
18 percent of $25,000 = 4,500	
30 percent of $25,000 = 7,500	
40 percent of $25,000 = 10,000	
46 percent of $550,000 = 253,000	
Actual tax liability $278,750	

As a result the corporation owes the federal government an additional $23,000 ($278,750 − $255,750) of income tax. The adjusting journal entry required to recognize the additional tax liability is:

GENERAL JOURNAL

DATE		ACCOUNT AND EXPLANATION	P.R.	DEBIT	CREDIT
1987					
Dec.	31	Income Tax		2 3 0 0 0 00	
		Income Tax Payable			2 3 0 0 0 00
		To record additional tax liability for 1987.			

The corporation can pay the additional tax liability in two install-ments of $11,500 each on March 15 and June 15, 1988. The entry to record each payment is:

GENERAL JOURNAL

DATE	ACCOUNT AND EXPLANATION	P.R.	DEBIT	CREDIT
1988				
	Income Tax Payable		1 1 5 0 0 00	
	Cash			1 1 5 0 0 00
	To record installment payment of one-half of additional tax liability for 1987.			

Closing entries for a corporation

At the end of each accounting period, after all necessary adjusting journal entries, including the income tax adjustment, have been re-corded, each expense and revenue account must be closed. In addition, the Income Tax account must be closed to the Income Summary account. Then the balance in the Income Summary account is trans-ferred to the Retained Earnings account. If a company has operated at a loss during the accounting period, the Summary account will have a debit balance before being closed to Retained Earnings. The Summary account is closed in this case by debiting Retained Earnings and crediting the Summary account. The debit will reduce Retained Earnings. If operations have been profitable, the Summary account will have a credit balance and will be closed by debiting the Summary account and crediting Retained Earnings. If the Retained Earnings account has a debit balance after closing the Income Summary ac-count, the debit balance is referred to as an operating **deficit** and is shown as a deduction in the owner's equity section of the balance sheet.

Here are the 1987 closing entries for the Rangle Corporation:

GENERAL JOURNAL					
DATE	ACCOUNT AND EXPLANATION	P.R.	DEBIT	CREDIT	
1987					
Dec. 31	Sales		80 0 0 0 0 00		
	Interest Revenue		2 0 0 0 00		
	Income Summary			80 2 0 0 0 00	
	To close revenue accounts.				
31	Income Summary		52 2 0 0 0 00		
	Selling Expense			32 0 0 0 0 00	
	Administrative Expenses			20 2 0 0 0 00	
	To close expense accounts.				
31	Income Summary		10 8 5 5 0 00		
	Income Tax			10 8 5 5 0 00	
	To close income tax account.				
31	Income Summary		17 1 4 5 0 00		
	Retained Earnings			17 1 4 5 0 00	
	To close income summary account.				

The credit of $171,450 to retained earnings represents Rangle's net income for the year. Rangle's 1987 income statement is:

RANGLE CORPORATION
Income Statement
For the Year Ended December 31, 1987

Revenues:		
Sales	$800,000	
Interest revenue	2,000	
Total revenues		$802,000
Expenses:		
Selling expenses	$320,000	
Administrative expenses	202,000	
Total expenses		522,000
Income before income taxes		$280,000
Income taxes		108,550
Net income.		$171,450

RETAINED EARNINGS

Retained earnings is an owner's equity account that represents accumulated earnings held by or reinvested in the business. In each period the retained earnings account is either credited for the amount of net income or debited for the amount of net loss. Other debits to retained earnings are appropriations of retained earnings for specific purposes and declarations of dividends to stockholders.

Appropriations of retained earnings

Net income can either be distributed to stockholders as dividends or retained in the business to finance growth. Most modern stockholders are aware that not all income will be distributed as dividends. In the past, boards of directors have made journal entries to transfer portions of retained earnings to **appropriations of retained earnings.** An appropriation of retained earnings has the purpose of reducing the amount of retained earnings available for dividends. The required entry is a debit to Retained Earnings and a credit to an appropriation account that reflects the reason for restricting distributions (for example, Appropriation for Plant Expansion). The appropriation does not set aside an amount of cash for the purpose indicated; it only lets stockholders know that a part of earnings will be reinvested in the company rather than distributed as dividends. The use of formal appropriations of retained earnings has virtually disappeared.

Statement of retained earnings

A **statement of retained earnings** is a corporate financial statement that explains the change in retained earnings that has occurred between two successive balance sheet dates. The statement starts with the retained earnings balance at the beginning of the period, adds net income or deducts a net loss, and deducts dividends to arrive at the retained earnings balance at the end of the period. The Rangle Corporation's statement of retained earnings is shown below:

RANGLE CORPORATION *similar to owners equity*
Statement of Retained Earnings
For the Year Ended December 31, 1987

Retained earnings, Jan. 1	$300,000
Add: Net income	171,450
	$471,450
Less: Dividends	63,640
Retained earnings, Dec. 31	$407,810

Retained earnings maintains a balance

DIVIDENDS

A dividend is a distribution by a corporation to its stockholders. The distribution may be in the form of cash, other assets, or the corporation's own stock.

Cash dividends

Cash dividends are the most common type and are usually stated as a number of dollars per share. For example, assume that a corporation declared a cash dividend of $1.25 per share of common stock. A stockholder who owns 100 shares will receive $125 ($1.25 × 100).

Three dates surround the declaration and distribution of a dividend: the date of declaration, the date of record, and the date of payment. The **date of declaration** is the date on which the corporation's board of directors votes to declare a dividend. Dividends become a legal liability on the date of declaration. The **date of record** is the date on which it is determined stockholders are entitled to receive the dividends. To receive a dividend, a stockholder's name must be registered in the corporation's stock records on the date of record. The time lag between the date of declaration and the date of record gives stockholders time to register their stock on the corporation's records, if they have not already done so. The **date of payment** is the date on which the dividends are distributed to the stockholders.

For example, assume that the board of directors of Scott Manufacturing Company declares a cash dividend of $1 per share on May 9, payable on May 25 to stockholders of record on May 20. Note that no entry is necessary on the date of record, May 20. Assuming that Scott Manufacturing Company has 10,000 shares of common stock outstanding, the entries in general journal form to record the declaration and subsequent payment are:

GENERAL JOURNAL

DATE 1987		ACCOUNT AND EXPLANATION	P.R.	DEBIT	CREDIT
May	9	Retained Earnings		1 0 0 0 0 00	
		Dividends Payable			1 0 0 0 0 00
		To record declared dividend.			
	25	Dividends Payable		1 0 0 0 0 00	
		Cash			1 0 0 0 0 00
		To record dividend payment.			

Between the date of declaration and the date of payment, the declared dividends are a current liability of the corporation. Before the board of directors can declare a cash dividend, the corporation must have an adequate amount of both retained earnings and cash.

Stock dividends

A **stock dividend** is a distribution of additional shares of a corporation's stock to the stockholders based on the number of shares they already own. Stock dividends may be issued because:

1. The corporation is short of cash but the board of directors wish to satisfy the stockholders by giving them something.
2. Stock dividends create more shares, and having more shares available tends to reduce a stock's market price. Lower priced shares are usually more easily marketable.
3. Stock dividends are not taxable income to stockholders, but cash dividends are.
4. The board of directors may wish to transfer a portion of a large Retained Earnings balance to permanent capital.

When a stock dividend is declared, a debit equal to the market value of the shares to be distributed is made to the Retained Earnings account. An amount equal to the par or stated value of the shares is credited to Stock Dividend Distributable. The excess of market value over par is credited to Premium on Common Stock. Alternatively, the excess of market value over stated value is credited to Paid-in Capital in Excess of Stated Value. In the case of no-par stock, the entire market value is credited to Stock Dividend Distributable. The Stock Dividend Distributable account is not a liability account because no money or other assets will be distributed. When the stock is distributed, the Stock Dividend Distributable account is debited and the Common Stock account is credited. Dates of declaration, record, and distribution (payment) may be used for a stock dividend just as they are for a cash dividend. If a balance sheet is constructed between the dates of declaration and distribution, the Stock Dividend Distributable account is shown as part of owner's equity. However, since no liability is created by the declaration of a stock dividend (no asset value will be paid out, only stock) frequently only one entry is made, on the date of payment.

For example, assume that the board of directors of the Shallow Mine Company declares a 20 percent common stock dividend on August 12 to be distributed on September 1 to stockholders of record on August 25. The 20 percent dividend means that one share will be distributed for every five (100% ÷ 20%) shares outstanding. Assuming that the common stock of Shallow Mine company has a par value of $10 and a market value of $15 and that 20,000 shares are outstanding, the following general journal entries are needed to record the declaration and distribution of the stock dividend:

GENERAL JOURNAL					
DATE 1987	ACCOUNT AND EXPLANATION	P.R.	DEBIT	CREDIT	
Aug. 12	Retained Earnings		6 0 0 0 0 00		
	Premium on Common Stock			2 0 0 0 0 00	
	Common Stock Dividend Distrib.			4 0 0 0 0 00	
	To record stock dividend of 4,000 shares				
	(0.20 × 20,000 = 4,000).				
Sept. 1	Common Stock Dividend Distributable		4 0 0 0 0 00		
	Common Stock			4 0 0 0 0 00	
	To record distribution of stock.				

Owners Equity account

If only one entry were made on the day of payment, it would be as follows:

GENERAL JOURNAL					
DATE 1987	ACCOUNT AND EXPLANATION	P.R.	DEBIT	CREDIT	
Sept. 1	Retained Earnings		6 0 0 0 0 00		
	Premium on Common Stock			2 0 0 0 0 00	
	Common Stock			4 0 0 0 0 00	
	To record and pay 20% stock dividend.				

A stock dividend does not affect a corporation's assets or liabilities. It only transfers part of the retained earnings to the invested capital accounts. A stock dividend does not increase owner's equity. It only changes the structure of the owner's equity section of the balance sheet. Because the increased number of shares issued represents the same amount of equity, stock dividends are not regarded as income to stockholders and are not included in their taxable income.

After a stock dividend, a stockholder's proportionate interest in the corporation remains unchanged. For example, assume that Lynn Steel owns 1,000 shares in a corporation that has 5,000 shares outstanding. Thus, she owns 20 percent of the stock. The corporation declares a 10 percent stock dividend and issues 500 (5,000 × 10%) new shares. Lynn receives 100 shares (20% × 500). After the dividend, Lynn still owns 20 percent (1,100 ÷ 5,500) of the corporation. She owns more shares, but the total book value of her shares does not change because owner's equity has not increased. The book value per share, however, decreases because more shares are outstanding.

Retained Earnings is debited for the market value of the shares issued only when stock dividends are 25 percent or less of the total stock outstanding. For stock dividends of more than 25 percent, Retained Earnings is debited for the par or stated value of the shares issued. A practical reason for this difference in treatment is that stock dividends of 25 percent or less rarely affect market value. Larger stock dividends will probably affect market value and so market value should not be entered into the accounts.

The above example of Lynn Steel illustrates the less than 25 percent rule. Assume that the market price is $27 per share and par value is $25. The 10 percent dividend of 500 shares (5,000 × 10%) is worth $13,500 (500 × $27). The following entry may be made on the payment date:

GENERAL JOURNAL

DATE		ACCOUNT AND EXPLANATION	P.R.	DEBIT	CREDIT
1988					
Jan.	15	Retained Earnings		13 500 00	
		Common Stock			12 500 00
		Premium on Common Stock			1 000 00
		To record the 10% stock dividend declared and paid.			

On the other hand, if the stock dividend is 30 percent, the entry is:

GENERAL JOURNAL

DATE		ACCOUNT AND EXPLANATION	P.R.	DEBIT	CREDIT
1988					
Jan.	15	Retained Earnings		37 500 00	
		Common Stock			37 500 00
		To record and pay the 30% stock dividend.			

The $37,500 debit to Retained Earnings is computed as follows:

$$5,000 \text{ shares} \times 30\% = 1,500 \text{ shares}$$
$$1,500 \text{ shares} \times \$25 \text{ par value} = \$37,500$$

Liquidating dividends

A **liquidating dividend** is a return *of* all or part of the stockholders' investment. It is different from an ordinary cash dividend which is a return *on* the stockholders' investment or a distribution of earnings. A liquidating dividend reduces permanent capital, while a cash dividend only reduces retained earnings.

A corporation pays liquidating dividends when it is reducing its size or when it is going out of business. Liquidating dividends are debited to paid-in capital accounts instead of Retained Earnings. To illustrate, assume that Fairbanks Company is liquidating. It returns all $500,000 of its stockholders' investment: $400,000 in the Common Stock account and $100,000 in the Premium on Common Stock account. The journal entry is:

GENERAL JOURNAL

DATE		ACCOUNT AND EXPLANATION	P.R.	DEBIT	CREDIT
1988					
June	15	Common Stock		40 0 0 0 0 00	
		Premium on Common Stock		10 0 0 0 0 00	
		Cash			50 0 0 0 0 00
		To record a 100% liquidating dividend.			

Stock split

A **stock split** is (1) a reduction in the par or stated value of shares and (2) the issuance of an increased number of shares. The balance in the Common Stock account remains the same after a stock split. For example, in a 2-for-1 stock split, the corporation doubles the number of shares outstanding but reduces the par value per share by one half. Assume that a corporation has 50,000 shares of $10 par value common stock outstanding. The company splits the stock 2 for 1. After the split, the corporation has 100,000 shares of $5 par value common stock outstanding. For each share of $10 par value stock owned, a shareholder receives two shares of $5 par value stock. The journal entry to record the stock split is:

GENERAL JOURNAL					
DATE 1988		ACCOUNT AND EXPLANATION	P.R.	DEBIT	CREDIT
June	15	Common Stock ($10 par) 150,000		50 0 0 0 0 00	
		Common Stock ($5 par) 100,000			50 0 0 0 0 00
		To record 2-for-1 stock split.			

The total book value of common stock outstanding remains the same, but the book value per share is less. Generally, the market value per share will be reduced by approximately one half. In fact, stock splits are used to increase the number of shares and reduce the market price per share in order to make the stock more marketable.

TREASURY STOCK

Treasury stock is stock that has been issued and reacquired by the corporation but has not been canceled and retired. Stock cannot be reissued if it has been canceled and retired. A corporation can reacquire stock by purchasing it in the open market. In addition, stockholders can donate stock to the corporation so that the corporation can resell it and obtain additional cash.

Treasury stock has no voting rights, no cash dividend rights, no preemptive right, and no right to share in assets upon corporate liquidation. Treasury stock can be sold at a price below par or stated value without the purchaser being held liable for the amount of the discount.

A corporation may decide to purchase its own stock for one or more of the following reasons:

1. The corporation may need shares of stock to give or sell to officers or employees under bonus agreements or stock option plans.
2. The corporation may want to stabilize the market price of its stock.
3. The corporation may have sold stock to employees under

an agreement to repurchase the stock upon termination of employment.
4. The corporation may need to have shares available in order to acquire other companies.
5. The corporation may wish to reduce the amount of stock outstanding.

Accounting for treasury stock transactions

When a corporation purchases its own stock, the cost is debited to a Treasury Stock account. When treasury stock is sold, Cash is debited for the selling price of the stock and Treasury Stock is credited for the cost of the stock to the corporation. Any excess of selling price over cost is credited to an account called Paid-in Capital from Sale of Treasury Stock. Any excess of cost over selling price is debited to Paid-in Capital from Sale of Treasury Stock to the extent of the account's credit balance from previous sales of treasury stock. Any additional excess of cost over selling price is debited to Retained Earnings.

To illustrate accounting for treasury stock transactions, assume that the Baker Corporation has the following owner's equity account balances at January 3, 1987:

Common stock, $10 par value (50,000 shares authorized;
40,000 shares issued) $400,000
Premium on common stock 100,000
Retained earnings 180,000
      Total owner's equity. $680,000

On January 14, the corporation purchases 5,000 shares of its common stock at $15 per share. The journal entry is:

GENERAL JOURNAL

DATE		ACCOUNT AND EXPLANATION	P.R.	DEBIT	CREDIT
1987					
Jan.	14	Treasury Stock		75000 00	
		Cash			75000 00
		To record purchase of 5,000 shares of common			
		stock at $15 per share.			

On February 10, the corporation sells 3,000 shares of treasury stock at $20 per share. On March 21, the corporation sells 1,700 shares of treasury stock at $9 per share. The journal entries to record these transactions are:

GENERAL JOURNAL

DATE		ACCOUNT AND EXPLANATION	P.R.	DEBIT	CREDIT
1987					
Feb.	10	Cash (3,000 × $20)		6 0 0 0 0 00	
		Treasury Stock (3,000 × $15)			4 5 0 0 0 00
		Paid-in Cap. from Sale of Treasury Stock			1 5 0 0 0 00
		To record sale of 3,000 shares of treasury			
		stock at $20 per share.			

GENERAL JOURNAL

DATE 1987		ACCOUNT AND EXPLANATION	P.R.	DEBIT	CREDIT
Mar.	21	Cash (1,700×$9)		1 5 3 0 0 00	
		Paid-in Cap. from Sale of Treasury Stock		1 0 2 0 0 00	
		Treasury Stock (1,700 × $15)			2 5 5 0 0 00
		To record sale of 1,700 shares of treasury			
		stock at $9 per share.			

Suppose that a shareholder donates 100 shares of common stock to the Baker Corporation on July 6 and the corporation sells the shares for a total of $1,200 on August 8. The journal entries to record these transactions are:

GENERAL JOURNAL

DATE		ACCOUNT AND EXPLANATION	P.R.	DEBIT	CREDIT
1987					
July	6	Memorandum Entry			
		Received 100 shares of common stock			
		as a donation from a stockholder.			
Aug.	8	Cash		1 2 0 0 00	
		Paid-in Capital from Donations			1 2 0 0 00
		To record sale of 100 shares of donated			
		treasury stock at $12 per share.			

After all the treasury stock transactions have been posted to the accounts, the owner's equity accounts appear as follows:

Common Stock		Premium on Common Stock	
	400,000		100,000

Treasury Stock			Paid-in Capital from Sale of Treasury Stock	
(5,000 shares) 75,000	(3,000 shares) 45,000			15,000
	(1,700 shares) 25,500		10,200	
Memo: 100 shares donated	Memo: 100 donated shares sold			4,800
(300 shares) 4,500				

Paid-in Capital from Donations		Retained Earnings	
	1,200		180,000

Owner's Equity:
  Paid-in Capital:
  Common stock, $10 par value
    (50,000 shares authorized;
    40,000 shares issued, of which
    300 shares are in the treasury) $400,000

Premium on common stock	100,000	$500,000
Paid-in capital from sale of treasury stock		4,800
Paid-in capital from donations		1,200
Total paid-in capital		$506,000
Retained earnings		180,000
		$686,000
Less: Treasury stock (300 shares at cost)		4,500
Total owner's equity		$681,500

The Treasury Stock account is shown as a deduction from owner's equity. It is *not* an asset account because a corporation cannot own a part of itself.

The account called Paid-in Capital from Donations is also credited when the corporation receives gifts, such as tracts of land from cities. For example, assume that the City of Glendale gives Baker Corporation a tract of land with a market value of $13,000 to induce the corporation to build a plant there. The journal entry is:

	GENERAL JOURNAL			
DATE 1987	ACCOUNT AND EXPLANATION	P.R.	DEBIT	CREDIT
Aug. 15	Land		1 3 0 0 0 00	
	Paid-in Capital from Donations			1 3 0 0 0 00
	To record gift of land from city of Glendale.			

RETIREMENT OF STOCK

A corporation can also purchase shares of its own common or preferred stock and permanently cancel and retire them. Such an action can be taken, however, only if it does not jeopardize the interests of creditors and other stockholders.

When a corporation purchases stock for retirement, Cash is credited for the cost of the stock and the paid-in capital accounts are debited for the price at which the stock was originally issued. If the corporation buys the stock for more than its original issue price, the difference is debited to Retained Earnings. If the corporation buys the stock for less than its original issue price, the difference is credited to Paid-in Capital from Retirement of Stock.

Accounting for retired stock

To illustrate accounting for the retirement of stock, assume that the Cadmium Corporation has outstanding 10,000 shares of $100 par value 8% preferred stock that were originally issued at $105 per share. Cadmium repurchased half the shares in the open market at $98 per share and retired them. There is a gain on retirement because the purchase price of $98 is less than the original issue price of $105. The journal entry to record the retirement is:

GENERAL JOURNAL								
DATE 1987		ACCOUNT AND EXPLANATION	P.R.	DEBIT		CREDIT		
Aug.	31	8% Preferred Stock		50 0 0 0 0 00			
		Premium on Preferred Stock		2 5 0 0 0 00			
		Cash				49 0 0 0 0 00	
		Paid-in Capital from Retirement of Stock				3 5 0 0 0 00	
		To record purchase and retirement of 5,000					
		shares of 8% preferred stock at $98 per share.					

The account called Paid-in Capital from Retirement of Stock is an owner's equity account.

At a later date, the Cadmium Corporation purchases the remaining 5,000 shares of preferred stock at $106 per share. The purchase price is higher than the original issuance price. The loss on retirement must be debited to Retained Earnings and reduces the balance in that account. The entry to record the retirement is:

GENERAL JOURNAL								
DATE 1987		ACCOUNT AND EXPLANATION	P.R.	DEBIT		CREDIT		
Sept.	30	8% Preferred Stock		50 0 0 0 0 00			
		Premium on Preferred Stock		2 5 0 0 0 00			
		Retained Earnings		5 0 0 0 00			
		Cash				53 0 0 0 0 00	
		To record purchase and retirement of 5,000					
		shares of 8% preferred stock at $106 per share.					

Corporation balance sheet illustrated

A comprehensive corporate balance sheet is illustrated on page 686 to review the new accounts discussed in this chapter and the previous chapter. The new accounts are:

1. Subscriptions Receivable, preferred stock.
2. Subscriptions Receivable, common stock.
3. Organization Costs.

4. Dividends Payable.
5. Income Tax Payable.
6. 7% Preferred Stock.
7. Preferred Stock Subscribed.
8. Discount on Preferred Stock.
9. Common Stock.
10. Stock Dividend Distributable.
11. Common Stock Subscribed.
12. Paid-in Capital in Excess of Stated Value. *sell stock at above stated value*
13. Paid-in Capital from Donations.
14. Paid-in Capital from Sale of Treasury Stock.
15. Paid-in Capital from Retirement of Stock.
16. Retained Earnings.
17. Treasury Stock.

POSTON CORPORATION
Balance Sheet
December 31, 1987

Assets

Current assets:			
Cash			$ 200,000
Accounts receivable	$1,000,000		
Less: Allowance for doubtful accounts	20,000	980,000	
① Subscriptions receivable, preferred stock		30,000	
② Subscriptions receivable, common stock		20,000	
Merchandise inventory		2,500,000	
Prepaid expenses		300,000	
Total current assets			$4,030,000
Plant assets:			
Equipment	$1,200,000		
Less: Accumulated depreciation	500,000	$ 700,000	
Building	$3,000,000		
Less: Accumulated depreciation	1,000,000	2,000,000	
Land		550,000	
Total plant assets			3,250,000
Intangible assets:			
③ Organization costs			7,000
Total assets			$7,287,000

Liabilities and Owner's Equity

Liabilities:
  Current liabilities:

	Notes payable	$ 50,000	
	Accounts payable	450,000	
	Interest payable	2,000	
	Accrued liabilities	100,000	
④	Dividends payable	250,000	
⑤	Income tax payable	48,000	
	Total current liabilities		$ 900,000

Long-term liabilities:

Mortgage note payable (due 1994)		500,000	
Total liabilities			$1,400,000

Owner's Equity:
  Paid-in capital:

⑥	7% preferred stock, $100 par value (10,000 shares authorized; 7,000 shares issued)	$ 700,000	
⑦	Preferred stock subscribed (500 shares)	50,000	
⑧	Less: Discount on preferred stock	(38,000)	$ 712,000
⑨	Common stock, $5 stated value (500,000 shares authorized; 250,000 shares issued, of which 50,000 are in the treasury)	$1,250,000	
⑩	Stock dividend distributable (20,000 shares)	100,000	
⑪	Common stock subscribed (5,000 shares)	25,000	
⑫	Paid-in capital in excess of stated value	2,200,000	3,575,000
⑬	Paid-in capital from donations		500,000
⑭	Paid-in capital from sale of treasury stock		100,000
⑮	Paid-in capital from retirement of stock		200,000
	Total paid-in capital		$5,087,000
⑯	Retained earnings		1,200,000
			$6,287,000
⑰	Less: Treasury stock (50,000 shares at cost)		(400,000)
	Total owner's equity		5,887,000
	Total liabilities and owner's equity		$7,287,000

SUMMARY

As a separate legal entity, a corporation is subject to income taxes. First, the corporation's income before tax is computed. Then graduated tax rates are applied to the current income to determine the corporation's tax liability. Corporations are required to make estimated quarterly payments of their income taxes. Once actual income is known, the final tax payment is adjusted.

At the end of the accounting period, the Income Tax account is closed to the Income Summary account, as are all the revenue and expense accounts. The Income Summary account is then closed to the **Retained Earnings** account.

The Retained Earnings account reflects the net accumulation of the corporation's earnings over time. Net income can be distributed to stockholders as dividends or retained in the business to finance business growth. A **Statement of Retained Earnings** is usually prepared at the end of an accounting period to show the changes in the Retained Earnings account for the fiscal period.

Dividends are distributions to stockholders. They may take the form of cash, other assets, or the corporation's own stock. Three important dates surround dividends: the **date of declaration,** the **date of record,** and the **date of payment.** The date of declaration is the date on which the board of directors formally states that a dividend will be paid. The date of record is the date on which stockholders must own the stock in order to receive the dividend when it is paid. The date of payment is when the dividend is paid to the stockholders.

A **stock dividend** is treated differently from other dividends. A corporation usually distributes stock when it is short of cash or when it wants to decrease the market value of its stock. A stock dividend is not taxable income for the stockholders. For the corporation it is simply a transfer from retained earnings to the stock accounts.

A corporation can also reacquire its own stock. The reacquired stock is known as treasury stock. It is recorded in a separate **Treasury Stock** account and is shown as a reduction in owner's equity on the balance sheet. When treasury stock is sold, any gain on the sale is credited to an account called Paid-in Capital from Sale of Treasury Stock. A loss on the sale is debited to the same account up to the balance in the account. Any additional loss is debited to Retained Earnings.

A corporation can also retire its own stock. When stock is retired, the corporation's assets are reduced by the amount it costs the corporation to repurchase the stock. The stock accounts are reduced by the amount at which the stock was issued. Any gain on retirement is credited to Paid-in Capital from Retirement of Stock and any loss is debited to Retained Earnings.

KEY TERMS

Appropriations of Retained Earnings—Retained earnings that are restricted in their use; they are unavailable for dividends.

Cash Dividend—A corporation's distribution of cash to its stockholders. It represents a return on investment.

Date of Declaration—The date on which a corporation's board of directors formally states that the corporation will pay a dividend.

Date of Payment—The date on which declared dividends will be paid.

Date of Record—The date on which the corporation will determine which stockholders will be eligible to receive dividends.

Deficit—A debit balance in the Retained Earnings account.

Liquidating Dividend—A return of part or all of the stockholders' investment in a corporation. It is paid when the corporation is going out of business or reducing its size.

Retained Earnings—An owner's equity account that represents accumulated earnings that have not been distributed to stockholders.

Statement of Retained Earnings—A corporate financial statement that explains the change in retained earnings that has occurred between two successive balance sheet dates.

Stock Dividend—A corporation's distribution of additional shares of stock to its stockholders. The distribution is proportional to stockholders' current holdings.

Stock Split—A reduction in the par or stated value of shares and the issuance of an increased number of shares such that the balance in the Common Stock account stays the same.

Treasury Stock—Stock that has been issued and reacquired by the corporation but has not been canceled and retired.

QUESTIONS AND EXERCISES

1. How does the determination of a corporation's net income differ from the determination of a proprietorship's or partnership's net income?
2. Corporations are required to remit quarterly estimates of their federal tax liability to the federal government. When the actual tax liability is computed, how is an overpayment of tax handled on the books? How is an underpayment handled?
3. Briefly describe the closing process for corporations.

4. The Nunn Corporation had retained earnings of $45,000 on January 1, 1987. During 1987, the corporation had net income of $70,000 and declared dividends of $32,000. Prepare a statement of retained earnings for the year ended December 31, 1987.

5. The Novak Company is authorized to issue 100,000 shares of $10 par value common stock. On December 8, the Novak Company has 80,000 shares of issued stock, 30,000 of which are in the treasury. On December 8, the board of directors declares a cash dividend of 50 cents per common share payable on January 30 to the stockholders of record on January 15. What journal entry should be made on each of the three mentioned dates?

6. Why might a company decide to distribute stock dividends?

7. The Wesley Corporation has 60,000 shares of $5 stated value common stock outstanding on January 15. The board of directors declares a 10 percent stock dividend on January 15, distributable on March 1 to the stockholders of record on February 5. The stock has a market price of $15 per share on January 15. What journal entries are needed to record the declaration and issuance of the dividend?

8. How does a liquidating dividend differ from an ordinary cash dividend?

9. Why might a corporation decide to purchase its own stock?

10. On July 1, the Phillips Corporation purchased 4,000 shares of its own common stock at $20 per share. On July 31, it sold 1,400 shares of its treasury stock at $23 per share. On August 15, it sold 700 shares of its treasury stock at $16 per share. Prepare journal entries to record the above transactions.

11. Monica Lane donated 200 shares of Tunnel Corporation's $10 par value common stock to the Tunnel Corporation. The corporation sold all the stock at $8 per share. Prepare journal entries to record these transactions.

12. The Vance Corporation has outstanding 15,000 shares of 10% preferred stock with a par value of $50. The shares were originally sold at $52 per share. What journal entry is required to cancel and retire the stock under each of the following conditions?
    a. The corporation purchases the stock in the open market at $48 per share.
    b. The corporation calls the stock at $54 per share.

13. The Anson Corporation has decided to retire some of its outstanding capital stock. It will purchase 2,500 shares at $65 per share. The stock is common stock with a par value of $50 per share

and an original premium of $12 per share. Record the journal entry for the retirement transaction.

PROBLEMS

22–1. On January 1, 1987, the Fricks Corporation estimated its income before taxes for 1987 would be $225,000. It then estimated its federal income tax liability and paid the liability in four equal quarterly installments.

On December 31, 1987, the corporation determined that its actual income before taxes was $260,000. Accordingly, the corporation's accountant adjusted the Income Tax account.

Required:

1. Compute the corporation's estimated federal income tax liability and its actual federal income tax liability. Assume the tax is 15 percent on the first $25,000, 18 percent on the second $25,000, 30 percent on the third $25,000, 40 percent on the fourth $25,000 and 46 percent on the remainder of income.
2. Prepare general journal entries to record the four installment tax payments.
3. Prepare a general journal entry to adjust the Income Tax account on December 31, 1987.

22–2. The Tucson Corporation had retained earnings of $200,000 on January 1, 1987. During 1987 the board of directors declared preferred stock dividends of $50,000 and common stock dividends of $25,000. The corporation generated total revenues of $500,000 and incurred total expenses (excluding income taxes) of $400,000.

Required:

1. Compute the corporation's net income. Assume the tax is 15 percent on the first $25,000, 18 percent on the second $25,000, 30 percent on the third $25,000, 40 percent on the fourth $25,000 and 46 percent on the remainder of income earned.
2. Prepare a statement of retained earnings for the year ended December 31, 1987.

22–3. On January 1, 1987, the Mulcahy Corporation has 75,000 shares of $20 par value 8% preferred stock outstanding and 400,000 shares of $10 par value common stock outstanding.

On July 1, the corporation declares an 8% cash dividend on the preferred stock and a $0.50 per share cash dividend on the common stock. The dividends are payable on August 5 to stockholders of record on July 20.

On September 1, the corporation declares a 5% stock dividend on the common stock. The market value of the common stock is $30 per share. The dividend is distributable on October 5 to stockholders of record on September 20.

On December 20, the corporation splits the common stock 2 for 1.

Required:

Prepare general journal entries to record the above transactions.

22–4. On January 1, 1987, the Kersey Corporation's owner's equity accounts have the following balances:

Common stock, $5 par value (100,000 shares authorized, 70,000 shares issued)	$350,000
Premium on common stock	280,000
Retained earnings	190,000

During the first quarter of 1987, the following owner's equity transactions occur:

1987
Jan. 10 Purchase 14,000 shares of common stock in the open market at $10 per share.
    31   Sell 6,000 shares of treasury stock at $12 per share.
Feb. 15 Declare an $0.80 per share cash dividend payable on March 15 to stockholders of record on February 28.
Mar. 15 Pay cash dividend declared on February 15.
    20   Sell 5,000 shares of treasury stock at $7 per share.

Required:

1. Prepare general journal entries to record the above transactions.
2. Prepare a schedule showing the owner's equity account balances after the above transactions have been posted.

22–5. The owner's equity section of the Lundquist Company's January 1, 1987, balance sheet is shown below:

Owner's equity:
  Paid-in capital:
    8% preferred stock, $50 par value
      (10,000 shares authorized;

6,000 shares issued)	$300,000		
Premium on preferred stock	30,000	$ 330,000	
Common stock, $10 par value			
(120,000 shares authorized;			
90,000 shares issued)	$900,000		
Premium on common stock.	270,000	1,170,000	
Total paid-in capital			$1,500,000
Retained earnings			600,000
Total owner's equity			$2,100,000

The following owner's equity transactions occurred during 1987:

Jan. 20   Purchased 10,000 shares of common stock in the open market at $16 per share.

Mar. 15   Declared an 8% cash dividend on the preferred stock. The dividend is payable on April 15 to stockholders of record on March 30.

Apr. 10   Sold 4,000 shares of treasury stock at $18 per share.

     15   Paid the cash dividend declared on March 15.

June 1   Declared a cash dividend of $1.00 per share on the common stock. The dividend is payable on July 2 to stockholders of record on June 15.

July 2   Paid the cash dividend declared on June 1.

     15   Received a donation of 300 shares of common stock from a stockholder.

Aug. 12   Sold the 300 shares of donated treasury stock at $17 per share.

Sept. 16   Sold 6,000 shares of treasury stock at $13 per share.

Oct. 20   Purchased and retired all the preferred stock at $54 per share.

Nov. 1   Received as a gift a tract of land valued at $22,000 from the city of Moreland.

     15   Declared a 20% common stock dividend distributable on December 20 to stockholders of record on December 5. The common stock has a market value of $20 per share.

Dec. 20   Distributed stock dividend declared on November 15.

     31   Closed the credit balance of $300,000 in the Income Summary account to Retained Earnings.

Required:

1. Prepare general journal entries to record the above transactions.

2. Prepare the owner's equity section of the December 31, 1987, balance sheet.

22–6. The balance sheet accounts of the Melton Corporation are shown below along with their December 31, 1987 balances:

Subscriptions receivable—preferred	$ 100,000
Subscriptions receivable—common	100,000
Treasury stock (100,000 shares at cost)	2,000,000
Organization costs	100,000
Cash	576,000
Accounts payable	1,000,000
Land	1,200,000
Accumulated depreciation, building	5,500,000
Equipment	6,000,000
Notes payable (due 1988)	500,000
Allowance for doubtful accounts	100,000
Merchandise inventory	5,000,000
Common stock dividend distributable (32,500 shares)	325,000
Paid-in capital from donations	200,000
Building	9,500,000
Mortgage note payable (due 1990)	1,000,000
Accounts receivable	3,100,000
Common stock subscribed (20,000 shares)	200,000
Accumulated depreciation, equipment	2,500,000
Common stock, $10 par value	7,500,000
Income tax payable	200,000
Premium on common stock	1,500,000
Dividends payable—common	325,000
7% preferred stock, $50 par value	1,750,000
Preferred stock subscribed (2,000 shares)	100,000
Retained earnings	5,000,000
Discount on preferred stock	74,000
Paid-in capital from sale of treasury stock	50,000

The corporation is authorized to issue 50,000 shares of 7% preferred stock and 1,000,000 shares of common stock.

Required:

Prepare a balance sheet for December 31, 1987.

22–7.

TUMBLER CORPORATION
Adjusted Trial Balance
December 31, 1987

	Debit	Credit
		Balance
Cash	$ 10,000	
Accounts receivable	20,000	
Allowance for doubtful accounts		$ 1,000
Subscriptions receivable	10,000	
Merchandise inventory	70,000	
Office supplies	1,000	
Prepaid rent	9,600	
Store equipment	25,000	
Accumulated depreciation, store equipment		5,000
Office furniture	20,000	
Accumulated depreciation, office furniture		2,500
Accounts payable		10,500
Notes payable		5,000
Interest payable		250
Income tax payable		1,270
Common stock, $5 stated value		40,000
Common stock subscribed		25,000
Common stock dividend distributable		4,000
Paid-in capital in excess of stated value		8,000
Retained earnings		47,435
Sales		497,000
Cost of goods sold	420,000	
Rent expense	9,600	
Salaries and wages expense	40,000	
Bad debts expense	2,500	
Depreciation expense	3,500	
Office supplies expense	2,000	
Interest expense	550	
Income tax	3,205	
	$646,955	$646,955

The Tumbler Corporation is authorized to issue 15,000 shares of common stock.

Retained earnings were $53,035 at January 1, 1987. During the year, the only debit to the Retained Earnings account was a $5,600 debit for the market value of the shares to be distributed as a stock dividend.

Required:

1. Prepare the necessary closing journal entries.
2. Prepare an income statement.
3. Prepare a statement of retained earnings.
4. Prepare a balance sheet.

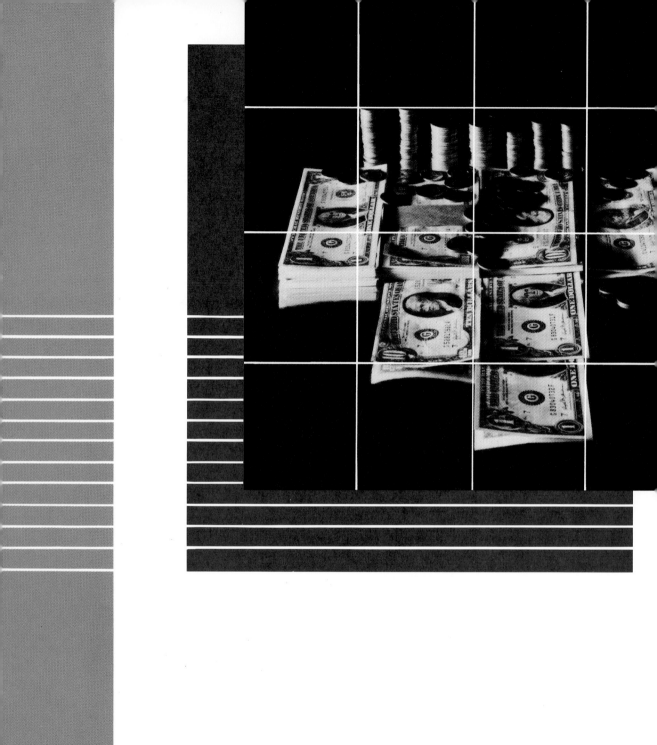

CHAPTER 23

Accrual accounting—
wholesale business

[handwritten notes:] p 909 910 read Cost of goods sold

[handwritten notes:] prove bank bal p 722 & 726 Petty cash over or short Payroll statement P 727 B 720

LEARNING OBJECTIVES

This chapter presents the day-by-day accounting procedures of a wholesale business. After studying this chapter, you should be able to:

1. Prepare journal entries for a wholesaler in the following books of original entry:
   Cash receipts journal.
   Cash disbursements journal.
   Sales register.
   Invoice register.

2. Foot and post transactions from the books of original entry to the proper ledgers.

3. Prepare a daily bank statement.

4. Prove the bank balance.

5. Record transactions in a petty cash disbursements record.

6. Record the entry to replenish the petty cash fund.

Wholesalers purchase products directly from manufacturers and importers. The **wholesaler** then sells the products to a retailer, who, in turn, sells them to individual customers. Because wholesalers facilitate trade between manufacturers and retailers, they are often referred to as middlemen. Since the wholesaler buys in large quantities, the goods are purchased at a lower cost per unit. The purchased products are then marked up and sold to retailers in smaller quantities. The markups of the wholesaler are often smaller than the markups of the retailer because wholesalers depend on volume rather than on large markups to produce revenue. Like retailers, wholesalers use cash to purchase and sell merchandise but they also use credit extensively. Because wholesalers use credit for both sales and purchases, an accrual system of accounting is used. As seen earlier in the text, only service types of businesses are likely to use a cash basis of accounting.

FACTORS THAT AFFECT ACCOUNTING RECORDS

A number of factors affect the books of original entry and the auxiliary records used in a wholesale business.

Type of business

A wholesale business may be operated as a sole proprietorship, a partnership, or a corporation. The records are basically the same for proprietorships and partnerships. But when a business is operated as a corporation, a **book of minutes,** a record of shares owned, and a **shareholders' ledger** are usually maintained.

The ownership structure of the business also has a direct impact on the accounts used. In a small proprietorship only two owner's equity accounts are necessary—one for the proprietor's capital and another for the proprietor's personal withdrawals. A partnership requires that separate capital and drawing accounts be maintained for each partner. When a wholesale business is operated as a corporation, separate accounts must be kept for various classes of stock, retained earnings, and dividends payable.

Business volume

In addition, the volume or potential volume of a business should be carefully considered when determining the kinds and number of accounts to be used. The accounting needs of an enterprise with sales of $10 million a year are very different from one with sales of $25,000 a year. As the volume of business increases, the need for additional accounts and adequate controls also increases. Such controls are often achieved through the use of statistical and analytical data. These controls further expand the number of records and the volume of paperwork.

The number of persons needed to keep a firm's accounting records depends on the size of the business and the extent to which accounting machines are used. When records are kept manually, the number of people engaged in the record-keeping is closely related to the size of the business. Separate records and books of original entry are maintained along with the appropriate ledgers. For example, special journals are kept for sales, purchases, cash receipts, and cash disbursements. A general journal is kept to record transactions not properly included in a special journal and to provide sufficient detail. Subsidiary ledgers are maintained for many of the general ledger accounts.

Dividing the accounting activities among the accounting employees:

1. Distributes work equitably.
2. Provides internal checks and controls.
3. Allows detailed classification of transactions in the books.
4. Permits transaction details to be summarized and posted to the general ledger on a periodic basis.

Office machines

With office machines replacing manual procedures, the accounting system is changing. Office equipment technology makes it possible for the small business executive to afford and operate various accounting machines. Although computers and posting machines have replaced manual operations, the need for separation of accounting procedures has not been eliminated. When computers are used, accounting controls are needed at the points of input and output in addition to the controls built into the computer itself.

The extent to which office machines are used does not reduce the need to adhere to the fundamental principles of record-keeping. Accounting theory must be applied whether office machines are used or not.

Desired information

An accounting system is of little value unless it provides management with the desired information needed to operate the business.

Management is interested in the financial position of the business as well as the results of operations from period to period. As mentioned earlier, statistical and analytical data may be desired in addition to traditional accounting information. Management may want information concerning inventory quantities as well as dollar amounts. Another important responsibility is providing information needed for federal, state, and local tax authorities. Also, if the company's stock is publicly traded, information required by the various regulatory agencies must be provided.

RECORDS AND CHART OF ACCOUNTS

Bailey and Brown are partners in the wholesale plumbing and electrical supply business. Plumbing supplies are handled in the plumbing department; electrical supplies are handled in the electrical department. All supplies and equipment are purchased on account from various manufacturers. Discounts on purchases range from 1 to 3 percent for cash paid in 10 to 30 days. Bailey and Brown sell to local dealers and distributors for cash or on account. Sales on account are given a 2 percent discount if paid within 10 days. Otherwise, the net amount is due within 30 days. These payment terms are usually referred to as 2/10, n/30.

Bailey and Brown maintain the following records:

1. Books of original entry:
   a. Sales register.
   b. Cash receipts journal.
   c. Invoice register.
   d. Cash disbursements journal.
   e. General journal.
2. Books of final entry:
   a. General ledger.
   b. Subsidiary ledgers.
      (1) Accounts receivable ledger.
      (2) Accounts payable ledger.
      (3) Operating expense ledger.
3. Supplementary records:
   a. Daily bank statement.
   b. Petty cash record.
   c. Insurance register.

    d. Notes receivable records.

    e. Inventory records.

    f. Plant asset record.

Sales register

Bailey and Brown use a sales register similar to the one shown in Illustration 23–1. The register provides columns for accounts receivable, customer, and sales by department. Columns are also provided for the date, invoice number, and miscellaneous debits and credits to the general ledger.

ILLUSTRATION 23–1

MONTH OF December 1987				SALES REGISTER							PAGE 12	
DEBIT							CREDIT					
GENERAL LEDGER			ACCTS. REC'BLE	DAY	NAME	SALE NO.	SALES		GENERAL LEDGER			
ACCT. NO.	AMOUNT	√					PLUMBING	ELECTRICAL	ACCT. NO.	AMOUNT	√	
			665 74	√	1	Sharp Contractors	220	482 60	183 14			
			67 42	√	1	B. L. Thompson	221		67 42			
			350 44	√	8	Peoples Hardware	227		345 60	6113	4 84	√
			6853 51					2591 75	4181 92		79 84	
			(130)					(410)	(420)		(√)	

Posting the sales journal. Items involving the General Ledger debit and credit columns are posted individually. These individual items are posted on a daily basis. Notice that the account number, not the account name, is used in recording transactions to the general ledger accounts. As each item is posted, a check mark is entered in the check (√) column beside the amount being posted. As a cross-reference the initials, SR, and the page number of the sales register are entered in the P.R. column of the general ledger account to which the amount is posted.

Summary totals of the remaining columns are posted on a monthly basis. The procedure is as follows:

    1. The Accounts Receivable column total is posted as a debit to Accounts Receivable, account no. 130, in the general ledger.

(Note: Postings to individual customer accounts are also made. A check mark is entered in the check (√) column beside the amount being posted.)

2. The sales columns are individually totaled and credited, respectively, to Sales—Plumbing Department, account no. 410, and Sales—Electrical Department, account no. 420, in the general ledger.

The account number should be recorded below the total in the sales register as each total is posted. As a cross-reference, the initials SR and the sales register page number are entered in the P.R. column of the general ledger account being posted. A check mark or other symbol should be recorded in the sales register below the totals of the General Ledger debit and credit columns. The check marks indicate that these totals are not to be posted since the items included in the totals were posted individually.

Cash receipts journal

Bailey and Brown's cash receipts journal is shown in Illustration 23–2. Debit columns are provided for general ledger, sales discount, and bank. Credit columns are used for accounts receivable, cash sales by department, and general ledger. All cash received is debited to the bank account. This procedure means that all receipts are deposited in the bank and that all disbursements, except petty cash, are made by check.

ILLUSTRATION 23–2

MONTH OF December, 1987 — CASH RECEIPTS JOURNAL — PAGE 12

DEBIT						CREDIT						
GENERAL LEDGER			SALES DISCOUNTS	BANK NET AMT.	DAY	RECEIVED FROM	ACCOUNTS RECEIVABLE	√	CASH SALES		GENERAL LEDGER		
ACCT. NO.	AMOUNT	√							PLUMBING	ELECTRICAL	ACCT. NO.	AMOUNT	√
			1 6 49	8 0 7 76	1	T. C. Scott	8 2 4 25	√					
				7 7 6 60	6	Cash sales			3 8 7 00	3 8 9 60			
				4 0 1 53	15	Discounted note					131	4 0 0 00	√
											710	1 53	√
			6 4 32	9 4 7 4 99			4 3 5 1 23		2 4 0 7 42	2 2 4 1 13		5 3 9 53	
			(4 2 2)	(1 1 0)			(1 3 0)		(4 1 0)	(4 2 0)		(√)	

The cash receipts journal may be proved daily or periodically by, footing the debit and credit columns and comparing the totals. If a page is filled before the journal is normally proved, the page should be footed and proved before starting a new page. The totals are written at the top of the new page. A new page is normally started at the beginning of each month for the Cash Receipts Journal and for each of the registers, records, and journals described in the following pages.

Posting the cash receipts journal. Items involving the General Ledger debit and credit columns are posted individually on a daily basis. Notice that the account number, not the account name, is used in recording transactions to the general ledger accounts. As each item is posted, a check mark is entered in the check (√) column beside the amount being posted. As a cross-reference the initials CR and the page number of the cash receipts journal are entered in the P.R. column of the general ledger account to which the amount is posted.

Summary totals of the remaining columns are posted on a monthly basis. The procedure is:

1. The Sales Discounts column is totaled and posted as a debit to Sales Discounts, account no. 422, in the general ledger.
2. The Bank column is totaled and posted as a debit to National Bank, account no. 110, in the general ledger.
3. The Accounts Receivable column total is posted as a credit to Accounts Receivable, account no. 130, in the general ledger. (Note: Postings to individual customer accounts are made when cash is received. A check mark is entered in the check (√) column beside the amount being posted.)
4. The Sales columns are individually totaled and credited, respectively, to Sales—Plumbing Department, account no. 410, and Sales—Electrical Department, account no. 420, in the general ledger.

The account number should be recorded below the total in the cash receipts journal as each total is posted. As a cross-reference, the initials CR and the cash receipts journal page number are entered in the P.R. column of the general ledger account being posted. A check mark or other symbol should be recorded in the cash receipts journal below the totals of the General Ledger debit and credit columns. The check marks indicate that these totals are not to be posted since the items included in the totals were posted individually.

The same general posting procedures are followed for the invoice register.

Invoice register

The invoice register used by Bailey and Brown is shown in Illustration 23–3. The register contains columns for purchases charged to the plumbing and electrical departments or to the general ledger accounts for nondepartmental purchases. Other columns are provided for the day of the month, invoice date, invoice number, creditor, and credits to accounts payable and general ledger accounts. (For an additional description of invoice register procedures, refer to Chapter 11.)

ILLUSTRATION 23–3

MONTH OF December, 1987					INVOICE REGISTER							PAGE 10	
DEBIT									CREDIT				
PURCHASES-SUPPLIES & PARTS		GENERAL LEDGER			DAY	DATE OF INV.	INV. NO.	NAME	ACCOUNTS PAYABLE	√	GENERAL LEDGER		
PLUMBING	ELECTRICAL	ACCT. NO.	AMOUNT	√							ACCT. NO.	AMOUNT	√
	3 4 5 00				3	12/2	649	National Electric Co.	3 4 5 00	√			
2 3 2 48					3	12/3	650	Southern Supply Co.	2 3 2 48	√			
		151	4 2 19	√	3	12/3	651	Bendix Office Supplies Co.	4 2 19	√			
		170	2 7 5 00	√	15	12/14	660	Owens Equipment Co.	2 7 5 00	√	170		
		171	1 2 5 00	√								1 2 5 00	
3 0 3 3 32	2 1 1 8 46		5 9 2 99						5 5 3 9 77			2 0 5 00	
(5 1 0)	(5 2 0)		(√)						(2 5 0)			(√)	

Cash disbursements journal

Bailey and Brown keep a record of checks drawn in a cash disbursements journal, as shown in Illustration 23–4. Debit columns are provided for general ledger, operating expenses, and accounts payable. A column for the payee and credit columns for general ledger, purchases discounts, and bank amount are also included. A column for recording the number of the check used to make the payment is provided to the left of the bank column. The cash disbursements journal should be footed and proved daily or periodically. The journal

ILLUSTRATION 23–4

MONTH OF December 1987						CASH DISBURSEMENTS JOURNAL							PAGE 21
DEBIT								**CREDIT**					
GENERAL LEDGER			OPERATING EXPENSES			ACCOUNTS PAYABLE	√	DAY	DRAWN TO THE ORDER OF	GENERAL LEDGER			PURCHASES DISCOUNTS	CH NO	BANK NET AMOUNT
ACCT NO.	AMOUNT	√	ACCT NO.	AMOUNT	√					ACCT NO.	AMOUNT	√			
			6125	250 00	√			1	Small Realtors					643	250 00
						556 88		2	Republic Elec. Co.				16 70	644	540 18
154	150 00	√						2	H. H. Insurance Co.					645	150 00
			6101	600 00				15	Payroll	210	83 85			654	2348 46
			6102	400 00						230	57 69				
			6103	440 00											
			6121	600 00											
			6122	450 00											
	741 67			3355 00		3214 67					199 00		162 68		6949 66
	(√)			(610)		(250)					(√)		(522)		(110)

is proved by comparing the debit footings with the credit footings. When a page is full, the columns are footed and a new page is started by entering the totals at the top of the next page.

Posting the cash disbursements journal. As with the cash receipts journal, the cash disbursements journal is posted both individually and in summary. Individual posting is required for the General Ledger debit and credit columns and for the Operating Expenses column. The individual posting is normally done daily. As each item is posted, a check mark is recorded in the check (√) column beside the amount being posted. To cross-reference the posting, the initials CD and the page number of the cash disbursements journal are recorded in the P.R. column of the ledger account being posted.

At the end of each month the summary posting is performed:

1. The Operating Expenses column is footed and posted as a debit to Operating Expenses, account no. 610, in the general ledger.
2. The Accounts Payable column total is posted as a debit to Accounts Payable, account no. 250, in the general ledger. (Note: Postings to individual creditors' accounts are performed when payment is made. A check mark is entered in the check (√) column when the posting is made.)
3. The Purchases Discounts column total is posted as a credit to Purchases Discounts, account no. 522, in the general ledger.

4. The Bank column total is posted as a credit to National Bank, account no. 110, in the general ledger.

When the column total is posted, the account number is written below the total to indicate that the total has been posted. The page number and initials CD are recorded in the P.R. column of the ledger account being posted as a cross-reference. A check mark is placed below the General Ledger debit and credit column totals in the cash disbursements journal. The check marks indicate that these totals are not to be posted.

General journal

Bailey and Brown use a general journal to record adjusting, closing, and reversing entries and transactions not recorded in the special journals.

Posting the general journal. Postings from the general journal must be made to both control and subsidiary ledger accounts. The subsidiary ledgers require individual posting to the appropriate accounts. Postings are usually made daily and are indicated by placing a check mark (√) the P.R. column in the general journal. The initial GJ and the general journal page number are entered in the P.R. column of the subsidiary ledger account being posted. Amounts may be posted to the general ledger accounts weekly or monthly. The account number should be entered in the P.R. column of the general journal, and the letter GJ and the page number of the general journal should be placed in the P.R. column of the general ledger account being posted. The general journal is shown in Illustration 23–14 on page 720.

General ledger

The general ledger accounts used by Bailey and Brown are shown in Illustration 23–5. The chart of accounts lists the general ledger accounts in numerical order. Several of these accounts need further explanation and are discussed below and on the following pages.

Government bonds, account no. 120. At present, Bailey and Brown are holding temporary investments in the form of U.S. government bonds. Whenever the partners have excess cash, they make temporary investments to add to earnings from normal operations.

ILLUSTRATION 23–5

BAILEY AND BROWN
General Ledger Chart of Accounts

Assets

Cash
- 110 National Bank
- 111 Petty Cash

Short-Term Investments
- 120 Government Bonds

Receivables
- 130 Accounts Receivable
- 131 Allowance for Doubtful Accounts
- 132 Notes Receivable
- 133 Accrued Interest Receivable

Merchandise Inventory
- 140 Merchandise Inventory—Plumbing Department
- 145 Merchandise Inventory—Electrical Department

Supplies and Prepayments
- 150 Store Supplies
- 151 Office Supplies
- 152 Advertising Supplies
- 153 Postage Stamps
- 154 Prepaid Insurance

Plant Assets
- 160 Store Equipment
- 161 Accumulated Depreciation—Store Equipment
- 170 Office Equipment
- 171 Accumulated Depreciation—Office Equipment
- 180 Delivery Equipment
- 181 Accumulated Depreciation—Delivery Equipment

Liabilities
- 210 FICA Taxes Payable
- 220 FUTA Taxes Payable
- 230 Income Taxes Payable—Federal—Employee
- 240 State Unemployment Taxes Payable
- 250 Accounts Payable
- 260 Notes Payable
- 270 Accrued Interest Payable

Owner's Equity

Owner's Equity
- 310 M. O. Brown, Capital
- 311 M. O. Brown, Drawing
- 320 W. E. Bailey, Capital
- 321 W. E. Bailey, Drawing
- 330 Income Summary

Revenues
- 410 Sales—Plumbing Department
- 411 Sales Returns and Allowances—Plumbing Department
- 420 Sales—Electrical Department
- 421 Sales Returns and Allowances—Electrical Department
- 422 Sales Discounts

Cost of Goods Sold
- 510 Purchases—Plumbing Department
- 511 Purchase Returns and Allowances—Plumbing Department
- 520 Purchases—Electrical Department
- 521 Purchase Returns and Allowances—Electrical Department
- 522 Purchases Discounts
- 540 Transportation-In—Plumbing Dept.
- 550 Transportation-In—Electrical Dept.
- 560 Cost of Goods Sold—Plumbing Dept.
- 570 Cost of Goods Sold—Electrical Dept.

Operating Expenses
- 610 Operating Expenses

Other Revenue
- 710 Interest Revenue

Other Expenses
- 810 Interest Expense
- 820 Collection Expense

Temporary investments of this type are of low risk and can be readily liquidated. Since they are held on a short-term basis, they are classified as current assets on the balance sheet.

Sales discounts, account no. 422. As an incentive for prompt payment of purchases, most wholesale businesses offer their customers a cash discount if payment is made within a certain period. The discount allowed by Bailey and Brown is 2 percent if the amount owed is paid within 10 days of the sale. Since Bailey and Brown have no way of knowing whether or not the customer will pay within the discount period, the sales are billed at the gross amount. If the customer pays within 10 days, the remittance is recorded by debiting National Bank for the amount received and Sales Discounts for the allowed discount and crediting Accounts Receivable for the gross amount. Even though sales discounts could be treated as an expense, the normal procedure is to subtract the discounts given along with sales returns and allowances to determine the amount of net sales on the income statement.

Cost of goods sold—plumbing department, account no. 560, and cost of goods sold—electrical department, account no. 570. These two accounts are used to close out the accounts needed to calculate cost of goods sold for each department. The debit balances of the beginning inventory of merchandise, transportation-in (discussed below), and purchases, and the credit balances of purchase returns and allowances and purchases discounts are closed to the appropriate department's cost of goods sold account. After the ending inventory is taken, it is credited to the Cost of Goods Sold account. The remaining balance represents the cost of goods sold for the department in question. The cost of goods sold balances are then closed to the Income Summary account.

Transportation-in—plumbing department, account no. 540, and transportation-in—electrical department, account no. 550. The freight charges on purchases by Bailey and Brown are charged to these two accounts. The year-end balances are transferred as debits to the cost of goods sold account.

Accounts receivable ledger

Bailey and Brown use the debit-credit-balance ledger form for accounts receivable. The Accounts Receivable control account (account no. 130) is kept in the general ledger. The individual ledger accounts are maintained in alphabetical order, and at the end of each month a **schedule of accounts receivable** is prepared. The schedule total should equal the Accounts Receivable control account balance in the general ledger.

Posting to the individual customer accounts may be done from the books of original entry, from the customer billing slip, or from other transaction documents. To lessen the probability of transcription errors, Bailey and Brown post from the transaction documents.

Accounts payable ledger

Bailey and Brown also use the debit-credit-balance form for the accounts payable ledger. The accounts are kept in alphabetical order and are represented in the general ledger by the Accounts Payable control account (account no. 250). A **schedule of accounts payable** is prepared at the end of each month and compared with the balance of the Accounts Payable control account in the general ledger.

Posting to the accounts payable ledger may be done from the books of original entry or from the transaction documents. Bailey and Brown post from the documents.

Operating expense ledger

Bailey and Brown's operating expense ledger is maintained in the debit-credit-balance form. The accounts are kept in numerical order as indicated in the operating expense chart of accounts in Illustration 23–6. The control account (account no. 610) for operating expenses is kept in the general ledger. At the end of each month, the subsidiary ledger balance is compared with the control account balance in the general ledger.

The books of original entry are used for posting to the Operating Expenses accounts. The page number and initials of the journal from which the posting is made are recorded in the **P.R.** column.

Supplementary records

Bailey and Brown maintain the following supplementary records: inventory records, a plant asset record, a daily bank statement, a petty cash record, an insurance register, and notes receivable records. Bailey and Brown's inventory record is shown in Illustration 23–7.

ILLUSTRATION 23–6

610 Control

BAILEY AND BROWN
Operating Expense Ledger Chart of Accounts

Selling Expenses		Administrative Expenses	
6101	M. O. Brown, Salary Expense	6121	W. E. Bailey, Salary Expense
6102	Truck Drivers' Wages Expense	6122	Office Salaries Expense
6103	Store Clerks' Salary Expense	6123	Power and Water Expense
6104	M. O. Brown, Travel Expense	6124	Telephone Expense
6105	Advertising Expense	6125	Rent Expense
6106	Garage Rent Expense	6126	Property Tax Expense
6107	Truck Repairs Expense	6127	Office Supplies Expense
6108	Truck Operating Expense	6128	Bad Debts Expense
6109	Shipping Expense	6129	Postage Expense (Administration)
6110	Merchandise Insurance Expense	6130	Office Equipment Insurance Expense
6111	Delivery Equipment Insurance Expense	6131	Payroll Taxes Expense
6112	Store Equipment Insurance Expense	6132	Depreciation of Office Equipment
6113	Postage Expense (Selling)	6133	Miscellaneous General Expense
6114	Store Supplies Expense		
6115	Depreciation of Store Equipment		
6116	Depreciation of Delivery Equipment		
6117	Miscellaneous Selling Expense		

ILLUSTRATION 23–7

INVENTORY RECORD

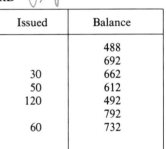

Perpetual

Date		Invoice No.	Received	Issued	Balance
Mar.	2				488
	3	1042	204		692
	4	667		30	662
	9	675		50	612
	10	683		120	492
	13	1050	300		792
	20	700		60	732

Article	Description	Minimum	Department
Light switches	White w/night light	500	Electrical

The daily bank statement and petty cash record are shown in Illustrations 23–8 and 23–9. The insurance register and notes receivable record are similar to those shown in Illustrations 17–1 and 15–3, respectively.

Inventory record.   Bailey and Brown use the **inventory record** shown in Illustration 23–7. The record provides inventory control and is used as an aid to good business management. The inventory record is particularly valuable in determining when to reorder. Although an inventory record is kept, a physical inventory count should be taken at least once each year to eliminate any differences between the records and the actual amounts on hand. Unless some form of inventory record or estimate is used, a physical count is required

ILLUSTRATION 23–8

Daily Bank Statement						
For Month of December 1987						
OUTSTANDING CHECKS		MEMORANDUM	DAILY BANK BALANCE			
CHECK NUMBER	AMOUNT					
		Balance-previous month	Day	Deposits	Checks	Balance
						8 4 2 5 16
			1	8 0 7 76	2 5 0 00	8 9 8 2 92
			2		6 9 0 18	8 2 9 2 74
			3			8 2 9 2 74
			4		3 4 8 98	7 9 4 3 76
			5			7 9 4 3 76
			6	7 7 6 60	1 8 2 14	8 5 3 8 22
			7			8 5 3 8 22
			8	4 8 2 33	3 1 5 77	8 7 0 4 78
			9	1 1 1 9 88	4 1 5 09	9 4 0 9 57
			1 0	4 9 3 32	3 1 4 82	9 5 8 8 07
			1 1	8 0 2 69	3 3 2 83	1 0 0 5 7 93
			1 2	2 3 8 14		1 0 2 9 6 07
			1 3	1 1 7 53		1 0 4 1 3 60
			1 4			1 0 4 1 3 60
			1 5	4 2 6 53	2 7 7 3 44	8 0 6 6 69
			3 1	1 2 1 0 32	2 6 9 2 64	8 4 6 1 10
				9 4 7 4 99	9 4 3 9 05	

when preparing interim statements (monthly or quarterly) and year-end reports. An inventory record allows the physical count to be taken in stages or in parts during the year. This is an advantage when preparing statements.

Information from the purchase invoices, sales invoices, sales returns, and purchase returns is used in maintaining the inventory record. Note that only quantities are recorded. When the minimum quantity is reached, a purchase order is prepared. Some inventory records provide columns for items on order but not yet received. The sum of quantities on order and quantities on hand is then used to determine when to reorder.

Plant asset record. Bailey and Brown maintain a separate account for each type of plant asset. As an asset is sold or traded, depreciation is brought up to date in order to determine the proper book value. This is not illustrated in this chapter.

ILLUSTRATION 23–9

	Petty Cash Disbursements Record					
	December 1987					

DAY	DESCRIPTION	VOUCHER NUMBER	TOTAL AMOUNT	6 1 0 5	6 1 0 7	6 1 0 0
	Balance $100.00					
9	Adding machine repairs	8 4	8 50			
9	Truck repair	8 5	1 4 15		1 4 15	
10	Newspaper advertisement	8 6	8 42	8 42		
10	Masking tape	8 7	7 14			5 00
11	Shipping labels	8 8	6 42			
11	Telephone bill	8 9	1 8 00			
11	Water bill	9 0	6 00			
15	Adding machine tape	9 1	6 8 63 / 2 65	8 42	1 4 15	5 00
31	Postage due	9 5	1 25			
			9 2 53	8 42	1 4 15	5 00
	Balance $7.47					
	Received 92.53					
	$100.00					

Daily bank statement. To keep track of the bank balance, Bailey and Brown use a **daily bank statement.** The statement is similar to the information kept on an individual's check stubs and is used to record the checks written and deposits made each day. The December statement is shown in Illustration 23–8. Since the statement is used to keep track of the daily bank balance, a running balance on the check stubs is not needed. Bailey and Brown use the check stubs to record information needed to maintain the record of checks drawn and for posting to the appropriate creditor accounts in the accounts payable ledger.

Petty cash disbursements record. A petty cash fund is maintained to keep track of small cash expenditures. The expenditures are recorded in a disbursements record, as shown in Illustration 23–9. Petty cash is replenished when the cash gets low and at the end of the period.

Page 12

| DISTRIBUTION CHARGES | | | | ACCOUNT | AMOUNT |
6 1 1 7	6 1 2 3	6 1 2 4	6 1 3 3		
			8 50		
			2 14		
6 42		1 8 00			
	6 00				
6 42	6 00	1 8 00	1 0 64	61 14	2 65
				61 29	1 25
1 5 32	6 00	1 8 00	2 1 74		3 90

ACCOUNTING PROCEDURE ILLUSTRATED

Bailey and Brown's records are kept on a calendar-year basis. The sales register, cash receipts journal, invoice register, cash disbursements journal, and general journal (the books of original entry) are shown in Illustrations 23–10, 23–11, 23–12, 23–13, and 23–14. The daily bank statement and the petty cash disbursement records are shown in Illustrations 23–8 and 23–9. The remaining supplementary records and the general and subsidiary ledgers are not shown. Bailey and Brown's transactions for December are described on the following pages:

BAILEY AND BROWN
Plumbing and Electrical Supply Wholesalers
Narrative of Transactions

December 1

Sales on account:

No. 220: Sharp Contractors, City; plumbing, $482.60; electrical, $183.14; terms, 2/10, n/30.

No. 221: B. L. Thompson, City; electrical, $67.42; terms, 2/10, n/30.

After the sale is made, the accountant obtains the necessary information from a carbon copy of the sales invoice prepared by the store clerk. As the amounts are entered in the sales register, a check mark is placed in the check ($\sqrt{}$) column to indicate that the amounts are being posted to the individual creditors' accounts. The invoices are then posted to the accounts receivable ledger. An additional copy of the sales invoice is used to make the appropriate entries in the inventory records (see inventory record shown in Illustration 23–7).

Issued check no. 643 for $250 to Small Realtors for the December rent.

Received a check for $807.76 from T. C. Scott for our invoice of November 25, $824.25, less than 2 percent discount.

To determine whether the discount and check amount were properly stated, the accountant examined the Accounts Receivable ledger account of T. C. Scott. The ledger showed that on November 25, Scott made purchases amounting to $824.25. Since payment was made

ILLUSTRATION 23–10

MONTH OF December 1987 SALES REGISTER PAGE

ACCT. NO.	AMOUNT	√	ACCTS. REC'BLE	√	DAY	NAME	SALE NO.	PLUMBING	ELECTRICAL	ACCT. NO.	AMOUNT	√
			665 74	√	1	Sharp Contractors	220	482 60	183 14			
			67 42	√	1	B. L. Thompson	221		67 42			
			132 14	√	4	Anderson Builders	222		132 14			
			243 00	√	4	Normal Hardware	223	243 00				
			325 00	√	5	McDonald Construction Co.	224		325 00			
			23 00	√	5	O. B. Smith	225	23 00				
			1456 30					748 60	707 70			
			389 05	√	8	Farmers Hardware	226	389 05				
			350 44	√	8	Peoples Hardware	227		345 60	6113	4 84	√
			143 18	√	8	Fred Smith	228		143 18			
			514 83	√	10	Sharp Contractors	229	208 88	305 95			
			408 15	√	10	Quick Contractors	230		408 15			
			88 09	√	13	B. L. Thompson	231		88 09			
			143 25	√	13	Anderson Builders	232		143 25			
			56 70	√	13	Green Plumbing Co.	233	56 70				
			3549 99					1403 23	2141 92		4 84	
			215 00	√	31	McDonald Construction Co.	250		215 00			
			88 52	√	31	Sturdy Builders	251	88 52			79 84	
			6853 51					2591 75	4181 92			
			(130)					(410)	(420)		(√)	

within 10 days, the discount was properly taken. The amount was verified as follows:

Invoice amount	$824.25
Less: 2% discount	16.49
Amount due	$807.76

After the check amount was verified, the check was entered in the cash receipts journal by debiting Sales Discounts for $16.49 and Bank for the amount of the check, $807.76, and by crediting Accounts Receivable for $824.25, the total invoice amount. The amount was then posted to T. C. Scott's account in the accounts receivable subsidiary ledger. A check mark was placed in the check mark column of the cash receipts journal to show that T. C. Scott's account had been posted.

At the close of each day, the total amount of checks issued and deposits made are recorded in the daily bank statement. Since Decem-

ILLUSTRATION 23–11

MONTH OF December, 1987						CASH RECEIPTS JOURNAL						PAGE 12	
DEBIT							**CREDIT**						
GENERAL LEDGER			SALES DISCOUNTS	BANK NET AMT.	DAY	RECEIVED FROM	ACCOUNTS RECEIVABLE	√	CASH SALES		GENERAL LEDGER		
ACCT. NO.	AMOUNT	√							PLUMBING	ELECTRICAL	ACCT. NO.	AMOUNT	√
			16 49	807 76	1	T. C. Scott	824 25	√					
				776 60	6	Cash sales			387 00	389 60			
			16 49	1584 36			824 25		387 00	389 60			
			9 84	482 33	8	George Glass	492 17						
			13 31	652 43	9	Sharp Contractors	665 74	√					
			1 35	66 07	9	B. L. Thompson	67 42	√					
				401 38	9	Cash sales			112 00	289 38			
				493 32	10	Cash sales			398 24	95 08			
			2 64	129 50	11	Anderson Builders	132 14	√					
				182 14	11	Slow Contractors	182 14	√					
				491 05	11	Cash sales			88 42	402 63			
			4 86	238 14	12	Normal Hardware	243 00	√					
				117 53	13	Cash sales			53 09	64 44			
			48 49	4838 25			2606 86		1038 75	1241 13			
				401 53	15	Discounted note					131	400 00	√
											710	1 53	√
				25 00	15	Interest revenue— govt. bonds					710	25 00	√
				668 67	31	Cash sales			668 67				
				408 15	31	Quick Contractors	408 15	√					
			2 72	133 50	31	Fred Smith	136 22	√					
			64 32	9474 99			4351 23		2407 42	2241 13		539 53	
			(422)	(110)			(130)		(410)	(420)		(√)	

ber 1 was the first working day of the month, the ending bank balance for November, $8,425.16, was forwarded to the top of the next page. The deposit of $807.76 and the check issued for $250 were entered in the daily bank statement, and the new balance was extended.

December 2

Issued checks as follows:

No. 644: Republic Electric Company, $540.18, in payment of its November 24 invoice for $556.88 less 3 percent discount.

No. 645: H. H. Insurance Company, $150, in payment for one-year policy on merchandise.

As the checks were drawn, check marks were placed in the check mark columns beside the Accounts Payable and General Ledger debit columns to show that the checks were posted to the proper subsidiary ledgers.

ILLUSTRATION 23–12

MONTH OF December, 1987 — INVOICE REGISTER — PAGE 10

PLUMBING	ELECTRICAL	ACCT. NO.	AMOUNT	√	DAY	DATE OF INV.	INV. NO.	NAME	ACCOUNTS PAYABLE	√	ACCT. NO.	AMOUNT	√
	345 00				3	12/2	649	National Electrical Co.	345 00	√			
232 48					3	12/3	650	Southern Supply Co.	232 48	√			
		151	42 19	√	3	12/3	651	Bendix Office Supplies Co.	42 19	√			
	245 18				4	12/3	652	Eastern Supply Co.	245 18	√			
232 48	590 18		42 19						864 85				
	308 14				10	12/9	653	Republic Electrical Co.	308 14	√			
440 15					10	12/8	654	Atlantic Manufacturing Co.	440 15	√			
		152	52 80	√	10	12/10	655	Peters Supply Co.	52 80	√			
		150	18 00	√	10	12/10	656	Butler and Sons Inc.	18 00	√			
	108 00				12	12/12	657	National Electrical Co.	108 00	√			
304 19					12	12/11	658	Southern Supply Co.	304 19	√			
208 01					12	12/10	659	Great Manufacturing Co.	208 01	√			
1184 83	1006 32		112 99						2304 14				
		170	275 00	√	15	12/14	660	Owens Equipment Co.	275 00	√	170		
		171	125 00	√								125 00	√
	112 14				31	12/30	681	National Electrical Co.	112 14	√			
348 49					31	12/29	682	Chattanooga Marble Co.	348 49	√			
3033 32	2118 46		592 99		31				5539 77			205 00	
(510)	(520)		(√)						(250)			(√)	

The total of the checks issued on December 2 was recorded on the daily bank statement, and the balance was extended.

December 3

Received the following invoices:

National Electrical Company, City; light fixtures, $345; terms, December 2—2/10, n/30.

Southern Supply Company, City; pipe fittings, $232.48; terms, December 3—2/10, n/30.

Bendix Office Supplies Company, City; office supplies, $42.19; terms, December 3—n/30.

As the invoices were received, they were numbered consecutively, beginning with No. 649, and were recorded in the invoice register. Check marks were placed in the check mark column to the right of the Accounts Payable credit column to show that the invoices were posted to the appropriate creditor accounts in the accounts

ILLUSTRATION 23-13

MONTH OF December 1987

CASH DISBURSEMENTS JOURNAL

PAGE 21

DEBIT — GENERAL LEDGER ACCT. NO.	AMOUNT	✓	DEBIT — OPERATING EXPENSES ACCT. NO.	AMOUNT	✓	ACCOUNTS PAYABLE	✓	DAY	DRAWN TO THE ORDER OF	CREDIT — GENERAL LEDGER ACCT NO	AMOUNT	✓	PURCHASES DISCOUNTS	CH. NO.	BANK NET AMOUNT
			6125	2 5 0 0 00	✓			1	Small Realtors					643	2 5 0 0 00
						5 5 6 88	✓	2	Republic Elec. Co.				1 6 70	644	5 4 0 18
154	1 5 0 00	✓						2	H. H. Insurance Co.					645	1 5 0 00
						3 5 6 10	✓	4	National Elec. Co.				7 12	646	3 4 8 98
						1 8 5 85	✓	6	E-Z Drain Manu. Co.				3 71	647	1 8 2 14
	1 5 0 00			2 5 0 00		1 0 9 8 83							2 7 53		1 4 7 1 30
						3 2 2 21	✓	8	Atlantic Manu. Co.				6 44	648	3 1 5 77
						4 2 3 56	✓	9	Copper Pipe Co.				8 47	649	4 1 5 09
						3 2 1 25	✓	10	National Elec. Co.				6 43	650	3 1 4 82
						2 3 2 48	✓	11	Southern Supply Co.				4 65	651	2 2 7 83
			6106	9 5 00	✓			11	Randall Company					652	9 5 00
153	1 0 00	✓						11	Postage					653	1 0 00
	1 6 0 00			3 4 5 00		2 3 9 8 33							5 3 52		2 8 4 9 81
			6101	6 0 0 00	✓			15	Payroll	210	8 3 85			654	2 3 4 8 46
			6102	4 0 0 00	✓					230	5 7 69				
			6103	4 4 0 00	✓										
			6121	6 0 0 00	✓										
			6122	4 5 0 00	✓										
								15	National Bank					655	4 2 4 98
210	3 0 9 60	✓				1 8 7 75	✓	31	Southern Supply Co.				3 75	667	1 8 4 00
230	1 1 5 38	✓				1 2 0 59	✓	31	West Manu. Co.				2 41	668	1 1 8 18
								31	Carried forward						
	7 4 1 62			3 3 5 5 00		3 2 1 4 67					1 9 9 00		1 6 2 68		6 9 4 9 61

718

CASH DISBURSEMENTS JOURNAL

DEBIT										CREDIT					
GENERAL LEDGER			OPERATING EXPENSES			ACCOUNTS PAYABLE	✓	DAY	DRAWN TO THE ORDER OF	GENERAL LEDGER			PURCHASES DISCOUNTS	CH. NO	BANK NET AMOUNT
ACCT. NO	AMOUNT	✓	ACCT. NO	AMOUNT	✓					ACCT. NO	AMOUNT	✓			
	741 62			3355 00		3214 67		31	Amts. brought forwd.		199 00		162 68		6949 61
180	42 00	✓						31	Ind. Supply Co.					669	42 00
			6101	600 00	✓			31	Payroll	210	83 85	✓		670	2348 46
			6102	400 00	✓					230	57 69	✓			
			6103	440 00	✓										
			6121	600 00	✓										
			6122	450 00	✓										
			6105	8 42	✓			31	Petty Cash					671	92 53
			6107	14 15	✓										
			6109	5 00	✓										
			6114	2 65	✓										
			6117	15 32	✓										
			6123	6 00	✓										
			6124	18 00	✓										
			6129	1 25	✓										
			6133	21 74	✓										
	783 62			5937 53		3214 67		31			340 54		162 68		9432 60
	(✓)			(610)		(250)					(✓)		(522)		(110)

ILLUSTRATION 23–14

		GENERAL JOURNAL			PAGE 55	
DATE		ACCOUNT AND EXPLANATION	P.R.	DEBIT	CREDIT	
1987						
Dec.	9	Sales Return and Allow.—Plumb. Dept.	411	9 83		
		Accounts Receivable—Normal Hard. √	130		9 83	
		Issued Credit Memo No. 128 for pipe returned.				
	10	Accounts Payable—Nat. Elec. Co. √	250	2 3 75		
		Purchase Returns and All.—Elec. Dept.	521		2 3 75	
		Issued charge—back invoice no. 10 for				
		electrical wire returned.				
	15	Depreciation of Office Equipment √	160	2 5 00		
		Accumulated Depreciation—Office Equipment	171		2 5 00	
		Depreciation on typewriter scrapped.				
	15	Payroll Taxes Expense √	610	1 2 7 70		
		FICA Taxes Payable	210		8 3 85	
		FUTA Taxes Payable	220		9 03	
		State Unemployment Taxes Payable	240		3 4 82	
		To record taxes for Dec. 1-15.				
	15	Depreciation of Store Equipment √	160	5 00		
		Accumulated Depreciation—Store Equipment	161		5 00	
		Depreciation on desk scrapped.				
	15	Accumulated Depreciation—Store Equipment	161	6 5 00		
		Store Equipment	160		6 5 00	
		Scrapped old desk.				
	15	Allowance for doubtful accounts	131	2 0 00		
		Accounts Receivable —J.J. Clark √	130		2 0 00	
		Uncollectible account written off.				
	15	Sales Returns and All.—Elec. Dept.	421	1 0 39		
		Accounts Receivable—B.L. Thompson √	130		1 0 39	
		Issued credit memo No. 129 for electrical				
		supplies returned.				
	31	Payroll Taxes Expense √	610	1 2 7 70		
		FICA Taxes Payable	210		8 3 85	
		FUTA Taxes Payable	220		9 03	
		State Unemployment Taxes Payable	240		3 4 82	
		To record taxes for Dec. 16-31.				

payable ledger. Invoices were also used to record relevant information on the inventory record cards.

December 4

Issued check no. 646 for $348.98 to National Electrical Company in payment of its November 27 invoice for $356.10 less 2 percent discount.

Received invoice from Eastern Supply Company, City; electric wire, $245.18; terms, December 3—2/10, n/30; shipped directly to Mc-Donald Construction Company, Monroe, freight collect.

Because of the warehouse limitations of Bailey and Brown, they do not stock the complete line of products carried by their suppliers. The above shipment of wire was of a special type which is not often requested. In such cases, Bailey and Brown instruct the supplier to bill them and ship the merchandise to the indicated address. When the invoice is received, Bailey and Brown's accountant posts it to the accounts payable ledger and bills the customer (McDonald Construction Company).

Made the following sales on account:

No. 222: Anderson Builders, City; electrical supplies, $132.14; terms, 2/10, n/30.

No. 223: Normal Hardware, City; plumbing fittings, $243; terms, 2/10, n/30.

December 5

Made the following sales on account:

No. 224: McDonald Construction Company, Monroe; electric wire, $325; terms, 2/10, n/30; shipped directly from Factory (see invoice of December 4 from Eastern Supply Company).

No. 225: O. B. Smith, City; pipe, $23; terms, 2/10, n/30.

December 6

Made the following cash sales:

No. 343: T. C. Owens; pipe fittings, $242.

No. 344: Moore Hardware; electrical supplies, $389.60.

No. 345: Benjimen Builders; plumbing supplies, $145.

At the close of each business day, the carbon copies of the cash sales tickets are analyzed to determine the total sales by department.

An entry is then made in the cash receipts journal debiting Bank and crediting the departments for the appropriate amounts.

Issued check no. 647 for $182.14 to E-Z Drain Manufacturing Company in payment for invoice of November 28 for $185.85 less 2 percent discount.

End-of-the-Week Accounting Procedures

1. Totaled the amount columns in the invoice register, sales register, cash receipts journal, and cash disbursements journal, and proved the footings.
2. Finished individual postings from books of original entry to the general and operating expense ledger accounts.
3. Proved the bank balance as follows:

Balance, December 1	$ 8,425.16
Add: Total receipts December 1–6 (cash receipts record).	1,584.36
Total	$10,009.52
Less: Checks issued December 1–6 (cash disbursements record).	1,471.30
Balance, December 6	$ 8,538.22

(Note balance of daily bank statement—December 6.)

December 8

Received a check for $482.33 from George Glass (plumber) for merchandise sold on November 29 amounting to $492.17, less 2 percent discount.

Made the following sales on account:

No. 226: Farmers Hardware, Winterville; plumbing supplies, $389.05; terms, 2/10, n/30.

No. 227: Peoples Hardware, City; electrical supplies, $345.60; postage, $4.84; terms, 2/10, n/30.

No. 228: Fred Smith (electrician), City; wire, fuse box, $143.18; terms, 2/10, n/30.

In recording Sales Invoice No. 227, the postage was charged to the Peoples Hardware account and credited to Postage Expense, account no. 6113.

Issued check no. 648 for $315.77 to the Atlantic Manufacturing Company in payment of November 29 invoice for $322.21 less 2 percent discount.

December 9

Issued check no. 649 for $415.09 to the Copper Pipe Company in payment of invoice of November 29 for $423.56 less 2 percent discount.

Received the following checks: Sharp Contractors, $652.43, in payment of merchandise sold on December 1 amounting to $665.74 less 2 percent discount; and B. L. Thompson, $66.07, in payment of merchandise sold on December 1 amounting to $67.42 less 2 percent discount.

Issued Credit Memorandum No. 128 to Normal Hardware, $9.83, for pipe returned.

Made the following cash sales:

No. 346: J. R. Reynold; plumbing, $112; electrical, $94.88.

No. 347: W. M. Stone; electrical, $194.50.

Made the following petty cash disbursements (petty cash has $100 balance):

Adding machine repairs, $8.50; voucher no. 84.

Repair on truck, $14.15; voucher no. 85.

December 10

Issued charge-back invoice no. 10 to National Electrical Company, $23.75, for electric wire returned; purchased on December 2.

Made the following cash sales:

No. 348: C. B. Clark; plumbing, $188.10.

No. 349: A. C. Maxwell; electrical, $95.08.

No. 350: N. L. Wilson; plumbing, $210.14.

Made the following petty cash disbursements:

Newspaper advertisement, $8.42, voucher no. 86.

Shipping expense, $5.00, and miscellaneous general expense, $2.14, voucher no. 87.

Made the following sales on account:

No. 229: Sharp Contractors, City; plumbing, $208.88; electrical $305.95; terms, 2/10, n/30.

No. 230: Quick Contractors, City; electrical, $408.15; terms, 2/10, n/30.

Issued check no. 650 for $314.82 to the National Electrical Company in payment of balance due on invoice of December 2, $321.25 less 2 percent discount.

In order to determine the amount due the National Electrical Company, it is necessary to refer to the accounts payable ledger. The amount payable was determined as follows:

Invoice of December 2	$345.00
Less: Merchandise returned on December 10 . .	23.75
Amount subject to discount.	$321.25
Less: 2% discount	6.43
Amount Due.	$314.82

Received the following invoices:

Republic Electrical Company, Atlanta; electrical supplies, $308.14; terms, December 9—2/10, n/30.

Atlantic Manufacturing Company, Boston; pipe fittings, $440.15; terms, December 8—2/10, n/30.

Peters Supply Company, City; advertising supplies, $52.80; terms, December 10—2/10, n/30.

Butler & Sons Inc., City; store supplies, $18; terms, December 10—2/10, n/30.

December 11

Issued the following checks:

No. 651: Southern Supply Company; $227.83 in payment of December 3 invoice for $232.48 less 2 percent discount.

No. 652: Randall Company; $95 in payment of December garage rent (due by 15th).

No. 653: $10 payable to Postage; cashed check at bank and purchased stamps.

Made the following petty cash disbursements:

Shipping labels, $6.42; voucher no. 88.

Telephone bill, $18; voucher no. 89.

Water bill, $6; voucher no. 90.

Received the following checks:

Anderson Builders, $129.50, in payment of merchandise sold December 4 amounting to $132.14 less 2 percent discount.

Slow Contractors, $182.14, in payment of merchandise sold on November 15 amounting to $182.14 (no discount).

Made the following cash sales:

No. 351: H. H. Banks; electrical, $170.45.

No. 352: Blank Hardware; electrical, $232.18.

No. 353: T. C. Owens; plumbing, $88.42.

December 12

Received the following invoices:

National Electrical Company, City; light switches, ground wire, $108; terms, December 12—2/10, n/30.

Southern Supply Company, City; bathroom fixtures, $304.19; terms, December 11—2/10, n/30.

Great Manufacturing Company, New York; plastic pipe and fittings, $208.01; terms, December 10—2/10, n/30.

Received a check from Normal Hardware for $238.14 in payment of merchandise sold on December 4 amounting to $243 less 2 percent discount.

December 13

Made the following sales on account:

No. 231: B. L. Thompson, City; electrical, $88.09; terms, 2/10, n/30.

No. 232: Anderson Builders, City; wire, $143.25; terms, 2/10, n/30.

No. 233: Green Plumbing Company, City; plumbing supplies, $56.70; terms, 2/10, n/30.

Made the following cash sales:

No. 354: O. R. Blair; plumbing, $53.09.

No. 355: H. B. Simpson; electrical, $64.44.

End-of-the-Week Accounting Procedures

1. Totaled the amount columns in the invoice register, sales register, cash receipts journal, petty cash disbursements record, and cash disbursements journal, and proved the footings.
2. Finished individual postings from books of original entry to the general and operating expense ledger accounts.

3. Proved the bank balance as follows:

Balance, December 8 . . . . $ 8,538.22
  Add: Total receipts December 8–13 (cash receipts
    record). 3,253.89
      Total $11,792.11
  Less: Checks issued December 8–13 (cash
    disbursements record). 1,378.51
Balance, December 13 . . . . $10,413,60

(Note balance of daily bank statement—December 13.)

December 15

Made a petty cash disbursement of $2.65 for adding machine tape—store, voucher no. 91.

Received invoice from Owens Equipment Company for cost of new typewriter, $275; terms, December 14—n/30.

The cost of the old typewriter was $125. Depreciation Expense in the amount of $25 is recorded in the General Journal. Since the old typewriter is fully depreciated, the transaction is recorded by debiting Office Equipment, account no. 170, for $275, the cost of the new typewriter; by debiting Accumulated Depreciation—Office Equipment, account no. 171, for $125, by crediting Office Equipment, account no. 170, for $125, the cost of the old typewriter; and by crediting Accounts Payable, account no. 250, for $275.

Discounted note from Able Contractors for $400 at the National Bank at 7 percent and deposited the proceeds which amounted to $401.53. The note had been held since November 25 (20 days).

Clipped interest coupons amounting to $25 from the government bonds and deposited them in the National Bank.

Issued check no. 654 payable to Payroll for $2,348.46.

Bailey and Brown pay their employees on the 15th and the last day of each month. Employee wages and salaries are subject to the following taxes and contribution requirements:

1. Federal Insurance Contribution Act—old-age benefits and hospital insurance, 6.5 percent (an assumed rate for computations).
2. Federal Unemployment Tax Act—unemployment insurance, 0.7 percent (an assumed rate for computations).
3. State unemployment compensation fund, 2.7 percent (an assumed rate).
4. Federal income tax.

In addition to the above deductions, Bailey and Brown have agreed that they are each to receive a monthly salary of $1,200, payable semimonthly. Although the partners' salaries are treated as a business expense, they do not represent "wages" as stated in the social security and income tax laws. Therefore, they are not subject to the above deductions. Partnership earnings are reported on each partner's individual tax return and taxed accordingly.

At the end of each pay period, the payroll statement is prepared:

Payroll Statement
December 1–December 15

Classification	Deductions			
	Gross Earnings	FICA Taxes	Federal Income Taxes	Net Amount Payable
Office salaries	$ 450.00	$29.25	$24.19	$ 396.56
Store clerk—salaries	440.00	28.60	19.42	391.98
Truck driver—wages	400.00	26.00	14.08	359.92
Partners' salaries:				
M. O. Brown	600.00	None	None	600.00
W. E. Bailey	600.00	None	None	600.00
	$2,490.00	$83.85	$57.69	$2,348.46

Employer's payroll taxes:			
FICA taxes			$ 83.85
Unemployment compensation taxes:			
State unemployment taxes		$34.82	
FUTA taxes		9.03	43.85
Total			$127.70

A check payable to Payroll was prepared and cashed at the National Bank. Currency was obtained in the proper denominations to meet individual payroll requirements. The accountant deposited the salaries of Bailey and Brown in their respective bank accounts and gave them duplicate deposit slips.

The payroll check was entered in the cash disbursements journal by debiting the proper payroll accounts and crediting the proper liability accounts for deductions and by crediting the bank account for the net payroll amount. The payroll taxes on the employer are recorded in the general journal by debiting Payroll Taxes Expense, account no. 610, and by crediting the appropriate liability accounts.

Issued check no. 655 for $424.98 to the National Bank in payment of the following taxes (the National Bank is a U.S. depository.)

Employees' federal income taxes		
(withheld during November)		$115.38
On employee (withheld during November)	$154.80	
On employer	154.80	309.60
Total		$424.98

Discarded desk in storage room. Additional depreciation expense of $5 is entered to bring depreciation up to date. Original cost was $65. Since the desk was completely depreciated, the transaction was recorded by debiting Accumulated Depreciation—Store Equipment, account no. 161, and by crediting Store Equipment, account no. 160, for $65.

Bailey and Brown decided that the $20 owed by J. J. Clark was uncollectible and wrote off the account. The entry was recorded by debiting Allowance for Doubtful Accounts, account no. 131, and by crediting Accounts Receivable, account no. 130.

Issued Credit Memorandum No. 129 to B. L. Thompson for electrical supplies returned. Credit amounted to $10.39.

(Transactions between December 15 and December 31 have been omitted.)

December 31

Received the following invoices:

National Electrical Company, City; electrical supplies, $112.14; terms, December 30—2/10, n/30.

Chattanooga Marble Company, Chattanooga; marble sink tops, $348.49; terms, December 29—2/10, n/30.

Made the following sales on account:

No. 250: McDonald Construction Company, Monroe; electrical, $215; terms, 2/10, n/30.

No. 251: Sturdy Builders, City; drain pipe, $88.52; terms, 2/10, n/30.

Made the following cash sales:

No. 376: A. A. Adams; plumbing, $214.99.

No. 357: O. J. Rich; plumbing, $175.50.

No. 378: J & J Hardware; plumbing, $278.18.

Made a petty cash disbursement of $1.25 for package received with postage due. Voucher No. 95 (charge to account no. 6129).

Issued the following checks:

No. 667: Southern Supply Company; $184 in payment of December 23 invoice for $187.75 less 2 percent discount.

No. 668: West Manufacturing Company, $118.18 in payment of December 22 invoice for $120.59 less 2 percent discount.

No. 669: Industrial Supply Company, $42. Cash purchase of two dollies for use in store and on delivery truck.

No. 670: Payroll, $2,348.46. Payroll is the same as for the first half of the month.

No. 671: $92.53 payable to Petty Cash to reimburse the petty cash fund.

December petty cash disbursements were as follows:

December Petty Cash Disbursements

Account No.	Account Title	Amount
6105	Advertising expense	$ 8.42
6107	Truck repairs expense	14.15
6109	Shipping expense	5.00
6114	Store supplies expense	2.65
6117	Miscellaneous selling expense	15.32
6123	Power and water expense	6.00
6124	Telephone expense.	18.00
6129	Postage expense (administrative)	1.25
6133	Miscellaneous general expense.	21.74
	Total disbursements	$92.53

Received the following checks:

Quick Contractors, $408.15, in payment of merchandise sold on December 10 amounting to $408.15.

Fred Smith, $133.50, in payment of merchandise sold on December 22 amounting to $136.22 less 2 percent discount.

End-of-the-Month Accounting Procedures

1. Proved the books of original entry and petty cash disbursements record by footing the amount columns and comparing totals.

2. Proved the bank balance as shown below:

Balance, December 1 . . . . $ 8,425.16
Add: Total receipts December 1–31 (cash receipts
record). 9,474.99
Total $17,900.15
Less: Checks issued December 1–31 (cash
disbursements record) 9,439.05
Balance, December 31 . . . . $ 8,461.10

(Note balance of daily bank statement—December 31.)

3. Finished posting from books of original entry to the general and operating expense ledger accounts.
4. Ruled all amount columns in books of original entry.
5. Posted totals from the appropriate columns of the books of original entry to the general ledger accounts.
6. Prepared trial balance of general ledger accounts.
7. Prepared schedules of accounts receivable, accounts payable, and operating expenses.

Steps 6 and 7 are ordinarily carried out at the end of each month. Since this is the end of the year for Bailey and Brown, additional procedures are performed. The trial balance and schedule of operating expenses are used to prepare worksheets to aid in preparation of financial statements for the year ending December 31. Additional procedures for preparing financial statements are discussed in the next chapter.

SUMMARY

A wholesaler's business is very similar to most other businesses. The major difference is the wholesaler's source of inventory. Inventory is bought directly from importers or manufacturers. The **wholesaler** then sells the products to a retailer who in turn sells them to individual customers.

In any enterprise the type of business, business volume, desired information, and available resources, such as office machines, affect the accounting system.

All accounting systems have three basic types of records: books of original entry, books of final entry, and supplementary records. These records vary from system to system.

Financial transactions are recorded first in the books of original entry. The most common books of original entry are a sales register, a cash receipts journal, an invoice register, a cash disbursements journal, and a general journal. Each journal has a specific purpose.

The books of final entry are a compilation of individual transactions from the books of original entry into meaningful financial data. The books of final entry include the general ledger and subsidiary ledgers.

Supplementary records include any extra records which are needed for management purposes. Examples are a **daily bank statement,** a petty cash record, and an insurance register.

The degree of complexity of the accounting system depends on management's needs and the operation of the business.

KEY TERMS

Book of Minutes—A record book in which actions taken at stockholders' and the board of directors' meetings are recorded.

Daily Bank Statement—A supplementary record which keeps track of an enterprise's bank balance on a daily basis.

Inventory Record—A supplementary record used in inventory control. It is particularly useful in determining physical inventory on hand when preparing interim financial statements.

Schedule of Accounts Payable—A list of all creditors' accounts in the subsidiary accounts payable ledger. Its total should equal the Accounts Payable control account balance in the general ledger.

Schedule of Accounts Receivable—A list of all customer accounts in the accounts receivable subsidiary ledger. Its total should equal the Accounts Receivable control account balance in the general ledger.

Stockholders' Ledger—A subsidiary ledger controlled by the capital stock account which shows the number of shares of stock held by each stockholder at any time.

Temporary Investments—Investments which will be converted into cash during the normal operating cycle of the business. Since they are held on a short-term basis, they are classified as current assets on the balance sheet.

Wholesalers—Businesses that purchase products directly from manufacturers and importers and then sell them to retailers who in turn sell them to individual customers.

QUESTIONS AND EXERCISES

1. Describe the operation of a wholesaler in the chain of product distribution.
2. What factors affect the accounting records to be used by a wholesaler?
3. What impact does the owner's equity structure of a business have on the accounts used?
4. What are the advantages of functionally dividing the accounting activities among the accounting employees?
5. List several books of original entry, books of final entry, and supplementary records that may be kept by a wholesaler.
6. When and why might a wholesale business buy U.S. government bonds? How would the government bonds be classified in the financial statements?
7. What are sales discounts? How are they treated in the financial statements?
8. What are some advantages of maintaining an inventory record?
9. On March 1, Ailene Barker purchased merchandise from Wistuff's Wholesale Company. The gross amount of the invoice was $1,950, and payment terms were 2/10, n/30. On March 9, Wistuff's Wholesale received a check from Ms. Barker. What should be the amount of the check if Ms. Barker wishes to take advantage of the cash discount?
10. If merchandise costing $420 was purchased on July 10 and $20 worth was returned on the fifteenth, how much cash should be remitted on July 19 if the terms are 2/10, n/30?
11. If merchandise costing $550 was purchased August 15 and $25 worth was returned on August 17, how much cash should be remitted on August 26 if the terms are 2/10, n/30?

PROBLEMS

23–1. Harley Richfield operates a wholesale jewelry and small appliance business. During the month of February 1987 Richfield completed the following transactions of sales on account:

1987
Feb. 2 No. 210: Axel Appliance Company; toasters, $75; wall clocks, $95; terms, 2/10, n/30.

1987

Feb. 4   No. 211: Hale's Jewelry; cocktail rings, $120; wire necklaces, $50; ladies' watches, $150; terms, 2/15, n/60.

      5   No. 212: Kohl & Sons; copper bracelets, $70; magnetic earrings, $80; terms, 2/10, n/60.

      7   No. 213: Hardy's Furnishings; blenders, $170; ice makers, $95; terms, 2/10, n/30.

      8   No. 214: Dietz Company; radios, $140; alarm clocks, $80; electric can openers, $105; terms, 2/20, n/60.

      9   No. 215: Jackson Fine Accessories, Inc.; earrings, $130; stickpins, $150; rings, $60; terms, 2/10, n/45.

   10   No. 216: Grey's Home Supplies; irons, $150; electric frying pans, $180; terms, 2/20, n/60.

   12   No. 217: Holmes, Inc.; electric mixers, $350; popcorn poppers, $200; terms, 2/10, n/30.

   14   No. 218: Bales Jewelry Outlet; pearl necklaces, $350; onyx tiepins, $200; terms, 2/10, n/30.

   15   No. 219: Shane's; ring sets, $320; watches, $180; earrings, $130; terms, 2/20, n/60.

   17   No. 220: Royal Appliances, Inc.; toaster ovens, $280; warming trays, $300; terms, 2/10, n/30.

   21   No. 221: Boyle's Jewelry; ladies' watches, $150; jade bracelets, $220; terms, 2/10, n/30.

   22   No. 222: Gunnar's Home Appliances; toasters, $170; alarm clocks, $120; terms, 2/20, n/60.

   23   No. 223: Alfred's, Inc.; juicers, $175; blenders, $215; mixers, $240; terms, 2/10, n/30.

   24   No. 224: Shelby Home-makers; crockery slow-cookers, $225; electric fondue pots, $190; terms, 2/20, n/60.

   26   No. 225: Myers Jewelry, Inc.; silver charms, $150; charm bracelets, $120; stickpins, $90; terms, 2/10, n/60.

   28   No. 226: Trainor's, Inc.; wire earrings, $95; adjustable rings, $105; bracelets, $120; terms, 2/10, n/30.

Required:

1. Record the transactions in a sales register like the one shown in Illustration 23–1 (have columns for (1) Appliances and (2) Jewelry).

2. Foot and rule the sales register.

23–2. James Hanley and Tom Bolton have just started a wholesale business which sells hardware and sporting goods. During their first month of operation, Hanley and Bolton completed the following selected transactions:

1987

May 1   James Hanley invested $12,000 cash and store equipment amounting to $750 in the business. Tom Bolton invested $15,000 in the business. Check no. 101 was issued to the Helman Company for May's rent, $400.

2   Issued check no. 102 to Bole's Equipment Company for store equipment, $1,050 and check no. 103 to the *Daily Pacer* for advertising, $95.

3   Issued check no. 104 for $1,700 for sporting goods to Haney Sports, Inc. and check no. 105 to Janson Manufacturing Company for hardware, $1,450.

6   Issued check no. 106 to Allen's Supply Company for store supplies, $500, and office supplies, $350.
Made the following cash sales:
No. 1: Jack Ruark; baseball mitts, $135.
No. 2: Frank Brown; tools, $85.

7   Made the following cash sales:
No. 3: Jane Wilson; tennis rackets, $160.
No. 4: Sam Leeds; saw, $40.

8   Made the following cash sales:
No. 5: John Anthony; garden tools, $95.
No. 6: Harold Myers; golf clubs, $250.

9   Issued the following checks:
No. 107: Rankin Sporting Goods Company for sporting goods, $800.
No. 108: U.S. Postal Service for stamps, $140.
No. 109: Shouts & Sons for office equipment, $750.

10   Made the following cash sales:
No. 7: Sandra Moore; lighting fixtures, $110.
No. 8: James Haskell; camping equipment, $240.
No. 9: Henry Pace; copper tubing, $30.

13   Issued check no. 110 for $735 to Hale's Hardware Company for invoice of May 3 for $750 less 2 percent discount. Received the following check: Jorgen's, Incorporated, $318.50 for merchandise sold on May 3 amounting to $325 less 2 percent discount.

14   Received the following checks: Robert Hull, $145.50 for merchandise sold on May 6 amounting to $150 less 3 percent discount; and May Willis, $436.50 for merchandise

1987

sold on May 7 amounting to $450 less 3 percent discount.

May 15   Issued the following checks:

No. 111: $230 to WFNR for television advertisements.

No. 112: $798.70 to Strang Manufacturers for its May 6 invoice amounting to $815 less 2 percent discount.

16   Made the following cash sales:

No. 10: Hank Phillips; sporting goods, $320.

No. 11: Pete Logan; hardware, $430.

Received a check for $360 from Marge Hansen for merchandise sold on May 3 amounting to $360.

17   Issued the following checks:

No. 113: $1,164 to Axel Products, Inc. for its May 9 invoice amounting to $1,200 less 3 percent discount.

No. 114: $300 to WFAM radio station for advertisements.

20   Made the following cash sales:

No. 12: Renee Recell; chain saws, $105.

No. 13: Ray Hardigree; power tools, $730.

Received the following check: Monty Haskell, $504.40 for merchandise sold on May 10 amounting to $520 less 3 percent discount.

21   Issued the following checks:

No. 115: $2,910 to Cooper Manufacturers for its May 13 invoice amounting to $3,000 less 3 percent discount.

No. 116: $125 to the United Fund.

22   Received a check for $610 from Jack North for merchandise sold on May 7 amounting to $610.

Issued check no. 117 to Sholes & Company for $1,750 for its May 8 invoice amounting to $1,750.

23   Made the following cash sale:

No. 14: Theresa Grey; sporting goods, $95.

24   Made the following cash sales:

No. 15: Ben Holcomb; tool box, $120.

No. 15: George Barnett; circular saws, $180.

27   Received a check for $315 from Eugene Kilpatrick for merchandise sold on May 13 amounting to $315. Issued check no. 118 for $70 to the March of Dimes.

28   Received the following checks: Craig Snyder, $210.70 for merchandise sold on May 20 amounting to $215 less 2 percent discount; and Brent Perry, $240.10 for merchandise sold on May 20 amounting to $245 less 2 percent discount.

1987

May 29 Made the following cash sale:

No. 17: Mike Holmes, tennis equipment, $70.

Issued the following check:

No. 119: Recreation Time, Inc., for sporting goods, $870.

30 Received a check for $1,096.10 from Harmony Company for merchandise sold on May 23 amounting to $1,130 less 3 percent discount.

31 Made the following cash sales:

No. 18: Norris Wells; work benches, $520.

No. 19: Jerry Hanes; baseball equipment, $324.

No. 20: Jim Bolton; power tools, $225.

Issued check no. 120 to Major Manufacturers, Inc., for sporting goods, $1,100.

Required:

1. Record the transactions in the appropriate book of original entry (cash receipts journal or cash disbursements journal).

2. Prepare a daily bank statement.

3. Foot and rule the books of original entry on May 31, 1987.

4. Prove the bank balance on May 31, 1987.

HANLEY AND BOLTON
Chart of Accounts (Partial)

Account No.	Account Title
101	Bank
111	Accounts Receivable
140	Office Equipment
150	Store Equipment
211	Accounts Payable
301	Tom Bolton, Capital
311	James Hanley, Capital
400	Sales—Hardware
410	Sales—Sporting Goods
413	Sales Discounts
500	Purchases—Hardware
510	Purchases—Sporting Goods
513	Purchases Discounts
600	Rent Expense
605	Advertising Expense
610	Office Supplies Expense
615	Store Supplies Expense
620	Postage Expense
625	Charitable Contributions Expense

23–3. James R. Buchanan runs a wholesale chemical supply store. On April 1, 1987, Mr. Buchanan created a $150 petty cash fund. During April the following disbursements were made from the petty cash fund:

1987
Apr. 3 Voucher no. 1: truck repairs, $20.
      6 Voucher no. 2: water bill, $12.
      8 Voucher no. 3: newspaper advertisement, $10.
    10 Voucher no. 4: telephone bill, $15.
    13 Voucher no. 5: postage stamps, $8.
    15 Voucher no. 6: truck repairs, $8.
    19 Voucher no. 7: electricity bill, $19.
    23 Voucher no. 8: newspaper advertisement, $10
    26 Voucher no. 9: adding machine repairs, $7.
    29 Voucher no. 10: typewriter repairs, $11.
    30 Voucher no. 11: postage stamps, $5.

The fund was replenished on April 30, 1987.

Required:

1. Prepare the general journal entry to establish the petty cash fund on April 1, 1987.
2. Record the above transactions in a petty cash disbursements record. The charges should be distributed among the following accounts:

6101   Truck Repairs Expense
6106   Power and Water Expense
6112   Advertising Expense
6118   Telephone Expense
6125   Miscellaneous Expense
6130   Postage Expense

3. Total the amount columns and prove the footings.
4. Prepare a general journal entry to replenish the fund on April 30, 1987.

The following chart of accounts is to be used in Problems 4 and 5:

**LEONARD'S WHOLESALE TV AND RADIO SUPPLIES
AND PARTS**
General Ledger Chart of Accounts

Assets		**Assets**	
101	Bank of Upson	121	Accounts Receivable
102	Petty Cash	122	Allowance for Doubtful Accounts
111	Marketable Securities	123	Notes Receivable

**LEONARD'S WHOLESALE TV AND RADIO SUPPLIES
AND PARTS** *(concluded)*
General Ledger Chart of Accounts

Assets

124	Accrued Interest Receivable
131	Merchandise Inventory—TV Supplies and Parts
132	Merchandise Inventory—Radio Supplies and Parts
141	Store Supplies
142	Office Supplies
143	Prepaid Insurance
151	Store Equipment
152	Accumulated Depreciation Store Equipment
153	Office Equipment
154	Accumulated Depreciation Office Equipment
155	Delivery Truck
156	Accumulated Depreciation—Delivery Truck

Liabilities

201	FICA Taxes Payable
202	FUTA Taxes Payable
203	Income Taxes Payable—Federal—Employee
204	State Unemployment Taxes Payable
211	Accounts Payable
212	Notes Payable
213	Accrued Interest Payable

Owner's Equity

301	G. R. Leonard, Capital
302	G. R. Leonard, Drawing
311	Income Summary

Revenues

401	Sales—TV Supplies and Parts
402	Sales Returns and Allowances—TV Supplies and Parts
411	Sales—Radio Supplies and Parts
412	Sales Returns and Allowances—Radio Supplies and Parts
421	Sales Discounts

Cost of Goods Sold

501	Purchases—TV Supplies and Parts
502	Purchase Returns and Allowances—TV Supplies and Parts
511	Purchases—Radio Supplies and Parts
512	Purchase Returns and Allowances—Radio Supplies and Parts
521	Purchases Discounts
531	Transportation-In—TV Supplies and Parts
541	Transportation-In—Radio Supplies and Parts
601	Operating Expenses
701	Interest Revenue
801	Interest Expense
811	Collection Expense

23–4. G. R. Leonard operates a wholesale store which sells TV and radio supplies and parts to retail stores. During the month of June 1987, Leonard completed the following purchases and sales transactions:

1987
June 1 Sales on account:

No. 106: Conyers Repair Shop, City; TV parts, $206; terms, 2/10, n/30.

1987

No. 107: Lance Denall, City; radio parts, $122; terms, 2/10, n/30.

June 2 Sales on account:

No. 108: Clay Dennis, Comer; TV supplies and parts, $400; terms, 2/10, n/30.

Received the following invoices:

No. 75: Helen Manufacturing Company, City; radio parts, $345; terms, June 2—2/10, n/30.

No. 76: Folk Manufacturing Company, Macon; TV parts, $690; terms, May 29—2/10, n/60.

No. 77: Reeves Supply Company, City; office supplies, $85; terms, June 2—2/10, n/30.

3 Received the following invoice:

No. 78: Haywood TV Company, Columbus; TV supplies and parts, $850; terms, May 28—2/10, n/60.

4 Sales on account:

No. 109: Love's Repair Service, City; radio parts and supplies, $110; terms, 2/10, n/30.

8 Sales on account:

No. 110: Lynn Eden, City; radio parts, $80; terms, 2/10, n/30.

No. 111: Henry Lovett, Monroe; TV parts and supplies, $175; terms, 2/10, n/30.

9 Sales on account:

No. 112: Huckleberry's Repair Company, Winder; radio parts and supplies, $125, and TV parts and supplies, $200; terms, 2/10, n/30.

10 Received the following invoice:

No. 79: Shaw's Equipment Company, Albany; typewriter, $300; terms, June 7—2/10, n/30.

11 Received the following invoices:

No. 80: Lloyd's Company, City; store supplies, $60; terms, June 11—n/30.

No. 81: Frank Baker, City; calculator, $90; terms, June 11—n/30.

15 Sales on account:

No. 113: Kathy Ryals, Bogart; radio supplies, $50; terms, n/30.

No. 114: Rhonda Hilley, Byron; radio supplies, $80, and TV supplies, $125; terms, 2/10, n/30.

1987

June 16 Sales on account:

No. 115: Mike's Repair Shop, Athens; TV parts and supplies, $290; terms, 2/10, n/30.

No. 116: Buford's Hardware Store, City; radio parts and supplies, $60; terms, n/30.

17 Sales on account:

No. 117: Yung's Supply Store, Augusta; radio supplies and parts, $160; terms, 2/10, n/30.

18 Received the following invoice:

No. 82: Calley's Equipment Company, City; store equipment, $200; terms, June 18—2/10, n/30.

22 Received the following invoices:

No. 83: Houston Supplies, Cordele; radio supplies and parts, $560; terms, June 18—2/10, n/60.

No. 84: Helen Manufacturing Company, City; radio supplies and parts, $300; terms, June 22—2/10, n/30.

No. 85: Roscoe's Radio Company, Forsyth; radio parts, $200; terms, June 19—2/10, n/30.

23 Sales on account:

No. 118: Buckley's Repair Shop, Shady Dale; TV supplies and parts, $150; terms, 2/10, n/30.

24 Sales on account:

No. 119: Michael Ware, City; TV parts, $50; terms, n/30.

No. 120: Phil Masten Company, Cairo; TV supplies and parts, $220; terms, 2/10, n/30.

Received the following invoices:

No. 86: Bobo Equipment Company, New York; multiple-purpose accounting machine, $1,800; terms, June 18—2/20, n/120.

No. 87: Lee Manufacturing Company, Dallas; radio supplies and parts, $400, and TV supplies and parts, $500; terms, June 20—2/10, n/90.

25 Sales on account:

No. 121: David Trice, Thomaston; radio supplies and parts, $80; terms, n/30.

29 Received the following invoices:

No. 88: Folk Manufacturing Company, Macon; TV parts, $400; terms, June 26—2/10, n/30.

1987

No. 89: Bates TV Company, Manchester; TV supplies and parts, $500; terms, June 26—2/10, n/30.

No. 90: T & R Manufacturing Company, Atlanta; TV parts, $250, and radio parts, $300; terms, June 27—2/10, n/30.

June 30   Sales on account:

No. 122: George Wells, Bishop; radio supplies, $75; terms, n/30.

No. 123: Heidi Kiger, Valdosta; TV supplies and parts, $325; terms, 2/10, n/30.

Received the following invoices:

No. 91: Huxley's, Columbus; radio supplies and parts, $510; terms, June 26—2/10, n/60.

No. 92: Windal's, Moultrie; TV supplies, $250; terms, June 27—2/10, n/30.

Required:

1. Prepare a sales register like the one shown in Illustration 23–1 for the month of June.

2. Prepare an invoice register like the one shown in Illustration 23–3 for the month of June.

3. Foot and rule the registers prepared in 1 and 2 above.

23–5.   G. R. Leonard (see Problem 23–4) completed the following selected transactions during the month of June 1987.

1987

June 1   Issued check no. 708 for $300 to Ruffin Realty Company for the June rent (account no. 6010). Issued check no. 709 for $240.10 to Deen Manufacturers in payment of its May 22 invoice for $245 less 2 percent discount.

2   Made the following cash sales:

No. 350: Leroy Allen; radio parts, $105.

No. 351: James Kellum; TV parts, $210.

No. 352: Charles Ford; radio supplies, $96.

Issued check no. 710 for $388 to Cordell Equipment Company in payment of its May 23 invoice for $400 less 3 percent discount.

3   Received a check for $318.50 from Carl Franko for mer-

1987

chandise sold on May 27 amounting to $325 less 2 percent discount. Made the following cash sales:

No. 353: Andy Melton; TV parts, $400.

No. 354: Stephen T. Hayes; TV parts, $160.

June 4   Issued check no. 711 for $666.40 to Mackey's Shack in payment of its May 26 invoice for $680 less 2 percent discount. Received a check for $176.40 from Troy Milsap for merchandise sold on May 27 amounting to $180 less 2 percent discount.

8   Made the following cash sales:

No. 355: Joe Garland; radio parts, $50, and television parts, $250.

No. 356: Terrell Wilson; TV supplies, $75.

9   Issued the following checks:

No. 712: $171.50 to Margot's Supply Company in payment of its May 31 invoice for $175 less 2 percent discount.

No. 713: $426.80 to Binet Manufacturing Company in payment of its May 31 invoice for $440 less 3 percent discount.

Made the following cash sale:

No. 357: Martin King; radio parts, $105.

10   Received the following checks: Conyers Repair Shop, $201.88, for merchandise sold on June 1 amounting to $206 less 2 percent discount; and Clay Dennis, $392, for merchandise sold on June 2 amounting to $400 less 2 percent discount.

Issued the following checks:

No. 714: $690 to Folk Manufacturing Company in payment of its May 29 invoice.

No. 715: $850 to Haywood TV Company in payment of its May 28 invoice.

11   Issued the following checks:

No. 716: $50 to *Sumter Journal* for local newspaper advertisements (account no. 6015).

No. 717: $212 to Hobo's Motor Company for repairs to the delivery truck (account no. 6019).

Received the following checks: Lance Denall, $119.56, for merchandise sold on June 1 amounting to $122 less 2 percent discount; and Kelly Potts, $218, for merchandise sold on May 15 amounting to $218.

1987

June 15   Received the following check: Love's Repair Service, $110 for merchandise sold on June 4 amounting to $110.

Issued the following checks:

No. 718: $345 to Helen Manufacturing Company in payment of its June 2 invoice.

No. 719: $85 to Reeves Supply Company in payment of its June 2 invoice.

16   Issued the following check:

No. 720: $294 to Shaw's Equipment Company in payment of its June 7 invoice for $300 less 2 percent discount.

17   Made the following cash sales:

No. 358: Richard Jones; TV parts, $300.

No. 359: Barbra Ronstall; radio parts, $175.

Issued the following checks:

No. 721: $60 to Lloyd's Company in payment of its June 11 invoice.

No. 722: $90 to Frank Baker in payment of his June 11 invoice.

18   Received the following checks: Lynn Eden, $78.40, for merchandise sold on June 8 amounting to $80 less 2 percent discount; Henry Lovett, $171.50, for merchandise sold on June 8 amounting to $175 less 2 percent discount. Huckleberry's Repair Company, $312, for merchandise sold on June 9 amounting to $325 less 4 percent discount.

Issued the following check:

No. 723: $125 to Southern Independence Telephone Company for the telephone bill (account no. 6020).

22   Made the following cash sales:

No. 360: Bill Brinkley; TV supplies, $85.

No. 361: Scott Alexander; radio parts, $75.

No. 362: Debbie Bell; radio parts, $50.

23   Received the following check: Kathy Ryals, $50 for merchandise sold on June 15.

Made the following cash sale:

No. 363: Tim Wheless; TV parts, $75.

24   Issued the following checks:

No. 724: $196 to Calley's Equipment Company in payment of its June 18 invoice for $200 less 2 percent discount.

1987

No. 725: $300 to G. R. Leonard for personal expenses. Received the following checks: Rhonda Hilley, $122.50, for merchandise sold on June 15 amounting to $125 less 2 percent discount; and Mike's Repair Shop, $284.20, for merchandise sold on June 16 amounting to $290 less 2 percent discount.

June 25   Received the following checks: Buford's Hardware Store, $60, for merchandise sold on June 16; and Yung's Supply Store, $156.80, for merchandise sold on June 17 amounting to $160 less 2 percent discount.

25   Issued the following check:

No. 726: $548.80 to Houston Supplies in payment of its June 18 invoice for $560 less 2 percent discount.

29   Issued the following check:

No. 727: $196 to Roscoe's Radio Company in payment of its June 19 invoice for $200 less 2 percent discount.

30   Issued the following check:

No. 728: $882 to Lee Manufacturing Company for its June 20 invoice of $900 less 2 percent discount.

Made the following cash sales:

No. 364: Byron Wells; TV supplies and parts, $206, and radio parts, $44.

No. 365: Satish Mehra; radio parts, $125.

Paid the payroll for the month of June with check nos. 729, 730, and 731. Payroll data is shown below:

Gross earnings		$2,400.00
Less: FICA Tax	$156.00	
Federal income tax	400.00	556.00
Net earnings		$1,844.00

Check No.	Employee	Net Earnings
729	Joseph French	$689.75
730	Faye Smothers	599.20
731	Adam Tucker	555.05

The employer's payroll tax expenses are also recorded in the cash disbursements journal.

(Salaries Expense—account no. 6030.)

(Payroll Tax Expense—account no. 6040.)

FICA tax—employer	$156.00
FUTA tax	16.80
State unemployment tax	64.80

Required:

1. Record each of the above transactions in either the cash receipts journal or the cash disbursements journal, whichever is correct.
2. Prepare a daily bank statement. (Cash balance, May 31, 1987— $6,411.65.)
3. Foot and rule the records prepared in 1 above.
4. Prove the bank balance on June 30, 1987.

23–6. Thomas Cooper and Laura Dooley own and operate C and D Wholesale House. The store is divided into two departments—Department C which sells clothing and Department G which sells groceries. During the month of February 1987, the C and D Wholesale House was involved in the following transactions:

1987

Feb. 2 Issued check no. 807 to Kendrick Realty Company for the February rent, $400.
Sales on account:
  No. 250: Tiller's Corner Grocery, City; groceries, $500; terms, 2/10, n/30.
  No. 251: Kemp's Variety Shop, City; groceries, $125; clothing, $300; terms, n/30.
  No. 252: Wayne's Market, City; groceries, $250; terms, n/30.

3 Received a check for $275 from Tim Gowan for merchandise sold on January 6 amounting to $275.
Made the following cash sale:
  No. 519: Goolsby Store; clothing, $275.

4 Received the following invoices:
  No. 400: Rice Manufacturing Company, Atlanta; clothing, $800; terms, February 2—2/10, n/30.
  No. 401: Ridley Brothers, City; groceries, $705; terms, February 4—2/10, n/30.
Issued check no. 808 to Independent Telephone Company for the January phone bill, $150.

5 Sales on account:
  No. 253: Hood's Clothes, City; clothing, $500; terms, 2/10, n/30.
  No. 254: Ford's Men's Store; clothing, $450; terms, n/30.

7 Issued the following checks:
  No. 809: $75 to Aubrey's Supply Company for office supplies.

1987

No. 810: $425 to Fleming Manufacturing Company in payment of its invoice of January 7 amounting to $425.

Made the following cash sales:

No. 520: Fred Fish; groceries, $300.

No. 521: Rebecca Fields; clothing, $215.

Received a check for $627.20 for Sikes' Grocery Store for merchandise sold on January 30 amounting to $640 less 2 percent discount.

Feb. 9 Received the following invoices:

No. 402: Griffin Manufacturing Company, Augusta; clothing, $650; terms, February 5—2/10, n/30.

No. 403: Lindsay Equipment Company, Detroit; office equipment, $750; terms, January 31—2/20, n/60.

Sales on account:

No. 255: Dorothy Cavan, City; groceries, $275; terms, n/30.

No. 256: Julian Liles, City; groceries, $580; terms, 2/10, n/30.

Made the following cash sale:

No. 522: Patrick Norton, Valdosta; clothing, $330.

10 Issued the following checks:

No. 811: $135 to Nunn Brothers for store supplies.

No. 812: $427.28 to Seabro Company in payment of its January 31 invoice of $436 less 2 percent discount.

Received a check for $478.24 from Howard Day for merchandise sold on January 12 amounting to $478.24.

11 Received the following invoices:

No. 404: Morrison Foods, Smithville; groceries, $585; terms, February 10—2/10, n/30.

No. 405: Henrietta's Cottons, Dallas; clothing, $759; terms, February 5—2/10, n/30.

12 Issued check no. 813 for $784 to Rice Manufacturing Company in payment of its February 2 invoice for $800 less 2 percent discount. Received a check for $490 from Tiller's Corner Grocery for merchandise sold on February 2 amounting to $500 less 2 percent discount.

14 Made the following cash sales:

No. 523: Mark Christo, City; groceries, $239.

No. 524: Dana Javo, City; clothing, $312.

1987

Issued the following checks:

No. 814 for $690.90 to Ridley Brothers in payment of its February 4 invoice for $705 less 2 percent discount.

No. 815 for $637 to Griffin Manufacturing Company in payment of its February 5 invoice for $650 less 2 percent discount.

No. 816 for $743.82 to Henrietta's Cottons in payment of its February 5 invoice for $759 less 2 percent discount.

Received a check for $490 from Hood's Clothes for merchandise sold on February 5 amounting to $500 less 2 percent discount.

Sales on account:

No. 257: James Turner, Thomasville; clothing, $650; terms, 2/10, n/30.

No. 258: Gerald Pierce, City; clothing, $180; groceries, $410; terms, 2/10, n/30.

Feb. 17   Made the following cash sales:

No. 525: Willis Hill, Americus; groceries, $267.

No. 526: Leslie Roper, City; clothing, $342.

18   Received the following invoices.

No. 406: Corbett's Groceries, City; groceries, $395; terms, February 18—n/30.

No. 407: Clinton's Clothing Company, Columbus; clothing, $562; terms, February 17—2/10, n/30.

Issued check no. 817 for $735 to Lindsay Equipment Company for its January 31 invoice of $750 less 2 percent discount.

19   Issued the following checks:

No. 818: $573.30 to Morrison Foods for its February 10 invoice amounting to $585 less 2 percent discount.

No. 819: $55 to *Times—Free Press* for local newspaper advertising.

Received a check for $568.40 from Julian Liles for merchandise sold on February 9 amounting to $580 less 2 percent discount.

21   Sales on account:

No. 259: Steve Sailors, City; clothing, $702; terms, 2/10, n/30.

1987

No. 260: Jack Trapnell, Leesburg; groceries, $610; terms, 2/10, n/30.

Received the following invoice:

No. 408: Rice Manufacturing Company, Atlanta; clothing, $700; terms, February 17—2/10, n/30.

Feb. 23 Received the following checks: Kemp's Variety Shop, $425, for merchandise sold on February 2 amounting to $425; and Wayne's Market, $250, for merchandise sold on February 2 amounting to $250.

Received the following invoice:

No. 409: Ridley Brothers, City; groceries, $911; terms, February 23—2/10, n/30.

24 Made the following cash sales:

No. 527: Kermit & Son, City; groceries, $308.

No. 528: Barbra Reinholt, City; clothing, $509.

25 Received the following checks: Ford's Men's Store, $450, for merchandise sold on February 5 amounting to $450; and Dorothy Cavan, $275, for merchandise sold on February 9 amounting to $275.

26 Received the following checks: James Turner, $637, for merchandise sold on February 16 amounting to $650 less 2 percent discount; and Gerald Pierce, $578.20, for merchandise sold on February 16 amounting to $590 less 2 percent discount.

Issued the following checks:

No. 820: $550.76 to Clinton's Clothing Company for its February 17 invoice of $562 less 2 percent discount.

No. 821: $686 to Rice Manufacturing Company for its February 17 invoice of $700 less 2 percent discount.

28 Issued the following check:

No. 822: $395 to Corbett's Groceries for its February 18 invoice of $395.

Required:

1. Record the transactions in the appropriate book of original entry— invoice register, sales register, cash receipts journal, or cash disbursements journal.
2. Prepare a daily bank statement for February. The bank balance was $3,417.54 on February 1.
3. Foot and rule the books of original entry.

4. Prepare a proof of the bank balance on February 28, 1987.

C AND D WHOLESALE HOUSE
Chart of Accounts (Partial)

Account No.	Account Title
100	Bank
120	Accounts Receivable
140	Store Supplies
142	Office Supplies
150	Store Equipment
160	Office Equipment
240	Accounts Payable
300	Thomas Cooper, Capital
301	Thomas Cooper, Drawing
310	Laura Dooley, Capital
311	Laura Dooley, Drawing
400	Sales—Department C
410	Sales—Department G
420	Sales Discounts
500	Purchases—Department C
510	Purchases—Department G
520	Purchases Discounts
610	Rent Expense
611	Telephone Expense
612	Advertising Expense

23–7. The petty cash fund of the Clarkston Wholesale Company was created on February 1, 1987 with the amount of $250. The following disbursements were made from the fund during February.

1987
Feb. 2 Voucher no. 1: postage stamps, $15.
      3 Voucher no. 2: typewriter repairs, $30.
      4 Voucher no. 3: telephone bill, $37.
      5 Voucher no. 4: electric bill, $21.
      8 Voucher no. 5: postage stamps, $15.
      9 Voucher no. 6: water bill, $12.
     14 Voucher no. 7: newspaper advertisement, $26.
     15 Voucher no. 8: pencil sharpener, $7.
     17 Voucher no. 9: typewriter repairs, $11.
     18 Voucher no. 10: postage stamps, $25.
     23 Voucher no. 11: newspaper subscription, $8.
     26 Voucher no. 12: newspaper advertisement, $19.

The fund was replenished on February 28, 1987.

Required:

1. Prepare the general journal entry on February 1, 1987, to establish the petty cash fund.

2. Record the above transactions using a petty cash disbursement record. The charges involve the following accounts:

   6111   Advertising Expense
   6117   Miscellaneous Expense
   6124   Office Machines Repair Expense
   6131   Postage Expense
   6138   Telephone Expense
   6145   Utilities Expense

3. Foot and rule the amount columns and prove the footings.

4. Prepare the February 28, 1987, general journal entry to replenish the petty cash fund.

CHAPTER 24

Year-end accounting procedures—
wholesale business

LEARNING OBJECTIVES

The material in Chapter 23 concerned the accounting for transactions for a wholesale business. In this chapter you will study the completion of the accounting cycle for a wholesale enterprise. After studying this chapter, you should be able to:

1. Prepare a 10-column worksheet.
2. Make adjusting entries.
3. Prepare closing entries.
4. Prepare reversing entries.
5. Prepare an income statement.
6. Prepare a balance sheet.
7. Prepare a schedule of operating expenses.
8. Prepare a post-closing trial balance.

Periodic financial reports are prepared to help management and other interested parties analyze the activities of a particular business. The preparation of financial statements is the end product of the accounting system. The statements are a primary reason for maintaining accounting records. Statement users require as a minimum that they be supplied with an income statement and a balance sheet. In order to collect and summarize the information necessary to prepare the statements, a **worksheet** is prepared. The worksheet has columns for the year-end trial balance and **adjusting entries.** After the accounts are adjusted, the amounts are extended to the appropriate financial statement columns. When the worksheet is completed, the data required to construct the various financial statements can be taken directly from the worksheet statement columns.

SUMMARY AND SUPPORTING WORKSHEETS

In the previous chapter, the transactions and related accounting procedures for the partnership of Bailey and Brown were illustrated. This chapter will be concerned with construction of year-end worksheets necessary to prepare statements for Bailey and Brown. The discussion will center around the use of a 10-column summary worksheet and a supporting three-column **operating expense worksheet.** The general ledger and operating expense account titles and numbers are the same as those used in the previous chapter (Illustrations 23–5 and 23–6, respectively). The transactions of Bailey and Brown in the previous chapter were for the month of December 1987, and were recorded in the books of original entry and other auxiliary records. The books of original entry were shown as they would appear after posting the transactions to the accounts. It may be assumed that a trial balance was taken upon completion of posting and that the general ledger accounts as well as the controlling and subsidiary ledger accounts were in balance.

Summary worksheet

The summary worksheet used by Bailey and Brown is shown in Illustration 24–1. After the trial balance is taken and the accounts are in balance, a worksheet is prepared. The worksheet provides spaces for each account title and number. All accounts are listed in order by account number except for Income Summary, account no. 330. It is not shown on the worksheet since it is used only in adjusting and closing the accounts. The cost of goods sold accounts (nos. 560 and 570) are used to combine several account balances into a single amount. The **cost of goods sold** is determined by combining:

1. Beginning inventory.
2. Purchases.
3. Transportation-in.
4. Purchase returns and allowances.
5. Purchases discounts.
6. Ending inventory.

As a part of the adjusting process, these amounts are combined into a single amount which is then extended to the Income Statement columns as the cost of goods sold. Because the combination of the above accounts involves several debits and credits, several lines are used on the worksheet for cost of goods sold. After the account balances are entered on the worksheet and shown to be in balance (total debits equal total credits), the worksheet is ready for the necessary adjustments to be made.

Adjustments to determine cost of goods sold. The following entries were used to adjust the inventory and inventory-related accounts to determine the cost of goods sold.

Adjustment (a): The beginning inventory for the plumbing department, $124,314.99, was transferred to Cost of Goods Sold—Plumbing Department by debiting account no. 560 and crediting Merchandise Inventory—Plumbing Department, account no. 140.

Adjustment (b): The beginning inventory for the electrical department, $78,705.10, was transferred to Cost of Goods Sold—Electrical Department by debiting account no. 570 and crediting Merchandise Inventory—Electrical Department, account no. 145.

Adjustment (c): Purchases of the plumbing department amounting to $376,867.25 were transferred to Cost of Goods Sold—Plumbing Department by debiting account no. 560 and crediting Purchases—Plumbing Department, account no. 510.

Adjustment (d): Purchases of the electrical department amounting to $235,334.71, were transferred to Cost of Goods Sold—Electrical Department by debiting account no. 570 and crediting Purchases—Electrical Department, account no. 520.

Adjustment (e): Transportation-in for the plumbing department

ILLUSTRATION 24–1

BAILEY AND BROWN
Worksheet
For the Year Ended December 31, 1987

ACCT. NO.	ACCOUNT NAME	TRIAL BALANCE DEBIT	TRIAL BALANCE CREDIT	ADJUSTMENTS DEBIT	ADJUSTMENTS CREDIT
110	National Bank	8 4 6 1 10			
111	Petty cash	1 0 0 00			
120	Government bonds	5 0 0 0 00			
130	Accounts receivable	2 6 5 9 2 67			
131	Allowance for doubtful accounts		1 1 6 1 88		v 7 7 7 39
132	Notes receivable	3 0 4 2 15			
133	Accrued interest receivable			l 4 2 81	
140	Merchandise inventory—plumbing dept.	12 4 3 1 4 99		j 12 5 2 1 8 67	a 12 4 3 1 4 99
145	Merchandise inventory—elec. dept.	7 8 7 0 5 10		k 8 0 0 1 5 11	b 7 8 7 0 5 10
150	Store supplies	3 0 1 6 75			n 2 9 4 0 87
151	Office supplies	2 2 2 4 18			o 2 1 7 6 17
152	Advertising supplies	8 4 7 19			p 7 6 9 44
153	Postage stamps	6 1 5 00			q 5 9 9 60
154	Prepaid insurance	8 0 4 72			r 4 4 5 39
160	Store equipment	3 2 5 5 70			
161	Accumulated depreciation—Store equipment		8 3 2 34		s 3 2 5 57
170	Office equipment	3 0 0 5 65			
171	Accumulated depreciation—Office equipment		7 8 9 83		t 2 7 5 35
180	Delivery equipment	5 7 9 0 12			
181	Accumulated depreciation—Del. equipment		3 4 9 50		u 5 7 4 51
210	FICA taxes payable		3 0 9 60		
220	FUTA taxes payable		5 3 28		
230	Employee's income taxes payable		1 1 5 38		
240	State unemployment taxes payable		9 7 72		
250	Accounts payable		8 9 4 2 78		w 1 1 5 50
260	Notes payable		2 4 0 0 00		
270	Accrued interest payable				m 2 6 83
310	M. O. Brown, capital		10 2 6 7 0 30		
311	M. O. Brown, drawing	1 7 9 4 5 88			
320	W. E. Bailey, capital		10 4 4 3 3 61		
321	W. E. Bailey, drawing	1 7 4 5 0 00			
410	Sales—plumbing dept		46 8 0 4 1 34		
411	Sales return and allowances—plumb. dept.	5 9 0 7 48			
420	Sales-electrical dept.		28 2 0 4 1 09		
421	Sales return and allowances—elec. dept.	2 1 1 9 62			
422	Sales discounts	8 3 7 1 44			
	Balance carried forward	31 7 5 6 9 74	97 2 2 3 8 65	20 5 2 7 6 59	21 2 0 4 6 71

	ADJUSTED TRIAL BALANCE		INCOME STATEMENT		BALANCE SHEET	
	DEBIT	CREDIT	DEBIT	CREDIT	DEBIT	CREDIT
	8 4 6 1 10				8 4 6 1 10	
	1 0 0 00				1 0 0 00	
	5 0 0 0 00				5 0 0 0 00	
	2 6 5 9 2 67				2 6 5 9 2 67	
		1 9 3 9 27				1 9 3 9 27
	3 0 4 2 15				3 0 4 2 15	
		4 2 81				4 2 81
	12 5 2 1 8 67				12 5 2 1 8 67	
	8 0 0 1 5 11				8 0 0 1 5 11	
		7 5 88				7 5 88
		4 8 01				4 8 01
		7 7 75				7 7 75
		1 5 40				1 5 40
		3 5 9 33				3 5 9 33
	3 2 5 5 70				3 2 5 5 70	
		1 1 5 7 91				1 1 5 7 91
	3 0 0 5 65				3 0 0 5 65	
		1 0 6 5 18				1 0 6 5 18
	5 7 9 0 12				5 7 9 0 12	
		9 2 4 01				9 2 4 01
		3 0 9 60				3 0 9 60
		5 3 28				5 3 28
		1 1 5 38				1 1 5 38
		9 7 72				9 7 72
		9 0 5 8 28				9 0 5 8 28
		2 4 0 0 00				2 4 0 0 00
		2 6 83				2 6 83
		10 2 6 7 0 30				10 2 6 7 0 30
	1 7 9 4 5 88				1 7 9 4 5 88	
		10 4 4 3 3 61				10 4 4 3 3 61
	1 7 4 5 0 00				1 7 4 5 0 00	
		46 8 0 4 1 34		46 8 0 4 1 34		
	5 9 0 7 48		5 9 0 7 48			
		28 2 0 4 1 09		28 2 0 4 1 09		
	2 1 1 9 62		2 1 1 9 62			
	8 3 7 1 44		8 3 7 1 44			
	31 2 8 9 4 77	97 4 3 3 3 80	1 6 3 9 8 54	75 0 0 8 2 43	29 6 4 9 6 23	22 4 2 5 1 37

ILLUSTRATION 24–1 (concluded)

BAILEY AND BROWN
Worksheet
For the Year Ended December 31, 1987

ACCT. NO.	ACCOUNT NAME	TRIAL BALANCE DEBIT	TRIAL BALANCE CREDIT	ADJUSTMENTS DEBIT	ADJUSTMENTS CREDIT
	Balance forward	317,569.74	972,238.65	205,276.59	212,046.71
510	Purchases—plumbing dept.	376,867.25			c 376,867.25
511	Purchases return and allowances— plumb. dept.		1,562.15	g 1,562.15	
520	Purchases—electrical dept.	235,334.71			d 235,334.71
521	Purchases return and allowances— elec. dept.		981.03	h 981.03	
522	Purchases discounts		10,183.88	i 10,183.88	
540	Transportation-in—plumbing dept.	2,563.07			e 2,563.07
550	Transportation-in— electrical dept.	1,218.60			f 1,218.60
560	Cost of goods sold—plumbing dept.			a 124,314.99 c 376,867.25 e 2,563.07	g 1,562.15 i 6,314.01 j 125,218.67
570	Cost of goods sold— electrical dept.			b 78,705.10 d 235,334.71 f 1,218.60	h 981.03 i 3,869.87 k 80,015.11
610	Operating expenses	51,258.45		(n-w) 8,999.79	l 42.81
710	Interest revenues		102.41		
810	Interest expense	204.05		m 26.83	
820	Collection expense	52.25			
		985,068.12	985,068.12	1,046,033.99	1,046,033.99
	Net income				

	ADJUSTED TRIAL BALANCE		INCOME STATEMENT		BALANCE SHEET	
	DEBIT	CREDIT	DEBIT	CREDIT	DEBIT	CREDIT
	312 894 77	97 433 3 80	1 6 398 54	75 0 0 82 43	29 6 496 23	22 4 251 37
	37 0 650 48		37 0 650 48			
	23 0 392 40		23 0 392 40			
	6 0 258 24		6 0 258 24			
		1 45 22		1 45 22		
		2 30 88		2 30 88		
		52 25		52 25		
	97 4 479 02	97 4 479 02	67 7 982 79	75 0 227 65	29 6 496 23	22 4 251 37
			7 2 244 86			7 2 244 86
			75 0 227 65	75 0 227 65	29 6 496 23	29 6 496 23

amounting to $2,563.07 was transferred to Cost of Goods Sold—Plumbing Department by debiting account no. 560 and crediting Transportation-In—Plumbing Department, account no. 540.

Adjustment (f):   Transportation-in for the electrical department amounting to $1,218.60 was transferred to Cost of Goods Sold—Electrical Department by debiting account no. 570 and crediting Transportation-In—Electrical Department, account no. 550.

Adjustment (g):   Purchase returns and allowances of $1,562.15 for the plumbing department were transferred to the related cost of goods sold account by debiting Purchase Returns and Allowances—Plumbing Department, account no. 511, and crediting Cost of Goods Sold—Plumbing Department, account no. 560.

Adjustment (h):   Purchase returns and allowances of $981.03 for the electrical department were transferred to the related cost of goods sold account by debiting Purchase Returns and Allowances—Electrical Department, account no. 521, and crediting Cost of Goods Sold—Electrical Department, account no. 570.

Adjustment (i):   During the year, purchases discounts amounting to $10,183.88 were taken. This amount was allocated between the cost of goods sold accounts in relation to the amount of purchases (less purchase returns and allowances) of the two departments. The following schedule was used in determining the allocation of purchases discounts:

Department	Purchases Less Returns	Percent	Purchases Discount	Department Allocation
Plumbing . . .	$375,305.10	62	× $10,183.88 =	$ 6,314.01
Electrical . . .	234,353.68	38	× 10,183.88 =	3,869.87
	$609,658.78	100		$10,183.88

Based on the above calculations, the purchases discounts were allocated to the cost of goods sold accounts by debiting Purchases Discounts, account no. 522, for $10,183.88, and by crediting Cost of Goods Sold—Plumbing Department, account no. 560, for $6,314.01, and Cost of Goods Sold—Electrical Department, account no. 570, for $3,869.87.

Adjustment (j):   On December 31, a physical inventory was taken and a cost of $125,218.67 was assigned to the merchandise inventory of the plumbing department. The inventory was recorded by debiting Merchandise Inventory—Plumbing Department, account no. 140, and crediting Cost of Goods Sold—Plumbing Department, account no. 560. Bailey and Brown use the first-in, first-out method for inventory costing purposes. A more accurate cost assignment to inventory could be made by including transportation-in and deducting purchases discounts associated with the inventory on hand. Since these amounts are small in relation to total inventory, they are ignored in determining inventory cost. After the physical inventory is taken, the inventory records are adjusted for any discrepancies between the stock records and the actual inventory counts.

Adjustment (k): The December 31 physical inventory assigned a cost of $80,015.11 to the merchandise inventory in the electrical department. The inventory was recorded by debiting Merchandise Inventory—Electrical Department, account no. 145, and crediting Cost of Goods Sold—Electrical Department, account no. 570.

Interest adjustments. The proper determination of both interest expense and interest revenue involves the use of accrual accounting. This occurs because all collections and payments of interest are not made on December 31. The schedule in Illustration 24–2 was prepared to determine the amount of accrued interest on notes receivable.

ILLUSTRATION 24–2

Schedule of Accrued Interest on Notes Receivable
For the Year Ended December 31, 1987
(assume a 365-day year)

No.	Principal Amount	Rate of Interest	Date of Note	Days Accrued	Accrued Interest
123	$ 800.00	12%	Nov. 2	59	$15.52
124	375.00	—	Nov. 8	—	—
130	725.00	12	Nov. 15	46	10.96
134	292.15	12	Dec. 17	14	1.34
135	850.00	12	Dec. 28	3	.84
	$3,042.15				$28.66

In addition, Bailey and Brown also own five $1,000 U.S. treasury bonds. Two of these bonds earn interest at a rate of 7.0 percent which was collected on December 15. Accrued interest on these bonds for 16 days amounts to $6.14. On December 18, three additional bonds were purchased (7.5 percent interest rate). Accrued interest on the December 18 bonds amounts to $8.01. Therefore, total accrued interest receivable on December 31 was $42.81 ($28.66 + $6.14 + $8.01).

Adjustment (l): Accrued interest receivable on December 31 was recorded by debiting account no. 133 for $42.81 and crediting Interest Revenue, account no. 710, for $42.81.

On December 31, Bailey and Brown had a single note outstanding amounting to $2,400. It was a 90-day 12 percent note dated November 27. As of December 31, the note had been outstanding for 34 days, and interest amounting to $26.83 had accrued.

Adjustment (m): The accrued interest payable was recorded by debiting Interest Expense, account no. 810, and by crediting Accrued Interest Payable, account no. 270, for $26.83.

Supporting worksheet—operating expenses

To make the general ledger more manageable, Bailey and Brown keep a subsidiary ledger for the various operating expense accounts. The subsidiary ledger is represented in the general ledger by the controlling account, Operating Expenses (no. 610). To bring the operating expense accounts up to date, a number of accounts must be adjusted. The adjustments involve debits to the subsidiary accounts and credits to the related general ledger accounts. The total debits to the subsidiary accounts are shown as a debit adjustment to the controlling account, Operating Expenses, in the general ledger.

Illustration 24–3 is the operating expense worksheet used by Bailey and Brown to adjust the operating expense accounts. Not only does the worksheet aid in adjusting the operating expense accounts, it also provides detailed information used in preparing the income statement and supporting schedule of operating expenses. An appropriate heading identifies the worksheet along with the period covered. Columns are provided for (1) the trial balance amounts, (2) adjustments, and (3) the adjusted trial balance amounts. As with the summary (general ledger) worksheet, the operating expense worksheet is prepared by listing the expense accounts by number as shown on the chart of accounts in Illustration 23–6. The trial balance amount for each account is entered in the Trial Balance column. It is noted that the trial balance contains a number of accounts with a zero balance. After the trial balance amounts are entered, the column is totaled and compared with the control account balance. If the total does not agree with the control account balance in the general ledger, the error would be corrected before making the adjustments.

ILLUSTRATION 24–3

BAILEY AND BROWN
Operating Expense Worksheet
For the Year Ended December 31, 1987

ACCT. NO.	ACCOUNT NAME	TRIAL BALANCE DEBIT	ADJUST- MENTS DEBIT	ADJUSTED TRIAL BAL. DEBIT
6101	M. O. Brown, salary expense	1 0 8 0 0 00		1 0 8 0 0 00
6102	Truck drivers' wages expense	5 1 6 0 00		5 1 6 0 00
6103	Store clerks' salary expense	6 0 0 0 00		6 0 0 0 00
6104	M. O. Brown, travel expense	9 4 3 18		9 4 3 18
6105	Advertising expense	2 1 0 5 54	(p) 7 6 9 44	2 8 7 4 98
6106	Garage rent expense	4 5 0 00		4 5 0 00
6107	Truck repairs expense	3 4 3 25	(w) 1 1 5 50	4 5 8 75
6108	Truck operating expense	1 6 8 8 19		1 6 8 8 19
6109	Shipping expense	2 5 00		2 5 00
6110	Merchandise ins. expense		(r) 2 0 1 19	2 0 1 19
6111	Delivery equip. ins. expense		(r) 1 5 2 40	1 5 2 40
6112	Store equip. ins. expense		(r) 5 4 92	5 4 92
6113	Postage expense (selling)		(q) 3 2 2 18	3 2 2 18
6114	Store supplies expense		(n) 2 9 4 0 87	2 9 4 0 87
6115	Depreciation of store equip.	5 00	(s) 3 2 5 57	3 3 0 57
6116	Depreciation of delivery equip.		(u) 5 7 4 51	5 7 4 51
6117	Miscellaneous selling expense	3 0 2 47		3 0 2 47
6121	W. E. Bailey, salary expense	1 0 8 0 0 00		1 0 8 0 0 00
6122	Office salaries expense	6 6 0 0 00		6 6 0 0 00
6123	Power and water expense	1 2 2 59		1 2 2 59
6124	Telephone expense	2 0 4 81		2 0 4 81
6125	Rent expense	3 0 0 0 00		3 0 0 0 00
6126	Property tax expense	4 2 5 70		4 2 5 70
6127	Office supplies expense		(o) 2 1 7 6 17	2 1 7 6 17
6128	Bad debts expense		(v) 7 7 7 39	7 7 7 39
6129	Postage expense (admin.)		(q) 2 7 7 42	2 7 7 42
6130	Office equip. ins. expense		(r) 3 6 88	3 6 88
6131	Payroll taxes expense	1 9 6 9 44		1 9 6 9 44
6132	Depreciation of office equip.	2 5 00	(t) 2 7 5 35	3 0 0 35
6133	Miscellaneous general expense	2 8 8 28		2 8 8 28
		5 1 2 5 8 45	8 9 9 9 79	6 0 2 5 8 24

Each of the adjusting entries involves debits to one or more operating expense accounts on the operating expense worksheet and credits to one or more general ledger accounts on the summary worksheet.

Supplies expense adjustments. Bailey and Brown maintain supplies accounts in the general ledger for (1) store supplies, (2) office supplies, (3) advertising supplies, and (4) postage stamps. All supplies are recorded as assets when purchased. At the end of the accounting period, a physical inventory of unused supplies and stamps is taken. The difference between each account balance and the amount on hand represents the amount charged as an expense in the adjusting entry. The schedule shown in Illustration 24–4 was used in determining the necessary adjustments.

ILLUSTRATION 24–4

Schedule of Supplies Used
For the Year Ended December 31, 1987

Asset	Acct. No.	Balance Dec. 31, 1987	On Hand Dec. 31, 1987	Expense for Year
Store supplies	150	$3,016.75	$75.88	$2,940.87
Office supplies	151	2,224.18	48.01	2,176.17
Advertising supplies	152	847.19	77.75	769.44
Postage stamps	153	615.00	15.40	599.60

After constructing the schedule, the following adjusting entries were made:

Adjustment (n): The store supplies expense for the year was recorded by debiting account no. 6114 and crediting Store Supplies, account no. 150, for $2,940.87.

Adjustment (o): The office supplies expense for the year was recorded by debiting account no. 6127 and crediting Office Supplies, account no. 151, for $2,176.17.

Adjustment (p): The advertising supplies expense for the year was recorded by debiting account no. 6105 and crediting Advertising Supplies, account no. 152, for $769.44.

Adjustment (q): During the year, postage stamps were used by both the selling and the administrative areas of the business. Upon examining the records kept by the mail clerk, it was determined that $322.18 was a selling expense and that $277.42 was an administrative expense. The postage expense was recorded by debiting Postage Expense (Selling), account no. 6113, for $322.18 and Postage Expense (Administrative), account no. 6129, for $277.42 and crediting Postage Stamps, account no. 153, for $599.60.

Insurance expense adjustments. Bailey and Brown account for prepaid insurance premiums by recording the amount paid as an asset. When payments are made, they are debited to Prepaid Insurance, account no. 154, in the general ledger. On December 31, the insurance expense for the year is calculated by examining each insurance policy to determine the proportion of the total term coverage that has expired during the year. The proportion expired is multiplied by the original premium to determine the dollar amount of insurance expense. Each policy is classified according to the type of asset insured so that the proper expense account is charged. Bailey and Brown maintain insurance expense accounts for merchandise, the delivery truck, store equipment, and office equipment in the operating expense ledger.

To determine the insurance expenses as of December 31, Bailey and Brown use an insurance register similar to the one shown in Illustration 17–1. This requisition simplifies the necessary calculations.

The following adjustment was prepared from the information presented in the schedule:

Adjustment (r): Insurance expense for the year was recorded by debiting Office Equipment Insurance Expense, account no. 6130, for $36.88; by debiting Store Equipment Insurance Expense, account no. 6112, for $54.92; by debiting Merchandise Insurance Expense, account no. 6110, for $201.19; by debiting Delivery Equipment Insurance Expense, account no. 6111, for $152.40; and crediting Prepaid Insurance, account no. 154, for $445.39. (See Illustration 24–5.)

**ILLUSTRATION
24–5**

**Schedule of Insurance Expense
For the Year Ended December 31, 1987**

Property Insured	Expense for Year
Office equipment	$ 36.88
Store equipment	54.92
Merchandise	201.19
Delivery equipment	152.40
Total	$445.39

Depreciation expense adjustment. As mentioned earlier, Bailey and Brown use the group method to account for and to depreciate plant assets. The general ledger contains asset accounts for office equipment, store equipment, and delivery equipment along with the related accumulated depreciation accounts. The operating expense ledger contains depreciation expense accounts for each of the plant assets mentioned above. For depreciation purposes, Bailey and Brown consider assets purchased on or before the 15th of the month to be owned for the whole month. Assets that are purchased after the 15th of the month are considered to have been purchased on the first day of the following month. Assets disposed of on or by the 15th are considered to be removed on the first day of the month, and those disposed of after the 15th are deemed to have been removed on the first day of the following month.

When office and store equipment were scrapped on December 14 and 15, an entry was made in the general journal to record depreciation for the year. Thus, Depreciation Expense—Store Equipment (account no. 6115) has a $5 debit balance on the operating expense worksheet. The account Depreciation Expense—Office Equipment (account no. 6132) also has a debit balance of $25 because of the earlier entry.

In determining the remaining amount of depreciation for the assets on hand it is necessary to review the asset accounts for any changes which occurred during the last month (particularly the last 15 days). Unless a review is made, depreciation expense may be misstated due to the improper inclusion or omission of assets. Based on the rules given above for including or excluding an asset when determining depreciation expense as described above, the Delivery Equipment account should be decreased by $45. This reduction is because of the purchase of two dollies on December 31.

The purchase of the typewriter for $275 on December 14 will require depreciation for only one month.

After making the necessary adjustments to calculate depreciation expense, the schedule in Illustration 24–6 was prepared.

The following adjustments were prepared from the schedule. Each adjustment involves a debit on the operating expense worksheet and a credit on the summary (general ledger) worksheet.

Adjustment (s): Depreciation of store equipment was recorded by debiting account no. 6115 and crediting Accumulated Depreciation—Store Equipment, account no. 161, for $325.57.

**ILLUSTRATION
24–6**

Schedule of Depreciation Expense—Straight Line
For the Year Ended December 31, 1987

Assets	Cost	Annual Rate of Depreciation	Depreciation Expense *debit*
Store equipment	$3,255.70	10%	$325.57
Office equipment	2,730.65*	10	273.06 *cr accumulated*
	275.00	10	2.29‡
Delivery equipment	5,745.12†	10	574.51

* $3,005.65 − $275.00 = $2,730.65.
† $5,790.12 − $45.00 = $5,745.12.
‡ $275 × 10% = $27.50 ÷ 12 = $2.29.

Adjustment (t):   Depreciation of office equipment was recorded by debiting account no. 6132 and crediting Accumulated Depreciation—Office Equipment, account no. 171, for $275.35.

Adjustment (u):   Depreciation of delivery equipment was recorded by debiting account no. 6116 and crediting Accumulated Depreciation—Delivery Equipment, account no. 181, for $574.51.

Bad debts expense adjustments.   Bailey and Brown have found from past experience that $\frac{4}{10}$ of 1 percent of credit sales are uncollectible. During the current year ended December 31, 1987, sales on account amount to $194,348.16 resulting in an estimated bad debts expense of $777.39 ($194,348.16 × 0.004). The following entry was made to record the bad debts expense.

Adjustment (v):   Debit Bad Debts Expense, account no. 6128, and credit Allowance for Doubtful Accounts, account no. 131, for $777.39.

Miscellaneous adjustments.   During the process of completing the operating expense worksheet, the accountant for Bailey and Brown discovered a bill for truck repairs of $115.50. The charge for repairs made on December 27 had not been recorded. Normally, this transaction would have been recorded before the trial balance was taken. The truck repairs expense was recorded by making the following adjustment:

Adjustment (w):   Debit Truck Repairs Expense, account no. 6107, and credit Accounts Payable, account no. 250, for $115.50.

Completion of worksheets

Operating expense worksheet.   To complete the operating expense worksheet, the amounts shown in the Trial Balance column were combined with amounts shown in the Adjustments column (if any) and entered in the Adjusted Trial Balance column. If there was no trial balance amount, the adjustment amount was simply extended to the Adjusted Trial Balance column.

After the Adjustments and Adjusted Trial Balance columns were totaled, the total of the first column $51,258.45 was added to the sum of the second column, $8,999.79 and compared with the total of the Adjusted Trial Balance column, $60,258.24. The fact that the sum of the first two columns equals the third column total does not necessarily indicate that the adjustments were properly made. Its equality only proves that the worksheet additions were correct.

Summary worksheet.   Note that all of the adjustments on the operating expense worksheet *(n–w)* were debits. Since Operating Expenses, account no. 610, is the control account for the subsidiary accounts shown on the operating expense worksheet, it was debited for the total amount of the operating expense adjustments, $8,999.79. The debit to the control account was identified as *(n–w)*, representing the total of adjustments *n* through *w* on the operating expense worksheet. This debit was offset by the credits entered on the summary worksheet as a result of each of the adjustments.

The next step is to total the Adjustments columns on the summary worksheet to prove their equality. The Adjusted Trial Balance column is completed by combining the amounts in the Trial Balance columns with the amounts shown in the Adjustments column. After combining the column amounts, the Adjusted Trial Balance columns are totaled to prove the equality of the debits and credits. Each of the amounts in the Adjusted Trial Balance columns is extended to the appropriate Income Statement or Balance Sheet column, depending on the nature of the account. The columns are then totaled. The excess of the Income Statement credit column total over the debit column total amounted to $72,244.86, representing the net income for the year. This amount is labeled as net income and entered as a debit in the Income Statement columns and as a credit in the Balance Sheet columns. The Income Statement and the Balance Sheet columns are then totaled to prove the equality of each statement's debit and credit columns. To complete the worksheet, each column is double ruled.

ILLUSTRATION 24–7

use total column

BAILEY AND BROWN
Income Statement
For the Year Ended December 31, 1987

	PLUMBING DEPARTMENT	ELECTRICAL DEPARTMENT	TOTAL
Sales	468,041.34	282,041.09	750,082.43
Less: Sales returns and allow.	(5,907.48)	(2,119.62)	(8,027.10)
Sales discounts	(5,190.29)	(3,181.15)	(8,371.44)
Net sales	456,943.57	276,740.32	733,683.89
Cost of goods sold:			
Merchandise inventory January 1	124,314.99	78,705.10	203,020.09
Purchases	376,867.25	235,334.71	612,201.96
Less: Purchase returns and allow.	(1,562.15)	(981.03)	(2,543.18)
Purchase discounts	(6,314.01)	(3,869.87)	(10,183.88)
Net purchases	368,991.09	230,483.81	599,474.90
Transportation-in	2,563.07	1,218.60	3,781.67
Merchandise available for sale	495,869.15	310,407.51	806,276.66
Less: Merchandise inventory, December 31	125,218.67	80,015.11	205,233.78
Cost of goods sold	370,650.48	230,392.40	601,042.88
Gross profit	86,293.09	46,347.92	132,641.01
Operating expenses			60,258.24
Net operating income			72,382.77
Other revenue			145.22
Interest revenue			72,527.99
Other expenses:			
Interest expense		230.88	
Collection expense		52.25	
Total other expenses			283.13
Net income			72,244.86

The income statement (Illustration 24–7) and the balance sheet (Illustration 24–8) are prepared from the summary worksheet. The operating expense schedule (Illustration 24–9) is prepared from the operating expense worksheet.

ADJUSTING ENTRIES—JOURNALIZING

The adjusting entries are made so that each account is properly stated as of December 31. Since the adjustments reflect actual changes in the accounts, the adjusting entries are recorded in the general journal. The general journal used by Bailey and Brown along with the adjusting entries *(a–w)* is shown in Illustration 24–10.

ILLUSTRATION
24–8

BAILEY AND BROWN
Balance Sheet
December 31, 1987

Assets

Current Assets:			
Cash		$ 8,561.10	
Government bonds		5,000.00	
Accrued interest receivable		42.81	
Notes receivable		3,042.15	
Accounts receivable	$ 26,592.67		
Less: Allowance for doubtful			
accounts	1,939.27	24,653.40	
Merchandise inventories:			
Plumbing department	$125,218.67		
Electrical department	80,015.11	205,233.78	
Supplies and prepayments:			
Store supplies	$ 75.88		
Office supplies	48.01		
Advertising supplies	77.75		
Postage stamps	15.40		
Prepaid insurance	359.33	576.37	
Total Current Assets			$247,109.61
Plant Assets:			
Store equipment	$ 3,255.70		
Less: Accumulated depreciation . .	1,157.91	$ 2,097.79	
Office equipment	$ 3,005.65		
Less: Acccumulated depreciation .	1,065.18	1,940.47	
Delivery equipment	$ 5,790.12		
Less: Accumulated depreciation . .	924.01	4,866.11	
Total Plant Assets			8,904.37
Total Assets			$256,013.98

Liabilities

Current Liabilities:		
F.I.C.A. taxes payable	$ 309.60	
F.U.T.A. taxes payable	53.28	
Income taxes payable—federal		
employee	115.38	
State unemployment taxes payable . .	97.72	
Accounts payable	9,058.28	
Notes payable	2,400.00	
Accrued interest payable	26.83	
Total Current Liabilities		$ 12,061.09

**ILLUSTRATION
24-8 (concluded)**

Owner's Equity

M. O. Brown Capital, January 1, 1987		$102,670.30	
Net income (½ of $72,244.86)	$36,122.43 . . .		
Less Withdrawals	17,945.88 . . .	18,176.55	
M. O. Brown Capital, December 31, 1987			$120,846.85
W. E. Bailey Capital, January 1, 1987		$104,433.61	
Net income (½ of $72,244.86	$36,122.43		
Less: Withdrawals	17,450.00 . . .	18,672.43	
W. E. Bailey Capital, December 31, 1987		123,106.04	
Total Owner's Equity. . . .			243,952.89
Total Liabilities and Owner's Equity . .			$256,013.98

**ILLUSTRATION
24-9**

**BAILEY AND BROWN
Schedule of Operating Expenses
For the Year Ended December 31, 1987**

Selling expenses:

M. O. Brown, salary expenses	$10,800.00
Truck drivers' wages expense	5,160.00
Store clerks' salary expense	6,000.00
M. O. Brown, travel expense	943.18
Advertising expense	2,874.98
Garage rent expense	450.00
Truck repairs expense	458.75
Truck operating expense	1,688.19
Shipping expense	25.00
Merchandise insurance expense	201.19
Delivery equipment insurance expense	152.40
Store equipment insurance expense	54.92
Postage expense (selling)	322.18
Store supplies expense	2,940.87
Depreciation of store equipment	330.57
Depreciation of delivery equipment	574.51
Miscellaneous selling expense	302.47
Total selling expenses	$33,279.21

**ILLUSTRATION
24–9
*(concluded)***

Administrative expenses:	
W. E. Bailey, salary expense	$10,800.00
Office salaries expense	6,600.00
Power and water expense	122.59
Telephone expense	204.81
Rent expense	3,000.00
Property tax expense.	425.70
Office supplies expense	2,176.17
Bad debts expense.	777.39
Postage expense (administrative)	277.42
Office equipment insurance expense.	36.88
Payroll taxes expense	1,969.44
Depreciation of office equipment.	300.35
Miscellaneous general expense	288.28
Total administrative expenses	$26,979.03
Total operating expenses	$60,258.24

The entries are journalized in alphabetical order *(a)* through *(w)* as shown on the related worksheets. Although journalizing in alphabetical order is not necessary, it helps to reduce the chance of omitting an entry.

ADJUSTING ENTRIES—POSTING

After the adjusting entries are journalized, the entries are posted to the appropriate accounts. As the entries are posted, the account number is placed in the posting reference column of the general journal. The posting is referenced in the general ledger and the operating expense ledger by recording the general journal page number (GJ56 or GJ57) by each posting.

The debits to the operating expense ledger are posted as a total, $8,999.79, to the Operating Expense Control account in the general ledger.

**ILLUSTRATION
24–10**

GENERAL JOURNAL					PAGE 56	

DATE		ACCOUNT AND EXPLANATION	P.R.	DEBIT	CREDIT
1987		Adjusting Entries			
Dec.	31	Cost of Goods Sold—Plumb. Dept.	560	12 4 3 1 4 99	
		Merchandise Inventory-Plumb. Dept.	140		12 4 3 1 4 99
	31	Cost of Goods Sold—Elec. Dept.	570	7 8 7 0 5 10	
		Merchandise Inventory—Elec. Dept.	145		7 8 7 0 5 10
	31	Cost of Goods Sold—Plumb. Dept.	560	37 6 8 6 7 25	
		Purchases—Plumb. Dept.	510		37 6 8 6 7 25
	31	Cost of Goods Sold—Elec. Dept.	570	23 5 3 3 4 71	
		Purchases—Elec. Dept.	520		23 5 3 3 4 71
	31	Cost of Goods Sold—Plumb. Dept.	560	2 5 6 3 07	
		Transportation-in—Plumb. Dept	540		2 5 6 3 07
	31	Cost of Goods Sold—Elec. Dept.	570	1 2 1 8 60	
		Transportation-in—Elec. Dept.	550		1 2 1 8 60
	31	Purchase Return and Allowances—Plumb. Dept.	511	1 5 6 2 15	
		Cost of Goods Sold—Plumb. Dept.	560		1 5 6 2 15
	31	Purchase Return and Allowances—Elec. Dept.	521	9 8 1 03	
		Cost of Goods Sold—Elec. Dept.	570		9 8 1 03
	31	Purchase Discounts	522	1 0 1 8 3 88	
		Cost of Goods Sold—Plumb. Dept.	560		6 3 1 4 01
		Cost of Goods Sold—Elec. Dept.	570		3 8 6 9 87
	31	Merchandise Inventory—Plumb. Dept.	140	12 5 2 1 8 67	
		Cost of Goods Sold—Plumb. Dept.	560		12 5 2 1 8 67
	31	Merchandise Inventory—Elec. Dept.	145	8 0 0 1 5 11	
		Cost of Goods Sold—Elec. Dept.	570		8 0 0 1 5 11
	31	Accrued Interest Receivable	133	4 2 81	
		Interest Revenue	710		4 2 81
	31	Interest Expense	810	2 6 83	
		Accrued Interest Payable	270		2 6 83
	31	Store Supplies Expense	6114	2 9 4 0 87	
		Store Supplies	150		2 9 4 0 87

ILLUSTRATION 24–10 (continued)

	GENERAL JOURNAL			PAGE 57	
DATE	ACCOUNT AND EXPLANATION	P.R.	DEBIT	CREDIT	
1987	Adjusting Entries				
Dec. 31	Office Supplies Expense	6127	2 1 7 6 17		
	Office Supplies	151		2 1 7 6 17	
31	Advertising Expense	6105	7 6 9 44		
	Advertising Supplies	152		7 6 9 44	
31	Postage Expense—Selling	6113	3 2 2 18		
	Postage Expense—Adm.	6129	2 7 7 42		
	Postage Stamps	153		5 9 9 60	
31	Office Equipment Insurance Expense	6130	3 6 88		
	Store Equipment Insurance Expense	6112	5 4 92		
	Merchandise Insurance Expense	6110	2 0 1 19		
	Delivery Equipment Insurance Expense	6110	1 5 2 40		
	Unexpired Insurance	154		4 4 5 39	
31	Depreciation Expense—Store Equip.	6115	3 2 5 57		
	Accumulated Depreciation—Store Equip.	161		3 2 5 57	
31	Depreciation Expense—Office Equip.	6132	2 7 5 35		
	Accumulated Depreciation—Office Equip.	171		2 7 5 35	
31	Depreciation Expense—Del. Equip.	6116	5 7 4 51		
	Accumulated Depreciation—Del. Equip.	181		5 7 4 51	
31	Bad Debts Expense	6128	7 7 7 39		
	Allowance for Doubtful Accounts	131		7 7 7 39	
31	Truck Repair Expense	6107	1 1 5 50		
	Accounts Payable	250		1 1 5 50	

CLOSING ENTRIES—JOURNALIZING

The required **closing entries** are shown in Illustration 24–10. The titles of those accounts which are credited are slightly indented. Although closing entries need not be journalized in any particular order, some logical sequence should be used to make sure that all accounts are closed. Quite often, the accounts are closed in the following order: (1) revenue accounts, (2) expense accounts, (3) income summary, (4) distribution of income, and (5) owner's drawing.

ILLUSTRATION 24–10 *(concluded)*

		GENERAL JOURNAL			PAGE 58
DATE		ACCOUNT AND EXPLANATION	P.R.	DEBIT	CREDIT
1987		Closing Entries			
Dec.	31	Sales—Plumbing Dept.	410	46 804 1 34	
		Sales—Electrical	420	28 204 1 09	
		Interest Revenue	710	1 45 22	
		Income Summary	330		75 0 22 7 65
	31	Income Summary	330	67 7 98 2 79	
		Sales Ret. and All.—Plumb.	411		5 9 07 48
		Sales Ret. and All.—Elec.	421		2 1 19 62
		Sales Discounts	422		8 3 71 44
		Cost of Goods Sold—Plumb.	560		37 0 65 0 48
		Cost of Goods Sold—Elec.	570		23 0 39 2 40
		Operating Expenses	610		6 0 25 8 24
		Interest Expense	810		2 3 0 88
		Collection Expense	820		5 2 25
	31	Income Summary	330	7 2 24 4 86	
		M.O. Brown, Capital	310		3 6 12 2 43
		W.E. Bailey, Capital	320		3 6 12 2 43
	31	M.O. Brown, Capital	310	1 7 94 5 88	
		M.O. Brown, Drawing	311		1 7 9 45 88
	31	W.E. Bailey, Capital	320	1 7 45 0 00	
		W.E. Bailey, Drawing	321		1 7 4 50 00

In the general journal shown in Illustration 24–10 which contains the closing entries, note that the expense accounts in the operating expense ledger are not credited in making the closing entries. Instead, the controlling account Operating Expenses, account no. 610, is credited for $60,258.24, the total of the adjusted account debits in the subsidiary ledger.

Even though the credits involved in closing the operating expense accounts are too numerous to record in the general journal, understand that all 30 of the subsidiary accounts must be closed. Whenever a controlling account is closed, the related subsidiary accounts should also be closed. Each of the subsidiary accounts are closed in a manner similar to Illustration 24–11 for Truck Repairs Expense, account no. 6107.

**ILLUSTRATION
24–11**

				GENERAL LEDGER				
				Truck Repairs Expense				ACCT. NO. 6107
DATE		EXPLANATION	P.R.	DEBIT	CREDIT	BALANCE		
						DEBIT	CREDIT	
1987								
Dec.	1	Balance	√			3 2 9 10		
	9		PC12	1 4 15		3 4 3 25		
	27		GJ57	1 1 5 50		4 5 8 75		
	31		GJ58		4 5 8 75	- 0 -		

CLOSING ENTRIES—POSTING

Postings are made to each of the accounts involved in the closing entries. A check mark (√) is placed in the check (√) column beside each amount that is posted. As a cross-reference, the general journal page (GJ58) is recorded in the P.R. column of each account posted. Refer to the Truck Repairs Expense account in Illustration 24–11 for an example of the cross-referencing used when posting the closing entries.

After posting the adjusting and closing entries, the Income Summary account (Illustration 24–12) and the two cost of goods sold accounts (Illustration 24–13) would appear as shown. These accounts are summary accounts and are used only at the end of the accounting period. When perpetual inventories are maintained, the cost of goods sold is recorded as each inventory unit is sold. This makes it possible to use the cost of goods sold account throughout the year. Since Bailey and Brown keep a perpetual inventory of quantities only, the cost of goods sold account is used as a summary account at the end of the period. Note that the Summary account is posted in detail (items representing the debits and credits in the closing entries are posted individually instead of in total).

POST-CLOSING TRIAL BALANCE

After all adjusting and closing entries are posted, a **post-closing trial balance** of the remaining general ledger accounts with balances (open) is taken. This is done to prove the equality of the debit and credit

ILLUSTRATION 24–12

GENERAL LEDGER

Income Summary   ACCT. NO. 330

DATE		EXPLANATION	P.R.	DEBIT	CREDIT	BALANCE
1987						
Dec.	31	Sales—plumbing department	GJ58		46 8 0 4 1 09	46 8 0 4 1 34
	31	Sales—electrical department	GJ58		28 2 0 4 1 09	75 0 0 8 2 43
	31	Interest revenue	GJ58		1 4 5 22	75 0 2 2 7 65
	31	Sales returns and allowances— plumbing	GJ58	5 9 0 7 48		74 4 3 2 0 17
	31	Sales returns and allowances— electrical	GJ58	2 1 1 9 62		74 2 2 0 0 55
	31	Sales discounts	GJ58	8 3 7 1 44		73 3 8 2 9 11
	31	Cost of goods sold—plumbing	GJ58	37 0 6 5 0 48		36 3 1 7 8 63
	31	Cost of goods sold—electrical	GJ58	23 0 3 9 2 40		13 2 7 8 6 23
	31	Operating expense	GJ58	6 0 2 5 8 24		7 2 5 2 7 99
	31	Interest expense	GJ58	2 3 0 88		7 2 2 9 7 11
	31	Collection expense	GJ58	5 2 25		7 2 2 4 4 86
	31	M. O. Brown, capital	GJ58	3 6 1 2 2 43		3 6 1 2 2 43
	31	W. E. Bailey, capital	GJ58	3 6 1 2 2 43		- 0 -

ILLUSTRATION 24–13

GENERAL LEDGER

Cost of Goods Sold—Plumbing Department   ACCT. NO. 560

DATE		EXPLANATION	P.R.	DEBIT	CREDIT	BALANCE DEBIT	BALANCE CREDIT
1987							
Dec.	31	Beginning inventory	GJ56	124 3 1 4 99		124 3 1 4 99	
	31	Purchases	GJ56	376 8 6 7 25		501 1 8 2 24	
	31	Transportation-in	GJ56	2 5 6 3 07		503 7 4 5 31	
	31	Purchase ret. and allowances	GJ56		1 5 6 2 15	502 1 8 3 16	
	31	Purchase discounts	GJ56		6 3 1 4 01	495 8 6 9 15	
	31	Ending inventory	GJ56		125 2 1 8 67	370 6 5 0 48	
	31	Income summary	GJ57		370 6 5 0 48	- 0 -	

GENERAL LEDGER

Cost of Goods Sold—Electrical Department   ACCT. NO. 570

DATE		EXPLANATION	P.R.	DEBIT	CREDIT	BALANCE DEBIT	BALANCE CREDIT
1987							
Dec.	31	Beginning inventory	GJ56	78 7 0 5 10		78 7 0 5 10	
	31	Purchases	GJ56	235 3 3 4 71		314 0 3 9 81	
	31	Transportation-in	GJ56	1 2 1 8 60		315 2 5 8 41	
	31	Purchase ret. and allowances	GJ56		9 8 1 03	314 2 7 7 38	
	31	Purchase discounts	GJ56		3 8 6 9 87	310 4 0 7 51	
	31	Ending inventory	GJ56		80 0 1 5 11	230 3 9 2 40	
	31	Income summary	GJ57		230 3 9 2 40	- 0 -	

ILLUSTRATION 24–14

BAILEY AND BROWN
Post-Closing Trial Balance
December 31, 1987

ACCT. NO.	ACCOUNT NAME	DEBIT	CREDIT
110	National Bank	8 4 6 1 10	
111	Petty cash	1 0 0 00	
120	Government bonds	5 0 0 0 00	
130	Accounts receivable	2 6 5 9 2 67	
131	Allowance for doubtful accounts		1 9 3 9 27
132	Notes receivable	3 0 4 2 15	
133	Accrued interest receivable	4 2 81	
140	Merchandise inventory—plumb. dept.	12 5 2 1 8 67	
145	Merchandise inventory—elec. dept.	8 0 0 1 5 11	
150	Store supplies	7 5 88	
151	Office supplies	4 8 01	
152	Advertising supplies	7 7 75	
153	Postage stamps	1 5 40	
154	Prepaid insurance	3 5 9 33	
160	Store equipment	3 2 5 5 70	
161	Accumulated depreciation—store equip.		1 1 5 7 91
170	Office equipment	3 0 0 5 65	
171	Accumulated depreciation—office equip.		1 0 6 5 18
180	Delivery equipment	5 7 9 0 12	
181	Accumulated depreciation—delivery equip.		9 2 4 01
210	FICA taxes payable		3 0 9 60
220	FUTA taxes payable		5 3 28
230	Income tax payable—federal employee		1 1 5 38
240	State unemployment taxes payable		9 7 72
250	Accounts payable		9 0 5 8 28
260	Notes payable		2 4 0 0 00
270	Accrued interest payable		2 6 83
310	M.O. Brown, capital		12 0 8 4 6 85
320	W.E. Bailey, capital		12 3 1 0 6 04
		26 1 1 0 0 35	26 1 1 0 0 35

balances of the general ledger accounts. The post-closing trial balance of Bailey and Brown is shown in Illustration 24–14.

Although a post-closing trial balance is not required, it is a desirable procedure. If a post-closing trial balance is taken, it can be used to help resolve any errors that might arise in the accounts at a later date.

REVERSING ENTRIES

In preparing the adjusting entries on December 31, two entries of the "accrual type" were made. **Reversing entries** enable the accountant to record payments (expenses) and receipts (revenues) in a consistent manner from period to period. Adjusting entries requiring reversal are normally reversed on the first day of the next accounting period. Bailey and Brown made two reversing entries—one for the accrued interest receivable of $42.81 and another for the accrued interest payable of $26.83. The reversing entries are shown in the general journal (Illustration 24–15).

ILLUSTRATION 24–15

	GENERAL JOURNAL			PAGE 1	
DATE	ACCOUNT AND EXPLANATION	P.R.	DEBIT	CREDIT	
1988	Reversing Entries				
Jan. 1	Interest Revenue	710	4 2 81		
	Accrued Interest Receivable	133		4 2 81	
1	Accrued Interest Payable	270	2 6 83		
	Interest Expense	810		2 6 83	

SUMMARY

Financial reports are required by management to help analyze the activities of a business. Also, financial statements are prepared at least annually. To facilitate the preparation of such reports, a **worksheet** summarizing financial data and allowing for adjusting data can be prepared.

Two common worksheets used are the summary worksheet which is used in preparing financial statements and the operating expense worksheet which often supports the summary worksheet.

The summary worksheet contains all of the accounts from the general ledger. First, a trial balance is taken to ensure that the overall debits and credits are in balance. Next, adjustments are made to account balances to bring them up to date so that the correct balances will be reflected in the financial statements. Some of the most common adjustments are for revenue and expense accruals.

Since operating expense accounts are often very numerous, a subsidiary ledger can be kept for them to make the general ledger more manageable. When this occurs, an **operating expense worksheet** is used to adjust the individual expense account balances as necessary so that the control account can be properly adjusted on the summary worksheet.

After all necessary adjustments are made on the summary worksheet, the beginning balance of each trial balance account, net of any adjustments made to it, is extended into the appropriate final columns as either an income statement item or a balance sheet item. All columns on the worksheet are added to ensure that everything is in balance. Then, the financial statements can be prepared.

The adjustments made on the worksheet must be reflected in the permanent accounting records. To do so, the adjustments are entered into the general journal and posted to the appropriate general ledger accounts.

The next step is to close out the nominal accounts, income and expenses. These accounts are found on the income statement and are closed to the Income Summary account. The next step is to record the distribution of profits or losses to the owners. If the business is a sole proprietorship or a partnership, the Income Summary account is closed to the capital account(s). If the wholesale business is a corporation, Income Summary is closed to Retained Earnings. In a corporation the closing of the Income Summary ends the closing process. However, in a sole proprietorship or partnership, the drawing accounts must be closed to the capital accounts. Entries are made in the general journal to accomplish this and then posted to the appropriate general ledger accounts. After the posting has been completed, the books are completely closed out and a new accounting period can begin.

KEY TERMS

Adjusting Entries—journal entries made at the end of an accounting period so that the accounts will reflect the correct balances in the financial statements. These entries are necessary because some transactions have an effect upon more than one accounting period, and their amounts must be apportioned over the accounting periods affected.

Bad Debts Expense—an expense incurred by a business when it grants credit to customers. It occurs because some customers fail to pay their accounts.

Closing Entries—those entries made at the end of an accounting period which transfer the balances in the expense and revenue accounts to the Income Summary account.

Cost of Goods Sold—an expense incurred consisting of the cost to the seller of goods sold to customers. It is computed as Beginning inventory + (Purchases + Transportation-in − Purchase returns and allowances − Purchase discounts) − Ending inventory.

Operating Expense Worksheet—a supporting worksheet used to adjust operating expense accounts.

Post-Closing Trial Balance—a trial balance taken after the expense and revenue accounts have been closed.

Reversing Entries—entries which enable the accountant to record payments and receipts in a consistent manner from period to period. Adjusting entries requiring reversal are normally reversed on the first day of the next accounting period.

Worksheet—an informal accounting statement which summarizes the trial balance and other information needed to prepare the financial statements and closing entries.

QUESTIONS AND EXERCISES

1. Why is the Income Summary account left out of the worksheet?
2. What account balances must be combined in order to determine the cost of goods sold?
3. The Huff Wholesale Store has two departments—A and B. During 1987, purchases for Department A totaled $425,000 and purchases for Department B totaled $282,000. Purchase returns and allowances amounted to $12,750 for Department A and $11,280 for Department B. Purchases discounts for 1987 amounted to $12,600. This amount is to be allocated between the cost of goods sold accounts in relation to the amount of purchases (less purchase returns and allowances) of the two departments. What general journal adjusting entry should be made to allocate the purchases discounts amount between the two departments?
4. On December 31, 1987, the Harbuck Wholesale Company had two notes receivable—an $850, 12 percent, 90-day note dated December 1, and a $360, 13 percent, 60-day note dated December 16. What adjustment is necessary to record accrued interest on December 31, 1987? (Assume a 360-day year.)

5. When would it be feasible to prepare a separate operating expense worksheet to be used in preparing the summary worksheet?

6. Store Supplies, account no. 125, has a balance of $3,725 on December 31, 1987. A physical inventory count reveals that $560 worth of store supplies are on hand at December 31, 1987. What adjustment is necessary to record store supplies expense for 1987?

7. The plant asset accounts of the J and S Wholesale Store have the following balances on December 31, 1987:

Store equipment $4,600
Office equipment   2,725
Delivery equipment   6,890

The annual rates of depreciation are 10 percent for store and office equipment and 20 percent for delivery equipment. What adjustments are necessary to record depreciation expense for 1987?

8. What is the sequence of events generally followed in making adjustments when a summary worksheet is used?

9. What logical sequence is often used to journalize closing entries?

10. What three amount columns appear on an operating expense worksheet?

11. Pessa and Miller have found from past experience that ½ of 1 percent of all credit sales become uncollectible. During the current year, credit sales amounted to $2,425,000. What adjustment is necessary to record the estimated bad debts expense?

12. Akins and Alexander have a single note payable outstanding on December 31. It is a $2,500, 90-day, 15 percent note dated November 16. What adjusting entry should be made on December 31, and what reversing entry should be made on January 1? (Assume a 360-day year.)

13. When is a post-closing trial balance prepared? What is its purpose?

PROBLEMS

24–1. Jack Holmes and Robert Hardin own and operate a wholesale sporting goods store. Holmes and Hardin's trial balance for the year ended December 31, 1987 is shown below:

work form income statement f worksheet

HOLMES AND HARDIN
Trial Balance
December 31, 1987

p ??? reversing entries acct that don't have a bal in trial Bal

Account No.	Account Title	Debit	Credit
102	First National Bank	$ 15,000	
106	Petty cash	150	
109	Accrued interest receivable		
111	Notes receivable	400	
113	Accounts receivable	19,600	
114	Allowance for doubtful accounts		$ 1,500
121	Merchandise inventory	93,000	
124	Office supplies	1,100	
127	Store supplies	1,500	
128	Postage stamps	1,800	
129	Prepaid insurance	2,500	
130	Store equipment	7,200	
131	Accumulated depreciation—store equipment		2,630
140	Office equipment	5,700	
141	Accumulated depreciation—office equipment		3,200
150	Delivery equipment	12,800	
151	Accumulated depreciation—delivery equipment		5,100
201	FICA taxes payable		820
203	Employees' income taxes payable		1,420
210	Accounts payable		19,700
301	Jack Holmes, capital		86,790
302	Jack Holmes, drawing	15,300	
311	Robert Hardin, capital		60,500
312	Robert Hardin, drawing	12,100	
401	Sales		883,000
402	Sales returns and allowances	9,750	
403	Sales discounts	7,250	
501	Purchases	750,000	
502	Purchases returns and allowances		6,900
503	Purchases discounts		10,200
505	Transportation-in	7,000	
520	Cost of goods sold		
601	Operating expenses	119,610	
701	Interest revenue		
		$1,081,760	$1,081,760

Holmes and Hardin maintain subsidiary ledgers for accounts receivable, accounts payable, and operating expenses. Below is a trial balance for the operating expense accounts:

Account No.	Account Title	Balance
6011	Salaries expense	$ 67,000
6012	Wages expense	22,800
6013	Travel expense	2,600
6014	Advertising expense	10,700
6015	Insurance expense	
6016	Rent expense	5,200
6017	Truck operating expense	1,400
6018	Truck repairs expense	700
6019	Shipping expense	1,300
6020	Postage expense	
6021	Office supplies expense	
6022	Store supplies expense	
6023	Depreciation expense	
6024	Utilities expense	2,400
6025	Telephone expense	450
6026	Bad debts expense	
6027	Payroll taxes expense	4,600
6028	Miscellaneous expense	460
		$119,610

Required:

Prepare (1) a 10-column worksheet for the year ended December 31, 1987 and (2) a supporting worksheet for operating expenses for the year ended December 31, 1987. (Note: Leave three lines for cost of goods sold.)

Information for adjustments is as follows:

Merchandise inventory, December 31, 1987, $87,000.
Office supplies on hand, December 31, 1987, $250.
Store supplies on hand, December 31, 1987, $320.
Postage stamps on hand, December 31, 1987, $400.
Prepaid insurance, December 31, 1987, $600.

Bad debts expense is estimated to be 3/10 of 1 percent of net sales. No new equipment was purchased after June 30, 1987. Therefore, one year's depreciation is to be taken on the equipment. Depreciation rates are 10 percent for office and store equipment and 15 percent for delivery equipment.

Holmes and Hardin own one note receivable. It is a $400, 8 percent, 60-day note dated November 16, 1987.

24–2. The worksheets completed in Problem 24–1 for Holmes and Hardin will be needed to work this problem.

Required:

1. Using a general journal, prepare the adjusting entries for the year ended December 31, 1987.
2. Prepare the closing entries on December 31, 1987. Distribute the Income Summary account balance equally between the partners.
3. Prepare the reversing entry on January 1, 1988.

24–3. Using the worksheets prepared in Problem 24–1 for Holmes and Hardin, prepare the following items:

1. Income statement.
2. Schedule of operating expenses.
3. Balance sheet.
4. Post-closing trial balance.

24–4. The Sasser Wholesale Corporation is divided into two departments—A and B. The corporation has just completed business for the year ended December 31, 1987. Susan Baker, an accountant for the corporation, has prepared the following trial balance:

THE SASSER WHOLESALE CORPORATION
Trial Balance
December 31, 1987

Account No.	Account Title	Debit	Credit
101	Second National Bank	$ 11,800	
102	Petty cash	100	
105	Marketable securities	1,200	
110	Accounts receivable	15,800	
111	Allowance for doubtful accounts		$ 400
114	Notes receivable	1,200	
115	Accrued interest receivable		
120	Merchandise inventory—Department A	40,000	
125	Merchandise inventory—Department B	32,000	
130	Store supplies	2,300	
132	Office supplies	1,800	
133	Prepaid insurance	3,600	

(continued)

THE SAASER WHOLESALE CORPORATION
Trial Balance
December 31, 1987

Account No.	Account Title	Debit	Credit
140	Store equipment	7,200	
141	Accumulated depreciation—store equipment		1,300
150	Office equipment	5,600	
151	Accumulated depreciation—office equipment		800
160	Delivery equipment	45,000	
161	Accumulated depreciation—delivery equipment		6,800
170	Building	82,000	
171	Accumulated depreciation—building		11,000
180	Land	10,000	
201	FICA taxes payable		1,100
202	FUTA taxes payable		150
203	Employees' income taxes payable		1,000
204	State unemployment taxes payable		250
210	Accounts payable		13,000
211	Notes payable		800
212	Accrued interest payable		
301	Common stock		80,000
302	Premium on common stock		48,000
305	Retained earnings		50,910
401	Sales—Department A		650,000
402	Sales returns and allowances—Department A	19,000	
410	Sales—Department B		480,000
411	Sales returns and allowances—Department B	8,000	
412	Sales discounts	20,000	
501	Purchases—Department A	529,000	
502	Purchase returns and allowances—Department A		20,000
510	Purchases—Department B	410,000	
511	Purchase returns and allowances—Department B		5,000
512	Purchases discounts		18,000
520	Transportation-in—Department A	3,100	
521	Transportation-in—Department B	1,600	
530	Cost of goods sold—Department A		
535	Cost of goods sold—Department B		
540	Operating expenses	138,200	
601	Interest revenue		30
701	Interest expense	40	
		$1,388,540	$1,388,540

Ms. Baker also prepared the following trial balance of operating expenses:

Operating Expenses Trial Balance

Account No.	Account Title	Balance
5400	Salaries expense (selling)	$ 40,000
5401	Wages expense	35,000
5402	Travel expense	3,000
5403	Advertising expense	4,500
5404	Truck repairs expense	1,400
5405	Truck operating expense	3,000
5406	Merchandise insurance expense	
5407	Delivery equipment insurance expense	
5408	Store equipment insurance expense	
5409	Building insurance expense	
5410	Postage expense (selling)	300
5411	Store supplies expense	
5412	Depreciation of store equipment	
5413	Depreciation of delivery equipment	
5414	Depreciation of building	
5415	Miscellaneous selling expense	100
5416	Office salaries expense	36,000
5417	Power and water expense	3,000
5418	Telephone expense	800
5419	Property tax expense	1,200
5420	Office supplies expense	
5421	Bad debts expense	
5422	Postage expense (administrative)	400
5423	Office equipment insurance expense	
5424	Payroll taxes expense	9,100
5425	Depreciation of office equipment	
5426	Miscellaneous general expense	400
		$138,200

Required:

Prepare (1) a 10-column worksheet for the year ended December 31, 1987, and (2) a supporting worksheet for operating expenses for the year ended December 31, 1987. (Note: Leave three lines for each cost of goods sold account.)

Data for adjustments is as follows:

Purchases discounts are to be allocated between the cost of goods sold accounts in relation to the amount of purchases (less purchase returns and allowances) of the two departments. Merchandise inventories, December 31, 1987:

Department A, $38,000.
Department B, $29,000.

Sixty days' interest at 10 percent has accrued on the notes receivable.
Ninety days' interest at 10 percent has accrued on the notes payable.

Supplies on hand, December 31, 1987:
  Store supplies, $500.
  Office supplies, $600.

The following amounts of insurance expired during 1987:

Merchandise insurance $200
Delivery equipment insurance 350
Store equipment insurance 200
Building insurance. 500
Office equipment insurance 150

No plant assets were purchased or disposed of during 1987. Depreciation rates are 10 percent for office and store equipment, 15 percent for delivery equipment, and 5 percent for building.
Bad debts expense is estimated to be $\frac{2}{10}$ of 1 percent of total net sales for 1987.

24–5. The worksheets completed in Problem 24–4 for the Sasser Wholesale Corporation will be needed to work this problem.

Required:

1. Using a general journal, prepare the adjusting entries for the year ended December 31, 1987.
2. Prepare the closing entries on December 31, 1987. (Income Summary is account no. 310.)
3. Prepare the reversing entries on January 1, 1988.

24–6. Using the worksheets prepared in Problem 24–4 for the Sasser Wholesale Corporation, prepare the following items:

1. Income statement.
2. Schedule of operating expenses.
3. Balance sheet.
4. Post-closing trial balance.

CHAPTER 25

Analyzing financial statements

Ratio & Trend %
P798

dif between quick & current ratio
" liquidity & profitability

LEARNING OBJECTIVES

In order to make sound decisions, investors and creditors need to know how to analyze and interpret financial statements. After studying this chapter, you should be able to:

1. Compute the dollar amount of increase or decrease and the percentage increase or decrease in two-year balance sheets and income statements.
2. Prepare common-size balance sheets and income statements.
3. Compute the following ratios:
   a. Current ratio.
   b. Quick ratio.
   c. Accounts receivable turnover.
   d. Average collection period for accounts receivable.
   e. Inventory turnover.
   f. Days in inventory.
   g. Owner's equity to debt.
   h. Times interest earned.
   i. Return on total assets.
   j. Return on owner's equity.
   k. Earnings per share.
   l. Book value of common stock.

Thus far, we have focused on recording transactions and accumulating and classifying this information to form the basic financial statements. This chapter is primarily concerned with *analyzing and interpreting* the information presented in the financial statements.

NEED FOR FINANCIAL STATEMENT ANALYSIS

Investors and creditors rely on the information contained in financial statements when making their investing and lending decisions. For the most part, they are concerned with measuring a company's liquidity and profitability. **Liquidity** is the ability of a company to pay its debts as they become due. **Profitability** is a company's ability to earn a reasonable return on its owner's investment.

Investors and creditors usually cannot gain enough information to make a sound decision by merely reading financial statements. They must carefully analyze and interpret the information. For example, assume that you are reading the income statement of a company in which you are considering investing and you see that the company had net income of $100,000 for the year. This tells you little about the financial condition of the company. The net income figure would mean more if you knew the total assets of the company or the amount of the prior year's net income. It might also be helpful to compare the net income figure with the net income of similar-sized companies in the same industry.

Thus, in financial statement analysis, there is a need to compare information. Comparisons may be made with information about the company from prior years and with information about companies in the same industry. To present information from prior years, comparative financial statements are used. **Comparative financial statements** present the same company's financial statements for two or more successive periods in side-by-side columns. Comparisons with companies in the same industry may be made by obtaining the other companies' published financial statements or by consulting an investment service publication. The most common methods of financial statement analysis include horizontal analysis, vertical analysis, trend percentages, and ratio analysis.

HORIZONTAL ANALYSIS

In **horizontal analysis** each item in the financial statements is analyzed to determine what changes have occurred from one accounting period to the next. Changes are usually reported in two ways: (1) absolute dollar changes, and (2) percentage changes. Such a review helps to detect variations in a company's performance and financial standing and may help to highlight trends.

To illustrate horizontal analysis, the current assets section of the Bright Company's comparative balance sheet is shown below. Columns 1 and 2 show the dollar amounts for the years 19X2 and 19X1 (the most recent year is usually presented in the first column). Column 3 contains the dollar amount of the increase or decrease from 19X1 to 19X2, while column 4 shows the percentage increase or decrease.

THE BRIGHT COMPANY
Comparative Balance Sheets
December 31, 19X1 and 19X2

	(1)	(2)	(3)	(4)
			Increase or Decrease*	
	December 31		19X2 over 19X1	
	19X2	19X1	Dollars	Percentages
Current assets:				
Cash	$ 80,200	$ 55,000	$25,200	45.8
Accounts receivable	124,200	132,600	8,400*	6.3*
Inventories	110,800	94,500	16,300	17.2
Total current assets. . . .	$315,200	$282,100	$33,100	11.7

Each amount in column 3 is found by subtracting the corresponding amount in column 2 from that in column 1. If a *positive* number results, this represents an *increase;* a *negative* result represents a *decrease.* For example, column 3 shows that Cash *increased* by $25,200 from 19X1 to 19X2. This was found by subtracting $55,000 (column 2) from $80,200 (column 1). Column 3 also shows that Accounts Receivable *decreased* by $8,400 (the asterisk means a decrease). Because $124,200 − $132,600 = −$8,400, a decrease is indicated.

Note from the illustration that the total of column 3 is $33,100

($25,200 − $8,400 + $16,300). The accuracy of this number can be checked by subtracting the total in column 2 from the total in column 1. Thus, $315,200 − $282,100 = $33,100.

The percentage change (column 4) for an item is calculated by dividing the dollar change (column 3) by the prior year's amount (column 2). Again, a positive result represents an increase, and a negative result represents a decrease.

The Bright Company reported a 45.8 percent *increase* in cash from 19X1 to 19X2. This was calculated as follows:

$$\text{Percentage change} = \frac{\text{Change}}{\text{Prior year}} = \frac{\$25,200}{\$55,000} = 45.8 \text{ percent increase}$$

The Accounts Receivable balance *decreased* by 6.3 percent, as follows:

$$\text{Percentage change} = \frac{-\$8,400}{\$132,600} = -6.3\%, \text{ or a } 6.3\% \text{ decrease}$$

VERTICAL ANALYSIS

Vertical analysis is the study of a financial statement for a single year. This method states each item in the financial statement as a percentage of some relevant total. In this way it is easy to see the relative importance of each item in the statement. For an income statement the base is usually net sales, while total assets is the typical base for a balance sheet. Vertical analysis of the income statement is quite useful for determining such information as the percentage of cost of goods sold or gross margin. Financial statements that show items as fractions of 100 percent are called **common-size statements.**

To illustrate the mechanics of vertical analysis, the partial balance sheet of the Bright Company is repeated on the next page, with items expressed as percentages of total assets. Total assets were $490,000 in 19X1 and $550,000 in 19X2 (see Illustration 25–1 on page 796).

The common-size percentages in columns 3 and 4 were derived by dividing each dollar amount by the total asset figure. For example, Cash has a balance of $80,200 for 19X2. The percentage for cash for 19X2 was determined as follows:

$$\text{Percentage} = \frac{\text{Item}}{\text{Base}}$$

$$\text{Percentage} = \frac{\text{Cash}}{\text{Total assets}} = \frac{\$80,200}{\$550,000} = 14.6\%$$

Total assets have a value of 100 percent.

BRIGHT COMPANY
Comparative Balance Sheets
December 31, 19X1 and 19X2

	(1)	(2)	(3)	(4)
			Percentage of Total Assets	
	December 31		December 31	
	19X2	19X1	19X2	19X1
Assets				
Current assets:				
Cash	$ 80,200	$ 55,000	14.6	11.2
Accounts receivable	124,200	132,600	22.6	27.1
Inventories	110,800	94,500	20.1	19.3
Total current assets.	$315,200	$282,100	57.3	57.6

HORIZONTAL AND VERTICAL ANALYSIS—AN ILLUSTRATION

Illustration 25–1 presents the Bright Company's comparative balance sheet for the years 19X1 and 19X2, while Illustration 25–2 shows the comparative income statement. In both illustrations, columns 1 and 2 contain the actual dollar amounts, columns 3 and 4 contain horizontal analysis information, and columns 5 and 6 show the common-size information for vertical analysis.

Analyzing the balance sheet

Analysis of the first three columns of the balance sheet in Illustration 25–1 reveals that current assets increased by $33,100, while current liabilities increased by only $21,400. At first glance, this would seem to be a good sign. However, the percentages in column 4 show that current assets increased 11.7 percent over 19X1, while current liabilities increased 20.2 percent. Current liabilities are therefore increasing faster than the current assets that will be used to pay them.

Another item highlighted by the horizontal analysis is the decrease in the mortgage note payable: a decrease of $17,200 in absolute dollars

ILLUSTRATION 25–1

BRIGHT COMPANY
Comparative Balance Sheets
December 31, 19X1 and 19X2

	(1)	(2)	(3)	(4)	(5)	(6)
			Increase or Decrease*		Percentage of Total Assets	
	December 31		19X2 over 19X1		December 31	
	19X2	19X1	Dollars	%	19X2	19X1
Assets						
Current assets:						
Cash	$ 80,200	$ 55,000	$25,200	45.8	14.6	11.2
Accounts receivable	124,200	132,600	8,400*	6.3*	22.6	27.1
Inventories	110,800	94,500	16,300	17.2	20.1	19.3
Total current assets	$315,200	$282,100	$33,100	11.7	57.3	57.6
Property, plant, and equipment:						
Land	$ 42,400	$ 42,400	–0–	0.0	7.7	8.7
Building	185,000	166,200	$18,800	11.3	33.6	33.9
Less: Accumulated depreciation . . .	(27,000)	(22,400)	(4,600)	20.5	(4.9)	(4.6)
Furniture and fixtures	50,200	30,800	19,400	63.0	9.2	6.3
Less: Accumulated depreciation . . .	(15,800)	(9,100)	(6,700)	73.6	(2.9)	(1.9)
Total	$234,800	$207,900	$26,900	12.9	42.7	42.4
Total assets	$550,000	$490,000	$60,000	12.2	100.0	100.0
Liabilities						
Current liabilities:						
Accounts payable.	$ 70,300	$ 60,400	$ 9,900	16.4	12.8	12.3
Notes payable	20,000	15,100	4,900	32.5	3.6	3.1
Accrued taxes	36,800	30,200	6,600	21.9	6.7	6.2
Total current liabilities	$127,100	$105,700	$21,400	20.2	23.1	21.6
Long-term liabilities:						
Mortgage note payable	$ 43,600	$ 60,800	$17,200*	28.3*	7.9	12.4
Total liabilities	$170,700	$166,500	$ 4,200	2.5	31.0	34.0
Owner's Equity						
Common stock, $10 par value	$180,000	$180,000	–0–	0.0	32.7	36.7
Retained earnings	199,300	143,500	$55,800	38.9	36.3	29.3
Total owner's equity	$379,300	$323,500	$55,800	17.2	69.0	66.0
Total liabilities and owner's equity.	$550,000	$490,000	$60,000	12.2	100.0	100.0

ILLUSTRATION 25-2

BRIGHT COMPANY
Comparative Income Statements
December 31, 19X1 and 19X2

	(1)	(2)	(3)	(4)	(5)	(6)
			Increase or Decrease* 19X2 over 19X1		Percentage of Net Sales, December 31	
	December 31					
	19X2	19X1	Dollars	Percent	19X2	19X1
Sales.	$940,000	$842,000	$98,000	11.6	104.4	102.7
Less: Sales returns and allowances	(40,000)	(22,000)	(18,000)	81.8	4.4	2.7
Net sales	$900,000	$820,000	$80,000	9.8	100.0	100.0
Cost of goods sold	575,000	515,000	60,000	11.7	63.9	62.8
Gross margin.	$325,000	$305,000	$20,000	6.6	36.1	37.2
Operating expenses:						
Selling	$101,700	$ 90,000	$11,700	13.0	11.3	11.0
Administrative	120,300	115,000	5,300	4.6	13.4	14.0
Total operating expenses	$222,000	$205,000	$17,000	8.3	24.7	25.0
Operating income	$103,000	$100,000	$ 3,000	3.0	11.4	12.2
Other expenses	12,200	10,100	2,100	20.8	1.4	1.2
Income before income taxes	$ 90,800	$ 89,900	$ 900	1.0	10.0R	11.0
Income taxes	35,000	36,500	1,500*	4.1*	3.9	4.5
Net income	$ 55,800	$ 53,400	$ 2,400	4.5	6.1R	6.5

R = Rounding difference.

and 28.3 percent in relative terms. This may indicate that in future years, interest expense will be lower, allowing for higher net income.

The vertical analysis in columns 5 and 6 shows each account as a percentage of total assets. In that way the relative importance of each item may be determined. For example, it may at first seem alarming that notes payable increased by 32.5 percent. However, considering that in 19X2 notes payable amounted to only 3.6 percent of total liabilities and owner's equity, the increase is probably not particularly significant.

Analyzing the income statement

In the income statement the most striking item is Sales Returns and Allowances. From 19X1 to 19X2 this item rose $18,000, an increase of 81.8 percent. Such an increase certainly merits closer inspection. It may suggest certain problems in the sales office, especially in light of the 13 percent increase in selling expenses, when compared to a modest 4.6 percent increase in administrative expenses.

Another area of concern may be indicated by the fact that net sales increased by almost 10 percent but gross margin increased by only 6.6 percent. As shown by the vertical analysis in columns 5 and 6, gross margin has fallen as a percentage of net sales. Because the drop is quite small, it is not a cause for immediate concern. But it should be kept in mind in case a trend develops.

Finally, other expenses grew at a rate of 20.8 percent. While this seems to be a rather large increase, other expenses make up only 1.4 percent of net sales. Therefore, this may not be a big problem.

TREND PERCENTAGES

Trend percentages are used to compare financial information covering a number of years. A base year is selected, and all items from other years' financial statements are compared to the base-year figure. The computations are as follows:

1. Select a base year (usually the earliest year).
2. Assign a base of 100 percent to *each* item appearing in the base-year financial statement.
3. Express each amount in the other years' financial statements as a percentage of the base-year amounts. The formula for this is:

$$\text{Percentage} = \frac{\text{Current amount}}{\text{Base year amount}} \times 100$$

For example, consider the following information:

	19X1	19X2	19X3	19X4
Sales	100	112	120	137
Cost of goods sold	100	112	122	133
Gross margin	100	107	118	141
Operating expenses	100	108	120	137
Net income.	100	104	100	128

The percentages were found by first dividing each years' sales by

$842,000; cost of goods sold by $515,000; gross margin by $305,000; operating expenses by $205,000; and net income by $53,400. The results were then multiplied by 100 to arrive at the figures presented. The computations of selected amounts are shown:

$$19\text{X2 sales} = \frac{19\text{X2 sales}}{19\text{X1 sales}} \times 100$$

$$= \frac{\$940,000}{\$842,000} \times 100$$

$$= 1.12 \times 100 = \underline{\underline{112}}$$

$$19\text{X2 gross margin} = \frac{19\text{X2 gross margin}}{19\text{X1 gross margin}} \times 100$$

$$= \frac{\$325,000}{\$305,000} \times 100$$

$$= 1.07 \times 100 = \underline{\underline{107}}$$

$$19\text{X2 net income} = \frac{19\text{X2 net income}}{19\text{X1 net income}} \times 100$$

$$= \frac{\$55,800}{\$53,400} \times 100$$

$$= 1.04 \times 100 = \underline{\underline{104}}$$

Referring to the full analysis in Illustration 25–2, note that there is only a horizontal relationship between the numbers. For example, look at the sales, cost of goods sold, and gross margin figures for the year 19X2. There is no *vertical* relationship between these numbers. That is, 112 (sales) minus 112 (cost of goods sold) does not equal 107 (gross margin). Only the figures within a category going from left to right across the columns are related. The sales figure of 112 in 19X2 means that sales increased by 12 percent (112 − 100) over 19X1. The 120 sales figure for 19X3 means that sales in 19X3 were 20 percent (120 − 100) greater in 19X3 than in 19X1. The value of 104 for net income for 19X2 means that net income *increased* by 4 percent (104 − 100 = 4) from 19X1 to 19X2.

Trend percentages show changes that are taking place in an organization and the *direction* of these changes.

RATIO ANALYSIS

Ratio analysis is the study of the logical relationships that exist between certain items in a company's financial statements. The items may be taken from a single financial statement or from two different statements. The relationship is usually expressed in the form of a fraction called a ratio.

Short-term liquidity ratios

Short-term creditors, such as bankers and suppliers, are primarily interested in a company's ability to pay its debts as they come due. They are especially interested in a company's ability to generate cash to pay debts that will come due in the next 12 to 18 months. Therefore, they tend to focus on ratios that measure short-term liquidity.

Current ratio. The **current ratio** indicates a company's ability to pay its current liabilities from its current assets. Recall that current liabilities must be paid within one year, while current assets are expected to be converted to cash within one year.

The current ratio is calculated using the formula:

$$\text{Current ratio} = \frac{\text{Current assets}}{\text{Current liabilities}}$$

The following information came from the Bright Company's balance sheet:

	19X2	19X1	Increase
Current assets	$315,200	$282,100	$33,100
Current liabilities	127,100	105,700	21,400
Working capital	$188,100	$176,400	$11,700
Current ratio	2.48:1	2.67:1	

The current ratios for 19X1 and 19X2 were calculated as follows:

$$19X1 = \frac{\$282,100}{\$105,700} = 2.668, \text{ or } 2.67:1$$

$$19X2 = \frac{\$315,200}{\$127,100} = 2.479, \text{ or } 2.48:1$$

The current ratio is usually stated in terms of current assets to current liabilities. For 19X2, Bright Company has $2.48 of current assets for each $1 of current liabilities. Note that, although Bright Company's working capital increased by $11,700 from 19X1 to 19X2, the current ratio fell from 2.67:1 to 2.48:1. Thus, the current ratio may be better than working capital as an indicator of a firm's ability to pay its current liabilities.

Quick ratio.   The **quick ratio** indicates a company's ability to pay its current liabilities from its *quick* assets. **Quick assets** are assets that can be quickly converted to cash. Quick assets include cash, marketable securities, and net receivables; prepaid expenses and inventories are excluded. The formula for the quick ratio is:

$$\text{Quick ratio} = \frac{\text{Quick assets}}{\text{Current liabilities}}$$

The Bright Company's quick ratios from 19X2 and 19X1 are:

	19X2	19X1
Quick assets	$204,400	$187,600
Current liabilities	127,100	105,700
Net quick assets	$ 77,300	$ 81,900
Quick ratio	1.61:1	1.77:1

These quick ratios were determined as follows:

$$19X1 = \frac{\$187,600}{\$105,700} = 1.774, \text{ or } 1.77:1$$

$$19X2 = \frac{\$204,400}{\$127,100} = 1.608, \text{ or } 1.61:1$$

For the Bright Company, for every $1 of current liabilities there are $1.77 and $1.61 "quick" dollars in 19X1 and 19X2, respectively. While this may appear favorable, a quick ratio of 1:1 is usually adequate. A quick ratio much higher than this may indicate that too many "idle" assets are on hand—assets that could be invested to produce additional income. Idle cash and accounts receivable do not produce income.

Accounts receivable turnover.   **Accounts receivable turnover** is the number of times per year that the average amount of accounts receivable is collected. It indicates how quickly a company collects its accounts receivable. **Turnover** reflects the relationship between an asset and its use. The higher the turnover, the more the asset was used.

The accounts receivable turnover is computed by the following formula:

$$\text{Accounts receivable turnover} = \frac{\text{Net credit sales}}{\text{Average net accounts receivable}}$$

Net credit sales rather than net sales is used so that all sales returns and allowances and cash sales are eliminated from the calculation. Net credit sales are the sales that are in accounts receivable. Total net sales may be used when cash sales are relatively small or their proportion to total sales is fairly constant. Often, cash sales and credit sales are not recorded separately, so that total net sales must be used.

Note that average accounts receivable, rather than ending accounts receivable, is used. A ratio involving both an income statement and a balance sheet amount should have the balance sheet amount stated as an average. Averaging balance sheet amounts is a means of "smoothing" fluctuations that may occur at year-end. A more accurate figure results when more observations are used in the calculation of the average. However, most financial statements provide only the beginning and ending balances.

The Bright Company's accounts receivable turnover figures for 19X1 and 19X2 are:

	19X2	19X1
Accounts receivable:		
Beginning	$132,600	$125,400
Ending	124,200	132,600
Total	$256,800	$258,000
Average accounts receivable	$128,400	$129,000
Net sales	$900,000	$820,000
Accounts receivable turnover	7.01	6.36

The accounts receivable turnover for each year was determined as follows:

$$19X1 = \frac{\$820,000}{\$129,000} = 6.356, \text{ or } 6.36 \text{ times}$$

$$19X2 = \frac{\$900,000}{\$128,400} = 7.009, \text{ or } 7.01 \text{ times}$$

These figures indicate that the average amount of accounts receivable was converted to cash 6.36 times during 19X1 and 7.01 times in 19X2. Thus, Bright Company collected their accounts receivable faster in 19X2 than in 19X1.

Average collection period for accounts receivable. The **average collection period for accounts receivable** is a measure of the average amount of time that passes from the date of sale to the day the receivable is collected. In other words, it is the amount of time that the average accounts receivable was on the books. The average collection period indicates the liquidity of accounts receivable; that is, how fast they are converted to cash.

The liquidity of accounts receivable is important for two reasons. First, accounts receivable must be converted to cash to pay current obligations as they come due. Second, the length of the collection period indicates how likely it is that the accounts receivable will be collected in full. Longer collection periods usually mean a lower likelihood of collection. It is helpful to compare the average collection period with the credit terms of the company. For example, an average collection period of 48 days would be better if a company's credit terms are 2/10, n/45 than if its terms are 2/10, n/30.

The average collection period for accounts receivable is computed by dividing the number of days in a year by the accounts receivable turnover.

$$\text{Average collection period} = \frac{365 \text{ days}}{\text{Accounts receivable turnover}}$$

The Bright Company's average collection periods for 19X1 and 19X2 are:

$$19\text{X}1 = \frac{365 \text{ days}}{6.36} = 57.3, \text{ or } 57 \text{ days}$$

$$19\text{X}2 = \frac{365 \text{ days}}{7.01} = 52.1, \text{ or } 52 \text{ days}$$

From 19X1 to 19X2, the average collection period decreased from 57 days to 52 days. Whether 52 days is too long for accounts receivable to be outstanding depends on the company's credit terms.

Inventory turnover. A firm's **inventory turnover** indicates the number of times its average inventory is sold during a year. It is calculated as follows:

$$\text{Inventory turnover} = \frac{\text{Cost of goods sold}}{\text{Average inventory}}$$

The Bright Company's inventory turnover rates for 19X1 and 19X2 are:

	19X2	19X1
Inventory:		
Beginning	$ 94,500	$ 98,200
Ending	110,800	94,500
Total	$205,300	$192,700
Average inventory	$102,650	$ 96,350
Cost of goods sold	$575,000	$515,000
Inventory turnover . . .	5.60	5.34

Note that the company's inventory turnover rate increased slightly from 19X1 to 19X2. The computations of the turnover rates for the two years are:

$$19X1 = \frac{\$515,000}{\$ 96,350} = 5.345, \text{ or } 5.34 \text{ times}$$

$$19X2 = \frac{\$575,000}{\$102,650} = 5.601, \text{ or } 5.60 \text{ times}$$

The inventory rate can be used to compute the number of days an average item remained in inventory. To do so, the number of days in the year is divided by the turnover rate. Here is the number of days an average item spent in inventory at the Bright Company:

$$\text{Days in inventory (19X1)} = \frac{365 \text{ days}}{5.34} = 68.35, \text{ or } 68 \text{ days}$$

$$\text{Days in inventory (19X2)} = \frac{365 \text{ days}}{5.60} = 65.17, \text{ or } 65 \text{ days}$$

The **days-in-inventory** calculation provides a measure of the length of time it takes a company to sell its inventory.

To maximize its sales performance, a company should try to keep inventory levels as low as possible without running out of goods to sell. Keeping low inventory levels will:

1. Minimize costs caused by obsolete or spoiled inventory.
2. Reduce storage costs.

Keeping inventory levels that are too low can:

1. Cause losses if sales are canceled due to stockouts.
2. Result in higher handling and ordering costs because items must be reordered more frequently.
3. Cause the firm to pay more for goods because inventory items must be purchased in smaller lots, resulting in lost quantity discounts.

Generally, a firm that is able to achieve a high turnover rate and thus keep inventory on hand for shorter periods of time will be more efficient. However, these measures must be kept within a reasonable range so that inventory levels do not fall too low.

Long-term liquidity ratios

Before making a lending decision, long-term creditors must analyze two aspects of a firm: (1) its ability to meet its debt-repayment obligations in the near future, and (2) its ability to repay its debt in the long run. Thus, long-term creditors use ratio analysis to assess both the short-term and the long-term liquidity positions of a firm. A long-term creditor, such as a mortgage holder or bondholder, is interested in a firm's short-term liquidity because mortgages and bonds often require periodic interest and principal payments. Also, a firm that is unable to pay its liabilities in the short run may not stay in business long enough to repay liabilities that are due several years in the future. Long-term creditors are also interested in a firm's long-term debt structure as an indicator of its ability to pay its obligations in the future.

Management and stockholders are also interested in a firm's liquidity position. A firm must be able to repay its debts in order to stay in business. It must also maintain a good credit standing in order to borrow funds in future years.

Owner's equity to debt ratio. From a lender's or investor's point of view, a company that is heavily in debt may be quite risky. The amount of debts a company can safely carry cannot be stated in absolute dollars, since the amount may vary with the size of both the company and the industry in which it operates. The **owner's equity to debt ratio** states the amount of owner's equity in relation to the total liabilities of a company. The calculation is as follows:

$$\text{Owner's equity to debt} = \frac{\text{Owner's equity}}{\text{Total liabilities}}$$

A company's assets come from its owners and creditors. Owners invest by giving the company assets in return for shares of stock, and by having the earnings retained in the firm rather than distributed as dividends. Creditors also invest in a company when they lend money. They give assets in return for the company's promise to return the assets, often with interest. Therefore, the owner's equity to debt ratio shows the relative investment of owners and creditors.

The Bright Company's owner's equity to debt ratios for 19X1 and 19X2 are:

	19X2	19X1
Owner's equity. . . .	$379,300	$323,500
Liabilities	$170,700	$166,500
Owner's equity to debt .	2.22:1	1.94:1

The ratios were calculated as follows:

$$19X1 = \frac{\$323,500}{\$166,500} = 1.943, \text{ or } 1.94:1$$

$$19X2 = \frac{\$379,300}{\$170,700} = 2.222, \text{ or } 2.22:1$$

These results show that, at the end of 19X2, for every dollar loaned by creditors the owners had invested $2.22. This amount increased from $1.94 in 19X1. The change resulted from the modest increase in total liabilities and a larger increase in owner's equity.

Creditors prefer a company to have a high proportion of owner's equity to debt. A higher proportion indicates that the creditors have a protective buffer if the company suffers a loss. Also, potential investors may think that a company with a low owner's equity to debt ratio is too risky an investment.

Times interest earned. A company that has outstanding long-term bonds or a mortgage must make interest payments on the debt. Creditors want to know about the company's ability to make the interest payments. **Times interest earned** is a measure of a company's ability to make periodic interest payments and provides a measure of the security of the debt. It is calculated by dividing income before interest and taxes by interest expense, as follows:

$$\text{Times interest earned} = \frac{\text{Net income} + \text{Interest} + \text{Income taxes}}{\text{Interest}}$$

Assume that interest expense for the Bright Company was $9,000 in 19X1 and $6,500 in 19X2. The times interest earned for these years is:

	19X2	19X1
Net income	$55,800	$53,400
Interest	6,500	9,000
Income taxes	35,000	36,500
Income before interest and taxes . . .	$97,300	$98,900
Times interest earned	15.0	11.0

The computations are as follows:

$$19X1 = \frac{\$98,900}{\$\ 9,000} = 10.988, \text{ or } 11 \text{ times}$$

$$19X2 = \frac{\$97,300}{\$\ 6,500} = 14.969, \text{ or } 15 \text{ times}$$

The ratio increased in 19X2 due to the decrease in interest expense. Interest was lower in 19X2 because the principal of the mortgage note decreased.

Profitability ratios

Although there are several measures of a company's operating success, perhaps the most important one is profitability. Again, it is desirable to know the firm's relative profitability rather than its absolute profitability. The aim is to see how well the company performed given the resources it had available.

Return on total assets. The **return on total assets** measures the firm's net income in relation to the total assets available for use. The formula for return on total assets is:

$$\text{Return on total assets} = \frac{\text{Net income}}{\text{Average total assets}}$$

Recall that when computing ratios that involve items from both the income statement and the balance sheet, the balance sheet item is stated as an average.

Assuming that on December 31, 19X0 the Bright Company's total assets amounted to $460,000, its return on total assets is:

	19X2	19X1
Total assets:		
Beginning	$ 490,000	$460,000
Ending	550,000	490,000
Total.	$1,040,000	$950,000
Average total assets. . . .	$ 520,000	$475,000
Net income	$ 55,800	$ 53,400
Return on total assets . . .	10.7%	11.2%

The return percentages were computed as follows:

$$19X1 = \frac{\$\ 53,400}{\$475,000} = .112, \text{ or } 11.2 \text{ percent}$$

$$19X2 = \frac{\$\ 55,800}{\$520,000} = .107, \text{ or } 10.7 \text{ percent}$$

Although the Bright Company's net income rose from 19X1 to 19X2, its profitability as measured by the return on total assets fell. This indicates that the Bright Company was not as efficient in using its available resources in the second year.

Return on owner's equity. From a stockholder's point of view, an important measure of a company's profitability is the relationship between net income and owner's equity. **Return on owner's equity** (sometimes called return on equity) is a measure of the return earned on each dollar invested by the owners. It is calculated by dividing net income by average owner's equity.

$$\text{Return on owner's equity} = \frac{\text{Net income}}{\text{Average owner's equity}}$$

Assume that the December 31, 19X0 owner's equity for the Bright Company was $270,100. Return on owner's equity can then be determined:

	19X2	19X1
Owner's equity:		
Beginning	$323,500	$270,100
Ending	379,300	323,500
Total	$702,800	$593,600
Average owner's equity . . .	$351,400	$296,800
Net income	$ 55,800	$ 53,400
Return on owner's equity . .	15.9%	18.0%

The percentage return for each year was computed as follows:

$$19X1 = \frac{\$\ 53,400}{\$296,800} = .179, \text{ or } 18.0 \text{ percent}$$

$$19X2 = \frac{\$\ 55,800}{\$351,400} = .158, \text{ or } 15.9 \text{ percent}$$

The same as the return on total assets, the return on owner's equity decreased despite the higher net income. The decrease indicates that the firm was less efficient in 19X2 at earning a return on its owner's investment.

Earnings per share. **Earnings per share** represents the amount of net income available to the common stockholders. The formula for earnings per share is:

$$\text{Earnings per share} = \frac{\text{Net income}}{\begin{array}{c}\text{Number of common} \\ \text{shares outstanding}\end{array}}$$

The Bright Company's earnings per share for 19X1 and 19X2 are shown below. There are 18,000 shares of common stock outstanding, calculated by dividing the common stock total by the $10 par value ($180,000/$10 = 18,000).

	19X2	19X1
Net income	$55,800	$53,400
Shares of common stock . . .	18,000	18,000
Earnings per share	$3.10	$2.97

The earnings per share figures were computed as follows:

$$19X1 = \frac{\$53,400}{18,000} = 2.966, \text{ or } \$2.97 \text{ per share}$$

$$19X2 = \frac{\$55,800}{18,000} = 3.100, \text{ or } \$3.10 \text{ per share}$$

When a company has issued preferred stock, the earnings per share computation is slightly more complicated. Because earnings per share measures the net income available to each share of common stock, preferred stock dividends must be subtracted from net income. These dividends must be subtracted even if they were not declared. Thus, if the Bright Company had issued 2,000 shares of $50 par value, 6 percent preferred shares, the earnings per share for 19X2 would be:

$$19\text{X2 EPS} = \frac{\$55,800 - \$6,000}{18,000} = 2.766, \text{ or } \$2.77 \text{ per share}$$

The $6,000 preferred stock dividend was calculated as $50 par value $\times$ .06 $\times$ 2,000.

Earnings per share must be published with each year's income statement. It is probably the most widely used measure of profitability. Actual and forecasted earnings per share figures, as well as period-to-period comparisons, are regularly included in the financial reports.

Book value of common stock. A company's long-term profitability may also be measured by its book value per share. Book value per share is calculated by dividing total owner's equity by the number of common shares outstanding. The formula is:

$$\text{Book value per share} = \frac{\text{Total owner's equity}}{\text{Common shares outstanding}}$$

Book values per share for the Bright Company for the years 19X1 and 19X2 are:

	19X2	19X1
Owner's equity	$379,300	$323,500
Common shares outstanding . . .	18,000	18,000
Book value per share	$21.07	$17.97

The amounts were computed as follows:

$$19\text{X1} = \frac{\$323,500}{18,000} = 17.972, \text{ or } \$17.97 \text{ per share}$$

$$19\text{X2} = \frac{\$379,300}{18,000} = 21.072, \text{ or } \$21.07 \text{ per share}$$

Book value per share increased from 19X1 to 19X2 as a result of the increase in retained earnings. When a company is first formed, its book value per share is equal to the amount paid for the stock. In later years, assuming no more stock is issued, book value per share increases if the company has net income and decreases if it has a net loss.

If the company has preferred stock outstanding, the computation of book value per share is slightly different. In that case, total owner's equity must be reduced by:

1. Liquidation value of the preferred shares (liquidation value per share × number of shares outstanding).
2. Preferred stock dividends from prior years that have not been declared, including those from the year just ended.

Assume that the Bright Company has 2,000 shares of $50 par value, cumulative 6 percent preferred stock with a liquidation value of $55 per share. Dividends were not declared in 19X1 or 19X2. Book value per share of common stock is:

	19X2	19X1
Owner's equity.	$379,300	$323,500
Less: Preferred stock liquidation value (2,000 × $55) . . .	110,000	110,000
Dividends in arrears		
2,000 × 2 × $50 × .06 . .	12,000	
2,000 × 1 × $50 × .06 . .		6,000
Adjusted owner's equity . . .	$257,300	$207,500
Common shares outstanding . .	18,000	18,000
Book value per common share .	$14.29	$11.53

The computations for the book value figures are:

$$19X1 = \frac{\$207,500}{18,000} = 11.527, \text{ or } \$11.53 \text{ per share}$$

$$19X2 = \frac{\$257,300}{18,000} = 14.294, \text{ or } \$14.29 \text{ per share}$$

Book value is not a liquidation value or the market value per share. When a company is liquidated, its stockholders rarely receive book value for their shares. The amount they receive depends on the amount of money that is raised when company assets are sold.

FINAL CONSIDERATIONS

In isolation, financial statements may not offer all the information needed to determine a company's financial situation. To obtain a more complete picture, the statements should be examined using horizontal, vertical, and ratio analysis. Illustration 25–3 contains a summary of the ratios discussed in this chapter. Above all, financial information needs to be compared. A company's financial data and ratios can be compared over time to determine trends. Also, the

ILLUSTRATION 25–3

Summary of Ratios

Short-term liquidity ratios:

1. $\text{Current ratio} = \dfrac{\text{Current assets}}{\text{Current liabilities}}$

2. $\text{Quick ratio} = \dfrac{\text{Quick assets}}{\text{Current liabilities}}$

3. $\text{Accounts receivable turnover} = \dfrac{\text{Net credit sales}}{\text{Average net accounts receivable}}$

4. $\text{Average collection period of accounts receivable} = \dfrac{365 \text{ days}}{\text{Accounts receivable turnover}}$

5. $\text{Inventory turnover} = \dfrac{\text{Cost of goods sold}}{\text{Average inventory}}$

6. $\text{Days in inventory} = \dfrac{365 \text{ days}}{\text{Inventory turnover}}$

Long-term liquidity ratios:

1. $\text{Owner's equity to debt} = \dfrac{\text{Owner's equity}}{\text{Total liabilities}}$

2. $\text{Times interest earned} = \dfrac{\text{Net income} + \text{Interest} + \text{Income taxes}}{\text{Interest}}$

Profitability ratios:

1. $\text{Return on total assets} = \dfrac{\text{Net income}}{\text{Average total assets}}$

2. $\text{Return on owner's equity} = \dfrac{\text{Net income}}{\text{Average owner's equity}}$

3. $\text{Earnings per share} = \dfrac{\text{Net income}}{\text{Number of common shares outstanding}}$

4. $\text{Book value per common share} = \dfrac{\text{Total owner's equity}}{\text{Common shares outstanding}}$

---

information can be compared with information for other companies in the same industry.

Finally, the limitations of financial statements must be taken into account. Sometimes a company may not disclose a condition that affects its financial statements. But if the information were available, it would change an analyst's interpretation. For example, a major supplier may have shut down, forcing the company to slow production or to buy elsewhere at higher costs. General economic conditions, such as inflation, may also affect financial statements. It is important to remember that some data cannot be discovered by using ratios and percentages. The possibility that unknown factors exist must be considered when analyzing financial statements.

SUMMARY

Investors and creditors analyze and interpret information in financial statements in order to make business decisions. Creditors and investors look at a company's **liquidity,** ability to pay liabilities, and **profitability,** the ability to earn a reasonable return on the owner's investments. Comparing financial data from different fiscal periods is another way of analyzing data. Companies often provide **comparative financial statements.**

Horizontal analysis is used to compare financial statements for two accounting periods. This type of analysis can be done by examining the absolute dollar change and the percentage change. Horizontal analysis is easily performed on comparative financial statements. It helps to detect changes in a company's performance and may reveal trends.

Vertical analysis is the study of a financial statement for a single year. Each item in the financial statement is reported as a percentage of a relevant total, such as total assets when analyzing the balance sheet or net sales when analyzing the income statement. Vertical analysis is quite useful in analyzing the income statement. Financial statements that show items as fractions of 100 percent are called **common-size statements.**

Trend percentages are also used to analyze financial data. A base year is established and all other years are compared to it in percentage terms. This method shows the relative amounts and the direction of changes.

Ratio analysis studies the logical relationships that exist between items in the financial statements. The relationships are usually expressed as a fraction, or ratio. There are two basic kinds of ratios: liquidity ratios and profitability ratios.

Liquidity ratios consist of short- and long-term ratios. Short-term liquidity ratios reflect a company's ability to generate cash to pay liabilities when they are due. The most common are the **current** ratio, quick ratio, accounts receivable turnover, average collection period for accounts receivable, inventory turnover, and days in inventory. Long-term liquidity ratios indicate a company's long-term ability to pay its debts. The most common are the owner's equity to debt ratio and times interest earned. These ratios are used most often by creditors.

Profitability ratios measure a company's operating success. The most common are return on total assets, return on owner's equity, earnings per share, and book value of common stock.

KEY TERMS

Accounts Receivable Turnover—Net credit sales ÷ average net accounts receivable; the number of times during the year that the average amount of accounts receivable is collected.

Average Collection Period for Accounts Receivable—365 days ÷ Accounts receivable turnover; measure of the average amount of time that elapses from a date of sale to the day the receivable is collected.

Book Value of Common Stock—Total owner's equity ÷ common shares outstanding; a measure of long-term profitability.

Common-Size Statements—Financial statements showing only percentages as opposed to dollar amounts.

Comparative Financial Statements—Financial statements of the same company for two or more successive periods, presented in side-by-side columns.

Current Ratio—Current assets ÷ current liabilities; indicates a company's ability to pay its current liabilities from its current assets.

Days in Inventory—365 days ÷ inventory turnover rate; indicates the number of days the average item remained in inventory.

Earnings per Share—(Net income − preferred stock dividends) ÷ number of common shares outstanding; represents the amount of net income available to common shareholders.

Horizontal Analysis—Method in which each item in the financial statements is analyzed for changes from one accounting period to the next.

Inventory Turnover—Cost of goods sold ÷ average inventory; indicates the number of times average inventory is sold during the year.

Liquidity—A company's ability to pay its debts as they come due.

Owner's Equity to Debt Ratio—Owner's equity ÷ total liabilities; indicates the amount of owners' investment in relation to total liabilities.

Profitability—A company's ability to earn a return on its owner's investment.

Quick Assets—Cash, marketable securities, and net receivables.

Quick Ratio—Quick assets ÷ current liabilities; tests a company's ability to pay its current liabilities from its quick assets.

Ratio Analysis—The study of the logical relationships that exist between items in a company's financial statements. The relationship is usually expressed as a fraction.

Return on Owner's Equity—Net income ÷ average owner's equity; measures the return earned on each dollar invested by owners.

Return on Total Assets—Net income ÷ average total assets; measures a firm's net income in terms of the total assets available for use.

Times Interest Earned—(Net income + interest + income taxes) ÷ interest; measures a company's ability to make periodic interest payments and provides a measure of the security of the debt.

Trend Percentages—A tool used to compare financial information covering a number of years. A base year is selected, and all items from other years' financial statements are expressed as percentages of the base-year amounts.

Turnover—The relationship between an asset and its use. The higher the turnover, the more the asset was used.

Vertical Analysis—The study of a financial statement for a single year by stating each item as a percentage of some relevant total.

QUESTIONS AND EXERCISES

1. Explain the difference between liquidity and profitability.
2. Explain the difference between horizontal and vertical analysis. What is the importance of each type of analysis?
3. What is the difference between comparative financial statements and common-size statements?

4. When vertical analysis is performed, what item in the income statement is normally assigned a base of 100? What item in the balance sheet is normally assigned a base of 100?

5. Explain how trend percentages are used to analyze financial statements. Which year is normally chosen as the base year?

6. Explain the difference between short-term liquidity ratios, long-term liquidity ratios, and profitability ratios. What does each type of ratio attempt to measure?

7. Ed's Auto Shop has $25,000 in current assets and $15,000 in current liabilities. What is the current ratio?

8. How does the quick ratio differ from the current ratio? Is a quick ratio of 2.03 good? Why or why not?

9. When computing a ratio involving both an income statement and a balance sheet amount, the balance sheet amount is normally stated as an average. Why is this so?

10. Why should a company try to keep inventory levels as low as possible? What are the disadvantages of keeping inventory levels too low?

11. What two aspects of a firm do long-term creditors analyze and why?

12. What are four common profitability ratios used in analyzing a company?

13. The following figures were taken from the financial statements of the Phillips Company for 1987:

Current assets	$27,000
Property, plant, and equipment	79,000
Current liabilities	14,700
Long-term liabilities	50,500
Common stock, $5 par	30,100
Retained earnings	10,700
Net income (included in retained earnings)	6,200

Required:

Compute: (1) owner's equity to debt ratio, (2) earnings per share, and (3) book value per share.

PROBLEMS

25–1. The comparative balance sheets for Mac's Hardware Store for 1986 and 1987 are presented below:

MAC'S HARDWARE STORE
Comparative Balance Sheets
December 31, 1986 and 1987

	1987	1986
Assets		
Cash	$15,000	$12,500
Accounts receivable	31,600	26,900
Inventories	23,200	26,000
Prepaid rent.	3,000	6,000
Total assets.	$72,800	$71,400
Liabilities		
Accounts payable	$18,000	$15,500
Notes payable	16,800	20,900
Total liabilities	$34,800	$36,400
Owner's equity		
Common stock, $10 par value. . . .	$10,000	$10,000
Retained earnings	28,000	25,000
Total owner's equity. . . .	$38,000	$35,000
Total liabilities and owner's equity . .	$72,800	$71,400

Required:

Compute the dollar amount of increase or decrease and the percentage increase or decrease from 1986 to 1987 for each item in the balance sheet.

25–2. The comparative income statements for Mac's Hardware Store for 1986 and 1987 are presented below.

MAC'S HARDWARE STORE
Comparative Income Statement
Years Ended December 31, 1986 and 1987

	1987	1986
Net sales	$55,000	$52,500
Less: Cost of goods sold . . .	41,000	40,000
Gross margin	$14,000	$12,500
Operating expenses	7,500	5,000
Operating income	$ 6,500	$ 7,500
Other expenses	1,000	500
Income before taxes	$ 5,500	$ 7,000
Income taxes	2,500	3,000
Net income	$ 3,000	$ 4,000

Required:

Compute the dollar amount of increase or decrease and the percentage increase or decrease from 1986 to 1987 for each item in the income statement.

25–3. The balance sheet for Fred's Appliance Store for 1987 is presented below.

FRED'S APPLIANCE STORE
Balance Sheet
December 31, 1987

Assets

Current assets:
Cash . . . . $ 15,000 _570_
Accounts receivable 32,000
Inventory. 25,200
Total current assets . . . . $ 72,200

Property, Plant and Equipment:
Land . . . . $ 50,000
Building 125,000
Less: Accumulated depreciation . . . . (10,000)
Furniture and fixtures 75,000
Less: Accumulated depreciation . . . . (12,000)
Total property, plant and equipment . . $228,000
Total assets $300,200

Liabilities

Current Liabilities:
Accounts payable . . . . $ 42,000
Notes payable 55,000
Total current liabilities. . . . . . . $ 97,000

Long-Term Liabilities:
Mortgage note payable 150,000
Total liabilities $247,000

Owner's Equity

Common stock, $15 par value . . . . . . $ 33,000
Retained earnings. 20,200
Total owner's equity . . . . . . $ 53,200
Total liabilities and owner's equity $300,200

Required:

Prepare a common-size 1987 balance sheet for Fred's Appliance Store using total assets as the base.

25–4. The income statement for Fred's Appliance Store for 1987 is presented below:

net sales is base

FRED'S APPLIANCE STORE
Income Statement
For the Year Ended December 31, 1987

Sales		$125,000
Less: Sales returns and allowances		15,100
Net sales		$109,900
Cost of goods sold		72,000
Gross margin		$ 37,900
Operating expenses:		
Selling	$6,800	
Administrative	4,900	
Total operating expenses		11,700
Operating income		$ 26,200
Other expenses		3,400
Income before income taxes		$ 22,800
Income taxes		10,260
Net income		$ 12,540

113.7%
-13.7%
100%

11.4%

Required:

Prepare a common-size 1987 income statement for Fred's Appliance Store using net sales as the base.

25–5. Presented below are the comparative income statements for the Steel Company for the periods 1984 to 1987.

STEEL COMPANY
Comparative Income Statements
Years Ended December 31, 1984, 1985, 1986, and 1987

	1984	1985	1986	1987
Net sales	$200,000	$350,000	$400,000	$550,000
Cost of goods sold	125,000	270,000	305,000	440,000
Gross margin	$ 75,000	$ 80,000	$ 95,000	$110,000
Operating expenses:				
Selling expenses	$ 27,000	$ 31,000	$ 38,000	$ 46,000
Administrative expenses	16,500	16,800	18,100	19,200
Total operating expenses	$ 43,500	$ 47,800	$ 56,100	$ 65,200
Income before taxes	$ 31,500	$ 32,200	$ 38,900	$ 44,800
Taxes	12,600	12,880	15,560	17,920
Net income	$ 18,900	$ 19,320	$ 23,340	$ 26,880

Required:

The owner of the Steel Company would like to see the trends occurring within each component in the above income statement.

Restate each year's income statement to show these trends. Use 1984 as the base year.

25–6. Presented below is the comparative balance sheet for Jim's Clothing Store for 1986 and 1987.

JIM'S CLOTHING STORE
Comparative Balance Sheet
December 31, 1986 and 1987

	1987	1986
Assets		
Cash	$18,000	$12,000
Accounts receivable.	29,500	32,100
Inventory	22,300	20,200
Marketable securities	5,000	5,000
Prepaid rent	6,000	9,000
Prepaid insurance	4,200	8,400
Total assets	$85,000	$86,700
Liabilities		
Accounts payable	$26,900	$30,700
Notes payable.	5,000	10,000
Total liabilities	$31,900	$40,700
Owner's Equity		
Jim Still, capital	53,100	46,000
Total liabilities and owner's equity. . .	$85,000	$86,700

Required:

1. Compute the current ratio for both years.
2. Compute the amount of working capital for both years.
3. Compute the quick ratio for both years.
4. Comment on the store's ability to meet its current debts as they become due.

25–7. Listed below are selected balances from the general ledger of the Hollowell Book Store at the years' end of 1986 and 1987, as well as the income statement for 1987.

	1987	1986
Cash	7,500	5,000
Accounts receivable	15,200	12,500
Marketable securities	7,500	7,500
Inventory	32,300	28,100
Prepaid expenses	2,000	1,000
Land	50,000	50,000
Building	250,000	250,000
Accumulated depreciation—building . . .	(100,000)	(90,000)

Furniture and fixtures	150,000	150,000
Accumulated Depreciation—furniture		
and fixtures	(30,000)	(25,000)
Accounts payable.	48,100	45,100
Notes payable (long term).	20,000	25,000
Mortgage payable	180,000	200,000
Common stock, $15 par value	87,000	75,000
Retained earnings.	49,400	44,000

HOLLOWELL BOOK STORE
Income Statement
For the Year Ended December 31, 1987

Net sales	$150,000
Cash sales, 25%	
Credit sales, 75%	
Cost of goods sold	125,000
Gross margin	$ 25,000
Operating expense	5,000
Interest expense	10,000
Income before taxes	$ 10,000
Income taxes	4,600
Net income	$ 5,400

Required:

Compute the 12 ratios discussed in this chapter for 1987.

CHAPTER 26

Accounting for a manufacturing business

Merchandising firms make money by selling goods that others have produced. Manufacturing businesses, on the other hand, personally produce the products that they sell. Consequently, manufacturing firms use some accounting procedures that are not needed in other kinds of businesses. In this chapter, you will learn the accounting for a manufacturing business. After studying this chapter, you should be able to:

1. Prepare a worksheet for a manufacturing business.
2. Journalize adjusting entries.
3. Journalize closing entries.
4. Post entries to the accounts.
5. Prepare a cost of goods manufactured statement.
6. Prepare an income statement.

In earlier chapters, we presented the accounting procedures used in merchandising firms and service enterprises. Because a manufacturing business makes, rather than purchases, articles for sale, its accounting processes are more elaborate. In this chapter we will discuss the way in which manufacturers determine the total cost of goods produced in each accounting period. We will also examine the financial statements and the worksheet of a manufacturing business.

COST OF MANUFACTURING

The three elements of manufacturing cost are materials, labor, and factory overhead.

Materials

Materials are used to manufacture products. Manufacturing materials may be classified as direct materials or indirect materials.

Direct materials enter into and become part of the finished product. They are physically identifiable with the finished product. An example would be the sheet steel used by an automobile company. Direct materials are also called raw materials.

Indirect materials include both materials used in the manufacturing process that do not become part of the finished goods, such as oil and grease used in machinery, and inexpensive items, such as nails and bolts, that do become part of the finished product. Since indirect materials have a relatively small cost, these materials are more easily accounted for as part of factory overhead. Indirect materials are also called factory supplies.

Labor

Labor, like materials, is also divided into direct and indirect portions. **Direct labor** consists of wages paid to factory employees who work directly on the materials to form a finished product. The workers may work on an assembly line or operate factory machinery. Their work is directly traceable to the finished product, and the cost varies directly with the level of production.

Indirect labor includes the wages of supervisors, inspectors, and others who work for the company but not directly on the product. Indirect labor is a part of factory overhead.

Factory overhead

Factory overhead consists of manufacturing costs that are not directly traceable to products. In addition to indirect materials and indirect labor, factory overhead includes items such as: (1) supervisors' salaries, (2) depreciation of factory buildings and equipment, (3) repairs and maintenance to factory buildings and equipment, (4) taxes on the factory payroll, (5) heat, power, and light, and (6) factory insurance expired. Each of these costs is generally recorded in a separate account, with the Factory Overhead account used as a control account.

Inventories

While a merchandising firm has one inventory—merchandise inventory—a manufacturing business generally has three inventories: (1) materials, (2) work in process, and (3) finished goods. To determine the **cost of goods manufactured** and **cost of goods sold,** it is necessary to know the beginning and ending amounts of all three inventories. The relationships are as follows:

Cost of Materials Used

$\dfrac{\begin{array}{l}\text{Beginning materials inventory}\\ +\ \text{Materials purchases}\end{array}}{}$
= Total cost of materials available for use
$\dfrac{-\ \text{Ending materials inventory}}{}$
= Cost of materials used

Cost of Goods Manufactured

$\dfrac{\begin{array}{l}\text{Beginning work in process inventory}\\ +\ \text{Cost of materials used}\\ +\ \text{Direct labor}\\ +\ \text{Factory overhead}\end{array}}{}$
= Total factory costs
$\dfrac{-\ \text{Ending work in process inventory}}{}$
= Cost of goods manufactured

Cost of Goods Sold

$\dfrac{\begin{array}{l}\text{Beginning finished goods inventory}\\ +\ \text{Cost of goods manufactured}\end{array}}{}$
= Cost of goods available for sale
$\dfrac{-\ \text{Ending finished goods inventory}}{}$
= Cost of goods sold

The computation of cost of goods sold for a manufacturer differs from that for a merchandiser in that cost of goods manufactured takes the place of purchases, and **finished goods inventory** takes the place of merchandise inventory.

STATEMENT OF COST OF GOODS MANUFACTURED

The statement of cost of goods manufactured for Henson's Manufacturing Company is shown in Illustration 26–1. Notice how the three elements of manufacturing cost are shown: direct materials, direct labor, and factory overhead. These elements are shown separately

ILLUSTRATION 26–1

HENSON'S MANUFACTURING COMPANY
Statement of Cost of Goods Manufactured
For The Year Ended December 31, 1987

Work in process inventory, January 1. . . .			$ 120,000
Direct materials:			
Materials inventory, January 1		$ 85,000	
Materials purchases (net)		215,000	
Cost of materials available.		$300,000	
Less: Materials inventory, December 31 . .		90,000	
Cost of materials used		$210,000	
Direct labor		550,000	
Factory overhead:			
Indirect materials.	$ 5,000		
Indirect labor	110,000		
Depreciation—factory equipment	40,000		
Depreciation—factory building	29,000		
Repairs and maintenance	22,000		
Factory insurance expired	17,000		
Heat, power, and light	100,000		
Miscellaneous factory costs	10,000		
Total factory overhead		333,000	
Total manufacturing costs			1,093,000
Total cost of work in process during period .			$1,213,000
Less: Work in process inventory, December 31			110,000
Cost of goods manufactured			$1,103,000

because investors and creditors find this added detail useful in assessing the firm's net cash inflows.

INCOME STATEMENT

An income statement for Henson's Manufacturing Company is shown in Illustration 26–2. The cost of goods manufactured figure is shown on the income statement as a part of cost of goods sold.

ILLUSTRATION 26–2

HENSON'S MANUFACTURING COMPANY
Income Statement
For the year ended December 31, 1987

Sales (net)		$2,000,000
Cost of goods sold:		
Finished goods inventory, January 1	$ 500,000	
Cost of goods manufactured	1,103,000	
Goods available for sale	$1,603,000	
Less: Finished goods inventory, December 31	280,000	
Cost of goods sold		1,323,000
Gross margin		$ 677,000
Operating expenses:		
Selling expenses	$ 351,000	
General expenses	179,000	
Total operating expenses		530,000
Income from operations		$ 147,000
Other expenses:		
Interest expense		22,000
Net income		$ 125,000

BALANCE SHEET

A balance sheet for Henson's Manufacturing Company is shown in Illustration 26–3. The ending balances of the firm's inventory accounts are included in the Current Assets section.

**ILLUSTRATION
26–3**

HENSON'S MANUFACTURING COMPANY
Balance Sheet
December 31, 1987

Assets

Current assets:

Cash		$ 15,000
Notes receivable		42,000
Accounts receivable	$150,000	
Less: Allowance for doubtful accounts .	3,000	147,000
Materials inventory		90,000
Work in process inventory.		110,000
Finished goods inventory		280,000
Prepaid insurance.		3,000
Total current assets		$ 687,000

Plant and equipment:

Factory equipment	$400,000		
Less: Accumulated depreciation	150,000	$250,000	
Office equipment	$ 70,000		
Less: Accumulated depreciation	42,000	28,000	
Factory building	$510,000		
Less: Accumulated depreciation	300,000	210,000	
Land		200,000	
Total plant and equipment			688,000
Total assets			$1,375,000

Liabilities

Current liabilities:

Accounts payable.	$ 80,000	
Notes payable	45,000	
Dividends payable	25,000	
Total current liabilities		$ 150,000
Long-term liabilities:		
Bonds payable (due December 31, 1989) . .		350,000
Total liabilities		$ 500,000

Owner's Equity

Paid in capital:

Common stock, $15 par (40,000 shares		
authorized, 30,000 shares issued). . . .	$450,000	
Premium on common stock	100,000	
Total paid in capital.	$550,000	
Retained earnings	325,000	
Total owner's equity		875,000
Total liabilities and owner's equity.		$1,375,000

WORKSHEET

Illustration 26–4 is the worksheet for Henson's Manufacturing Company. Look at the Trial Balance column. First, it is necessary to make adjusting entries including adjusting entries for the three inventory accounts. The beginning inventories must be closed out and the ending inventories added. To adjust Materials and Work in Process, the Manufacturing Summary account is used. To adjust Finished Goods, the Income Summary account is used. The adjusting entries are as follows:

Adjustments:

(a) Beginning materials inventory, $85,000.
(b) Ending materials inventory, $90,000.
(c) Beginning work in process inventory, $120,000.
(d) Ending work in process inventory, $110,000.
(e) Beginning finished goods inventory, $500,000.
(f) Ending finished goods inventory, $280,000.
(g) Depreciation of factory equipment, $40,000.
(h) Depreciation of factory building, $29,000.
(i) Expired factory insurance, $17,000.
(j) Depreciation of office equipment, $4,000.
(k) Estimated uncollectible accounts, $1,000.

The adjusting entries are journalized directly from the Adjustments column of the worksheet.

ILLUSTRATION 26–4

HENSON'S MANUFACTURING COMPANY
Worksheet
For the Year Ended December 31, 1987

ACCOUNT NAME	TRIAL BALANCE DEBIT	TRIAL BALANCE CREDIT	ADJUSTMENTS DEBIT	ADJUSTMENTS CREDIT
Cash	15,000.00			
Accounts receivable	150,000.00			
Notes receivable	42,000.00			
Allowance for doubtful accounts		2,000.00		(k) 1,000.00
Materials inventory	85,000.00		(b) 90,000.00	(a) 85,000.00
Work in process inventory	120,000.00		(d) 110,000.00	(c) 120,000.00
Finished goods inventory	500,000.00		(f) 280,000.00	(e) 500,000.00
Prepaid insurance	20,000.00			(i) 17,000.00
Factory equipment	400,000.00			
Accumulated depreciation—Factory equipment		110,000.00		(g) 40,000.00
Office equipment	70,000.00			
Accumulated Depreciation—Office equipment		38,000.00		(j) 4,000.00
Factory building	510,000.00			
Accumulated depreciation—Factory building		271,000.00		(h) 29,000.00
Land	200,000.00			
Notes payable		45,000.00		
Accounts payable		80,000.00		
Dividends payable		25,000.00		
Bonds payable		350,000.00		
Common stock		450,000.00		
Premium on common stock		100,000.00		
Retained earnings		200,000.00		
Sales (net)		2,000,000.00		
Materials purchases	215,000.00			
Direct labor	550,000.00			
Indirect materials	5,000.00			
Indirect labor	110,000.00			
Repairs and maintenance	22,000.00			
Heat, power, and light	100,000.00			
Miscellaneous factory costs	10,000.00			
Selling expenses (control)	350,000.00		(k) 1,000.00	
General expenses (control)	175,000.00		(j) 4,000.00	
Interest expense	22,000.00			
	3,671,000.00	3,671,000.00		
Manufacturing summary			(a) 85,000.00	(b) 90,000.00
			(c) 120,000.00	(d) 110,000.00
Income summary			(e) 500,000.00	(f) 280,000.00
Depreciation—Factory equipment			(g) 40,000.00	
Depreciation—Factory building			(h) 29,000.00	
Factory insurance expense			(i) 17,000.00	
			1,276,000.00	1,276,000.00
Cost of goods manufactured				
Net income				

	STATEMENT OF COST OF GOODS MANUFACTURED		INCOME STATEMENT		BALANCE SHEET	
	DEBIT	CREDIT	DEBIT	CREDIT	DEBIT	CREDIT
					15 0 0 0 00	
					150 0 0 0 00	
					42 0 0 0 00	
						3 0 0 0 00
					90 0 0 0 00	
					110 0 0 0 00	
					280 0 0 0 00	
					3 0 0 0 00	
					400 0 0 0 00	
						150 0 0 0 00
					70 0 0 0 00	
						42 0 0 0 00
					510 0 0 0 00	
						300 0 0 0 00
					200 0 0 0 00	
						45 0 0 0 00
						80 0 0 0 00
						25 0 0 0 00
						350 0 0 0 00
						450 0 0 0 00
						100 0 0 0 00
						200 0 0 0 00
				2000 0 0 0 00		
215 0 0 0 00						
550 0 0 0 00						
5 0 0 0 00						
110 0 0 0 00						
22 0 0 0 00						
100 0 0 0 00						
10 0 0 0 00						
		351 0 0 0 00			
		179 0 0 0 00			
		22 0 0 0 00			
85 0 0 0 00	90 0 0 0 00				
120 0 0 0 00	110 0 0 0 00				
		500 0 0 0 00	280 0 0 0 00		
40 0 0 0 00					
29 0 0 0 00					
17 0 0 0 00					
1303 0 0 0 00	200 0 0 0 00				
	1103 0 0 0 00	1103 0 0 0 00			
1303 0 0 0 00	1303 0 0 0 00	2155 0 0 0 00	2280 0 0 0 00	1870 0 0 0 00	1745 0 0 0 00
		125 0 0 0 00			125 0 0 0 00
		2280 0 0 0 00	2280 0 0 0 00	1870 0 0 0 00	1870 0 0 0 00

GENERAL JOURNAL						
DATE		ACCOUNT AND EXPLANATION	P.R.	DEBIT	CREDIT	
1987		Adjusting Entries				
Dec.	31	(a) Manufacturing Summary		8 5 0 0 0 00		
		Materials Inventory			8 5 0 0 0 00	
		Close beginning materials inventory.				
	31	(b) Materials Inventory		9 0 0 0 0 00		
		Manufacturing Summary			9 0 0 0 0 00	
		Set up ending materials inventory.				
	31	(c) Manufacturing Summary		12 0 0 0 0 00		
		Work in Process Inventory			12 0 0 0 0 00	
		Close beginning work in process inventory.				
	31	(d) Work in Process Inventory		11 0 0 0 0 00		
		Manufacturing Summary			11 0 0 0 0 00	
		Set up ending work in process inventory.				
	31	(e) Income Summary		50 0 0 0 0 00		
		Finished Goods Inventory			50 0 0 0 0 00	
		Close beginning finished goods inventory.				
	31	(f) Finished Goods Inventory		28 0 0 0 0 00		
		Income Summary			28 0 0 0 0 00	
		Set up ending finished goods inventory.				
	31	(g) Depreciation Expense—Factory Equipment		4 0 0 0 0 00		
		Accumulated Depreciation—Factory Equip.			4 0 0 0 0 00	
		Depreciation expense—factory equipment.				
	31	(h) Depreciation Expense—Factory Building		2 9 0 0 0 00		
		Accumulated Depreciation—Factory Bldg.			2 9 0 0 0 00	
		Depreciation expense—factory building.				
	31	(i) Factory Insurance Expense		1 7 0 0 0 00		
		Prepaid Insurance			1 7 0 0 0 00	
		Factory insurance expired.				
	31	(j) General Expenses (control)		4 0 0 0 00		
		Accumulated Depreciation—Office Equip.			4 0 0 0 00	
		Depreciation expense—office equipment.				
	31	(k) Selling Expenses (control)		1 0 0 0 00		
		Allowance for Doubtful Accounts			1 0 0 0 00	
		Bad debts expense recorded.				

The closing entries must now be journalized.

(a) Close the cost of goods manufactured accounts to the Manufacturing Summary account.

	GENERAL JOURNAL				
DATE	ACCOUNT AND EXPLANATION	P.R.	DEBIT	CREDIT	
1987	*Closing Entries*				
Dec. 31	Manufacturing Summary		109 8 0 0 0 00		
	Materials Purchases			21 5 0 0 0 00	
	Direct Labor			55 0 0 0 0 00	
	Indirect Materials			5 0 0 0 00	
	Indirect Labor			11 0 0 0 0 00	
	Repairs and Maintenance			2 2 0 0 0 00	
	Heat, Power, and Light			10 0 0 0 0 00	
	Miscellaneous Factory Costs			1 0 0 0 0 00	
	Depreciation Expense—Factory Equipment			4 0 0 0 0 00	
	Depreciation Expense—Factory Building			2 9 0 0 0 00	
	Factory Insurance Expense			1 7 0 0 0 00	

(b) Close the Manufacturing Summary account into the Income Summary account.

(c) Close the revenue accounts to the Income Summary account.

	GENERAL JOURNAL				
DATE	ACCOUNT AND EXPLANATION	P.R.	DEBIT	CREDIT	
31	Income Summary		110 3 0 0 0 00		
	Manufacturing Summary			110 3 0 0 0 00	
31	Sales (net)		200 0 0 0 0 00		
	Income Summary			200 0 0 0 0 00	

(d) Close the expense accounts to the Income Summary account.

(e) Close the Income Summary account into Retained Earnings.

	GENERAL JOURNAL				
DATE	ACCOUNT AND EXPLANATION	P.R.	DEBIT	CREDIT	
31	Income Summary		55 2 0 0 0 00		
	Selling Expenses (control)			35 1 0 0 0 00	
	General Expenses (control)			17 9 0 0 0 00	
	Interest Expense			2 2 0 0 0 00	
31	Income Summary		12 5 0 0 0 00		
	Retained Earnings			12 5 0 0 0 00	

The T accounts for the Manufacturing Summary and Income Summary account are shown below.

Manufacturing Summary

Materials inventory, 1/1	85,000	Materials inventory, 12/31	90,000
Work in process inventory, 1/1	120,000	Work in process inventory,	
Materials purchases	215,000	12/31	110,000
Direct labor	550,000	Balance (to income summary)	1,103,000
Indirect materials	5,000		
Indirect labor	110,000		
Depreciation expense—factory			
equipment	40,000		
Depreciation expense—factory			
building	29,000		
Repairs and maintenance	22,000		
Factory insurance expense	17,000		
Heat, power, and light	100,000		
Miscellaneous factory costs	10,000		
	1,303,000		1,303,000

Income Summary

Finished goods inventory, 1/1	500,000	Finished goods inventory, 12/31	280,000
(From manufacturing summary)	1,103,000	From revenue accounts	2,000,000
From expense accounts	552,000		
Balance (to			
retained earnings)	125,000		
	2,280,000		2,280,000

ACCOUNTING CYCLE FOR A MANUFACTURING FIRM

In this chapter, three of the four formal financial statements were presented prior to the worksheet for the sake of clarity. The usual sequence of accounting for a manufacturing firm is a series of nine steps:

1. Journalize the transactions.
2. Post to the ledger accounts.
3. Prepare the trial balance.
4. Determine the adjustments.

5. Complete the worksheet.
6. Prepare the four financial statements (statement of cost of goods manufactured, income statement, statement of owner's equity, and balance sheet).
7. Journalize and post adjusting entries.
8. Journalize and post closing entries.
9. Prepare a post-closing trial balance.

VALUATION OF INVENTORIES

The costs of the ending inventories for materials, work in process, and finished goods are first listed in the Adjustments column of the worksheet and then carried forward to the Balance Sheet columns. In assigning costs to ending inventories, one of the bases listed below must be used:

1. Cost basis.
   a. First-in, first-out (FIFO) cost.
   b. Average cost.
   c. Last-in, first-out (LIFO) cost.
2. The lower of cost (FIFO or average) or market (cost to replace).

A manufacturer may use any of these methods to allocate the cost of materials purchased between the materials used and those that are still on hand at the end of the period. For the work in process and finished goods inventories, cost includes (1) direct materials cost, (2) direct labor cost, and (3) factory overhead associated with the production of goods.

The full cost accounting procedures necessary for valuation of inventories are beyond the scope of this book. Generally, however, factory overhead is apportioned on some reasonable basis, such as in proportion to direct labor. For example, assume that a manufacturer's accounts show the following information at year-end:

Cost of work in process, beginning	$ 20,000
Cost of direct materials used during year	72,000
Cost of direct labor for year	108,000
Factory overhead for year	86,400

Factory overhead amounted to 80 percent of direct labor ($86,400 ÷ $108,000). If the cost of direct labor in the work in process inventory at year-end is $20,000, it may be reasonable to estimate that $16,000 (80% of $20,000) of factory overhead relates to those goods. If the cost of direct materials in work in process is $22,000, the allocation between finished goods and work in process is as follows:

	Total	Cost Apportioned to Finished Goods	Cost Apportioned to Work in Process
Beginning work in process	$ 20,000	$ 20,000	—
Direct materials used	72,000	50,000	$22,000
Direct* labor	108,000	88,000	20,000
Factory overhead	86,400	70,400*	16,000†
	$286,400	$228,400	$58,000

* $88,000 × .80
† $20,000 × .80

SUMMARY

Manufacturing firms use certain accounting procedures that differ from those of other businesses. The main difference centers on determining the value of total **cost of goods manufactured** during each accounting period.

The three elements of manufacturing costs are materials, labor, and factory overhead. Materials consist of **direct materials** and **indirect materials.** Labor consists of **direct labor** and **indirect labor.** Both indirect materials and indirect labor are part of **factory overhead.** Factory overhead also consists of other costs not directly attributable to the manufacturing process.

A manufacturing firm generally has three separate inventories: **materials, work in process,** and **finished goods.** Materials are transferred into work in process. When the manufacturing process is complete, the products are transferred to finished goods.

A statement of cost of goods manufactured is included as part of the calculation of cost of goods sold shown in the income statement.

A manufacturing business has an accounting cycle as does any enterprise. To ensure that correct and complete financial statements are prepared, a systematic series of accounting procedures should be adopted.

Each form of inventory must be valued at the end of the accounting period. The company can use any of the three cost valuation methods: FIFO cost, average cost, or LIFO cost; or it can use the lower of cost (FIFO or average) or market (cost to replace).

KEY TERMS

Cost of Goods Manufactured—Beginning work in process + cost of materials used + direct labor + factory overhead − ending work in process. This is the value of the products that were completed during an accounting period.

Cost of Goods Sold—Beginning finished goods inventory + cost of goods manufactured − ending finished goods inventory. This is the cost of the goods sold to customers during an accounting period.

Cost of Materials Used—Beginning materials inventory + materials purchased − ending materials inventory. This is the value of the materials placed into production during an accounting period.

Direct Labor—Wages paid to factory employees who work directly on the materials that form a finished product.

Direct Materials—Materials that become part of the finished product and are physically identifiable with the finished product.

Factory Overhead—All manufacturing costs except direct labor and direct materials.

Finished Goods Inventory—The finished products held by a manufacturing company for sale.

Indirect Labor—Wages paid to workers who are not directly involved with production.

Indirect Materials—Materials used in manufacturing that either do not become part of the finished product or are inexpensive and more easily accounted for as factory overhead.

Materials Inventory—The raw materials held by a manufacturing company that will be used in manufacturing a product.

Work in Process—The unfinished products of a manufacturing company that are in process at a point in time.

QUESTIONS AND EXERCISES

1. What are the three elements of manufacturing cost?
2. Generally, how many inventories does a manufacturing firm have and what are they called?
3. What is the formula for determining cost of materials used?
4. From the following balances, determine the cost of materials used:

   Materials purchases. $9,000
   Materials inventory, June 30. . . . 1,500
   Materials inventory, June 1 900

5. What is the formula for determining cost of goods manufactured?
6. What is the formula for determining Cost of Goods Sold?
7. Prepare a statement of Cost of Goods Manufactured using the following account balances:

   Materials purchases . . . . $ 900
   Work in process inventory, July 1 350
   Materials inventory, July 1 75
   Materials inventory, July 31 100
   Finished goods inventory, July 31 170
   Work in process inventory, July 31. . . . 315
   Finished goods inventory, July 1 175
   Direct labor 1,150
   Factory overhead. 890

8. From the data in Exercise 7, compute the Cost of Goods Sold.
9. From the following balances, determine the Cost of Goods Manufactured:

   Cost of goods sold $1,490
   Finished goods inventory, August 1 310
   Finished goods inventory, August 31. . . . 298

10. From the following, calculate the cost of ending work in process, which contains the following elements:

    Direct materials used $105
    Direct labor 172
    Factory overhead (82 percent of direct labor)

11. Cost may be assigned to ending inventories using cost or the lower of cost or market. What are two methods of determining cost?

PROBLEMS

26–1. Following is a statement of cost of goods manufactured for Jones Manufacturing Company:

JONES MANUFACTURING COMPANY
Statement of Cost of Goods Manufactured
For the Year Ended December 31, 1987

Work in process inventory, January 1		$130,000
Direct materials:		
Materials inventory, January 1	$270,000	
Materials purchases (net)	405,000	
Cost of materials available	$675,000	
Less: Materials inventory,		
December 31	275,000	
Cost of materials used	$400,000	
Direct labor	620,000	
Factory overhead:		
Indirect labor	$120,000	
Depreciation—factory equipment	72,000	
Heat, light, and power	25,000	
Depreciation—factory building	21,500	
Factory insurance expired	9,300	
Miscellaneous factory overhead	5,200	
Total factory overhead		253,000
Total manufacturing costs		1,273,000
Total cost of work in process during the period . .		$1,403,000
Less: Work in process inventory, December 31 . .		280,000
Cost of goods manufactured		$1,123,000

Required:

1. Journalize the adjusting entries for the materials inventory and the work in process inventory.
2. Journalize the closing entries for manufacturing costs.
3. Post the entries to the Manufacturing Summary account.
4. Journalize and post the entry to close the Manufacturing Summary account.

26–2. Following is the trial balance of the Above Products Corporation as of December 31:

ABOVE PRODUCTS CORPORATION
Trial Balance
December 31, 1987

Account Titles	Debit	Credit
Cash	$ 8,100	
Accounts receivable	72,000	
Allowance for doubtful accounts.		$ 2,300
Materials inventory	80,000	
Work in process inventory	151,400	
Finished goods inventory	139,300	
Prepaid factory insurance	4,000	
Machinery	172,000	
Accumulated depreciation, machinery		86,000
Accounts payable		54,200
Common stock.		225,000
Paid-in capital in excess of par value		50,000
Retained earnings		142,500
Sales		1,390,000
Materials purchases	120,000	
Direct labor	515,000	
Indirect labor	182,000	
Utilities	46,500	
Maintenance and repairs	22,000	
Selling expenses (control)	293,000	
General expenses (control)	132,300	
Income tax	12,400	
	$1,950,000	$1,950,000

For the adjustments the following information is given.

(a) Ending inventories: materials, $74,000; work in process, $142,800; finished goods, $142,000.

(b) Allowance for doubtful accounts to be increased by $1,800.

(c) Estimated depreciation of factory machinery, $18,400.

(d) $2,500 of factory insurance expired this year.

(e) Additional income tax is $14,000.

Required:

1. Prepare a worksheet.

2. Prepare a statement of cost of goods manufactured.

3. Prepare an income statement.

26–3. Following are the adjusting and closing entries appearing on the books of Williams Manufacturing Company at the end of the fiscal year, June 30.

Adjusting Entries

1987				
June 30	Manufacturing Summary	. . . . . .	85,000	
	Materials Inventory.	. . . . . .		85,000
30	Materials Inventory	. . . .	80,000	
	Manufacturing Summary .	. . . .		80,000
30	Manufacturing Summary	. . . . .	120,000	
	Work in Process Inventory	. . . .		120,000
30	Work in Process Inventory .	. . . . .	190,000	
	Manufacturing Summary .	. . . .		190,000

Closing Entries

30	Manufacturing Summary	. . . . . .	1,082,000	
	Materials Purchases	. . . . . .		200,000
	Indirect Materials	. . . . . .		12,000
	Direct Labor .	. . . .		625,000
	Indirect Labor	. . . .		115,000
	Depreciation, Machinery .	. . . .		30,000
	Depreciation, Building.	. . . . .		45,000
	Utilities.	. . . .		26,000
	Repairs and Maintenance.	. . . .		13,000
	Property Tax, Building	. . . .		5,500
	Factory Insurance Expired	. . . .		2,500
	Miscellaneous Factory Costs.	. . . .		8,000
30	Income Summary		1,017,000	
	Manufacturing Summary .	. . . .		1,017,000

Required:

Prepare a statement of cost of goods manufactured for the year.

26–4. The worksheet columns which reflect the statement of cost of goods manufactured and the income statement are shown below, as of December 31, the end of the fiscal year. The beginning inventory for materials is $72,450; the beginning inventory for work in process is $128,300.

Account Name	Statement of Cost of Goods Manufactured		Income Statement	
	Debit	Credit	Debit	Credit
Sales				2,300,000
Sales returns and allowances			10,500	
Sales discounts			9,800	
Selling expenses (control)			292,000	
General expenses (control)			76,200	
Materials purchases	392,000			
Direct labor	516,000			
Indirect materials	12,300			
Indirect labor	122,200			
Heat, power, and light	28,000			
Repairs and maintenance	32,000			
Miscellaneous factory costs	14,500			
Depreciation—machinery	16,000			
Factory insurance expired	4,200			
Interest expense			5,000	
Income tax			361,420	
Manufacturing summary	72,450	102,000		
	128,300	143,000		
Income summary			520,000	610,000
	1,337,950	245,000		
Cost of goods manufactured		1,092,950	1,092,950	
	1,337,950	1,337,950	2,367,870	2,910,000
Net income			542,130	
			2,910,000	2,910,000

Required:

1. Prepare a statement of cost of goods manufactured.
2. Prepare an income statement.
3. Journalize the adjusting entries for the inventories.
4. Journalize the closing entries.

26–5. Following are the adjusting and closing entries that appear on the books of Jamestown Marine Corporation at the end of the fiscal year, December 31.

Dec. 31	Manufacturing Summary	. . .	82,000	
	Materials inventory .	. . .		82,000
31	Materials inventory	. . . . .	75,000	
	Manufacturing summary	. .		75,000
31	Manufacturing summary.	. . .	132,900	
	Work in process inventory	.		132,900
31	Work in process inventory .	. .	152,000	
	Manufacturing summary .	. .		152,000

Closing Entries

31	Manufacturing Summary	. . . . . .	815,500	
	Materials Purchases	. . . . . .		112,000
	Direct Labor . .	. . . . . .		492,000
	Indirect Materials	. . . . . .		9,800
	Indirect Labor .	. . . . . .		115,000
	Utilities . .	. . . . . .		42,200
	Maintenance and Repairs	. . . .		18,000
	Depreciation Expense—Machinery	.		23,000
	Factory Insurance Expired .	. . .		3,500
31	Income Summary . .	. . . . . .	803,400	
	Manufacturing Summary .	. . . .		803,400

Required:

1. Post the adjusting and closing entries in T accounts for Materials Inventory, Work in Process Inventory, Manufacturing Summary, and Income Summary.
2. Prepare a statement of cost of goods manufactured.

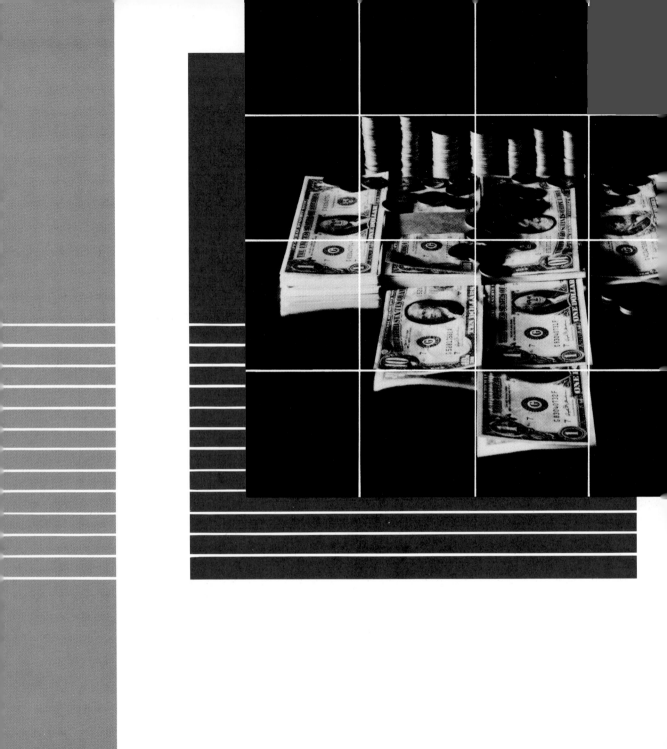

CHAPTER 27

Cost accounting

LEARNING OBJECTIVES

The basic accounting system described in previous chapters does not always provide enough information to control and manage resources effectively. A study of this chapter will provide a basic understanding of cost accounting systems which are used to control and manage resources. After studying this chapter, you should be able to:

1. Allocate joint costs using the physical quantities method and the relative sales value method.
2. Prepare journal entries for a job order cost system.
3. Compute under-or overapplied overhead.
4. Compute equivalent units of production for a process cost system.
5. Prepare a cost production report.

The term **cost accounting** originally referred to the accumulation and assignment of manufacturing costs to units of output for the purposes of inventory valuation and net income determination. Today, the term *cost accounting* is often used interchangeably with the terms **management accounting** and **managerial accounting.** Management accounting, in turn, is broadly defined as the process of providing a wide range of information useful for management decision making. Management decision making includes both short-run and long-run planning and control decisions.

This chapter will focus on cost accounting narrowly defined as the use of accounting information for product costing purposes. Product cost information is useful for determining the selling price of a product. As stated above, product cost information is necessary for measuring inventory and net income.

There are two basic types of cost accounting systems: (1) **job order cost accounting** systems and (2) **process cost accounting** systems. The characteristics of both systems are described in this chapter. Examples are given to illustrate the flow of costs through each system and the journal entries required in each system.

JOB ORDER COST ACCOUNTING SYSTEMS

In a job order cost accounting system, costs are accumulated separately for each individual job or order. A job may consist of a single physical unit or a distinct batch of similar units. Job order systems are typically used if products are made to customers' specifications or are produced in identifiable batches. Such systems are often used by print shops, the construction industry, and manufacturers of custom-made furniture, aircraft, and machinery.

The basic document in a job order system is a **job cost sheet.** A job cost sheet is a form or record on which the manufacturing costs of a particular job are recorded and summarized. One type of job cost sheet is shown in Illustration 27–1. Each individual job has its own job cost sheet which is identified by the job number. The costs of direct materials and direct labor applicable to the job are entered on the job cost sheet. Factory overhead allocable to the job is also recorded on the job cost sheet. When the job is completed, the total cost of the job is computed in the cost summary section. Then the total cost is divided by the number of units in the job to determine

ILLUSTRATION 27–1

JOB COST SHEET								

Product _____

Quantity _____

For _____

Job. No. _____

Date Wanted _____

Date Started _____

Date Completed _____.

Direct Materials			Direct Labor			Factory Overhead	
Date	Requisition Number	Amount	Date	Hours	Amount	Date	Amount

Cost Summary _____

Direct Materials _____

Direct Labor _____

Factory Overhead _____

Total _____

Cost per Unit _____

the cost per unit. Recall from Chapter 26 that direct materials and direct labor are materials and labor that are clearly identifiable with or traceable to a particular job. Factory overhead costs include indirect materials and labor; depreciation of factory buildings and equipment; repairs, insurance, and property taxes applicable to factory buildings and equipment; factory supplies; and heat, light, and power.

All the job cost sheets taken together make up the **job ledger.** The job ledger is a subsidiary ledger to the general ledger account called **Work in Process.** The balance in the Work in Process account should equal the total of all costs charged on the job cost sheets.

Accounting for materials

In general, perpetual inventory records are kept when cost accounting systems are used. The general ledger contains a control account called Materials or Stores (an inventory account). A subsidiary materials ledger contains an inventory card for each different type of material.

Purchases of materials are placed in the storeroom and are debited to the appropriate subsidiary materials ledger cards and to the Materials control account. The storekeeper issues materials to the production departments upon receipt of an approved **materials requisition,** such as the one shown in Illustration 27–2. The materials requisition authorizes the storekeeper to issue materials and serves as a source document for recording the movement of materials. The amounts on the materials requisitions serve as the basis for debits in the job ledger (for direct materials), debits in the factory overhead ledger (for indirect materials) and credits in the stores ledger. Summary totals of the amounts on the requisitions provide the debit to the Work in Process account, the debit to the Factory Overhead control account, and the credit to the Materials control account.

Accounting for labor costs

The procedures involved in accounting for payroll have been described elsewhere in this text. The basic procedures of accounting for earnings, payroll deductions, and wage and salary payments are applicable to a job order cost system. However, more detailed records must be kept in a job order cost system to permit the separation of direct labor costs from indirect labor costs. Earnings of workers who provide indirect labor services should be charged to the appropriate Factory Overhead accounts. Earnings of workers who provide direct labor services should be charged to the jobs on which they worked.

Work tickets are generally used to record the amount of time spent on each job by each worker. A work ticket is shown in Illustration 27–3. The amount of direct labor cost chargeable to each job is also indicated on the work ticket. The work tickets of all workers

ILLUSTRATION 27–2

MATERIALS REQUISITION

Job No. _____   Requisition No. _____

Deliver to _____   Date_____

Charge to _____

Description	Quantity	Unit Cost	Extension

Requested by   Approved by   Issued by

may be summarized daily, weekly, or monthly to determine the direct labor cost of each job.

Accounting for factory overhead costs

Factory overhead costs were discussed in Chapter 26. Since it is difficult to trace factory overhead costs directly to individual jobs, some method is required to allocate reasonable amounts of factory overhead to the jobs. Factory overhead is usually allocated to jobs by using a **predetermined overhead rate.** The rate is generally determined at the beginning of the accounting period using the following formula:

$$\text{Predetermined overhead rate} = \frac{\text{Estimated factory overhead costs}}{\text{Estimated activity}}$$

ILLUSTRATION 27-3

```
                              WORK TICKET

    Date _____        Employee No. _____

    Time Started _____    Job. No. _____

    Time Stopped _____    Department _____

    Hours Worked _____    Pieces Completed _____

    Rate _____           Amount _____


    _____              _____
      Employee Signature                 Approved by
```

The denominator, estimated activity, can be direct labor hours, machine hours, direct labor costs, material costs, or units of production. Suppose that direct labor cost is selected as the activity base. At the beginning of the year, a company estimates total factory overhead at $2,500,000 and total direct labor costs at $2,000,000. The predetermined overhead rate is 125 percent ($2,500,000/$2,000,000). As each job is completed, overhead is assigned to it at the rate of 125 percent of direct labor costs. Thus, if a job includes $120 of direct labor, $150 (125% of $120) of factory overhead is assigned to the job. At the end of the year, overhead is assigned to unfinished jobs at the rate of 125 percent of the direct labor costs incurred to date for those jobs.

Actual overhead costs incurred are debited to the appropriate factory overhead subsidiary ledger accounts and to the Factory Overhead control account. Overhead applied to jobs on the basis of the predetermined overhead rate is entered on the job cost sheets and is debited to Work in Process and credited to **Factory Overhead Applied.** Factory Overhead Applied is a contra account to Factory Overhead.

If actual overhead costs or actual direct labor costs (or direct labor hours or machine-hours) differ from the estimated costs, then the amount of overhead assigned to jobs will differ from the amount of overhead costs incurred. If actual factory overhead exceeds factory overhead applied, overhead is said to be **underapplied** or **underabsorbed.** If factory overhead applied exceeds actual factory overhead,

overhead is said to be **overapplied** or **overabsorbed.** In theory, the underapplied or overapplied overhead should be apportioned among the jobs worked on during the year. In practice, the underapplied or overapplied overhead is generally insignificant in amount and is assigned to the cost of goods sold.

There are two types of overhead—fixed and variable. A controversy exists in accounting for fixed overhead costs (costs that do not vary with the level of production). Proponents of **direct costing** argue that fixed costs should be treated as period costs and not as product costs. Under direct costing, only variable overhead costs are assigned to units of product. Fixed overhead costs are expensed as incurred. Direct costing is not acceptable for either external reporting or income tax purposes. For those purposes, both fixed and variable overhead costs must be assigned to units of product. This method is called **full costing** or **absorption costing.**

Job order cost accounting illustrated

This section illustrates the flow of costs through the accounts in a job order cost accounting system. The basic journal entries in job order costing are presented for the Barstow Manufacturing Company for the month of January. The company uses a voucher system. The inventory accounts had the following balances on January 1:

General Ledger Accounts		Subsidiary Ledger Accounts	
		Materials Ledger:	
		Material A	$ 3,000
Materials	$10,000	Material B	5,000
		Material C	2,000
		Job Ledger:	
		Job no. 301	$ 4,000
Work in Process.	13,000	Job no. 302	9,000
		Finished Goods Ledger:	
Finished Goods	32,000	Product Y	$12,000
		Product Z	20,000

Notice that the beginning balances in the general ledger accounts agree with the totals of the subsidiary ledger accounts. Journal entries for the transactions that occurred during January are shown on pages 852 through 855. The flow of costs is traced through the general ledger accounts in Illustration 27–4. Postings to the subsidiary ledger accounts are shown in Illustration 27–5. Notice that the ending balances in the general ledger accounts also agree with the totals of the subsidiary ledgers.

ILLUSTRATION 27-4   Flow of Costs through General Ledger Accounts in a Job Order Cost System

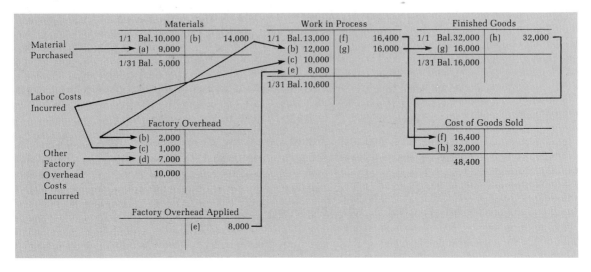

Journal entries for January transactions

(a) The company purchased $8,000 of direct materials ($4,000 of material A and $4,000 of material B) and $1,000 of indirect material C.

Materials	9,000*	
Vouchers Payable.		9,000

* In materials ledger:

Material A	$4,000
Material B	4,000
Material C	1,000

(b) The following amounts of materials were requisitioned from stores and issued to the jobs indicated:

Issued to	Material A	Material B	Material C (Indirect)
Job no. 301	$2,000	$1,000	$1,000
Job no. 302	–0–	2,000	–0–
Job no. 303	4,000	3,000	1,000

ILLUSTRATION 27–5   Flow of Costs through Subsidiary Ledger Accounts in a Job Order Cost System

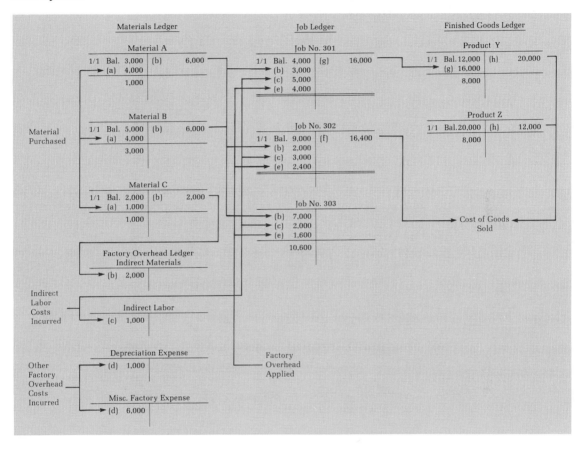

Work in Process	12,000*	
Factory Overhead	2,000†	
Materials		14,000‡

* In job ledger:

Job no. 301.	$3,000
Job no. 302.	2,000
Job no. 303.	7,000

† In factory overhead ledger:

Indirect Materials	$2,000

‡ In materials ledger:

Materials A	$6,000
Materials B	6,000
Materials C	2,000

(c) The following amounts of factory labor cost were incurred:

Work in Process $10,000*
Factory Overhead. . . . .   1,000†
    Vouchers Payable, etc. . . . .   11,000‡

* In job ledger:
  Job no. 301 . . . . $5,000
  Job no. 302   3,000
  Job no. 303   2,000
† In factory overhead ledger:
  Indirect Labor $1,000
‡ Direct labor:
  Job no. 301 . . . . $5,000
  Job no. 302   3,000
  Job no. 303   2,000
Indirect labor: 1,000

(d) The company incurred $1,000 of depreciation on factory buildings and equipment and $6,000 of miscellaneous factory expenses:

Factory Overhead 7,000*
    Accumulated Depreciations—
      Factory Buildings and Equipment   1,000
      Vouchers Payable, Prepaid Insurance, etc. . . .   6,000

* In factory overhead ledger:
  Depreciation expense $1,000
  Miscellaneous factory expense   6,000

(e) Overhead is applied to jobs using a predetermined overhead rate of 80 percent of direct labor costs:

Work in Process ($10,000 × .80) 8,000*
    Factory Overhead Applied.   8,000

* In job ledger:
  Job no. 301 ($5,000 × .80) $4,000
  Job no. 302 ($3,000 × .80)   2,400
  Job no. 303 ($2,000 × .80)   1,600

(f) Job no. 302 was completed and shipped directly to the customer. The total cost of the job was $16,400 and the selling price was $21,000:

Cost of Goods Sold 16,400*
    Work in Process   16,400
Accounts Receivable 21,000
    Sales   21,000

* In job ledger:
  Job no. 302 . . . . $16,400

(g) Job no. 301 was finished and placed in the finished goods storeroom. The job consisted of product Y and had a total cost of $16,000.

Finished Goods	16,000*	
Work in Process		16,000

* In finished goods ledger:
  Product Y $16,000

† In job ledger:
  Job no. 301 . . . . $16,000

(h) $20,000 of product Y were sold for $24,000 while $12,000 of product Z were sold for $15,000.

Cost of Goods Sold	32,000	
Finished Goods		32,000*
Accounts Receivable	39,000	
Sales		39,000

* In finished goods ledger:
  Product Y. $20,000
  Product Z. 12,000

PROCESS COST ACCOUNTING SYSTEMS

A process cost accounting system is used when identical units of product are produced continuously as in mass production or assembly-line processing. Continuous production usually passes through a series of departments, operations, or processes. In a process cost system, manufacturing costs are accumulated for each process for a period of time such as a week or a month. The total costs for a period are divided by the number of units that pass through the process during the period to determine the average unit cost of production. For example, assume that 10,000 units are started and finished in the cutting department during May. There are no beginning or ending work-in-process inventories. Total costs charged to the department in May amount to $21,000. Thus, the average cost per unit is $2.10 ($21,000 ÷ 10,000). The unit cost will increase as additional costs are added in subsequent departments.

Process cost accounting systems are often used to account for such homogeneous products as flour, cement, sugar, chemicals, oil, paint, steel, glass, and rubber. The units of measurement may be gallons, barrels, square feet, pounds, or tons.

In a process cost system, each process or department has its own Work in Process account. The cost of materials, labor, and factory overhead chargeable to each department is debited to its Work in Process account in the general ledger.

Accounting for materials

Accounting for materials in a process cost system is similar to accounting for materials in a job order cost system. Perpetual inventory systems are generally used, and a subsidiary materials ledger is maintained if there are many different types of materials. Material requisitions may also be used in a process cost system. Only the amount and total cost of each material issued to each process must be known. No distinction is required between direct and indirect materials since the costs of all materials issued to a process are debited to the Work in Process account for that process.

Accounting for labor costs

Accounting for labor costs is generally easier in a process cost system than in a job order cost system. Most workers are involved with only one process or department and their services are direct labor with respect to that process. As with materials, the distinction between direct and indirect labor costs is of minor importance in process cost accounting. However, some labor costs, such as those of the plant manager and custodial staff, are not clearly identifiable with individual processes. Such indirect labor costs must be allocated to the processes in a reasonable manner.

Accounting for factory overhead costs

In a job order cost system, overhead is applied to individual jobs on the basis of a predetermined overhead rate. In process cost systems, actual overhead can be charged to each process in some cases. If the level of production and the level of fixed costs do not vary a great deal from period to period, actual overhead can be charged to processes. Otherwise, overhead must be applied to processes.

Computing equivalent units of production

The computation of average cost per unit on page 855 ignored the existence of work in process inventories. In most continuous production processes, the Work in Process Inventory accounts have beginning and ending balances. At any point in time, there are units in process at different stages of completion. The production of some units may have just started; other units may be almost finished. In such cases, the average degree of completion of the units in process must be estimated so that the partially completed units can be expressed in *equivalent units of production.*

To illustrate the key concept of equivalent units, assume the following facts with respect to the cutting department:

> Work in process, beginning of month:
> 10,000 units, 100% complete as to materials, 25% complete as to labor and overhead
>
> Units both started and finished this month:
> 12,000 units
>
> Work in process, end of month:
> 5,000 units, 100% complete as to materials, 20% complete as to labor and overhead

The equivalent units of production are computed below:

	Materials	Labor and Overhead
Beginning work in process:		
(10,000 × 0).	–0–	
(10,000 × 75%)		7,500
Started and finished:		
(12,000 × 100%)	12,000	12,000
Ending work in process:		
(5,000 × 100%)	5,000	
(5,000 × 20%)		1,000
Equivalent units of production	17,000	20,500

The beginning work in process was 100 percent complete as to materials at the start of the month. Thus, no materials were added this month. The ending work in process was 100 percent complete as to materials at the end of the month. Thus, all of its materials were added during the month.

The beginning work in process was 25 percent complete as to labor and overhead at the start of the month. Thus, 75 percent of the labor and overhead was added to the 10,000 units during the month. Seventy-five percent completion of 10,000 units is equivalent to 100 percent completion of 7,500 units. The ending work in process consisted of 5,000 units 20 percent completed, which is equivalent to 1,000 units 100 percent completed.

Computing unit costs

To continue the illustration, assume that $10,000 of cost had been assigned to the beginning work in process inventory as of the start of the month and that the following costs were added in the cutting department during the month:

Materials	$17,000
Labor	41,000
Factory overhead	32,800

Since the number of equivalent units has already been computed, the costs per equivalent unit can be determined as follows:

Costs per equivalent unit:

Material ($17,000 ÷ 17,000)	$1.00
Labor ($41,000 ÷ 20,500)	2.00
Factory overhead ($32,800 ÷ 20,500) . .	1.60

The total cost of $100,800 ($10,000 + $17,000 + $41,000 + $32,800) is accounted for in the following cost summary:

	Total	Per Unit
Cost of beginning inventory of work in process (10,000 units)	$ 10,000	
Costs to complete:		
Labor (7,500 equivalent units × 2.00)	15,000	
Factory overhead (7,500 equivalent units × $1.60)	12,000	
Total	$ 37,000	$3.70
Cost to start and finish 12,000 units:		
Materials (12,000 × $1.00)	$ 12,000	
Labor (12,000 × $2.00).	24,000	
Factory overhead (12,000 × $1.60)	19,200	
Total	$ 55,200	$4.60
Cost assigned to 22,000 units completed and transferred	$ 92,200	
Cost assigned to ending inventory of work in process (5,000 units):		
Materials (5,000 × $1.00)	$ 5,000	
Labor (1,000 equivalent units × $2.00)	2,000	
Factory overhead (1,000 equivalent units × $1.60)	1,600	
Total	$ 8,600	
Total cost accounted for	$100,800	

Process cost accounting illustrated

This section illustrates the flow of costs through the accounts in a simple process cost accounting system. The basic journal entries in process cost accounting are presented for the Meju Manufacturing Company for the month of January. Meju uses two types of material—P and Q—to manufacture a single product which passes through two production departments—assembly and finishing. The company does not use subsidiary ledgers. All factory overhead is charged to the Work in Process accounts. A voucher system is used.

On January 1, the inventory accounts had the following balances:

Material P	$10,000
Material Q	8,000
Work in Process—Assembly Department	
(5,000 units complete as to both materials P and Q	
and 90% complete as to labor and overhead)	20,000
Work in Process—Finishing Department	
(2,000 units 25% complete as to labor	
and overhead)	9,000
Finished Goods	
(8,000 units at $5.00)	40,000

All materials are added in the assembly department. Thus, only labor and overhead are added in the finishing department.

Journal entries for transactions that occurred during January are shown on pages 859 and 863. The flow of costs is traced through the accounts in Illustration 27–6.

Journal entries for January transactions

(a) The company purchased $20,000 of material P and $10,000 of material Q:

Material P	20,000	
Material Q	10,000	
Vouchers Payable		30,000

(b) The following amounts of material were added in the assembly department: Material P, $13,200, and material Q, $5,500:

Work in Process—Assembly Department	18,700	
Material P.		13,200
Material Q		5,500

ILLUSTRATION 27–6   Flow of Cost through Accounts in a Process Cost System

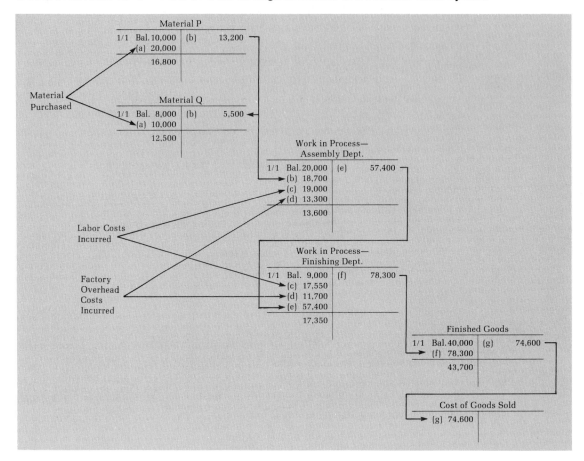

(c) The following amounts of factory labor costs were charged to the departments: Assembly department, $19,000, and finishing department, $17,550:

Work in Process—Assembly Department	19,000	
Work in Process—Finishing Department	17,550	
Vouchers Payable, FICA Taxes		
Payable, etc.		36,550

(d) The assembly department was charged with $13,300 of factory overhead costs and the finishing department was charged with $11,700 of factory overhead costs:

Work in Process—Assembly Department	13,300	
Work in Process—Finishing Department	11,700	
Accumulated Depreciation, Factory Supplies,		
Vouchers Payable, etc.		25,000

(e) During January, 12,000 units were *completed* in the assembly department and transferred to the finishing department. The cost of these units, $57,400, is computed in the cost of production report in Illustration 27–7. (The next section on page 865, describes how to prepare this report.)

Work in Process—Finishing Department	57,400	
Work in Process—Assembly Department		57,400

ILLUSTRATION 27–7

MEJU MANUFACTURING COMPANY
Cost of Production Report
Assembly Department
For the Month of January

Quantities

Units in process at beginning of month	5,000
Units started during month	11,000
Units to be accounted for	16,000
Units completed and transferred	
during month	12,000
Units still in process at end of	
month	4,000
Units accounted for	16,000

Costs to Be Accounted for

Beginning balance of work in process	$20,000
Costs added during month:	
Material P	13,200
Material Q	5,500
Labor	19,000
Factory overhead	13,300
Total costs to be accounted for	$71,000

**ILLUSTRATION
27–7
(concluded)**

	Total	Per Unit

Costs Accounted for

Beginning work in process inventory (5,000 units):

Cost at beginning of month $20,000

Cost to complete:

Labor (500 × $2.00). 1,000

Factory overhead (500 × $1.40). 700

    Total $21,700 $4.34

Cost of 7,000 units started and finished:

Material P (7,000 × $1.20) . . . . $ 8,400

Material Q (7,000 × $0.50) 3,500

Labor (7,000 × $2.00) 14,000

Factory overhead (7,000 × $1.40) 9,800

    Total $35,700 $5.10

Cost of 12,000 units completed and transferred
to finishing department. $57,400

Ending inventory of work in process (4,000 units):

Material P (4,000 × $1.20) . . . . $ 4,800

Material Q (4,000 × $0.50) 2,000

Labor (2,000 × $2.00) 4,000

Factory overhead (2,000 × $1.40) 2,800

    Total $13,600

Total costs accounted for $71,000

Additional Computations

	Materials	Labor and Overhead

Equivalent Units

Beginning work in process:

(5,000 × 0) . . . . –0–

(5,000 × 10%) 500

Started and finished:

(7,000 × 100%) 7,000   7,000

Ending work in process:

(4,000 × 100%) 4,000

(4,000 × 50%) 2,000

Equivalent units of production 11,000   9,500

Costs per equivalent unit:

Material P. . . . . $13,200 ÷ 11,000 = $1.20

Material Q. . . . . $ 5,500 ÷ 11,000 = 0.50

Labor . . . . $19,000 ÷ 9,500 = 2.00

Factory overhead . . . . $13,300 ÷ 9,500 = 1.40

(f) During January, 11,000 units were completed in the finishing department and transferred to the finished goods storeroom. The cost of these units, $78,300, is computed in the cost of production report in Illustration 27–8.

Finished Goods.	78,300	
Work in Process—Finishing Department		78,300

(g) The company sold 13,000 units with a total cost of $74,600 for a selling price of $93,250. The company uses the first-in, first-out method of inventory valuation. Thus, units having the following costs were sold during January:

Cost of Goods Sold	74,600*	
Finished Goods		74,600
Accounts Receivable	93,250	
Sales.		93,250

* Costs of units sold:

8,000 units at $5.0000	$40,000
2,000 units at $6.3750	12,750
3,000 units at $7.2833	21,850
13,000	$74,600

At the beginning of January, there were 5,000 partially completed units in the assembly department. During January, 11,000 units were

---

ILLUSTRATION 27–8

MEJU MANUFACTURING COMPANY
Cost of Production Report
Finishing Department
For the Month of January

Quantities

Units in process at beginning of month	2,000
Units started during month	12,000
Units to be accounted for	14,000
Units completed and transferred	
during month	11,000
Units still in process at end of month.	3,000
Units accounted for	14,000

Costs to Be Accounted for

Beginning balance of work in process	$ 9,000
Costs transferred in from assembly	
department (Illustration 27–7)	57,400
Costs added during month:	
Labor.	17,550
Factory overhead.	11,700
Total costs to be accounted for	$95,650

**ILLUSTRATION
27–8
(concluded)**

	Total	Per Unit
Costs Accounted for		
Beginning work in process inventory (2,000 units):		
Cost at beginning of month	$ 9,000	
Cost to complete:		
Labor (1,500 × $1.50)	2,250	
Factory overhead (1,500 × $1.00)	1,500	
Total	$12,750	$6.375
Cost of 9,000 units started and finished:		
Assembly department costs $\left(\$57,400 \times \dfrac{9,000}{12,000}\right)$. . .	$43,050	
Labor (9,000 × $1.50)	13,500	
Factory overhead (9,000 × $1.00)	9,000	
Total	$65,550	$7.2833
Cost of 11,000 units completed and transferred to finished goods storeroom	$78,300	
Ending inventory of work in process (3,000 units):		
Assembly department costs $\left(\$57,400 \times \dfrac{3,000}{12,000}\right)$. . .	$14,350	
Labor (1,200 × $1.50).	1,800	
Factory overhead (1,200 × $1.00)	1,200	
Total	$17,350	
Total costs accounted for	$95,650	

	Labor and Overhead
Additional Computations Equivalent Units	
Beginning work in process:	
(2,000 × 75%).	1,500
Started and finished:	
(9,000 × 100%)	9,000
Ending work in process:	
(3,000 × 40%).	1,200
Equivalent units of production	11,700
Costs per equivalent unit:	
Labor . . . . $17,550 ÷ 11,700 = $1.50	
Factory overhead . . . . 11,700 ÷ 11,700 = 1.00	

started in production. At the end of January, 4,000 units 100 percent complete as to materials and 50 percent complete as to labor and overhead were still in the department. Thus, 12,000 units (5,000 + 11,000 − 4,000) were completed and transferred to the finishing department during January. Of these 12,000 units, 5,000 represent the beginning inventory and 7,000 represent units started and finished this month.

There were 2,000 partially completed units in the finishing department at the beginning of January. During January, 12,000 units were transferred to the finishing department from the assembly department, and 11,000 units were completed and transferred to the finished goods storeroom. Of these 11,000 units, 2,000 were in the beginning inventory and 9,000 were started and finished in January. At the end of January, 3,000 units 40 percent complete as to labor and overhead were still in the department.

COST OF PRODUCTION REPORT

The **cost of production report** summarizes the costs charged for a period to a department or process and apportions the costs between the units completed and transferred out of the department and the units still in process. The first section of the report is called Quantities. This section accounts for the physical flow of units into and out of a process or department. The units in process at the beginning of the period plus the units started during the period should equal the units completed and transferred out plus the units in process at the end of the period.

The second section of the cost of production report details the costs to be accounted for by the department. These costs include the cost of beginning work in process inventory plus any costs transferred in from previous departments plus costs (material, labor, and overhead) added in the department during the period.

The third section of the report accounts for the disposition of the costs charged to the department. The costs are allocated among the beginning work in process inventory, the units started and finished during the period, and the ending work in process inventory. The total costs accounted for should equal the total costs to be accounted for.

The last section of the report contains the computation of equivalent units of production and costs per equivalent unit. Actually, these computations are made before the third section of the report is prepared.

Standard costs

Standard costs are carefully predetermined product costs. They are goals that should be attained under reasonably ideal conditions. Standard costs form the foundation of a budgeting and feedback system. They indicate how a product should be produced—that is, how much material, labor, and overhead should be used—and how much that product should cost.

Standard costs are used to help management control costs. The actual costs incurred can be compared with the standard costs to determine inefficiencies in purchasing and production methods. The process of comparing actual costs with standard costs is referred to as a **variance analysis.** Standard costs can be used in both process cost and job order cost systems.

Joint products and by-products

In some industries, such as chemicals, petroleum, lumber, and meatpacking, a company must produce several products at the same time in order to produce any one of the products. In such cases, two or more products produced in large quantities and having significant sales values are referred to as **joint products** or main products. Products produced in smaller quantities and having smaller market values than joint products are referred to as **by-products.** In the meat-packing industry, roasts, steaks, ribs, and ground beef are considered joint products whereas cattle bones and hair are considered by-products. Often, the distinction or dividing line between joint products and by-products is not clear cut.

In addition to joint products and by-products, manufacturing operations often result in waste and scrap. **Waste** such as gases, smoke, and unsalable materials has no measurable sales value and may even entail a disposal cost. **Scrap,** such as sawdust, odd pieces of lumber, and remnants of cloth, has a nominal sales value and may be sold or reused. Usually no cost is assigned to scrap. Proceeds from the sale of scrap should be accounted for: (1) as a reduction in total manufacturing costs, or (2) as other revenue.

Many different methods are used to account for by-products. By-products may or may not be assigned part of total manufacturing costs. Thus, by-product inventory accounts may or may not be formally established. The costs assigned to the by-products should not exceed their **net realizable value**—selling price less costs of completion and disposition. The proceeds from the sale of by-products are generally treated: (1) as reductions of total manufacturing costs or cost of goods sold, or (2) as additional sales revenue or other revenue.

Joint products require simultaneous common processing until a certain point in production called the **split-off point.** Separate products do not emerge until the split-off point. Costs incurred prior to the split-off point are known as **joint costs.** Joint costs must be allocated among joint products on some arbitrary basis. Two bases of joint cost allocation are physical quantities and relative sales values.

To illustrate the allocation of joint costs assume that 2,000 pounds of Product A and 3,000 pounds of Product B are produced during a month. Also assume that Product A has a sales value of $1.50 per pound and Product B has a sales value of $1.00 per pound. Joint costs total $4,000. Under the physical quantities method, joint costs are allocated as follows:

$$\text{To Product A: } \$4,000 \times \frac{2,000}{5,000} = \$1,600$$

$$\text{To Product B: } \$4,000 \times \frac{3,000}{5,000} = \$2,400$$

Under the relative sales value method, joint costs are allocated as follows:

Total Sales Value:
2,000 × $1.50 = $3,000
3,000 × $1.00 = 3,000
                $6,000

Allocation of Joint Costs:

$$\text{To Product A: } \$4,000 \times \frac{\$3,000}{\$6,000} = \$2,000$$

$$\text{To Product B: } \$4,000 \times \frac{\$3,000}{\$6,000} = \$2,000$$

Under the relative sales value method, the two products have the same gross margin percentages.

SUMMARY

The term **cost accounting** is often used interchangeably with the terms **management accounting** and **managerial accounting.** There are two basic types of cost accounting systems: (1) **job order** systems and (2) **process cost** systems.

In a job order cost system, costs are accumulated separately for each individual job or order. A job order system is used if products are made to customers' specifications or are produced in identifiable batches. Costs are accumulated on job order cost sheets. All the job costs sheets taken together make up the job subsidiary ledger to the Work in Process account in the general ledger. The job order system must account for materials, labor, and factory overhead.

Fixed overhead costs can be treated as period costs with direct costing or assigned to units of production with full or absorption costing. Direct costing cannot be used for external reporting or income tax purposes.

A process cost accounting system is used when identical units of a product are produced continuously, as in mass production or assembly-line processing. In a process cost system, each process or department has its own Work in Process account. As in a job order system, materials, labor, and overhead must be accounted for. The actual amount of factory overhead can be charged to each process if production and fixed costs do not vary a great deal. Otherwise, overhead must be applied to each process.

In a process cost system, each work in process inventory has a beginning and an ending amount. At the end of a period, units are at different stages of completion. Equivalent units of production must be computed in order to compute unit costs.

The cost of production report is an important part of a process cost system. The report is divided into three sections which account for: (1) the physical flow of units in and out of a process or department, (2) the costs to be accounted for by the department, and (3) the disposition of costs charged to the department.

Standard costs are carefully predetermined product costs. They represent goals that should be attained in ideal conditions. Standard costs are compared to actual costs in a process known as **variance analysis.** Such analysis helps management control costs.

Joint products and **by-products** are common in manufacturing entities. Two or more products produced in large quantities and having significant sales values are joint products. Products produced in smaller quantities and having smaller market values than joint products are by-products. Costs must be allocated among joint products and by-products. Manufacturing operations often produce **waste** and **scrap.** Neither should be assigned a cost. Waste has no measurable sales value. Scrap is usually sold and treated as a reduction in total manufacturing costs or as other revenue.

KEY TERMS

Absorption Costing—The process of charging all fixed and variable manufacturing costs to units of product. Also called full costing.

By-product—A product with a limited sales value that is produced at the same time as a main product but in smaller quantities.

Cost Accounting—The accumulation and assignment of manufacturing costs to units of product.

Cost of Production Report—A report that accounts for the physical flow of units into and out of a department (or process), summarizes the costs charged to a department for a period, and apportions the costs between the units completed and transferred out of the department and the units still in process.

Direct Costing—The process of treating fixed overhead costs as period costs and charging only variable costs (direct materials, direct labor, and variable overhead) to units of product.

Equivalent Units of Production—The number of whole physical units that could have been produced during a period. Partially completed units at the beginning and end of a period are multiplied by their percentage of completion and added to units started and finished during the period.

Factory Overhead Applied—A contra account to Factory Overhead in which the overhead applied to production using a predetermined overhead rate is accumulated.

Full Costing—Same as absorption costing.

Job Cost Sheet—The basic document in a job order cost system on which the manufacturing costs of a particular job are recorded and summarized.

Job Ledger—A subsidiary ledger to the general ledger control account Work in Process. It contains the job cost sheets of all jobs currently in process.

Job Order Cost Accounting—A system of product cost accounting in which costs are accumulated separately for each individual job or order.

Joint Costs—Costs incurred prior to the split-off point in the production of two or more products that must be produced simultaneously.

Joint Products—Main products of a production process that are produced simultaneously. Joint products are produced in large quantities and have significant sales values.

Management (or Managerial) Accounting—The process of providing a wide variety of information for management decision-making purposes.

Materials Requisition—A form that authorizes the storekeeper to release materials. It is used as the source document for charging materials to individual jobs and overhead.

Net Realizable Value—Selling price less costs of completion and disposition.

Overapplied (or Overabsorbed) Overhead—The amount by which applied overhead exceeds actual overhead.

Predetermined Overhead Rate—The rate used to apply overhead to products or departments. It is determined at the beginning of a period by dividing estimated factory overhead costs by estimated activity.

Process Cost Accounting—A system of product costing in which costs are accumulated for each department or process and are allocated among the units completed and transferred and the units still in process.

Scrap—A product that occurs in the production of other products and has a nominal sales value. It may be sold or reused.

Split-off Point—The point in production at which joint products separate from each other.

Standard Costs—Carefully predetermined product costs that represent goals that should be attained under reasonably ideal conditions.

Underapplied (or Underabsorbed) Overhead—The amount by which actual overhead exceeds applied overhead.

Variance Analysis—The process of comparing actual costs and standard costs and investigating discrepancies.

Waste—A product, such as gases or smoke, that occurs in the production of other products but has no measurable sales value.

Work in Process—An inventory account that contains the costs charged or assigned to partially completed units of product.

Work Ticket—A form used to record the amount of time spent on each job by each worker. It serves as a source document for charging direct labor to individual jobs.

QUESTIONS AND EXERCISES

1. Why is product cost information necessary and useful?
2. Describe the conditions under which job order cost systems and process cost systems are generally used. Give examples of industries that might use each system.
3. How is a job ledger related to the Work in Process account in a job cost system?
4. On January 1, 1987, the Benton Manufacturing Company estimated that it would use 400,000 direct labor hours during the year and that it would incur $300,000 of factory overhead costs. The company applies overhead to jobs on the basis of direct labor hours. During January, the company used 33,000 direct labor hours and incurred factory overhead costs of $28,000. Compute the following:
   a. The predetermined overhead rate.
   b. The amount of overhead applied during January.
   c. The amount of overapplied or underapplied overhead for January.
5. What is the difference between *direct costing* and *full costing*?
6. Describe the steps that should be followed in preparing a cost of production report.
7. Compute equivalent units of production for each of the following situations:
   a. Beginning work in process inventory: 10,000 units, 100 percent complete as to materials, 80 percent complete as to labor and overhead.
   Units started during month: 25,000.
   Ending work in process inventory: 8,000 units, 100 percent

complete as to materials, 30 percent complete as to labor and overhead.

b. Beginning work in process inventory: 14,000 units, 0 percent complete as to materials, 90 percent complete as to labor and overhead.

Units completed and transferred during month: 26,000.

Ending work in process inventory: 6,000 units, 0 percent complete as to materials, 40 percent complete as to labor and overhead.

8. What are standard costs? How are standard costs used?

9. Distinguish among the following:

    a. Waste.

    b. Scrap.

    c. By-product.

    d. Joint products.

10. The Carson Chemical Company incurred joint costs of $12,000 in the production of chemicals A, B, and C. The quantities and sales values of the chemicals are as follows:

	Number of Units	Sales Value per Unit
Chemical A	3,000	$5.00
Chemical B	6,000	3.00
Chemical C	9,000	3.50

Allocate the joint costs among the chemicals using *(a)* the physical quantities method and *(b)* the relative sales value method.

PROBLEMS

27–1. At the beginning of March, the inventory accounts of the Reagan Manufacturing Company had the following balances:

General Ledger Accounts		**Subsidiary Ledger Accounts**	
		Materials Ledger:	
Materials	$ 9,000	Material R	$3,000
		Material S	4,000
		Material T	2,000
		Job Ledger:	
Work in Process.	13,000	Job no. 605	$5,000
		Job no. 606	8,000
		Finished Goods Ledger:	
Finished Goods	10,000	Product A	$4,000
		Product B	6,000

The following transactions occurred during March:

a. Purchased $12,000 of material R, $10,000 of material S, and $3,000 of material T. Materials R and S are direct materials whereas material T is an indirect material. A voucher system is used.

b. The following materials were issued to individual jobs:

	Material R	Material S	Material T
Issued to:			
Job no. 605	2,000	3,000	–0–
Job no. 606	1,000	2,000	1,000
Job no. 607	5,000	2,000	1,000

c. The following factory labor costs were incurred:

Direct labor:
Job no. 605	$3,000
Job no. 606	4,000
Job no. 607	7,000
Indirect labor	2,000

d. Depreciation on factory buildings and equipment is $2,000 per month. Other factory overhead costs incurred during March total $9,000.

e. Overhead is applied to jobs using a predetermined overhead rate of 90 percent of direct labor costs.

f. Job no. 606 was completed and shipped directly to the customer at a selling price of $23,000.

g. Job no. 605, which consists entirely of Product B, was finished and placed in the finished goods storeroom.

h. During March, $2,000 of Product A was sold for $2,400 while $11,000 of Product B was sold for $13,500.

Required:

1. Set up T accounts similar to the ones in Illustrations 27–4 and 27–5 on pages 852 and 853.
2. Prepare journal entries to record the above transactions for March.
3. Post the journal entries to the T accounts.

27–2. The Farr Furniture Company manufactures furniture to customers' specifications. At the beginning of 1987, the company's inventory consisted solely of $12,000 of materials. During the first quarter of 1987, the company engaged in the following activities:

a. Purchased $20,000 of materials. The company uses a voucher system.

b. Issued the following direct materials to jobs:

Job no. 355. . . .	$5,000
Job no. 356. . . .	4,000
Job no. 357. . . .	7,000
Job no. 358. . . .	6,000

c. Issued $3,000 of indirect materials to production departments.

d. Incurred the following factory labor costs:

Direct labor:

Job no. 355. . . .	$2,000
Job no. 356. . . .	4,000
Job no. 357. . . .	3,000
Job no. 358. . . .	5,000
Indirect labor. . . .	2,000

e. Incurred $17,000 of miscellaneous factory overhead expenses and accrued $3,000 of depreciation expense on the factory building and equipment.

f. Applied overhead to production on the basis of a predetermined overhead rate based on direct labor costs. At the beginning of 1987, the company estimated factory overhead costs at $80,000 and direct labor costs at $100,000.

g. Job nos. 356 and 358 were completed and shipped to customers at sales prices of $14,500 and $18,000, respectively.

Required:

1. Prepare journal entries to record the above transactions. The job ledger and factory overhead ledger are the only subsidiary ledgers used.

2. Determine the balance in the Work in Process account at the end of the period.

3. Determine the amount of over- or underapplied overhead for the period.

27–3. Compute equivalent units of production in each of the following situations:

a. Beginning inventory of work in process:

> 7,000 units complete as to materials and 75 percent complete as to labor and overhead
> Units started and finished: 15,000.

Ending inventory of work in process:

   5,000 units complete as to materials and 30 percent complete as to labor and overhead

b. Beginning inventory of work in process:

   100 percent complete as to materials and 60 percent complete as to labor and overhead
   Units started: 20,000.
   Units completed: 25,000.

   Ending inventory of work in process:

   6,000 units complete as to materials and 80 percent complete as to labor and overhead

c. Beginning inventory of work in process:

   2,000 units 0 percent complete as to materials and 90 percent complete as to labor and overhead
   Units completed and transferred: 14,000.

   Ending inventory of work in process:

   3,000 units 0 percent complete as to materials and 40 percent complete as to labor and overhead.

27–4. The Ridgefield Company manufactures a single product, Product XYZ. At the beginning of July, 20,000 units of Product XYZ were in process, 100 percent complete as to materials and 25 percent complete as to labor and overhead. During July, 50,000 units were started in process and 55,000 units were completed and transferred to the finished goods stockroom. At the beginning of July, the Work in Process account had a balance of $56,000. During July, the following costs were charged to Work in Process:

Materials	$ 70,000
Labor	242,000
Factory overhead. . . .	151,250

Required:

   Prepare a cost of production report for the month of July. Assume that the ending work in process inventory is 100 percent complete as to materials and 70 percent complete as to labor and overhead.

27–5. The Heule Manufacturing Corporation produces a single product which passes through two departments—A and B. The following information is available for the month of April:

Units	Dept. A	Dept. B
Beginning work in process inventory:		
Dept. A: 100 percent complete as to materials, 90 percent complete as to labor and overhead	9,000	
Dept. B: 75 percent complete as to labor and overhead		5,000
Started in process during April	40,000	
Received from Dept. A		42,000
Completed and transferred to finished goods		40,000
Ending work in process inventory:		
Dept. A: 100 percent complete as to materials, 20 percent complete as to labor and overhead	7,000	
Dept. B: 80 percent complete as to labor and factory overhead		7,000

Costs	Dept. A	Dept. B
Beginning work in process inventory	$ 96,480	$65,875
Transferred from Dept. A	—	?
Materials	80,000	—
Labor	176,500	83,700
Overhead	141,200	41,850

Required:

Prepare cost of production reports for *(a)* department A and *(b)* department B for the month of April.

27–6. The Rossi Manufacturing Company incurred joint costs of $30,000 in the production of products A, B, C, and D. The quantities and sales values of the products are as follows:

	Number of Units	Sales Value per Unit
Product A	10,000	$2.00
Product B	15,000	1.50
Product C	20,000	2.50
Product D	5,000	3.00

Required:

Allocate the joint costs among the products using *(a)* the physical quantities method and *(b)* the relative sales value method.

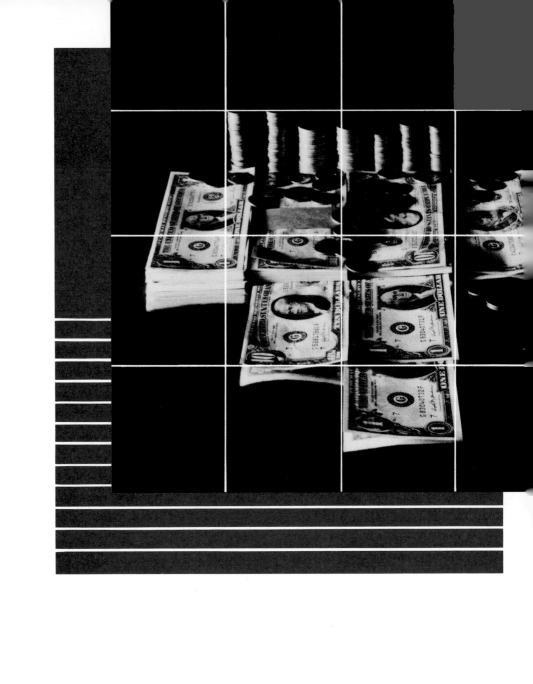

CHAPTER 28

Inflation accounting—changing prices

LEARNING OBJECTIVES

Many users of financial statements believe that information based on historical cost loses some of its relevance during periods of changing prices. By studying this chapter, you will learn how changing prices affect the information shown in financial statements. After studying this chapter, you should be able to:

1. Prepare constant dollar balance sheets and income statements.
2. Compute purchasing power gains or losses.
3. Prepare current cost balance sheets and income statements.
4. Calculate realized and unrealized holding gains.

Generally accepted accounting principles require that historical costs be used in the preparation of financial statements. This means that land acquired for $50,000 in 1984 would be reported on the 1987 balance sheet at that cost, even though the land may have increased in value. During the 1970s, the United States experienced high inflation. Inflation is a rise in the prevailing level of prices, caused by an increase in the money supply and an increase in credit availability. High inflation makes it difficult for investors to evaluate companies that have purchased identical assets but in different years. Since financial statements are prepared using historical costs, each company's assets may be reported at different amounts, even if they are identical and are worth the same amount today. In 1979, the FASB issued Statement 33, which includes procedures to be used to account for the effects of changing prices. Uniform procedures were necessary so that information provided in the financial statements would be more meaningful to users. This chapter discusses the two methods recommended to account for changing prices: constant dollar accounting and current cost accounting.

PRICE CHANGES

There are two kinds of price changes, general and specific. General price changes are changes in the prices of all goods because of inflation. For example, an increase of 15 percent in the general price level means that the cost of a collection of goods has increased by 15 percent. In that case, goods that cost $200 a year ago would cost $230 today.

One of the most common measures of general price changes is the consumer price index (CPI). The CPI measures the change in prices for a collection of goods defined by the Department of Labor. This collection of goods is also known as a **market basket.** The Department of Labor publishes the CPI monthly. To index prices, a **base year** is chosen and given a value of 100. For example, if 1986 is selected as the base year, it is given a value of 100. If inflation during the year is 15 percent, the CPI on January 1, 1987, will be 115.

Specific price changes are changes in the price of a particular good or service. This can occur whether inflation is low or high and reflects changes in supply and demand. For example, assume that a car cost $6,000 in 1986 and $7,000 in 1987 but inflation during the year was zero. The price change of $1,000, or 17 percent, is a **specific price change.** Of course, some goods are affected by both general and specific price changes. However, general and specific price indexes measure different kinds of price changes and cannot substitute for each other.

CONSTANT DOLLAR ACCOUNTING

Constant dollar accounting is a method of reporting elements of financial statements in dollars that have the same general purchasing power.[1] This method is used to reflect general price changes. Certain asset, owner's equity, revenue, and expense accounts are multiplied by the appropriate conversion factor. The **conversion factor** is determined by the fraction:

$$\frac{\text{CPI at balance sheet date}}{\text{CPI at date of acquisition}}$$

The numerator is the consumer price index as of the date of restatement, which is usually the balance sheet date. The denominator is the Consumer Price Index for the date of acquisition. Use of the indexes is required by FASB Statement 33. For example, assume that a machine was purchased for $10,000 in May 1986 when the CPI was 110. A supplementary balance sheet is prepared on December 31, 1987, when the CPI is 125. The machine is reported on the supplementary balance sheet at $11,364 ($10,000 × 125/110).

Monetary items

The monetary items on the balance sheet are not restated. **A monetary asset** is money or a claim to receive money, such as accounts receivable. **A monetary liability** is an obligation to pay a sum of money, such as a note payable. These items are reported at their *historical amounts.* All other items are nonmonetary and are restated to end-of-the-year dollars. A nonmonetary item does not reflect a fixed amount to be paid or received. The real value of these items can change. All income statement amounts are nonmonetary.

---

[1] FASB Statement 33, paragraph 22.

To illustrate constant dollar accounting, we will consider the Whatley Company's balance sheet and income statement for the year ended December 31, 1987. The figures are converted to end-of-the-year dollars using constant dollar accounting and the following general price indexes:

$$
\begin{array}{ll}
1/1/86 & 100 \\
12/31/86 & 105 \\
12/31/87 & 115 \\
\text{Average for 1987} & 110 \\
\end{array}
$$

The purpose of distinguishing between monetary and nonmonetary items is to state all items in terms of current purchasing power. Monetary items by their nature require no restatement because they already reflect current purchasing power. However, nonmonetary items must be restated to convert each historical cost dollar to its equivalent amount of current purchasing power. The restatement is accomplished through the conversion factor.

The following facts were used to convert the balance sheet amounts to December 31, 1987 dollars, as shown in Illustration 28–1. The circled numbers in the illustration correspond to the numbered explanations as follows:

1. Monetary assets and liabilities are not restated because they are already expressed in December 31, 1987 dollars.
2. Ending inventory is considered to have been purchased evenly throughout the year, so the denominator of the conversion factor is the average price index for 1987.
3. The land was purchased on January 1, 1986, so the denominator for the conversion factor is 100.
4. The building was also purchased on January 1, 1986, so the building and its accumulated depreciation are restated using 100 as the denominator in the conversion factor.
5. The equipment was purchased on December 31, 1986, so the denominator for the conversion factor is 105.
6. The common stock was issued on January 1, 1986, so the conversion factor has a denominator of 100.
7. The retained earnings amount is a balancing figure and therefore no conversion factor is used.

The following facts were used to convert the income statement amounts to December 31, 1987 dollars as shown in Illustration 28–2. The circled numbers correspond to the numbered explanations as follows:

**ILLUSTRATION
28–1**

**WHATLEY COMPANY
Balance Sheet—Constant Dollar
December 31, 1987**

	Historical Cost	Conversion Factor			Constant Dollars	
Assets						
Cash.	$ 80,000				$ 80,000	①
Accounts receivable.	100,000				100,000	①
Inventory	90,000	×	115/110	=	94,091	②
Land	150,000	×	115/100	=	172,500	③
Buildings	200,000	×	115/100	=	230,000	④
Accumulated depreciation— buildings	(20,000)	×	115/100	=	(23,000)	④
Equipment.	75,000	×	115/105	=	82,143	⑤
Accumulated depreciation— equipment	(15,000)	×	115/105	=	(16,429)	⑤
Total assets	$660,000				$719,305	
Liabilities and Owner's Equity						
Accounts payable	$ 40,000				$ 40,000	①
Notes payable	20,000				20,000	①
Bonds payable	300,000				300,000	①
Common stock	215,000	×	115/100	=	247,250	⑥
Retained earnings	85,000				112,055	⑦
Total liabilities and owner's equity.	$660,000				$719,305	

1. It is assumed that sales were made evenly throughout the year. Therefore the denominator of the conversion factor is the average price index for 1987.
2. In cost of goods sold, $50,000 was beginning inventory, purchased on December 31, 1986 so the 1986 CPI must be used to convert the beginning inventory to constant dollars: $50,000 × 115/105 = $54,762. The remaining $250,000 of cost of goods sold represents goods purchased evenly throughout the year. Therefore the conversion factor includes the average CPI for 1987 and the computation is: $250,000 × 115/110 = $261,364. The sum of the two conversions is the constant dollar amount reported on the income statement as cost of goods sold ($54,762 + $261,364 = $316,126).
3. The depreciation expense must be divided into building depreciation ($10,000) and equipment depreciation ($15,000). These

ILLUSTRATION 28-2

WHATLEY COMPANY
Income Statement—Constant Dollars
For the Year Ended December 31, 1987

	Historical Cost	Conversion Factor	Constant Dollars
Sales	$500,000	115/110	$522,727 ①
		($50,000 × 115/105 +	
Cost of goods sold	300,000	$250,000 × 115/110) =	316,126 ②
Gross margin	$200,000		$206,601
Operating expenses:			
Depreciation—building	10,000 ×	115/100 =	11,500 ③
Depreciation—equipment	15,000 ×	115/105 =	16,429 ③
Other expenses	60,000 ×	115/110 =	62,727 ④
Income before taxes	$115,000		$115,945
Income taxes	40,000 ×	115/110 =	41,818 ④
Income before purchasing power gain or loss			$74,127
* Purchasing power gain			16,645
Net income	$ 75,000		$ 90,772

* Purchasing power gain(loss) is explained in the following section.

amounts are then converted using the same factors that were used for converting the related assets on the balance sheet.

4. Other expenses and income taxes are considered to have been incurred evenly throughout the year.

Gains and losses in purchasing power

During times of inflation more cash is needed to maintain the same level of purchasing power. For example, assume that inflation is 20 percent and a company has $100 at the beginning of the year. To have the same purchasing power at the end of the year, the company must have $120. When a company holds *net monetary assets* for the year (that is, when its monetary assets exceed its monetary liabilities), the company experiences a loss in purchasing power. The loss occurs because monetary assets are fixed sums of money and prices are increasing. To illustrate, consider a company that has net monetary assets of $2,000 at the beginning of a year. If the annual inflation rate is 10 percent, in order to maintain the same purchasing power, the company should have net monetary assets of $2,200 at the end of the year. If the company still has only $2,000, it suffers a purchasing power loss of $200 ($2,200–$2,000).

If a company holds *net monetary liabilities* (that is, if its monetary liabilities exceed its monetary assets) during periods of inflation, the company enjoys a gain in its purchasing power. The gain occurs because while prices are increasing, the debt remains fixed. For example, consider a company that holds net monetary liabilities of $3,000 when inflation is 10 percent. At the end of the year, it will take $3,300 to have the same purchasing power as the $3,000 in liabilities. The company thus has a purchasing power gain of $300 ($3,300–$3,000), because it will only have to pay $3,000. Illustration 28–3 shows the calculation of the Whatley Company's gain in purchasing power during 1987.

To determine the purchasing power gain, it is necessary to calculate the gain from holding the net monetary liabilities of $170,000 for the entire year plus the gain from holding the $10,000 increase in liabilities during the year. At the end of 1987, the Whatley Company would need to pay $186,190 in order for creditors to have the same purchasing power as the $170,000 it held at the beginning of the year. To calculate the purchasing power gain on the $10,000 increase,

---

ILLUSTRATION 28–3	WHATLEY CORPORATION Calculation of Purchasing Power Gain

January 1, 1987:

Cash	$ 90,000	
Accounts receivable	80,000	$170,000
Accounts payable	$ 30,000	
Notes payable	10,000	
Bonds payable	300,000	340,000
Net monetary liabilities		$170,000 × 115/105 $186,190

December 31, 1987:

Cash	$ 80,000	
Accounts receivable	100,000	180,000
Accounts payable	40,000	
Notes payable	20,000	
Bonds payable	300,000	360,000
Net monetary liabilities		$180,000

Increase in net monetary liabilities $10,000 × 115/110	10,455
Net monetary liabilities restated in December 31, 1987 dollars	$196,645
Actual amount of net monetary liabilities at December 31, 1987	180,000
Purchasing power gain	$ 16,645

we must assume that the increase occurred evenly throughout the year. Thus the denominator of the conversion factor is 110, the average price index for 1987. As shown, it would require $10,455 in year-end dollars to have the same purchasing power as the $10,000 increase that occurred during the year. The total number of year-end-purchasing-power dollars needed to equal the net monetary liabilities held by the Whatley Company at December 31, 1987 is $196,645. Since the Whatley Company has net monetary liabilities of $180,000 at December 31, 1987, the purchasing power gain is $16,645. The purchasing power gain is added to net income in calculating restated net income, as shown in Illustration 28–2.

CURRENT COST ACCOUNTING

Current cost accounting measures the current value of financial statement items at the balance sheet date or when the goods or services were sold or used; that is, current cost accounting reflects specific price changes. This method shows the costs that a company would incur if the goods consumed were purchased at the current price. To use this method, the company must determine the current cost of its assets, liabilities, and owner's equity for the balance sheet. On the income statement, most of the items are already expressed at current costs. For example, wages expense is the current cost of paying employees for their services. Two items on the income statement that must be restated are cost of goods sold and depreciation expense because they were incurred in the past and consumed at a later date.

To illustrate current cost accounting, we will again use the Whatley Company's balance sheet and income statement. The following facts were used to restate the balance sheet, shown in Illustration 28–4. The circled numbers correspond to the numbered explanations:

1. Monetary assets and liabilities do not have to be restated because they are already current amounts.
2. The current cost of the inventory was determined from the vendor's price list and is $120,000.
3. An independent appraiser valued the land at $200,000 and the building at $250,000. The building was purchased on January 1, 1986, and is depreciated using the straight-line method

ILLUSTRATION
28–4

WHATLEY COMPANY
Balance Sheet
December 31, 1987

	Historical Cost	Current Cost	
Assets			
Cash	$ 80,000	$ 80,000	①
Accounts receivable	100,000	100,000	①
Inventory	90,000	120,000	②
Land	150,000	200,000	③
Buildings.	200,000	250,000	③
Accumulated depreciation—buildings	(20,000)	(25,000)	③
Equipment	75,000	90,000	④
Accumulated depreciation—equipment.	(15,000)	(18,000)	④
Total assets	$660,000	$797,000	
Liabilities and Owner's Equity			
Accounts payable	$ 40,000	$ 40,000	①
Notes payable	20,000	20,000	①
Bonds payable	300,000	300,000	①
Common stock.	215,000	215,000	⑤
Retained earnings	85,000	222,000	⑥
Total liabilities and owner's equity	$660,000	$797,000	

with a useful life of 20 years and no salvage value. The annual depreciation charge is $12,500 ($250,000/20). The accumulated depreciation is $25,000, which covers 1986 and 1987.

4. The equipment was purchased on January 1, 1987, and has a current cost of $90,000. It is being depreciated over five years using the straight-line method and has no salvage value. The annual depreciation charge is $18,000 ($90,000/5). Because the asset was purchased in 1987, accumulated depreciation is $18,000.

5. The common stock is not restated. Retained earnings is the only owner's equity item that is restated.

6. Retained earnings is a balancing figure. It can also be calculated by adding the increased value of the assets to the beginning balance of retained earnings. Illustration 28–4 shows the Whatley Company's balance sheet with historical and current costs.

The following adjustments were necessary to convert Whatley's income statement to current dollars, as shown in Illustration 28–5. The circled numbers correspond to the numbered explanations:

1. The cost of goods sold had a current value of $350,000 when the goods were sold; this value is assumed.
2. The restated depreciation amounts are based on the current cost of the assets. For the building, depreciation is $12,500 ($250,000/20). For the equipment, it is $18,000 ($90,000/5).
3. The current operating profit is the profit the company would have earned if it had had to pay current prices. This is an important number because assets consumed will have to be replaced at the current price.
4. The realized holding gain is the portion of the increase in

---

ILLUSTRATION 28–5

WHATLEY COMPANY
Income Statement
For the Year Ended December 31, 1987

	Historical Cost		Current Cost	
Sales		$500,000		$500,000
Cost of goods sold		300,000		350,000 ①
Gross margin		$200,000		$150,000
Operating expenses:				
Depreciation—building . .	$10,000		$12,500 ②	
Depreciation—equipment .	15,000		18,000 ②	
Other operating expenses: .	60,000	85,000	60,000	90,500
Current operating profit . .				$ 59,500 ③
Realized holding gain:				
Inventory			$50,000 ④	
Building			2,500 ④	
Equipment			3,000 ④	55,500
Income before income taxes .		$115,000		$115,000
Income tax.		40,000		40,000
Realized income				$ 75,000
Unrealized holding gain:				
Inventory			$30,000 ⑤	
Land			50,000 ⑤	
Building			45,000 ⑤	
Equipment			12,000 ⑤	137,000
Net Income		$ 75,000		$212,000

values that is recognized in the current year. Simply stated, realized holding gains are the difference between the current costs and the historical costs of assets consumed during the period. The $50,000 of inventory represents the increase in the value of cost of goods sold. The $2,500 for the building is the increase in depreciation expense, as is the $3,000 for the equipment.

5. The unrealized holding gain is the portion of the increase in value that is not recognized currently. The gains are not recognized because these assets were not consumed during the period. The $30,000 for inventory is the increase in value of the ending inventory. The land has increased $50,000 in value. For the building, the $45,000 is the increase in book value [($250,000 − $25,000) − ($200,000 − $20,000)]. The unrealized gain of $12,000 for the equipment is determined the same way [($90,000 − $18,000) − ($75,000 − $15,000)].

CONSTANT DOLLAR VERSUS CURRENT COST ACCOUNTING

The effects of general price changes on the financial statements are shown by using constant dollar accounting. Current cost accounting deals with specific price changes. Any disclosure of constant dollar and current cost financial statements are *supplementary to the principal financial statements* which are still prepared using historical cost information. Statement 33 applies only to certain large enterprises. Large enterprises are defined as those having (1) property, plant, and equipment of $125 million or more before deducting accumulated depreciation, and (2) total assets of $1 billion or more after deducting accumulated depreciation.

Accounting for the effects of changing prices is still at an early stage. FASB Statement 33 is an experimental standard. The FASB has been studying the information disclosed by large enterprises since Statement 33 was released in 1979 to see which method, constant dollar or current cost, provides more useful information. Some people believe that requiring two methods is confusing. They say either constant dollar accounting or current cost accounting should be eliminated. Others believe a combination of the two methods is useful because it shows the effects of both general and specific price changes.

In December 1984, the FASB decided in Statement 82 that the presentation of current cost data would probably be more helpful to the readers of financial statements. Constant dollar data is no longer required. Both approaches are presented in this chapter as background to the changing price problem. Further study will be continued and additional alternatives may occur in the future.

SUMMARY

Financial statements are prepared using **historical costs.** However, beginning in 1979, FASB Statement 33 requires certain large enterprises to present supplementary information showing the effects of changing prices. Two methods were required: **constant dollar accounting** and **current cost accounting.** Only current cost is required at the present time.

There are two kinds of price changes, general and specific. **General price changes** reflect the overall shift in prices of a **market basket** of goods caused by inflation. **Specific price changes** are changes in the prices of specific items and reflect changes in supply and demand. The most common general price change measurement is the **consumer price index.**

Constant dollar accounting is a method of reporting elements of financial statements in dollars that have the same general purchasing power. To obtain the constant dollar values, **nonmonetary items** stated at **historical cost** are multiplied by the following **conversion factor:**

$$\frac{\text{Consumer price index (at the balance sheet date)}}{\text{Consumer price index (at the date of acquisition)}}$$

Monetary items (cash, accounts receivable, and accounts payable for example) are not restated on the Balance Sheet. These items are already reported at their current purchasing power value and therefore do not require restatement.

When **monetary items** are restated, **purchasing power gains** and **losses** occur and are reported in the constant dollar income statement. A purchasing power gain occurs when a company holds net **monetary liabilities** during periods of inflation. A purchasing power loss occurs when a company holds net **monetary assets** during periods of inflation.

Current cost accounting measures the current cost of financial statement items at the balance sheet date. The method reflects the costs that would be incurred if goods consumed were purchased at current prices. Many income statement items are already reported at their current values and do not require restatement. On the balance sheet, monetary items are not restated. When current cost accounting is used, unrealized holding gains and losses occur and are reported in the current value income statement.

The basic financial statements are presented at historical cost. However, FASB Statement 33 requires supplementary disclosures, using the current cost method to reflect specific price changes. Statement 33 applies only to large enterprises and is an experimental standard. The requirements may be changed when experience shows which method of accounting for price changes provides the most useful information.

KEY TERMS

Base Year—In constant dollar accounting, the year that has an index of 100, or the initial-year index.

Constant Dollar Accounting—A method of converting financial statement items to dollars that have the same general purchasing power.

Consumer Price Index—A measure of the change in prices of a collection of goods over a period of time. It is a common measure of general price change.

Conversion Factor—The fraction used to convert historical costs to constant dollar amounts. The fraction is the consumer price index at the balance sheet date divided by the consumer price index at the date when the asset was acquired.

Current Cost Accounting—A method of converting financial statement items to their current value at the balance sheet date. The method reflects the costs that would be incurred if goods consumed were purchased at current prices.

Current Operating Profit—In current cost accounting, the profit a company would have earned if current prices had been paid.

General Price Changes—Changes in the general price level of goods and services. These changes are measured by the consumer price index.

Historical Cost—The cost at which a transaction is originally recorded.

Market Basket—A collection of goods defined by the Department of Labor. The change in the prices of these goods is used to construct the consumer price index.

Monetary Asset—The right to receive a definite sum of money. Net monetary assets exist when monetary assets exceed monetary liabilities.

Monetary Liability—The obligation to pay a definite sum of money. Net monetary liabilities exist when monetary liabilities exceed monetary assets.

Nonmonetary Items—Items whose values change as a result of changes in the general price level.

Purchasing Power Gain—In constant dollar accounting, a purchasing power gain occurs if a company holds net monetary liabilities during periods of inflation.

Purchasing Power Loss—In constant dollar accounting, a purchasing power loss occurs if a company holds net monetary assets during periods of inflation.

Realized Holding Gain—The difference between the current cost and the historical cost of assets consumed during the current period.

Specific Price Changes—Changes in the prices of specific goods or services.

Unrealized Holding Gain—In current cost accounting, the portion of the increase in values that is not recognized currently. These gains are the increases in the current cost of assets held during the entire period.

QUESTIONS AND EXERCISES

1. What does historical cost mean?
2. Distinguish between general price increases and specific price increases.
3. During the year inflation was 15 percent. If a company had $40,000 at the beginning of the year, how much money would be needed at the end of the year to have the same purchasing power?

4. What does constant dollar accounting mean?

5. A company purchases inventory evenly throughout the year. The average price index is 110 and the year-end price index is 120. If the company has $50,000 of ending inventory, what is the constant dollar value of the inventory?

6. Define monetary assets and monetary liabilities. How are these items reported?

7. A company has $20,000 of monetary assets and $15,000 of monetary liabilities. Inflation for the year was 5 percent. Would the company have a purchasing power gain or loss? Why?

8. Which of the following are monetary items? Why?

Cash	Accounts payable
Inventory	Bonds payable
Notes receivable	Retained earnings
Accounts receivable	Equipment
Land	

9. What is meant by the term *current cost accounting?*

10. Land was purchased in 1986 for $100,000 when the price index was 100. In 1987 the index was 110. An independent appraiser valued the land at $115,000. What is the current cost of the land?

11. What type of price change does constant dollar accounting deal with? Current cost? Which method should be used per the FASB?

PROBLEMS

28–1. The following is a condensed comparative balance sheet for the Martin Company for December 31, 1987.

MARTIN COMPANY
Condensed Balance Sheet
December 31, 1986 and 1987

	1987	1986
Assets		
Cash	$ 75,000	$ 50,000
Accounts receivable	60,000	40,000
Inventory	80,000	70,000
Land	100,000	100,000
Buildings	200,000	200,000
Accumulated depreciation—buildings	(25,000)	(20,000)
Equipment	50,000	50,000
Accumulated depreciation—equipment	(10,000)	(5,000)
Total assets.	$530,000	$485,000

	1987	1986
Liabilities and Owner's Equity		
Accounts payable.	$ 50,000	$ 30,000
Notes payable	40,000	40,000
Common stock	300,000	300,000
Retained earnings.	140,000	115,000
Total liabilities and owner's equity	$530,000	$485,000

Additional data:

1. The price index on December 31, 1986 was 115.
2. The average price index for 1987 was 120.
3. The price index on December 31, 1987 was 125.
4. The land and building were purchased five years ago when the price index was 100.
5. The equipment was purchased January 1, 1986 when the index was 110.
6. The ending inventory was purchased evenly throughout the year.
7. The common stock was issued when the price index was 100.

Required:

Prepare a constant dollar balance sheet for December 31, 1987.

28–2. Using the information in Problem 1, compute the purchasing power gain or loss for 1987.

28–3. The following is a partial income statement for the Martin Company for the year ended December 31, 1987.

MARTIN COMPANY
Partial Income Statement
For the Year Ended December 31, 1987

Sales		$400,000
Cost of goods sold		250,000
Gross margin		$150,000
Operating expenses:		
Depreciation—bldg.	$ 5,000	
Depreciation—equipment	5,000	
Other expenses.	90,000	100,000
Income before income taxes		$ 50,000
Income taxes		25,000
Net income.		$ 25,000

$70,000 of the cost of goods sold was beginning inventory that was purchased when the price index was 115. The remaining cost of goods sold were purchased evenly throughout the year.

Required:

Using the above income statement and the data given in Problems 1 and 2, prepare a constant dollar income statement.

28–4. The following is a comparative balance sheet and an income statement for the Hayes Company for December 31, 1987.

HAYES COMPANY
Balance Sheet
December 31, 1986 and 1987

	1987	1986
Assets		
Cash	$ 50,000	$ 40,000
Accounts receivable	40,000	35,000
Inventory	35,000	20,000
Land	75,000	75,000
Buildings	100,000	100,000
Accumulated depreciation—buildings	(20,000)	(16,000)
Total assets	$280,000	$254,000
Liabilities and Owner's Equity		
Accounts payable	$ 20,000	$ 10,000
Notes payable	50,000	50,000
Common stock	150,000	150,000
Retained earnings	60,000	44,000
Total liabilities and owner's equity	$280,000	$254,000

HAYES COMPANY
Income Statement
For the Year Ended December 31, 1987

Sales		$200,000
Cost of goods sold		120,000
Gross margin		$ 80,000
Operating expenses:		
Depreciation	$ 4,000	
Other expenses	50,000	54,000
Income before taxes		$ 26,000
Income tax		10,000
Net income		$ 16,000

Additional Information:

1. Average price index for 1987 was 110.
2. Price index on December 31, 1987 was 115.
3. Building and land were purchased when the index was 100.
4. Ending inventory was purchased evenly throughout the year.
5. Of the cost of goods sold, $20,000 was purchased on December 31, 1986 when the price index was 105, the remaining amount was purchased evenly throughout the year.
6. The common stock was issued when the price index was 100.

Required:

Prepare constant dollar financial statements for the Hayes Company.

28–5. The following information pertains to the Winslow Corporation:

Account balances at year-end:

Inventory	$ 50,000
Buildings.	200,000
Accumulated depreciation—buildings	(40,000)
Land	100,000
Equipment	60,000
Accumulated depreciation—equipment. . . .	(6,000)

1. The current value of the inventory is $75,000.
2. The current value of the building is $225,000.
3. The land is currently worth $150,000.
4. The equipment is currently worth $70,000.
5. The building is being depreciated over 20 years using the straight-line method with no salvage value.
6. The equipment is being depreciated over 10 years using the straight-line method with no salvage value.
7. The actual cost of goods sold for the year was $300,000. The current value at the time of the sale was $375,000.

Required:

a. Calculate the realized holding gain.
b. Calculate the unrealized holding gain.

28–6. The following information is for the Hartley Corporation.

HARTLEY CORPORATION
Balance Sheet
December 31, 1987
Assets

Cash	$150,000
Accounts receivable	95,000
Inventory	120,000
Land	200,000
Buildings	300,000
Accumulated depreciation—buildings	(45,000)
Equipment	140,000
Accumulated depreciation—equipment	(28,000)
Total assets	$932,000

Liabilities and Owner's Equity

Accounts payable	$110,000
Bonds payable	250,000
Common stock	400,000
Retained earnings	172,000
Total liabilities and owner's equity	$932,000

HARTLEY COMPANY
Income Statement
For the Year Ended December 31, 1987

Sales		$625,000
Cost of goods sold		400,000
Gross margin		$225,000
Operating expenses:		
Depreciation	$29,000	
Other expenses	80,000	109,000
Income before taxes		$116,000
Income tax		50,000
Net income		$ 66,000

Additional information:

1. The current value of the ending inventory is $150,000.
2. The current value of the land is $275,000.
3. The current value of the building is $400,000. The building is being depreciated over 20 years using the straight-line method.
4. The current value of the equipment is $160,000. The equipment is being depreciated using the straight-line method over a period of 10 years.
5. The value of the cost of goods sold at the time the goods were sold was $475,000.

Required:

Prepare financial statements using current cost accounting.

APPENDIX A

Accounting and computers

In many companies the computer has replaced the manual accounting system. There have been two reasons for this change. First, changes in business transactions, tax laws, and financial disclosure requirements have forced companies to find new ways to manage the large amounts of data required to meet these new standards. Second, with the advent of the microcomputer, the cost of computers has fallen sharply. Many small businesses can now enjoy the time and cost savings that were previously reserved for larger companies. The computer is now prevalent in most types of businesses, and it is becoming the primary medium of accounting. For this reason, each student should become familiar with computers and should understand to some degree how they work. To aid the student in understanding how computers interact with accounting, a computerized practice set to accompany this text has been prepared. The purpose of this appendix is to provide the student with the basic concepts necessary to understand what a computer is and how it functions.

Hardware

Hardware is the electronic components of the computer. The name comes from the fact that electronic parts are hard to the touch and not easily changed. The components that make up the hardware of a computer basically consist of (1) a central processing unit (CPU) and (2) input/output devices such as a video display terminal (VDT) and printer. The CPU is the part of the computer that performs the required operations. It is made up of three parts—memory, arithmetic logic unit, and a control unit. The input and output devices allow the CPU to interact with people and other machines. The VDT, for example, allows people to direct the operations of the computer and to give it the data needed to perform the operations requested. The functions of directing operations of the computer and providing data for the computer to perform operations on are known as the input cycle. Printers are used to produce "hardcopy" or paper versions of the information generated by the computer. The printing of hardcopy is an example of an output cycle. Certain devices or pieces of equipment perform both input cycles and output cycles. The most common occurrence of this is related to the storage of data. The data used by the CPU is usually stored on some form of magnetic medium, such as a magnetic tape or magnetic disk. The disks can be either hard or soft. Bigger computers generally use hard disks because each hard disk can store large amounts of data and because information can be retrieved from the hard disk much more quickly than from soft disks or other types of magnetic medium. Hard disks are quite costly, however, so their use is usually restricted to larger computers and to other applications requiring rapid access to very large amounts of data. Many smaller computers use the soft disks called "floppy" disks. Floppy disks are much slower than hard disks in retrieving stored data and do not provide as much space to store the data, but they are also much less costly than hard disks. Regardless of the storage medium used, extreme care should be taken to provide for a backup or copy of the data stored. Data lost because of a medium failure is just as irretrievable as data on paper lost in a fire.

Software

A set of instructions is needed to make the electronic components function in a meaningful and useful manner. These instructions are called software, and logical groupings of the software are called programs. Programs are written in special languages that the computer can understand much the same way as a person from Mexico would understand Spanish. The software is loaded into the computer by an input device, such as floppy disk, and then the instructions are executed by the computer. It is important to realize that the software controls the operation of the hardware. The hardware itself cannot be used without appropriate software.

Types of computers

Microcomputers.   Microcomputers are relatively low-cost computers generally used by a single user. Microcomputers typically consist of the following hardware: (1) CPU, (2) VDT, (3) keyboard, and (4) printer. A typical microcomputer is pictured below.

Since the microcomputer has all of the necessary components to perform its operations, it can be used in a "standalone" environment, which means it operates without another computer. Alternatively, a microcomputer can operate as a piece of a larger computer system

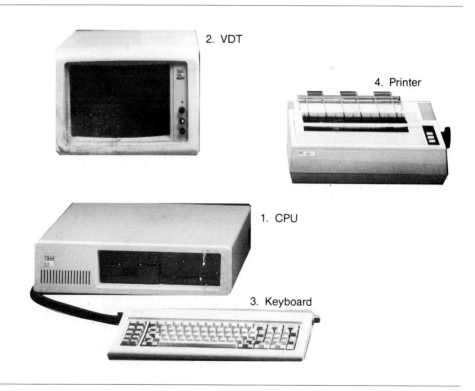

known as a network. The microcomputer does not require a specially constructed room in which to operate, and it uses little space. Usually the microcomputer is located on a desk, although some models are portable.

Most of the software for microcomputers is application software. Application software is packaged software written by software companies to solve a particular problem. For the accountant, the most common of these problems are letter writing and spreadsheet analysis. Other common uses of application software are for replacing manual ledgers and for assisting in the preparation of tax returns. Many small companies now use microcomputers to process accounts receivable and payable, prepare payrolls, record general ledger transactions, and provide up-to-date financial statements. A complete applications software package consists of floppy disks that hold the program for the computer to use and documentation on how to use the program.

Minicomputers. Minicomputers are usually somewhat larger than microcomputers and often have the capability to allow a number of people to use the computer at the same time. The minicomputer's hardware may require a special room to accommodate its large size and special environmental requirements. Usually, the hardware for a minicomputer consists of a large CPU, one or more disk drives,

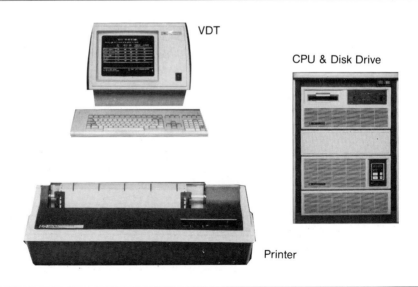

VDT

CPU & Disk Drive

Printer

several VDTs, and one or more printers. Minicomputers typically use hard disks to store and retrieve large amounts of data. A fast and reliable method of backing up the disk drives is needed, and this is usually accomplished with a magnetic tape drive. The information on the disk drives is transferred to magnetic tape, which can be stored in a secure and fireproof vault to ensure adequate records are properly preserved. Magnetic tapes can also be used to transfer data between two different minicomputers. The main disadvantage of magnetic tapes is that someone must mount each tape on the tape drive before any data on that tape can be accessed. Above is a picture of a typical minicomputer.

Minicomputers are used mostly by mid-sized companies with limited financial resources that prevent the purchase of a larger and more powerful mainframe computer. The minicomputer usually requires a person to oversee its maintenance and upkeep, whereas a microcomputer does not.

Mainframe computers. The first computers made were mainframes. They are very powerful and can be used by a large number of people at the same time, simultaneously storing and retrieving

A mainframe computer contains several large units operated by a team of people.

data and executing up to 100 million operations per second. The hardware and software required by mainframe computers is essentially the same as for microcomputers and minicomputers except that it is more sophisticated and expensive to develop and build. Their large physical size and special environmental requirements make mainframe computers very expensive. For these reasons, the U.S. government and large corporations are the primary users of mainframes.

ELECTRONIC DATA PROCESSING

Electronic data processing (EDP) refers to the using of computers to collect and store raw data and to process that raw data into useful information. Four elements form the building blocks of the EDP system. Those elements are: (1) the system that stores the data; (2) the hardware and software to process the data, i.e., the computer; (3) the personnel who run the computers; and (4) the users who use the information.

The data gathering system is the starting point of any EDP system. Raw data and some forms of preprocessed information are gathered in some manner and arranged in a way that can be entered into the computer for additional processing. For larger companies, the information gathering system can be very sophisticated and can consist of many policies and procedures. In contrast, a small company may keep handwritten notes and figures to be entered on a microcomputer for analysis. These notes and figures are an information gathering system. Although the small company may be totally unaware that it operates an information gathering system, the system does exist.

The second element of an EDP system is the hardware and software needed to process the data—the computer. Before the data can be processed by the computer, it must be entered into the computer in some manner. The data may be input into the computer at a location far from where the computer is located. This method is called remote data entry. Remote data entry is often used by large organizations located in a wide geographical area. A good example of remote data entry is an airline reservation system. The computer is usually located at the home office—Atlanta, Georgia, for instance—and a reservationist in a distant city, like New York, can enter data into the computer located in Atlanta. Data can be entered into the computer locally as well.

Related to the location of data entry is the form of the data when it is input into the computer. One type of input data is known as "batch." Batch data processing occurs when large quantities of data of a similar nature are "batched" together for processing at one time. In older computer systems, the information was keypunched onto cards that were batched together for processing. Batch processing is currently being replaced by a more efficient type of data entry known as "on-line" data entry. On-line data entry occurs when a person enters data into the computer as that information becomes available. On-line data entry results in up-to-date information being available. The airline reservation system used in an example above is a type of on-line data entry system. By contrast, under batch processing transactions, data is collected and stored until the next batch processing is scheduled to occur. The information in the system is only updated periodically as each batch job is run.

In most instances, a mainframe computer functions as part of a larger EDP system and not as a system in itself. For example, the parts department of a car dealership may use a minicomputer to handle inventory. This information could be communicated to the mainframe of a large corporation that owns many dealerships, each with its own minicomputer in the parts department. The information for the whole corporation is collected on the mainframe and processed further for use by corporate management. When the EDP system is organized like the one mentioned above, it is called a distributed processing system. In a centralized data processing system, by contrast, the data is entered at remote terminals, but all processing occurs on one or more mainframe computers located at a centralized location. All aspects of the centralized data processing system are located in one place and administered and maintained by EDP personnel.

The next vital element of the EDP system is the EDP personnel, the people who make the EDP system work. Management, accountants, and other users of the EDP system must be able to communicate their needs to the EDP personnel so that the most efficient and best system is designed and implemented in the organization. Most likely the accountant or other user will consult an EDP person called a systems analyst to determine what the system must do to meet the need of the users. When the systems analyst and the users of the EDP system agree on the needs of the users, the systems analyst will design the system. The design is broken down into separate sets of instructions. These sets of instructions are then assigned to a programmer. A programmer is also an EDP person who usually works for the systems analyst. The programmer takes the set of instructions and codes them into a language that the computer can understand. When all of the individual programs are working properly, the system is implemented or installed within the organization, and the accountant and other users are able to extract the information they need to perform their jobs. After the users have used the EDP system for a while, the systems analyst will consult with some of the users to determine if their needs are being met or if a better way of meeting those needs is available. At this point, the systems analyst is back to where he started, and the process begins once again. Thus, the design and implementation of an EDP system is evolutionary and cyclical.

In the previous paragraph the users of the EDP system were mentioned briefly but were never really explained. Who are the users of an EDP system and what are their needs? Obviously a user is anyone who inputs data into the system or retrieves data from the system. But some method of classification is needed to aid the systems analyst in the design of the EDP system. Currently, two methods of classification are being used by EDP personnel to classify users. They are classification by function and classification by level.

The first and most common classification of EDP users is by function. Before the advent of the computer, all data was processed manually by whoever required the information. Since almost all companies at that time were organized by function, data was processed by the appropriate function. These functions consisted primarily of accounting and finance, personnel, production, marketing, and purchasing. When the computer entered the business environment, electronic data processing naturally evolved along the functional lines that had existed prior to the computer. One systems analyst would assist the accounting and finance departments in designing and implementing a system that only processed data of a financial nature. At the same time, another systems analyst would assist the production department with the design of a manufacturing system.

The second method of classifying EDP users resulted from the widespread changes in the organization structure of many companies during the 1970s. Organization by function was replaced with the matrix organization, which gave certain managers a little piece of each of the functions. By changing the organizational structure of the company, information provided by the EDP systems of the past was no longer useful. A new way of classifying the users was needed. To solve this problem, EDP personnel determined that the users should be classified by the level of their decision-making authority. At the lowest level are the operational users. These users need information to perform the daily operations of the company. The information required by operational users usually is obtained from analysis of a large quantity of detailed data relating to day-to-day operations. The second level is the managerial level. Since the managers have several operational users under them, they could use the information available to their subordinates. However, managers often do not want or need the information that the operational users need. Managers need a summary of all the operations under their control so they can exercise effective control and manage resources in the most efficient manner possible. The final level is the strategic level. Users of information at the strategic level are the top decision makers of an organization. Their decisions often affect the course the organization will take in the years to come. Because of their need for abstract and long-range information, information which differs greatly from that needed at the managerial level, strategic users are classified separately from the other users. The method of classifying users is an important part of designing and implementing the EDP system because the system is created for the benefit of those users.

EDP: INTERNAL VERSUS EXTERNAL

As with many services, electronic data processing can be provided by a department within the company or through a data processing service, which will charge the company a fee to perform the data processing activities. The advantages of in-house data processing relate mainly to the control the company has over its data. Because the data never leaves the company, security is better maintained. Also, the priority of processing the data is in the control of the company itself, not a third party. The disadvantages of in-house data processing are cost, lack of expertise, and the risk of obsolescence of the hardware and of the system itself. Engaging a data processing service to design, build, and operate a data processing system for the company will overcome many of the disadvantages associated with an in-house EDP system. However, the involvement of an outside, third party reduces the company's degree of control and the level of security associated with the system. The choice is best made in view of what is most important to each individual firm.

SUMMARY

For the accountant to understand the world of computers, he or she must first have a general knowledge of what a computer consists of and how the computer operates. Basically, the computer is made of electronic parts known as hardware that are controlled by sets of instructions called software. The computer is used in the accumulation of information by a process known as an electronic data processing system. This system is run by people who assist the users of the information generated by the EDP system. Finally, the EDP system can be run by a department within the company or a data processing service outside the company.

APPENDIX B

Statement of changes in financial position

Generally Accepted Accounting Principles require that published financial reports include a *balance sheet, income statement,* and a *statement of changes in financial position.* This appendix provides a brief discussion of the statement of changes in financial position.

The balance sheet provides an indication of the resources, obligations, and ownership interests of an enterprise as of a moment in time. The income statement provides an indication of the firm's profitability over a period of time, generally one year. While both statements provide useful information to present and potential investors and creditors, the two statements leave certain questions unanswered. For example, how can a firm that operated at a net loss afford to pay dividends? Were additional investments in plant and equipment made during the period, and, if so, how were the investments financed? Most important, how much cash or working capital (current assets minus current liabilities) were generated from operations? The information contained in the statement of changes in financial position is intended to aid investors and creditors in answering these and similar questions.

Generally speaking, the statement of changes in financial position is intended to show the effects of all significant financing and investing activities on the firm's cash or working capital position. For example, suppose a firm purchased a new building for $50,000 cash during the current year. The increase in the asset account *Buildings* would be readily apparent from comparative balance sheets. The method of financing the purchase would not be easily determinable from comparative balance sheets alone, however. The statement of changes in financial position would show that the building purchase resulted in a $50,000 decrease in cash (or working capital), and therefore it gives a more complete picture of the financing *and* investing activities of the firm. Thus, the statement of changes in financial position can be considered as a linkage between beginning and ending amounts in the balance sheet accounts. That is, it shows the financing *and* investing activities together in one statement.

The statement of changes in financial position also enhances the information provided in the income statement. Recognition of revenues and expenses may not coincide with the associated cash inflows and outflows. Consider the $50,000 building mentioned earlier. While the cash outflow associated with the purchase of the building may occur today, the related depreciation expense will be recognized periodically over the building's useful life. The timing of the expense recognition and the cash outflow differ, and the statement of changes in financial position highlights these differences. Hence, the statement of changes in financial position will help users answer such questions as how a firm can pay dividends when operating at a loss.

THE CONCEPT OF FUNDS

The statement of changes in financial position may be prepared using either of two definitions of funds; working capital or cash. Working capital is defined as current assets minus current liabilities. A firm is said to have a positive working capital position if the amount of current assets exceeds current liabilities. The major difference between statements prepared on the cash basis versus statements prepared on the working capital basis is the level of detail presented in the statement. A cash basis statement is more detailed than a statement prepared on the working capital basis.

A statement prepared on the working capital basis includes any transaction that affects the amount of working capital. The advantage of using the working capital basis is the exclusion of many routine transactions. Consider, for example, the collection of a $10 accounts receivable. This transaction would not appear on the working capital basis statement since the amount of working capital is not affected (the current asset Cash increases by $10 while the current asset Accounts Receivable decreases by $10—there is no net change in the amount of working capital). But consider the purchase of the $50,000 building mentioned earlier. There is a net decrease in working capital of $50,000 because of this transaction (the current asset Cash was decreased by $50,000). This transaction does affect the amount of working capital and would therefore be included in the working capital basis statement.

The statement of changes in financial position prepared on the cash basis would include any transaction that affected cash. Both of the transactions mentioned above would be included in a cash basis statement. These two examples illustrate that the information reported on either basis is the same, differing only in the level of detail. Each shows the effect of significant financing and investing activities.

Because of the similarities between the statements prepared on either basis, the remainder of this discussion will concentrate on the working capital basis statement. However, there is significant movement in the accounting profession towards the cash basis statement. The concepts in the following sections hold regardless of the definition of funds being used.

Primary sources of funds

Despite the variety and complexity of financing alternatives available today, sources of funds (financing) can be classified into one of four major types.

1. **Operations:** The primary source of funds for an established firm should be from operations. In order to survive in the long run, a firm must generate inflows of funds from selling goods or services greater than the outflow of funds required to produce those goods and services. As indicated earlier, funds generated from operations may differ from net income.
2. **Investments by owners:** Owners frequently contribute cash or other current assets to the business for a variety of reasons, such as to promote the firm's growth.
3. **Sale of plant and equipment:** Businesses often sell depreciated or obsolete plant assets. For example, a firm may sell an outdated facility in order to move to a more efficient facility.

If the old facility is sold for cash, working capital is increased, and the sale constitutes a source of funds.

4. **Long-term debt:** Businesses frequently finance new investments by issuing long-term debt such as bonds. When bonds are sold for cash, working capital is increased. The sale of bonds is therefore a source of funds. Long-term borrowing from a bank is essentially the same as issuing bonds.

Primary uses of funds

Uses of funds (investing) can be classified into three major categories:

1. **Distributions to owners:** Investors purchase an interest in corporations in hopes of receiving dividends in the future. Dividends paid to shareholders are distributions to owners and constitute a primary use of funds.

2. **Purchases of plant and equipment:** In order to remain competitive in the long run, firms must replace worn or outdated physical assets. Long-term physical assets must also be purchased in order to take advantage of new opportunities. When cash or other current assets are exchanged for long-term assets, working capital will be reduced.

3. **Repayment of long-term debt:** Repayment of long-term debt usually requires the use of cash or other current assets, which reduces working capital.

In addition to these major uses of funds, operations could result in a net decrease in working capital. If the outflow of funds required to produce goods and services exceeds the inflow of funds from the sale of these goods and services, operations are said to require the use of working capital. Recall that net income (net loss) is not synonymous with operations being a source (use) of funds.

PREPARATION OF THE STATEMENT OF CHANGES IN FINANCIAL POSITION: AN ILLUSTRATION

There are numerous acceptable approaches to preparing a statement of changes in financial position. For a complex organization that typically engages in a wide variety of complex transactions, it may be beneficial to prepare a worksheet. For firms engaging in fairly routine transactions on a regular basis, direct preparation of the statement without a worksheet is usually most efficient. We will use the direct approach to illustrate the preparation of a working capital basis statement. The financial statements on which this illustration is based, along with the completed statement of changes in financial position, will be presented at the end of the appendix.

Regardless of the approach taken (worksheet or direct), the first step is to compute the net change in working capital for the period. Current liabilities at the end of the period are subtracted from the current assets of the same date. This gives the net working capital position as of the end of the period. The working capital for the Ball Company is $39,000 ($90,000 − $51,000) as of the end of the year. The ending working capital position minus the beginning working capital position yields the net change in working capital for the year. Note that the Butch Company has a decrease in working capital of $3,000 for the year. This is an important first step because the statement of changes in financial position is intended to explain (or isolate the factors contributing to) the $3,000 decrease in working capital. The bottom line of the statement of changes in financial position for the Butch Company indicates a net decrease in working capital of $3,000.

The direct approach to preparing a statement of changes in financial position begins with net income for several reasons. Beginning with net income provides a readily apparent link between the income statement and the statement of changes in financial position.

More important, recall that operations is the primary (recurring) source of funds for the business. Funds provided by (or applied to) operations are required to be shown as a line item on the statement. Since most transactions affecting net income affect working capital in a similar fashion, it is a simple exercise to begin with net income and make adjustments for the transactions that affect net income and working capital differently (the timing differences mentioned in the introduction to this appendix).

For example, consider the following transactions (as if each were the only transaction for the firm during the entire year):

(1) Cash	15	
Sales.		15
Cost of Goods Sold	10	
Inventory		10

(2) Salary Expense. 4	
Cash.	4
(3) Advertising Expense 2	
Cash.	2

If transaction number (1) was *the only transaction for the year,* net income would be $5 computed as follows:

Sales	$15
Cost of goods sold	10
Net income	$ 5

Working capital would be increased by $5 as well (the current asset cash increases by $15, while the current asset inventory decreases by $10—a net change of $5).

Considered *alone,* transaction (2) would result in net income of −$4 computed as follows:

Sales	$ 0
Salary expense	4
Net loss	$(4)

The net effect of transaction (2) on working capital is also a net decrease of $4 (the current asset cash is reduced by $4, no other current accounts are affected). Transaction (3) is similar in that the effects on income and working capital are identical (a $2 decrease in each). These three examples are typical of the majority of transactions entered into by most firms in that most transactions related to operations affect working capital and income in the same way. Hence, it simplifies our task a great deal to begin the statement of changes in financial position with net income and adjust for the few transactions that affect net income and working capital differently. Transactions that decrease net income but do not affect working capital are referred to as "nonworking capital charges."

The most common nonworking capital charge is depreciation expense. Consider the journal entry for recording depreciation expense for the year:

Depreciation Expense 10	
Accumulated Depreciation	10

Since accumulated depreciation is not a current asset, working capital is not affected by this journal entry. But net income is reduced by

$10. Because we are beginning with net income and working towards *funds provided by operations,* we must add the amount of depreciation expense to net income to arrive at funds from operations. This is entry A in the statement of changes provided at the end of the appendix.

Many people believe that because depreciation expense is added to net income in determining funds provided by operations, depreciation expense is a source of funds. Depreciation is *not* a source of funds. Depreciation is added to net income because it did not require the outlay of funds but was deducted in arriving at net income.

Another common nonworking capital charge similar to depreciation expense is the expense associated with the amortization of intangibles (patents, goodwill, etc.). Amortization of intangibles will not be mentioned further except to note that it is treated exactly like depreciation expense.

After all nonworking capital charges have been identified (the information is usually available from the income statement), funds provided by operations is readily determinable.

The remaining entries in the statement of changes in financial position are determined by examining the comparative balance sheets. Since we are still concerned with the working capital provided section, we look for changes in noncurrent account balances that would likely cause an increase in working capital. For example, the first noncurrent account listed is *Property and Equipment.* This account shows an increase of $42,000. It is unlikely that we could acquire $42,000 of property and equipment and increase working capital at the same time. It is also unlikely that we could reduce *bonds payable* by $10,000 while increasing working capital. It will be shown that these two changes reduce working capital and therefore belong in the *working capital applied* section of the statement.

This leads us to the *Common Stock* equity account in our example. Consider the type of transaction that would increase Common Stock by $5,000. It is probably something similar to the following:

Cash	5,000	
Common Stock		5,000

This transaction increases working capital by $5,000 (the current asset cash is increased by $5,000, the Common Stock account is an equity account). Hence, the issuance of common stock provides $5,000 in working capital. This is labeled entry B in the illustration. Having identified all possible sources of working capital, we can now turn to the applications (uses) of working capital.

The purchase of equipment was identified earlier as a primary use of working capital. In this example, the company's Property and Equipment account increased by $42,000—a use of funds labeled entry C. Repayment of long-term debt is also a use of funds—labeled entry D. Finally the declaration of dividends (entry E) constitutes a use of funds. Consider the journal entry made at the time dividends are declared:

Retained Earnings 4,000
    Dividends Payable 4,000

Dividends payable is a current liability and is being increased while Retained Earnings is not a current account (Retained Earnings is an equity account). Thus, working capital is reduced by $4,000 due to the above transaction—a use of funds.

Since the effect of the changes in all noncurrent accounts on working capital have been isolated, the statement is complete. Note the correspondence between the $3,000 decrease on the statement and the $3,000 decrease computed directly from the working capital accounts.

The statement indicates that although the Ball Company earned a reasonable profit and generated an acceptable amount of funds from operations, most of the funds were used to finance plant expansion and to retire a portion of the company's outstanding debt.

This example illustrates how the statement of changes in financial position highlights financing *and* investing activities (the funds were generated primarily by operations and used to expand facilities and retire debt). It also provides investors with the information necessary to evaluate the firm's dividend policy.

Also notice that the change in each noncurrent account from the beginning to the end of the year is explained by the statement of changes in financial position.

Finally, when a statement of changes in financial position is prepared on the working capital basis, a supporting *schedule of changes in working capital components* must also be presented. This schedule is simply a formal presentation of the information derived in the first step of this illustration. The beginning and ending balance of each current account (assets and liabilities) and the corresponding increase or decrease in each account are listed to provide a check figure ($3,000 decrease in our example) for the statement of changes in financial position. A schedule of changes in working capital components is presented with the completed statement of changes in financial position for the Ball Company.

The following is a summary of the steps used to prepare a statement of changes in financial position:

1. Begin with net income.
2. Add back nonworking capital charges (items that reduce net income while not affecting working capital). This yields funds provided by operations.
3. Examine the comparative balance sheets for changes in all noncurrent accounts. If the change resulted in an increase in working capital, enter the transaction under "other resources provided." If the change resulted in a decrease in working capital, enter the transaction as "working capital applied."
4. Construct a *schedule of changes in working capital components* to provide a check figure.

BALL COMPANY
Comparative Balance Sheets

	December 31	
	1987	1986
Assets		
Cash	$ 26,000	$ 25,000
Accounts receivable	35,000	30,000
Inventory	29,000	34,000
Total current assets	$ 90,000	$ 89,000
Property and equipment	110,000	68,000
Less: Accumulated depreciation	(45,000)	(35,000)
Total assets	$155,000	$122,000
Liabilities and Stockholder's Equity		
Accounts payable	$ 32,000	$ 25,000
Accrued liabilities	19,000	22,000
Total current liabilities	$ 51,000	$ 47,000
Bonds payable	10,000	20,000
Common stock ($10 par)	50,000	45,000
Retained earnings	44,000	10,000
Total liabilities and stockholder's equity	$155,000	$122,000

BALL COMPANY
Income Statement
For the Year Ended December 31, 1987

Sales		$150,000
Cost of goods sold		80,000
Gross profit		$ 70,000
Operating expenses:		
Salaries	$15,000	
Rent	7,000	
Depreciation	10,000	32,000
Net income		$ 38,000

BALL COMPANY
Statement of Retained Earnings
For the Year Ended December 31, 1987

Beginning retained earnings.	$10,000
Add: Net income	38,000
Less: Dividends declared.	(4,000)
Ending retained earnings.	$44,000

BALL COMPANY
Statement of Changes in Financial Position
Working Capital Basis
For the Year Ended December 31, 1987

Working capital provided by:			
Operations:			
Net income.	$38,000		
Add: Nonworking capital charges:			
Depreciation expense	10,000	(A)	
Working capital provided by operations . . .	$48,000		
Other sources of working capital:			
Issuance of common stock.	5,000	(B)	
Total working capital provided			$53,000
Working capital applied:			
Purchase of equipment.	$42,000	(C)	
Retirement of equipment	10,000	(D)	
Declaration of dividends	4,000	(E)	
Total working capital applied			56,000
Net decrease in working capital			$ 3,000

BALL COMPANY
Schedule of Changes in Working Capital Components

	1987	1986	Increase (Decrease)
	December 31		
Cash	$26,000	$25,000	$1,000
Accounts receivable	35,000	30,000	5,000
Inventory	29,000	34,000	(5,000)
Accounts payable	32,000	25,000	(7,000)
Accrued liabilities	19,000	22,000	3,000
Net decrease in working capital . . .			($3,000)

PROBLEMS

1. Given the following information, complete the net change in working capital for the year 1987.

	December 31	
	1987	1986
Cash	$40,000	$30,000
Accounts receivable	70,000	75,000
Inventory	60,000	62,000
Buildings.	90,000	95,000
Accounts payable	41,000	30,000
Wages payable	17,000	13,000
Common stock	60,000	60,000
Retained earnings	40,000	28,000

ANN CORPORATION
Comparative Balance Sheets

	December 31	
	1987	1986
Assets		
Cash	$ 4,000	$ 3,000
Accounts receivable	11,000	15,000
Inventory	17,000	14,000
Equipment	65,000	60,000
Accumulated depreciation—equipment	(18,000)	(10,000)
Total assets	$79,000	$82,000
Liabilities and Stockholder's Equity		
Accounts payable	$ 6,000	$ 9,000
Accrued liabilities	7,000	5,000
Bonds payable	10,000	10,000
Common stock	15,000	12,000
Retained earnings	41,000	46,000
Total liabilities and stockholder's Equity	$79,000	$82,000

Additional data:
   Net income for the year was $2,000.
   Depreciation expense was $8,000.
   Equipment was purchased for cash.
   Common stock was issued for cash.
   Dividends of $7,000 were declared.

Required:
   Prepare a statement of changes in financial position (working capital basis) for the year 1987. (Include a schedule of changes in working capital components.)

Index

This book has been set VideoComp in 11 point Times Roman (set 12 on 13) and 10/12 point Times Roman. Chapter numbers are 24 point Avant Garde Medium and 64 point Avant Garde Bold; chapter titles are 18/19 Avant Garde Medium. The size of the type page is 36 by 47 picas.